Using the Housing Act 2004

Published by
Jordan Publishing Limited
21 St Thomas Street
Bristol BS1 6JS

Whilst the publishers and the author have taken every care in preparing the material included in this work, any statements made as to the legal or other implications of particular transactions are made in good faith purely for general guidance and cannot be regarded as a substitute for professional advice. Consequently, no liability can be accepted for loss or expense incurred as a result of relying in particular circumstances on statements made in this work.

British Library Cataloguing-in-Publication Data

A catalogue record for this book is available from the British Library.

ISBN 978 1 84661 100 1

Typeset by Letterpart Ltd, Reigate, Surrey

Printed in Great Britain by Antony Rowe Limited, Chippenham, Wiltshire

Using the Housing Act 2004

Helen Carr
Senior Lecturer in Law, University of Kent; part-time Chair, Residential Property Tribunal

Stephen Cottle
Barrister, Garden Court Chambers

David Ormandy
Professor and Principal Research Fellow, Warwick Law School

JORDANS

PREFACE

In the Foreword to *The Housing Act 2004: A Practical Guide* published in 2005, Professor Burridge observed that it 'is a work that will inevitably spawn further editions as regulations and ... guidance add detail to the main framework'. Here is a further edition with a narrower scope.

This book came about for two reasons.

First, time has elapsed to enable assessment of the early signs of how the Act is bedding in and the overall picture has been completed with the implementation of all the regulations and guidance, a process also marked by relevant appeal decisions reaching the Residential Property Tribunal.

Second, we have fresh input from David Ormandy of the Safe and Healthy Housing Unit, Warwick Law School, who, whilst working with others, was responsible for developing the key concepts and methodology of the HHSRS. This we feel, has produced a more focused book that omits chapters on Home Information Packs, Mobile Homes and the wider cover of the Housing Act 2004. Instead we concentrate on just those aspects of the legislation required for those dealing with standards of housing and for those responsible for aspects of residential property management who find themselves necessarily using the Housing Act 2004.

We hope, subject to the humble rider that we have endeavoured to avoid and would apologise for any remaining mistakes, to facilitate a better understanding for those already familiar with housing law. As important, we aim also to make using the Act accessible for those having to use 'law' for the first time, with a book, also containing as it does the necessary provisions, regulations and selected guidance.

The views expressed in this book are the authors' own personal views and not that of any organisation to which they are affiliated.

Helen Carr
Stephen Cottle
David Ormandy
February 2008

CONTENTS

Part V
Management Orders and EDMOs

TABLE OF CASES

References are to paragraph numbers.

TABLE OF RESIDENTIAL PROPERTY TRIBUNAL DECISIONS

References are to paragraph numbers.

TABLE OF STATUTES

References are to paragraph numbers.

TABLE OF STATUTORY INSTRUMENTS

References are to paragraph numbers.

Part I

INTRODUCTION

Chapter 1

THE LEGAL ENVIRONMENT

INTRODUCTION

1.1　The purpose of Chapter 1 is to provide an overview of the English legal system.

1.2　The Housing Act 2004 (the Act), like all other statutes, operates within our legal framework. In order to use the Act successfully you need to have an understanding of that legal framework and how law operates within England and Wales. We will focus on those elements which are most relevant to the operation of the Act, such as public law, the use of discretion and the operation of the tribunal system. The chapter is designed to provide the background information which complements the detailed explanations of the operation of the Act which are provided in later chapters.

1.3　Devolution is of increasing relevance to the operation of law in England and Wales. Devolution in the UK involves the transfer of some legislative power from Parliament to Scotland, Northern Ireland and Wales. The legislative basis for devolution is set out in the Scotland Act 1998, the Government of Wales Act 1998 and the Northern Ireland Act 1998. There is also a non-legislative framework of agreements between government departments and the devolved institutions. Certain areas of responsibility are devolved, ie have been passed to the new political bodies. Other matters are reserved for the UK Parliament.

1.4　The consequences of devolution are that in some areas, such as university fees, there are different policies in the different parts of the UK.

1.5　This book only covers the law in England and Wales. However, because housing is a devolved matter there may well be distinctions between the ways in which the law operates in England and Wales. For further up-to-date information on the detailed operation of the law in Wales check the website of the National Assembly: www.wales.gov.uk/.

1.6　This chapter will provide you with an introduction to:

- the sources of law;

- reading statutes;

- public law;

- human rights;

- the court system;

- tribunals.

THE SOURCES OF LAW

1.7 The rule of law is a crucial feature of our democracy. It means that no one is above the law. However much they may disagree with the way in which it operates they are bound to obey it. So, for instance, an environmental health officer who is making a decision about what action to take in response to defects in a property must make his decision in accordance with the law. Therefore, the law that governs decisions needs to be found, and needs to be understood.

1.8 The law is found in statutes and in the common law. Common law is most simply explained as judge-made law. Judges make decisions which derive from precedents – legal principles established in earlier cases. This is quite distinct from statute law, which is law that has been passed by Parliament. The term 'common law' is also used to distinguish legal rules from the operation of equity. Equity is the umbrella term for the principles which were developed by the Courts of Chancery which were designed to mitigate the harshness of the common law. Most law encountered will be statute law. However, common law is still relevant in England and Wales – murder for instance is a common law offence. Equity has a more specialised role. However, it is still important in family law work. It is equity, for instance, which decides how the family home is divided when the house is in the husband's name but both husband and wife have contributed to it. Equity is also relevant in the operation of certain legal remedies, such as injunctions, which are used, for instance, to prevent a landlord from harassing a tenant.

1.9 Statutes – Acts of Parliament – start life as Bills. These may be bills sponsored by government ministers, or private members' bills. Private members' bills are, as the name suggests, bills sponsored by ordinary backbench Members of Parliament. Most bills are government bills. One important piece of legislation which started as a private members' bill is the Homeless Persons Act 1977. The statutory framework it established forms the basis of our current homelessness legislation.

1.10 Often the subject matter of a bill is discussed extensively before it gets to Parliament. Sometimes the government may publish a Green Paper which will set out a number of proposals to change the law and ask for comments. Green Papers got their name because in the past they were published with green covers. Following this consultation process the government may set out its revised policy objectives in a White Paper. White Papers were originally published with white covers.

1.11 The draft bill procedure is a relatively recent innovation whereby the government publishes a bill in draft form, before it is introduced in Parliament as a formal bill. This enables consultation and pre-legislative scrutiny before it is issued formally. The Housing Act 2004 was originally published as a draft bill and was extensively debated prior to its introduction to parliament.

1.12 The formal parliamentary process starts when a bill is presented to Parliament, generally by the minister responsible for it. There are a series of readings, scrutiny by committee, and debates on the bill. There are frequently amendments to the bill – for instance the tenancy deposit scheme was introduced into the Housing Bill at a late stage. The debates can also prove helpful in explaining why particular provisions are contained within the statute. Eventually the bill reaches its final form – the Act of Parliament.

1.13 Acts of Parliament are also described as primary legislation. Even when the Act receives the Royal Assent there is often a long delay before particular sections are brought into effect.

1.14 Most Acts of Parliament contain provisions which allow for delegated legislation. These provisions give power to some person or body to pass legislation that has the same effect as if it had been passed by Parliament through its normal process of legislation. Legislation passed in this way is known as delegated or secondary legislation. Usually it is the relevant minister or the National Assembly for Wales who are empowered to develop the detail necessary to ensure that the Act will work.

1.15 For delegated legislation to come into force, normally it must be 'laid before Parliament'. This requires a copy of the proposed delegated legislation to be placed (or laid) in the House of Commons and the House of Lords for a specified number of days. After that the legislation comes into force. It may require a vote without a debate. The alternative form is where it comes into effect by 'negative resolution'. This means that it will come into force unless sufficient members of Parliament require a vote to be taken.

1.16 Delegated legislation is often enacted as statutory instruments. Statutory instruments come in two forms – Regulations and Orders.

1.17 In certain areas of law, in particular social services and social welfare law, government gives extensive guidance on the implementation of legislation. The Housing Act 2004 is no exception. The status of guidance can be confusing. Statutory guidance – that is guidance published in pursuit of a statutory power – does not have the full force of a statute, but it must be followed unless there are justifiable reasons for not doing so. On the other hand, following statutory guidance does not guarantee that actions are lawful.

Guidance issued by a government department will always only amount to a view of what the department thinks the law is. It is perhaps the clearest expression of the government's wish as to what the law should mean. However, it remains the function of the court to actually decide what legislation means.

1.18 Not all guidance is statutory. You can only discover the status of guidance by reading it. Guidance which is not statutory is persuasive only. However, public officials who do not follow guidance are leaving themselves open to criticism, and must always be ready to justify their actions.

1.19 One example drawn from the Act may be helpful to explain these distinctions. Part 1 of the Act provides for the introduction of the Housing Health and Safety Rating System (HHSRS) which is an evidence-based system for local authorities to adopt as the basis for enforcement against bad housing conditions. Part 1 is primary legislation. It sets out the legislative framework but does not give the level of detail necessary for practical implementation. The HHSRS regulations prescribe the method of inspections and assessment of hazards. The regulations are delegated or secondary legislation. These must be followed by local authorities as if they were primary legislation. Operating Guidance has also been published in connection with this Part of the Act. This provides detailed guidance on hazard assessments. This guidance is not statutory and is designed to provide helpful assistance to local authorities in carrying out their responsibilities under the legislation.

READING STATUTES

1.20 To be successful in using the framework of the Act you must learn how to read it. The best way to explain how to read statutes is to explain the features of statutes using the Housing Act 2004 as an example. The date 2004 is the year that the Act received royal assent. It was not the year the statute came into force. Many statutes contain complex provisions which need to be prepared for. The delegated legislation is published after the Act has completed the parliamentary process. In the case of a complex piece of legislation, like the Housing Act 2004, different parts of the Act have different commencement dates. Explanatory notes have been produced to assist in the understanding of this Act and are available separately. This is a relatively recent innovation. The explanatory notes provide a really useful source of information about the provisions of the Act which may help to understand their meaning.

1.21 Looking more closely at this particular Act it can be seen that it is divided into seven parts and 270 sections which makes it a very large Act.

1.22 Looking at one section, for example section 212, the typical layout for a section of an Act can be seen. The section has a heading, in this case 'Tenancy deposit schemes'. It is then divided into nine subsections which are numbered in brackets. To refer to a particular subsection you would say section two hundred and twelve subsection one. If you are referring to this subsection in writing you would write s 212(1).

1.23 Not everything is contained in the body of the statute. Most Acts have schedules attached which contain further material, usually of a more detailed kind. This Act has 16 schedules. They are listed beneath the contents of the Act. Schedules are set out slightly differently from the main body of the Act. If you turn to Schedule 1 you will see its title, 'Procedures and Appeals relating to improvement notices'. In small script to the right of the title there is a section number, section 18. This is the section in the Act which gives effect to the Schedule. The Schedule is then set out in paragraphs and subparagraphs. If you wish to refer to a paragraph within a Schedule then you refer to it as paragraph 1(2) of Schedule 1 to the Act. We say 'to' the Act rather than 'of' the Act because the Schedule is attached to the Act.

1.24 Frequently statutes contain provisions which amend the provisions of earlier statutes. An example within the Housing Act 2004 is contained in section 181 of the Act.

This provides:

'In Schedule 5 to the Housing Act 1985 (exceptions to the right to buy) paragraph 11 (single dwelling-house particularly suitable for elderly persons) is amended as follows.

In sub-paragraph (4) questions arising under paragraph 11 to be determined by the Secretary of State), for the "Secretary of State" (in both places) substitute "the appropriate tribunal or authority".'

1.25 What this means is that from the commencement date of this provision of the 2004 Act, that particular paragraph of Schedule 5 to the Housing Act 1985 has to be read in the new way.

1.26 Acts can do more than amend particular sections. They can introduce new sections into other Acts. In the Housing Act 2004, new provisions in relation to the exercise of the right to buy are introduced into the Housing Act 1985. The new sections are introduced by section 183 of the Housing Act 2004, but they will become sections 138A–138C of the Housing Act 1985. You will always recognise sections of legislation which have been introduced by subsequent legislation because of the use of the capital letter.

1.27 Now you have some idea of the geography of the statute, you need to pay more attention to the detail of the provisions. That means you must read them so that you understand exactly what they are saying.

1.28 There are certain hints we can give you to help you understand statutory language. First of all every word of a section is important, so do not overlook any word used. That can be difficult – most of us tend to skim read technical information. Resist that by reading sections which are important to you out loud.

1.29 Secondly, definitions sections within statutes are extremely important aids to understanding meaning. So if we look at sections 261–263 of the Act we find some very useful general interpretative provisions which provide definitions of 'appropriate national authority' 'local housing authority', 'lease', 'tenancy', 'occupier', 'owner', 'person having control' and 'person managing'. These definitions will help you understand those sections of the Act which use those particular words.

1.30 Thirdly, you will find commentaries on sections helpful in understanding meaning so, if you are in difficulty, use our commentary on the Housing Act 2004 to see if it provides any help with the words you are struggling with. Certain commentaries, such as Current Law are regularly updated and can provide insight into the way that courts have decided upon the meaning of statutes.

1.31 Finally, accept that reading statutes is a skill. It is not intuitive but improves with practice. Moreover, the meaning of certain words and phrases will be contested as there will be more than one view on meaning. Your understanding, even if it is disputed, may be right. The important thing is that it is based upon the actual words of the statute and not upon some notion of what you think – or have been told – that the statute says.

POWERS AND DUTIES

1.32 Something that you must notice when you read statutes is whether the statute provides you with a duty to act or a power to act. The distinction is relatively straightforward. Where a statute imposes a duty on a person or a body then they have to carry out that duty. There is no choice, however hard the carrying out of the duty may be. Lack of finance, for instance, is not an acceptable reason for not carrying out the duty. Where a statute gives a person or a body a power to do some act, the person or the body may exercise that power but they are not obliged to do so.

1.33 The distinction is important for a number of reasons. First, it sets your priorities. If Parliament has considered that carrying out a particular action is so significant that it should be a duty upon a local authority then it is a course of action which must be given priority. Secondly, it is significant when a person is disgruntled by the behaviour of a statutory person or body. If there is a duty then, in general, the disgruntled person will be able to take court action to enforce that duty. If there is only a power, then it is unlikely that there will be any legal redress – although, if the person can show that the way in which the power was exercised was unreasonable, that could be challenged by a judicial review which we discuss below at **1.49**.

1.34 However, it is important to read the scope of the duty in the statute carefully. The law has distinguished between general or target duties which are expressed in broad terms, leaving the public authority with a wide measure of latitude over the steps to be taken to perform the duty owed to the relevant section of the public and personal or particular duties which are specific and precise and which are owed to each individual member of a relevant section of the public. Target duties must be performed, notwithstanding their general nature, and they must be discharged in accordance with the principles of public law and they can be enforced like powers through judicial review. However, the public authority has discretion in how it delivers services under the duty and individuals have no personal right of action.

1.35 The duty on local housing authorities to review housing conditions in their districts which is set out in section 3 of the Act is an example of a general or target duty.

1.36 If we look at section 80 of the Act we can demonstrate the difference between powers and duties. Section 80 is headed 'designation of selective licensing areas'. Subsection one provides local housing authorities with a power to designate areas as areas for selective licensing. What it says is:

'(1)   A local housing authority may designate either –
  (a)   the area of their district, or
  (b)   an area in their district,
  as subject to selective licensing, if the requirements of subsections (2) and (9) are met.'

1.37 The crucial word in the subsection is 'may'.

1.38 If we look at subsection (2) we find a different formulation. It states:

'(2)   The authority must consider that –
  (a)   the first or second set of general conditions mentioned in subsection (3) or (6) or
  (b)   any conditions specified in an order under subsection (7) as an additional set of conditions
  are satisfied in relation to the area.'

1.39 What this means is that once the local housing authority has decided to exercise its discretion then it must take heed of particular sets of conditions.

1.40 These subsections also demonstrate two other points about reading statutory materials. First, as we pointed out above, the general definition sections are very important. So you need to know the definition of local housing authority. Secondly, you frequently need to refer to other subsections in order to fully understand the requirements of the provision. So here you need to read subsections 3, 6, 7 and 9, in addition to 1 and 2, in order to fully understand the provision.

STATUTORY INTERPRETATION

1.41 Unfortunately, but unavoidably, the meaning of statutory provisions is not always clear. The courts have an important role in deciding the meaning of statutes when these are in dispute. This process is called statutory interpretation. This is not the book to explain in detail how courts interpret statutes. If you are interested in learning more you may enjoy *Learning Legal Rules'* by James Holland and Julian Webb (OUP, 2006).

1.42 Statutory interpretation has evolved over centuries. When courts have had to decide what a statute says, there has developed a series of so called 'rules' that guide the courts. Their effect is to set out the approach that should be adopted by the courts. There are three main 'rules'. First, the 'literal rule', which says that the words in a statute are taken to have their literal meaning unless such an interpretation produces a nonsensical result. In that case, the 'golden rule' applies which says that if the literal meaning produces an absurd result then you look at it in the overall context of the statute. If these two 'rules' do not help then the 'mischief rule' is applied. This rule states that you interpret the meaning of the word in the light of what the problem or mischief was that the statute was passed to deal with.

CIVIL LAW AND CRIMINAL LAW

1.43 The state sets out rules which define certain types of unacceptable behavior as criminal. These rules form the criminal law. It is the state which has the main responsibility for enforcing those rules and punishing infringements of the rules. The criminal justice system is the mechanism by which action is taken to deal with those suspected of committing offences. People can be convicted only where the evidence points to guilt 'beyond reasonable doubt'. This is described as the criminal burden of proof. The parties to proceedings are the prosecution and the defence. There are a number of criminal offences within the Housing Act 2004. For instance, it is a criminal offence if a person controlling or managing a house in multiple occupation to do so without a licence. The criminal offences within the Housing Act 2004 are enforced through the magistrates' court.

1.44 In contrast, the civil law is not concerned with punishment but with remedies. The law provides certain rules for individuals and organisations to regulate their behaviour and relationships, for instance determining when contracts have been breached. However, breaches of these rules are not crimes and it is for individuals and organisations to decide whether to take action when these rules have been breached.

1.45 Certain behaviour may constitute both a criminal offence and a breach of civil law. Civil action can be taken against someone whose behaviour apparently constitutes a criminal offence, even if the evidence is not strong enough to result in a criminal conviction. The burden of proof in the civil courts is lower than in the criminal courts – the claimant in a civil case only has to demonstrate that it is more likely than not that the breach took place. In other words the burden of proof is the balance of probabilities.

PUBLIC LAW AND PRIVATE LAW

1.46 So far we have highlighted the distinction between courts and Parliament, between common law and statute, and between criminal law and civil law. There is another distinction within civil law which is important – that between public and private law. Public law cases are cases brought by public authorities, such as local authorities. Private law cases are cases brought by private individuals. For example, Housing Act cases are an area of public law. Public law proceedings, because they involve public authorities interfering with the way individuals live their lives, are required to conform to certain standards. Those standards are achieved through the operation of the law. The particular area of the law which performs this function is administrative law which we discuss below.

1.47 In contrast, an example of private law would be a dispute between a car owner and a garage over the quality of a repair to the car. If the owner refuses to pay the bill because of dissatisfaction with the quality of the repair, the garage may sue the car owner in the County Court. How the dispute is to be resolved by the court is set out in the law of contract and the rules of court. The outcome of the case, though, is not of interest to society as a whole, only to the parties to the dispute.

ADMINISTRATIVE LAW

1.48 The state is very powerful and well resourced in comparison with an individual. Administrative law attempts to ensure that justice is done between the state and the individual by embracing particular principles which operate to restrain arbitrary or wrong decision making by the state. These principles are openness (often described as transparency by lawyers and public administrators), fairness, rationality (including giving reasons for decisions), impartiality (which means that decision takers should be independent), accountability, the control of discretion, consistency, participation, efficiency, equity, and equal treatment. These principles can be collectively described as the requirements necessary for fairness, and are often referred to as the requirements of 'natural justice'. Sometimes these principles conflict, and then the decision maker must weigh up the various principles and make the best decision he or she can in the circumstances.

1.49 Natural justice means that whatever the law is, citizens are entitled to have the law applied fairly, in accordance with common law, and the courts will uphold that right. The mechanism available for people who believe that they have not been treated fairly by the state is to apply for judicial review. Judicial review is the process by which the courts oversee decisions made by public officials and ensure that they have been made fairly. Applications for judicial review are made to the Administrative Court which is a branch of the High Court. They must be made within three months of the decision which is being complained about.

1.50 It is possible that your decisions will be challenged by way of judicial review. Of course judicial review is also open to you as a remedy, if you feel that for instance a tribunal has behaved improperly, you can apply to the High Court for a judicial review of the proceedings.

1.51 In general judges will not substitute their decision for the public official's decision. What they will consider is the process of decision making. This means that you must ensure that your decision making process is open to scrutiny. Ask yourself – have you made a fair decision taking into account all relevant issues, and not being distracted by irrelevant ones? Has there been an opportunity for the other side to respond to your decision? Have you given clear reasons for the decision you have reached? The best way to ensure that your decisions can withstand judicial scrutiny is to record not only the decision, but the decision making process and the reasons upon which you based your decision.

THE HUMAN RIGHTS ACT

1.52 The legal responsibilities of public bodies are enhanced by the Human Rights Act 1998 (HRA). The HRA was one of the first pieces of legislation enacted by the incoming Labour Government in 1997. It was implemented on 2 October 2000 after a two year period for the training of the judiciary and public authorities. Its primary purpose is to enable the individual rights which are provided in the European Convention on Human Rights (ECHR) to be enforced through the UK courts. It provides a legal check based on human rights principles on the activities of Parliament and public bodies.

1.53 The HRA builds upon the mechanisms in the ECHR which recognises that a balance has to be reached between rights and responsibilities. Not all rights are absolute and frequently practitioners are required to balance competing rights. The ECHR provides practitioners with the tools of proportionality, necessity and legitimacy to enable them to reach decisions in individual cases.

1.54 The Act can be found on the web at www.opsi.gov.uk/ACTS/acts1998/19980042.htm.

The Ministry of Justice provides an excellent user friendly guide to the Human Rights Act see www.justice.gov.uk/docs/hr-handbook-introduction.pdf and further details are on the Ministry of Justice website www.justice.gov.uk/guidance/humanrights.htm.

1.55 Whilst we can provide only a brief overview of the workings of the HRA there are some important concepts with which you should be familiar.

1.56 Firstly only victims of breaches of Convention rights can bring proceedings under the Human Rights Act. So only the person who has been affected by an act or decision of a public authority can take action, in relation to that act or decision. This means that pressure groups cannot initiate legal proceedings, although they can help individual victims pursue their case.

1.57 Whilst the courts have to consider the Convention rights in all cases even if they do not involve a public authority, a victim can only bring a case under the Act if the act or decision in questions is one of a public authority. A public authority is a broader concept than you might think. It is best understood as a body carrying out a governmental or public function. Local authorities and their environmental health departments are public bodies. Other examples include schools, departments of central government such as the Home Office, hospitals and prisons. Private companies that exercise public functions, such as organisations that run private prisons are also public authorities under the Act.

1.58 Some bodies have mixed public and private functions. Many housing associations, for instance, carry out functions which courts may decide are public functions. However, other functions they carry out are clearly private functions.

1.59 The courts are still trying to get to grips with the meaning of public body at a time when there is an increasing privatisation of public functions. The latest significant decision was by the House of Lords in *L v Birmingham City Council* [2007] UKHL 27. In this case, a woman with Alzheimer's disease, aged 84 years, was threatened with eviction from the private care home where she was living because of what was said to be the bad behaviour of her family when they visited her. Medical opinion was that the person would be put at considerable risk if she were moved. Lawyers for the woman, known as YL to protect her privacy, issued proceedings arguing that it was a breach of YL's Human Rights (Article 8 – see **1.67**) if she was evicted. They argued in the House of Lords that the private care home was exercising the functions of a public body because the local authority had funded YL's placement there after assessing that she was in need of care because of her condition. The private care home argued that it was not carrying out public functions but was a private body, and it said that the funding source of any individual service user is irrelevant. The House of Lords decided that the provision of care services by a private body did not engage the provisions of the Human Rights Act, even in circumstances where a public body was paying the fees of the service user.

1.60 The European Court of Human Rights will allow domestic courts some space to make decisions which reflect their national domestic concerns, rather than impose its interpretation on the way the articles should operate. This leeway is described as the margin of appreciation. This is particularly relevant when the courts have to weigh up competing priorities, for instance individual liberty and national security. Of course the margin of appreciation can only go so far; the European Court of Human Rights does ensure some consistency in the interpretation of the Convention.

1.61 Rights are formulated in different ways under the Convention. Some rights are so fundamental that they are absolute. These rights include the right to protection from torture, inhuman and degrading treatment and the prohibition on slavery. Others, such as the right to liberty, are limited under explicit and finite circumstances that are set out in the Convention itself. Finally certain rights are qualified which means that interference with these rights is permissible only if the interference is:

- justified in law;

- is done with a permissible aim set out in the Convention;

- is necessary in a democratic society which means that it must fulfil a pressing social need, pursue a legitimate aim and be proportionate to the aims being pursued.

1.62 Proportionality is a particularly important requirement. Interference with rights is not justified if the means used to achieve the aim are disproportionate.

1.63 The convention rights which are most relevant to your work are summarised below.

1.64 Article 2 establishes a right to life. Examples of cases where breaches of Article 2 have been claimed included destitute asylum seekers who could not access health care or subsistence and prisoners forced to share cells with violent cellmates who may place their life in jeopardy. Failure to use powers to protect life could provoke a claim under the HRA. This could be relevant to, for instance, decisions about taking action on hazards or on granting a licence to an HMO.

1.65 Article 3 is the right not to be subjected to inhuman or degrading treatment, and could again be relevant to a number of decisions you have to take in connection with the Act. For instance, if you fail to take action in particular circumstances it may mean that a tenant is forced to live in degrading circumstances. However, you should note that the threshold for breach of the Article is high – so not all treatment that we might consider to be degrading would breach the Article.

1.66 Article 6, right to a fair trial, refers to the requirement for civil rights to be fairly determined, and criminal trials to contain full safeguards. The basic right is to a fair and public hearing within a reasonable time by an independent and impartial tribunal established by law. The way you decide to use your statutory powers under the Act could be challenged under this Article.

1.67 Article 8 provides a right to respect for family life and private life; any interference with this right must be both lawful and necessary, and proportionate. It is clear that preventing a landlord from using his property in the way he chooses could engage Article 8 by interfering with the landlord's private life. If the interference is carried out within the legal framework provided by the legislation the first test for interference – lawfulness – is satisfied. You must be careful to ensure that your actions are also necessary and proportionate. For instance it may be consistent with the legal framework and therefore legitimate to insist on categorising a particular risk within a property as Category 1. However, you must also be sure that such action is necessary and that the remedial action you require is proportionate to the risk which is being addressed.

1.68 One relevant example of where the HRA proved effective for a tenant is *R (Bernard) v Enfield LBC* [2002] EWHC 2282 (Admin). Here the High Court considered the application of Mrs Bernard, a severely disabled wheelchair user who lived with her family in inappropriate local authority accommodation. Despite the social services department having assessed her needs and recommending special adaptations, so that, for instance, Mrs Bernard could access the bathroom, the local authority failed to respond to the family's needs. The High Court found that the local authority had positive obligations to enable the family to live as normal a life as possible and to secure Mrs Bernard's physical integrity and human dignity. The lack of action by the local authority was a breach of Mrs Bernard's right to respect for family life, under Article 8 of the Convention.

1.69 Article 14 of the ECHR prohibits discrimination in the enjoyment of Convention rights. The grounds for discrimination are very broad; the article forbids on any ground such as sex, race, colour, language, religion, political or other opinion, national or social origin, association with a national minority, property, birth or other status. There is one important limit; it can only be invoked when there has been a breach of another article of the Convention. In effect, it piggybacks upon the other articles of the Convention. It means, for instance, it is illegal to treat landlords from one minority group differently from others if that treatment engages any of their Convention rights.

1.70 Article one of protocol one provides for the protection of property. This is described as the right to the peaceful enjoyment of possessions. It means that public authorities cannot usually interfere with the ownership or use of property except in when it is in accordance with law and in the public interest to do so. Empty Dwelling Management Orders could potentially be in breach of article one of protocol one. However action can be justified on the basis that it is in accordance with a statutory scheme which has as its purpose the public interest in the effective use of property. Nonetheless human rights principles demand that EDMOs are only made when it is proportionate and necessary – so you must be prepared to argue this in any tribunal.

THE LEGAL MECHANISMS FOR ENFORCING HUMAN RIGHTS

1.71 Generally when someone has been the victim of a potential breach of their convention rights the appropriate legal action will be judicial review of the public body's action by the High Court. Such cases usually have to be taken with one year of the action complained of.

1.72 When the court considers the human rights issue raised it will review the law to see if the public authority had any choice about the action it took. It will try to interpret the legislative basis of the public authority's action to see if it can be interpreted in a way which is compatible with Convention rights. If the legislation can be interpreted compatibly and the public authority is found to have acted in breach then the court can remedy that breach using its usual powers.

1.73 The Human Rights Act also gives the courts a power to grant damages for breach of Convention rights. However, the courts are reluctant to do this, and where they have made an award, the levels of damages have been quite small.

1.74 The greater political significance of the Human Rights Act lies in the actions the courts can take if the legislation cannot be interpreted compatibly. The court's powers depend upon the type of legislation that forms the basis of the public authority's action. If the legislation was secondary legislation then the court may quash or disapply that legislation. If the breach arises out of primary legislation – Acts of Parliament – then the court cannot quash the legislation. This is because the Human Rights Act maintains the supremacy of Parliament that must be recognised by the courts. Instead, what the courts can do, is to make a declaration of incompatibility. Such a declaration will not make that Act invalid and the public authority involved will not be acting unlawfully in applying the legislation. However, any declaration of incompatibility makes it clear to the government that there is a problem with the legislation and provides support for the victim in taking their challenge to Strasbourg.

1.75 There is another mechanism built into the Human Rights Act which is designed to ensure that all new legislation takes the European Convention into account. A minister who is introducing a Bill into Parliament has to make a statement as to whether or not the Bill is compatible with Convention rights and to highlight those provisions of the Bill which are relevant. All Bills are scrutinised by the Joint Parliamentary Committee on Human Rights which has considerable expertise in Human Rights law and is able to make proposals as to how a Bill can be made more compatible with Convention rights.

THE COURT STRUCTURE

1.76 Figure 1.1 gives an overall picture overview of the court system. Courts are arranged in a hierarchical structure. This means that a lower court must follow decisions of any court higher than itself in the judicial 'ladder' and that there is also a system of appeals against the decision of one court from one level to another. Cases begun in the lower courts can, normally, work their way up to the highest court, by way of appeal.

Figure 1.1

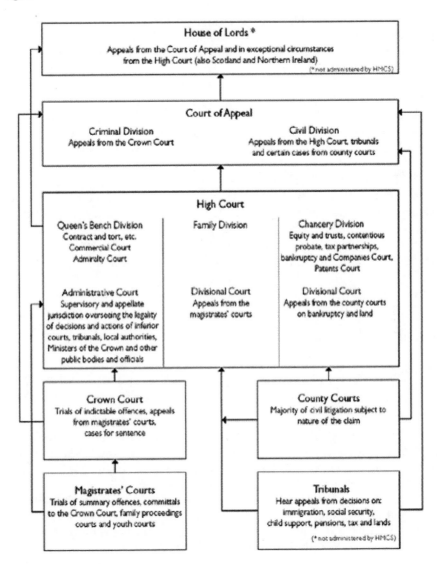

1.77   In the following sections we provide an outline of the operations of those courts which you are most likely to use in the course of your work.

CRIMINAL PROCEEDINGS IN THE MAGISTRATES' COURT

1.78   The magistrates' court is divided into different parts. There is the division into the criminal and civil, but there is also the distinction in criminal proceedings between the adult and youth courts, which deal with juveniles under the age of 18. The criminal functions of the magistrates' court are exercised by both the adult and the youth court benches. The magistrates also have important family (civil) functions. This account concentrates on criminal proceedings as it is this aspect of the work of the magistrates which you are most likely to encounter.

1.79   All criminal cases begin in the magistrates' court. The vast majority (95%) start there and stay there. They stay there because either there are no powers for the cases to be transferred anywhere else or the person involved (the defendant) agrees to the case being dealt with by the magistrates.

1.80   The magistrates' courts are the mainstay of the criminal justice system. Cases are heard either by three lay magistrates or one District Judge. The lay magistrates, or 'Justices of the Peace', as they are also known, are local people who volunteer their services. They have no formal legal qualifications, but are given legal and procedural advice by qualified clerks. District Judges are legally qualified, paid, full-time professionals and are usually based in the larger cities.

1.81   There are three types of criminal offences which are heard in the magistrates' court. These are:

(a)   summary offences;

(b)   indictable offences;

(c)   either way offences.

1.82   Summary offences are the most common types of offence. Examples include common assault, less serious criminal damage, and taking a motor vehicle without consent (this offence is known by the acronym 'TWOC'). They can normally be dealt with only in the magistrates' court. Therefore, the court has the limited powers of sentence which we describe below. The offences created by the Housing Act 2004 are summary offences, see for instance section 72 which sets out the offences in relation to licensing of houses in multiple occupation (HMOs). If we look at section 72(7) we see that someone who commits an offence by failing to comply with the conditions of his or her licence is liable on summary conviction to a fine.

1.83 Indictable only offences are cases that are 'just passing through' the magistrates' court. They are the serious offences, such as murder, rape, and arson that, for an adult (over 18), can be dealt with only by the Crown Court.

1.84 Either way offences are hybrid offences which, as the name implies, can be dealt with either by the magistrates' court or by the Crown Court before a judge and jury. An example of such an offence is theft.

1.85 Magistrates have restricted powers in relation to the sentences that they can impose. Many of the offences dealt with by the magistrates' court carry no power of imprisonment, and the heaviest penalty then can only be a fine or perhaps a community rehabilitation order. The statutorily prescribed penalty for the offences in relation to the licensing of HMOs (discussed above) is a fine not exceeding level 5 on the standard scale.

1.86 Where the magistrates have the power to imprison a person the maximum length of the sentence will be governed by the statute. Even where an offence might carry a maximum penalty of several years' imprisonment if it were dealt with by the Crown Court, the magistrates are limited in the length of sentence they can impose. For any one offence committed by an adult they can impose a maximum of only 6 months' imprisonment, assuming the offence merits such a sentence. In addition, if a person has committed more than one offence, each of which is an either way offence and each of which could have a 6 month sentence imposed for it, then the total maximum sentence the magistrates could impose is 12 months' imprisonment (ie two 6 month sentences to run consecutively). If the magistrates think that their powers, in relation to either way offences only, are inadequate, then after conviction they can commit the person to the Crown Court for sentence.

TRIBUNALS

1.87 A great deal of dispute resolution within the English legal system is carried out by tribunals. They hear a large number and a great variety of cases. Most are disputes, generally between the citizen and the state, such as in Appeals Service Tribunals which general hears social security appeals; but they also hear citizen against citizen disputes, as in Employment Tribunals.

1.88 Tribunals are created by statute and are administered by the relevant government department. Tribunals generally consist of three people, with only the chair being legally qualified. Their numbers have dramatically increased over the last 50 years. Currently there are about 80 types.

1.89 Their purpose is to provide a quicker and less formal forum than the courts and to allow cases to be adjudicated on by people with an expertise in the particular jurisdiction, so for instance psychiatrists sit on Mental Health Review Tribunals and surveyors on Residential Property Tribunals.

1.90 The advantages of the tribunal system are that they provide speedier and more cost-effective dispute resolution. In addition they can be argued to have the advantages of:

- informality;

- flexibility;

- specialisation;

- relief of congestion in the ordinary courts;

- awareness of policy in particular areas;

- a more private forum for the resolution of disputes.

1.91 The tribunal system is criticised on a range of issues. Tribunals may not be, or be seen to be, clearly independent of the government body whose decision is being challenged. Procedures and the quality of decision making vary enormously. Informality and simplicity of procedure is difficult to achieve in many of the complex social welfare fields in which tribunals operate, so that unrepresented parties feel themselves to be at a disadvantage, yet in the vast majority of tribunals there is no publicly funded legal help available (exceptions being the Mental Health Review Tribunal and the Immigration Appeal Tribunal) to pay for lawyers. As the Legal Action Group points out, those who are unrepresented encounter pitfalls, such as being unaware that an application is without merit, misunderstanding tribunal procedures, preparing inadequately for the hearing, or putting forward irrelevant facts and arguments.

1.92 The Government set up a comprehensive review of the tribunal system in June 2000 (the Leggatt Review). The report was published in August 2001, entitled *Tribunals for Users: One System, One Service.* It addresses many concerns about the tribunal service – the need for an enhanced role for the Council on tribunals, a greater standardisation of tribunal procedures, better judicial training, and clearer separation from government departments. The report can be found on the Department of Constitutional Affairs web site: www.dca.gov.uk.

1.93 The Government intends to create an 'increasingly unified tribunal system' with most tribunals brought together under the umbrella of the Department of Constitutional Affairs. It published a White Paper, *Transforming Public Services: Complaints, Redress and Tribunals* in July 2004. This goes beyond the Leggatt Review suggesting that a much more radical approach to the reform of dispute resolution is needed, one which concentrates on the needs of the users of the system and on proportionate dispute resolution.

1.94 In July 2004, the government published a White Paper, *Transforming Public Services: Complaints, redress and tribunals*. This forms the basis of Part 1 of the Tribunals, Courts and Enforcement Act 2007.

1.95 The main features of Part 1 of the Tribunals, Courts and Enforcement Act 2007 are:

- A new simplified statutory structure for tribunals, with two tiers of tribunals, the First Tier Tribunal and the Upper Tribunal.

- The Lord Chancellor will have the power to transfer existing tribunals to the new structure.

- A new judicial office – the Senior President of Tribunals – to oversee tribunal judiciary.

- New provisions for tribunal membership, rights of appeal from tribunals and new tribunal rules.

- The Upper Tribunal will have certain powers of judicial review.

- The Administrative Justice and Tribunals Council will replace the current Council on Tribunals and have a broader remit over the whole of the administrative justice system.

1.96 We will look in detail at the operation of the Residential Property Tribunal Service in Chapter 17 of this book. This is the tribunal with which you are likely to become most familiar.

SUMMARY

1.97 This introductory chapter is designed as an introduction to the legal environment for those readers who have little familiarity with it, and a reminder/reference point for other readers. We hope that you will turn to it when a general question, for instance about judicial review, or about the sentencing powers of magistrates, occurs to you when reading the rest of the book.

1.98 Our following chapters concentrate on the detailed operation of the Housing Act 2004.

Part II

HOUSING STANDARDS AND THE NEW HHSRS

Chapter 2

ENFORCEMENT OF HOUSING STANDARDS

2.1 Part 1 of the Act provides a simple framework. There is the Act. There are the Regulations. There is the Guidance. All three are required to use Part 1 of the Act. Then there is the case law. Part 1 of the Act introduces the Housing Health and Safety Rating System (HHSRS), an evidence-based system for assessing housing conditions. The new system is described as: 'a means of identifying faults in dwellings and of evaluating the potential effect of any faults on the health and safety of the occupants or visitors.' The underlying principle is that any residential premises should provide a safe and healthy environment.[1]

OUTLINE TO PART 1

2.2 The Act announces that the HHSRS will operate by reference to the existence of category 1 or category 2 hazards in residential premises. The Act provides that:

> '"category 1 hazard" means a hazard of a prescribed description which falls within a prescribed band as a result of achieving, under a prescribed method for calculating the seriousness of hazards of that description, a numerical score of or above a prescribed amount;
>
> "category 2 hazard" means a hazard of a prescribed description which falls within a prescribed band as a result of achieving, under a prescribed method for calculating the seriousness of hazards of that description, a numerical score below the minimum amount prescribed for a category 1 hazard of that description; . . .'

2.3 The Act imposes a duty on local authorities to take enforcement action where a category 1 hazard exists and gives discretion to take action where a category 2 hazard exists. Sections 2 and 4 of the Act provide for regulations to be made to prescribe descriptions of hazards, the method for assessing the seriousness of hazards and the manner and extent of inspections of residential premises to see whether category 1 or 2 hazards exist. Part 1 of the Act replaces the previous test for unfitness and requires that the HHSRS is to be used in conjunction with new kinds of enforcement action, in addition to demolition orders and slum clearance declarations which are two means of enforcement

---

[1] Paragraph 1.12 of the Operating Guidance.

retained from Part 9 of the 1985 Act. The new kinds of enforcement action are described in part 1 and in Schedules 1 to 3 of the Act including, where applicable, the means for suspension, variation, revocation and appeal. Part 1 of the Act also imposes a duty to keep housing conditions under review and provides in what circumstances a local housing authority must inspect or arrange for inspection of residential premises. The Act also puts the duty to give reasons for taking enforcement action on a statutory footing describing what the reasons for taking a chosen action must address.[2]

2.4   The available enforcement measures centre on the improvement notice, the prohibition order and the hazard awareness notice, the key characteristics of which are contained in the following table. Emergency measures[3] and default action[4] are based on the improvement notice and the prohibition order. There is good reason to believe that the hazard awareness notice may be the course of action that local housing authorities most frequently use. Such a notice advises of the existence of the hazard and gives details of what remedial action (if any) the LHA consider would be practicable and appropriate. The following table lists in relation to improvement notices, prohibition orders and hazard awareness notices (i) the premises in relation to which each may be served, (ii) the necessary circumstances which must exist and (iii) who must be served:

Improvement Notice

The premises in relation to which an improvement notice may be served	The notice may require action to be taken in relation to the dwelling or HMO containing the residential premises on which the hazard (irrespective of which category the hazard is) exists.[5]
	If the residential premises on which the hazard exists are one or more flats or on the common parts of a building containing one or more flats then the notice can require action to be taken in relation to any part of the building.[6]
	If the deficiency from which the hazard arises is situated in any part of a building, containing one or more flats, or its common parts, that is not included in any residential premises, then the improvement notice may only require remedial action to be taken in relation to those non residential parts if it is necessary for the action to be taken in order to protect the health and safety of any actual or potential occupiers of one or more of the flats.[7]
Circumstances for service of an improvement notice	(1) Where the authority are satisfied that a category 1 hazard exists;[8] or

---

[2]   Section 8(3).
[3]   Emergency remedial action and the emergency prohibition order.
[4]   Either taken with or without agreement: see Schedule 3.
[5]   Sections 11(3)(a) and 12(3).
[6]   Sections 11(3)(b), 12(3).
[7]   Sections 11(3)(c), (4), 12(3).
[8]   Section 11(1)(a).

Improvement Notice

	(2) where the authority are satisfied a category 2 hazard exists;[9] and
	(3) where there is no interim or final management order in existence;[10] and
	(4) where the notice is not in respect of land which has been approved by the authority for re-development by the owner and the re-development is being proceeded with, within any specified time limit;[11] and
	(5) where such relevant guidance as may be issued pursuant to section 9 has been expressly considered by the authority.[12]
Who must be served with an improvement notice	(1) In relation to licensed dwellings and licensed HMOs the notice should be served on the licence holder.[13]
	(2) If the dwelling or HMO is not licensed then the notice has to be served on the person having control or if an HMO then on the person having control or the person managing the HMO.[14]
	(3) In the case of an HMO, which is a flat, the local housing authority must serve either the owner or the person managing the flat.[15]
Who must be served with a copy of the improvement notice	Every person who to the local housing authority's knowledge has a relevant interest (freehold, mortgage or lease) or is an occupier of the premises specified in the notice.[16]

Prohibition Order

The premises which a prohibition order may prohibit use of	(1) If the residential premises on which the hazard exists are a dwelling or HMO, the order may prohibit use of the dwelling or HMO.[17]
	(2) If those premises on which the hazard exists are one or more flats it can prohibit use of the building containing the flats or any part of the building or any external parts.[18]
	(3) If those premises are the common parts of a building containing one or more flats it can prohibit use of the building containing the flats or any part of the building or any external parts.[19]

---

[9]   Section 12(1)(a).
[10] Sections 11(1)(b), 12(1)(b). If an improvement notice has been served and a management order comes into force the improvement notice is treated as not served, if the notice is operative when a management order comes into force then the notice ceases to have effect: see section 39. For the time when an improvement notice becomes operative see section 15 which provides that the notice is operative, subject to it being suspended and subject to whether or not the notice is subject of an appeal, 21 days after service.
[11] Section 39(5).
[12] Section 9(2).
[13] Schedule 1, paragraph 1.
[14] Schedule 1, paragraph 2.
[15] The owner can only be the person served if the authority believe that the owner ought to take the action specified in the notice; see the word 'and' at the end of Schedule 1, paragraph 3(3)(a).
[16] Schedule 1, paragraph 5.
[17] Sections 20(3)(a), 21(3).
[18] Sections 20(3)(b), 21(3).

Improvement Notice

	(4) However, use of parts of a building (which comprise flats) or its external parts which are not included in any residential premises, cannot be subject of prohibition in the order unless the authority are satisfied that it is necessary for the action to be taken in order to protect the health and safety of any actual or potential occupiers of one or more of the flats.[20]
Circumstances for service of a valid prohibition order	(1) Where a category 1 hazard exists;[21] or
	(2) where a category 2 hazard exists;[22] and
	(3) where there is no interim or final management order in existence.[23]
	(4) Where the order is not in respect of land which has been approved by the authority for re-development by the owner and the re-development is being proceeded with;[24] and
	(5) where such relevant guidance as may be issued pursuant to section 9 has been expressly considered by the authority.[25] The current draft guidance points to a number of matters which should be addressed including the availability of local accommodation for re-housing of any displaced occupants.
Who must be served with a prohibition order	(1) Every person who the authority knows is an owner or occupier of any part of the premises;[26]
	(2) every person the authority knows is entitled or authorised to permit persons to occupy the whole or part of the premises;[27] or
	(3) every known mortgagee of the whole or part of the premises.[28] Each person falling in to any of the above three categories has to be served within 7 days of the order being made.[29]
Who must be served with a copy of the prohibition order	Not applicable because the category of persons who have to be served with the prohibition order is so wide.

Hazard Awareness Notice

---

[19] Sections 20(3)(c), 21(3).
[20] Sections 20(4)(b), 21(3).
[21] Section 20(1)(a).
[22] Section 21(1)(a).
[23] Sections 20(1)(b), section 21(1)(b). If a prohibition order has been served and a management order comes into force the order is treated as not served, see section 39(2)(b); if the order is already operative when a management order comes into force then the notice ceases to have effect; see section 39(2)(a). For the time when a prohibition order becomes operative see section 24 which provides that the order is operative, subject to it being suspended and subject to whether or not the order is subject of an appeal, 28 days after service.
[24] Section 39(5).
[25] Section 9(2).
[26] Schedule 2, paragraph 1(2)(a).
[27] Schedule 2, paragraph 1(2)(b).
[28] Schedule 2, paragraph 1(2)(c).
[29] Schedule 2, paragraph 1(3).

Improvement Notice

The premises in respect of which a hazard awareness notice may be served	(1) If the residential premises on which the hazard exists are a dwelling or HMO which is not a flat, it may be served in respect of the dwelling or the HMO.[30] (2) If those premises are one or more flats it may be served in respect of the building containing the flat or flats or any part of the building or any external parts.[31] (3) If those premises are the common parts of a building containing one or more flats it may be served in respect of the building or any part of the building or any external parts.[32] However, the notice may not be served in respect of any part of a building (which comprise flats) or its external parts which are not included in any residential premises on which the hazard exists, unless the authority are satisfied (a) that the deficiency from which the hazard arises is situated there, and (b) that it is desirable for the notice to be served in the interests of the health and safety of any actual or potential occupiers of one or more of the flats.[33]
Circumstances for service of a valid hazard awareness Order	(1) Where category 1 hazard exists;[34] or (2) where category 2 hazard exists;[35] and (3) where there is no interim or final management order in existence;[36] and (4) where such relevant guidance as may be issued pursuant to section 9 has been expressly considered by the authority.[37]
Who has to be served with the notice	(1) In relation to licensed dwellings and licensed HMOs the notice should be served on the licence holder.[38] (2) If the dwelling or HMO is not licensed then the notice has to be served on the person having control or if an HMO then on the person having control or the person managing the HMO.[39] (3) In the case of a dwelling which is unlicensed or an HMO, which is also unlicensed, and is a flat; the local housing authority has a choice of who to serve, either the owner, the person managing the flat or the person who in the authority's opinion ought to take the action specified.[40]
To whom copies must also be sent	(1) Every person who to the local housing authority's knowledge has a relevant interest (freehold, mortgage or lease) or is an occupier of the premises specified in the notice.[41] (2) These 'copy' notices must be served within seven days of the service of the actual notice.[42]

2.5 Part 1 also specifies when a local housing authority must consult the fire and rescue authority for the area.[43] The relevant provision[44] together with the

---

[30] Section 28(3)(a).
[31] Section 28(3)(b).
[32] Section 28(3)(c).
[33] Section 28(4).
[34] Section 28(1).
[35] Section 29(1).
[36] Sections 28(1)(b), 29(1)(b).
[37] Section 9(2).
[38] Sections 28(7), 29(7) and Schedule 1, paragraph 1.
[39] Sections 28(7), 29(7) and Schedule 1, paragraph 2.
[40] Sections 28(7), 29(7) and Schedule 1, paragraph 3.
[41] Sections 28(7), 29(7) and Schedule 1, paragraph 5.
[42] Schedule 1, paragraph 5(4).
[43] See 'Protocol between LHAs and FRA to improve fire safety' published by the CIEH.

comprehensive changes to fire safety law introduced by the regulations,[45] place differing responsibilities on local housing authorities and on fire and rescue authorities. A fire hazard for the purposes of section 10 is one where the risk of harm arises from exposure to uncontrolled fire and associated smoke.[46]

2.6   In discharging the duty in relation to category 1 hazards, where there is a choice of enforcement action, the authority must take the action which they consider to be the most appropriate.[47] But beyond that the Act says very little about the workings and method of the rating system it has introduced, instead leaving the detail to the relevant Regulations and to the Guidance.

THE REGULATIONS

2.7   The Act provides that Regulations will prescribe a method for calculating the seriousness of hazards and that Regulations may prescribe the manner and the extent to which premises are to be inspected and the manner in which the assessments of hazards are to be made. The relevant Regulations are The Housing Health and Safety Rating System (England) Regulations 2005, SI 2005/3208 and The Housing Health and Safety Rating System (Wales) Regulations 2006, SI 2006/1702.

THE METHOD[48]

2.8   The task on inspection is to assess the likelihood of an occurrence, deriving from any of the 29 prescribed hazards, that could cause harm and to assess the probable severity of the outcome, if it did happen. Probable severity is divided into four different classes of harm which are specified in Schedule 2 to the HHSRS Regulations.[49] The calculation of a hazard score also includes appraisal of the likelihood of the feared potential occurrence occurring over the next 12 months.[50] Once the score has been decided it is given a banding[51] which in turn decides the category the hazard is placed in. Except in relation to a perceived harm arising from a lack of adequate space for living and

---

[44]   Section 10.
[45]   Regulatory Reform (Fire Safety) Order 2005, SI 2005/1541. For Wales see paragraph 2(b) of The National Assembly for Wales (Transfer Of Functions) Order 2006, SI 2006/1458.
[46]   Regulation 4 in SI 2005/3208, which for Wales is SI 2006/1702.
[47]   Section 5(4).
[48]   The term 'method' is used in section 2(3).
[49]   The Housing Health and Safety Rating System (England) Regulations 2005, SI 2005/3208 and The Housing Health and Safety Rating System (Wales) Regulations 2006, SI 2006/1702.
[50]   See Regulation 5(2) of the HHSRS Regulations.
[51]   The different bands are set out in Regulation 6 of the HHSRS Regulations.

sleeping,[52] the assessment of the likelihood and severity of harm from the prescribed hazard is not just to actual occupier but also to a deemed potential occupier.[53]

THE GUIDANCE

2.9 In addition to providing the legal framework and containing the workings of the different enforcement measures, Part 1 of the Act provides for the issue of binding regulations, and thirdly, mandates[54] local housing authorities to have regard to guidance when exercising their functions in relation to inspections, the assessment of hazards and in relation to the taking of any enforcement action.

2.10 The statutory guidance comes into two main documents: the Operating Guidance covering inspections and the assessment of hazards and the Enforcement Guidance.

2.11 The Operating Guidance, published by the ODPM in February 2006 comprises five chapters and substantial annexes taking it in total to 185 pages. The stated aim of the Guidance is to provide guidance on the technical aspects of the HHSRS assessment and to assist in the correct understanding and application of the HHSRS.

2.12 A brief look at the content to the Operating Guidance best demonstrates how essential it is to practitioners:
Chapter 1
Introduction and Background
Chapter 2
Terminology, and Extent and Purpose of the Guidance
Chapter 3
Overview of Rating Hazards
The HHSRS Formula
Judging the Likelihood
Judging the Spread of Harm outcomes
Generating a Hazard Score
The Hazard Bands

---

[52] Specified as a prescribed hazard in paragraph 11 of Schedule 1 to the HHSRS Regulations.

[53] Regulation 2 of the HHSRS Regulations therefore broadens the statutory definition of occupier, which otherwise operates in the rest of Part 1 by virtue of sections 53 and 262(6) to include a potential occupier. The definition of occupier in section 262(6) apparently excludes trespassers but includes a licensee and occupiers with an estate eg a tenant, or interest in the premises. A legal interest would include a right to occupy under section 12 of the Trusts of Land and Appointment of Trustees Act 1996 that applies to those with a beneficial interest in a trust for sale in respect of the occupied premises. Case law may have to determine whether a trespasser who occupies for long enough might be said to acquire a right to respect for his or her home and whether that could amount to an interest for the purposes of section 262(6) of the Act.

[54] Section 9(2).

2.13 The Enforcement Guidance is slimmer and aimed at helping local housing authorities decide which is the appropriate enforcement action under section 5 and how they should exercise their discretionary powers under section 7.[55] In doing so it replaces the Guidance contained in Annex B of Circular 17/96 which gave a strategic approach to private sector renewal and also replaces the guidance in Circular 12/92 which gave authorities guidance on standards of fitness in HMOs.[56]

2.14 In practice it is the Enforcement Guidance which is more likely to be in issue when it comes to challenging enforcement action by way of appeal to the Residential Property Tribunal. This is so because, save in the exceptional case of irrational and obvious error in calculation or in banding, the scope for challenging the assessment of the hazard by reference to the Operating Guidance will arise far less frequently than the scope for asking the tribunal to choose, at a *de novo* hearing, what it considers to be the most appropriate course of action on the given facts of an agreed assessment.

---

[55] Paragraph 1.1 of the Enforcement Guidance ODPM Feb 2006.
[56] Paragraph 1.2 of the Enforcement Guidance.

STATUS OF THE STATUTORY GUIDANCE

2.15 Since section 9 requires an authority to have regard to such guidance it is a statutory document and although the Guidance does not say so failure to follow it would be a highly relevant matter to a Tribunal's decision. In judicial review terms parties affected would have a legitimate expectation that the housing authority would correctly apply the Guidance. Whereas Regulations specify the way inspections and assessments are to be carried out[57] the Guidance does not have the same binding effect.

2.16 Any local housing authority should consider with great care both the Operating Guidance and the Enforcement Guidance, from which it should depart only in exceptional circumstances and where it has cogent reasons for doing so. In theory the Guidance does not rule out a reasoned but significant departure where there are compelling individual facts. However, there is no scope to disregard it because an authority disagrees with the government's advice. It follows that there is no general discretion to depart from the Guidance where an authority thinks it expedient to do so.[58] On the contrary, the tribunal will expect them to follow it.[59] If there has been a procedural error in not specifically having referred to the applicable guidance, this may not be fatal if in substance the Guidance expected consideration of the very same issues which an authority did address, and so the procedural error made no difference.[60]

---

[57] See section 4(5) in conjunction with regulations 4-7 and schedules 1 and 2 of SI 2005/3208 and for Wales: SI 2006/1702.

[58] However, even if the HHSRS Guidance has greater weight than may be accorded to planning policy guidance (now called statements) which sometimes can be departed from where material considerations indicate otherwise, what has been said in relation to this PPGs is still relevant to housing authorities and not just in the context of housing enforcement matters. The following quote is useful if the various references to 'planning' are read as housing enforcement and the references to the 'PPGs' are read as the Guidance: 'PPGs are not delegated legislation and do not have the force of statute. They are guidance and not tramlines. They do not purport to deal definitively with every situation which may arise. They are important because they represent government policy in relation to planning, because by the fact of planning authorities having regard to them a desirable consistency of approach to planning matters nationwide is promoted and because they inform the Secretary of State when he makes those planning decisions which fall to him to be made and when, for example, a planning authority decides to refuse an application it is desirable it has in mind the policy approach which is likely to be considered in the event of an appeal' per Jowitt J in *R v Wakefield Metropolitan District Council Ex Parte Pearl Assurance plc* (1997) 11 EG 32.

[59] An example where departure from guidance was permitted is *R (on the application of Munjaz) v Mersey Care NHS Trust* [2006] 4 All ER 736 HL, the facts of which concerned the seclusion of a prisoner transferred to a high security hospital whose status was subject to less frequent reviews than the Government guidance required, but where there were other monitoring, notification and appeal procedures which the House of Lords considered, in context, would prevent breach of rights under the ECHR.

[60] A possibility contemplated by Carnwath J as he then was in *R v Newham Borough Council, ex p Bones* (1993) 25 HLR 357 but on the facts, found not to have been the case.

Chapter 3

THE HOUSING HEALTH AND SAFETY
RATING SYSTEM (HHSRS)

INTRODUCTION

3.1   In April 2006,[1] the Housing Health and Safety Rating System was introduced as the statutory method for assessing housing conditions for the purposes of Part 1 of the Housing Act 2004. It is a risk assessment approach, focusing on the potential threats to health and safety.

3.2   The principle underlying the System is that a dwelling, including the structure, associated outbuildings, garden, yard or other amenity space, and means of access, should provide a safe and healthy environment for the occupants and any visitors. However, this principle is impossible to satisfy completely as some hazards are necessary and even desirable – eg electricity, gas, stairs, windows, and cooking facilities – so these necessary and unavoidable hazards should be as safe as possible.

3.3   The HHSRS lists 29 'Hazards' that, to a greater or lesser extent, can be attributed to the state and condition of the dwelling (see Table 3.1). The nature of the hazards differs widely, as does the type of health outcome that they can cause.[2] The effect of some hazards, such as excess cold and dampness, will be slow and insidious, while for others, such as the fall hazards, the effect will be almost instantaneous. The outcomes from hazards can be physical injuries, illnesses and other health conditions. To allow the different types of outcomes to be compared, the possible outcomes are classified according the degree of incapacity the victim will suffer (see Table 3.1 for examples of the four Classes of Harm). In addition, the severity of the outcome will vary; some hazards such as asbestos and radon can cause death, while for others, such as noise, death is very unlikely. The HHSRS limits the health outcomes to four 'Classes of Harm', all serious enough for the victim to seek medical attention. It does not cover minor health outcomes, such as minor cuts and bruising, where the victim is likely to self-help.

---

[1]   Housing Health and Safety Rating System (England) Regulations 2005, SI 2005/3208. In Wales, June 2006 by Housing Health and Safety Rating System (Wales) Regulations 2006, SI 2006/1702 (W164).

[2]   Profiles describing each hazard, their public health importance, and the dwelling characteristic that influence them are given in Annex D of *Housing Health and Safety Rating System: Operating Guidance* (ODPM, 2006).

3.4 To give a truer indication of the importance of a hazard, the System is design to take account of both the frequency of a hazardous occurrence and the potential severity of the outcome. For example, a relatively infrequent occurrence that results in a very severe or fatal outcome may be more significant than an occurrence which happens frequently but causes a relatively minor outcome.

3.5 The System also recognises that there are a range of possible outcomes that could result from a hazardous occurrence. For example, below a window there may be soft earth on one side and spiked railings on the other; so there would be a 50% chance of bruising and a 50% chance of serious puncture wounds from a fall out of that window.

Table 3.1: HHSRS Potential Housing Hazards

Physiological Requirements	**Protection Against Infection**
Damp and mould growth etc	Domestic hygiene, pests and refuse
Excessive cold	Food safety
Excessive heat	Personal hygiene, sanitation and
Asbestos etc	drainage
Biocides	Water supply
CO and fuel combustion productions	
Lead	
Radiation	
Uncombusted fuel gas	
Volatile organic compounds	
Psychological Requirements	**Protection Against Accidents**
Crowding and Space	Falls associated with baths etc
Entry by intruders	Falling on level surfaces
Lighting	Falling on stairs etc
Noise	Falling between levels
	Electrical hazards
	Fire
	Flames, hot surfaces etc
	Collision and entrapment
	Explosions
	Position and operability of amenities etc
	Structural collapse and falling elements

CLASS I

This covers the most extreme harm outcomes. It includes: death from any cause; lung cancer; mesothelioma and other malignant lung tumours; permanent paralysis below the neck; regular severe pneumonia; permanent loss of consciousness; 80% burn injuries.

CLASS II

This class includes severe conditions, including: cardio-respiratory disease; asthma; non-malignant respiratory diseases; lead poisoning; anaphylactic shock; crytosporidiosis; legionnaires disease; myocardial infarction; mild stroke; chronic confusion; regular severe fever; loss of a hand or foot; serious fractures; serious burns; loss of consciousness for days.

CLASS III

This class includes serious conditions such as: eye disorders; rhinitis; hypertension; sleep disturbance; neuro-pyschological impairment; sick building syndrome; regular and persistent dermatitis, including contact dermatitis; allergy; gastro-enteritis; diarrhoea; vomiting; chronic severe stress; mild heart attack; malignant but treatable skin cancer; loss of a finger; fractured skull and severe concussion; serious puncture wounds to head or body; severe burns to hands; serious strain or sprain injuries; regular and severe migraine.

CLASS IV

This Class includes moderate harm outcomes which are still significant enough to warrant medical attention. Examples are: pleural plaques; occasional severe discomfort; benign tumours; occasional mild pneumonia; broken finger; slight concussion; moderate cuts to face or body; severe bruising to body; regular serious coughs or colds.

To enable the severity of the risk from each of the 29 hazards to be compared, the HHSRS uses a numerical score generated by a formula (see Table 3.2). The formula requires three sets of numbers: the likelihood expressed as a ratio; the spread of outcomes expressed as percentages; and a Class of Harm weighting to reflect the degree of incapacity. The first two figures are based on the assessor's judgments; the weightings are fixed.

Table 3.2: Examples of Health Outcomes in the Four HHSRS Classes of Harm

		Class of Harm Weighting		Likelihood		Spread of Harm
SI	=	10,000	X	$\dfrac{1}{L}$	X	O1
SII	=	1,000	X	$\dfrac{1}{L}$	X	O2
SIII	=	300	X	$\dfrac{1}{L}$	X	O3
SIV	=	10	X	$\dfrac{1}{L}$	X	O4

Hazard Score = (SI+SII+SIII+SIV)

Where:

L = the Likelihood of an occurrence

O = the Outcome expressed as a percentage for each Class of Harm

S = the row product for each Class of Harm.

(Based on Figure 1 in *Housing Health and Safety Rating System, Operating Guidance* (ODPM, 2006)

3.6   As it would be very time-consuming to have to assess each of the 29 hazards at each dwelling, national averages have been calculated for each hazard. The national averages were calculated by matching data on housing conditions from sources such as the English House Condition Survey,[3] with data on reported injuries, illnesses and other health conditions from sources such as the Hospital Episode Statistics and the Home Accident Surveillance System.[4] These enabled averages to be calculated, generally, for four age bands of dwellings and both for single household house and for other dwellings.[5]

---

[3]   See CLG website at www.communities.gov.uk/housing/housingresearch/housingsurveys/ englishhousecondition/.

[4]   Now archived at www.rospa.com/hassandlass/.

[5]   See *Statistical Evidence to Support the Housing Health and Safety Rating System* (2003) ODPM. The national averages are given in the hazard profiles of the Operating Guidance, op cit, n 4.

3.7 This means that the full assessment of a hazard is only necessary where a hazard is significantly worse than average.[6] This approach has meant that even in dwellings in very poor condition it is very unusual to have to assess fully more than five hazards.

3.8 As well as calculating national averages, it was possible from the statistical evidence to calculate whether an age group of the population was more vulnerable to a particular hazard than the rest of the population. In the majority of cases where there was a vulnerable age group is was generally either the very young, 0–5 years old, or the elderly, 60 years and over.

THE ASSESSMENT PROCESS

3.9 The assessment process consists of four stages:

- A full survey of the dwelling

- Determine which hazards any deficiencies contribute

- Judge whether the deficiencies make a hazard significantly worse than the average

- For those hazards significantly worse than average, judge whether the deficiencies increase the likelihood; and whether the deficiencies increase the severity of the outcome.

DWELLING SURVEY

3.10 A full inspection should be carried out to identify all deficiencies.[7] A deficiency is an unsatisfactory condition arising from an inherent defect, or from deterioration and a lack of repair. To determine whether a there is a deficiency it is necessary to understand the basic functions of each element (ie each part of the structure and each amenity and facility) are intended to perform.

3.11 A full survey is necessary to ensure all deficiencies that could contribute to hazards are identified. As it is the potential effect of a deficiency that is important under the HHSRS, even minor deficiencies should be noted – those defects which could easily and cheaply be remedied. The inspection should be

---

6   See HHSRS Regs, reg 6(1)(b).
7   Note that unless it is an emergency, the owner and occupier of the premises should be informed that an inspection is to be carried out: see section 239(5) of the Housing Act 2004.

carried out having regard to guidance given[8] and an accurate record, in written or electronic form, of the state of the dwelling based on the inspection must be kept.[9]

ATTRIBUTING DEFICIENCIES TO HAZARDS

3.12 Attributing the deficiencies to hazards is necessary as it is a whole dwelling assessment and it is the cumulative effect that is assessed.

3.13 A single deficiency could contribute to several hazards, and several deficiencies could be contributing to a single hazard. Also, there may be deficiencies in several locations contributing to the same hazard. For example, there may be dampness present in several rooms, or there may be several sets of steps and stairs.

JUDGING WHETHER A HAZARD IS SIGNIFICANTLY WORSE THAN AVERAGE

3.14 The hazard profiles given in the *Operating Guidance* include 'National Average Likelihoods', 'Spread of Harm Outcomes', and 'Hazard Scores' for up to eight dwelling types (see Table 3.3 for an example). The inspector should determine whether, for the particular age and type of dwelling surveyed, any of the hazards are significantly worse than the average.

3.15 While hazards are present in every dwelling (doors, heating systems, windows etc) in the majority of cases most hazards will be around the average. As the likelihood, spread of outcomes and hazard score is known for the hazards judged 'average', only those hazards which are significantly worse than average need to be fully assessed.

---

[8]   Currently, the *Housing Health and Safety Rating System: Operating Guidance* (2006), op cit, n 2. See in particular Chapters 4 and 5, and Annex B.
[9]   HHSRS Regulations, reg 5.

Table 3.3: Falling on stairs: average likelihood and health outcomes for all persons aged 60 years and over, 1997–1999

Dwelling type and age		Average Likeli-hood 1 in	Spread of health outcomes				Average HHSRS scores
			Class I %	Class II %	Class III %	Class IV %	
Houses	Pre 1920	218	2.2	7.7	22.1	68.0	170
	1920–45	226	2.1	7.4	20.5	70.0	156
	1946–79	256	1.6	6.6	21.6	70.2	116
	Post 1979	256	1.4	6.3	25.3	67.0	112
Flats	Pre 1920	214	3.9	8.0	19.3	68.8	249
	1920–45	263	1.6	2.8	20.1	75.5	97
	1946–79	410	2.8	5.3	17.7	74.2	96
	Post 1979	409	2.6	5.2	19.4	72.8	92
	All	245	1.9	6.7	21.7	69.7	134

(Based on Table in Housing Health and Safety Rating System, Operating Guidance (ODPM, 2006))

ASSESSING THE SIGNIFICANTLY WORSE THAN AVERAGE HAZARDS

3.16   For the assessment, the current occupiers, if any, are disregarded, and the assessment is made on the basis of the age group most vulnerable to the particular hazard being assessed. There are three good reasons for this:

- It is the dwelling that is being assessed, not the dwelling as occupied. If it was the dwelling as occupied, then a further assessment would be needed as soon as the occupation changed.

- If the dwelling is assessed as safe for the vulnerable age group, then it will be safe for all.

• It is possible to assess an empty dwelling.

3.17 Taking account of all the deficiencies contributing to the hazard, the inspector first judges the likelihood of a hazardous occurrence over the next 12 months that could result in harm to a member of the age group most vulnerable to that hazard.

3.18 A precise judgment of likelihood is not required, but a range: eg in the range 1 in 24 to 1 in 42, or in the range 1 in 75 to 1 in 130. However, while it is a range that is to be judged by the inspector, the HHSRS formula uses a 'Representative Scale Point'. This means that the formula will use 1 in 32 to represent the range of 1 in 24 to 1 in 42.[10]

3.19 Judging the likelihood involves taking account of the location and severity of the deficiency(ies) contributing to the hazard. For example, anyone entering a dwelling will be exposed to some damp and mould growth in an entrance hall, but that exposure will be for a short period on entering and leaving. The same amount of dampness and mould growth in a small bedroom (likely to be occupied by a child, a member of the vulnerable age group) will mean exposure everyday of the year for around 8 hours every night.

3.20 The next stage is to judge whether there are any deficiencies that mean that the spread of outcomes will be different from the national average. For falls out of windows, for example, most are from first floor window and this is reflected in the national average. So, the outcomes from a fall from a ground floor window will be better than the average as it is not likely to result in death, but a fall from a window on the fifth floor is likely to result in more serious outcomes.

3.21 While for injury hazards there may be good reasons for altering the spread of outcomes, this is not the case for many of the other hazards. So for damp and mould growth etc, it is very unlikely that the outcomes would change. An increase in mould or exposure means an increase in the likelihood of the same outcomes.

3.22 As for likelihood, the inspector is not expected to give an exact figure, but a range. Again, however, the HHSRS formula uses a representative scale point for that range.[11]

3.23 This process is repeated for each hazard significantly worse than average.

---

[10] The ranges and the Representative Scale Points are given in the HHSRS Regs at reg 6 Table 1 in Box 3 of the Operating Guidance.

[11] The ranges and the Representative Scale Points are given in the HHSRS Regs at reg 6 Table 2 and in Box 5 of the Operating Guidance.

GENERATING A HAZARD SCORE

3.24 Three ways were produced by central government to generate a 'Hazard Score' using the HHSRS formula (a paper scoring form), a software program for handheld computers (PDAs), and a software program for PCs. Both the software programs calculate the hazard score automatically when the likelihood and the spread of outcomes has been entered.

HAZARD BANDS

3.25 While numbers are necessary for the formula, the resulting hazard score suggests precision. It also suggests that there is a meaningful difference between a score of (say) 255 and one of 300. To make the hazard scores more manageable, the HHSRS uses ten bands: band J being the safest and band A the most dangerous risk[12] (see Table 3.4).

Table 3.4: HHSRS Hazard Scores and Bands

Hazard Score	HHSRS Band
5,000 or more	A
2,000 to 4,999	B
1,000 to 1,999	C
500 to 999	D
200 to 499	E
100 to 199	F
50 to 99	G
20 to 49	H
10 to 19	I
9 or less	J

(Based on Box 8, Housing Health and Safety Rating System, Operating Guidance (ODPM, 2006))

---

[12] The bands and hazards scores are given in the HHSRS Regs at reg 7 Table 3 and in Box 8 of the Operating Guidance.

HAZARD PROFILE

3.26 Once all significantly worse than average hazards have been assessed and the bands generated, a 'Hazard Profile' has been produced. This shows which hazards are average for a dwelling of that type and age, and the bands for each hazard fully assessed by the inspector.

3.27 It should be noted that the hazard scores are not summed to give a single score for the dwelling. The resulting number would not give an indicator of whether there were two hazards in band C, or six hazards in band E.

DETERMINING REMEDIAL ACTION

3.28 The next stage is to determine what remedial action would reduce the hazard. This is something to judged by the inspector taking account of the deficiencies contributing to the hazard and the nature and form of the design and construction of the dwelling elements. In many cases, although the hazard score is very high, the remedial action may be relatively easy and cheap, eg, fitting a smoke detector, and a safety catch to a window. In some cases it may not be possible to reduce the hazard to the average for that type and age of dwelling, but it may still be possible to reduce it from a very high score (make it safer). This may be the case with dangerous stairs where the layout of the dwelling means it is not feasible to redesign the stairs.

3.29 The aim should be to determine the remedial action to reduce the non-average hazards, but also, where possible, determine whether any of the average hazards could be reduced (made safer).

Chapter 4

HHSRS – OPTIONS FOR ACTION

4.1 The HHSRS assessment does not determine the enforcement action to be taken, but the result of the assessment does determine whether the local housing authority is under a duty or has a power to take action.

4.2 The HHSRS Regulations state that a hazard falling into band A, B or C is a 'category 1 hazard', and a hazard falling into any other band is a 'category 2 hazard'.[1] Also, the Act[2] states that a local housing authority is under a duty to take action under Part 1 of the Act in the case of a dwelling where there is at least one category 1 hazard[3] and has power to take action in the case of a dwelling where there is no category 1 hazard but there are category 2 hazards.[4]

4.3 The enforcement options available to the local housing authority under Part 1 of the Act are:

- hazard awareness notice (sections 28 and 29);

- improvement notice (sections 11–19);

- emergency remedial action (section 40);

- prohibition order (section 20);

- emergency prohibition order (section 43);

- demolition order (section 265 of the Housing Act 1985 as amended);

- clearance area (section 289 of the Housing Act 1985 as amended).

4.4 Each of these is outlined below, followed by a discussion on factors relevant to determining which is the appropriate action.

---

[1] HHSRS Regs, reg 8.
[2] Section 2.
[3] Section 5.
[4] Section 7.

HAZARD AWARENESS NOTICE

4.5   A hazard awareness notice is a notice advising the addressee that one or more category 1 hazards exist,[5] and/or one or more category 2 hazards exist.[6]

4.6   There is no sanction or enforcement option associated with a hazard awareness notice. However, if the hazard still exists at a later date, the authority may consider taking another action if they determine that the remedial action should be taken and has not.[7]

IMPROVEMENT NOTICE

4.7   An improvement notice is a notice requiring the addressee to take remedial action to deal with one or more category 1 hazards,[8] and/or one or more category 2 hazards.[9] The notice must specify a date when the remedial action is to be started (which cannot be less than 28 days from the date of service) and the period within which the action is to be completed, or the periods within which each part of that action is to be completed.

4.8   An improvement notice may be suspended until a specified time or a specified event.[10] The specified time may be when a person of a description (eg, a person of 60 years or over, or a child under 5) moves into or moves out of the premises. The event may be a breach of an undertaking.

EMERGENCY REMEDIAL ACTION

4.9   In some cases, there may be one or more category 1 hazards existing that pose an imminent risk of serious harm to occupiers and where action should be taken immediately. In such cases, a local housing authority can take emergency remedial action.[11] Under this provision the authority can take the action they consider necessary to remove the imminent risk of serious harm and recover the expenses reasonably incurred afterwards.[12]

4.10 Emergency remedial action is not available where only category 2 hazards are present.

---

5   Section 28.
6   Section 29.
7   Section 5(5).
8   Section 11(2) and (6).
9   Section 12(2) and (4).
10   Section 14(1).
11   Section 40(1) and (4).
12   Section 42.

PROHIBITION ORDER

4.11 Where one or more category 1 hazards and/or one or more category 2 hazards exist, and the authority consider that requiring remedial action is inappropriate, they may make a prohibition order.[13]

4.12 The order may prohibit the use of all or part of the premises, for any purpose of for a particular purpose[14] (eg, it may prohibit the use for human habitation only, so allowing the use for storage purposes). Alternatively, the order may prohibit the occupation by more than a specified number of households or persons, or by a particular description of persons.[15] The former is a method of dealing with crowding. The latter provides a means of dealing with dwellings that while otherwise satisfactory may be unsuitable for occupation by a particular category of individual (eg a dwelling on the fourth floor of a walk-up block may be considered unsuitable for occupation by the elderly or by a household with young children).

4.13 The order may be suspended until a specified time or a specified event.[16] It may be appropriate to suspend an order that prohibits the occupation by more than a specified number or by a certain category of individual where the dwelling is currently occupied in excess of that number or by that category of individual. In such a case, the specified time for the suspension to end could be when the current occupier(s) leave the premises.

EMERGENCY PROHIBITION ORDER

4.14 A prohibition order does not become operative until 28 days after the date it was made. There may be situations where one or more category 1 hazards exist that pose an imminent risk of serious harm to occupiers.[17] In such cases the authority can make an emergency prohibition order, which takes effect immediately.

DEMOLITION ORDER

4.15 As an alternative to a prohibition order, and where the premises could be safely demolished, the authority may make an order requiring that demolition.[18]

---

[13] Sections 20 and 21.
[14] Section 22(4).
[15] Section 22(5).
[16] Section 23.
[17] Section 43.
[18] Section 46, amending section 265, Housing Act 1985.

CLEARANCE AREA

4.16 Where the authority is satisfied that there is an area of residential buildings, and each of those buildings contains a category 1 hazard, then the authority may declare that area a clearance area.[19] If the area contains any other non-residential buildings, the authority must be satisfied that those buildings are dangerous or harmful to the health and safety of the inhabitants of the area.

4.17 In certain circumstances a clearance area can be declared where each residential building contains a category 2 hazard.

4.18 Declaring a clearance area enables the local housing authority to ensure that all the buildings within the area are demolished.

DETERMINING THE APPROPRIATE ACTION

4.19 There is a range of factors that will influence the decision on the most appropriate action.[20] This will include:

- the potential imminence and severity of the threat to health;

- the extent and feasibility of the remedial action;

- the expected life of the premises;

- the characteristics of the occupants;

- the views of the occupants.

4.20 Where the threat to health is judged to be serious, ie hazard bands C and above, and it judged that there is an imminent likelihood of harm occurring, then the appropriate action is more like to be one of the emergency options: emergency remedial action or emergency prohibition order.

4.21 The extent and feasibility of the remedial action considered necessary to reduce the hazard(s) will influence whether a hazard awareness notice, an improvement notice, or prohibition order is appropriate. A hazard awareness notice may be appropriate where the remedial action is likely to be extensive but the hazard is low scoring. Alternatively, where the remedial action is likely to be extensive but the hazard is severe, ie B and C and above, then a prohibition order may be appropriate.

---

[19] Section 47, amending section 289, Housing Act 1985.

[20] See *Housing Health and Safety Rating System: Enforcement Guidance – Housing Act 2004, Part 1; Housing Conditions* (2006) ODPM. Available at www.communities.gov.uk/publications/housing/housingact2 (accessed 21 November 2007).

4.22 Where premises are scheduled for clearance, say to make way for a new road, and that clearance is within a relatively short period, then it may be more appropriate to make a prohibition order rather than requiring costly remedial action.

4.23 Where the premises are occupied by a household that includes a member of the age group vulnerable to the particular hazard(s) identified, that should influence the type of action and the speed within which the action should be started and completed. The characteristics of the occupiers may also influence whether the action should be suspended.

4.24 The premises, whatever the condition, constitutes the 'home' for the occupiers, and their views on what should happen to their home should be taken into account. Their views may again influence whether the action should be suspended.

4.25 Whatever decision is made, the action should be proportionate as well as appropriate.

4.26 A local housing authority cannot take more than one action simultaneously for the same hazard. However, the same or another course of action can be taken to deal with a hazard where the first course failed to reduce that hazard.[21]

---

[21] Section 5.

Chapter 5

CONTENTS OF NOTICES AND ORDERS

REASONS

5.1   To be valid an improvement notice, a prohibition order and a hazard awareness notice must be accompanied by a statement of reasons which explain why the authority decided to take the action it did, rather than use any other kind of enforcement measure available to them.[1]

REQUIREMENTS FOR A VALID IMPROVEMENT NOTICE

5.2   In addition to the reasons requirement, an improvement notice must, according to section 13, specify in relation to the hazard or to each of the hazards to which it relates:

- whether the notice is served under section 11 or 12; telling the recipient whether the hazard is assessed as category 1 or 2, ie whether it is served pursuant to a power or a duty;

- the nature of the hazard and the residential premises on which it exists;

- the deficiency giving rise to the hazard;

- the premises in relation to which the remedial action is to be taken;

- and the nature of that remedial action;

- the date when the remedial action is to be started, which cannot be earlier than the 28th day after that on which the notice is served;

- the period within which the remedial action is to be completed;

- information about the right to appeal under Part 3 of Schedule 1;

- the period within which an appeal may be made.[2]

---

[1]   See sections 8 and 29(5)(d).
[2]   21 days see Schedule 1, paragraph 14(1).

CONTENTS OF A VALID PROHIBITION ORDER

5.3   A prohibition order, apart from the reasons requirement and spelling out the prohibitions, must by virtue of section 22, specify a number of matters which are also required, for a valid emergency prohibition order; see section 44.

In relation to the hazard or to each of the hazards to which the prohibition order or emergency prohibition order relates:

- whether the order is served under section 20 or 21; again telling the recipient whether the hazard is assessed as category 1 or 2;[3]

- the nature of the hazard and the residential premises on which it exists;

- the deficiency giving rise to the hazard;

- the premises in relation to which prohibitions are imposed;

- any remedial action, which the authority consider would, if taken in relation to the hazard, result in their revoking the order;

- information about the right to appeal under Part 3 of Schedule 2;

- the period within which an appeal may be made;[4]

- specify the date on which the order is made.

REQUIREMENTS FOR A VALID HAZARD AWARENESS NOTICE

5.4   A Hazard Awareness Notice must according to section 28(6) specify:

- the nature of the hazard and the residential premises on which it exists;

- the deficiency giving rise to the hazard;

- the premises in relation to which the remedial action is to be taken;

- the authority's reasons for deciding to serve the notice including the reasons for deciding it is the most appropriate course of action;

- details of the remedial action (if any) which the authority consider that it would be practicable and appropriate to take in relation to the hazard.

---

[3]   Not required for a valid emergency prohibition order which is dependent on the existence of a category 1 hazard – see section 43(1).

[4]   28 days see Schedule 2, paragraph 10.

REQUIREMENTS FOR REMEDIAL ACTION WITHOUT AGREEMENT

5.5 Before a LHA can take direct action and carry out works in default a notice pursuant to paragraph 4(2) of Schedule 3 must be served which specifies:

- the improvement notice to which it relates;

- the premises and the hazard concerned;

- that the authority intends to enter the premises;

- the action which the authority intend to take on the premises;

- the power under which the authority intend to enter the premises and take the action.

REQUIREMENTS FOR EMERGENCY REMEDIAL ACTION

5.6 Before commencing emergency remedial action a notice complying with section 41 must be served, which specifies:

- the nature of the hazard and the residential premises on which it exists;

- the deficiency giving rise to the hazard;

- the premises in relation to which emergency remedial action has been (or is to be) taken;

- the nature of the remedial action;

- the power under which that remedial action authority has been (or is to be) taken;

- the date when that remedial action was (or is to be) started.

REQUIREMENTS FOR A VALID DEMOLITION ORDER

5.7 Once operative then a notice must be served stating:

- the effect of the order;

- specifying the date by which the order requires the building to be vacated;

- that the person served is required to vacate the building before that date or before the expiration of 28 days from the service of the notice, whichever may be the later.

Part III

HMOS AND OVERCROWDING

Chapter 6

THE MEANING OF HOUSE IN MULTIPLE OCCUPATION

INTRODUCTION

6.1   A study for the Campaign for Bedsit Rights estimated that the chances of being killed or injured by fire in an HMO are 28 times higher than for residents of other dwellings. A report to the DETLR in 1997 confirmed the risk to occupants of HMOs from fire. HMOs have long been regarded as being of higher risk to health and safety than dwellings built for single households.[1] The Court of Appeal has stated: 'It is of the greatest importance to the good of the occupants that houses which ought to be treated as HMOs do not escape statutory control'.[2]

6.2   In the repealed[3] Part 11 of the Housing Act 1985[4] multiple occupation was defined[5] but little else.

6.3   It was left to case law to search out the wider context for deciding whether or not the house was an HMO.[6] The new Act has tried to fill some of

---

[1]   Paragraph 6.6 of the Enforcement Guidance.

[2]   *Rodgers v Islington LBC* (1999) 32 HLR 138 an HMO case, where Nourse LJ acknowledged in relation to the test for what is and what is not an HMO: 'the dangers inherent in seeking to further define the indefinable'. The facts of the case concerned a three storey house with ten bedrooms on four floors where the residents were not a preformed group, but stayed over dissimilar periods.

[3]   See section 266 and Schedule 16 to the Act. The Housing Act 2004 (Commencement No 5 and Transitional Provisions and Savings) (England) Order 2006, SI 2006/1060 commenced Parts 2 and 4 of the Act, with savings. It also commenced section 266 insofar as it related to certain repeals, including the repeals in Part 11 of the Housing Act 1985 concerning HMO registration schemes, which are replaced by the licensing provisions in Part 4 of the Act. Part 2 of the Schedule to SI 2006/1060 provides that the repeal of certain sections of the Housing Act 1985 does not have effect in respect of a relevant converted block of flats until regulations made under section 61(5) of the Housing Act 2004 come into force. The Modifications Regulations, therefore, trigger the repeal of the Housing Act 1985 provisions that are saved in relation to relevant converted blocks of flats.

[4]   Part 11 included the power to require execution of works to render premises fit and/or to comply with a management code (the now repealed section 352 and 372) and the control provisions in section 348.

[5]   A house occupied by persons who do not form a single household.

[6]   In *Simmons v Pizzey* [1979] AC 37 the House of Lords set its face against a single test when it decided a women's refuge was not a single household, being occupied by a fluctuating population who used the premises as 'a temporary harbour in a storm', by holding that membership and household were questions of fact and degree. In *Barnes v Sheffield CC* (1995)

the gaps setting out detailed conditions for what is and what is not an HMO and when persons are to be regarded as forming a single household and treated as occupying premises as their only or main residence.[7] The Act however retains to the national authority[8] the power[9] to add to or to subtract from the category of buildings or part of buildings which are to be treated as HMOs.

6.4   Not all HMOs are HMOs for the purposes of the Act. Furthermore, not all HMOs for the purposes of the Act have to have a licence. It is therefore possible to divide types of house in multiple occupation into the following four broad groups:

- The first group includes those houses occupied by persons who do not form a single household (ie the house is in multiple occupation) but which nevertheless, although not specifically excluded by Schedule 14, are not HMOs which the Act recognises as a house in multiple occupation.[10] The fact of multiple occupation would still be relevant to Part 1.

- The second group comprises those which the Act says are HMOs for the purposes of the Act. A neat definition of those HMOs covered by the Act are those not excluded, that meet one of three tests[11] or is deemed or is declared to be one.

- The third group, even though those within it fall within the second group, are the particular HMOs which attract or can attract a licensing requirement, that is covered by Statutory Instruments SI 2006/371, and in Wales SI 2006/1712, or subject to additional or selective licensing.[12]

- The fourth group comprise those HMOs, which although not necessarily subject to licensing, are in any event caught by management regulations

---

27 HLR 719; Bingham LJ as he then was, set out a number of factors relevant to determining if a house was in multiple occupation and decided that a house there used by four or five students was not a HMO.

[7]   Section 258 sets out when persons are not to be regarded as forming a single household and see section 259 which deems certain types of occupation (even temporary harbour in a storm cases) as occupying as only or main residence. These categories were further built upon to include certain employees (nannies, carers, butler, cook or cleaner etc) within the employer's single household and to deem migrant or seasonal worker as occupying premises as their only or main residence. See 3,4 and 5 of The Licensing and Management of Houses in Multiple Occupation and Other Houses (Miscellaneous Provisions) (England) Regulations 2006, SI 2006/373.

[8]   Secretary of State or national assembly.

[9]   See section 254(6).

[10]   For example, if no rent was payable or other consideration was provided by any of the occupants it could not be an HMO for the purposes of the Act nor could accommodation which was not solely used as living accommodation qualify.

[11]   An essential limb of each of the three tests is that the accommodation is occupied by persons who do not form a single household.

[12]   The conditions for designating an area for selective licensing in Wales are different to that in England; see notes 9 and 10 to paragraphs 11.6 and 11.7.

made pursuant to section 234, covered by Statutory Instruments SI 2006/372 and in Wales SI 2006/1535.

6.5   Dividing the types of HMO in this way is consistent with the statutory definition of HMO for the purposes of the Act being wider than the type of HMO which is or can be made the subject of licensing.

6.6   The Housing Health and Safety Rating System set out in Part 1 of the Act, applies to residential premises[13] irrespective of whether they are a HMO, irrespective of whether the HMO is an HMO for the purposes of the Act or not, irrespective of whether the HMO is unoccupied, and irrespective of whether the HMO is one to which the licensing or management provisions would, could or do apply. That said, the juxtaposition of licensing control and potential for enforcement under the HHSRS, in respect of the same matter; is a more difficult area which is not unrelated to the intention of the legislation that no HMO which is licensable requires action to be taken concerning a category 1 or 2 hazard.

HMOS WHICH THE ACT SAYS ARE HMOS FOR THE PURPOSES OF THE ACT

6.7   As set out above a building or part of a building is an HMO for the purposes of the Act if it meets one of the three statutory tests, or it is deemed to be an HMO by virtue of there being a declaration to that effect[14] or it is deemed to be an HMO by virtue of section 257. The three tests are:

- the standard test;

- the self-contained test; and

- the converted building test.

Converted building and the meaning of self contained flat are defined.[15]

6.8   For any purposes of the Act, other than for the purposes of Part 1, a building or part of a building cannot be an HMO if it is listed in Schedule 14.[16]

---

[13]   Defined in section 1(4) as including a dwelling, an HMO, unoccupied HMO accommodation and any common parts of a building containing one or more flats.

[14]   See section 255.

[15]   Section 254(8); a building in which one or more of the living units has been created since the building or part was constructed is a converted building. A self contained flat contains a toilet, washing facilities and cooking facilities, forms part of a building and either the whole of it or a material part of the accommodation lies above or below some other part of the building.

[16]   Section 254(5).

THOSE SPECIFICALLY EXCLUDED BY SCHEDULE 14

6.9   A building occupied by only two persons who form separate households is exempt from being considered an HMO. Some of the exemptions focus on different categories of persons managing the premises.[17] If an HMO is managed by any of six types of public authority listed in paragraph 2, it cannot be an HMO for the purposes of the Act (save for the purposes of Part 1).[18] The authorities listed include the police, a health service body, a fire and rescue authority and more contentiously a registered social landlord. HMOs managed by local housing authorities[19] are also exempt. In the same vein,[20] if a specified person or an educational institution, manage any building occupied by students of that institution, who live there for the purposes of undertaking a full time course, then it will be exempt.[21] Religious community HMOs may also be exempt. But this is subject to it not being a deemed HMO under section 257 and subject to the authority being satisfied that the main purpose for occupation of the building is prayer, contemplation, education or the relief of suffering. Also exempt, unless the building is a deemed HMO under section 257, are buildings occupied by owners or by long leaseholders.[22] A building occupied by owners or by long leaseholders may still be exempt if the numbers of non leaseholder or non owners does not exceed a number specified by regulations.

THE STANDARD TEST

6.10   A building cannot meet the standard test if it is a building which consists of flats or self-contained flats. Neither can a building or part of it meet the standard test if it is exempt under Schedule 14. A building or part of it[23] meets the standard test if:

(i)   it is occupied by more than one household (the Act sets out when persons are not to be regarded as forming a single household);[24]

---

[17]   See paragraphs 2, 3 and 4.

[18]   These categories include occupation regulated by a clutch of different provisions, e g section 87 of the Children Act 1989 listed in Schedules 1 to The Licensing and Management of Houses in Multiple Occupation and Other Houses (Miscellaneous Provisions) (England) Regulations 2006, SI 2006/373; and to The Licensing and Management of Houses in Multiple Occupation and Other Houses (Miscellaneous Provisions) (Wales) Regulations 2006, SI 2006/1715.

[19]   Defined in section 261. Specified educational institutions are dealt with in England in SI 2006/1707 and in Wales by SI 2007/2601.

[20]   According to paragraph 3 of Schedule 4.

[21]   Paragraph 4 of Schedule 14.

[22]   Over 21 years: see paragraph 6 of Schedule 14.

[23]   See section 254(2).

[24]   See section 258 which sets out when persons are to be regarded as not forming a single household.

(ii) each household occupy their respective accommodation as their only or main residence,[25] or if not occupying as their only or main residence is occupied by persons escaping domestic violence,[26] is occupied by students[27] during term time or is occupied for some other purpose prescribed by regulations[28] and are thereby treated as occupying as their only or main residence;[29]

(iii) the occupation of the living accommodation use must constitute the only use of the accommodation;[30]

(iv) rents or other consideration is provided;[31]

(v) more than one household shares a basic[32] amenity or the living accommodation is lacking in one or more of the basic amenities.[33]

THE SELF CONTAINED TEST

6.11 The first prohibition for the standard test falls away because this test is only met if part of the building consists of a self contained flat. A self contained flat cannot be in use as an HMO for the purposes of the Act if it is exempt under Schedule 14. Otherwise all of the five requirements for the standard test, apply – save the reference to living accommodation in (iii) above, is to be read as reference to the flat.[34]

THE CONVERTED BUILDING TEST

6.12 The first prohibition for the standard test operates here,[35] thus a building cannot meet the converted building test if it is a building which consists of flats or self-contained flats. Furthermore, the building cannot meet the converted building test if it is exempt under Schedule 14.[36] The converted building test

---

[25] Occupying as only or main residence (as opposed to occupying as only or principal home which is found in the tenant condition in section 81 of the Housing Act 1985) is defined in section 259.

[26] Catching the facts of *Simmons v Pizzey*: see section 259(2)(b).

[27] Potentially catching the facts of *Barnes v Sheffield CC* query the effect of occupation during vacation as well. See section 259(2)(a).

[28] By migrant or seasonal workers: Regulation 5 of The Licensing and Management of Houses in Multiple Occupation and Other Houses (Miscellaneous Provisions) (England) Regulations 2006, SI 2006/373.

[29] Section 254(2)(c) read in conjunction with section 259.

[30] Section 254(2)(d).

[31] Section 254(2)(e).

[32] Defined in section 254(8) as a toilet, personal washing facilities or cooking facilities.

[33] Section 254(2)(f).

[34] Section 254(3)(b).

[35] Section 254(4)(b).

[36] Section 254(5).

varies from the standard test because the sharing criteria in (v) above is omitted and there is an additional criteria for the converted building test that the building or part of a building is a converted building.[37] Otherwise, the criteria (i) to (iv) inclusive which apply to both the standard test and the self contained test also have to be met to satisfy the converted building test.[38]

SECTION 257 (DEEMED) HMO

6.13 A building is an HMO if it comprises entirely of converted self contained flats and the standards of conversion does not meet that required by the 1991 Building Regulations[39] and at least one third[40] of the flats are occupied under short tenancies.

6.14 If the reference to short tenancies was not there and the premises were occupied by long leaseholders the premises would be exempt.[41] The Act has been modified in its operation in respect of section 257 HMOs by regulations which came into force on 1 October 2007.[42] Furthermore, the Additional Provisions Regulations[43] apply minimum standards of management to all section 257 HMOs. These are based upon the Management of Houses in Multiple Occupation (England) Regulations 2006, but are modified to meet the policy objective that HMO regulations should not apply to such parts of the HMO, eg flats held on long leaseholds, where the manager cannot reasonably be expected to exercise control.

THOSE HMOS NOT OTHERWISE HMOS FOR THE PURPOSES OF THE ACT, WHICH MAY BE DECLARED TO BE HMOS BY THE ACT

6.15 Where a building or part of a building is partly occupied but there is an element[44] of mixed use, such that the occupation of the living accommodation is not solely used by the persons,[45] so that the criteria in (ii) and (iii) of paragraph 3.10 above are not met; eg holidaymakers are also staying there or

---

[37] Section 254(4)(a).

[38] See section 254(4)(c) to (f) inclusive.

[39] SI 1991/2768 prescribed matters including means of escape in event of fire, internal and external fire spread, access and facilities for the fire service, ventilation, sanitary conveniences and washing facilities, bathrooms and heat producing appliances.

[40] See section 257(2)(b).

[41] See paragraph 6 of Schedule 14.

[42] The Houses in Multiple Occupation (Certain blocks of flats) (Modifications to the Housing Act 2004 and Transitional Provisions for Section 257 HMOs) (England) Regulations 2007, SI 2007/1904.

[43] The Licensing and Management of Houses in Multiple Occupation (Additional Provisions) (England) Regulations 2007, SI 2007/1903.

[44] If the extent of such use renders the occupation by those occupying as a sole residence marginal and insignificant, then the power does not arise: see the last line of section 255(2).

[45] But their use remains significant.

B&B premises occupied otherwise than as a residence, then the local housing authority may serve a notice declaring the building to be an HMO.[46]

6.16 The third group of HMOs are those that attract or can attract a licensing requirement. These are the following:

(i)   HMOs for the purposes of Part 2 of the Act and which qualify for mandatory licensing;

(ii) HMOs for the purposes of Part 3 of the Act and which do not qualify for mandatory licensing but are in an area designated for selective licensing of the Act.

HMOS FOR THE PURPOSES OF PART 2

6.17 Mandatory licensing under Part 2 applies to HMOs of a prescribed description set out in the relevant regulations and to those which the LHA have decided, by imposition of a scheme of additional licensing, must be licensed under Part 2. The power to designate a scheme of additional licensing can be exercised in such a way that it applies to all HMOs in the authority's district.[47] When an authority designates an area subject to additional licensing then already registered HMOs[48] are passported directly into a licensing scheme.[49]

6.18 The prescribed description of HMOs,[50] which must be licensed even if the LHA has not made any additional designation under Part 2 or designated an area for selective licensing under Part 3, are those which satisfy the following conditions:

(a)   the HMO or any part of it comprises three stories or more;

(b)   it is occupied by five or more persons;

(c)   it is occupied by persons living in two or more single households.

HMOS FOR THE PURPOSES OF PART 3

6.19 Part 3 of the Act deals with selective licensing. Selective licensing applies to HMOs which are not otherwise subject to mandatory licensing, through either of the two routes identified under Part 2, and which are in an area which

---

[46]   Section 255(1) and (2).
[47]   Section 56(4).
[48]   Prior to commencement – see **10.4**.
[49]   Paragraph 4 to Part 2 of the Schedule, pursuant to Article 3 of SI 2006/1060; Welsh SI 2006/1535.
[50]   Regulation 3 of The Licensing of Houses in Multiple Occupation (Prescribed Descriptions) (England) Order 2006, SI 2006/371.

the local has designated as subject to selective licensing.[51] Conditions have to be met before an authority is entitled to so designate.

HMOS CAUGHT BY MANAGEMENT REGULATIONS MADE PURSUANT TO SECTION 234

6.20 The last group of HMOs is the broadest. This group goes wider than those subject to licensing under Parts 2 and 3.

6.21 Section 234 enables regulations in respect of any HMO to be made for the purpose of ensuring there are satisfactory management arrangements in place in respect of every HMO, of a description specified in the regulations. In particular the regulations[52] impose duties on the managers to repair and maintain the fabric of the building and facilities and equipment within it and upon the occupiers not to frustrate the manager in exercising his duties under the regulations

6.22 The management regulations requirement applies to any HMO other than a converted block of flats to which section 257 of the Act applies.[53] Failure to comply with the regulations is a criminal offence.[54]

---

[51]   See sections 85(1)(a), 79(2) and 80(1).
[52]   The Management of Houses in Multiple Occupation (England) Regulations 2006 SI 2006 No 372. The Management of Houses in Multiple Occupation (Wales) Regulations 2006, SI 2006/1713.
[53]   Article 1 of SI 2006/372 and SI 2006/1713.
[54]   Section 234(5).

Chapter 7

HMOS – INTERRELATIONSHIP WITH HHSRS

INTRODUCTION

7.1   The HHSRS was developed over a period of several years and was designed to allow the assessment of potential hazards that may be found in any dwelling.[1] The HHSRS[2] defines a dwelling as:

'... any form of accommodation which is used for human habitation, or intended or available for such use. It includes:

(a)   what is commonly known as a "house", whether it is detached, semi-detached or terraced;

(b)   what is commonly known as a "flat", "maisonette" or "apartment"; that is a self-contained dwelling on one or more floors in a building containing other dwellings or other types of accommodation (eg shops or offices); and

(c)   what may be known as a "bedsit'", or "flat", and which is not self-contained, and where there is the shared use with other dwellings of some facilities such as a bath or shower-room, sanitary accommodation, or kitchen.'

7.2   The guidance also states that included as part of the dwelling are the means of access to the dwelling, such as paths, rooms, passageways, circulation areas, and facilities that are shared or used in common with others.[3]

7.3   This enables a dwelling of any type to be assessed, and where the risk of a particular hazard is judged to be increased because, for example, facilities are shared, then it can be taken into account. Similarly, occupants of a dwelling on a top floor of a five storey block may be judged to be more at risk from fire than the occupants of a dwelling on the ground floor. To take account of differences between houses and flats, bedsits etc, the Operating Guidance includes guidance and advice on the assessment of potential hazards in such dwellings.[4]

---

[1]   For a description of the HHSRS assessment process, see Part 3.
[2]   See Housing Health and Safety Rating System: Operating Guidance (ODPM, 2006), paragraph 2.04, p 10.
[3]   See ibid paragraph 2.05, p 10.
[4]   See ibid Chapter 5, p 32.

7.4   The guidance advises:[5]

'Assessments using the Rating System, therefore, include:

(a)   those rooms and areas of the dwelling which are in exclusive occupation (ie, not shared in common with others);

(b)   any rooms or areas (whether internal or external) which are shared with others;

(c)   the means of access to the dwelling; and

(d)   the building associated with the dwelling.'

7.5   However, Part 1 of the 2004 Act refers to 'residential premises' rather than dwelling and goes on to define this term as 'a dwelling', 'an HMO', and 'any common parts of a building containing one or more flats'.[6] As the HHSRS is designed to allow the assessment of an empty property,[7] it was necessary to include in the definition of residential premises an 'unoccupied HMO accommodation'. This reference to residential premises implies that the whole of an HMO should be inspected before decisions on the appropriate action should be taken. However, as an HMO will contain two or more dwellings and as each individual dwelling within the HMO should be assessed separately following the HHSRS process, providing that each individual dwelling can be clearly identified (eg flat 2 or ground floor front bedsit), there is nothing to prevent action being taken in respect of each dwelling.

7.6   The Act makes it quite clear that authorities must proceed on the basis that they should seek to remove or reduce category 1 or category 2 hazards by exercising their functions under Part 1 and not by means of licence conditions.[8]

7.7   In August 2007, local housing authorities were reported to have received 22,314 applications from landlords operating licensable HMOs affecting 111,570 tenants.[9] Where a local authority receives an application for a licence, it is under a duty[10] to satisfy itself that there are no Part 1 functions that ought to be exercised by it in relation to the premises. If the authorities were to carry out a full inspection of every HMO for which a licence application is received, this would cause considerable delay. To avoid this, a main concern[11] in the Enforcement Guidance is that authorities do not delay the processing of applications. However, where there is concern in relation to the need for possible restriction on occupancy the guidance makes an exception to such advice, and the government anticipates the licensing application may be dealt with subsequently to deciding if a prohibition notice is appropriate.

---

[5]   See ibid paragraph 5.3, p 33.

[6]   Housing Act 2004, section 1(4).

[7]   See Operating Guidance, Part II, Chapter 3, paragraph 3.17.

[8]   Housing Act 2004, Part 2, section 67(4)(a).

[9]   Evaluating the impact of houses in multiple occupation and selective licensing (CLG August 2007).

[10]   Housing Act 2004, section 55(5)(c).

[11]   In accordance with the 5-year period given in section 55(6)(b).

7.8 There is a complication in relating to fire safety in HMOs and the Guidance is confusing. For example where, although a relatively high but still category 2 hazard in respect of fire safety has been identified and the authority has decided to take no action, then consultation is not necessary. But where the authority has decided to take action for that category 2 hazard, including a hazard awareness notice, consultation is necessary.[12]

7.9 Although the HHSRS is the prescribed process for the purposes of Part 1 of the Act, this does not mean that it cannot be used to assess conditions for other purposes. For example, it could be used to support decisions on standards for facilities in relation to section 65 of the Act (Licensing) and on the threats to health and health for the purposes of section 104 (IMOs).

---

[12] Enforcement Guidance, paragraph 6.18.

Chapter 8

OVERCROWDING –
INTERRELATIONSHIP OF THE
PROVISIONS

INTRODUCTION

8.1   There are three sets of provisions dealing with crowding of residential premises:

- Part X of the Housing Act 1985;

- Chapter 3 of Part 2 of the Housing Act 2004;

- The HHSRS and Part 1 of the Housing Act 2004.

Here, after briefly summarising the provisions, the relationship between them is discussed.

PART X OF THE HOUSING ACT 1985

8.2   These provisions give a procedure for determining the maximum number of persons that may sleep in a dwelling. The provisions were first set down in the Housing Act 1935, and have not been updated but repeated in the subsequent Acts.

8.3   There are two parts to these provisions. The first is a method for calculating the 'permitted number' based on the size and number of rooms available in the dwelling. The permitted number approach requires all living rooms and bedrooms to be taken into account, and treats a child between 1 year and 10 years as half a unit, and disregards any child under the age of 1 year. The second part is a prohibition on sexual overcrowding, defined as when two persons over the age of 10 years, of opposite sex, and not normally living together as husband and wife, are forced to sleep in the same room (note the word 'forced').

8.4   A criminal offence is committed under these provisions where the number of persons exceeds the permitted number or sexual overcrowding cannot be avoided. The only defence given is where children pass the age of 1 or

10 years so increasing the number of 'units', provided that the occupier applies to the local housing authority for rehousing.

8.5   It should be noted that there is provision in the 2004 Act for the repeal of Part X.[1] In addition, the government has been consulting on options for replacing these provisions.[2]

CHAPTER 3 OF PART 2 OF THE HOUSING ACT 2004

8.6   These provisions give local housing authorities powers to issue an 'Overcrowding Notice' in respect of a house in multiple occupation.[3] The notice must state in respect of each room in the HMO the maximum number of persons who may sleep in the room at any one time, or whether the room is not suitable for use as sleeping accommodation.[4] The notice may also give a special maximum if the persons using the room for sleeping are under a specified age.

8.7   Contravention of the notice is a criminal offence,[5] as is allowing sexual overcrowding to occur[6] (defined the same as under Part X of the 1985 Act).

THE HHSRS AND PART 1 OF THE HOUSING ACT 2004

8.8   One of the 29 hazards under the HHSRS is crowding and space.[7] This covers hazards associated with a lack of space within the dwelling for living, sleeping and normal family or household life.

8.9   The assessment of hazards using the HHSRS is dealt with in Part II, Chapter 3. However, for crowding and space (and only for this hazard) a supplemental assessment stage is necessary. For all the other 28 hazards, the current occupants are disregarded in scoring the hazard.[8] However, as crowding is a result of a mismatch between the dwelling and the occupying household, it is necessary to reassess the likelihood and outcomes taking account of the current occupants to generate an adjusted hazard score and band.[9]

8.10   The courses of action available where it is determined that the hazard of crowding and space is significantly worse than average are as described in paragraphs 8.12–8.14. As this hazard does not involve problems with the state

---

[1]   Housing Act 2004, section 216.
[2]   *Tackling Overcrowding in England: A Discussion paper* (CLG, 2006); and *Tackling Overcrowding in England: An Action Plan* (CLG, 2007).
[3]   As defined by Housing Act 2004, sections 254–259.
[4]   Housing Act 2004, section 140.
[5]   Section 139(7).
[6]   Section 141.
[7]   See Housing Health and Safety Rating System: Operating Guidance (ODPM, 2006), p 91.
[8]   See Operating Guidance, paragraph 4.29.
[9]   See Operating Guidance, paragraphs 4.30 and 4.31, pp 30 and 31.

and condition of the dwelling, probably the most appropriate course of action is the making of a prohibition order,[10] prohibiting the occupation by more than a specified number of persons[11] (a 'human' response rather than a 'building' response). To avoid making the current occupants guilty of contravening the order, the order could be suspended[12] until a specified time or until the current occupants can be rehoused.

RELATIONSHIP BETWEEN THE PROVISIONS

8.11 Part X of the 1985 Act applies to all dwellings, including houses in multiple occupation. It sets a bedrock standard, albeit an appalling low standard and one that relates only to sleeping, taking no account of the space necessary for living and recreation.

8.12 While the HMO overcrowding notice provisions under Chapter 3 of Part 2 of the 2004 Act allow local housing authorities to specify the number of persons that may use a room for sleeping, that number cannot exceed the permitted number calculated in accordance with the provisions of Part X. The provisions also enable an authority to prohibit the use of a room for sleeping purposes, but not for any other purpose (unlike the prohibition order provisions under Part 1 of the 2004 Act).

8.13 The HHSRS deals with the space available for living and normal household life as well as space for sleeping. While the other two provisions are more properly described as dealing with density, this allows for consideration of the space needed for social interaction between individuals and for somewhere to go for private time away from others. It also recognises that there are cultural and age elements to a sense of crowding, so that adolescents may need more space that the elderly, and children need space for play.[13]

8.14 Part X remains an obsolete bedrock standard, and the HMO overcrowding notice provisions seem unnecessary as they are limited and duplicate only part of the options available using the HHSRS and Part 1 of the 2004 Act. It also seems that the HHSRS and Part 1 provide for a more human and humane approach compared to the criminal basis of Part X and the HMO overcrowding provisions.

---

[10]   Sections 20 and 21.
[11]   Section 22(5).
[12]   Section 23.
[13]   See Operating Guidance, Annex D paragraphs 11.08 and 11.09, p 92.

Part IV

LICENSING

Chapter 9

WHO NEEDS A LICENCE?

9.1   Those controlling or managing premises which are required to be licensed under either Part 2 or Part 3 need a licence.[1] Where licensing would otherwise be required a property may be exempt by one of a number of routes.[2] Licences are non-transferable and property specific.[3] Licensing can be extended beyond the scope of mandatory licensing not just in respect of HMOs by way of additional licensing under Part 2 but also by way of selective licensing under Part 3 of the Act, which can include non HMOs. Part 3 of the Act contains provisions in relation to selective licensing that can cover houses, defined as buildings or part of a building consisting of one or more dwellings[4] as well as of Houses in Multiple Occupation.[5] The LHA is required to promote the implementation of licensing[6] and is under a duty to take reasonable steps to ensure that applications for licences are made on behalf of all relevant houses and HMOs in their area (that do not already have a licence).[7] The Act also requires LHAs to keep an up-to-date register of all the licences and of all temporary exemption notices under both Parts.[8]

9.2   Under both Parts 2 and 3 the LHA must grant a licence if:

- the proposed licence holder is a fit and proper person as well as being the most appropriate person to be granted a licence, ie they have management responsibility and are locally resident – this is intended to ensure that unfit landlords cannot use front men to apply for licences;

---

[1]   The Department of Communities and Local Government has published helpful guidance for landlords and managers and separate guidance for tenants.

[2]   There are three routes to exemption under Part 2 see section 61. These are if a temporary exemption notice is in force or it is subject to an IMO or FMO. A temporary exemption notice is defined in sections 62 and 86. The routes to exemption under Part 3 are wider. The same three grounds for exemption under Part 2 are available under Part 3 plus no licence will be required in respect of selective licensing if (1) there is in force an interim or final empty dwelling order under Chapter 2 of Part 4 of the Act; or (2) the whole of the house is occupied under a single exempt tenancy or licence. Categories of exempt tenancy and licence are set out in Article of SI 2006/370 in England and SI 2006/2825 Wales.

[3]   Section 68(1)and (6) and 91(1) and (6).

[4]   Section 99.

[5]   For the definition of HMO see Chapter 6.

[6]   Section 55(5)(a).

[7]   Sections 61(4) and 85(4).

[8]   Section 232, the register must be available for inspection at all reasonable times.

- the proposed manager of the house is the person having control of the house or an agent or employee of that person and is also a fit and proper person;[9]

- the proposed management arrangements are satisfactory.

9.3   Under Part 2[10]there is an additional requirement:

- the house is suitable for occupation by a certain number of persons or households as specified in the application or by the LHA, or can be rendered suitable for that number by imposition of conditions in the licence.

9.4   Save in respect of transitional provisions peculiar to Part 2 and although Part 2 and Part 3 of the Act contain different regimes for licensing, each Part of the Act shares a similar format, with almost mirror provisions set out in sixteen respective sections and a respective definition section:

Quick reference guide to
licensing of HMOs and
houses legislation

	RELEVANT PROVISION IN PART 2 (MANDA- TORY & ADDI- TIONAL LICENSING)	REL- EVANT PROVI- SIONS IN PART 3 (SELEC- TIVE LICENS- ING)	RELEVANT REGS (England)	REL- EVANT REGS (Wales)
DEFINITION SECTION	77	99		
WHAT REQUIRES TO BE LICENCED	61	85		
LICENSING TO WHICH THIS PART APPLIES (Pt 2)	55		SI 2006/371	SI 2006/ 1712
LICENSING TO WHICH THIS PART APPLIES (Pt 3)		79	SI 2006/370	SI 2006/ 2824
DESIGNATION	56 & 57	80 & 81		SI 2006/ 2825
APPROVAL	58	82		
NOTIFICATION REQUIREMENT	59	83	SI 2006/373	SI 2006/ 1715
DURATION REVIEW AND REVOCATION OF DESIGNATIONS	60	84	SI 2006/373	SI 2006/ 1715

[9]   For fit and proper person see **10.10**.
[10]   Section 65 for the tests of suitability.

Quick reference guide to licensing of HMOs and houses legislation				
TEMPORARY EXEMPTION	62	86	SI 2006/370	
APPLICATION FOR LICENCES	63	87	SI 2006/373; SI 2007/1903	SI 2006/ 1715
GRANT OR REFUSAL OF LICENCES	64	88	SI 2006/373 SI 2007/1903	
TESTS AS TO SUITABILITY FOR MULTIPLE OCCUPATION	65			
TESTS FOR FITNESS AND SATISFACTORY MANAGEMENT ARRANGEMENTS	66	89		
LICENCE CONDITIONS	67	90		
MODIFIED LICENCE CONDITIONS IN RELATION TO S.257 HMOs			SI 2007/1904	
GENERAL REQUIREMENTS AND DURATION OF LICENCES	68 & Pt 1 of SCHEDULE 5	91 & Pt 1 of SCHED-ULE 5		
VARIATION OF LICENCES	69 & Pt 2 of SCHEDULE 5	92 & Pt 2 of SCHED-ULE 5		
REVOCATION OF LICENCES	70 & Pt 2 of SCHEDULE 5	93 & Pt 2 of SCHED-ULE 5		
APPEALS AGAINST LICENCE DECISIONS	71 & Pt 3 of SCHEDULE 5	94 & Pt 3 SCHED-ULE 5		

9.5   According to the transitional provisions[11] relating to Part 2 only, a licence is deemed to have been granted in relation to: a non section 257 HMO which is an HMO which is a prescribed HMO or situated in an area of additional licensing (and a designation under section 56 of an area of additional licensing is deemed to have been made in respect of any area for which a local housing authority have made a registration scheme containing any of the control provisions described in sections 347 to 348F of the Housing

---

[11]   Section 76 provides that an order made under section 270 may make provision for HMOs that are part of a registration scheme with control provisions (under Part 11 of the Housing Act 1985) when the licensing provisions commence. This is designed to smooth the process of licensing for LHAs who run registration schemes for HMOs by allowing them to passport registered HMOs directly into a licensing scheme. Such an Order has been made see Regulation 4(4) The Housing Act 2004 (Commencement No 5 and Transitional Provisions and Savings) (England) Order 2006, SI 2006/1060, Welsh SI 2006/1535.

Act 1985, and it was granted to a person who before the commencement date was recorded on the register of a relevant registration scheme[12] as the person managing the HMO).

WHAT A LICENCE DOES

9.6   The effect of being licensed is that it gives the LHA a certain amount of control which can be exercised by the use of the licence conditions[13] and the penalties for non-compliance. Furthermore, the effect of a licence is to authorise occupation of the HMO caught by Part 2[14] and to authorise occupation of the house subject to selective licensing under Part 3.[15] Under Part 2 a licence authorises occupation of the HMO concerned by no more than a maximum number of households or persons specified in the licence. Schedule 4 of the Act sets out mandatory conditions that are to be attached to licences granted under both Part 2 and Part 3. These[16] require the licence holder to:

- produce an annual gas safety certificate;

- keep electrical appliances and furniture supplied by the landlord in a safe condition and to supply declarations of their safety to the local council on demand;

- install smoke alarms and keep them in proper working order and to supply to the local council, on demand, a declaration of their positioning and condition; and

- give the occupiers a statement of the terms on which they occupy the HMO.

9.7   In addition and the most important thing a licence does, where one is required, is that having one protects against the penalties for not having one, which include being liable to:

- a fine of up to £5000 or up to £20,000 for different offences;[17]

---

[12]   Prepared under section 346 of the Housing Act 1985: see paragraph 2 of Part 2 of The Housing Act 2004 (Commencement No 5 and Transitional Provisions and Savings) (England) Order 2006 prepared under section 346 of the Housing Act 1985.

[13]   Some conditions are imposed by statute, others will be imposed by the LHA – see sections 67 and 90 and see **10.4** in relation to deemed areas of additional licensing.

[14]   Section 61(2).

[15]   Section 85(2).

[16]   Which can be added to by Regulations made by the national authority: see paragraph 3 of Schedule 4.

[17]   Sections 71(1) and 95(1): not having a licence; section 72(2) permitting excessive occupation; section 72(3) and 95(2) failing to comply with the terms of the licence, for which offence the fine is limited to £5000: see section 72(7).

- a rent repayment order;[18]

- loss of the right to automatic possession by use of section 21 of the 1988 Housing Act in relation to assured shorthold tenancies.[19]

---

[18] Sections 73 and 96.
[19] Sections 75 and 98.

Chapter 10

MANDATORY AND ADDITIONAL LICENSING UNDER PART 2 OF THE ACT

HMOS FOR THE PURPOSES OF PART 2

10.1 The Act provides that every HMO to which this part applies must be licensed unless a temporary exemption notice is in force or an 'interim management order' or 'final management order' is in force.[1]

10.2 Mandatory licensing applies to those which are statutorily required to be licensed and those that the statute allows the LHA to say must be licensed.

10.3 The Act does not say which HMOs are statutorily required to be licensed other than saying that Part 2 applies to those HMOs which fall within any prescribed description.[2] The prescribed description are those HMOs of three storeys or more which are occupied by five or more persons (who form two or more households), but not HMOs that comprise entirely of self contained flats.[3]

10.4 Mandatory licensing also applies to HMOs located in areas that are for the time being designated by the local housing authority under section 56 of the Act as being an area that is subject to additional licensing. In such cases it is the designation that describes the HMOs that are the subject of the additional licensing. Additional licensing applies to any other type of HMO where the local housing authority has identified a significant problem with the management of that type of HMO. Before making a designation[4] the authority must consult with local stakeholders, consider their representations and obtain approval from the Secretary of State or from the national assembly.[5]

---

[1] Section 61.

[2] Section 55(2)(a).

[3] Paragraph 3 of The Licensing of Houses in Multiple Occupation (Prescribed Descriptions) (England) Order 2006, SI 2006/371 – see Appendix 2.

[4] This requirement to consult is disapplied in relation to deemed areas of additional licensing. Deeming occurs by virtue of paragraph 3(2) of Part 2 of the Schedule to The Housing Act 2004 (Commencement No 5 and Transitional Provisions and Savings) (England) Order 2006, SI 2006/1060. An area is deemed to be designated if it is an area for which the local authority have a registration scheme made under section 346 of the 1985 Act containing any of the control provisions or special control provisions described in sections 347, 348, 348A, 348B, 348C, 348D, 348E or 348F of that Act.

[5] Sections 56–58.

10.5 There are five requirements before an HMO which must have a licence, can be licensed.[6] If an LHA is not satisfied that there is a reasonable prospect of an HMO, which requires to be licensed, ever being licensed then it is under a duty to make an interim management order.[7] The five requirements are:

- that the house is reasonably suitable for occupation by not more than the maximum number of households or persons, or that it can be made so suitable by the imposition of conditions under section 67;

- that the proposed licence holder and proposed manager of the house are both fit and proper persons;

- that the proposed licence holder is the most appropriate person;

- that the proposed manager of the house is either the person having control of the house, or a person who is an agent or employee of the person having control of the house; and

- that the proposed management arrangements for the house are otherwise satisfactory.

10.6 The first requirement is that a housing authority may grant a licence if it is satisfied that the house is reasonably suitable for occupation by not more than the maximum number of households or persons that is either specified in the application, or decided by the authority, or that it can be made so suitable by the imposition of conditions. This comprises two limbs. The first concerns how many households or persons are to occupy the house. The second concerns the number type and quality of facilities which should therefore be available in the particular circumstances.

10.7 The Act provides that a local housing authority cannot be satisfied that a house is reasonably suitable for occupation by a particular maximum number of households or persons if they consider that it fails to meet prescribed standards ('amenity standards') for occupation by that number of households or persons.[8] But the authority may decide that it is not reasonably suitable for occupation by that maximum number even if it does meet the standards.

10.8 The relevant regulations specifying:

- the standards as to the number, type and quality of bathrooms, toilets, washbasins and showers, areas for food storage, preparation and cooking and laundry facilities which should be available in particular circumstances; and

---

6 Section 64.
7 Section 102(2).
8 Section 65.

- standards as to the number, type and quality of other facilities or equipment which should be available in certain circumstances,

are the Licensing and Management of Houses in Multiple Occupation and Other Houses (Miscellaneous Provisions) (England) Regulations 2006, SI 2006/373 and the Licensing and Management of Houses in Multiple Occupation and Other Houses (Miscellaneous Provisions) (Wales) Regulations 2006, SI 2006/1715. Regulation 8 and Schedule 3 to both sets of regulations prescribe the standards, which the regulations make a statutory precondition, for premises being reasonably suitable for use as an HMO.[9] Schedule 3 provides:

'Schedule 3

Prescribed standards for deciding the suitability for occupation of an HMO by a particular maximum number of households or persons.

Heating

1. Each unit of living accommodation in an HMO must be equipped with adequate means of space heating.

Washing Facilities

2.—(1) Where all or some of the units of living accommodation in an HMO do not contain bathing and toilet facilities for the exclusive use of each individual household—

(a)   there must be an adequate number of bathrooms, toilets and wash-hand basins suitable for personal washing) for the number of persons sharing those facilities; and
(b)   where reasonably practicable there must be a wash hand basin with appropriate splash back in each unit other than a unit in which a sink has been provided as mentioned in paragraph 4(1),

having regard to the age and character of the HMO, the size and layout of each flat and its existing provision for wash-hand basins, toilets and bathrooms.]

(3) All baths, showers and wash hand basins in an HMO must be equipped with taps providing an adequate supply of cold and constant hot water.

(4) All bathrooms in an HMO must be suitably and adequately heated and ventilated.

(5) All bathrooms and toilets in an HMO must be of an adequate size and layout.

---

9   Regulation 8 was amended in respect of standards prescribed for section 257 HMOs by The Licensing and Management of Houses in Multiple Occupation (Additional Provisions) (England) Regulations 2007, SI 2007/1903.

(6) All baths, toilets and wash hand basins in an HMO must be fit for the purpose.

(7) All bathrooms and toilets in an HMO must be suitably located in or in relation to the living accommodation in the HMO.

Kitchens

3. Where all or some of the units of accommodation within the HMO do not contain any facilities for the cooking of food—

(a)   there must be a kitchen, suitably located in relation to the living accommodation, and of such layout and size and equipped with such facilities so as to adequately enable those sharing the facilities to store, prepare and cook food;

(b)   the kitchen must be equipped with the following equipment, which must be fit for the purpose and supplied in a sufficient quantity for the number of those sharing the facilities—

(i)   sinks with draining boards;
(ii)   an adequate supply of cold and constant hot water to each sink supplied;
(iii)   installations or equipment for the cooking of food;
(iv)   electrical sockets;
(v)   worktops for the preparation of food;
(vi)   cupboards for the storage of food or kitchen and cooking utensils;
(vii)   refrigerators with an adequate freezer compartment (or, where the freezer compartment is not adequate, adequate separate freezers);
(viii) appropriate refuse disposal facilities;
(ix)   appropriate extractor fans, fire blankets and fire doors.

Units of living accommodation without shared basic amenities

4.—(1) Where a unit of living accommodation contains kitchen facilities for the exclusive use of the individual household, and there are no other kitchen facilities available for that household, that unit must be provided with—

(a)   adequate appliances and equipment for the cooking of food;
(b)   a sink with an adequate supply of cold and constant hot water;
(c)   a work top for the preparation of food;
(d)   sufficient electrical sockets;
(e)   a cupboard for the storage of kitchen utensils and crockery; and
(f)   a refrigerator.

(1A) The standards referred to in paragraphs (a) and (f) of sub-paragraph (1) shall not apply in relation to a unit of accommodation where—

(a)   the landlord is not contractually bound to provide such appliances or equipment;
(b)   the occupier of the unit of accommodation is entitled to remove such appliances or equipment from the HMO; or
(c)   the appliances or equipment are otherwise outside the control of the landlord.

(2) Where there are no adequate shared washing facilities provided for a unit of living accommodation as mentioned in paragraph 2, an enclosed and adequately laid out and ventilated room with a toilet and bath or fixed shower supplying adequate cold and constant hot water must be provided for the exclusive use of the occupiers of that unit, either—

(a)   within the living accommodation; or

(b)   within reasonable proximity to the living accommodation.

Fire precautionary facilities

5. Appropriate fire precaution facilities and equipment must be provided of such type, number and location as is considered necessary.'

10.9   As soon as reasonably practicable[10] as the authority are in receipt of an application for a licence for an HMO, and in addition to being satisfied in relation to suitability and management issues[11] the Act requires the local housing authority to satisfy themselves that it does not have a duty or a power to take enforcement action in relation to the premises, under Part 1 of the Act.[12] This read too literally could lead authorities to want to inspect the premises which are the subject of the application, before granting a licence, but section 55(6)(b) removes the justification for such a stance by stipulating that the duty to be satisfied no action is required under Part 1 must be met before the end of five years after the date of the application. This indicates that processing of the application should not be put on hold pending an inspection although if the duty to inspect under section 4 of Part 1 was independently triggered by any other circumstance (and that could be done quite quickly) then delay in issue of a licence may be appropriate.

FIT AND PROPER PERSON

10.10 Section 66 provides for the tests of fitness and management arrangements. This section sets out the evidence and issues that must be considered by a local housing authority when determining whether a person is or is not fit and proper to hold a licence or be a manager of an HMO. The Regulations[13] make it a statutory requirement that the applicant must supply as a part of his application:

'(a)   details of any unspent convictions that may be relevant to the proposed licence holder's fitness to hold a licence, or the proposed manager's fitness to manage the HMO or house, and, in particular any such conviction in respect

---

[10]   Section 55(5)(c).

[11]   Spelt out under section 64(3).

[12]   Section 55(5)(c) and 55(6)(a).

[13]   See Regulation 7 and Schedule 2 to The Licensing and Management of Houses in Multiple Occupation and Other Houses (Miscellaneous Provisions) (England) Regulations 2006, SI 2006/373 and The Licensing and Management of Houses in Multiple Occupation and Other Houses (Miscellaneous Provisions) (Wales) Regulations 2006, SI 2006/1715.

of any offence involving fraud or other dishonesty, or violence or drugs or any offence listed in Schedule 3 to the Sexual Offences Act 2003[26];

(b)   details of any finding by a court or tribunal against the proposed licence holder or manager that he has practised unlawful discrimination on grounds of sex, colour, race, ethnic or national origin or disability in, or in connection with, the carrying on of any business;

(c)   details of any contravention on the part of the proposed licence holder or manager of any provision of any enactment relating to housing, public health, environmental health or landlord and tenant law which led to civil or criminal proceedings resulting in a judgement being made against him.

(d)   information about any HMO or house the proposed licence holder or manager owns or manages or has owned or managed which has been the subject of:

   (i)   a control order under section 379 of the Housing Act 1985[27] in the five years preceding the date of the application; or

   (ii)   any appropriate enforcement action described in section 5(2) of the Act.

(e)   information about any HMO or house the proposed licence holder or manager owns or manages or has owned or managed for which a local housing authority has refused to grant a licence under Part 2 or 3 of the Act, or has revoked a licence in consequence of the licence holder breaching the conditions of his licence; and

(f)   information about any HMO or house the proposed licence holder or manager owns or manages or has owned or managed that has been the subject of an interim or final management order under the Act.'

10.11 In one Court of Appeal case[14] it was recorded that although under the 1985 Act there was no definition nor guidance regarding the meaning of fit and proper person, the authority were entitled to stipulate its own conditions for registration of HMOs under a scheme made pursuant to Part 11. The claimant in that case, wishing to register his premises failed to answer the question 'Is the landlord known to have been convicted for non compliance with enforcement notices under section 352?' even though he had a number of convictions and had been fined over £5000 for previous offences in relation to just such offence concerning HMOs. The Court of Appeal allowed the authority's appeal against the judge at first instance who had allowed an appeal against the authority's rejection of his application. The court found that it was impossible to see how the necessary precaution of refusal of registration can be withheld if a person was unfit. Yet the court still managed to replace the order of the judge at first instance with an order requiring the authority to approve the application subject to the appointment by the claimant of a manager whose terms of appointment were acceptable to the authority. This approach ties in with the guidance given to landlords in relation to licensing of HMOs: 'The council must be satisfied that the licence holder is the most appropriate person to hold the licence. There is a presumption in the Act that this will be the landlord. However, if the council does not consider that he or she is suitable to hold the licence, eg because he is not fit and proper or the management arrangements

14   *Brent LBC v Reynolds* [2002] HLR 15.

are inadequate, it can agree that the licence be held by someone more appropriate, such as a managing agent'.

CRITERIA FOR GRANT OF LICENCE FOR A SECTION 257 HMO

10.12 According to the Licensing and Management of Houses in Multiple Occupation (Additional Provisions) (England) Regulations 2007[15] the LHA must be satisfied of the following matters before a section 257 (which must be licensed if any part of it comprises three storeys or more; and it is occupied by five or more persons; and it is occupied by persons living in two or more single households) can be issued with a licence:

'(a) that all bathrooms and toilets contained in each flat must be of an adequate size and layout, and all wash-hand basins must be suitably located and be fit for purpose, having regard to the age and character of the HMO, the size and layout of each flat and its existing provision for wash-hand basins, toilets and bathrooms;

(b) those standards set out in paragraph 4(1) of Schedule 3, in so far as it is reasonably practicable to comply with them; and

(c) those standards set out in paragraph 5 of Schedule 3.'

10.13 Paragraph 5 of Schedule 3 concerns fire precautionary facilities and applies to all licensable HMOs under Part 2, including s 257 HMOs caught by Part 2.[16]

10.14 Before examining what of Paragraph 4 of Schedule 3 (which concerns an HMO with no shared facilities so that what is in the unit of accommodation is all that the residents have to use) can be applied to section 257 HMOs it is worth remembering the significant feature of a section 257 HMO is that it comprises entirely of converted self contained flats; (and the standards of conversion does not meet that required by the 1991 Building Regulations and at least one third[17] of the flats are occupied under short tenancies). A converted house of three storeys or more with a number of self contained flats occupied by at least five people in three or more separate households should therefore have, unless it is not reasonably practical, the facilities specified in Paragraph 4 of Schedule 3 which are:

---

[15] Regulation 12 of SI 2007/1903 which modifies Regulation 8 of SI 2006/373 by inserting a new 8(2).

[16] Part 3 which governs selective licensing does not have an equivalent provision to section 65 which stipulates the tests for suitability of multiple occupation, because Part 3 can apply to houses which are not in multiple occupation. The statutory prescription of number type and quality of bathrooms, toilets, washbasins, showers, areas for food storage, facilities for preparation of food and laundry facilities concern only HMO's subject to mandatory licensing under Part 2.

[17] See section 257(2)(b).

'4. — (1) Where a unit of living accommodation contains kitchen facilities for the exclusive use of the individual household, and there are no other kitchen facilities available for that household, that unit must be provided with —

(a)   adequate appliances and equipment for the cooking of food;
(b)   a sink with an adequate supply of cold and constant hot water;
(c)   a work top for the preparation of food;
(d)   sufficient electrical sockets;
(e)   a cupboard for the storage of kitchen utensils and crockery;
(f)   a refrigerator.

(2)Where there are no adequate shared washing facilities provided for a unit of living accommodation as mentioned in paragraph 2, an enclosed and adequately laid out and ventilated room with a toilet and bath or fixed shower supplying adequate cold and constant hot water must be provided for the exclusive use of the occupiers of that unit either —

(a)   within the living accommodation; or
(b)   within reasonable proximity to the living accommodation.'

10.15 The caveat of not having to have these facilities if it is not reasonably practical to provide them in the section 257 HMO will be dealt with on a case by case basis and no doubt what is reasonable will be relative to the facility and the costs in issue, e g if an enclosed and adequately ventilated room with a toilet and bath or shower cannot be provided within reasonable proximity but can be provided further away, how much expense and building work is reasonable, before the LHA decide it is appropriate to grant a licence, given the distances otherwise involved and bearing in mind that it concerns accessibility to the bathroom?

10.16 Another important distinction concerning section 257 HMOs is that the Additional Provisions Regulations specify manager's duties which are only applicable 'in relation to such parts of the HMO over which it would be reasonable to expect the licence holder, in all the circumstances, to exercise control'.

10.17 According to Regulation 11 every occupier of a section 257 HMO would be in breach of statutory duty if they don't:

•   avoid conduct which would (knowingly) hinder or frustrate the manager in the performance of his duties;

•   allow access to the manager at all reasonable times for any purpose connected with the carrying out of any of the duties which the regulations impose;

•   provide such information as may reasonably be required for the purpose of carrying out any such duty;

- take reasonable care to avoid damaging anything which the manager is under a duty to supply, maintain or repair;

- store and dispose of litter in accordance with the arrangements made by the manager pursuant to the Regulations; and

- comply with reasonable instructions in relation to fire safety.

10.18 As well as being in breach of the Regulations an occupier who defaults in any of the above, without reasonable excuse, may face a fine of up to £5,000, since section 234(2) of the Act allows the regulations to impose duties on persons occupying the house and section 234(3) makes it an offence not to comply with a regulation under this section.

10.19 The manager of a section 257 HMO must:

- provide his contact details and ensure they are prominently displayed in the common parts;

- take fire safety measures, eg ensuring means of escape are free from obstruction and equipment, and alarms are maintained in good working order;

- take all such measures as are reasonably required to protect occupiers from injury including in relation to (a) an unsafe roof or balcony; and (b) windows near ground level;

- maintain clean and proper water supply and drainage;

- discharge duties in relation to the supply and maintenance of installations for the supply of gas and electricity;

- maintain common parts, fixtures, fittings and appliances, including banisters, lights and stair coverings;

- maintain in good repair, clean condition and good order any outbuildings, yards and forecourts, including fences and railings;

- maintain, save in relation to those items the occupier is entitled to remove, the living accommodation including windows and other means of ventilation, save that the manager is not required to repair any item which has been damaged by un-tenantlike or unreasonable behaviour; and

- maintain waste disposal facilities.

Chapter 11

SELECTIVE LICENSING

INTRODUCTION

11.1 Selective licensing is a form of LHA control imposed through use of licence conditions.

11.2 Selective licensing contained in Part 3 applies to those houses which are both in an area of designation and which require to be licensed.[1]

11.3 Designation is only possible with confirmation or approval and once designation is made there are notification requirements.[2]

11.4 In areas of designation, those houses which must be licensed are those which are occupied under a non-exempt single tenancy or licence or where a house is occupied under two or more tenancies or licences, none of those tenancies or licences are exempt.[3]

11.5 The categories of exemption are set out in the Act[4] and in the Regulations[5] and comprise the following:

(i)   houses subject to prohibition orders because of the existence of a category 1 hazard;

(ii) business and agricultural tenancies and licensed premises;

(iii) houses managed or controlled by local housing authorities, police authorities and similar bodies;

(iv) certain houses which would be HMOs but for being excluded (eg, student halls of residence);

(v)   houses let under tenancies for 21 years or more which cannot be ended earlier by the landlord except in the case of forfeiture and which are

---

[1]   See section 79(1).
[2]   Section 82.
[3]   Section 79(2).
[4]   Sections 79(3) and 79(4).
[5]   SI 2006/370; see Appendix 2. Similar provisions are contained in the Selective Licensing of Houses (Specified Exemptions) (Wales) Order 2006, SI 2006/2824.

occupied by the person to whom the tenancy was granted or by their successor in title or a family member of such a person;

(vi) tenancies granted to family members for them to occupy as their only or main residence where the person granting the tenancy is the freeholder (or has a lease for more than 21 years which cannot be ended earlier except in the case of forfeiture);

(vii) holiday homes;

(viii) tenancies under which any accommodation is shared with the landlord or a member of the landlord's family;

(ix) tenancies or licences granted by a registered social landlord;[6]

(x) houses which are HMOs to which Part 2 applies;

(xi) a temporary exemption notice is in force;[7]

(xii) a management order is in force.[8]

11.6 Designation is possible for an area, where the objective of designation is consistent with the authority's overall housing strategy; and the LHA are satisfied that the area:

(a) is, or is likely to become, an area of low housing demand;

(b) is experiencing a significant and persistent problem caused by anti-social behaviour;

(c) is affected by matters which subsequent regulations specify as criteria for selective licensing.[9]

11.7 Only in Wales have any additional conditions (for making a designation of an area for selective licensing) been made.[10] These are:

'3. — (1) Subject to paragraph (2), for the purposes of section 80(2)(b) of the Act either the first or second condition applies —

    (a)   the first condition is that, either
           (i)   a local housing authority has declared an area as a renewal area under section 89 of the 1989 Act; or

---

[6]   See Part 1 of the Housing Act 1996.

[7]   Such a notice tells the LHA that the person having control or managing a Part 3 house intends to take particular steps to securing that the house is no longer required to be licensed: see section 86.

[8]   Section 85(1)(c).

[9]   Section 80(7).

[10] SI 2006/2825.

(ii)   a local housing authority has provided assistance to any person in accordance with an adopted and published policy under articles 3 and 4 of the 2002 Order in that area (power of local housing authorities to provide assistance);

(b)   The second condition is that the area of their district or area in their district comprises a minimum of 25% of housing stock let by private sector landlords.'

PRE-CONDITIONS

11.8   There are four prior conditions to valid designation:

(1)   The LHA have considered whether there are any other courses of action available to them (of whatever nature) that might provide an effective method of achieving the objective or objectives that the designation would be intended to achieve, and they consider that making the designation will significantly assist them to achieve the objective or objectives (whether or not they take any other course of action as well).[11]

(2)   The LHA must have taken reasonable steps to consult[12] persons likely to be affected by the designation.

(3)   The LHA must have the necessary authority specifically confirmed by the national authority or the designation must fall within a general description of designations which has been given a general approval by the national authority.[13]

(4)   As soon as a designation is confirmed or made the LHA must publish the fact of the notification.[14]

LOW HOUSING DEMAND

11.9   Additionally the LHA must be satisfied that by making a designation the designation will, when combined with other measures taken in the area by the

---

[11]   Section 81(4).

[12]   In *R (on the app of Fudge) v SWSHA* [2007] EWCA Civ 803 at 50, the ambit of consultation was summarized: first, consultation must be undertaken at a time when proposals are still at a formative stage; secondly, sufficient reasons must be provided for particular proposals so as to permit those consulted to give intelligent consideration and response; thirdly, adequate time must be given; and fourthly, the product of consultation must be conscientiously taken into account when the ultimate decision is taken (see *R v Brent London Borough Council ex p Gunning* (1985) 84 LGR 168 approved in *R v London Borough of Barnet ex p B* [1994] ELR 357 and *R v North and East Devon Health Authority ex p Coughlan* [2001] QB 213). The duty to consider representations is expressly provided for in section 80(9)(b).

[13]   Section 82.

[14]   See sections 83 and 83(4) and Licensing and Management of Houses in Multiple Occupation and Other Houses (Miscellaneous Provisions) (England) Regulations 2006, SI 2006/373, Regulation 9 – see Appendix 2.

local housing authority, or by other persons together with the local housing authority, contribute to the improvement of the social or economic conditions in the area.

11.10 Factors relevant to deciding whether an area is likely to become, an area of low housing demand are set out in section 80(4). These include comparative value, turnover of occupation and the number of residential premises on the market and for the length of time they remain vacant.

SIGNIFICANT AND PERSISTENT PROBLEM CAUSED BY ANTI-SOCIAL BEHAVIOUR

11.11 The LHA must be satisfied that some or all of the private sector landlords who have let premises in the area (whether under leases or licences) are failing to take action to combat persistent anti-social behaviour and that making a designation will, when combined with other measures taken in the area by the local housing authority, or by other persons together with the local housing authority, lead to a reduction in, or the elimination of, the problem.[15]

SELECTIVE LICENCE CONDITIONS

11.12 Schedule 4 also includes mandatory conditions which apply to any licence granted under Part 3. These are that the licence holder must:

(1) produce an annual gas safety certificate;

(2) keep electrical appliances and furniture supplied by the landlord in a safe condition and to supply declarations of their safety to the local council on demand;

(3) install smoke alarms and keep them in proper working order and to supply to the local council, on demand, a declaration of their positioning and condition; and

(4) give the occupiers a statement of the terms on which they occupy the house or HMO; and

(5) demand references from persons wishing to occupy the house.

Regulations have not yet spelt out any further mandatory licence conditions.

11.13 When formulating its list of intended licence conditions for a house in an area designated for selective licensing the authority must proceed on the basis

---

[15]   Section 80(6)(c).

that, in general, they should seek to identify, remove or reduce category 1 or category 2 hazards in the house by the exercise of Part 1 functions and not by means of licence conditions.[16]

11.14 Under section 90(7) a LHA cannot make it a condition of licence that existing tenancy agreements are altered. Nor can the LHA seek to impose restrictions or obligations on a particular person other than the licence holder unless that person has consented to the imposition of the restrictions or obligations.

11.15 Licence may include such conditions:

- as the local housing authority consider appropriate for regulating the management, use or occupation of the house concerned;

- conditions imposing restrictions or prohibitions on the use or occupation of particular parts of the house by persons occupying it;

- conditions requiring the taking of reasonable and practicable steps to prevent or reduce anti-social behaviour by persons occupying or visiting the house;

- conditions requiring facilities and equipment to be made available in the house for the purpose of meeting standards prescribed for the purposes of this section by regulations made by the appropriate national authority;

- conditions requiring such facilities and equipment to be kept in repair and proper working order;

- conditions requiring, in the case of any works needed in order for any such facilities or equipment to be made available or to meet any such standards, that the works are carried out within such period or periods as may be specified in, or determined under, the licence.[17]

---

[16] Section 90(5)(a). There is a rider to this which appears in section 90(5)(b) to the effect that it is not wrong to impose an otherwise permissible condition requiring installation or maintenance of facilities or equipment even if the same result could be achieved by use of powers under Part 1.

[17] Section 90(3).

Part V

MANAGEMENT ORDERS AND EDMOS

Chapter 12

MANAGEMENT ORDERS

INTRODUCTION

12.1 Part 4 of the Act contains mechanisms which allow the local housing authority in particular circumstances to step into the shoes of a failing landlord and manage the rented house. These measures, known as management orders, are not designed primarily to punish the landlord but to ensure that the property is managed responsibly and safely for the benefit of occupiers or potential occupiers and others living or owning property in the vicinity.

12.2 There are two forms of management order: interim management orders which last for a maximum of 12 months, and final management orders which can last up to 5 years. The statutory provisions covering management orders are:

Interim management orders	sections 101–112 of the Act
Final management orders	sections 113–122 of the Act
General operational provisions relating both to interim and final management orders	sections 123–131 and Schedule 6

12.3 Interim and final management orders act to supplement licensing powers, and they are generally used when authorities consider that there is no reasonable prospect of granting a licence for a property. In addition, in a really quite remarkable extension to the powers of local housing authorities to intervene in the business of private landlords, in limited circumstances they provide a mechanism for ensuring appropriate management of properties which are not licensable.

12.4 This chapter outlines the legal framework of management orders. We begin by describing the statutory provisions relating to interim and then final management orders, we then consider the general obligations both orders impose upon local authorities.

INTERIM MANAGEMENT ORDERS

12.5 Table 12.1 summarises the statutory provisions on interim management orders.

Table 12.1: Interim management orders

Section	Provision	Comment
101(1)–(3), (5)–(7)	Introduces and describes interim management orders	Lasts a maximum of 12 months. Designed to ensure immediate steps are taken to protect the health, safety or welfare of occupiers or neighbours, and other interim measures are taken appropriate for proper management pending a longer-term solution.
102	Describes the duties and powers of local housing authorities to make interim management orders	Duties relate to unlicensed Part 2 and Part 3 houses or in certain circumstances Part 2 and Part 3 houses where the licence is to be revoked. Powers relate to HMOs which fall outside the mandatory licensing scheme in Part 2 and to properties to which section 99 (special interim management orders) apply. Housing authorities use of discretion overseen by Residential Property Tribunal.
103	Special interim management orders	Applies to a particular category of tenancies which are not exempt[1] from Part 3 of the Act.
104	The health and safety condition	Covers occupiers and others occupying or having an estate or interest in any premises in the vicinity and justifies interference with property rights of the landlord.
105	Operation of interim management orders	This deals with the appropriate dates for the commencement and cessation of the interim management order.
106	Local housing authority's duties during interim management orders	Sets out specific duties on local housing authorities, firstly to protect the health safety or welfare of the occupiers and then to organise the proper management of the house.
107–110	General effect of interim management orders	Sets out the balancing exercise between the need to ensure the effective management of the house by the local housing authority and the appropriate respect for landlord's ownership of the house.
111–112	Variation and revocation of interim management orders	Provides a procedure for the variation and revocation of interim management orders by both the local housing authority and the landlord. The procedure is subject to appeal to the Residential Property Tribunal.

---

[1]   Exempt tenancies are defined in section 79(3), (4) of the Act and include tenancies where the landlord is a registered social landlord and other tenancies prescribed by the relevant national authorities.

12.6 Local housing authorities can make interim management orders to ensure that:

- immediate steps are taken to protect the health, safety or welfare of the occupiers of a house; or

- immediate steps are taken to protect the health, safety or welfare of the other occupiers or landowners in the neighbourhood; and

- any other appropriate steps are taken to ensure the proper management of the house pending further action.[2]

12.7 Further action means:

- the grant of a licence under Part 2 or Part 3 of the Act;

- the making of a final management order;

- the revocation of the interim management order.[3]

12.8 A local housing authority can use interim management orders to respond to the need for protection over and beyond the needs of occupiers of the house. It can consider the needs of others in the vicinity whether neighbouring occupiers or people 'with an estate or interest in any premises'. Thus landlords, mortgagees and others living nearby are covered.

12.9 Interim management orders are therefore temporary measures – designed to last a maximum of 12 months – to protect occupiers and others from risks to their health, safety or welfare and to give the local housing authority a breathing space to work on a more permanent solution to the property management problems whilst ensuring proper management of the house in the meantime.

THE DUTY TO MAKE INTERIM MANAGEMENT ORDERS

12.10 Local housing authorities have a duty to make interim management orders in two sets of circumstances.

12.11 First where an HMO which is subject to mandatory licensing or a Part 3 house:

- does not have the requisite licence under Part 2 or Part 3 of the Act; and

---

[2]   Section 101(3).
[3]   Section 101(3)(b).

- either there is no prospect of it being licensed in the near future; or

- the health and safety condition is satisfied.[4]

12.12 Second where either an HMO which is subject to mandatory licensing or a Part 3 house:

- does have the requisite licence under Part 2 or Part 3 of the Act; and

- the local housing authority has revoked the licence but the revocation has not yet come into force; and

- either once the revocation comes into force there is no prospect of the house being licensed in the near future; or

- when the revocation comes into force the health and safety condition will be satisfied.[5]

12.13 In other words, if a property must be licensed as a result of the provisions in Parts 2 or 3 of the Act, it must either have a licence or be subject to a management order (either interim or final) unless it has been temporarily exempted. Licensing is the first route for local housing authorities to achieve the aim of the legislation. However, where that is not possible then interim management orders provide the safety net.

12.14 The health and safety condition is satisfied if the making of an interim management order is required to protect the health (including mental health), safety or welfare of the occupiers, or people occupying neighbouring properties, or with an estate or interest in neighbouring properties.[6]

12.15 The local housing authority has the discretion (but not the duty) to treat a threat to evict the occupiers in order to avoid the licensing requirements of Part 2 of the Act as a threat to the welfare of the occupiers.[7] This is potentially an important protection for occupiers of HMOs whose occupation may well be at risk as a result of licensing requirements. The power is limited to Part 2 licensing because of the more severe potential impact of evicting a number of tenants from an HMO.

12.16 Note that where the local housing authority are required to take enforcement action in respect of category 1 hazards in relation to the house, or would be so required if they revoked the licence, and such action would protect the health, safety or welfare of the occupiers, then the health and safety condition is not satisfied.[8]

---

[4]   Section 102(2).
[5]   Section 102(3).
[6]   Section 104.
[7]   Section 104(3).
[8]   Section 104(5), (6).

DISCRETIONARY AND SPECIAL INTERIM MANAGEMENT ORDERS

12.17 The local housing authority also has discretion to apply to the Residential Property Tribunal (RPT) for an interim management order in other circumstances. The power is available if the property concerned is an HMO which does not require licensing under Part 2 of the Act[9] or if the property is one to which special interim management orders apply.[10]

12.18 Special interim management orders apply to houses which would not be exempt from Part 3 of the Act[11] if they were in an area of selective licensing and are not in multiple occupation.

12.19 A Residential Property Tribunal can only approve the making of an interim management order if:

- it complies with 'categories of circumstances' prescribed by the appropriate national authority[12]

- the making of an order is necessary for the protection of the health, safety or welfare of the occupiers or visitors or others engaged in lawful activities in the vicinity of the house.[13]

12.20 If the property is an HMO which does not require licensing the Residential Property Tribunal must take into account, in any decision to authorise the interim management order, the extent to which the landlord or manager has in the past complied with a code of conduct approved under the Act.[14]

12.21 The relevant circumstances, which are set out in the Housing (Interim Management Orders) (Prescribed Circumstances) England) Order 2006, SI 2006/369 are:

'(a)   the area in which the house is located is experiencing a significant and persistent problem caused by anti-social behaviour;

(b)   that problem is attributable, in whole or in part, to the anti-social behaviour of an occupier of the house;

(c)   the landlord of the house is a private sector landlord;

(d)   the landlord of the house is failing to take action to combat that problem that it would be appropriate for him to take; and

---

[9]   Section 102(4).
[10]   Section 103.
[11]   See section 79(3).
[12]   Section 103(3).
[13]   Section 103(4).
[14]   Section 102(6).

(e)   the making of an interim management order, when combined with other measures taken in the area by the local housing authority, or by other persons together with the local housing authority, will lead to a reduction in, or elimination of, that problem.'

12.22 Special interim management orders therefore enable local housing authorities to respond to anti-social behaviour in the private rented sector in areas not covered by selective licensing. Where a privately rented house is the source of anti-social behaviour, the landlord fails to take appropriate action to deal with it and the consequences are serious enough, then an order can be made to protect the health, safety or welfare of people occupying, visiting or engaged in lawful activities in the locality of the house. This is a significant extension of the power of local housing authorities over properties in their area – which is why it needs authorisation from an RPT.

12.23 The situation is quite distinct from the operation of interim management orders where properties are licensable. In such circumstances the local housing authority is under a duty to make an interim management order and there is no need to apply to the Residential Property Tribunal. The extensive rights of appeal granted to a landlord if he or she disagrees with the decision to make an interim management order provide sufficient protection for the landlord. For those reasons it is unnecessary for the legislation to require the local housing authority to apply to the Residential Property Tribunal service for all interim management orders.

URGENT APPLICATIONS TO THE RPT

12.24 There will be some exceptional circumstances when the local housing authority needs to apply to the RPT as a matter of urgency. Regulation 9 of the RPT (Procedure) (England) Regulations (SI 2006/831) provide a mechanism for this.

12.25 The tribunal can hold an urgent oral hearing if the circumstances are that:

'(a)   there is an immediate threat to the health and safety of the occupiers of the house or to persons occupying or having an estate or interest in any premises in the vicinity of the house; and

(b)   by making the interim management order as soon as possible (together where applicable with such other measures as the LHA intends to take) the LHA will be able to take immediate appropriate steps to arrest or significantly reduce the threat.'[15]

12.26 If the RPT decides to hold an urgent hearing then it must as soon as practicable notify the parties and each interested person it has knowledge:

---

[15]   Regulation 9(3).

'(a) that the application is being dealt with as a matter of urgency under this regulation;

(b) of the reasons why it appears to the tribunal that the exceptional circumstances exist;

(c) of any requirement to be satisfied by a party before the hearing; and

(d) of the date on which the urgent oral hearing will be held.'[16]

12.27 The hearing must be held within 4 days of the notification from the authority, and can be heard by a single panel member.

COMMENCEMENT AND EXPIRY OF INTERIM MANAGEMENT ORDERS

12.28 An interim management order comes into force on the date it is made unless it is made when a licence has been revoked but the revocation has not yet come into effect. In those circumstances the interim management order comes into effect when the revocation of the licence becomes effective.[17]

12.29 An interim management order lasts a maximum of 12 months.[18] If the order does not provide an earlier expiry date then it will cease to have effect after 12 months. Orders made when a licence has been revoked but the revocation has not yet come into effect must contain a provision for an expiry date which is no more than 12 months after the coming into force of the order.[19]

12.30 The Act provides for certain circumstances when an interim management order can be extended. These circumstances are limited to appeals against the imposition of final management orders and enable the interim management order to continue as temporary measure until the appeal process is complete.

12.31 What is required in the case of mandatory interim management orders is that:

- the local housing authority has made a final management order but the order has not come into force because of an appeal to a Residential Property Tribunal;

- the house is one which would be required to be licensed under Part 2 or Part 3 of the Act if it were not for the existence of the interim management order;

---

[16] Regulation 9(4).
[17] Section 105.
[18] Section 105(4).
[19] Section 105(6).

- the date on which the final management order, any licence under Part 2 or 3 of the Act or another interim management order comes into force in relation to the house following the appeal is later than the expiry date of the interim management order.[20]

12.32 Where the appeal is against the imposition of a final management order, and the interim management order was discretionary, the local housing authority has to apply to the Residential Property Tribunal for the interim management order to continue in force beyond its expiry date pending the disposal of the appeal. The tribunal is able to make the order to extend the life of the interim management order.[21]

DUTIES ON LOCAL HOUSING AUTHORITIES

12.33 Local housing authorities have a number of duties imposed upon them once an interim management order is in force. These are set out in Table 12.2. Note that we discuss administrative requirements such as notification duties at **12.78**.

Table 12.2: Local housing authority duties during an interim management order

Section 106, sub-section	The local housing authority must	Comment
(2)	First take any immediate steps necessary for the purpose of protecting the health, safety or welfare of occupiers or of occupiers or owners of property in the vicinity.	This requirement emphasises that the prime purpose of interim management orders is the occupiers' or neighbours' health, safety or welfare.
(3)	Take steps to ensure the proper management of the house pending the grant of a licence or the making of a final management order or the revocation of the interim management order.	The duty includes ensuring that the house has fire insurance in place.

---

[20] Section 105(9).
[21] Section 105(10).

Section 106, sub--section	The local housing authority must	Comment
(4)	If the house would require a licence under Part 2 or Part 3 but for the existence of the interim management order then the local housing authority must decide either to grant a licence or to make a final management order.	The grant of a licence includes the serving of a temporary exemption notice. The normal course of events would be to organise the licensing of the property. A final management order is a last resort.
(5)	If the house does not require a licence under Part 2 or Part 3 then the authority must decide either: • to make a final management order; or • to revoke the order without taking any further action.	The only long term solution for such properties is the final management order.

THE EFFECT OF INTERIM MANAGEMENT ORDERS

12.34 The authority has the power:

- to manage the house (subject to the rights of existing occupiers);[22]

- to authorise a manager to do so on its behalf;[23]

- to permit others to take up occupation of the premises, but only with the written consent of the legal owners.[24]

12.35 The local authority:

- does not acquire the legal estate;[25]

- is not to be treated as managing or providing the housing for the purpose of any other statutory provisions.[26]

---

[22] Section 107(3).
[23] Section 107(3).
[24] Section 107(4).
[25] Section 107(5).
[26] Section 107(8).

12.36 What this means is that the occupiers cannot acquire the status of secure tenants of the local authority. Nor have they got the status of legal tenancies or licences, because the authority would require the legal estate in order to create such a status.

12.37 However, if an authority does create what appear to be tenancies and licences using its powers in a management order, those agreements are to be regarded as legal leases, binding on any future owner of the property[27] and, in appropriate circumstances, registrable at the local Land Registry.[28] This will not give powers to local housing authorities to create legal leases, but any lease they do create must be treated as if it were such a lease.

12.38 The immediate landlord[29] cannot:

- receive any rent;

- manage the house; or

- create any lease or licence or other right to occupy it.[30]

12.39 The order does not affect the validity of a mortgage on the house, or of a superior lease on the house. The rights and remedies available to the mortgagee or the superior landlord continue to be available limited only in so far as such rights would prevent the local authority creating any occupancy agreements for the house.[31] If a dispute about these rights and remedies reaches the court, it may make any order in connection with the interim management order that it thinks appropriate, which includes an order quashing the interim management order.[32]

12.40 The landlord can, however, sell or otherwise dispose of the house.[33] The local housing authority cannot.

FINANCIAL ARRANGEMENTS

12.41 The effect of the interim management order is to place the local housing authority into the shoes of the landlord.[34] The occupiers therefore pay their rent to the local housing authority. When a local housing authority incurs reasonable expenditure in the management of the house under the interim

---

[27] Section 108(2).
[28] Section 107(10).
[29] The immediate landlord is defined in section 109(6) as the owner or lessee of the house and someone who would be entitled to receive rent from the occupiers of the house if the order was not in existence.
[30] Section 109(2).
[31] Section 109(4).
[32] Section 109(4).
[33] Section 109(3).
[34] Section 124(4).

management order then it can use the rent it collects to cover that expenditure.[35] This would include, for example, expenditure on routine repairs, capital expenditure, administrative costs and building insurance.

12.42 The rent can also cover the payment of any compensation payable to a third party in connection with the interim management order.[36]

12.43 The local authority is required, having deducted the relevant expenditure, to pay the relevant landlord the balance of any rents received at such intervals as it considers appropriate.[37] If there is more than one landlord the local authority can allocate the payment of the balance of rent in the proportions it considers appropriate.[38] In addition, when appropriate, it must pay interest at a reasonable rate that it has determined on such sums.[39] If the interim management order does not set out the rate of interest payable and the frequency of payment of interest the landlord can appeal to the residential tribunal.[40] Finally, it must keep proper accounts of its income and expenditure and must make them available for inspection or verification by the relevant landlord.[41]

12.44 The landlord has the right to apply to the Residential Property Tribunal for an order declaring that the relevant expenditure has not been reasonably incurred, and to ask the tribunal to require the authority to make financial adjustments reflecting the tribunal's declaration.[42]

12.45 A problem may arise when money is owed by the landlord to the local housing authority at the end of the interim management order. The minister explained in committee that:

> 'a series of possibilities might apply. If the conclusion at the end of the interim management order is that a final management order is needed, the debt would carry through and become part of the accounting machine under the final management order. It would continue to be a carried-over debt against which the ongoing rent under the final management order could be charged to repay it before any surplus income appeared down the line. Alternatively, there could be a charge on the property or, if a licence were granted, there could be a condition attached saying that the money should be repaid within a certain period, because it would have been used for work to make a property fit for human habitation, and to make it a safe, licensable property on which a landlord could earn rent.'[43]

---

[35] Section 110(3).
[36] See section 128 and **12.97** below.
[37] Section 110(4).
[38] Section 110(4).
[39] Section 110(4).
[40] Section 110(5) and Schedule 6, paragraph 24(3).
[41] Section 110(6).
[42] Section 110(7).
[43] *Hansard*, Commons Committee, vol 417, col 373 (3 February 2004).

Local authorities therefore have sufficient flexibility to recoup their money in the most effective manner.

12.46 A further potential problem is where the landlord resides in part of the house that is subject to the interim management order. Again the local housing authority has flexibility whether to extend the scope of the interim management order to the part of the house occupied by the landlord,[44] although that flexibility is constrained by the landlord's right to appeal to the Residential Property Tribunal.

VARIATION AND REVOCATION

12.47 Interim management orders can be varied or revoked either on the initiative of the local authority[45] or following an application by a 'relevant' person – an owner or manager of a house.[46] 'Relevant' person expressly excludes tenants with a remaining interest in the property of less than 3 years. So short-term fixed term tenants are excluded, as are periodic tenants.

12.48 The local housing authority has to consider that it is appropriate to vary or revoke the order.[47] The local housing authority is specifically given the power to revoke interim management orders where:

- the house ceases to be an HMO to which Part 2 of the Act applies, or ceases to be subject to Part 3 of the Act (selective licensing);

- a licence is going to come into force on the house under either Part 2 or Part 3 of the Act;

- a final management order is made to replace the interim management order.[48]

12.49 A variation or revocation will not come into effect until the period for appealing against it has expired or the process of appeal has been concluded.[49] Appeals are discussed at paragraphs **12.108–12.113**.

FINAL MANAGEMENT ORDERS

12.50 Table 12.3 summarises the provisions on final management orders.

---

[44] Section 102(8).
[45] Section 111(3).
[46] Section 111(3), (4).
[47] Sections 111(1), 112(1)(d).
[48] Section 112(1).
[49] Section 112(2).

Table 12.3: Final management orders

Section	Provision	Comment
101(4)	Definition of final management order	Makes clear that the purpose is to secure the proper management of the house on a long term basis in accordance with a management scheme.
113	Describes the duty and the power to create final management orders and sets out their relationship with interim management orders	The duty relates to circumstances where: • there is an interim management order; • the property must be licensed under the Act; but • the authority are unable to grant a licence to replace the interim management order.
114	Describes effective dates of commencement and cessation of final management orders	Final management orders last a maximum of 5 years.
115	Describes the duties on a local housing authority when a final management order is in force	The duties reflect the role of local housing authority as a manager of the property and require the local housing authority to review the operation of the order from time to time.
116–118	Sets out the general effects of a final management order	These effects are similar to the effects of the interim management order.
119–120	Sets out the requirement for a management scheme and accounts and provides a mechanism for the enforcement of the management scheme by the landlord	The management scheme is embedded into the order. This requires the local housing authority to be explicit about the management plan for the house and the financial arrangements. If the local housing authority deviates from the scheme then the landlord can apply to the Residential Property Tribunal either for an order requiring compliance with the scheme or for the final management order to be revoked.
121–122	Variation and revocation of final management orders	Provides a system for variation and revocation of final management orders similar to that provided for local housing authorities and landlords under interim management orders. The procedures are subject to appeal.

12.51 Final management orders are designed to secure the proper management of a house in the longer term[50] and as a replacement for the short-term interim management orders. They cannot be created except to replace an interim management order from its expiry date.[51]

12.52 The local housing authority must make a final management order if:

• the house requires licensing under Part 2 or Part 3 of the Act;

---

[50] Section 101(4).
[51] Section 113(1).

- the authority considers that it is unable to grant a licence under Part 2 or Part 3 to replace the interim management order.[52]

12.53 The local housing authority must also make a final management order where it is necessary to replace an existing final management order when it expires if the house is one which requires licensing under Part 2 or Part 3 of the Act and it is still unable to grant a licence.

12.54 The local housing authority has the power to create a final management order to replace an interim management order when it expires or an existing final management order if:

- the house does not require licensing under Part 2 or Part 3 of the Act; and

- the authority considers that making the final management order is necessary for the purpose of protecting the health, safety or welfare of the occupiers or neighbouring occupiers or property owners on a long-term basis.[53]

12.55 Final management orders come into effect only after periods for appeals have expired or the process of appeal is completed.[54] In general their duration is 5 years,[55] but can be for a shorter period if the order provides for a different expiry date.[56] There are provisions for lengthening the period where a replacement order is being appealed. If the house requires a licence under either Part 2 or Part 3 of the Act and without an extension of the duration of the final management order the continuation of the appeals process would result in the house being unlicensed and not subject to a management order, then the order continues in force until the appeals process is complete.[57] Otherwise the authority must apply to the tribunal for an extension of the existing order.[58]

12.56 The local housing authority's duties under the final management order are set out in Table 12.4.

---

[52]   Section 113(2).
[53]   Section 113(3), (6).
[54]   Section 114(2).
[55]   Section 114(3).
[56]   Section 114(4).
[57]   Section 114(6).
[58]   Section 114(7).

Table 12.4: Local housing authority duties during a final management order

Section 115, sub-section	The local authority must	Comment
(2)	Take such steps as it considers appropriate to ensure the proper management of the house in accordance with the management scheme.	This includes ensuring provision for fire and other insurance. Management schemes are discussed below.
(3)	From time to time review: • the operation of the order and the management scheme; • whether keeping the order in place is the best alternative.	The order should only remain if it provides the best means of dealing with the problem. No time interval specified for the review.
(4)	Vary the order if on review it considers that variations should be made.	If on the review action is considered to be necessary then that action must be taken.
(5)	Grant a licence under Part 2 or Part 3 of the Act if on review it considers that is the best available alternative. Revoke the order if on review it considers that is the best available alternative.	

12.57 The effect of a final management order is similar to the effect of an interim management order. However, the local housing authority has the power to create more extensive rights to occupy the property reflecting the longer term nature of the final management order. The provisions are written in such a way that registered social landlords or other appropriate bodies will be able to carry out the management of the properties on behalf of the local authority.

12.58 The authority has the right:

• to possession of the house (subject to the rights of existing and future occupiers)[59]

• to manage the house[60]

---

[59] Section 116(3)(a).
[60] Section 116(3)(b).

- to authorise a manager to do so on its behalf[61]

- to create occupation rights similar to leases or licences.[62]

12.59 There are limits on the occupation rights which can be created by the authority.[63] It cannot create occupation rights without the consent of the landlord:

- for fixed terms which will expire after the date of expiry of the final management order;

- which require more than four weeks notice to terminate.

12.60 It can, however, create assured shorthold tenancies without the landlord's consent as long as the mandatory 6-month period, during which time there are only limited grounds for eviction and in particular the notice only ground is not available, will expire before the end of the final management order.[64]

12.61 Therefore local housing authorities can create, without consent, rights similar to leases and licences which are excluded from the requirements of the Protection from Eviction Act 1977, and assured shorthold tenancies for occupiers of the house. What they cannot do is to create occupancy rights which will bind the landlord after the expiry of the final management order without the landlord's consent.

12.62 The local authority:

- does not acquire the legal estate and therefore cannot sell the property;[65]

- is not to be treated as managing or providing the housing accommodation for the purpose of any other statutory provisions.[66]

12.63 Therefore the occupiers cannot acquire the status of secure tenants of the local authority. Nor have they got the status of legal tenants or licencees, because the authority would require the legal estate in order to create such a status.

12.64 However, if an authority does create what appear to be tenancies and licences using its powers in a management order, those agreements are to be regarded as legal leases, binding on any future owner of the property and, in appropriate circumstances, registrable at the local Land Registry. This will not

---

[61] Section 116(3)(b).
[62] Section 116(3)(c).
[63] Section 116(4).
[64] Section 116(4)(b).
[65] Section 116(5).
[66] Section 116(8).

give powers to local housing authorities to create legal leases, but any lease they do create must be treated as if it were such a lease.[67]

12.65 A final management order is a local land charge and the local authority can enter a restriction in the Land Register in respect of it. This is designed to prevent the landlord creating new interests in the property.[68]

12.66 During a final management order the immediate landlord[69] cannot:

- receive any rent;

- manage the house; or

- create any lease or licence or other right to occupy it.[70]

12.67 The order does not affect the validity of a mortgage on the house, or of a superior lease on the house. The rights and remedies available to the mortgagee or the superior landlord continue to be available, limited only insofar as such rights would prevent the local authority creating any occupancy agreements for the house. If a mortgagee or a superior landlord take proceedings for enforcing their rights the court may make orders which vary or quash the final management order.[71]

12.68 The landlord can, however, sell or otherwise dispose of the house.[72]

MANAGEMENT SCHEMES

12.69 A key difference between an interim management order and a final management order is that a final management order must contain a management scheme.[73]

12.70 A management scheme is a scheme setting out the details of the intentions of the local housing authority in managing the house.[74] It provides an opportunity for the landlord to see what the local housing authority's intentions are for the house, and enables him or her to enforce those intentions.

12.71 Management schemes are divided into two parts. Part 1 of the scheme provides the financial details of the management plan. Table 12.5 sets out the

---

[67] Section 117(2).
[68] Section 116(9), (10).
[69] The immediate landlord is defined in section 118(6) as the owner or lessee of the house and someone who would be entitled to receive rent from the occupiers of the house if the order was not in existence.
[70] Section 118(2).
[71] Section 118(4).
[72] Section 118(3).
[73] Section 119(1).
[74] Section 119(2).

mandatory information requirements for the plan. Table 12.6 sets out the discretionary requirements. Basically the provisions ensure that the landlord is given sufficient information to understand the financial implications of the local housing authority's intentions.

Table 12.5: Management scheme Part 1 mandatory requirements under section 119(4)

Section 119(4)	The scheme must include
(a)	Details of any works that the authority intend to carry out
(b)	An estimate of the capital and other expenditure to be incurred by the authority
(c)	The amount of rent or other payments that the authority will be seeking, taking into account the condition of the house
(d), (e)	The amount of and provision for the payment of compensation payable to a third party whose rights are interfered with in connection with the final management order[75]
(f)	Provision for payments to the landlord of rent etc that remain after the deduction of: • relevant expenditure • amounts of compensation
(g)	Explanation of how the authority will pay the landlord outstanding rent etc due following the termination of the final management order following deduction of: • relevant expenditure • amounts of compensation
(h)	Explanation of how the authority will pay a third party any outstanding compensation due following the termination of the final management order.

---

[75] The payment of compensation is dealt with in section 128.

Table 12.6: Management scheme Part 1 discretionary provisions under section 119(5)

Section 119(4)	The scheme may include	Comment
(a)	Information about how the authority intends to use the rent to meet relevant expenditure.	These provisions amplify the mandatory requirements.
(b)	Information about how the authority intend to deal with interest which accrues on the rent etc.	
(c), (d)	Information about the authority's intentions to disapply section 129 (2)–(5), ie the authority's intention to 'roll over' into the new order any excess of rent over expenditure and compensation, any deficit of compensation to a third party, any deficit owed by a landlord to the authority or any overpayment of compensation by the authority to a third party following the termination of a previous management order.	The standard provisions are in section 129(2)–(5) which provide either: • that the landlord or a third party must be paid the amounts due following the termination of a management order; or alternatively • that the authority has the right to recover any deficit due from the landlord or a third party. Where, however, a management order is replacing a previous management order, the authority may disapply those sections[76] and 'roll over' the excess of income over expenditure or the deficit.
(e)	Information about how the authority intends to recoup from a landlord expenditure over and above what can be recovered from the rent etc.	

12.72 Part 2 of the management scheme is designed to address the reasons for the imposition of the final management order. The local authority must give an explanation as to how it intends to respond to the particular problems of the house.[77] The response may include:

---

76 Under section 129(6).
77 Section 119(6).

- the steps it intends to make to ensure that the occupiers comply with their tenancy obligations[78] (another reference to anti-social behaviour);

- a description and explanation of the necessary repairs.[79]

12.73 In addition, the authority must keep full accounts in respect of the house and allow the landlord and any other owner of the house reasonable opportunity to inspect, copy and verify the accounts.[80]

12.74 The management scheme is extremely important. It justifies the intervention by the local housing authority and limits the scope of that intervention. Its significance is underpinned by the right of the landlord[81] (or a third party[82] whose rights have been affected by the final management order) to apply to the Residential Property Tribunal for an order requiring the local housing authority to manage the house in accordance with the management scheme.[83] Following an application, the tribunal has extensive powers to ensure that the house is managed in accordance with the scheme. It can set out the steps which the authority must take to fulfill the requirements of the scheme,[84] it can vary the final management order[85] and it can order the payment of damages to the applicant. Alternatively it can revoke the final management order.[86] Ultimately then the Residential Property Tribunal can provide very detailed supervision of the local housing authority's management of the house.

VARIATION AND REVOCATION

12.75 Final management orders can be varied[87] or revoked[88] either on the initiative of the local authority or following an application by a 'relevant' person – an owner or manager of a house.[89] 'Relevant' person expressly excludes tenants with a remaining interest in the property of less than three years.[90] So short-term fixed-term tenants are excluded, as are periodic tenants. At first sight this may appear counterintuitive but it is consistent with the concept of the local housing authority stepping into the shoes of the landlord. The provisions are not about providing extra rights to tenants to manage their property.

---

[78]   Section 119(6)(a).
[79]   Section 119(6)(b).
[80]   Section 119(7).
[81]   That is, an immediate landlord as defined in section 119(8).
[82]   Section 120(4)(b).
[83]   Section 120(1).
[84]   Section 120(3)(a).
[85]   Section 120(3)(b).
[86]   Section 120(2)(b).
[87]   Section 121.
[88]   Section 122.
[89]   Sections 121(3), 122(3).
[90]   Sections 121(4), 122(4).

12.76 The local housing authority has to consider that it is appropriate to vary or revoke the order.[91] Examples of when the local housing authority would have the power to revoke are:

- if the house ceases to be an HMO to which Part 2 of the Act applies, or ceases to be subject to Part 3 of the Act (selective licensing);[92]

- if a licence is going to come into force on the house under either Part 2 or Part 3 of the Act;[93]

- if a further final management order is made to replace the existing final management order.[94]

12.77 A variation or revocation will not come into effect until the period for appealing against it has expired or the process of appeal has been concluded. Appeals are discussed at **12.108–12.113**.

GENERAL PROVISIONS – INTERIM AND FINAL MANAGEMENT ORDERS

12.78 The Act sets out some general provisions relating to the practical implications of both interim and final management orders. These relate to the impact of the orders upon occupiers, agreements and legal proceedings arising from the agreements or from the statutory provisions, furnishings and third parties. The provisions also provide a power of entry to carry out work and set out the financial and legal consequences of the termination of the orders.

12.79 The rights of existing occupiers – occupiers whose occupation of the house was created prior to or at the time of the interim or final management order coming into force and who are not resident landlords[95] – are not affected by the imposition of an order on the house.[96] Whilst the order is in force the local housing authority is substituted for any non-residential lessor or licensor.[97]

12.80 The rights of new occupiers – occupiers whose occupation rights are created during the course of an interim or final management order[98] – are not affected by the creation of a final management order.

---

[91] Sections 121(1), 122(1)(d).
[92] Section 122(1)(a).
[93] Section 122(1)(b).
[94] Section 122(1)(c).
[95] Section 124(2).
[96] Section 124(3).
[97] Section 124(4).
[98] Section 124(2).

12.81 The exclusions of local authority landlords from the statutory protections offered by the Rent Act 1977, the Rent (Agriculture) Act 1976 and the HA 1988 do not apply to occupation rights under interim and final management orders.[99]

12.82 If an existing occupier has the benefit of a protected or statutory tenancy under the Rent Act 1977, the Rent (Agriculture) Act 1976 or an assured tenancy (which includes an assured shorthold tenancy) or assured agricultural occupancy under the HA 1988 then those benefits continue unaffected by the operation of the management orders.[100]

12.83 The occupiers do not become secure or introductory tenants under the HA 1985.[101]

AGREEMENTS AND LEGAL PROCEEDINGS

12.84 Certain agreements between the landlord and another party which are in existence during the interim or final management order will operate as if the rights and liabilities of the landlord under the agreement are the rights and liabilities of the local housing authority. This only applies to agreements which:

- are effective at the commencement of the order;[102]

- relate to the house, either in connection with its management[103] or the provision of services or otherwise;[104]

- are specified within the order, either specifically or generally;[105]

- the local housing authority have notified the parties in writing that it is in effect adopting the agreement.[106]

12.85 The local housing authority therefore only becomes burdened with agreements that are relevant, that it knows about and that it chooses to adopt. This provision does not include superior leases of the house to which the landlord is a party,[107] or any permitted disposition of the house by the landlord.[108] Nor does it include any lease or licence granting occupation rights

---

[99] Section 124(7).
[100] Section 124(10).
[101] Section 124(9).
[102] Section 125(2)(a).
[103] Management includes repair, maintenance, improvement and insurance – section 125(7).
[104] Section 125(2)(c).
[105] Section 125(2)(d).
[106] Section 125(2)(e).
[107] Section 125(3)(a).
[108] Section 125(3)(b).

to an occupier of the house.[109] The local authority has no choice but to step into the shoes of the landlord in that situation.[110]

12.86 Legal proceedings in connection with such an agreement may be instituted by or against the local housing authority instead of by or against the landlord if the proceedings:

- originated prior to the imposition of the order;

- relate to the house;

- are specifically or generally described within the order;

- a notice has been served on all parties stating that this applies.[111]

12.87 When the interim or final management order is terminated and is not replaced by a further order then the status quo before the imposition of the management order is restored, ie the original landlord of the house or his successor in title is substituted for the local housing authority.[112]

12.88 If the local housing authority has created agreements to occupy the house which are in effect leases or licences during the course of the interim or final management order, the landlord is substituted for the local housing authority in those agreements.[113]

12.89 The local housing authority is liable for any liability to a superior landlord that a landlord who is a lessee may have for anything done during the interim or final management order.[114] Where other agreements have been entered into by the local housing authority in performance of its duties under the interim or final management order, the landlord will be substituted for the housing authority.[115] However, this will only apply if the authority serves a notice on the other party or parties to the agreement that the provision is to apply.[116]

12.90 The local authority may also serve a notice on all interested parties[117] that:

- the rights or liabilities arising either as a result of the operation of interim or final management orders or under any agreement where the landlord

---

[109] Section 125(3)(c).
[110] Section 124(4).
[111] Section 124(4), (5).
[112] Section 130(1), (2).
[113] Section 130(2).
[114] Section 130(3).
[115] Section 130(4).
[116] Section 130(5).
[117] Section 130(7).

has been substituted for the local housing authority are to be treated as the rights and liabilities of the substituted landlord[118]

- any proceedings arising from the statutory provisions or from any agreement commenced or continued by or against the local authority may be commenced or continued by the substituted landlord instead.[119]

12.91 If the result of this transfer of rights or liabilities to the landlord is that the landlord is required to pay damages in respect of anything done or omitted to be done by the local housing authority, then the authority must reimburse the landlord.[120]

FURNITURE ETC

12.92 Any furniture, fittings or other articles which are included in the tenancy agreement become the responsibility of the local housing authority for the duration of the interim or final management order.[121] This is important because the state of repair of furniture can be crucial to the health, safety or welfare of the occupiers.

12.93 The owner of the furniture can apply in writing to the authority to reclaim the furniture and the authority can accept that application in writing with 2 weeks' notice.[122] If there is a dispute between two or more owners of the furniture about their respective rights and liabilities then one of the furniture owners can apply to the Residential Property Tribunal to adjust those rights and liabilities. Any order the tribunal makes can include awards of compensation or damages.[123]

12.94 The local housing authority can supply the house with the necessary furniture and the expenses incurred in doing so can be recouped since they are a necessary part of properly managing the house.[124]

COMPENSATION TO THIRD PARTIES

12.95 Any third party who considers that his or her rights have been affected as a result of the interim or final management order has the right to apply to the local housing authority requesting it to consider payment of compensation.[125]

---

[118] Section 130(6)(a).
[119] Section 130(6)(b).
[120] Section 130(8).
[121] Section 126(1), (2).
[122] Section 126(3).
[123] Section 126(5), (6).
[124] Section 127.
[125] Section 128(1).

12.96 The local housing authority must then:

- notify the third party of its decision as soon as possible

- if it decides to pay compensation then it must vary the management scheme both to specify the amount of compensation and set out how it is to be paid.[126]

FINANCIAL ARRANGEMENTS FOLLOWING THE TERMINATION OF THE MANAGEMENT ORDER

12.97 At the termination of the management order the local housing authority may be owed money or may owe money. The Act provides for different methods of balancing the financial position and the local housing authority is given enforcement powers to recover any money owed to it. These provisions are summarised in Table 12.7.

Table 12.7: Financial arrangements following the termination of management orders – section 129

	Financial position	Interim management order	Final management order	Comment
129(2)	The total amount of rent collected exceeds the total amount of expenditure by the local housing authority including the payment of compensation payable.	The local housing authority must as soon as possible pay the balance to the relevant landlord.		

---

[126] Section 128(2), (3).

	Financial position	Interim management order	Final management order	Comment
129(3)	The total amount of rent collected is less than the total amount of expenditure by the local housing authority including the payment of compensation payable.	The difference is recoverable by the local housing authority. The recoverable sum is a local land charge on the house which takes effect on the termination of the order.[127] The authority has the powers and remedies available to it as if it were a mortgagee by deed having powers of sale and lease, or accepting surrenders of leases and appointing a receiver.[128]	Not applicable.	Where the interim management order is followed by a final management order then the local authority can disapply the provision as long as the management scheme so provides and roll over the debt.[129] If the order is followed by a licence then the licence conditions can include conditions on repayment of the debt.[130]
129(5)	Money is owed to the local authority in accordance with the management scheme.		The money is recoverable by the local housing authority in accordance with the scheme as a local land charge on the house which takes effect on the termination of the order.[131] The authority has the powers and remedies available to it as if it were a mortgagee by deed having powers of sale and lease, or accepting surrenders of leases and appointing a receiver.[132]	Where the final management order is followed by another final management order then the local authority can disapply the provision as long as the management scheme so provides and roll over the debt.[133] If the order is followed by a licence then the licence conditions can include conditions on repayment of the debt.[134]

---

[127] Section 129(7), (8).
[128] Section 125(9).
[129] Section 129(6).
[130] Section 129(11).

	Financial position	Interim management order	Final management order	Comment
129(5)	Money is owed to a third party or to a landlord in accordance with the management scheme.	The section does not provide for the payment of compensation awards made as a result of the imposition of an interim management order. However, section 110 (3) enables the authority to pay the compensation out of the rent paid.	The money must be paid in accordance with the management scheme.	Where the final management order is followed by another final management order then the local authority can disapply the provision as long as the management scheme so provides and roll over excess.[135]

POWER OF ENTRY TO CARRY OUT WORK

12.98 The statute provides the local housing authority with a power of entry to the house for the purpose of carrying out work.[136] The right is exercisable at all reasonable times and against tenants or licensees. If part of the house is excluded from the scope of the interim or final management order because of the occupation of a resident landlord the right of entry is limited in that part of the house to a right to enter to carry out work in the part of the house subject to the order.[137] The government suggested some examples where an enforceable right of entry may be required against a resident landlord:

> 'the resident landlord may resent the local authority having taken away his management of the property and may just want to make things difficult and be a member of the awkward squad; or the landlord may not care and make life difficult, for example, if certain communal features were in his flat and in disrepair.'[138]

12.99 If someone refuses entry after receiving reasonable notice then the authority may obtain an access order from the magistrates' court enforcing the power.[139] Failure to comply with the court order is an offence[140] and on

---

[131] Section 129(7), (8).
[132] Section 129(9).
[133] Section 129(6).
[134] Section 129(11).
[135] Section 129(6).
[136] Section 131(2).
[137] Section 131(3).
[138] *Hansard*, HL Committee, vol 664, col 903 (13 September 2004).
[139] Section 131(4).

summary conviction the person who refused entry is liable to a fine not exceeding level 5 on the standard scale.[141]

PROCEDURAL REQUIREMENTS FOR INTERIM AND FINAL MANAGEMENT ORDERS

12.100 There are important and extensive requirements set out in Schedule 6 to the Act to ensure that the landlord has sufficient opportunity to express his or her views about the imposition of management orders. These requirements parallel the notification requirements for selective licensing under Part 3 of the Act.

12.101 Table 12.8 sets out the requirements before the making of a final management order which are detailed in paragraphs 1–6 of Part 1 of Schedule 6. The requirements only apply to final management orders because interim management orders require speedy imposition.

Table 12.8: Schedule 6, Part 1, paragraphs 1–6: notification requirements prior to making final management orders

When	Served on	Information	Together with	Consultation requirements
Before making a final management order	Each relevant person	Reasons for making the order. Main terms of proposed order. End of the consultation period.	Copy of proposed order	Must consider representations made in accordance with the notice and not withdrawn. The consultation period must be at least 14 days.
After considering representations and when proposing to make a modified order	Each relevant person	The proposed modifications. The reasons for them. The end of the consultation period.		Must consider representations made in accordance with the notice and not withdrawn The consultation period must be at least seven days.

12.102 The requirement to renotify relevant people of modifications to the proposed final management order does not apply if the local housing authority considers that the proposed modifications are not material in any respect.

12.103 Table 12.9 sets out the notification requirements following the making of interim or final management orders which are set out in paragraph 7 of Part 1 of Schedule 6.

---

[140] Section 131(5).
[141] Section 131(6).

Table 12.9: Schedule 6, Part 1, paragraph 7: notification requirements following making interim or final management orders

When	Served on	Information	Together with
As soon as practicable after making an interim or a final management order	The occupiers of the house	Reasons for making the order. The date it was made. The general effect of the order. Date it will cease to have effect. For final management orders – a general description of the way the house is to be managed by the authority in accordance with the management scheme.	Copy of the order (which in the case of final management orders will contain the management scheme).
Within seven days of the making of the order	Relevant persons	As above plus: • the decision of the authority whether to pay compensation to a third party; • the amount of the compensation if any; • rights of appeal; • the period within which the appeal must be made.	Copy of the order (which in the case of final management orders will contain the management scheme).

12.104 People are 'relevant persons' if they are owners or managers of the property. Owners are defined as people who have an estate or interest in the property but excludes those who have a lease with an unexpired term of 3 years or less.

12.105 Regulations provide (in England) that an additional notice must be served as soon as the order is made where the house is subject to a lease and the authority step into the position of the lessee[142]. That notice must inform the lessor of:

(a)   the type of order by reference to the relevant provision of the Act under which it has been made

(b)   the date the order comes into force

(c)   a summary of the effect the order has on the validity of the lease, by reference to the relevant provision of the Act

---

[142]   Regulation 3 Housing (Management Orders and Empty Dwelling Management Orders) (Supplemental Provisions) (England) Regulations 2006, SI 2006/368.

(d) the name and address of the local housing authority or any person authorised to receive on their behalf any future demand for ground rent, service charges or other charges due, or any notices or other documents in respect of the premises.

12.106 The regulations also provide that from the date of the order the authority has the liability to pay sums such as ground rent and service charges due under the lease.[143]

12.107 Similar procedural requirements apply to the variation or revocation of interim and final management orders. The provisions are set out in Part 2 of Schedule 1 to the Act – paragraphs 9–23. They are summarised in Table 12.10.

Table 12.10: Schedule 6, Part 2: procedural requirements for the variation or revocation of management orders

When	Served on	Information	Together with	Consultation requirements
Before varying the interim or final management order	Each relevant person	Statement that the authority is proposing a variation. The effect of the variation. The reasons for the variation. The end of the consultation period.		Must consider representations made in accordance with the notice and not withdrawn.
Following a decision to vary the interim or final management order and within seven days of the decision	Each relevant person	The reasons for the decision. The date on which it was made. The right of appeal. The period within which an appeal may be made.	A copy of the decision to vary the interim or final management order.	

---

[143] Regulation 3 Housing (Management Orders and Empty Dwelling Management Orders) (Supplemental Provisions) (England) Regulations 2006, SI 2006/368.

When	Served on	Information	Together with	Consultation requirements
Before refusing to vary the interim or final management order	Each relevant person	Statement that the authority are proposing to refuse to vary the interim or final management order. The reasons for the refusal. The end of the consultation period.		Must consider representations made in accordance with the notice and not withdrawn.
Following refusal to vary the interim or final management order and within seven days of the decision	The licence holder and each relevant person	The authority's decision not to vary the interim or final management order. The reasons for the decision. The date upon which it was made. The right of appeal. The period within which an appeal may be made.		
Before revoking the interim or final management order	Each relevant person	Statement that the authority are proposing to revoke the interim or final management order. The reasons for the revocation. The end of the consultation period.		Must consider representations made in accordance with the notice and not withdrawn.
Following the decision to revoke the interim or final management order and within seven days of the decision	Each relevant person	The reasons for the decision. The date on which it was made. The right of appeal against the decision. The period within which an appeal may be made.	Copy of the decision to revoke the interim or final management order.	

When	Served on	Information	Together with	Consultation requirements
Before refusing to revoke the interim or final management order	Each relevant person	Statement that the authority is refusing to revoke the interim or final management order. The reasons for refusal. The end of the consultation period.		Must consider representations made in accordance with the notice and not withdrawn.
Following refusal and within seven days of the decision	Each relevant person	The reasons for the decision and the date on which it was made. The right of appeal against the decision. The period within which an appeal may be made.	Copy of the decision not to revoke the interim or final management order.	

APPEALS

12.108 If a landlord disagrees with the local authority's decision to make an interim or final management order or with the terms of a management scheme, he can appeal against the decision to the Residential Property Tribunal. The tribunal has wide powers and considerable discretion in such circumstances and can confirm the order with or without amendments to the terms (including where relevant the terms of the management scheme) or revoke it and order that a licence should be granted or a temporary exemption notice issued.

12.109 There are three rights of appeal. These are the right to appeal against:

- the making of the order which can be appealed by a relevant person;

- the variation or revocation of an order or the refusal to vary or revoke and order which can be appealed by a relevant person;

- decisions in respect of compensation payable to third parties – appealable by the third party.

12.110 There is also an extremely limited right of appeal against the failure of an interim management order to provide for the payment of interest on any surpluses of income over expenditure when the interim management order has been made by the tribunal.

12.111 A relevant person is an owner or a manager of the house or part of the house. Tenants with unexpired terms of 3 years or less are specifically excluded from the definition of relevant person.[144] Providing tenants with rights of appeal was specifically rejected by the government as both inappropriately time consuming and opening those tenants to the risk of retaliatory action by the landlord.[145]

12.112 The details are set out in Part 3 of Schedule 6 to the Act and summarised in Table 12.11.

Table 12.11: Schedule 6, Part 3: appeals against decisions relating to management orders

Paragraph	The right to appeal against	The appellant	Time limits	Powers of the RPT	Additional comments
1(a)	The decision of the housing authority to make an interim or final management order. This right of appeal does not include a right of appeal against a discretionary interim management order[146] or an interim management order made by the tribunal in accordance with Schedule 6, paragraph 26(5).[147]	A relevant person	28 days (or longer if RPT is satisfied of good reason for the failure to appeal before the end of the period (and for any delay in applying for permission to appeal out of time).	The RPT may confirm or vary or revoke the order. If the RPT revokes an interim or final management order and the house requires licensing under Part 2 or Part 3 then RPT must either direct the local housing authority to grant a licence on terms it directs or make an interim management order on terms it directs[148] or direct the local housing authority to serve a temporary exemption notice in respect of the house. There is a limited right of appeal against the terms of such an interim management order dealt with in paragraph 24(2).	Operates as a rehearing but can take into account matters of which the authority was unaware. The effective date of the confirmation, variation or revocation is the date specified in the tribunal order or (in the case of a final management order) as from the tribunal's order. If no appeal is brought within the time limit the order is final and conclusive as to the matters which could have been raised on appeal.

---

[144] Paragraph 35 of Part 3 of Schedule 6.
[145] See *Hansard*, HL, vol 664, col 763 (9 September 2004).
[146] That is, one made under section 102(4) or (7).
[147] That is, one made by the tribunal on the revocation of a final management order.
[148] The tribunal can do this despite section 102(9) which provides that nothing in section 102 'requires or authorises the making of an interim management order in respect of a house if (a)

Para-graph	The right to appeal against	The appel-lant	Time limits	Powers of the RPT	Additional comments
24(1)(b)	The terms of the interim or final management order (including for final orders the terms of the management scheme).	A relevant person	At any time the order is in force	The RPT is limited to determining whether the order should be varied by the tribunal so as to include a term providing for the matter in question and (if so) what provision should be made by the term.	Operates as a rehearing but can take into account matters of which the authority was unaware.
24(2)	The decision of the tribunal to make an interim management (either on revocation of a management order or as a result of an application by the local housing authority) the right of appeal is limited to the failure of the order to provide for the rate of interest and the intervals at which payment of interest on the surplus of rent over expenditure is paid to the landlord.[149]	A relevant person			
28	The decision or refusal to vary or revoke an interim management order or a final management order.	A relevant person	28 days (or longer if RPT is satisfied of good reason for the failure to appeal before the end of the period (and for any delay in applying for permission to appeal out of time).	The tribunal may confirm, reverse or vary the decision of the local housing authority. If the appeal is against a decision of the authority to refuse to revoke the order, the tribunal may make an order revoking the order as from a date specified in its order.	Operates as a rehearing but can take into account matters of which the authority was unaware.

an interim management order has been previously made in respect of it and (b) the authority have not exercised any relevant function in respect of the house at any time after the making of the order'.

[149] This appeal right is specifically mentioned in section 110(5)(a) and (b).

Para-graph	The right to appeal against	The appel-lant	Time limits	Powers of the RPT	Additional comments
32	A local housing authority decision not to pay compensation to a third party in respect of any interference with his rights as a result of the interim or final management order or the decision as to the amount of compensation.	The third party	28 days from the date when the authority notifies the third party of its decision in relation to compensation.[150]	The tribunal may confirm, reverse or vary the decision of the local housing authority. Where the tribunal reverses or varies the decision in respect of a final management order it must vary the management scheme accordingly.	Operates as a rehearing but can take into account matters of which the authority was unaware.

12.113 The availability of a right to appeal has additional significance because it determines the operative periods of orders under the Act. The time period during which an appeal right remains outstanding and an order not operative under the Act is set out in Table 12.12.

Table 12.12: Schedule 6, Part 3: the operative time of orders

For the purposes of	If . . .	The operative time is
The coming into force of final management orders[151]	No appeal is made under paragraph 24 before the end of 28 days.	28 days after the date of the order.
	An appeal is made under paragraph 24 and a decision of the RPT is made which confirms the order.[152]	The expiry of the period within which an appeal may be made to the Lands Tribunal if an appeal is not made within that period; or if an appeal to the Lands Tribunal is made the time when a decision is made by the Lands Tribunal to confirm the order.
	The appeal is withdrawn – this operates as a decision to confirm the order.	

---

[150] Under section 128(2).
[151] Under section 114(2) The operative period is set out in Schedule 6, Part 3, paragraph 27.
[152] A decision which confirms the order includes a decision which confirms it with variation.

For the purposes of	If . . .	The operative time is
The variation or revocation of interim or final management orders[153]	No appeal is made under paragraph 28 before the end of 28 days.	28 days after the decision to vary or revoke or to refuse to vary or revoke the interim or final management order.
	An appeal is made under paragraph 28 and a decision of the RPT is made which confirms the variation or revocation.	The expiry of the period within which an appeal may be made to the Lands Tribunal if an appeal is not made within that period; or if an appeal to the Lands Tribunal is made the time when a decision is made by the Lands Tribunal to vary or revoke the order.
	The appeal is withdrawn – this operates as a decision to vary or revoke the order appealed against.	

CONCLUSION

12.114 Interim and final management orders provide local housing authorities with mechanisms to ensure necessary improvements in the physical conditions, the management of the rented accommodation and the behaviour of the occupiers where there is no available 'fit and proper' person to take on the responsibilities of a licence in areas where licensing is required under Part 2 or Part 3 of the Act. They also provide local housing authorities with the power to impose measures in response to the needs of the occupiers or the neighbours of 'problem' housing which falls outside of the requirements of Part 2 and Part 3 in certain limited circumstances.

12.115 The provisions are arguably either over-bureaucratic because of the need to constrain the local housing authority in dealing with someone else's property and are destined be used very little or they represent a major step towards a national system of licensing for all private rented housing. To date there has been little evidence of local authority activity, but it remains early days.

---

[153] Under sections 111(2), 112(2), 121(2) or 122(2). The operative period is set out in Schedule 6, Part 3, paragraph 31.

TIPS AND TRAPS

12.116 The biggest challenge for local authorities in making management orders is to appreciate the tension between the need to take action, without dispossessing the owner of the property.

12.117 The provisions of the Act attempt to balance the needs of the authority to manage the property appropriately with the fact that the order is short term, does not equate with ownership of the property and is not meant to disturb the status quo of property ownership, particularly in relation to other parties' interests, such as mortgagees and superior landlords. As the minister explained in committee, 'We are seeking to provide a power that will allow the local authority to manage the property effectively. That is not dispossessing the owner of all of his rights.'[154]

12.118 Interim management orders in particular have limits to reflect their temporary nature. As the government minister explained:

> 'It is important that local authorities do not see the making of an interim management order as giving them a green light to act as if they owned the property for all time. I believe that there are already adequate safeguards to protect against this. First, the authority is under a duty to sort out the long-term management of the house as soon as practicable. It will hardly fulfil this obligation if it is embarking on an extensive programme of unnecessary works. Secondly, and most importantly, the landlord can appeal to the Residential Property Tribunal against any unreasonable expenditure incurred. If the local authority were to attempt to take unreasonable actions under the interim management order, it would find itself landed with the bill for doing so.'[155]

12.119 Clearly the greatest potential infringement of property rights lies in the special interim management orders. It is for this reason that they can only be made following authorisation from the RPT.

12.120 At the time of writing there have been no reported decisions on special interim management orders. However, it is possible to draw lessons from other applications/appeals to the RPT as to the potential pitfalls of applications.

12.121 In particular authorities should pay close attention to paragraphs 27–37 of the Schedule to the Residential Property Tribunal Procedure (England) Regulations 2006.[156] These require the authority to provide copies of the draft order, and most importantly a statement demonstrating that the authority has satisfied all of the statutory requirements under the Act.

---

[154] *Hansard*, Commons Committee, vol 417 col 362 (3 February 2004).
[155] *Hansard*, HL Committee, vol 664, col 804, (9 September 2004).
[156] SI 2006/831.

Chapter 13

EMPTY DWELLING MANAGEMENT ORDERS

INTRODUCTION

13.1 The statutory scheme for Empty Dwelling Management Orders (EDMOs) was developed in response to concerns about empty properties in England and Wales. The consultation paper *Empty Homes: temporary management, lasting solutions*[1] set out measures to bring more unoccupied privately owned homes back into use. The consultation paper set two specific objectives:

- to provide a mechanism for bringing empty homes back into use that complements voluntary leasing arrangements and is not as protracted and over-prescriptive as existing enforcement powers;

- to provide a mechanism for bringing dilapidated empty homes back into use that does not require owners to fund renovation from their own resources.

13.2 The consultation and the ODPM's risk assessment of the proposals for reform considered that an empty home was a wasted resource both for the owner, who could otherwise make financial gains by letting or selling the property, and for those who are in need of housing. In addition, it was considered that empty homes may have negative impacts particularly with regard to antisocial behaviour both on neighbouring residents and the wider community.

13.3 According to Government statistics the number of privately owned empty homes has been decreasing since the early 1990s. Nonetheless numbers still remain significant. It was estimated that in 2003 there were 308,000 long-term[2] empty dwellings in the private sector across England.[3] The private sector, which accounts for 80% of the dwelling stock in England, accounted for nearly 84% of empty homes.

---

[1] ODPM (May 2003).
[2] A long-term empty dwelling refers to a dwelling that has remained vacant for more than 6 months.
[3] Local Authority Housing Investment Programme returns, April 2003.

13.4 The proposals for EDMOs were introduced late in the parliamentary process. Their statutory shape is similar to management orders. In essence EDMOs allow a local housing authority to step into the shoes' of the owner of a privately owned unoccupied dwelling and secure its occupation and proper management. However, the ownership of the property is not transferred to the housing authority, rather it manages the property. The housing authority meets its management costs from the income produced by letting out the dwelling.

13.5 There are two forms of EDMO: the interim EDMO and the final EDMO. Interim orders can only be made with the authorisation of the RPT. They assume some form of co-operation between the owner and the housing authority, as the property can only be let with the owner's consent. Final orders allow the authority to let without the owner's consent. Final EDMOs do not require the authorisation of the RPT. However, the owner can appeal to the tribunal against the making of the order.

THE LEGISLATIVE FRAMEWORK

13.6 Table 13.1 summarises the provisions on EDMOs.

Table 13.1: Empty Dwelling Management Orders

Section Number	Summary	Comment
132	EDMOs: introductory	Defines interim and final EDMOs, provides other relevant definitions and makes reference to Schedule 7 where more detailed requirements are set out
133	Making interim EDMOs	Details the conditions which an authority must meet before applying to an RPT for an interim EDMO
134	Authorisation of the making of interim EDMOs	Specifies the role of the RPT in authorising interim EDMOs and sets out the matters about which the authority must satisfy the RPT before making an interim EDMO

135	Local authority's duties once interim EDMOs in force	Describes the duties on local housing authorities to ensure the occupation and proper management of the dwelling pending the making of a final EDMO or the revocation of the interim EDMOs
136	Making final EDMOs	Details the conditions necessary before a final EDMO can be made
137	Local authority's duties once final EDMOs in force	Sets out the duties relating to final EDMOs, including the necessity for a management scheme
138	Compensation: third parties	Sets out the arrangements for claims and payments of compensation to third parties in respect of any interference with rights in respect of the dwelling.

13.7 Certain definitions are crucial to the operation of EDMOs. First, the statutory scheme applies only to a dwelling, which is defined in section 132(4)(a) as:

'(i) a building intended to be occupied as a separate dwelling, or
(ii) a part of a building intended to be occupied as a separate dwelling which may be entered otherwise than through any non-residential accommodation in the building.'

13.8 Secondly, the scheme provides particular protections to 'relevant' proprietors and third parties. A 'relevant proprietor' is the freeholder or, if the property is subject to a lease or a chain of leases, the person who has the shortest unexpired term.

13.9 A third party is a person who has an estate or interest in the dwelling who is neither the relevant proprietor, nor someone who has been granted a tenancy of the dwelling by the local housing authority under the EDMO provisions.[4]

EFFECT ON OWNERSHIP RIGHTS

13.10 When an EDMO is in force, the local housing authority takes over most of the rights and responsibilities of the relevant proprietor and may exercise

---

4   Section 132(4)(d).

them as if it were the relevant proprietor. For example, it has the right to possession of the dwelling whilst the order is in force. However, the local housing authority does not become the legal owner of the property and cannot sell the property or mortgage it.

13.11 A relevant proprietor is not entitled to receive any rent or other payments from anyone occupying the dwelling and may not exercise any rights to manage the dwelling whilst an EDMO is in force. Nevertheless, the relevant proprietor retains their right to dispose of their interest in the property.

13.12 The validity of a mortgage or superior lease of the property and any rights or remedies available to the mortgage lender or lessor are unaffected by the EDMO, except where they would prevent the local housing authority exercising its power to grant a tenancy or some other right to occupy the dwelling.

13.13 An EDMO is classified as a local land charge and the local housing authority may apply to have details of it entered on the Land Registry. Any sum of money recoverable from the relevant proprietor under an EDMO is, until recovered, a charge on the dwelling.

INTERIM EDMOS

13.14 The first, and most scrutinised step in the process of taking control of an empty dwelling, is the interim EDMO. Local authorities are made aware of empty properties either through council tax records, or through complaints about properties being at risk or causing a nuisance from neighbours.

13.15 The interim EDMO procedure provides a mechanism to prompt the owner into ensuring the property becomes occupied, or allows a local housing authority to take steps to ensure that a dwelling becomes, and continues to be, occupied.

13.16 Whilst it is the local housing authority which makes the interim EDMO, it must first seek the authorisation of the RPT. Before applying to a RPT for authorisation to make an interim EDMO, a local housing authority must make reasonable efforts to contact the owner and find out if he has any intentions to bring the dwelling back into occupation.[5]

13.17 In addition the local authority must consider the balance of interests between the rights of the relevant proprietor and the interests of the wider community.[6]

13.18 The tribunal will scrutinise both of these steps.

---

[5]   Section 133(3).
[6]   Section 133(4).

13.19 Before a Residential Property Tribunal can authorise the making of an interim EDMO it must be satisfied that:

- the property has been wholly unoccupied for at least the prescribed period of time (the minimum period is currently 6 months);[7]

- that there is no reasonable prospect that the dwelling will become occupied in the near future;[8]

- there is a reasonable prospect that the property will become occupied if an interim EDMO is made;[9]

- the local housing authority has complied with its duties in seeking to make an interim EDMO, including any matters that may be set out in regulations.[10]

13.20 In authorising an interim EDMO the RPT must take account of the interests of the wider community and the effect on third parties.[11] The RPT must also be satisfied that the case does not come within any exempt category that may be provided by the appropriate national authority (the Secretary of State in England or the National Assembly in Wales).[12]

13.21 The exempt categories are set out in The Housing (Empty Dwelling Management Orders) (Prescribed Exceptions and Requirements) (England) Order 2006.[13]

13.22 A dwelling is exempt if:

'(a) it has been occupied solely or principally by the relevant proprietor and is wholly unoccupied because —
  (i) he is temporarily[14] resident elsewhere;
  (ii) he is absent from the dwelling for the purpose of receiving personal care by reason of old age, disablement, illness, past or present alcohol or drug dependence or past or present mental disorder;
  (iii) he is absent from the dwelling for the purpose of providing, or better providing, personal care for a person who requires such care by reason of old age, disablement, illness, past or present alcohol or drug dependence or past or present mental disorder; or
  (iv) he is a serving member of the armed forces and he is absent from the dwelling as a result of such service;

---

7   Section 134(1), (2)(a).
8   Section 134(2)(b)
9   Section 134(2)(c).
10 Section 134(2)(d).
11 Section 134(3)(a), (b), (4).
12 Section 134(5).
13 SI 2006/367.
14 There is no indication how long an absence can be before it ceases to be temporary. In case no CAM260/UK/HYI/2006/0002 there was a suggestion that 3 years absence was possibly too long, however the case turned on other facts.

(b)   it is used as a holiday home (whether or not it is let as such on a commercial basis) or is otherwise occupied by the relevant proprietor or his guests on a temporary basis from time to time;

(c)   it is genuinely on the market for sale or letting;[15]

(d)   it is comprised in an agricultural holding within the meaning of the Agricultural Holdings Act 1986 or a farm business tenancy within the meaning of the Agricultural Tenancies Act 1995;

(e)   it is usually occupied by an employee of the relevant proprietor in connection with the performance of his duties under the terms of his contract of employment;

(f)   it is available for occupation by a minister of religion as a residence from which to perform the duties of his office;

(g)   it is subject to a court order freezing the property of the relevant proprietor;

(h)   it is prevented from being occupied as a result of a criminal investigation or criminal proceedings;

(i)   it is mortgaged, where the mortgagee, in right of the mortgage, has entered into and is in possession of the dwelling; or

(j)   the person who was the relevant proprietor of it has died and six months has not elapsed since the grant of representation was obtained in respect of such person.'

The Regulations – at paragraph 4 – require the housing authority to provide certain information to the RPT in connection with the prescribed exemptions. This includes:

(1)   details of the efforts they have made to notify the relevant proprietor that they are considering making an interim empty dwelling management order in respect of his dwelling, as required under section 133(3)(a) of the Act;

(2)   details of the enquiries they have made to ascertain what steps (if any) the relevant proprietor is taking, or is intending to take, to secure that the dwelling is occupied, as required under section 133(3)(b) of the Act;

(3)   details of any advice and assistance they have provided to the relevant proprietor with a view to the relevant proprietor securing that the dwelling is occupied;

(4)   all information they have that suggests that the dwelling may fall within one of the exceptions described in Article 3, whether available from the authority's own enquiries or from representations made to it by the relevant proprietor; and

(5)   the classification of the dwelling for council tax purposes under the Local Government Finance Act 1992; and where the relevant proprietor —

---

[15]   This is another area which has received attention in the decisions. They suggest it is unlikely that hand written postcards stating 'To Let' and providing a mobile phone number are genuine efforts at sale or letting.

(i) has undertaken or is undertaking repairs, maintenance or improvement works; or

(ii) has applied to a local planning authority or other authority for permission to make structural alterations or additions to the dwelling and he awaits the decision of a relevant authority on the application,

(6) the local housing authority must give reasons to the tribunal why it considers that an EDMO is required to secure occupation of the dwelling.

13.23 An interim EDMO comes into force as soon as it has been authorised and can last for a maximum of 12 months.[16] Once an interim EDMO is in force, a local housing authority must take steps to secure occupation and proper management of the property.[17] Nevertheless, the local housing authority may only grant a tenancy (or some other right of occupation) to someone with the consent of the relevant proprietor.[18]

FINAL EDMOS

13.24 A local housing authority may make a final EDMO either to replace an interim EDMO or a previous final EDMO if the local housing authority considers the property would otherwise become or remain unoccupied.[19] This might happen, for example, if the relevant proprietor refused to allow a tenancy to be granted under an interim EDMO and the local housing authority considered that once the order ceased to have effect the property would be likely to remain unoccupied. In such circumstances the local housing authority might decide to revoke the interim EDMO early and make a final EDMO to replace it.

13.25 If a property that is subject to a final EDMO is unoccupied, a local housing authority may make a new final EDMO to replace it provided that the local housing authority is satisfied it has taken all steps it was appropriate for it to take to secure occupation of the property.[20]

13.26 In this process the local housing authority must consider that making a final EDMO is the most appropriate course of action when taking account of the interests of the community and the effect the final EDMO will have on the rights of the relevant proprietor and any third parties to the EDMO.[21]

13.27 A local housing authority does not need to obtain authorisation from a RPT to make a final EDMO. However, this makes the RPT particularly

---

[16] Section 135(1), Schedule 7, Part 1, paragraph 1.
[17] Section 135(2)–(4).
[18] Section 135, Schedule 7, paragraph 7.
[19] Section 136(1)(a), (b).
[20] Section 136(2).
[21] Section 136(3)–(5).

assiduous in checking the procedural formalities required for an interim EDMO. There are also rights to appeal in connection with both final and interim EDMOs.

13.28 Subject to any appeal, a final EDMO comes into force no earlier than the day after the period for appealing has expired and lasts for the period specified in the order, which can be up to 7 years.

APPEALS

13.29 A person who is affected by an EDMO may appeal to a RPT against:[22]

- a decision of a local housing authority to make a final EDMO;

- the terms of a final EDMO (including the terms of a management scheme see below);

- the terms of an interim EDMO (relating to payment of any balance of rent left after deduction of relevant expenditure and any compensation payable to a third party or a dispossessed landlord or tenant);

- a decision of the local authority to vary or revoke an interim or final EDMO or its refusal to vary or revoke an interim or final EDMO.

ARRANGEMENTS FOR COMPENSATION

13.30 A third party may apply to the RPT for an order requiring a local housing authority to pay them compensation for any interference with their rights in respect of a property on which an application for authorisation of an interim EDMO is made.

13.31 A third party may also request a local housing authority to pay compensation for interference with their rights in respect of a dwelling on which a final EDMO is made and they may appeal to a RPT if the local housing authority refuses to pay compensation or they consider the amount is inadequate.

TERMINATION OF LEASES

13.32 When applying for authorisation to make an interim EDMO, or in making a final EDMO, a local housing authority may apply to a RPT for an order to terminate an existing lease or licence of the property. This allows for the termination of a lease or licence where the property is not being occupied.

---

[22] See Schedule 7, Part 4.

13.33 If the local housing authority is unable to terminate an occupation arrangement by serving notice to quit, the RPT may make an order of termination provided it is satisfied the dwelling is not being occupied under a lease or licence and the local housing authority requires possession of it to secure occupation.

13.34 In making an order terminating a lease or licence, a RPT may require the local housing authority to pay compensation to the dispossessed person.[23] Compensation paid out by the local housing authority can be recovered out of any surplus rent obtained under the EDMO.[24]

DUTIES ON THE LOCAL HOUSING AUTHORITY

13.35 Once a final EDMO is in force the local housing authority has a number of duties.[25] A local housing authority is under a duty to review the operation of a final EDMO from time to time.[26] If the property is unoccupied, the local housing authority must consider whether there are any steps it could take to secure occupation or whether it is necessary to keep the EDMO in force. If the local housing authority concludes that there are no steps it could take to secure occupation, or that keeping the order in force is not necessary, the local housing authority must revoke the EDMO.[27]

The most important duty on the local housing authority is to draw up a management scheme.

MANAGEMENT SCHEME

13.36 A final EDMO must contain a management scheme setting out how the local housing authority intends to carry out its duties and how it will account for moneys expended and collected whilst it is operative. The local housing authority must keep full accounts of income and expenditure and provide anyone with a relevant interest in the dwelling reasonable access to inspect them.[28]

13.37 The management scheme must include details of the following:[29]

- work the local housing authority intends to carry out to the dwelling and an estimate of expenditure;

---

23   Schedule 7, paragraph 22(6).
24   Schedule 7, paragraph 23.
25   Section 137(1).
26   Section 137(4).
27   Section 137(6)(a).
28   Schedule 7, Part 3, paragraph 13.
29   Schedule 7, Part 3, paragraph 13.

- the rent the dwelling might be expected to fetch on the open market and the rent the local housing authority will seek to obtain;

- any compensation payable to third parties;

- where the amount of rent payable is less than the open market rent, the management scheme must account for the difference. For example, the local housing authority is permitted to charge a sub-market rent, but it must make up any shortfall out of its own resources.

13.38 The management scheme must also include details of how the local housing authority intends to pay the relevant proprietor, any surplus remaining after deduction of its relevant expenditure and any compensation payable.[30]

13.39 The management scheme may also state if the local housing authority intends to carry over any surplus to a subsequent final EDMO or, where there is a deficit, how it intends to recover the deficit under a subsequent final EDMO.[31]

13.40 Anyone affected by a management scheme who considers the local housing authority is not managing the dwelling in accordance with the management scheme may apply to a Residential Property Tribunal for an order requiring the local housing authority to do so.[32]

NOTIFICATION PROCEDURES

13.41 Before making a final EDMO, a local housing authority must serve a copy of the proposed order on all relevant persons and a notice stating the reason for making the order and the main terms of it. The notice must also invite representations about the proposal (which the local housing authority must consider).[33]

13.42 When an interim or final EDMO is made the local housing authority must, within 7 days, serve a copy of the order and a notice on the relevant proprietor and other persons with an interest in the dwelling.[34]

13.43 The notice must state:[35]

- the reason for making the order and the date on which it is made;

- the general effect of the order;

---

[30] Schedule 7, Part 3, paragraph 13.
[31] Schedule 7, Part 3, paragraph 13.
[32] Schedule 7, Part 3, paragraph 14.
[33] Schedule 7, Part 3, paragraph 14.
[34] Schedule 7, Part 3, paragraph 14.
[35] Schedule 7, Part 3, paragraph 14.

- the date on which it is proposed the order will cease to have effect.

In addition, the notice must advise of any right to appeal against the order.[36]

VARIATION AND REVOCATION OF EDMOS

13.44 A relevant proprietor or someone else with an interest in the dwelling is entitled to ask the local housing authority to vary or revoke an interim or final EDMO at any time.[37]

13.45 The terms of an interim or final EDMO (including the terms of a management scheme) may be varied if the local housing authority considers it appropriate to do so. A person with an interest in the dwelling may request a variation and may appeal to a RPT against a decision of the local housing authority to vary or, as the case may be, refusal to vary the order.[38]

13.46 A local housing authority may revoke an EDMO if:[39]

- it concludes that there are no steps it can take to secure occupation of the dwelling;

- it is satisfied that the dwelling will become or continue to be occupied following revocation;

- it is satisfied that the dwelling is to be sold;

- a final EDMO (or subsequent final EDMO) has been made to replace the order;

- it concludes that it should revoke the order so it does not interfere with the rights of a third party;

- in any other circumstance it considers it appropriate to do so.

13.47 However, if the dwelling is occupied at the time the revocation is proposed, the local housing authority may only revoke with the consent of the relevant proprietor (unless the revocation is necessary so that a final EDMO may be made). This restriction is provided so that the relevant proprietor is not left to manage tenancies he did not enter into. Therefore, if the local housing authority decides to revoke the order and hand back responsibility for the dwelling to the relevant proprietor, it must first bring to an end any occupation, unless the relevant proprietor is willing for the occupation to continue.[40]

---

[36] Schedule 7, Part 3, paragraph 14.
[37] Schedule 7, Part 3, paragraph 15 et seq.
[38] Schedule 7, Part 3, paragraph 15 et seq.
[39] Schedule 7, Part 3, paragraph 15, et seq.
[40] Schedule 7, Part 3, paragraph 15, et seq.

13.48 The local housing authority may make revocation subject to payment of any expenditure incurred by it that has not already been recouped from rental income. It might also refuse to revoke the order on the grounds that the property would be likely to be left vacant.

13.49 Where revocation is refused, a right of appeal to a Residential Property Tribunal is provided.

MONEY MATTERS

13.50 A local housing authority may use any rent collected from a person occupying the dwelling to meet its expenditure and to pay any compensation it is required to pay to a third party. When an EDMO ceases to have effect, the local housing authority must pay the relevant proprietor any surplus after deduction of such relevant sums (and if appropriate interest on the balance). However, in the case of an interim EDMO, a local housing authority is not required to pay any surplus to the relevant proprietor if the order is followed by a final EDMO.

13.51 If, when an EDMO ceases to have effect, there is a deficit rather than a surplus after deduction of relevant sums, the local housing authority cannot recover the amount from the relevant proprietor unless:

- he has agreed to pay it, for example, as a condition for revoking the order early;

- it is an amount equivalent to a service charge paid by the local housing authority;

- in the case of an interim EDMO, the local housing authority considers the relevant proprietor unreasonably refused consent to allow it to grant a tenancy.

13.52 If a final EDMO is made to replace either an interim EDMO or a previous final EDMO, any deficit may be carried over and recovered from income under the subsequent order.

APPEALS

13.53 A third party may appeal to a RPT against a decision of a local housing authority not to pay compensation to him, or a decision relating to the amount of compensation payable.[41]

---

[41]   Schedule 7, Part 3, paragraph 15 and section 138.

REPAIRS AND RENOVATION WORKS

13.54 There are no restrictions on the works of repair or renovation a local housing authority may undertake under an EDMO.[42] However, the work must be commensurate with the income it is likely to receive during the lifetime of the order. As an interim EDMO can only last for 12 months, it is unlikely that a local housing authority would expend larger sums of money to renovate a dwelling without obtaining the relevant proprietor's consent to the grant of a tenancy.

13.55 A local housing authority is more likely to consider undertaking significant work under a final EDMO as it would have up to 7 years to recoup the cost from rental income. Details of any work the local housing authority intends to carry out must be contained in the management scheme. Someone with an estate or interest in the dwelling may object to such provision in the management scheme and appeal against the terms of it to a Residential Property Tribunal.

FURNITURE

13.56 A local housing authority has the right to possession of furniture or other articles in a dwelling that is owned by the relevant proprietor whilst the order is in force. But the relevant proprietor may request possession of the furniture. A local authority may renounce the right to possession of such furniture by notifying the relevant proprietor. If so, the authority must store the furniture at its own cost.[43]

13.57 A local authority may supply furniture to a dwelling subject to an interim or final EDMO and can recover the cost of it as relevant expenditure.[44]

POWERS OF ENTRY

13.58 A local housing authority has the right to enter a dwelling subject to an EDMO to survey its condition or to carry out works. Any occupier who prevents an officer, employee, agent or contractor of a local housing authority from carrying out their duties may be ordered to stop by a magistrate's court. Failure to comply with an order of the court is an offence.[45]

13.59 A local housing authority may apply to a court for a warrant to authorise entry to a dwelling subject to an EDMO.[46]

---

[42] See Schedule 7.
[43] Schedule 7, paragraphs 20 and 21.
[44] Schedule 7, paragraphs 20 and 21.
[45] Schedule 7, paragraph 25.
[46] Schedule 7, paragraph 25(3).

Part VI

ENFORCEMENT AND SANCTIONS

Chapter 14

ENFORCEMENT AND SANCTIONS IN RELATION TO THE HHSRS/CONSEQUENCES OF NON-COMPLIANCE WITH ENFORCEMENT ACTION UNDER PART 1

INTRODUCTION

14.1　This chapter will look at the sanctions which can be imposed in relation to enforcement action under Part 1. There are two conditions precedent to imposition of any sanction: (i) the particular method of enforcement has become operative and (ii) the period for completion of the action required by the improvement notice or the time for compliance with the prohibition order has expired.[1]

14.2　At the point the notice or order is operative it is final and conclusive as to matters which could have been raised on appeal.[2] This ouster prevents arguments relating to the merits of the enforcement action being raised in the magistrates' court. Since the jurisdiction of the Residential Property Tribunal on appeal from an improvement notice or against a prohibition order is so wide it will be questionable as to what scope, if any, there remains for a collateral challenge defending any sanction on the basis that the enforcement action was not lawful and a nullity.[3]

---

[1]　Subject to the authority not being satisfied that reasonable progress is being made towards completing the remedial work specified in the notice; see paragraph 3(3) of Schedule 3 and section 30(2).

[2]　Section 15(6) and 24(6).

[3]　Eg pursuant to a decision tainted by illegality, irrationality or procedural impropriety. In *BTP v Boddington* [1999] 2 AC 143/153 The House of Lords allowed someone prosecuted for smoking on south east trains to defend the case against him on the grounds that the relevant byelaws were introduced pursuant to an unlawful decision. Under the Town and Country Planning Act 1990 the statutory grounds for appeal against an enforcement notice are spelt out under section 174. There is also an ouster in the 1990 Act in broadly equivalent terms to section 15(6). The grounds under section 174 do not embrace that the enforcement action is a nullity. In *R v Wicks* [1998] AC 92 the House of Lords, having considered the purpose of the ouster in section 285 of the 1990 Act) held that an argument of alleged nullity could not be relied on as a defence in the magistrates court, instead the matter could only be raised by judicial review. An attempt to judicially review enforcement action under Part 1 would be scrutinised to see if the complaint could not be aired by way of statutory appeal, because if it could then permission might well be refused, since judicial review is meant to be a remedy of last resort. See also the judgment in *Palacegate Properties Limited v Camden LBC*

14.3 There are three methods of sanction. The first is prosecution. The second is default action.[4] The third, acting like a carrot and stick (to encourage prompt steps being taken to reduce, if not altogether stop, mounting costs and expenses being incurred by the LHA) is that costs and expenses can be recovered by way of legal charge on the premises.

PROSECUTIONS

14.4 These are the main criminal offences which may be committed for non compliance with enforcement action under Part 1:

- Failure to comply with an improvement notice: section 30;

- Failure to comply with a prohibition order: section 32;

- Preventing the owner or person having control or their respective representative[5] from taking action required by an improvement notice or prohibition order, and which has been authorised by a court order made pursuant to section 35(2): section 35(4);

- Preventing direct action by the local housing authority and which has been authorised by a court order made pursuant to section 35(3): section 35(4);

- Entering into occupation of a property subject to a demolition order: section 270(5) of the Housing Act 1985.

14.5 In the event that none of the above offences 'fit the crime' there is a further catch all offence[6]:

- Obstructing a relevant person[7] in the performance of anything which by virtue of any of Parts 1 to 4, they are required or authorised to do: section 241.

14.6 This catch all offence under section 241 is specifically said to have been committed where a person obstructs default action under paragraph 3 of

---

CO/2503/1999 4 PLR 59 which Lord Justice Laws began: 'The case requires the court to revisit well-trodden ground: how far may a defendant challenge, by way of defence to a criminal prosecution, the instrument or order which founds the prosecution against him on grounds which could have been raised upon an application for judicial review? For convenience I will call this the collateral challenge issue.'

4   Schedule 3, Part 2, paragraph 3.
5   Defined in section 35(8) as any officer, employee, agent or contractor of that person.
6   Which would equally apply to the offences under section 35(4).
7   Defined in section 241(4): as an officer of a local housing authority or any person authorised to enter premises by virtue of Parts 1 to 4 or section 239 (powers of entry) or 240 (warrant to authorise entry).

Schedule 3.[8] Section 241 may have numerous uses but particularly where under section 239 there is a power of entry, and under section 40 and paragraph 3(4) of Schedule 3 where there is a right of entry, and it is obstructed. Further, under paragraph 5 of Schedule 3, a person is to be treated as if they have offended under section 241 where entry into premises (in respect of which default works have already begun) has taken place, in order to carry out works.

14.7 The power of entry under section 239 is subject to notice to both owner (if known) and occupier (if any).[9] The power may arise where any of the following conditions is met:[10]

- a survey or examination of premises is necessary in order to carry out an inspection under section 4(1);

- an inspection is required pursuant to section 4(2);

- the premises are specified by an improvement notice or prohibition order; or

- a management order is in force.

14.8 If the LHA considers that premises need to be entered to ascertain if an offence of having control or managing unlicensed premises[11] or to ascertain if an offence of breach of management regulations has taken place[12] then entry may be without prior notice, but still only at any reasonable time.[13]

14.9 Additionally there are further generic offences:

- Failing to produce documents reasonably required in connection with exercise of the authority's functions and specified in a notice served pursuant to section 235;

- Knowingly or recklessly supplying false or misleading information in connection with exercise of any of the housing authority's functions under Parts 1 to 4 and Part 7 (section 238).

14.10 The penalties, two of which[14]are subject to a power to up-rate if the Secretary of State considers there has been a change in the value of money;[15] are as follows:

---

[8] See paragraph 5 of Schedule 3.
[9] Section 239(5).
[10] Section 239(1) and (2).
[11] Offences in relation to Parts 2 and 3 of the Act under sections 72(1) and 95(1).
[12] Section 234(3).
[13] Section 239(7).
[14] The offences under sections 32 and 35.
[15] Section 252.

Provision	Offence	Penalty
30	Failing to comply with Improvement Notice	Level 5: £5,000
32	Failing to comply with Prohibition Order	Level 5: £5,000 and a fine of up to £20 in respect of each day, or part of a day, which the offender uses or permits the premises to be used after conviction
35(4)	Failing to comply with Court Order made under either 35(2) or 35(3)[16]	Fine of up to £20 in respect of each day, or part of a day, the failure continues
270(5) HA 1985	Entering or permitting another to enter into occupation of premises knowing that a demolition order has become operative and applies to the premises	Level 5 and a daily fine in respect of each day, or part of a day, on which occupation continues after conviction
241	Obstruction	Level 4: £2,500
236(1)	Failing to provide specified information	Level 5: £5,000
236(4)	Intentionally altering suppressing or destroying any document required to be produced under section 235	Statutory maximum or on conviction on indictment, to a fine
238	Supplying false or misleading information	Level 5; £5,000

14.11 It will be a defence that the person charged had a reasonable excuse for:

(a) failing to comply with the improvement notice;[17]

(b) for using the premises or permitting them to be used in contravention of the prohibition order;[18]

(c) for failing to comply with the order which authorised the action to be taken;[19]

(d) failing to provide the specified information required under section 235;[20]

(e) obstructing the relevant person.[21]

---

[16] Section 35(2) and 35(3) make it an offence, if respectively an occupier and a relevant person, despite having received reasonable notice, prevents action being taken by the persons specified in the respective sub-sections.

[17] Section 30(4).

[18] Section 32(3).

[19] Section 35(5).

[20] Section 236(2).

[21] Section 241(2).

14.12 There is a statutory defence to the offence of obstruction under section 241 when charged in relation to entering for the purpose of doing works premises that were already the subject of default action, which is that there was an urgent necessity for the works in order to prevent danger to persons occupying the premises.[22]

DEFAULT ACTION

14.13 There is action by agreement[23] which is to be contrasted with default (remedial) action without agreement required by an improvement notice which has become operative.[24] There is also emergency remedial action, which maybe with or without agreement, in relation to a category 1 hazard which involves an imminent risk of serious harm to the health and safety of occupiers of any residential premises.[25]

14.14 In relation to the action by agreement, the Act permits a local housing authority to take any action required to be taken by the person served with an improvement notice, if the person served agrees for the work to be done, understanding that the cost of such work as the authority carries out is at his or her expense.[26]

14.15 Before default action is taken without agreement, the local housing authority must first serve a notice.[27] The notice has to contain certain information. The notice must[28] identify the premises and the hazard concerned, the notice has to state that the authority intends to enter the premises, it has to specify the action the authority intends to take and finally it must set out the power[29] which it relies on to enter the premises, and which enables it to take the default action.

RECOVERING COSTS AND EXPENSES

14.16 The act deals with recovery of costs and expenses in relation to Part 1 in two places: (i) sections 49 and 50 and (ii) in Part 3 of Schedule 3. The former concern administrative and other expenses incurred in relation to serving and making notices and orders in relation to all types of enforcement action including the taking of emergency remedial action. Part 3 of Schedule 3 deals with recovery of expenses reasonably incurred in carrying out default action.

---

22   Paragraph 5(2) of Schedule 3.
23   Paragraph 1 of Schedule 3.
24   Paragraph 3 of Schedule 3.
25   Section 40.
26   Schedule 3, Part 1,
27   Schedule 3, paragraph 4.
28   Schedule 3, paragraph 4(2).
29   Contained in paragraph 3(4) of Schedule 3.

14.17 Once the authority has correctly demanded their recoverable sum[30] and the demand has become operative,[31] the charge becomes a charge on the premises concerned.[32]

14.18 The Local Land Charges Act 1975 requires[33] an authority to enter an enforceable charge on the local land charges register. If there was a delay by a local housing authority in entering the charge on the local land charges register[34] there is apparently the possibility of a purchaser buying premises subject of a charge which has arisen by virtue of section 50(9) of the Act, before the charge has been registered.[35] The charge takes effect as if registered by legal mortgage. This means that the authority have the same powers and remedies as if mortgagees with the power of sale.[36]

14.19 The Act permits a Residential Property Tribunal (which allows an appeal against the underlying notice or order) to require the authority to repay any amounts already extracted under the power to charge.[37]

SERVING A RECOVERY NOTICE ON TENANTS OR LICENSEES OF THE PERSON SERVED WITH A DEMAND FOR RECOVERY OF EXPENSES

14.20 Once the demand is operative the authority can require all future payments by tenants or licensees, 'whether already accrued due or not', to be made to them instead of being paid to the landlord.[38] This power is hedged about by the need to serve a recovery notice which has the effect of transferring to the authority the right to recover, receive and give a discharge for rent or sums paid in the nature of rent.[39]

---

[30]   For which see section 50 and paragraphs 8, 9 and 12 of Part 3 of Schedule 3.

[31]   No amount is recoverable until the operative time. Provisions governing the operative time have to be understood in the context of the right of appeal to the Residential Property Tribunal. The operative time is after the time for appealing has expired. If there is an unsuccessful appeal the operative time will not be until the time for appealing to the Lands Tribunal has expired or if there is such a second appeal, the date the decision is given by the Lands Tribunal confirming the authority's decision.

[32]   Section 50(9) and paragraph 13 of Schedule 3.

[33]   Section 5 of LLCA 1975.

[34]   Section 50(10).

[35]   If the property is charged before the charge is registered, and a purchase takes place during the intervening period, then a purchaser who had inquired of the authority's register prior to purchase may seek compensation under section 10 of the Local Land Charges Act 1975.

[36]   Section 50(11).

[37]   Section 49(7).

[38]   Schedule 3, paragraph 12(2).

[39]   Schedule 3, paragraph 12(4).

RECOVERY FROM THIRD PARTIES

14.21 If the authority finds itself in the situation that expenses are unlikely to be recovered and a person is profiting as a result of the default action, e g obtaining rents which would not otherwise have been obtainable, then the authority can seek an order from the Residential Property Tribunal that that person pays to the authority such amount as the tribunal considers to be just.[40]

APPEALING A DEMAND FOR RECOVERY OF EXPENSES

14.22 An appeal must be made within 21 days[41] of service of a demand for the payment of expenses. The appeal is to be made to the Residential Property Tribunal who can confirm, vary or quash the demand as it considers appropriate.[42] The scope of the appeal jurisdiction would therefore be like an assessment of costs, encompassing a dispute relating to the amount of costs as well as whether or not the sums were reasonably incurred, provided such argument does not require challenge to the works specified in the improvement notice, because that would be foreclosed, only arguable on appeal against the notice itself.[43]

14.23 If reasonable progress towards completing the remedial work was not being made and a person authorised by the authority carried out the work and expenses are demanded, there is an additional specified ground for appeal. The recipient of the demand may defeat the demand by persuading the tribunal on appeal that reasonable progress was being made towards compliance with the improvement notice.[44]

---

[40]   Schedule 3, paragraph 14.
[41]   Schedule 3, paragraph 11(2).
[42]   Schedule 3, paragraph 11(5).
[43]   Section 15(6).
[44]   Schedule 3, paragraph 11(4).

Chapter 15

ENFORCEMENT AND SANCTIONS IN RELATION TO UNLICENSED HMOS AND OTHER HOUSES UNDER PARTS 2 AND 3

INTRODUCTION

15.1 This chapter will look at the sanctions which can be imposed in relation to unlicensed houses under Parts 2 and 3. There are four methods of sanction.

(i)   The first is prosecution.

(ii) Secondly, where there has been a conviction the stream of income from the premises is jeopardised and such rent that is paid is recoverable by an occupier.[1]

(iii) Thirdly, management of the premises is hampered. A landlord who is required to have a licence for an HMO but, in fact, does not have one, loses the right to automatic possession of property rented under an assured shorthold lease under the Housing Act 1988. There is a prohibition on service of notices of intention to seek possession, under section 21 of the 1988 Act. This restriction[2] on the use of section 21 ceases when a landlord makes an application for a licence or for a temporary exemption notice.

(iv) Fourthly, irrespective of whether the person has been charged or convicted,[3] where the local housing authority makes an application to the Residential Property Tribunal and subject to certain notice requirements[4] a landlord is at risk of being subject to a rent repayment order requiring him or her to repay housing benefit Where a landlord is actually convicted of an offence   the Tribunal must,[5] subject to exceptional circumstances, reasonableness and the 'rent total', make a rent repayment order requiring repayment to the authority of the total amount of housing benefit paid whilst an offence was committed.

---

[1]   Section 73(5)and (8); section 96(5) and (8).
[2]   Which does not affect in relation to section 257 HMOs , the right of any other person (who is not the person having control) to serve such a notice – see Regulation 8 of SI 2007/1904.
[3]   Sections 73(6)(a) and 96(6).
[4]   Sections 73(7) and 96(7).
[5]   Sections 74(2) and 97(2).

PROSECUTIONS

15.2 These are the main criminal offences which may be committed for breach of licence conditions and for operating unlicensed houses under Parts 2 and 3:

(1) controlling or managing an HMO which is required to be licensed under Part 2 but is not licensed without a reasonable excuse: section 72(1);

(2) permitting occupation by more persons than are permitted under the licence: section 72(2);

(3) failure to comply with a condition of licence required under part 2: section 72(3);

(4) controlling or managing an HMO which is required to be licensed under Part 3 but is not licensed without a reasonable excuse: section 95(1); and

(5) failure to comply with a condition of licence required under part 3: section 95(2).

15.3 Additionally there is the offence of breach of management regulations: section 234.

15.4 Then there are the further generic offences:

(1) Failing to produce documents reasonably required in connection with exercise of the authority's functions and specified in a notice served pursuant to section 235; and

(2) Knowingly or recklessly supplying false or misleading information in connection with exercise of any of the housing authority's functions under Parts 1 to 4 and Part 7: section 238.

15.5 The penalties, are as follows:

Provision	Offence	Penalty
72(1)	Having control or managing unlicensed premises that are required to be licensed under Part 2	£20,000
72(2)	Permitting over occupation	£20,000
72(3)	Breach of terms of licence	Level 5: £5,000
95(1)	Having control or managing unlicensed premises that are required to be licensed under Part 3	£20,000

Provision	Offence	Penalty
95(2)	Breach of terms of licence	Level 5: £5,000
234(3)	Failure to comply with management regulations	Level 5: £5,000
236(1)	Failing to provide specified information	Level 5: £5,000
236(4)	Intentionally altering suppressing or destroying any document required to be produced under section 235	Statutory maximum or on conviction on indictment, to a fine
238	Supplying false or misleading information	Level 5: £5,000

15.6 It will be a defence for the person charged under sections 72(1) or 95(1) that there is an effective application outstanding with the LHA for the grant of a licence or for a temporary exemption notice.[6]

15.7 Additionally, each of the six offences under sections 72, 95 and 234 are subject to the defence that the person had reasonable excuse.[7]

15.8 There is a peculiar defence to the offence under section 72(2) in relation to an HMO when it becomes licensed for the first time, if more persons occupy it than the licence permits, and the over occupation is pursuant to contracts entered into before the licence came into force. In those circumstances it is a defence that the licence holder is taking reasonable steps to reduce the number of occupants in order to comply with the terms of the licence.[8]

RENT REPAYMENT ORDERS

15.9 Rent Repayment Orders (RPOs) form part of the array of measures designed to dissuade owners and their agents from non compliance with the requirements of Parts 2 and 3 which each have their respective provisions for rent repayment orders. The respective sections,[9] comprising in total 53 subsections, are a mirror image of each other save that Part 2 concerns licensable HMOs and Part 3 concerns houses in an area of selective licensing.

15.10 The RPO must be seen in context of freezing the reliance on use of s 21 notices so a landlord cannot recover possession against an assured shorthold tenant except by serving a section 8 notice and proving a ground for possession.

---

[6]   Sections 72(4) and 95(3.)
[7]   Sections 72(5) and 95(4).
[8]   Section 76(4).
[9]   Sections 73 and 74 in Part 2 and sections 95 and 96 in Part 3.

15.11 By way of somewhat mysterious preamble there is exclusion of the common law rule of illegality,[10] which thus paves the way for taking steps in relation to what otherwise might be viewed as an unenforceable contract.

15.12 Who Can Apply? The local authority and or an occupier can apply for an RPO, but only in respect of an unlicensed HMO or house which is required to be licensed and there is no existing effective application for a licence nor existing and effective notification for temporary exemption. The application is made by applying to the Residential Property Tribunal, the procedure for which is governed by Schedule 13

15.13 Occupiers can only apply for a rent repayment order to cover rent that they have actually paid during the period the premises were not licensed when they were meant to be and which was not covered by housing benefit.[11] There is no prior notice requirement imposed on an individual occupier. The individual needs to be armed with a memorandum of conviction or a copy of a rent repayment order which has already been made. If there has been no conviction then the occupier's position is entirely dependent on the authority having already obtained a rent repayment order against the appropriate person – normally the landlord – who was entitled to the rent payable in connection with his or her occupation.

15.14 The occupier's application must be made within 12 months of the date of the conviction or the rent repayment order whichever was later.

15.15 A LHA seeking an order, does not have to demonstrate that there has been a criminal charge or a conviction for the offence before an application can be made. But an authority must also show that the application is made in time. A LHA has a 12-month window, within which to reclaim housing benefit paid out on unlicensed premises where were required to be licensed. The criteria are:

- That a notice has first been served on the appropriate person of intended proceedings which conforms with the statutory requirements and the period for representations by that person set out in the notice has expired; and that those representations have been considered. The notice must set out the reasons for proposing to make an application, the amount that the authority will seek to recover and a copy must also be served on the relevant department responsible for housing benefit.

- That at any time in the preceding 12 months the appropriate person who has control of or manages an HMO to which Part 2 applies or a house to which Part 3 has, to the satisfaction of the Tribunal, committed an offence under section 72(1) or 95(1) of operating unlicensed premises whether or not charged or convicted.

---

[10] Demonstrated in *Taylor v Bhail* (1996) Con LR 70. The rule is more fully explained in *Hewison v Meridian Shipping PTE* [2002] EWCA Civ 1821.

[11] Sections 73(4), 96(4), 73(8)(b), 96(8)(b), 73(11)(b) and 96(11)(b).

- That housing benefit has been paid to anyone in connection with the occupation of the premises during any period which it appears to the tribunal that such an offence was committed.

MANDATORY ORDERS

15.16 If a LHA applies for a rent repayment order following a conviction for controlling or managing without a licence an HMO or a Part 3 house, which requires licensing and the tribunal is satisfied that housing benefit was paid to anybody in connection with the occupation of those premises whilst the offence was being committed, then the tribunal must make the order.

THE VALUE OF AN RPO

15.17 The rent repayment order is for an amount, which is reasonable in the circumstances but cannot be for payment of housing benefit paid more than 12 months before the application to the tribunal. In deciding what is a reasonable amount the tribunal must take into account:

- the total amount of housing benefit and rent paid during the period of the offence;

- the extent to which that amount derived from housing benefit;

- the amount which was actually received by the appropriate person;

- whether the appropriate person has previously been convicted of an offence of managing or controlling a house which requires a licence without a licence; and

- the conduct and financial circumstances of the appropriate person.

ENFORCEMENT

15.18 From the point of view of the individual occupier any amount payable by virtue of a rent repayment order is recoverable as a debt due to him from the appropriate person. From the authority's point of view until recovered any amount payable is a local land charge which is secured on the property giving the authority the same powers as if they were mortgagees,[12] including appointment of a receiver. Alternatively, if the authority subsequently grant a

---

[12] Sections 74(10) and 97(10).

licence[13] or makes a management order, the order may[14] stipulate for recovery of the amounts due. Once paid, the sums do not constitute an amount of recovered housing benefit.

REGULATIONS

15.19 In England regulations[15] have been issued pursuant to sections 74(15) and 97(15) which do three things:

- allow LHAs to amend the amount of the RPO which they seek to include amounts of housing benefit properly payable;

- allow LHAs to use the proceeds of the RPO towards defraying costs and expenses (administrative and legal) covering all aspects of the LHA's work in relation to the premises in connection with Parts 2, 3 and 4, including dealing with any application for a licence and costs incurred in carrying out works while an interim management order was in force;[16] and

- requires a LHA to pay into the consolidated fund amounts not applied for a purpose specified under Regulation 3.

15.20 In relation to HB payments in connection with occupation of a part of a section 257 HMO (section 257(5) contemplates flats in a section 257 HMO which are themselves in use as an HMO) the Houses in Multiple Occupation (Certain Converted Blocks of Flats) (Modifications to the Housing Act 2004 and Transitional Provisions for section 257 HMOs) (England) Regulations 2007, SI 2007/1904, alter the meaning of appropriate person in section 73(10) from the person who was entitled to receive the rent to the person (a) having control of the HMO and (b) entitled to receive the rent on his own account.

15.21 The same regulations also prohibit any ground rent, service charge or insurance charge paid under the terms of a lease in respect of a flat within a section 257 HMO from being counted as rent for the purpose of RPOs.

---

[13] Sections 74(12) and 97(12).
[14] Sections 74(13) and 97(13).
[15] The Rent Repayment Orders (Supplementary Provisions) (England) Regulations 2007.
[16] Regulation 3 of SI 2007/572.

Chapter 16

REVOCATION, SUSPENSION AND VARIATION

REVOCATION OF AN IMPROVEMENT NOTICE

16.1   Revocation does not have to be of the whole notice if the subject notice related to a number of hazards.[1] A notice must be revoked if the notice has been complied with.[2] However, there is a discretion to revoke where the notice was served in respect of a category 1 hazard under section 11 of the Act, and the authority considers that there are special circumstances making it appropriate to revoke the notice.[3] Revocation can be sought by the person served or done by the LHA on its own initiative.[4]

16.2   Special circumstances are not required to revoke a notice in respect of a category 2 hazard. A notice can be revoked where the notice was served in respect of a category 2 hazard merely if the authority considers that it is appropriate to revoke the notice.

16.3   How 'special', special circumstances have to be, before a notice, served in respect of a category 1 hazard, can be revoked is not dealt with by the Act.

16.4   The enforcement guidance was an opportunity to throw light on what might be regarded as special circumstances in order to achieve some consistency of approach. The guidance gives two examples, one of which is where the category 1 hazard has ceased to exist, the notice has not been fully complied with, but the authority do not intend to take further action. The other example is where the improvement notice dealt with a number of both category 1 and 2 hazards, and the notice can be revoked in relation to certain hazards and varied in relation to the rest.[5]

---

[1]   Section 16(3)(a).
[2]   Section 16(1).
[3]   Section 16(2)(a).
[4]   Section 16(8).
[5]   Paragraph 5.10.

REVOCATION OF A PROHIBITION ORDER

16.5 Revocation can be sought by the person served or done by the LHA on its own initiative.[6]

16.6 Paragraphs 30 and 31 of Schedule 15 insert new sections 584A and 584B into the Housing Act 1985 which govern payment and re-payment of compensation if a prohibition order is, respectively, made or revoked. The compensation is calculated by reference to diminution of the compulsory purchase value of the owner's interest in the premises caused by the making of the prohibition order. Since it is possible that a prohibition order may relate to a number of hazards, it follows that revocation need not be of the whole order. This could lead to some complicated sums in order to arrive at the figure to be repaid.

16.7 A prohibition order can be revoked in three different circumstances:

(1)   where the authority is satisfied that the hazard in respect of which the order was made no longer exists on the specified premises; in which case the order must be revoked;[7]

(2)   where the order was served in respect of a category 1 hazard, if the authority considers that there are special circumstances making it appropriate to revoke the order;[8] and

(3)   where the order was served in respect of a category 2 hazard under section 20 of the Act if the authority considers that it is appropriate to revoke the order.

16.8 The enforcement guidance is silent as to when it might be appropriate to revoke a prohibition order in respect of a category 2 hazard, which is perhaps a reflection of the fact that an operative prohibition order would more often than not be in existence on account of category 1 hazards.

SUSPENDED IMPROVEMENT NOTICES AND SUSPENDED PROHIBITION ORDERS

16.9 The Act allows for situations when an improvement notice or a prohibition order may be suspended. The first situation envisaged by the Act is for the notice or order to be suspended until a specified time; the second is until the occurrence of an event specified in the notice.[9]

---

6   Section 25(8).
7   Section 25(1).
8   Section 25(2)(a).
9   Sections 14(1) and 22(1).

16.10 Once served, the local housing authority has the power to review a suspended improvement notice or prohibition order at any time.[10] On a review, there is a notification requirement with which the authority must comply. Copies of the authority's decision on such a review must be served on the person on whom the notice or order was served and in relation to an improvement notice also on every person on whom a copy of the notice was required to be served.[11]

16.11 The enforcement guidance offers guidance in relation to a decision to suspend an improvement notice or prohibition order.[12] In relation to category 1 hazards the authority is advised to consider very carefully whether a suspended notice is the appropriate way of responding.[13]

16.12 How long a notice or order may be suspended, is hinted at by the provision which requires that an authority must review the suspension of an improvement notice one year after the date of service and at subsequent intervals of not more than one year. Once a notice or order is suspended, it can then be varied to alter the time or the events by reference to which the suspension is to come to an end.

16.13 Should the notice or order be suspended generally then it would fail to comply with the requirement that it only be suspended until a time or until the occurrence of an event. If that is true, then the suggestion in the guidance that enforcement action may safely be postponed while a more strategic approach to area renewal is considered, would require that there be some idea when the purpose of the period of suspension would be fulfilled, for example, a specified date for the anticipated adoption of the strategy. Otherwise the suspension might be too uncertain.

16.14 The guidance states that suspension of an improvement notice may be appropriate where the hazard is not sufficiently minor to be addressed by a

---

[10]   See paragraph 5.30 of the Enforcement Guidance.
[11]   Sections 17(3) and 27(3).
[12]   Paragraphs 5.24–5.29.
[13]   In one Residential Property Tribunal decision, reference number CHI/00HB/HOPO/2007/0005 a suspended prohibition order served on account of a category 1 hazard caused by overcrowding was varied from when there was a change of tenancy (which might not have been for a very long time) to a period of 9 months or a change in occupancy whichever occurs first. The LHA sought permission to appeal on the basis that the Tribunal had erred in its construction of the order as being in effect suspended indefinitely, alternatively if the period of suspension of the SPO was to end after 9 months then that deprived the LHA of its discretion to prolong the period of suspension on any review. The President of the Lands Tribunal, Mr Bartlett QC, refused permission for both of the grounds. He stated 'The fact that the council may vary the order under section 25(4)(a) does not mean, as is contended in the alternative, that the insertion of a date for termination of the suspension is otiose. The council may or may not decide to vary the order at some point before the termination date. If it does not, the RPT's variation will clearly not have been otiose; and if it considers varying the order the RPT's decision will be a material consideration.' The Tribunal also dealt with the issue of its jurisdiction to hear an appeal against a suspended prohibition order (if the Tribunal had been wrong about that, the alternative remedy would be judicial review).

hazard awareness notice.[14] The Act gives the example of a specified time for suspension as the date that persons of a certain description begin to use or cease to occupy any premises. In the guidance the Government advises that a suspended notice may require a landlord to notify the authority of a change of occupancy.[15]

16.15 The example of a specified event, given by the Act in relation to both notices and orders, is when the authority notifies a person who has previously given the authority an undertaking that he has failed to comply with the terms of the undertaking.[16] The offer of an undertaking to carry out steps which would otherwise be required by an improvement notice or prohibition order can only be properly accepted 'for the purposes of this section' if the terms of the undertaking not only govern the procedure for notification in case of breach but also specify that the notice will cease to be suspended if there is an act or omission which the authority considers to be a breach and which is notified to the person on whom the notice is served.[17]

16.16 In relation to a decision to suspend a prohibition order in circumstances of a category 1 crowding and space hazard, the Residential Property Tribunal have held[18] that the following were relevant:

(1) the seriousness of the hazard, and whether the seriousness requires the operation of the prohibition order to have immediate effect;

(2) the impact on the occupants of the immediate operation of the prohibition order, including, again, non-exhaustively, the following factors:

    (a) the length of time that the occupants have occupied the premises whilst the hazard has existed;

    (b) whether or not the occupants are members of a vulnerable group, to the extent, if any, that that factor has not already been taken into account in the assessment of the seriousness of the hazard;

    (c) the effect, if any, of the hazard on the occupants' physical and psychological health, to the extent, if any, that that effect has not already been taken into account in the assessment of the seriousness of the hazard;

    (d) the ages and genders of the occupants, to the extent, if any, that their ages and genders have not already been taken into account in the assessment of the seriousness of the hazard, or in the assessment of whether the occupants are members of a vulnerable group;

    (e) any other relevant personal circumstances of the occupants;

    (f) the state of repair of the premises;

---

[14] Paragraph 5.24.
[15] Paragraph 5.27.
[16] Sections 14(3) and 23(3).
[17] Sections 14(4) and (5) and 23(3) and (4).
[18] CHI/00HB/HOPO/2007/0005; see note 13 above.

(g) the likelihood or otherwise of any of the occupants voluntarily moving out of the premises, and, if so, whether the move is likely to be temporary or permanent, and the date when each move is likely to take place;

(h) the likelihood or otherwise of other occupants moving into the premises;

(i) the availability of suitable alternative accommodation for those occupants who are unlikely to be voluntarily moving out of the premises;

(3) the wishes of the occupants;

(4) the question whether the consequences of the immediate operation of, or the suspension of, the Prohibition Order would result in a breach of Article 8 ECHR.

VARIATION OF IMPROVEMENT NOTICES AND PROHIBITION ORDERS BY CONSENT

16.17 The Act permits variation of an operative improvement notice[19] by consent of the person on whom the notice was served. If the premises are caught by Parts 2 or 3 that person will be the licence holder. Otherwise that person will be the person having control or in the case of an HMO, the person managing it unless the premises are a flat[20] in which case the person, who could consent, would be either the owner or the person who the authority believes ought to take the action specified in the improvement notice. But a suspended improvement notice can also be varied by the local housing authority unilaterally. The scope of the variation would be to alter the time or events by reference to which the suspension is to come to an end.[21] The enforcement guidance does not expressly suggest that before the varied notice is issued, some prior discussion takes place with those likely to be affected by the intended variation in order to avert appeals under paragraph 13(1)(b) of Schedule 1 but the guidance does repeatedly[22] advise that LHAs consider the circumstances of the tenants and owner occupiers.

16.18 The Act also caters for variation of a prohibition order by consent.[23] The necessary consent is of every person on whom copies of the notice were

---

[19] Section 16(4)(a).

[20] Paragraph 3 of Part 1 to Schedule 1.

[21] Section 16(4)(b).

[22] Paragraphs 4.9-4.15 and 5.11. The guidance is peppered with reference to 'occupancy factors' in relation to enforcement decisions. Consequences for the individuals concerned could be relevant to a decision to vary.

[23] Section 25(4)(a). Approval of a prohibited use may also be sought: see section 22(4), (7) and (8).

required to be served.[24] According to paragraph 1(2) of Schedule 2 copies of a prohibition order have to be served on the owner or occupier, persons permitted to occupy and any mortgagee of whom the authority is aware. This category of person who have to be served, are the same group described by paragraph 16 of Part 3 of Schedule 2 as relevant persons, who can appeal. So unsurprisingly they also have standing to apply to vary.[25]

16.19 The local housing authority has the power to vary an improvement notice or a prohibition order either on application made by the person on whom the notice was served or, provided the proposed change is subsequently agreed, or relates to a suspended notice or order, of its own initiative.[26]

16.20 If everyone agrees the variation takes effect at the time of the agreement.[27]

16.21 When considering variation of a prohibition order also relevant is the fact that the order may prohibit uses except to the extent they are approved. In those circumstances approval for part of the previously prohibited use may be sought and given. Secondly, if that approval is refused the person who sought the approval may appeal within 28 days. The Act sets out what might have been taken for granted: that once an approval is sought the local housing authority must act reasonably in deciding whether or not to grant the approval. The Act nevertheless spells out that the authority cannot unreasonably withhold its approval.[28]

UNILATERAL VARIATION OF SUSPENDED IMPROVEMENT NOTICES OR OF SUSPENDED PROHIBITION ORDERS

16.22 The Act only deals with one scenario for unilateral variation, namely to alter the time or event which was specified for the suspension to end.[29] The enforcement guidance talks in terms of variation in 'other circumstances' than partial compliance with the original notice or order being possible but does not elaborate.[30]

16.23 If variation takes place without the agreement of the person on whom the suspended improvement notice or suspended prohibition order was served,

---

[24] Schedule 2 lists the persons who have to be served, the references for which are given in footnotes 177 to 180 in Table 2.6 which appears at **2.97** below.
[25] Section 25(4)(a).
[26] Sections 16(8) and 25(8).
[27] Sections 16(6) and 25(6).
[28] Section 22(7).
[29] See sections 14(4)(b) re improvement notices and 25(4)(b) in relation to prohibition notices.
[30] Paragraphs 5.10.

the variation takes effect when the time for appealing expires or, if there is an appeal, the date the decision to vary is confirmed, if it is confirmed, on appeal.[31]

REVOCATION AND VARIATION OF LICENCES OBTAINED PURSUANT TO PART 2 (MANDATORY AND ADDITIONAL) AND PART 3 (SELECTIVE) LICENSING

16.24 According to sections 70 and 93 licences granted under either Part 2 or 3 can be revoked on the following grounds:

(1)   if the LHA does so with the agreement of the licence holder;

(2)   where the authority consider that the licence holder or any other person has committed a serious breach of a condition of the licence or repeated breaches of such a condition;

(3)   where the authority no longer consider that the licence holder is a fit and proper person to be the licence holder;

(4)   where the authority no longer consider that the management of the house is being carried on by persons who are in each case fit and proper persons to be involved in its management;

(5)   where the HMO to which the licence relates ceases to be an HMO to which this Part applies; and

(6)   where the authority consider at any time that, were the licence to expire at that time, they would, for a particular reason relating to the structure (ie what it comprises, e g facilities in relation to numbers of occupants) of the HMO, refuse to grant a new licence to the licence holder on similar terms in respect of it.

16.25 Additionally a licence granted in relation to a house, which is an HMO in area designated for selective licensing may be revoked if the HMO becomes subject to mandatory licensing under Part 2.

16.26 Revocation of licences (for trading in public places) has historically been a fertile area of judicial review, from which elementary principles and standards of fairness have been regularly restated. Now paragraph 22 of Part 2 to schedule 5 mandates LHAs who are contemplating a revocation to serve a notice on the licence holder stating the reasons for the intended revocation, the right of appeal, the time for appealing and the time by which any

---

[31]   Sections 16(7) and 25(7).

representations opposing the revocation should be received. The authority is then enjoined to consider any representation made in accordance with the notice.

16.27 Further grounds for revocation may be specified in regulations made by the appropriate national authority.[32]

16.28 Variation is also provided for by a similar pattern of provisions to both Parts 2 and 3.

16.29 Sections 69 and 92 empower the LHA to vary the terms of a licence with the agreement of the licence holder or without their agreement of it appears to the local housing authority that circumstances have changed concerning the relevant house or HMO. A change in circumstances contemplates (but is not restricted to) new information.[33]

16.30 The change in circumstances that a local housing authority may consider relate, in particular, to the number of persons or households that are permitted to occupy the HMO; or the standards of the accommodation required for a particular number of occupants.

16.31 A variation of the licence made with the agreement of the licence holder takes effect immediately. If the variation is made without an agreement it does not come into effect until the time limit for appealing the decision has expired, or any appeal against the decision has been disposed of in favour of the local housing authority or the appeal has been withdrawn.

---

[32] Sections 73(1)(d), 93(1)(d) and 261.
[33] Section 69(1) and 92(1).

Part VII

TRIBUNAL PRACTICE AND PROCEDURE

Chapter 17

USING THE RESIDENTIAL PROPERTY TRIBUNAL

INTRODUCTION

17.1 The Housing Act 2004 gives jurisdiction to Residential Property Tribunals (RPTs) to deal with appeals and applications in relation to:

- housing conditions under Part 1 of the Act;

- licensing of Houses in Multiple Occupation under Part 2 of the Act;

- selective licensing of other residential accommodation under Part 3 of the Act; and

- management orders under Part 4 of the Act.

It also transfers jurisdiction from the county court to the RPT for proceedings relating to demolition orders under the Housing Act 1985.

17.2 RPTs were given the jurisdiction for a number of reasons including:

- the expertise of the tribunal in property matters;

- the power open to the tribunal to inspect premises; and

- the informal and flexible approach that is the hallmark of tribunal proceedings.

It was anticipated that RPTs would produce speedier decisions than the county court and that parties would feel able to take and defend proceedings without legal representation.

17.3 The RPT is likely to be an unfamiliar forum for many environmental health officers and other local housing authority officers who may be required to present cases. The purpose of this chapter therefore is to familiarise readers with both the procedures and the practice of the RPT and to highlight what is necessary to ensure effective presentation of the local housing authority case.

17.4   In the first part of the chapter we explain in outline the operations of the RPT, the regulations which govern hearings under the Housing Act and provide an outline of the normal progress of a case including appeals. In the second half of the chapter we will consider the decisions of the RPT. We provide a summary of the cases heard to date, and then extract some principles from these decisions. Finally we provide you with some practical tips to help you both with avoiding and preparing for hearings.

THE RESIDENTIAL PROPERTY TRIBUNAL SERVICE

17.5   The Residential Property Tribunal Service (RPTS) is the administrative body which runs RPTs as well as other tribunals and committees. It is made up of five regional offices called Rent Assessment Panels. Each panel has a President who is assisted by one or more Vice Presidents.

17.6   The range of tribunals and committees run by the RPTS are:

•   Rent Assessment Committees which hear disputes about fair and market rents in the private residential sector;

•   Leasehold Valuation Tribunals which hear disputes involving leasehold property; and

•   Residential Property Tribunals.

17.7   Each tribunal and committee is a quasi-judicial body which means that it has been set up by statute to determine disputes which would otherwise be decided by the courts. They are independent decision making bodies which have no links with the parties appearing before them.

17.8   The website of the RPTS can be found at www.rpts.gov.uk/. The site contains extensive useful information including the contact details of the regional panels and application forms. In particular, the RPTS provides useful – and user friendly – guidance on applications and appeals under the Act.

RESIDENTIAL PROPERTY TRIBUNALS

17.9   RPTs make decisions on applications under the Housing Act 2004 and demolition notices under the Housing Act 1985. The decision making process includes case management powers, the power to make directions, the power to inspect relevant premises, the power to make decisions on written submissions only, as well as decisions made following oral hearings of applications.

17.10 Members of the RPT include chairmen and ordinary members. Chairmen are appointed by the Lord Chancellor and are responsible for the effective running of the proceedings and for writing up the reasons for the tribunal decision. They are usually lawyers or surveyors. They can sit alone to exercise tribunal powers relating to procedural and other matters.

17.11 Other members are appointed by the Department of Communities and Local Government. They can be lawyers, surveyors or other professional experts such as environmental health officers or lay people.

THE PROCEDURAL REGULATIONS

17.12 Schedule 13 to the Housing Act 2004 gives the Secretary of State the power to make procedural regulations. The Residential Property Tribunal Procedure (England) Regulations 2006 (SI 2006/831) govern the procedures used at RPTs.

17.13 The regulations – at paragraph 4 – provide that their interpretation and the exercise of any powers given by them should meet the overriding objective of dealing fairly and justly with applications.

17.14 This includes:

'(a)   Dealing with applications in ways which are proportionate to the complexity of the issues and to the resources of the parties;

(b)   Ensuring, so far as practicable, that the parties are on an equal footing procedurally and are able to participate fully in the proceedings;

(c)   Assisting any party in the presentation of his case without advocating the course he or she should take;

(d)   Avoiding delay, so far as is compatible with proper consideration of the issues.'

In the following paragraphs we explain the main provisions of the regulations and follow the progress of a standard case. We provide only a synopsis of the procedural requirements and it is important to check the regulations when you are running a case.

APPLICATIONS

17.15 The decision making process commences when someone makes an application to the RPT. The person who makes the application is known as an applicant or an appellant. Normally that person is someone on whom a statutory notice under the Act has been served. Applications can also be made by the local housing authority in pursuit of their statutory powers.

17.16 Applications must be in writing and include:

•   the applicant's name and address;

- the name and address of the respondent where known to the applicant, or where not known a description of the respondent's connection with the premises;

- the address of the premises;

- the applicant's connection with the premises;

- the applicant's reasons for making the application including the remedy sought; where known to the applicant;

- a statement that the applicant believes that the facts stated in the application are true.

17.17 For most applications a fee of £150 is payable. The Residential Property Tribunal (Fees) (England) Regulations (SI 2006/830) govern the payment of fees. Fees can be waived when the applicant or their partner is in receipt of certain benefits. A written application (on a form available from the RPTS) must be made for waiver of fees.

17.18 The regulations provide[1] that where a fee is not paid within a period of 14 days from the date on which the application is received, the application shall be treated as withdrawn unless the tribunal is satisfied that there are reasonable grounds not to do so.

17.19 Not all applications attract fees. The explanatory note to the fees regulations explains that it is inappropriate for a fee to be charged when a local housing authority is exercising its duties and powers under the Act and is therefore obliged to go to the tribunal. Fees are also not payable when persons are trying to enforce rights granted to them by that Act.

17.20 The fees regulations also give power to the RPT to require a party to proceedings to reimburse any other party to the proceedings, the whole or part of any fees paid.

17.21 Applications must be made with specified time limits which are set out in the statute. The relevant chapters of this book explain the time limits.

17.22 In most cases applications can be made out of time if the RPT is satisfied that there is a good reason for the failure to appeal before the end of that period (and for any delay since then in applying for permission to appeal out of time). Any request must be in writing, signed and dated, giving reasons for the delay, and be accompanied by a completed application form. The request must include a statement that the person making the request believes that the facts stated in it are true. The decisions indicate that RPTs are prepared

---

[1]   Regulation 12.

to agree to extensions when it is consistent with the overriding objective of dealing fairly and justly with applications to do so.

17.23 Applications relating to the declaration of a premises as an HMO cannot be made out of time. Neither the statute nor the regulations provide the tribunal with any discretion to extend the period of time for appeal.

17.24 Once the tribunal receives an application, it must acknowledge it and send a copy to the person against whom it is made.

FRIVOLOUS AND VEXATIOUS APPLICATIONS

17.25 A tribunal may dismiss an application which it considers to be frivolous and vexatious. However, before it can do so, it must give notice to the applicant of the grounds on which it is minded to do so. The applicant must be given an opportunity to be heard by the tribunal on the matter.

17.26 The tribunal also has the power to award costs against a party it considers has behaved in a frivolous and vexatious manner – see **17.47**.

RESPONDENTS

17.27 The person or body against whom an application is made is described as the respondent. Generally local housing authorities are the respondents to applications. Respondents do not have to pay fees.

17.28 Unless the application is an urgent Interim Management Order and the tribunal decides that an urgent oral hearing is necessary,[2] the respondent must inform the tribunal whether or not he intends to oppose the application, provide the names and address of any other interested persons known to the respondent, and provide a dress to which documents should be sent for the purposes of the proceedings.

CASE MANAGEMENT POWERS

17.29 The next stage of the tribunal process is the organisation of the case in a way which ensures that it is properly prepared for determination. The RPT will make directions, which are orders, to ensure that the relevant information is provided to the tribunal, and exchanged with other parties. Applicants and respondents can ask the tribunal to make specific directions.

17.30 Failure to comply with directions may enable the tribunal to make a costs order against that party – see **17.47**.

---

[2] For details of this procedure see Chapter 12.

17.31 The RPT has the power to hold a case management conference. This is a hearing on at least 7 days notice at which parties may be represented if they wish. Usually one procedural chairman only will hear from the parties. He will identify the issues which are in dispute, make directions about the inspection of the premises, the provision of expert evidence and other relevant matters. A timetable will be agreed along with a hearing date.

17.32 The powers of the RPT at the case management conference are broad. The regulations[3] state that the tribunal may order the parties to take such steps to do such things as appear to it to be necessary or desirable for securing the just, expeditious and economical determination of the application.

17.33 You should try to spend some time before the case management conference considering what evidence you intend to present at the final hearing, what would be an appropriate timetable for preparation, including taking leave commitments into account, and any other matters you think are relevant for the tribunal to take into consideration. This will help focus your preparation and ensure you get the directions you want from the case management conference.

EXPERT EVIDENCE

17.34 Some cases before the RPT will involve the presentation of expert evidence. For instance, an applicant may want to dispute the evidence of the EHO by adducing (producing) alternative evidence. The regulations give parties the power to do this.

17.35 An expert, for the purpose of the regulations, is an independent expert who is not an employee of a party. A written summary of the expert's report must be provided to the tribunal and to each other party at least 7 days before the determination of the matter.

17.36 Expert evidence must be addressed to the tribunal,[4] include details of the expert's qualifications, and contain a statement that the expert understands and has complied with his duty to assist the tribunal on the matters within his expertise, overriding any obligation to the person who has commissioned the report.

17.37 Failure to comply with these requirements is likely to lead to the tribunal refusing to take the evidence into account in making its decision. See case number LON/00AL/HPO/2006/0001.

---

[3] Regulation 23.
[4] Regulation 22.

INSPECTION

17.38 The tribunal has the power to inspect the premises or any other premises which may be useful to inspect, and the locality of the premises.[5]

17.39 Parties may attend the inspection. Inspections can only take place if appropriate consents are given. In particular, an owner, or a tenant is able to refuse access to the premises. Parties can point out any physical aspect of the premises that they wish the tribunal to see, but they must not make representations during the inspection.

17.40 The tribunal has the power to decide when it will inspect the premises. If it does this after the hearing, and as a result learns of matters which are relevant to its decision, then it may re-open the hearing to consider these matters.

THE HEARING

17.41 The RPT is a much more flexible forum than the county court. The tribunal has, subject to the regulations, the power to determine its own procedure. The tribunal may receive evidence even if it would be inadmissible in a court of law. It can allow a party to rely on reasons not previously stated and on evidence not previously available, as long as it considers that it is just and reasonable to do so. This flexibility is particularly useful to unrepresented parties who may for instance not understand fully the legal basis for their appeal against a decision of the local housing authority.

17.42 Hearings are in public unless the tribunal is satisfied that it is appropriate that the hearing – or part of it – should be held in private. Even though most cases are in public, they do not generally attract an audience other than law students or housing officials wanting to learn about procedures.

17.43 The tribunal has the power to proceed with the hearing if a party does not turn up as long as it is satisfied that that party has had notice and there is no evidence of good reason for the failure to appeal.

17.44 Parties can give evidence, call witnesses, question witness and address the tribunal on the evidence and law and generally on the subject matter of the application.

17.45 The hearing is inquisitorial in form. This means that the tribunal is likely to intervene with its own questions, and will order the proceedings in a way which is most helpful to it in reaching a decision. Do not forget that the tribunal is both an expert and specialist tribunal, so expect questions which

---

[5]   Regulation 21.

reflect this. However, this expertise should be helpful to you – the tribunal will be familiar with the language and concepts of environmental health.

17.46 The tribunal can give its decision orally at the end of the hearing. The normal practice is to give a written decision within 4 to 6 weeks of the hearing.

COSTS

17.47 The RPT has the power to make an order for costs in exceptional circumstances. Paragraph 12 of Schedule 13 to the Act gives power to the tribunal to order one party to pay a contribution to the costs incurred by another party in certain circumstances. These circumstances are:

- that party has failed to comply with an order made by the tribunal;

- that party has failed to comply with a requirement imposed by regulations;

- the tribunal dismisses the whole or part of an application or appeal made by that party to the tribunal; or

- that party has, in the opinion of the tribunal, acted frivolously, vexatiously, abusively, disruptively or otherwise unreasonably in connection with the proceedings.

17.48 The limit to the costs which can be awarded against a party is currently £500.

APPEALS

17.49 RPTs do not have the power to reconsider their own decisions. However, if you are dissatisfied with the decision of the tribunal, you can appeal the decision to the Lands Tribunal. Appeals can only be heard if permission to appeal has been granted by the RPT or the Lands Tribunal.

17.50 You must request permission to appeal from the RPT within 21 days of the decision – although that time can be extend in exceptional circumstances. If the tribunal refuses permission, the parties have a further 28 days to seek permission to appeal from the Lands Tribunal itself.

JUDICIAL REVIEW

17.51 It is possible to judicially review the decision of an RPT when there has been procedural irregularities, or when the requirements of natural justice have not been met. The High Court exercises a supervisory jurisdiction over all tribunals. However, it is unlikely to provide an appropriate form of redress in most cases since the role of the High Court is not to substitute its decision for that of the tribunal but to ensure that decisions are made properly.

DECISIONS OF THE RPT

17.52 Decisions of the RPT are published on its website. Decisions are organised under type of application and region. There is a useful search engine which will produce links to decisions following insertion of a word such as dangerous or mandatory.

17.53 Decisions are also summarised and published on the LACORs website. LACORS (the Local Authorities Coordinators of Regulatory Services) provides advice and guidance to help support local authority regulatory and related services. LACORS is a local government central body created by the UK local authority Associations which comprise of the Local Government Association (LGA), Welsh Local Government Association (WLGA), Convention of Scottish Local Authorities (COSLA) and Northern Ireland Local Government Association (NILGA).

17.54 Full access to the LACORs website is only available by subscription. However, the decisions of the RPT and the commentary are publicly available on www.lacors.gov.uk.

17.55 Decisions are relatively easy to read. Usefully many of the decisions provide a statement of the decision at the beginning, before explaining the reasoning of the tribunal. This is very helpful in understanding the reasoning. If the decision is not organised in that way, we suggest that you look at the end of the decision to see what determination was made, before reading the reasoning.

17.56 Note that decisions of individual tribunals are not binding upon other tribunals. However, they are persuasive and it is worth drawing the attention of the tribunal to any decision that determines issues which are relevant to your case. There are examples within several cases discussed below of the tribunal being referred to decisions of other tribunals.

17.57 Tribunals are bound by decisions of the Lands Tribunal. To date no Housing Act case has been appealed to the Lands Tribunal.

17.58 We have summarised the decisions made by the RPT up to the time of writing. The cases are discussed in two ways. First we consider the decisions grouped under types of application. We make some general points about these and then provide a brief summary. We then draw some general principles from the decisions which may provide a useful insight into the evolving approach that the RPT takes to Housing Act matters.

IMPROVEMENT NOTICES

17.59 The first group of decisions we consider are improvement notices. Whilst the majority of decisions of local housing authorities have been confirmed by the RPT, there are some general points to note.

17.60 First paragraphs 1–4 of the Schedule to the regulations sets out additional details which must be complied with in connection with improvement notices. It is important to ensure that all the required documents are provided to the tribunal.

17.61 The decisions demonstrate the importance that the RPT attaches to the statutorily prescribed procedural requirements. Housing authorities should ensure that these are meticulously observed. In particular, it is important that the statement of reasons for the improvement notice is provided, together with a statement which sets out the authority's reasons for considering that an improvement notice is the best course of action in relation to the hazard when the applicant has challenged that decision.

17.62 Secondly, the RPT is reluctant to uphold requirements which are disproportionate to the aim of the notice. Therefore housing authorities should pay close attention to demonstrating that the requirements, including their cost, are proportionate to the outcome. Think about the impact of the requirement on both the occupier and the landlord. This is particularly necessary when requirements cover central heating and double glazing.

17.63 Finally, it is important to remember that the hearings are actually rehearings. Therefore the requirements must be appropriate at the time of the tribunal. If work has been done to the property so that there is no longer a justification for the requirements in the notice, then the notice will be quashed. Check through the crucial points the day before the hearing. Is the situation still the same as when you made your decision? If not, you may need to reconsider.

17.64 The table below summarises the decisions to the time of writing.

Improvement Notices	Region and Local authority	Outcome	Commentary
LON/00AG/HIN/2007/009 Appeal by landlord against service of an improvement notice	**LONDON CAMDEN**	Improvement notice quashed Application fee reimbursed	This case presented two problems to the tribunal. First the notice was found to be invalid because neither the owners nor the occupiers of the flat had been given notice of the local housing authority's intention to inspect under section 239 of the Act.
			Secondly the property had been substantially rebuilt around its original façade, yet the authority had used the original date of construction as the basis for the calculation of the hazard score. The tribunal considered that this led to a 'disproportionate, misleading and unjustified result'. The tribunal also considered that the hazard would more properly have been dealt with by the service of a hazard awareness notice and the installation of secondary glazing to the remaining windows and the provision of a more efficient slim line electric heating system would have been a proportionate response to the problem of excess cold.
LON/00AG/HIN/2007/0011 Appeal by landlord against the requirement of improvement notice to install double glazing	**LONDON CAMDEN**	Notice varied to delete requirement for central heating and to substitute a requirement for roof insulation and remedial work to the windows	The case turned on its particular facts and the tribunal stressed that it was not a precedent for arguing that when a requirement to install central heating was imposed, that there was no necessity for double glazing

Improve-ment Notices	Region and Local authority	Outcome	Commentary
LON/00AY/ HIN/2007/ 0010 Appeal by landlord against service of an improve-ment notice	**LONDON LAMBETH**	Appeal dismissed and improvement notice confirmed	The decision is robust in its response to the applicant's argument that the hazards in the property are the responsibility of the tenant
LON/00AY/ HIN/2006/ 0001 Appeal by landlord against the requirement of improve-ment notice to fit a particular type of heat and smoke detector	**LONDON LAMBETH**	Appeal dismissed and improvement notice confirmed	The local authority application to have the appeal dismissed because it was out of time had to be withdrawn as it was unable to substantiate its statement that there was precedent for the date of service of the notice being the date of postage
			The appeal was dismissed following consideration by the tribunal because the works required were reasonable in relation to the hazard
LON/00BK/ HIN/2007/ 0003 Appeal by landlord against the service of an improve-ment notice. Appeal was also against a suspended prohibition order	**LONDON WESTMINSTER**	Appeal dismissed and improvement notice and suspended prohibition order confirmed	This case concerned a basement flat with very little natural light

Improve-ment Notices	Region and Local authority	Outcome	Commentary
			The appellant's main argument was that the combination of an improvement notice and suspended prohibition order was unreasonable because it required works to be done to the flat, but if the current tenant left, then the prohibition order would cease to be suspended and the flat could not be re-let.
			The decision suggests a procedure for dealing with these sorts of cases (see paragraph 46 for procedure)
MAN/ 20UE/HIN/ 2006/0002 Claim for costs by landlord following revocation of improve-ment notice by local authority	NORTHERN DURHAM	Application for costs dismissed	The tribunal found nothing in the process to suggest that the local authority had behaved unreasonably either in the service of the notice or its revocation. In particular, the error in the Revocation Notice was rectified as soon as it was brought to the attention of the local authority and the postponement of the hearing did not cause the appellant to incur any additional significant costs
MAN/ 00BN/HIN/ 2006/0009 Appeal by landlord against one of the requirements of the improve-ment notice	NORTHERN MANCHESTER	The improvement notice confirmed and the appeal dismissed	The local authority neither submitted written representations nor attended the hearing. In the absence of either party the tribunal resolved the matter on the basis of written evidence, the inspection and its own expertise
			It found that the requirement to do works which was challenged was appropriate and reasonable

Improve-ment Notices	Region and Local authority	Outcome	Commentary
MAN/00CJ/ HIN/2006/ 0003 Appeal by landlord against the service of an improve-ment notice	NORTHERN NEWCASTLE	The improvement notice quashed	Appeal allowed out of time because the appellant had not been notified of the details of the tribunal in particular its address
			Matter considered on written representations
			A great deal of work had been carried out to the property since the original inspection
			The tribunal did not recalculate hazard scores it was decided that this was not appropriate. The notice was quashed on the basis that 'so clearly were the respondent's justifications not or no longer applicable that there is no possibility of any of the identified hazards being classified as category 1'
BIR/44UD/ HIN/2006/ 0003 Appeal by landlord against the service of an improve-ment notice	MIDLANDS RUGBY	Improvement notice quashed	This decision emphasises the importance of procedural requirements (see below). The notice failed to conform to the requirements of section 8 of the Act. The tribunal determined that therefore it was invalid despite the fact that the appellant did not appeal on the basis of procedural irregularities. The tribunal decided that the procedural requirements were crucial to the right to a fair hearing under Article 6 of the ECHR. There were other defects in the notice. Moreover the tribunal recalculated the hazard scores and reclassified the hazards as category 2 rather than category 1

Improve-ment Notices	Region and Local authority	Outcome	Commentary
BIR/41UH/ HIN/2007/ 0001 Appeal by landlord against service of an improve-ment notice	**MIDLAND STAFFORD-SHIRE MOORLANDS**	Improvement notice confirmed	All of the hazards identified in the notice existed and there was no reason for varying the notice
BIR/00GF/ HIN/2007/ 0003 Appeal by landlord against service of an improve-ment notice	**MIDLAND TELFORD AND WREKIN**	Improvement notice confirmed subject to some variation to the requirements	Written submissions only
			A category 1 hazard was found to exist because of a very inadequate boundary wall leading to the dwelling being at risk to intruders.
			The period for compliance with the notice was extended from 7 to 28 days
CAM/ 44UD/HIN/ 2007/0001 Appeal by landlord against a requirement of the improve-ment notice	**EASTERN**	The requirement to install double glazed windows to the property varied so that new windows (single or double glazed) need only be fitted in the bathroom or toilet	Appeal accepted out of time due to 'exceptional reasons'
			The tribunal expressed some reservations about whether double glazing could ever, on its own, be appropriate works for a category 1 hazard

Improvement Notices	Region and Local authority	Outcome	Commentary
			The tribunal considered that the EHO had fallen into the trap of not assessing the actual risk to the property. He started off with the national average likelihood tables, assumed that this applied to all average properties in his area and moved directly from this to assuming that the rating applied to this property
			The tribunal concluded that a remedy for excess cold was required and therefore the improvement notice was justified. However, the actual proposed remedy was not justified and it was therefore varied
CHI/23UB/ HIN/2007/ 0002 Appeal by regulated tenant against the service of an improvement notice	SOUTHERN CHELTENHAM	No jurisdiction to hear appeal	The regulated tenant was served a copy of the improvement notice in accordance with the requirements of paragraph 5 of Schedule 1 to the Act. Those who statute requires to be served with the actual improvement notice can appeal to the tribunal. However, there is a distinction between those people and others who are served only with a copy of the notice, who have no right to appeal
CHI/23UE/ HIN/2007/ 0004 Appeal by owner occupier against the service of an improvement notice	SOUTHERN GLOUCESTER	Improvement notice confirmed	The applicant had lived in the flat as an owner occupier for 17 years. The tribunal endorsed the local authority view that a category 1 hazard existed to the whole building so long as the flat was not adequately alarmed or hard wired to the main fire alarm and smoke detection system covering the entire building. This meant that the authority was under a duty to serve the improvement notice

Improvement Notices	Region and Local authority	Outcome	Commentary
CHI/18UG/ HIN/2007/ 0005 Appeal by landlord against the service of an improvement notice	SOUTHERN SOUTH HAMS	Improvement notice confirmed	Appeal accepted out of time – reference made to the overriding objective of justice
			The appellant did not turn up at the hearing, and had done nothing in response to the problems in the property identified by the authority seven months previously. Appealing out of time, and subsequently failing to pursue the appeal in any meaningful way, appears to have been a deliberate strategy for further delay to carrying out the repairs
CHI/00MS/ HIN/2006/ 0002 Appeal by landlord against the service of an improvement notice	SOUTHERN SOUTHAMP-TON	Half of the £150 application fee reimbursed to the applicant	No oral hearing, the tribunal determined the matter on the basis of written representations
			Complex situation involved works to a listed building where there appears to have been faults on both sides
			The tribunal comments on the difficulties involved in resolving evidential issues on the basis of papers alone. Typing inaccuracies to the notice and delay in providing the landlord with advice caused particular problems

PROHIBITION ORDERS

17.65 The biggest difficulties faced by local housing authorities in connection with prohibition orders relate to proportionality and demonstrating that the prohibition order, rather than for example an improvement notice, is the correct course of action.

17.66 It is important to pay attention to the requirements of paragraph 5–8 of the Schedule to the regulations.

17.67 The table below summarises the decisions.

Prohibition orders	Region & Local authority	Outcome	Commentary
LON/00AL/HPO/ 2006/0001 Landlord's appeal against the making of a prohibition order	**LONDON GREENWICH**	Prohibition order confirmed and appeal dismissed	The tribunal exercised its discretion to allow the appeal out of time
			However, the appellant's expert evidence was excluded from the bundle of documents. It was undated and unsigned, had not been served on the respondent's the requisite 7 days before the hearing, it did not contain a statement of the expert's overriding duty to the tribunal as required by the regulations and did not contain a copy of an initial report which was referred to in the expert evidence. The tribunal determined that the breach of regulation 22 was serious and to allow the evidence would be prejudicial to the respondents

Prohibition orders	Region & Local authority	Outcome	Commentary
			The flat was in very poor condition and the appellant accepted that there were three category 1 hazards to the premises. In all the circumstances the decision to serve a probation order was not disproportionate
MAN/00EY/HPO/ 2007/0001 Landlord's appeal against the making of a prohibition order	**NORTHERN BLACKPOOL**	The prohibition order confirmed subject to a variation to exclude the commercial part of the premises	Taking into account the number and continuing effect of the category 1 and 2 hazards to the property, the health and safety issues and implications for the occupiers the tribunal determined that it was appropriate that the local authority chose to exercise its power to make a prohibition order. The tribunal also took into account the period of time that the property had been the subject of local authority concerns
			The applicant's assertion that his lack of information about the process of scoring the hazards made him believe that the process was stilted against him was rejected. The tribunal saw no reason to believe that the decisions were anything other than objective

Prohibition orders	Region & Local authority	Outcome	Commentary
MAN/32UB/HPO/ 2006/0004 Landlord's appeal against the making of a prohibition order	NORTHERN BOSTON	Prohibition order quashed	The property was accessed via an external steel staircase. It satisfied building regulations. However, the local authority at the time of inspection considered that it was a category 1 hazard and only work which enclosed the staircase would move it below this category. At the hearing the local authority conceded that there was the possibility of works being carried out other than enclosure which would reduce the risk of harm. The tribunal determined that an improvement notice was the most appropriate form of enforcement action. The applicant was not awarded costs nor reimbursed with his fee for the application
BIR/17UB/HPO/ 2006/0002 Owner occupier's appeal against prohibition order	MIDLAND AMBER VALLEY	Prohibition order confirmed save for operative time	No oral hearing
			The applicant occupied a semi-derelict grade 2 listed building. The tribunal determined that there were category 1 hazards at the premises. An improvement notice would not be an acceptable alternative form of action. The operative time in the order did not conform to the statutory requirements and was therefore varied

Prohibition orders	Region & Local authority	Outcome	Commentary
CAM/26UG/HPO/ 2006/0002 Owner occupier's appeal against prohibition order	EASTERN ST ALBANS	Prohibition order invalid	The order was not valid because it failed to specify in sufficient detail the work which would be necessary to enable the authority to revoke the order in accordance with the statutory requirement. In addition the local authority had failed to provide the statutorily required statement explaining the decision to take the particular form of action. This is necessary for Article 6 of the HER – right to a fair hearing. The tribunal indicated that it would have confirmed the order if it had been valid, although it expressed some disquiet that the statute does not allow for two forms of action in response to hazards, as in this case this would have been helpful
CAM/26UG/HPO/ 2006/0002 Landlord's appeal against prohibition order	EASTERN HUNGERFORD	Prohibition order varied to the extent that the property is not to be occupied by more than two adults under the age of 60 and one child over the age of 10	Case determined on the papers
			Prohibition order originally prevented use of the second floor (top floor) of the property for residential use because of the unsafe nature of internal staircase and lack of headroom on staircase and second floor. The property a flat above commercial premises in a grade 2 listed building and the appellant's case was that it was not be practicable to make the required alternations

Prohibition orders	Region & Local authority	Outcome	Commentary
			This was a difficult case involving accommodation around 300 years old. The tribunal considered that there was a category 1 hazard from the staircase, but not from the low ceilings. The tribunal considered that prohibiting the residential use of the second floor was neither appropriate nor reasonable
			It decided that the most appropriate response was to exclude the most vulnerable groups from exposure to the hazard by preventing the occupation of the accommodation of the property by adults over 60 or children under 10

Prohibition orders	Region & Local authority	Outcome	Commentary
CHI/00HB/HPO/ 2007/0005 Tenant's application against the suspension of prohibition order	SOUTHERN BRISTOL	The suspension of the prohibition order was confirmed but a time limit of was placed on the suspension	This unusual case was an appeal not against the imposition of a prohibition order but against its suspension. Moreover, the applicant was the tenant. The tribunal did not consider the standing of the tenant to make the application, but note the decision in CHI/23UB/HIN/2007/ 0002. The applicant was concerned that the suspension of the order prevented her from being found to be statutorily homeless. The tribunal found that in these particular circumstances the applicant wishes should be given little weight. Nonetheless, the tribunal imposed a time limit on the suspension to reflect the seriousness of the hazard caused by the overcrowding in the property

Prohibition orders	Region & Local authority	Outcome	Commentary
CHI/00MR/HPO/ 2007/0001, 0002, 0003, 0004 Landlord's appeal against prohibition orders relating to four flats in one building	SOUTHERN SOUTHSEA	Prohibition orders confirmed	The four flats had been created by converting the ground floor of a terraced house. The prohibition orders arose from the flats being too small to accommodate the necessary facilities. Two applications were withdrawn on the day of the tribunal. The landlord's appeal was not based on a challenge to the calculation of the hazard scores; rather it argued that improvement notices were a more appropriate course of action. It was quite clear to the tribunal that the floor area of the flats was too small and that the only way to remove the hazards was to increase the floor area which required work which was over and above the remit of an improvement notice
CHI/00MR/HPO/ 2007/0001, 0002, 0003, 0004	SOUTHERN SOUTHSEA		

EMERGENCY NOTICES AND ORDERS

17.68 These cases seem to prove particularly difficult for local housing authorities. They appear to involve landlords who are particularly ignorant of the law, or where the authority has had a long standing difficult relationship with the landlord.

17.69 Nonetheless it is important not to let the frustrations that housing authorities understandably feel cloud their judgment.

17.70 It is particularly important in these cases to be able to demonstrate that taking emergency action was the most appropriate course in the circumstances, and that is was proportionate to the risk posed by the properties.

17.71 It is also important to be able to justify the money spent by the local housing authority in responding to the emergency. All expenditure should be documented and officers should be prepared to explain both how costs were calculated. This includes the administrative costs incurred in organising the repairs.

17.72 Finally ensure that you pay attention to the requirements of paragraphs 9–11 of the Schedule to the Regulations.

17.73 The table below summarises the decisions on interim EDMOs.

Emergency notices and orders	Region & Local authority	Outcome	Commentary
MAN/00FB/HED/2006/0001 Appeal by landlord against the costs of the emergency remedial works	MANCHESTER BRIDLING-TON	Appeal allowed in part. Sum demanded of £8723 reduced to £6962	The applicant disputed all of the sum demanded by the local authority. The tribunal determined that the costs demanded in connection with the rehousing of vulnerable occupiers in bed and breakfast accommodation during the execution of the remedial works were not costs incurred in taking remedial action because those occupiers had been relocated prior to the commencement of the emergency remedial action process

Emergency notices and orders	Region & Local authority	Outcome	Commentary
			The tribunal found that all the other costs were reasonable and recoverable. This included the sum of £1152.03 for administrative costs. Because of the harassing conduct of the applicant towards council officers they were obliged to visit the premises on numerous occasions and in pairs
			Nonetheless the tribunal found these to be necessary and proportionate to the process of ensuring that the category 1 hazard was removed
MAN/3OUJ/HER/2007/0001 Appeal by landlord against the decision to take emergency remedial works	NORTHERN NELSON	Decision to take emergency remedial action confirmed	A category 1 hazard (a defective gas supply) was present on the property and the hazard involved an imminent risk of serious harm to the occupants. The local authority acted appropriately and reasonably in response

Emergency notices and orders	Region & Local authority	Outcome	Commentary
CAM/00KA/HER/2007/0001	**EASTERN LUTON**	The emergency remedial action was invalid because of failure to follow the correct procedures. In the alternative the course of action taken by the local authority was not the most appropriate of those available. The tribunal reversed the decision of the local authority	Whilst the tribunal determined that there was a category 1 hazard in the premises, the local authority had failed to carry out a proper inspection of the premises or to prepare a written report which properly considered the range of actions which might be appropriate. This meant that it could not be satisfied to the extent that the statute demands that emergency remedial action was appropriate. The tribunal pointed out that the safeguards in the statute are necessary to prevent inappropriate exercises of power against property owners
			The effect of the emergency remedial action was to leave an occupier in an upper floor flat without a fire alarm creating a risk of death through fire.

Emergency notices and orders	Region & Local authority	Outcome	Commentary
			Whilst emergency action was justified the correct course of action was an emergency prohibition order. This would remove all occupiers and visitors from risks of hazards, prevent any further occupation of the property and would not have created other potential hazards
CHI/00MS/HIN/2006/0002 Appeal by landlord against the costs of the emergency remedial works	SOUTHERN SWINDON	Applicant liable to pay costs of emergency remedial works	There was a history of poor property management including fires and fire alarm failures to the premises. The landlord did not appeal against the emergency remedial action notice but against the demand for reimbursement of costs. The tribunal found that the local authority was justified in getting the work done because the landlord had not provided evidence that he would ensure that the work on the fire alarm system would be carried out imminently

Emergency notices and orders	Region & Local authority	Outcome	Commentary
			Indeed there was no requirement to allow the landlord any time at all to do the works. The tribunal found that the work done was reasonably necessary. Although the cost of the work was on the high side it was still reasonable (if on the high side of reasonable) considering the premium paid for priority work

MANDATORY LICENSING

17.74 The table below summarises the decisions on Mandatory Licensing.

Mandatory licensing	Region & Local authority	Outcome	Commentary
LON/00AG/HMV/2007/0003 Appeal by landlord against an HMO declaration notice	LONDON CAMDEN	The HMO declaration notice was confirmed and the appeal disallowed	The landlord's case was that the property was not a house in multiple occupation because it was a guesthouse and there was only one long term resident, the other being in the process of moving out. The tribunal determined on the basis of the evidence before it that the property had a long history of an HMO with people using it as their main residence. Although the appellants were in the process of selling the building and winding down the business it remained an HMO. The tribunal does comment that it would have been more difficult to find that a significant use had been established if the tribunal were only considering the situation as at the date of the hearing

Mandatory licensing	Region & Local authority	Outcome	Commentary
LON/00AH/HMV/2007/0002 Appeal by landlord against the fee demanded for the grant of an HMO licence	**LONDON CROYDON**	A temporary exemption notice issued. The applicant's fee ordered to be reimbursed by the local authority	The property was one which was registrable under Croydon's own HMO scheme, rather than the national mandatory scheme. Following inspection by the local authority the applicant was told that the property had to be licensed and work would have to be done to the property. The applicant's response was to tell the local authority that she might sell the property or do the works depending on the costs of the works. The applicant then put the property on the market. The licence was granted on 4 April 2007. On 22 May the applicant completed the sale of the property. She objected to having to pay for a 5-year licence which was otiose for most of the period. The tribunal decided that once a clear intention to sell property had been communicated to the local authority it should have considered the grant of a temporary exemption notice. If it had then decided not to grant the temporary exemption notice then it the applicant would have been entitled to know the reasons for the decision and to appeal against it. Because the hearing operates as a re-hearing and because the applicant has now sold the property the tribunal determined that the authority must issue a temporary exemption notice from the date when the licence was granted

Mandatory licensing	Region & Local authority	Outcome	Commentary
LON/00AG/HMD/2007/0002 Landlord's appeal against declaration of an HMO	LONDON HACKNEY	Appeal dismissed because application to tribunal made out of time	Appeals against the authority's decision must be made within 28 days of its decision. There is no express power to extend the time for appeal against declarations of an HMO
LON/00AV/HMT/2007/0002 Landlord's appeal against refusal of the authority to grant a temporary exclusion notice	LONDON ISLINGTON	Appeal confirmed the decision of the authority not to grant a temporary exclusion notice quashed	The decision that the property was an HMO was not in dispute. The appellant also made no criticism of the original decision of the authority not to grant a temporary exclusion notice. However, at the time of the appeal – which proceeds by rehearing – the tenants of the property had been given notice to vacate the property and it was likely that the property would be empty before the expiry of the 3 months of the temporary exclusion notice. Because the tenants paid too high a rent to fall within the scope of the assured tenancy status of the Housing Act 1988, there was no need for a 2-month notice period. Therefore, although the original appeal had been based on the proposed conversion works which would have taken longer than 4 months and could not therefore have been upheld, the decision of the authority was quashed on the basis of the new facts available to the tribunal

Mandatory licensing	Region & Local authority	Outcome	Commentary
MAN/13UE/HMV/2007/0002 Landlord's appeal against condition in a licence	NORTHERN ELLESMERE PORT	The decision of the local housing authority confirmed that the date by which the condition is to be complied with is varied to 6 months from the date of the decision of the tribunal	In contrast with the position in LON/00AG/HMD/2007/0002 there is a discretion given to tribunals to allow applications out of time when the appeal is against conditions within licences. The tribunal chose to exercise its discretion in this case
			The HMO in question had eight rooms each accommodating a single resident. The residents shared a kitchen and two bathrooms (each of which contains a toilet). The authority required the applicant to provide an additional WC and wash hand basin within 6 months of the date of the licence. The appellant objected to this condition
			The case turned on the interpretation of paragraph 2(1) (b) of Schedule 3 to SI 2006/373 which prescribes the minimum amenity standards required of a licensable HMO. The tribunal had no hesitation in holding that the appellant's submission that the same requirement applies to an HMO whether it has 5, 6, 7, 8 or 9 occupants is incorrect. It agreed with the LHA contention that the reference in the paragraph of the schedule to 'every five' means that there is a step change in the requirements at 5, 6–10 etc. The tribunal struggled more with the meaning of the word 'separate'

Mandatory licensing	Region & Local authority	Outcome	Commentary
			In essence the appellant's argument was that by providing two bathrooms each with a toilet, the toilets are separate from each other by virtue of being in different (bath)rooms. The local authority argued that 'separate' means separate from any other room including a bathroom. The logic of the local authority position was that there should be two additional toilets provided by the appellant, and not the one required by the condition of the licence. They argued a complex hybrid interpretation based on the DCLG guidance
			The tribunal accepted the authority's position, and pointed out that whether or not it is correct, it would not be unreasonable for the LHA to require that where there are eight units of accommodation there should be at least one toilet that is in a separate room from the two bathrooms. This is because the policy of the Act is to raise standards and not to derogate from pre-Act amenity norms

Mandatory licensing	Region & Local authority	Outcome	Commentary
MAN/30UK/HML/2007/0001 Landlord's appeal against the requirements of the licence	NORTH-ERN PRESTON	The decision of the local housing authority to require the fitting of fire doors to three shower rooms was quashed	The tribunal accepted that it was legitimate for the local authority to decide to impose licensing conditions on the basis of plans of the accommodation rather than an inspection. It was concerned that the authority had applied a 'one size fits all' approach. If the authority had made inquiries it would have learned that the showers provided were not electrical showers and that extractor fans were provided in only two of the three bathrooms. It pointed out that the authority must exercise its discretion reasonably and that the greater the risk the greater the requirements to be imposed. No evidence was produced of the likelihood of fires in extractor fans or of the risk of injury or death by fire in these circumstances. Therefore the requirement for fire doors to the shower rooms was untenable

Mandatory licensing	Region & Local authority	Outcome	Commentary
BIR/00FY/HML/2007/0002/01 Landlord's appeal against the requirement of a licence	**MIDLANDS NOTTING-HAM**	The authority's decision confirmed and the appeal dismissed	This appeal appears to have been taken on a point of principle that the mandatory conditions that wash hand basins are provided in every unit of accommodation are inappropriate and that environmental health officers should be allowed some discretion. As there is no discretion, the tribunal had no alternative but to confirm the requirement. However, the tribunal did observe that if there were discretion it would not require a wash hand basin where there was a shower in a room, and it would not require two wash hand basins in a shared bathroom
CAM/38UB/HML/2007/0001 Landlord's appeal against the licensing of an HMO and the conditions imposed	**EASTERN CHERWELL**	The authority's decision to grant the licence affirmed. The conditions to the licence varied	This was a trenchant attack by a landlord on the imposition of a license and the conditions imposed by that licence. First, the landlord challenged the validity of the licence. This was based on the fact that the licence was addressed just to him, and not to his wife who was the joint owner and manager of the property

Mandatory licensing	Region & Local authority	Outcome	Commentary
			However, it transpired that the application for the licence to the authority had been made only in the landlord's name – in order to avoid double penalties for failing to comply with conditions – and therefore the authority were entitled to rely on that information. The landlord also raised issues connected to the 'passporting' of licenses granted under the discretionary licensing scheme. He argued that a licence without conditions should be granted because of the transitional arrangements
			However, the tribunal found that the authority's previous scheme was not one to which passporting applied. The appellant further challenged the conditions relating to inspection of the fire precautions, the washing/toilet facilities, and the timeframe for compliance. The tribunal did not consider that the requirement for inspection was unduly onerous, although it tightened the wording as to who should be considered competent to inspect. The appellant failed on his argument that the property did not provide six separate units of accommodation and therefore the regulations applied. The regulations were mandatory, and even if arguably onerous had to be applied by the authority

Mandatory licensing	Region & Local authority	Outcome	Commentary
			Finally the appellant argued that the 3 years he was given to carry out the works to the property was too short a time. The tribunal concluded that it was a reasonable time frame. The tribunal also considered the matter of the appellant's request that the property should be licensed for eight as opposed to six occupants. The authority had no objection to this, subject to ensuring that certain bedrooms were reserved for single occupation. The tribunal therefore made the appropriate amendments to the conditions
CAM/42UD/HML/2006/0001 Landlord's appeal against conditions imposed by a licence	EASTERN IPSWICH	Appeal allowed and the authority directed to grant to the appellant a licence permitting the premises to be used as an HMO by up to a maximum of eight occupants at any one time	The authority granted the appellant a licence limiting occupation of the premises to six persons. This was because the authority considered that the kitchen and dining facilities were poorly laid out. The landlord wanted the licence to allow him six households and eight tenants. The tribunal considered that the dining facilities were sufficiently capacious for a maximum of eight persons and made its order accordingly
CAM/33UG/HMO/2006/0001 Landlord's appeal against notice designating the premises as an HMO	EASTERN NORWICH	The appeal failed and the decision of the authority upheld	The landlord's appeal was that the premises were a guest house and not an HMO, and therefore that no-one who resided there did so as their only or main residence

Mandatory licensing	Region & Local authority	Outcome	Commentary
			The tribunal inspected the property and concluded that it had the characteristics of a hostel rather than a guest house or a hotel. The facilities were very basic and the house rules were consistent with long term residence. The tribunal found that whilst the landlord may have had an intention to change the use from an HMO (which he admitted it was in 2005) he had not carried through his intentions and provided sufficient safeguards to prevent people occupying it as their only or main residence. It also observed that although the hearing was a rehearing, it was important to take into account the use of the premises over a period of time, otherwise an unscrupulous landlord could simply ensure that on the date of the inspection there was no occupation other than by those who had other main residences
CHI/OOHN/HMJ/2007/ 0001 Landlord's appeal against the refusal of the authority to grant a further temporary extension notice	SOUTHERN BOURNE-MOUTH	Decision of the authority upheld	This case appears only to have been made on the papers. Although there was a suggestion that there were no longer four residents in the premises this was not pursued by the tribunal. It found as a matter of law that a further temporary extension notice could not be granted as two had already been granted

Mandatory licensing	Region & Local authority	Outcome	Commentary
CHI/000HB/HML/2007/0004 Landlord's appeal against a requirement of a licence	SOUTHERN BRISTOL	Decision of the authority upheld	The landlord's appeal was against the requirement to provide an additional WC to the premises. The landlord was represented by Mr Adrian Thompson of the Guild of Residential Landlords. The appellant's case was that he was fully compliant with the regulations because he provides two bathrooms for the six occupants to the property and that each occupant has a key to one specific property so that three occupants have the use of one bathroom and three of the other. The authority replied that if this were the case the occupiers would be deprived of access to one of the bathrooms, in breach of the licence condition that all occupiers have 24 hour access to all toilet, washing and cooking facilities, which cannot have been the intention of the regulations. The appellant did not challenge this condition. Moreover if the appellant's interpretation was correct there would be no need for the regulations to specify different levels of facilities for every five occupants. The tribunal preferred the arguments of the authority and confirmed its decisions

Mandatory licensing	Region & Local authority	Outcome	Commentary
CHI/000HB/HML/2007/ 0005 Landlord's appeal against a requirement of a licence	SOUTHERN BRISTOL	Decision of the authority upheld	This application was concerned with the same issue as the preceding case, although the premises and the appellant were different. The landlord was represented by Mr Adrian Thompson of the Guild of Residential Landlords. The reasoning and decision of the tribunal were as above
CHI/18UC/HML/2006/ 0001 Landlord's appeal against a requirement of a licence	SOUTHERN EXETER	Decision of the authority upheld save that the requirement to provide a combination microwave oven was varied to provide a microwave oven	The issue here was the provision of kitchen facilities for the six occupiers of an HMO. The authority's position was that where six or seven people were sharing a kitchen it required two sinks or a sink and a dishwasher and in addition to a four-ringed hob and oven a two-ringed hob and oven or a combination microwave. The appellant's argument was that the facilities provided were adequate, if not wonderful. The tribunal was satisfied that there was a requirement for an additional sink or dishwasher. It also considered that there was a need for a microwave oven. The appellant provided a microwave oven, but not a combination one. The tribunal considered that nothing material was added by the requirement that the microwave oven was provided

Mandatory licensing	Region & Local authority	Outcome	Commentary
CHI/00MR/HML/2007/0001 Landlord's appeal against the limitation in the licence granted to him and certain conditions of the licence	SOUTHERN PORT-SMOUTH	The authority directed to grant a licence to the landlord limiting the occupation of the HMO to nine instead of seven, and deleting the conditions relating to occupation of rooms 3 and 6 of the premises	The landlord had let out rooms in the premises since the 1970s. The premises had nine separate bed sitting rooms. The authority decided that two of the rooms were too small for occupation. The tribunal decided that room size was not on its own sufficient to determine whether a room was reasonably suitable for occupation. Other facilities such as natural lighting, layout, etc should be considered. The tribunal also noted that the Act used the words 'reasonably suitable' rather than good or ideal. The tribunal considered that taken as a whole the premises provided reasonable accommodation, that rooms 3 and 6, whilst having small floor areas had natural light and high ceilings, that there was no evidence of detriment to the health and safety of the occupiers and that the provision of additional accommodation for communal facilities was not necessary for the protection of occupiers' health and safety

RENT REPAYMENT ORDERS

17.75 With so few cases it is difficult to make useful general observations. However, the observation of the tribunal in BIR/44UF/HMA/2007/0001 and 0002 that rent repayment orders are a useful enforcement tool for HMO licensing, and that landlords should not be able to effectively disregard licensing by paying a relatively small fine is useful for applicants to bear in mind.

17.76 The tribunal in LON/00BB/HSR/2007/0001 provides some important guidance on how RROs should be approached when there has been no criminal conviction of the respondent. The decision points to the need of the applicant to be meticulous in documenting its claim. This decision should be read carefully by any local housing authority intending to make an application in similar circumstances.

17.77 The table below sets out the relevant cases.

Rent repayment orders	Region & Local authority	Outcome	Commentary
BIR/44UF/HMA/2007/ 0001 & 0002	MIDLANDS WARWICK	Rent repayment order made for 50% of rent paid for the period during which the property was unlicensed.	The application for a rent repayment order was made by the tenants and former tenants of properties owned by a landlord who was convicted of operating HMOs which were required to be licensed without a licence. The application is limited to the period during which time the applicants lived in the property and the time when the landlord applied for a license. During this time the applicants had benefited from above average student accommodation although they had also had a 'poor experience' with the landlord being unresponsive to problems with the accommodation. The tribunal in deciding what proportion of the rent paid should be reimbursed were mindful of avoiding a windfall gain to the applicants, yet at the same time noted the conduct of the landlord who was a 'professional' in failing to obtain licenses for his properties. It therefore made a rent repayment order of 50% of the rent paid for the relevant period

Rent repayment orders	Region & Local authority	Outcome	Commentary
LON/00BB/HSR/2007/ 0001 Application by the local authority for a rent repayment order in respect of housing benefit paid to the respondent in connection with occupation of parts of the premises	**LONDON NEWHAM**	RRO made but for a lesser amount than claimed	The tribunal gave less than 21 days notice of hearing because it accepted that there were exceptional circumstances, namely that the ability of some of the former occupiers of the property to apply for their own RRO depended on the outcome of this application and that delay could prejudice them
			The decision provides some important guidance on principles for RROs when there has been no criminal conviction of the respondent
			The standard of proof required to satisfy itself that an offence had been committed, given no conviction or prosecution had taken place. Counsel, on behalf of the applicant conceded that the tribunal should apply the higher criminal test so that we should be satisfied beyond reasonable doubt

Rent repayment orders	Region & Local authority	Outcome	Commentary
			There are practical difficulties in applying the higher standard in the absence of the ability to take evidence under oath. No procedural regulations have yet been made to include administration of oaths to witnesses. The tribunal therefore considered that it should require cogent and persuasive evidence to find that an offence had been committed
			A defence is available that at the material time an application for a licence had been duly made. Counsel for the applicant submitted that the respondent needed to argue this defence. The tribunal disagreed. 'He is an unrepresented party faced with new and complex legislation and there was evidence of his sending in the form'. For a restricted period therefore the respondent had a defence to the applicant's claim
			The applicant could only demonstrate that it had paid housing benefit to five or more individuals for a restricted period
			The tribunal therefore decided that a rent repayment order should be made but for a lesser amount than claimed

EMPTY DWELLING MANAGEMENT ORDERS

17.78 All but one of the applications made by local housing authorities were granted by the tribunal. The one that was not made was due to exceptional circumstances that were not known to the applicant at the time of the application. This would suggest that local housing authorities are exercising due care in making what is potentially a draconian application.

17.79 There are a couple of points to bear in mind. It is important that the application addresses all of the statutory requirements specifically. By their nature it is likely that such applications will not attract a coherent response, and therefore the tribunal will be assiduous in ensuring the statutory requirements are demonstrably present. The applicant should pay particular attention to paragraph 38 to 47 of the Schedule to the regulations.

17.80 Secondly, there are some 'rogue' commercial forms containing draft orders which do not comply with the legal requirements. Applicants should check that their forms are legally correct.

17.81 The table below sets out the applications and their outcomes.

Empty Dwelling Management Orders	Region & Local authority	Outcome	Commentary
LON/00AZ/HYI/2007/0004 Application by local authority for an interim empty dwelling management order	LONDON LEWISHAM	The tribunal granted the authorisation in the form submitted by the applicant subject to some variations	Application proceeded on the basis of written representations. The parties were agreed that the property had been empty for at least 6 months. Council tax records show it has been empty since 1 April 2004 although some illegal occupation has taken place since then

Empty Dwelling Management Orders	Region & Local authority	Outcome	Commentary
			The tribunal was satisfied that the dwelling has been wholly unoccupied for at least 6 months, that there is no reasonable prospect that it will become occupied in the near future, but that once an interim EDMO is made there is a reasonable prospect that it will become occupied. The tribunal accepts that the applicant has complied with the statutory provisions and that no prescribed exceptions apply. The tribunal took into account the interest of the community and the effect the order would have on the respondents
LON/OOAZ/HYI/2007/0003 Application by local authority for an interim empty dwelling management order	LONDON LEWISHAM	The tribunal granted the authorisation	The property had sat empty for many years. Council tax arrears have accumulated of over £9000. Land Registry searches revealed that the property was owned by a father and son. The first named respondent was served with a copy of the application and has not made any representations. The whereabouts of the second named respondent are unknown

Empty Dwelling Management Orders	Region & Local authority	Outcome	Commentary
			The tribunal was satisfied that the property had remained empty and that given the lack of cooperation by the first (sic) named respondent, there was little prospect that the property would become occupied in the near future. The tribunal was also satisfied that there was a reasonable prospect that the property would become occupied if it authorised the making of an interim EDMO. The tribunal noted that although the totality of the documentary evidence and material before it was sufficient to enable the tribunal to be satisfied of the matters contained in the Act and that it was satisfied that the case did not fall within the category of exceptions, the applicant's witness statement did not address the above matters. The tribunal pointed out that it was important that the warren evidence specifically addressed the matters
MAN/16UD/HYI/2007/0001 Application by local authority for an interim empty dwelling management order	NORTHERN CARLISLE	The tribunal granted the authorisation for the interim EDMO	The tribunal found that the property had been empty since 1992 when the respondent's mother died. Several complaints were made about the condition of the property which was in serious disrepair and possibly dangerous. The tribunal found that the statutory and regulatory requirements had been complied with and therefore made the order

Empty Dwelling Management Orders	Region & Local authority	Outcome	Commentary
CAM/33UG/HYI/2007/0001 Application by local authority for an interim empty dwelling management order	EASTERN NORWICH	The tribunal granted the authorisation. for the interim EDMO	The facts were not in dispute. The owner of the property agreed that it was problematic, and that he would like to see it occupied, but he could not afford to do the repairs so he was happy for an interim EDMO to be made and for the applicant to take over the management of the property. The tribunal found that the statutory and regulatory requirements had been complied with and therefore made the order
CAM/00JA/HYI/2007/0002 Application by local authority for an interim empty dwelling management order	EASTERN PETERBOR-OUGH	The tribunal granted the authorisation in the form submitted by the applicant subject to some variations	The tribunal concluded from the evidence that the property had been unoccupied for at least 6 months, although not the 7 years asserted by the applicant. The applicant had certainly been concerned about the property for some time. The respondent provided no written representations on the matter. The tribunal found that the statutory and regulatory requirements had been complied with and therefore made the order. It expressed concern that the draft order had been produced by a commercial firm and it contained legal inaccuracies. It corrected those inaccuracies in its decision, however, asked the applicant to inform the provider of the forms of the errors. The form used seems to have been identical to the form used in LON/00AZ/HYI/2007/0004 and CAM/38UD/HYI/2006/0001

Empty Dwelling Management Orders	Region & Local authority	Outcome	Commentary
CAM/38UD/HYI/2006/0001 Application by local authority for an interim empty dwelling management order	EASTERN SOUTH OXFORD- SHIRE	The tribunal granted the authorisation in the form submitted by the applicant subject to some variations	The tribunal found that the property had been empty for at least 5 years, that none of the exceptions applied, and that the local community was concerned about the risks of fire and burglary. The second respondent in this matter was the mortgagee who urged the tribunal not to make an interim order as it might result in the first respondent ceasing to make her mortgage payments. The tribunal pointed out that the EDMO does not affect the validity of the mortgage nor the mortgagee's ability to enforce those terms. No compensation was ordered for the second respondent as it was unlikely to suffer any loss as a result of the EDMO

Empty Dwelling Management Orders	Region & Local authority	Outcome	Commentary
CAM/26UK/HYI/2006/0002 Application by local authority for an interim empty dwelling management order	EASTERN WATFORD	The tribunal refused authorisation for an interim EDMO	Whilst the matter was dealt with on the basis of written representations, and no written representations were received from the respondent, the respondent's sister had contacted the tribunal to inform them that 4 years earlier the respondent's daughter had a serious accident in France and had been in and out of hospital ever since. The respondent was currently living with her elderly mother. The sister suggested that the respondent had had a mental breakdown. The respondent intended to return to the property to live but agreed that in the meantime it should be let. No order can be made whilst the owner is temporarily absent or whilst he is caring for someone because of old age, illness or disability. The tribunal concluded that the applicant was not aware of the information about the respondent when it made its application and that therefore it was justified in making the application. The tribunal declined to make the order because there was a reasonable prospect of the property becoming occupied in the near future
CHI/29UM/HYI/2007/0001 Application by local authority for an interim empty dwelling management order	SOUTHERN SWALE	The tribunal granted the authorisation for the interim EDMO	At the time of writing the full reasons of the tribunal had not been published

PRINCIPLES EMERGING FROM THE DECISIONS

17.82 Whilst it is very helpful to draw conclusions from decisions that are closely related to any application you are considering, it is also useful to consider any general emerging principles from the RPT decisions. This is particularly so if you are responding to or making an application in an area where there have been no published decisions. We have, therefore, drawn some general principles from the decisions.

17.83 Tribunals should be respectful of the local housing authority view on matters of local housing conditions and slow to disagree with its conclusions. For instance, in an appeal against an HMO Declaration Notice (1 Grafton Road London: LON/00AG/HMV/2007 0003) the tribunal emphasised that it was proper that in 'this important area of social housing policy' that it paid 'considerable attention to the view of the local housing authority and to be slow to disagree with it unless of course the facts as found warrant such disagreement'.

17.84 Procedural matters are particularly important. The failure of the local housing authority to consider the issue of a temporary exemption notice in a case where the landlady had provided clear notification of her intention to sell the property was strongly criticised in 89 Temple Road Croydon LON/00AH/HMV/2007/0002. The tribunal points out that accepting that there has been notification of an intention to sell does not mean that a temporary exemption notice must be issued but it does mean that it should be considered. If it is refused then the authority must issue a notice explaining the reasons for the refusal and giving the recipient an opportunity to challenge it before the tribunal. The tribunal emphasises the importance of this – 'An authority should never underestimate the value of such a notice – even if an HMO owner has no real prospect of persuading an authority or a Tribunal that a temporary exemption notice should be issued, he is entitled to know why and to have an opportunity both to consider and to put his case'.

17.85 The particular importance of procedural matters was also made clear in 145 Clifton Road BIR/44UD/HIN/2006/0003. Here the tribunal determined that the improvement notice was invalid because it failed to comply with the requirements of section 8 of the Act. These matters were not raised by the applicant. However, the tribunal emphasised the significance of Article 6 of the ECHR – the right to a fair trial. The failure of the local authority to prepare a statement of reasons for their decision to take particular action was fatal to the notice. This failure was exacerbated by mistakes in the calculation of the hazard scores such that the tribunal determined that the hazards were category 2 rather than category 1. In the view of the tribunal this made it even more important to provide an explanation of the required action as category 2 hazards open for consideration by the authority a wider range of possible action, including of course, the possibility of no action at all.

17.86 The tribunal has generally taken a purposive construction to the legislation. For instance, in 43 Whitby Road MAN/13UE/HMV/2007/0002 the tribunal observed that 'the purpose of the 2004 Act is to raise standards in HMOs and it is consistent with that purpose to interpret the reference to the need for one separate toilet and one bathroom for "every five" occupiers to men that no more than five occupiers should be required to share a single bathroom and a single separate toilet'.

17.87 Decisions made by local housing authorities in connection with the Act need to be proportionate. This is illustrated in 73 Dallas Street MAN where the requirement to install fire doors to shower rooms was found to be disproportionate to any risk posed to the occupiers. Significantly the authority provided evidence relating only to the risk posed by electrical showers. In the case the showers provided were not electric, which the authority would have found out if it had inspected the premises or made inquiries of the landlord. The authority provided no evidence of the fire risk imposed by extractor fans in bathrooms, which was the relevant electrical equipment in the case.

17.88 Certain problems appear to be caused by the fact that the hearing at the tribunal operates as a rehearing. So, for instance, a property may be occupied by several people when the housing authority makes its decision on whether it is a HMO, but by the time the tribunal inspects, it is occupied by only one or two tenants. This was one of the issues in 1 Grafton Road, LON/00AG/HMV/ 2007 0003 (see **17.83**). The tribunal decided that for the purposes of section 255(2) of the Act, 'the proper approach was to look at the matter in the round, considering the position both in the past and as at the date of the hearing'.

17.89 There is some suggestion in the cases that economic realities will influence decision making. So, for instance, in an appeal against conditions imposed by the local authority in a House in Multiple Occupation Licence (8 Burrell Road Suffolk Cam/42UD/HML/2006/0001) the decision states: 'It would be a pity if unnecessary restrictions made the provision of such a service uneconomic'.

17.90 Tribunals seem to be well aware of the burden placed upon landlords by the fees that are charged for HMO licences. So, for instance, in one appeal discussed above (1 Grafton Road London: LON/00AG/HMV/2007/0003) the tribunal expressed disquiet that a local authority was charging a fee for each of two adjoining properties. The decision suggests that it is 'highly irregular that the Appellants who ran the two properties under one business would be required to pay two HMO licence fees in respect of the same business'. The tribunal hoped that commonsense would prevail and that the council would now not require the appellants to pay an additional HMO licence fee in respect of 3 Grafton Road if that property also proved to be an HMO. In the appeal concerning the failure to consider a temporary exemption notice (LON/00AH/ HMV/2007/0002) the basis of the appellant's dissatisfaction with the actions of the local housing authority was that she would be liable for a fee of £750 for a licence which would run for 6 years when in fact she had sold the property within 2 months of the issue of the licence. There appears to have been some disquiet at the possibility that the underlying reason for not considering the exemption notice was the authority's desire to recoup its costs of licensing via the fee.

PRACTICAL TIPS FOR SUCCESS

17.91 In general it appears that local housing authorities are acquitting themselves well at the tribunal. Their use of the law, and in particular the hazard scoring system, appears to be robust. However, there are some problems which can be avoided. In this final section of the chapter we suggest some tips:

(i)   for avoiding appeals;

(ii)   helping you prepare for those which are unavoidable; and

(iii) for ensuring that you make the best possible impression on the tribunal if you do have to go to a hearing.

17.92 The best way to avoid hearings is to gather together appropriate evidence and communicate fully the reasons for your actions to those upon whom they will impact, therefore:

- carry out good and thorough inspections of premises and take relevant photographs;

- demonstrate that you have carefully considered all the available options and provide a statement that you have done so;

- ensure that you have thought through the rationale for your actions, and considered the impact of your decision on the parties;

- do a final check – is the action necessary and proportionate;

- keep good records of all decisions and compliance with statutory requirements;

- ensure that you have complied with the HHSRS guidance;

- ensure that you have complied with any local authority protocol or concordat on legal proceedings which should ensure that you have achieved the necessary transparency.

17.93 When preparing for a hearing:

- create a check list of the statutory requirements of the action you are taking;

- note when you complied with the action, and ensure you have evidence that you did so;

- satisfy yourself before the hearing that you can meet each requirement in the legislation;

- remember that the hearing operates as a rehearing, so just before the hearing double check that the statutory requirements are still satisfied. For instance if the number of residents in a building falls below the statutory minimum then it no longer qualifies as an HMO;

- use the case management conference to assist in your preparation;

- request any orders that will assist you at the case management conference and ensure that you comply with any directions that it makes;

- consider carefully whether or not you require a lawyer. For some cases it is best to be represented by a solicitor or a barrister if possible as the law is new and, in parts, complex and found in different parts of the Act. However, the decisions demonstrate that environmental health officers have been effective at hearings so, if you are sure you have met the legal requirements, be confident in representing the authority yourself;

- go and observe a Housing Act hearing (or if that is not possible any kind of hearing at RPTS). This will familiarise you with the procedures and the balance of formality/informality;

- know that you can phone the clerk at RPTS for guidance about procedure (but not the law);

- prepare your bundle carefully. Badly arranged/incomplete bundles will irritate the tribunal and suggest that you are not prepared. Ensure that you use dividers to organise the material, and paginate the bundle;

- produce a chronology of events which you agree with the other side. This will help the tribunal follow events;

- consider producing something along the lines of a Scott Schedule. This means that you list your points and next to your point you make reference to the page in the bundle which contains the evidence that supports your point.

17.94 At the hearing:

- stay calm;

- bring your witnesses if you need them, as written statements may not be sufficient;

- bring a colleague for support;

- remember the hearings are in public;

- remember that you will have to present the case orally but your life will be easier the more that you have clearly set out in writing for the tribunal to read in advance;

- note that if you produce documents at the hearing which the other side has not seen this might mean there has to be an adjournment. Try to avoid this, it increases your costs, might lead to a costs penalty, and looks unprofessional;

- address the chair of the tribunal as Mr Chairman, or Madame Chairman and the other members as Sir;

- be familiar with your bundle, use your pre-prepared chronology of events, and refer to the exact page of the bundle which supports your point as you make it.

Appendix 1

HOUSING ACT 2004

Chapter 34

ARRANGEMENT OF SECTIONS

PART 1
HOUSING CONDITIONS

Chapter 1
Enforcement of Housing Standards: General

Chapter 2
Improvement Notices, Prohibition Orders and Hazard Awareness Notices

PART 4

ADDITIONAL CONTROL PROVISIONS IN RELATION TO RESIDENTIAL ACCOMMODATION

Chapter 1

Interim and Final Management Orders

Introductory

An Act to make provision about housing conditions; to regulate houses in multiple occupation and certain other residential accommodation; to make provision for home information packs in connection with the sale of residential properties; to make provision about secure tenants and the right to buy; to make provision about mobile homes and the accommodation needs of gypsies and travellers; to make other provision about housing; and for connected purposes.

[18th November 2004]

BE IT ENACTED by the Queen's most Excellent Majesty, by and with the advice and consent of the Lords Spiritual and Temporal, and Commons, in this present Parliament assembled, and by the authority of the same, as follows: –

PART 1
HOUSING CONDITIONS

Chapter 1
Enforcement of Housing Standards: General

New system for assessing housing conditions

1   New system for assessing housing conditions and enforcing housing standards

(1) This Part provides—

  (a)   for a new system of assessing the condition of residential premises, and
  (b)   for that system to be used in the enforcement of housing standards in relation to such premises.

(2) The new system—

  (a)   operates by reference to the existence of category 1 or category 2 hazards on residential premises (see section 2), and
  (b)   replaces the existing system based on the test of fitness for human habitation contained in section 604 of the Housing Act 1985 (c 68).

(3) The kinds of enforcement action which are to involve the use of the new system are—

  (a)   the new kinds of enforcement action contained in Chapter 2 (improvement notices, prohibition orders and hazard awareness notices),
  (b)   the new emergency measures contained in Chapter 3 (emergency remedial action and emergency prohibition orders), and
  (c)   the existing kinds of enforcement action dealt with in Chapter 4 (demolition orders and slum clearance declarations).

(4) In this Part "residential premises" means—

  (a)   a dwelling;
  (b)   an HMO;
  (c)   unoccupied HMO accommodation;
  (d)   any common parts of a building containing one or more flats.

(5) In this Part—

  "building containing one or more flats" does not include an HMO;
  "common parts", in relation to a building containing one or more flats, includes—
     (a)   the structure and exterior of the building, and
     (b)   common facilities provided (whether or not in the building) for persons who include the occupiers of one or more of the flats;

"dwelling" means a building or part of a building occupied or intended to be occupied as a separate dwelling;

"external common parts", in relation to a building containing one or more flats, means common parts of the building which are outside it;

"flat" means a separate set of premises (whether or not on the same floor)—

    (a)   which forms part of a building,

    (b)   which is constructed or adapted for use for the purposes of a dwelling, and

    (c)   either the whole or a material part of which lies above or below some other part of the building;

"HMO" means a house in multiple occupation as defined by sections 254 to 259, as they have effect for the purposes of this Part (that is, without the exclusions contained in Schedule 14);

"unoccupied HMO accommodation" means a building or part of a building constructed or adapted for use as a house in multiple occupation but for the time being either unoccupied or only occupied by persons who form a single household.

(6) In this Part any reference to a dwelling, an HMO or a building containing one or more flats includes (where the context permits) any yard, garden, outhouses and appurtenances belonging to, or usually enjoyed with, the dwelling, HMO or building (or any part of it).

(7) The following indicates how this Part applies to flats—

    (a)   references to a dwelling or an HMO include a dwelling or HMO which is a flat (as defined by subsection (5)); and

    (b)   subsection (6) applies in relation to such a dwelling or HMO as it applies in relation to other dwellings or HMOs (but it is not to be taken as referring to any common parts of the building containing the flat).

(8) This Part applies to unoccupied HMO accommodation as it applies to an HMO, and references to an HMO in subsections (6) and (7) and in the following provisions of this Part are to be read accordingly.

2   Meaning of "category 1 hazard" and "category 2 hazard"

(1) In this Act—

"category 1 hazard" means a hazard of a prescribed description which falls within a prescribed band as a result of achieving, under a prescribed method for calculating the seriousness of hazards of that description, a numerical score of or above a prescribed amount;

"category 2 hazard" means a hazard of a prescribed description which falls within a prescribed band as a result of achieving, under a prescribed method for calculating the seriousness of hazards of that description, a numerical score below the minimum amount prescribed for a category 1 hazard of that description; and "hazard" means any risk of harm to the health or safety of an actual or potential occupier of a dwelling or HMO which arises from a deficiency in the dwelling or HMO or in any building or land in the vicinity (whether the deficiency arises as a result of the construction of any building, an absence of maintenance or repair, or otherwise).

(2) In subsection (1)—

"prescribed" means prescribed by regulations made by the appropriate national authority (see section 261(1)); and
"prescribed band" means a band so prescribed for a category 1 hazard or a category 2 hazard, as the case may be.

(3) Regulations under this section may, in particular, prescribe a method for calculating the seriousness of hazards which takes into account both the likelihood of the harm occurring and the severity of the harm if it were to occur.

(4) In this section—

"building" includes part of a building;
"harm" includes temporary harm.

(5) In this Act "health" includes mental health.

Procedure for assessing housing conditions

3 Local housing authorities to review housing conditions in their districts

(1) A local housing authority must keep the housing conditions in their area under review with a view to identifying any action that may need to be taken by them under any of the provisions mentioned in subsection (2).

(2) The provisions are—

(a) the following provisions of this Act—
   (i)   this Part,
   (ii)   Part 2 (licensing of HMOs),
   (iii) Part 3 (selective licensing of other houses), and
   (iv)   Chapters 1 and 2 of Part 4 (management orders);
(b) Part 9 of the Housing Act 1985 (c 68) (demolition orders and slum clearance);
(c) Part 7 of the Local Government and Housing Act 1989 (c 42) (renewal areas); and
(d) article 3 of the Regulatory Reform (Housing Assistance) (England and Wales) Order 2002 (SI 2002/1860).

(3) For the purpose of carrying out their duty under subsection (1) a local housing authority and their officers must—

(a) comply with any directions that may be given by the appropriate national authority, and
(b) keep such records, and supply the appropriate national authority with such information, as that authority may specify.

4   Inspections by local housing authorities to see whether category 1 or 2 hazards exist

(1) If a local housing authority consider—

    (a)   as a result of any matters of which they have become aware in carrying out their duty under section 3, or

    (b)   for any other reason,

that it would be appropriate for any residential premises in their district to be inspected with a view to determining whether any category 1 or 2 hazard exists on those premises, the authority must arrange for such an inspection to be carried out.

(2) If an official complaint about the condition of any residential premises in the district of a local housing authority is made to the proper officer of the authority, and the circumstances complained of indicate—

    (a)   that any category 1 or category 2 hazard may exist on those premises, or

    (b)   that an area in the district should be dealt with as a clearance area,

the proper officer must inspect the premises or area.

(3) In this section "an official complaint" means a complaint in writing made by—

    (a)   a justice of the peace having jurisdiction in any part of the district, or
    (b)   the parish or community council for a parish or community within the district.

(4) An inspection of any premises under subsection (1) or (2)—

    (a)   is to be carried out in accordance with regulations made by the appropriate national authority; and

    (b)   is to extend to so much of the premises as the local housing authority or proper officer (as the case may be) consider appropriate in the circumstances having regard to any applicable provisions of the regulations.

(5) Regulations under subsection (4) may in particular make provision about—

    (a)   the manner in which, and the extent to which, premises are to be inspected under subsection (1) or (2), and

    (b)   the manner in which the assessment of hazards is to be carried out.

(6) Where an inspection under subsection (2) has been carried out and the proper officer of a local housing authority is of the opinion—

    (a)   that a category 1 or 2 hazard exists on any residential premises in the authority's district, or

    (b)   that an area in their district should be dealt with as a clearance area,

the officer must, without delay, make a report in writing to the authority which sets out his opinion together with the facts of the case.

(7) The authority must consider any report made to them under subsection (6) as soon as possible.

Enforcement of housing standards

5 Category 1 hazards: general duty to take enforcement action

(1) If a local housing authority consider that a category 1 hazard exists on any residential premises, they must take the appropriate enforcement action in relation to the hazard.

(2) In subsection (1) "the appropriate enforcement action" means whichever of the following courses of action is indicated by subsection (3) or (4)—

(a) serving an improvement notice under section 11;
(b) making a prohibition order under section 20;
(c) serving a hazard awareness notice under section 28;
(d) taking emergency remedial action under section 40;
(e) making an emergency prohibition order under section 43;
(f) making a demolition order under subsection (1) or (2) of section 265 of the Housing Act 1985 (c 68);
(g) declaring the area in which the premises concerned are situated to be a clearance area by virtue of section 289(2) of that Act.

(3) If only one course of action within subsection (2) is available to the authority in relation to the hazard, they must take that course of action.

(4) If two or more courses of action within subsection (2) are available to the authority in relation to the hazard, they must take the course of action which they consider to be the most appropriate of those available to them.

(5) The taking by the authority of a course of action within subsection (2) does not prevent subsection (1) from requiring them to take in relation to the same hazard—

(a) either the same course of action again or another such course of action, if they consider that the action taken by them so far has not proved satisfactory, or
(b) another such course of action, where the first course of action is that mentioned in subsection (2)(g) and their eventual decision under section 289(2F) of the Housing Act 1985 means that the premises concerned are not to be included in a clearance area.

(6) To determine whether a course of action mentioned in any of paragraphs (a) to (g) of subsection (2) is "available" to the authority in relation to the hazard, see the provision mentioned in that paragraph.

(7) Section 6 applies for the purposes of this section.

6 Category 1 hazards: how duty under section 5 operates in certain cases

(1) This section explains the effect of provisions contained in subsection (2) of section 5.

(2) In the case of paragraph (b) or (f) of that subsection, the reference to making an order such as is mentioned in that paragraph is to be read as a reference to making instead a determination under section 300(1) or (2) of the Housing Act 1985 (c 68) (power to purchase for temporary housing use) in a case where the authority consider the latter course of action to be the better alternative in the circumstances.

(3) In the case of paragraph (d) of that subsection, the authority may regard the taking of emergency remedial action under section 40 followed by the service of an improvement notice under section 11 as a single course of action.

(4) In the case of paragraph (e) of that subsection, the authority may regard the making of an emergency prohibition order under section 43 followed by the service of a prohibition order under section 20 as a single course of action.

(5) In the case of paragraph (g) of that subsection—

(a) any duty to take the course of action mentioned in that paragraph is subject to the operation of subsections (2B) to (4) and (5B) of section 289 of the Housing Act 1985 (procedural and other restrictions relating to slum clearance declarations); and

(b) that paragraph does not apply in a case where the authority have already declared the area in which the premises concerned are situated to be a clearance area in accordance with section 289, but the premises have been excluded by virtue of section 289(2F)(b).

7   Category 2 hazards: powers to take enforcement action

(1) The provisions mentioned in subsection (2) confer power on a local housing authority to take particular kinds of enforcement action in cases where they consider that a category 2 hazard exists on residential premises.

(2) The provisions are—

(a) section 12 (power to serve an improvement notice),
(b) section 21 (power to make a prohibition order),
(c) section 29 (power to serve a hazard awareness notice),
(d) section 265(3) and (4) of the Housing Act 1985 (power to make a demolition order), and
(e) section 289(2ZB) of that Act (power to make a slum clearance declaration).

(3) The taking by the authority of one of those kinds of enforcement action in relation to a particular category 2 hazard does not prevent them from taking either—

(a) the same kind of action again, or
(b) a different kind of enforcement action,

in relation to the hazard, where they consider that the action taken by them so far has not proved satisfactory.

8 Reasons for decision to take enforcement action

(1) This section applies where a local housing authority decide to take one of the kinds of enforcement action mentioned in section 5(2) or 7(2) ("the relevant action").

(2) The authority must prepare a statement of the reasons for their decision to take the relevant action.

(3) Those reasons must include the reasons why the authority decided to take the relevant action rather than any other kind (or kinds) of enforcement action available to them under the provisions mentioned in section 5(2) or 7(2).

(4) A copy of the statement prepared under subsection (2) must accompany every notice, copy of a notice, or copy of an order which is served in accordance with—

    (a)   Part 1 of Schedule 1 to this Act (service of improvement notices etc),

    (b)   Part 1 of Schedule 2 to this Act (service of copies of prohibition orders etc), or

    (c)   section 268 of the Housing Act 1985 (service of copies of demolition orders),

in or in connection with the taking of the relevant action.

(5) In subsection (4)—

    (a)   the reference to Part 1 of Schedule 1 to this Act includes a reference to that Part as applied by section 28(7) or 29(7) (hazard awareness notices) or to section 40(7) (emergency remedial action); and

    (b)   the reference to Part 1 of Schedule 2 to this Act includes a reference to that Part as applied by section 43(4) (emergency prohibition orders).

(6) If the relevant action consists of declaring an area to be a clearance area, the statement prepared under subsection (2) must be published—

    (a)   as soon as possible after the relevant resolution is passed under section 289 of the Housing Act 1985, and

    (b)   in such manner as the authority consider appropriate.

9 Guidance about inspections and enforcement action

(1) The appropriate national authority may give guidance to local housing authorities about exercising—

    (a)   their functions under this Chapter in relation to the inspection of premises and the assessment of hazards,

    (b)   their functions under Chapter 2 of this Part in relation to improvement notices, prohibition orders or hazard awareness notices,

    (c)   their functions under Chapter 3 in relation to emergency remedial action and emergency prohibition orders, or

    (d)   their functions under Part 9 of the Housing Act 1985 (c 68) in relation to demolition orders and slum clearance.

(2) A local housing authority must have regard to any guidance for the time being given under this section.

(3) The appropriate national authority may give different guidance for different cases or descriptions of case or different purposes (including different guidance to different descriptions of local housing authority or to local housing authorities in different areas).

(4) Before giving guidance under this section, or revising guidance already given, the Secretary of State must lay a draft of the proposed guidance or alterations before each House of Parliament.

(5) The Secretary of State must not give or revise the guidance before the end of the period of 40 days beginning with the day on which the draft is laid before each House of Parliament (or, if copies are laid before each House of Parliament on different days, the later of those days).

(6) The Secretary of State must not proceed with the proposed guidance or alterations if, within the period of 40 days mentioned in subsection (5), either House resolves that the guidance or alterations be withdrawn.

(7) Subsection (6) is without prejudice to the possibility of laying a further draft of the guidance or alterations before each House of Parliament.

(8) In calculating the period of 40 days mentioned in subsection (5), no account is to be taken of any time during which Parliament is dissolved or prorogued or during which both Houses are adjourned for more than four days.

10 Consultation with fire and rescue authorities in certain cases

(1) This section applies where a local housing authority—

    (a)   are satisfied that a prescribed fire hazard exists in an HMO or in any common parts of a building containing one or more flats, and

    (b)   intend to take in relation to the hazard one of the kinds of enforcement action mentioned in section 5(2) or section 7(2).

(2) Before taking the enforcement action in question, the authority must consult the fire and rescue authority for the area in which the HMO or building is situated.

(3) In the case of any proposed emergency measures, the authority's duty under subsection (2) is a duty to consult that fire and rescue authority so far as it is practicable to do so before taking those measures.

(4) In this section—

    "emergency measures" means emergency remedial action under section 40 or an emergency prohibition order under section 43;

    "fire and rescue authority" means a fire and rescue authority under the Fire and Rescue Services Act 2004 (c 21);

    "prescribed fire hazard" means a category 1 or 2 hazard which is prescribed as a fire hazard for the purposes of this section by regulations under section 2.

Chapter 2
Improvement Notices, Prohibition Orders and Hazard Awareness Notices

Improvement notices

11 Improvement notices relating to category 1 hazards: duty of authority to serve notice

(1) If—

    (a)   the local housing authority are satisfied that a category 1 hazard exists on any residential premises, and

    (b)   no management order is in force in relation to the premises under Chapter 1 or 2 of Part 4,

serving an improvement notice under this section in respect of the hazard is a course of action available to the authority in relation to the hazard for the purposes of section 5 (category 1 hazards: general duty to take enforcement action).

(2) An improvement notice under this section is a notice requiring the person on whom it is served to take such remedial action in respect of the hazard concerned as is specified in the notice in accordance with subsections (3) to (5) and section 13.

(3) The notice may require remedial action to be taken in relation to the following premises—

    (a)   if the residential premises on which the hazard exists are a dwelling or HMO which is not a flat, it may require such action to be taken in relation to the dwelling or HMO;

    (b)   if those premises are one or more flats, it may require such action to be taken in relation to the building containing the flat or flats (or any part of the building) or any external common parts;

    (c)   if those premises are the common parts of a building containing one or more flats, it may require such action to be taken in relation to the building (or any part of the building) or any external common parts.

Paragraphs (b) and (c) are subject to subsection (4).

(4) The notice may not, by virtue of subsection (3)(b) or (c), require any remedial action to be taken in relation to any part of the building or its external common parts that is not included in any residential premises on which the hazard exists, unless the authority are satisfied—

    (a)   that the deficiency from which the hazard arises is situated there, and

    (b)   that it is necessary for the action to be so taken in order to protect the health or safety of any actual or potential occupiers of one or more of the flats.

(5) The remedial action required to be taken by the notice—

    (a)   must, as a minimum, be such as to ensure that the hazard ceases to be a category 1 hazard; but

(b) may extend beyond such action.

(6) An improvement notice under this section may relate to more than one category 1 hazard on the same premises or in the same building containing one or more flats.

(7) The operation of an improvement notice under this section may be suspended in accordance with section 14.

(8) In this Part "remedial action", in relation to a hazard, means action (whether in the form of carrying out works or otherwise) which, in the opinion of the local housing authority, will remove or reduce the hazard.

12 Improvement notices relating to category 2 hazards: power of authority to serve notice

(1) If—

(a) the local housing authority are satisfied that a category 2 hazard exists on any residential premises, and

(b) no management order is in force in relation to the premises under Chapter 1 or 2 of Part 4,

the authority may serve an improvement notice under this section in respect of the hazard.

(2) An improvement notice under this section is a notice requiring the person on whom it is served to take such remedial action in respect of the hazard concerned as is specified in the notice in accordance with subsection (3) and section 13.

(3) Subsections (3) and (4) of section 11 apply to an improvement notice under this section as they apply to one under that section.

(4) An improvement notice under this section may relate to more than one category 2 hazard on the same premises or in the same building containing one or more flats.

(5) An improvement notice under this section may be combined in one document with a notice under section 11 where they require remedial action to be taken in relation to the same premises.

(6) The operation of an improvement notice under this section may be suspended in accordance with section 14.

13 Contents of improvement notices

(1) An improvement notice under section 11 or 12 must comply with the following provisions of this section.

(2) The notice must specify, in relation to the hazard (or each of the hazards) to which it relates—

(a) whether the notice is served under section 11 or 12,

(b) the nature of the hazard and the residential premises on which it exists,

(c)   the deficiency giving rise to the hazard,

(d)   the premises in relation to which remedial action is to be taken in respect of the hazard and the nature of that remedial action,

(e)   the date when the remedial action is to be started (see subsection (3)), and

(f)   the period within which the remedial action is to be completed or the periods within which each part of it is to be completed.

(3) The notice may not require any remedial action to be started earlier than the 28th day after that on which the notice is served.

(4) The notice must contain information about—

(a)   the right of appeal against the decision under Part 3 of Schedule 1, and

(b)   the period within which an appeal may be made.

(5) In this Part of this Act "specified premises", in relation to an improvement notice, means premises specified in the notice, in accordance with subsection (2)(d), as premises in relation to which remedial action is to be taken in respect of the hazard.

14   Suspension of improvement notices

(1) An improvement notice may provide for the operation of the notice to be suspended until a time, or the occurrence of an event, specified in the notice.

(2) The time so specified may, in particular, be the time when a person of a particular description begins, or ceases, to occupy any premises.

(3) The event so specified may, in particular, be a notified breach of an undertaking accepted by the local housing authority for the purposes of this section from the person on whom the notice is served.

(4) In subsection (3) a "notified breach", in relation to such an undertaking, means an act or omission by the person on whom the notice is served—

(a)   which the local housing authority consider to be a breach of the undertaking, and

(b)   which is notified to that person in accordance with the terms of the undertaking.

(5) If an improvement notice does provide for the operation of the notice to be suspended under this section—

(a)   any periods specified in the notice under section 13 are to be fixed by reference to the day when the suspension ends, and

(b)   in subsection (3) of that section the reference to the 28th day after that on which the notice is served is to be read as referring to the 21st day after that on which the suspension ends.

15 Operation of improvement notices

(1) This section deals with the time when an improvement notice becomes operative.

(2) The general rule is that an improvement notice becomes operative at the end of the period of 21 days beginning with the day on which it is served under Part 1 of Schedule 1 (which is the period for appealing against the notice under Part 3 of that Schedule).

(3) The general rule is subject to subsection (4) (suspended notices) and subsection (5) (appeals).

(4) If the notice is suspended under section 14, the notice becomes operative at the time when the suspension ends.

This is subject to subsection (5).

(5) If an appeal against the notice is made under Part 3 of Schedule 1, the notice does not become operative until such time (if any) as is the operative time for the purposes of this subsection under paragraph 19 of that Schedule (time when notice is confirmed on appeal, period for further appeal expires or suspension ends).

(6) If no appeal against an improvement notice is made under that Part of that Schedule within the period for appealing against it, the notice is final and conclusive as to matters which could have been raised on an appeal.

16 Revocation and variation of improvement notices

(1) The local housing authority must revoke an improvement notice if they are satisfied that the requirements of the notice have been complied with.

(2) The local housing authority may revoke an improvement notice if—

   (a) in the case of a notice served under section 11, they consider that there are any special circumstances making it appropriate to revoke the notice; or

   (b) in the case of a notice served under section 12, they consider that it is appropriate to revoke the notice.

(3) Where an improvement notice relates to a number of hazards—

   (a) subsection (1) is to be read as applying separately in relation to each of those hazards, and

   (b) if, as a result, the authority are required to revoke only part of the notice, they may vary the remainder as they consider appropriate.

(4) The local housing authority may vary an improvement notice—

   (a) with the agreement of the person on whom the notice was served, or

   (b) in the case of a notice whose operation is suspended, so as to alter the time or events by reference to which the suspension is to come to an end.

(5) A revocation under this section comes into force at the time when it is made.

(6) If it is made with the agreement of the person on whom the improvement notice was served, a variation under this section comes into force at the time when it is made.

(7) Otherwise a variation under this section does not come into force until such time (if any) as is the operative time for the purposes of this subsection under paragraph 20 of Schedule 1 (time when period for appealing expires without an appeal being made or when decision to vary is confirmed on appeal).

(8) The power to revoke or vary an improvement notice under this section is exercisable by the authority either—

(a) on an application made by the person on whom the improvement notice was served, or

(b) on the authority's own initiative.

17 Review of suspended improvement notices

(1) The local housing authority may at any time review an improvement notice whose operation is suspended.

(2) The local housing authority must review an improvement notice whose operation is suspended not later than one year after the date of service of the notice and at subsequent intervals of not more than one year.

(3) Copies of the authority's decision on a review under this section must be served—

(a) on the person on whom the improvement notice was served, and

(b) on every other person on whom a copy of the notice was required to be served.

18 Service of improvement notices etc and related appeals

Schedule 1 (which deals with the service of improvement notices, and notices relating to their revocation or variation, and with related appeals) has effect.

19 Change in person liable to comply with improvement notice

(1) This section applies where—

(a) an improvement notice has been served on any person ("the original recipient") in respect of any premises, and

(b) at a later date ("the changeover date") that person ceases to be a person of the relevant category in respect of the premises.

(2) In subsection (1) the reference to a person ceasing to be a "person of the relevant category" is a reference to his ceasing to fall within the description of person (such as, for example, the holder of a licence under Part 2 or 3 or the person managing a dwelling) by reference to which the improvement notice was served on him.

(3) As from the changeover date, the liable person in respect of the premises is to be in the same position as if—

    (a)   the improvement notice had originally been served on him, and

    (b)   he had taken all steps relevant for the purposes of this Part which the original recipient had taken.

(4) The effect of subsection (3) is that, in particular, any period for compliance with the notice or for bringing any appeal is unaffected.

(5) But where the original recipient has become subject to any liability arising by virtue of this Part before the changeover date, subsection (3) does not have the effect of—

    (a)   relieving him of the liability, or

    (b)   making the new liable person subject to it.

(6) Subsection (3) applies with any necessary modifications where a person to whom it applies (by virtue of any provision of this section) ceases to be the liable person in respect of the premises.

(7) Unless subsection (8) or (9) applies, the person who is at any time the "liable person" in respect of any premises is the person having control of the premises.

(8) If—

    (a)   the original recipient was served as the person managing the premises, and

    (b)   there is a new person managing the premises as from the changeover date,

that new person is the "liable person".

(9) If the original recipient was served as an owner of the premises, the "liable person" is the owner's successor in title on the changeover date.

Prohibition orders

20 Prohibition orders relating to category 1 hazards: duty of authority to make order

(1) If—

    (a)   the local housing authority are satisfied that a category 1 hazard exists on any residential premises, and

    (b)   no management order is in force in relation to the premises under Chapter 1 or 2 of Part 4,

making a prohibition order under this section in respect of the hazard is a course of action available to the authority in relation to the hazard for the purposes of section 5 (category 1 hazards: general duty to take enforcement action).

(2) A prohibition order under this section is an order imposing such prohibition or prohibitions on the use of any premises as is or are specified in the order in accordance with subsections (3) and (4) and section 22.

(3) The order may prohibit use of the following premises—

    (a)   if the residential premises on which the hazard exists are a dwelling or HMO which is not a flat, it may prohibit use of the dwelling or HMO;

    (b)   if those premises are one or more flats, it may prohibit use of the building containing the flat or flats (or any part of the building) or any external common parts;

    (c)   if those premises are the common parts of a building containing one or more flats, it may prohibit use of the building (or any part of the building) or any external common parts.

Paragraphs (b) and (c) are subject to subsection (4).

(4) The notice may not, by virtue of subsection (3)(b) or (c), prohibit use of any part of the building or its external common parts that is not included in any residential premises on which the hazard exists, unless the authority are satisfied—

    (a)   that the deficiency from which the hazard arises is situated there, and

    (b)   that it is necessary for such use to be prohibited in order to protect the health or safety of any actual or potential occupiers of one or more of the flats.

(5) A prohibition order under this section may relate to more than one category 1 hazard on the same premises or in the same building containing one or more flats.

(6) The operation of a prohibition order under this section may be suspended in accordance with section 23.

21 Prohibition orders relating to category 2 hazards: power of authority to make order

(1) If—

    (a)   the local housing authority are satisfied that a category 2 hazard exists on any residential premises, and

    (b)   no management order is in force in relation to the premises under Chapter 1 or 2 of Part 4,

the authority may make a prohibition order under this section in respect of the hazard.

(2) A prohibition order under this section is an order imposing such prohibition or prohibitions on the use of any premises as is or are specified in the order in accordance with subsection (3) and section 22.

(3) Subsections (3) and (4) of section 20 apply to a prohibition order under this section as they apply to one under that section.

(4) A prohibition order under this section may relate to more than one category 2 hazard on the same premises or in the same building containing one or more flats.

(5) A prohibition order under this section may be combined in one document with an order under section 20 where they impose prohibitions on the use of the same premises or on the use of premises in the same building containing one or more flats.

(6) The operation of a prohibition order under this section may be suspended in accordance with section 23.

22   Contents of prohibition orders

(1) A prohibition order under section 20 or 21 must comply with the following provisions of this section.

(2) The order must specify, in relation to the hazard (or each of the hazards) to which it relates—

   (a)   whether the order is made under section 20 or 21,

   (b)   the nature of the hazard concerned and the residential premises on which it exists,

   (c)   the deficiency giving rise to the hazard,

   (d)   the premises in relation to which prohibitions are imposed by the order (see subsections (3) and (4)), and

   (e)   any remedial action which the authority consider would, if taken in relation to the hazard, result in their revoking the order under section 25.

(3) The order may impose such prohibition or prohibitions on the use of any premises as—

   (a)   comply with section 20(3) and (4), and

   (b)   the local housing authority consider appropriate in view of the hazard or hazards in respect of which the order is made.

(4) Any such prohibition may prohibit use of any specified premises, or of any part of those premises, either—

   (a)   for all purposes, or

   (b)   for any particular purpose,

except (in either case) to the extent to which any use of the premises or part is approved by the authority.

(5) A prohibition imposed by virtue of subsection (4)(b) may, in particular, relate to—

   (a)   occupation of the premises or part by more than a particular number of households or persons; or

   (b)   occupation of the premises or part by particular descriptions of persons.

(6) The order must also contain information about—

(a)   the right under Part 3 of Schedule 2 to appeal against the order, and

(b)   the period within which an appeal may be made,

and specify the date on which the order is made.

(7) Any approval of the authority for the purposes of subsection (4) must not be unreasonably withheld.

(8) If the authority do refuse to give any such approval, they must notify the person applying for the approval of—

(a)   their decision,

(b)   the reasons for it and the date on which it was made,

(c)   the right to appeal against the decision under subsection (9), and

(d)   the period within which an appeal may be made,

within the period of seven days beginning with the day on which the decision was made.

(9) The person applying for the approval may appeal to a residential property tribunal against the decision within the period of 28 days beginning with the date specified in the notice as the date on which it was made.

(10) In this Part of this Act "specified premises", in relation to a prohibition order, means premises specified in the order, in accordance with subsection (2)(d), as premises in relation to which prohibitions are imposed by the order.

23   Suspension of prohibition orders

(1) A prohibition order may provide for the operation of the order to be suspended until a time, or the occurrence of an event, specified in the order.

(2) The time so specified may, in particular, be the time when a person of a particular description begins, or ceases, to occupy any premises.

(3) The event so specified may, in particular, be a notified breach of an undertaking accepted by the local housing authority for the purposes of this section from a person on whom a copy of the order is served.

(4) In subsection (3) a "notified breach", in relation to such an undertaking, means an act or omission by such a person—

(a)   which the local housing authority consider to be a breach of the undertaking, and

(b)   which is notified to that person in accordance with the terms of the undertaking.

24   Operation of prohibition orders

(1) This section deals with the time when a prohibition order becomes operative.

(2) The general rule is that a prohibition order becomes operative at the end of the period of 28 days beginning with the date specified in the notice as the date on which it is made.

(3) The general rule is subject to subsection (4) (suspended orders) and subsection (5) (appeals).

(4) If the order is suspended under section 23, the order becomes operative at the time when the suspension ends.

This is subject to subsection (5).

(5) If an appeal is brought against the order under Part 3 of Schedule 2, the order does not become operative until such time (if any) as is the operative time for the purposes of this subsection under paragraph 14 of that Schedule (time when order is confirmed on appeal, period for further appeal expires or suspension ends).

(6) If no appeal against a prohibition order is made under that Part of that Schedule within the period for appealing against it, the order is final and conclusive as to matters which could have been raised on an appeal.

(7) Sections 584A and 584B of the Housing Act 1985 (c 68) provide for the payment of compensation where certain prohibition orders become operative, and for the repayment of such compensation in certain circumstances.

25   Revocation and variation of prohibition orders

(1) The local housing authority must revoke a prohibition order if at any time they are satisfied that the hazard in respect of which the order was made does not then exist on the residential premises specified in the order in accordance with section 22(2)(b).

(2) The local housing authority may revoke a prohibition order if—

  (a) in the case of an order made under section 20, they consider that there are any special circumstances making it appropriate to revoke the order; or
  (b) in the case of an order made under section 21, they consider that it is appropriate to do so.

(3) Where a prohibition order relates to a number of hazards—

  (a) subsection (1) is to be read as applying separately in relation to each of those hazards, and
  (b) if, as a result, the authority are required to revoke only part of the order, they may vary the remainder as they consider appropriate.

(4) The local housing authority may vary a prohibition order—

  (a) with the agreement of every person on whom copies of the notice were required to be served under Part 1 of Schedule 2, or
  (b) in the case of an order whose operation is suspended, so as to alter the time or events by reference to which the suspension is to come to an end.

(5) A revocation under this section comes into force at the time when it is made.

(6) If it is made with the agreement of every person within subsection (4)(a), a variation under this section comes into force at the time when it is made.

(7) Otherwise a variation under this section does not come into force until such time (if any) as is the operative time for the purposes of this subsection under paragraph 15 of Schedule 2 (time when period for appealing expires without an appeal being made or when decision to revoke or vary is confirmed on appeal).

(8) The power to revoke or vary a prohibition order under this section is exercisable by the authority either—

(a)   on an application made by a person on whom a copy of the order was required to be served under Part 1 of Schedule 2, or

(b)   on the authority's own initiative.

26   Review of suspended prohibition orders

(1) The local housing authority may at any time review a prohibition order whose operation is suspended.

(2) The local housing authority must review a prohibition order whose operation is suspended not later than one year after the date on which the order was made and at subsequent intervals of not more than one year.

(3) Copies of the authority's decision on a review under this section must be served on every person on whom a copy of the order was required to be served under Part 1 of Schedule 2.

27   Service of copies of prohibition orders etc and related appeals

Schedule 2 (which deals with the service of copies of prohibition orders, and notices relating to their revocation or variation, and with related appeals) has effect.

Hazard awareness notices

28   Hazard awareness notices relating to category 1 hazards: duty of authority to serve notice

(1) If—

(a)   the local housing authority are satisfied that a category 1 hazard exists on any residential premises, and

(b)   no management order is in force in relation to the premises under Chapter 1 or 2 of Part 4,

serving a hazard awareness notice under this section in respect of the hazard is a course of action available to the authority in relation to the hazard for the purposes of section 5 (category 1 hazards: general duty to take enforcement action).

(2) A hazard awareness notice under this section is a notice advising the person on whom it is served of the existence of a category 1 hazard on the residential premises concerned which arises as a result of a deficiency on the premises in respect of which the notice is served.

(3) The notice may be served in respect of the following premises—

(a) if the residential premises on which the hazard exists are a dwelling or HMO which is not a flat, it may be served in respect of the dwelling or HMO;

(b) if those premises are one or more flats, it may be served in respect of the building containing the flat or flats (or any part of the building) or any external common parts;

(c) if those premises are the common parts of a building containing one or more flats, it may be served in respect of the building (or any part of the building) or any external common parts.

Paragraphs (b) and (c) are subject to subsection (4).

(4) The notice may not, by virtue of subsection (3)(b) or (c), be served in respect of any part of the building or its external common parts that is not included in any residential premises on which the hazard exists, unless the authority are satisfied—

(a) that the deficiency from which the hazard arises is situated there, and

(b) that it is desirable for the notice to be so served in the interests of the health or safety of any actual or potential occupiers of one or more of the flats.

(5) A notice under this section may relate to more than one category 1 hazard on the same premises or in the same building containing one or more flats.

(6) A notice under this section must specify, in relation to the hazard (or each of the hazards) to which it relates—

(a) the nature of the hazard and the residential premises on which it exists,

(b) the deficiency giving rise to the hazard,

(c) the premises on which the deficiency exists,

(d) the authority's reasons for deciding to serve the notice, including their reasons for deciding that serving the notice is the most appropriate course of action, and

(e) details of the remedial action (if any) which the authority consider that it would be practicable and appropriate to take in relation to the hazard.

(7) Part 1 of Schedule 1 (which relates to the service of improvement notices and copies of such notices) applies to a notice under this section as if it were an improvement notice.

(8) For that purpose, any reference in that Part of that Schedule to "the specified premises" is, in relation to a hazard awareness notice under this section, a reference to the premises specified under subsection (6)(c).

29   Hazard awareness notices relating to category 2 hazards: power of authority to serve notice

(1) If—

    (a)   the local housing authority are satisfied that a category 2 hazard exists on any residential premises, and

    (b)   no management order is in force in relation to the premises under Chapter 1 or 2 of Part 4,

the authority may serve a hazard awareness notice under this section in respect of the hazard.

(2) A hazard awareness notice under this section is a notice advising the person on whom it is served of the existence of a category 2 hazard on the residential premises concerned which arises as a result of a deficiency on the premises in respect of which the notice is served.

(3) Subsections (3) and (4) of section 28 apply to a hazard awareness notice under this section as they apply to one under that section.

(4) A notice under this section may relate to more than one category 2 hazard on the same premises or in the same building containing one or more flats.

(5) A notice under this section must specify, in relation to the hazard (or each of the hazards) to which it relates—

    (a)   the nature of the hazard and the residential premises on which it exists,

    (b)   the deficiency giving rise to the hazard,

    (c)   the premises on which the deficiency exists,

    (d)   the authority's reasons for deciding to serve the notice, including their reasons for deciding that serving the notice is the most appropriate course of action, and

    (e)   details of the remedial action (if any) which the authority consider that it would be practicable and appropriate to take in relation to the hazard.

(6) A notice under this section may be combined in one document with a notice under section 28 where they are served in respect of the same premises.

(7) Part 1 of Schedule 1 (which relates to the service of improvement notices and copies of such notices) applies to a notice under this section as if it were an improvement notice.

(8) For that purpose, any reference in that Part of that Schedule to "the specified premises" is, in relation to a hazard awareness notice under this section, a reference to the premises specified under subsection (5)(c).

Enforcement: improvement notices

30   Offence of failing to comply with improvement notice

(1) Where an improvement notice has become operative, the person on whom the notice was served commits an offence if he fails to comply with it.

(2) For the purposes of this Chapter compliance with an improvement notice means, in relation to each hazard, beginning and completing any remedial action specified in the notice—

(a)   (if no appeal is brought against the notice) not later than the date specified under section 13(2)(e) and within the period specified under section 13(2)(f);

(b)   (if an appeal is brought against the notice and is not withdrawn) not later than such date and within such period as may be fixed by the tribunal determining the appeal; and

(c)   (if an appeal brought against the notice is withdrawn) not later than the 21st day after the date on which the notice becomes operative and within the period (beginning on that 21st day) specified in the notice under section 13(2)(f).

(3) A person who commits an offence under subsection (1) is liable on summary conviction to a fine not exceeding level 5 on the standard scale.

(4) In proceedings against a person for an offence under subsection (1) it is a defence that he had a reasonable excuse for failing to comply with the notice.

(5) The obligation to take any remedial action specified in the notice in relation to a hazard continues despite the fact that the period for completion of the action has expired.

(6) In this section any reference to any remedial action specified in a notice includes a reference to any part of any remedial action which is required to be completed within a particular period specified in the notice.

31   Enforcement action by local housing authorities

Schedule 3 (which enables enforcement action in respect of an improvement notice to be taken by local housing authorities either with or without agreement and which provides for the recovery of related expenses) has effect.

Enforcement: prohibition orders

32   Offence of failing to comply with prohibition order etc

(1) A person commits an offence if, knowing that a prohibition order has become operative in relation to any specified premises, he—

(a)   uses the premises in contravention of the order, or
(b)   permits the premises to be so used.

(2) A person who commits an offence under subsection (1) is liable on summary conviction—

(a)   to a fine not exceeding level 5 on the standard scale, and
(b)   to a further fine not exceeding £20 for every day or part of a day on which he so uses the premises, or permits them to be so used, after conviction.

(3) In proceedings against a person for an offence under subsection (1) it is a defence that he had a reasonable excuse for using the premises, or (as the case may be) permitting them to be used, in contravention of the order.

33 Recovery of possession of premises in order to comply with order

Nothing in—

(a) the Rent Act 1977 (c 42) or the Rent (Agriculture) Act 1976 (c 80), or

(b) Part 1 of the Housing Act 1988 (c 50),

prevents possession being obtained by the owner of any specified premises in relation to which a prohibition order is operative if possession of the premises is necessary for the purpose of complying with the order.

34 Power of tribunal to determine or vary lease

(1) Subsection (2) applies where—

(a) a prohibition order has become operative, and

(b) the whole or part of any specified premises form the whole or part of the subject matter of a lease.

(2) The lessor or the lessee may apply to a residential property tribunal for an order determining or varying the lease.

(3) On such an application the tribunal may make an order determining or varying the lease, if it considers it appropriate to do so.

(4) Before making such an order, the tribunal must give any sub-lessee an opportunity of being heard.

(5) An order under this section may be unconditional or subject to such terms and conditions as the tribunal considers appropriate.

(6) The conditions may, in particular, include conditions about the payment of money by one party to the proceedings to another by way of compensation, damages or otherwise.

(7) In deciding what is appropriate for the purposes of this section, the tribunal must have regard to the respective rights, obligations and liabilities of the parties under the lease and to all the other circumstances of the case.

(8) In this section "lessor" and "lessee" include a person deriving title under a lessor or lessee.

Enforcement: improvement notices and prohibition orders

35 Power of court to order occupier or owner to allow action to be taken on premises

(1) This section applies where an improvement notice or prohibition order has become operative.

(2) If the occupier of any specified premises—

(a)   has received reasonable notice of any intended action in relation to the premises, but

(b)   is preventing a relevant person, or any representative of a relevant person or of the local housing authority, from taking that action in relation to the premises,

a magistrates" court may order the occupier to permit to be done on the premises anything which the court considers is necessary or expedient for the purpose of enabling the intended action to be taken.

(3) If a relevant person—

(a)   has received reasonable notice of any intended action in relation to any specified premises, but

(b)   is preventing a representative of the local housing authority from taking that action in relation to the premises,

a magistrates" court may order the relevant person to permit to be done on the premises anything which the court considers is necessary or expedient for the purpose of enabling the intended action to be taken.

(4) A person who fails to comply with an order of the court under this section commits an offence.

(5) In proceedings for an offence under subsection (4) it is a defence that the person had a reasonable excuse for failing to comply with the order.

(6) A person who commits an offence under subsection (4) is liable on summary conviction to a fine not exceeding £20 in respect of each day or part of a day during which the failure continues.

(7) In this section "intended action", in relation to any specified premises, means—

(a)   where an improvement notice has become operative, any action which the person on whom that notice has been served is required by the notice to take in relation to the premises and which—

(a)   (in the context of subsection (2)) is proposed to be taken by or on behalf of that person or on behalf of the local housing authority in pursuance of Schedule 3, or

(b)   (in the context of subsection (3)) is proposed to be taken on behalf of the local housing authority in pursuance of Schedule 3;

(b)   where a prohibition order has become operative, any action which is proposed to be taken and which either is necessary for the purpose of giving effect to the order or is remedial action specified in the order in accordance with section 22(2)(e).

(8) In this section—

"relevant person", in relation to any premises, means a person who is an owner of the premises, a person having control of or managing the premises, or the holder of any licence under Part 2 or 3 in respect of the premises;

"representative" in relation to a relevant person or a local housing authority, means any officer, employee, agent or contractor of that person or authority.

36 Power of court to authorise action by one owner on behalf of another

(1) Where an improvement notice or prohibition order has become operative, an owner of any specified premises may apply to a magistrates" court for an order under subsection (2).

(2) A magistrates" court may, on an application under subsection (1), make an order enabling the applicant—

    (a)   immediately to enter on the premises, and

    (b)   to take any required action within a period fixed by the order.

(3) In this section "required action" means—

    (a)   in the case of an improvement notice, any remedial action which is required to be taken by the notice;

    (b)   in the case of a prohibition order, any action necessary for the purpose of complying with the order or any remedial action specified in the order in accordance with section 22(2)(e).

(4) No order may be made under subsection (2) unless the court is satisfied that the interests of the applicant will be prejudiced as a result of a failure by another person to take any required action.

(5) No order may be made under subsection (2) unless notice of the application has been given to the local housing authority.

(6) If it considers that it is appropriate to do so, the court may make an order in favour of any other owner of the premises which is similar to the order that it is making in relation to the premises under subsection (2).

Supplementary provisions

37 Effect of improvement notices and prohibition orders as local land charges

(1) An improvement notice or a prohibition order under this Chapter is a local land charge if subsection (2), (3) or (4) applies.

(2) This subsection applies if the notice or order has become operative.

(3) This subsection applies if—

    (a)   the notice or order is suspended under section 14 or 23, and

    (b)   the period for appealing against it under Part 3 of Schedule 1 or 2 has expired without an appeal having been brought.

(4) This subsection applies if—

    (a)   the notice or order is suspended under section 14 or 23,

    (b)   an appeal has been brought against it under Part 3 of Schedule 1 or 2, and

(c)   were it not suspended—
    (i)   the notice would have become operative under section 15(5) by virtue of paragraph 19(2) of Schedule 1 (improvement notices: confirmation on appeal or expiry of period for further appeal), or
    (ii)   the order would have become operative under section 24(5) by virtue of paragraph 14(2) of Schedule 2 (prohibition orders: confirmation on appeal or expiry of period for further appeal).

38   Savings for rights arising from breach of covenant etc

(1) Nothing in this Chapter affects any remedy of an owner for breach of any covenant or contract entered into by a tenant in connection with any premises which are specified premises in relation to an improvement notice or prohibition order.

(2) If an owner is obliged to take possession of any premises in order to comply with an improvement notice or prohibition order, the taking of possession does not affect his right to take advantage of any such breach which occurred before he took possession.

(3) No action taken under this Chapter affects any remedy available to the tenant of any premises against his landlord (whether at common law or otherwise).

39   Effect of Part 4 enforcement action and redevelopment proposals

(1) Subsection (2) applies if—

    (a)   an improvement notice or prohibition order has been served or made under this Chapter, and
    (b)   a management order under Chapter 1 or 2 of Part 4 comes into force in relation to the specified premises.

(2) The improvement notice or prohibition order—

    (a)   if operative at the time when the management order comes into force, ceases to have effect at that time, and
    (b)   otherwise is to be treated as from that time as if it had not been served or made.

(3) Subsection (2)(a) does not affect any right acquired or liability (civil or criminal) incurred before the improvement notice or prohibition order ceases to have effect.

(4) Subsection (5) applies where, under section 308 of the Housing Act 1985 (c 68) (owner's re-development proposals), the local housing authority have approved proposals for the re-development of land.

(5) No action is to be taken under this Chapter in relation to the land if, and so long as, the re-development is being proceeded with (subject to any variation or extension approved by the authority)—

    (a)   in accordance with the proposals; and

(b) within the time limits specified by the local housing authority.

Chapter 3
Emergency Measures

Emergency remedial action

40 Emergency remedial action

(1) If—

    (a) the local housing authority are satisfied that a category 1 hazard exists on any residential premises, and

    (b) they are further satisfied that the hazard involves an imminent risk of serious harm to the health or safety of any of the occupiers of those or any other residential premises, and

    (c) no management order is in force under Chapter 1 or 2 of Part 4 in relation to the premises mentioned in paragraph (a),

the taking by the authority of emergency remedial action under this section in respect of the hazard is a course of action available to the authority in relation to the hazard for the purposes of section 5 (category 1 hazards: general duty to take enforcement action).

(2) "Emergency remedial action" means such remedial action in respect of the hazard concerned as the authority consider immediately necessary in order to remove the imminent risk of serious harm within subsection (1)(b).

(3) Emergency remedial action under this section may be taken by the authority in relation to any premises in relation to which remedial action could be required to be taken by an improvement notice under section 11 (see subsections (3) and (4) of that section).

(4) Emergency remedial action under this section may be taken by the authority in respect of more than one category 1 hazard on the same premises or in the same building containing one or more flats.

(5) Paragraphs 3 to 5 of Schedule 3 (improvement notices: enforcement action by local authorities) apply in connection with the taking of emergency remedial action under this section as they apply in connection with the taking of the remedial action required by an improvement notice which has become operative but has not been complied with.

But those paragraphs so apply with the modifications set out in subsection (6).

(6) The modifications are as follows—

    (a) the right of entry conferred by paragraph 3(4) may be exercised at any time; and

    (b) the notice required by paragraph 4 (notice before entering premises) must (instead of being served in accordance with that paragraph) be served on every person, who to the authority's knowledge—

        (i) is an occupier of the premises in relation to which the authority propose to take emergency remedial action, or

    (ii)   if those premises are common parts of a building containing one or more flats, is an occupier of any part of the building; but

(c)   that notice is to be regarded as so served if a copy of it is fixed to some conspicuous part of the premises or building.

(7) Within the period of seven days beginning with the date when the authority start taking emergency remedial action, the authority must serve—

    (a)   a notice under section 41, and

    (b)   copies of such a notice,

on the persons on whom the authority would be required under Part 1 of Schedule 1 to serve an improvement notice and copies of it.

(8) Section 240 (warrant to authorise entry) applies for the purpose of enabling a local housing authority to enter any premises to take emergency remedial action under this section in relation to the premises, as if—

    (a)   that purpose were mentioned in subsection (2) of that section, and

    (b)   the circumstances as to which the justice of the peace must be satisfied under subsection (4) were that there are reasonable grounds for believing that the authority will not be able to gain admission to the premises without a warrant.

(9) For the purposes of the operation of any provision relating to improvement notices as it applies by virtue of this section in connection with emergency remedial action or a notice under section 41, any reference in that provision to the specified premises is to be read as a reference to the premises specified, in accordance with section 41(2)(c), as those in relation to which emergency remedial action has been (or is to be) taken.

41 Notice of emergency remedial action

(1) The notice required by section 40(7) is a notice which complies with the following requirements of this section.

(2) The notice must specify, in relation to the hazard (or each of the hazards) to which it relates—

    (a)   the nature of the hazard and the residential premises on which it exists,

    (b)   the deficiency giving rise to the hazard,

    (c)   the premises in relation to which emergency remedial action has been (or is to be) taken by the authority under section 40 and the nature of that remedial action,

    (d)   the power under which that remedial action has been (or is to be) taken by the authority, and

    (e)   the date when that remedial action was (or is to be) started.

(3) The notice must contain information about—

    (a)   the right to appeal under section 45 against the decision of the authority to make the order, and

    (b)   the period within which an appeal may be made.

42 Recovery of expenses of taking emergency remedial action

(1) This section relates to the recovery by a local housing authority of expenses reasonably incurred in taking emergency remedial action under section 40 ("emergency expenses").

(2) Paragraphs 6 to 14 of Schedule 3 (improvement notices: enforcement action by local authorities) apply for the purpose of enabling a local housing authority to recover emergency expenses as they apply for the purpose of enabling such an authority to recover expenses incurred in taking remedial action under paragraph 3 of that Schedule.

But those paragraphs so apply with the modifications set out in subsection (3).

(3) The modifications are as follows—

(a) any reference to the improvement notice is to be read as a reference to the notice under section 41; and

(b) no amount is recoverable in respect of any emergency expenses until such time (if any) as is the operative time for the purposes of this subsection (see subsection (4)).

(4) This subsection gives the meaning of "the operative time" for the purposes of subsection (3)—

(a) if no appeal against the authority's decision to take the emergency remedial action is made under section 45 before the end of the period of 28 days mentioned in subsection (3)(a) of that section, "the operative time" is the end of that period;

(b) if an appeal is made under that section within that period and a decision is given on the appeal which confirms the authority's decision, "the operative time" is as follows—

(i)   if the period within which an appeal to the Lands Tribunal may be brought expires without such an appeal having been brought, "the operative time" is the end of that period;

(ii) if an appeal to the Lands Tribunal is brought, "the operative time" is the time when a decision is given on the appeal which confirms the authority's decision.

(5) For the purposes of subsection (4)—

(a) the withdrawal of an appeal has the same effect as a decision which confirms the authority's decision, and

(b) references to a decision which confirms the authority's decision are to a decision which confirms it with or without variation.

Emergency prohibition orders

43 Emergency prohibition orders

(1) If—

(a) the local housing authority are satisfied that a category 1 hazard exists on any residential premises, and

(b) they are further satisfied that the hazard involves an imminent risk of serious harm to the health or safety of any of the occupiers of those or any other residential premises, and

(c) no management order is in force under Chapter 1 or 2 of Part 4 in relation to the premises mentioned in paragraph (a),

making an emergency prohibition order under this section in respect of the hazard is a course of action available to the authority in relation to the hazard for the purposes of section 5 (category 1 hazards: general duty to take enforcement action).

(2) An emergency prohibition order under this section is an order imposing, with immediate effect, such prohibition or prohibitions on the use of any premises as are specified in the order in accordance with subsection (3) and section 44.

(3) As regards the imposition of any such prohibition or prohibitions, the following provisions apply to an emergency prohibition order as they apply to a prohibition order under section 20—

(a) subsections (3) to (5) of that section, and

(b) subsections (3) to (5) and (7) to (9) of section 22.

(4) Part 1 of Schedule 2 (service of copies of prohibition orders) applies in relation to an emergency prohibition order as it applies to a prohibition order, but any requirement to serve copies within a specified period of seven days is to be read as a reference to serve them on the day on which the emergency prohibition order is made (or, if that is not possible, as soon after that day as is possible).

(5) The following provisions also apply to an emergency prohibition order as they apply to a prohibition order (or to a prohibition order which has become operative, as the case may be)—

(a) section 25 (revocation and variation);

(b) sections 32 to 36 (enforcement);

(c) sections 37 to 39 (supplementary provisions); and

(d) Part 2 of Schedule 2 (notices relating to revocation or variation);

(e) Part 3 of that Schedule (appeals) so far as it relates to any decision to vary, or to refuse to revoke or vary, a prohibition order; and

(f) sections 584A and 584B of the Housing Act 1985 (c 68) (payment, and repayment, of compensation).

(6) For the purposes of the operation of any provision relating to prohibition orders as it applies in connection with emergency prohibition orders by virtue of this section or section 45, any reference in that provision to the specified premises is to be read as a reference to the premises specified, in accordance with section 44(2)(c), as the premises in relation to which prohibitions are imposed by the order.

44 Contents of emergency prohibition orders

(1) An emergency prohibition order under section 43 must comply with the following requirements of this section.

(2) The order must specify, in relation to the hazard (or each of the hazards) to which it relates—

    (a)   the nature of the hazard concerned and the residential premises on which it exists,

    (b)   the deficiency giving rise to the hazard,

    (c)   the premises in relation to which prohibitions are imposed by the order (see subsections (3) and (4) of section 22 as applied by section 43(3)), and

    (d)   any remedial action which the authority consider would, if taken in relation to the hazard, result in their revoking the order under section 25 (as applied by section 43(5)).

(3) The order must contain information about—

    (a)   the right to appeal under section 45 against the order, and

    (b)   the period within which an appeal may be made,

and specify the date on which the order is made.

Appeals

45 Appeals relating to emergency measures

(1) A person on whom a notice under section 41 has been served in connection with the taking of emergency remedial action under section 40 may appeal to a residential property tribunal against the decision of the local housing authority to take that action.

(2) A relevant person may appeal to a residential property tribunal against an emergency prohibition order.

(3) An appeal under subsection (1) or (2) must be made within the period of 28 days beginning with—

    (a)   the date specified in the notice under section 41 as the date when the emergency remedial action was (or was to be) started, or

    (b)   the date specified in the emergency prohibition order as the date on which the order was made,

as the case may be.

(4) A residential property tribunal may allow an appeal to be made to it after the end of that period if it is satisfied that there is a good reason for the failure to appeal before the end of that period (and for any delay since then in applying for permission to appeal out of time).

(5) An appeal under subsection (1) or (2)—

    (a)   is to be by way of a re-hearing, but

(b)   may be determined having regard to matters of which the authority were unaware.

(6) The tribunal may—

(a)   in the case of an appeal under subsection (1), confirm, reverse or vary the decision of the authority;

(b)   in the case of an appeal under subsection (2), confirm or vary the emergency prohibition order or make an order revoking it as from a date specified in that order.

(7) Paragraph 16 of Schedule 2 applies for the purpose of identifying who is a relevant person for the purposes of subsection (2) in relation to an emergency prohibition order as it applies for the purpose of identifying who is a relevant person for the purposes of Part 3 of that Schedule in relation to a prohibition order.

Chapter 4
Demolition Orders and Slum Clearance Declarations

Demolition orders

46   Demolition orders

For section 265 of the Housing Act 1985 (c 68) substitute—

"265   Demolition orders

(1) If—

(a)   the local housing authority are satisfied that a category 1 hazard exists in a dwelling or HMO which is not a flat, and

(b)   this subsection is not disapplied by subsection (5),

making a demolition order in respect of the dwelling or HMO is a course of action available to the authority in relation to the hazard for the purposes of section 5 of the Housing Act 2004 (category 1 hazards: general duty to take enforcement action).

(2) If, in the case of any building containing one or more flats—

(a)   the local housing authority are satisfied that a category 1 hazard exists in one or more of the flats contained in the building or in any common parts of the building, and

(b)   this subsection is not disapplied by subsection (5),

making a demolition order in respect of the building is a course of action available to the authority in relation to the hazard for the purposes of section 5 of the Housing Act 2004.

(3) The local housing authority may make a demolition order in respect of a dwelling or HMO which is not a flat if—

(a)   they are satisfied that a category 2 hazard exists in the dwelling or HMO,

(b)   this subsection is not disapplied by subsection (5), and

(c) the circumstances of the case are circumstances specified or described in an order made by the Secretary of State.

(4) The local housing authority may make a demolition order in respect of any building containing one or more flats if—

(a) they are satisfied that a category 2 hazard exists in one or more of the flats contained in the building or in any common parts of the building,

(b) this subsection is not disapplied by subsection (5), and

(c) the circumstances of the case are circumstances specified or described in an order made by the Secretary of State.

(5) None of subsections (1) to (4) applies if a management order under Chapter 1 or 2 of Part 4 is in force in relation to the premises concerned.

(6) This section also has effect subject to section 304(1) (no demolition order to be made in respect of listed building).

(7) In this section "HMO" means house in multiple occupation.

(8) An order made under subsection (3) or (4)—

(a) may make different provision for different cases or descriptions of case (including different provision for different areas);

(b) may contain such incidental, supplementary, consequential, transitory, transitional or saving provision as the Secretary of State considers appropriate; and

(c) shall be made by statutory instrument which shall be subject to annulment in pursuance of a resolution of either House of Parliament.

(9) Sections 584A and 584B provide for the payment of compensation where demolition orders are made under this section, and for the repayment of such compensation in certain circumstances."

Slum clearance declarations

47   Clearance areas

In section 289 of the Housing Act 1985 (c 68) (declaration of clearance area) for subsections (2) and (2A) substitute—

"(2) If the local housing authority are satisfied, in relation to any area—

(a) that each of the residential buildings in the area contains a category 1 hazard, and

(b) that the other buildings (if any) in the area are dangerous or harmful to the health or safety of the inhabitants of the area,

declaring the area to be a clearance area is a course of action available to the authority in relation to the hazard or hazards for the purposes of section 5 of the Housing Act 2004 (category 1 hazards: general duty to take enforcement action).

(2ZA) The local housing authority may declare an area to be a clearance area if they are satisfied that—

(a) the residential buildings in the area are dangerous or harmful to the health or safety of the inhabitants of the area as a result of their bad arrangement or the narrowness or bad arrangement of the streets; and

(b)   that the other buildings (if any) in the area are dangerous or harmful to the health or safety of the inhabitants of the area.

(2ZB) The local housing authority may declare an area to be a clearance area if they are satisfied that—

(a)   that each of the residential buildings in the area contains a category 2 hazard,

(b)   that the other buildings (if any) in the area are dangerous or harmful to the health or safety of the inhabitants of the area, and

(c)   the circumstances of the case are circumstances specified or described in an order made by the Secretary of State.

Subsection (8) of section 265 applies in relation to an order under this subsection as it applies in relation to an order under subsection (3) or (4) of that section.

(2ZC) In this section "residential buildings" means buildings which are dwellings or houses in multiple occupation or contain one or more flats.

This is subject to subsection (2ZD).

(2ZD) For the purposes of subsection (2) or (2ZB)—

(a)   subsection (2ZC) applies as if "two or more flats" were substituted for "one or more flats"; and

(b)   a residential building containing two or more flats is only to be treated as containing a category 1 or 2 hazard if two or more of the flats within it contain such a hazard.

(2ZE) Subsections (2) to (2ZB) are subject to subsections (2B) to (4) and (5B)."

Appeals

48   Transfer of jurisdiction in respect of appeals relating to demolition orders etc

(1) Part 9 of the Housing Act 1985 (c 68) (slum clearance) is further amended as follows.

(2) In section 269 (right of appeal against demolition order etc)—

(a)   in subsection (1), for "the county court" substitute "a residential property tribunal";

(b)   in subsection (3), for "court" substitute "tribunal"; and

(c)   in subsection (6)(a) and (b), for "Court of Appeal" substitute "Lands Tribunal".

(3) In section 272 (demolition orders)—

(a)   in subsection (2), for "the court" in the first place it appears substitute "a residential property tribunal", and in the second place it appears substitute "such a tribunal";

(b)   in subsection (5), for the words from the beginning to "and has" substitute "A residential property tribunal has jurisdiction to hear and determine proceedings under subsection (1) (as well as those under subsection (2)), and a county court has"; and

(c)   in subsection (6), for "the court" substitute "a tribunal or court".

(4) In section 317 (power of court to determine lease where premises demolished etc)—

    (a)   in subsection (1), for "the county court" substitute "a residential property tribunal"; and

    (b)   in subsections (2) and (3), for "court" substitute "tribunal".

(5) In section 318 (power of court to authorise execution of works on unfit premises or for improvement)—

    (a)   in the sidenote, for "court" substitute "tribunal";

    (b)   in subsection (1), for "the court" in the first place it appears substitute "a residential property tribunal", and in the second place it appears substitute "the tribunal";

    (c)   in subsections (2) and (3), for "court" substitute "tribunal"; and

    (d)   omit subsection (4).

Chapter 5
General and Miscellaneous Provisions Relating to Enforcement Action

Recovery of expenses relating to enforcement action

49 Power to charge for certain enforcement action

(1) A local housing authority may make such reasonable charge as they consider appropriate as a means of recovering certain administrative and other expenses incurred by them in—

    (a)   serving an improvement notice under section 11 or 12;

    (b)   making a prohibition order under section 20 or 21;

    (c)   serving a hazard awareness notice under section 28 or 29;

    (d)   taking emergency remedial action under section 40;

    (e)   making an emergency prohibition order under section 43; or

    (f)   making a demolition order under section 265 of the Housing Act 1985 (c 68).

(2) The expenses are, in the case of the service of an improvement notice or a hazard awareness notice, the expenses incurred in—

    (a)   determining whether to serve the notice,

    (b)   identifying any action to be specified in the notice, and

    (c)   serving the notice.

(3) The expenses are, in the case of emergency remedial action under section 40, the expenses incurred in—

    (a)   determining whether to take such action, and

    (b)   serving the notice required by subsection (7) of that section.

(4) The expenses are, in the case of a prohibition order under section 20 or 21 of this Act, an emergency prohibition order under section 43 or a demolition order under section 265 of the Housing Act 1985, the expenses incurred in—

    (a)   determining whether to make the order, and

(b)   serving copies of the order on persons as owners of premises.

(5) A local housing authority may make such reasonable charge as they consider appropriate as a means of recovering expenses incurred by them in—

(a)   carrying out any review under section 17 or 26, or
(b)   serving copies of the authority's decision on such a review.

(6) The amount of the charge may not exceed such amount as is specified by order of the appropriate national authority.

(7) Where a tribunal allows an appeal against the underlying notice or order mentioned in subsection (1), it may make such order as it considers appropriate reducing, quashing, or requiring the repayment of, any charge under this section made in respect of the notice or order.

50   Recovery of charge under section 49

(1) This section relates to the recovery by a local housing authority of a charge made by them under section 49.

(2) In the case of—

(a)   an improvement notice under section 11 or 12, or
(b)   a hazard awareness notice under section 28 or 29,

the charge may be recovered from the person on whom the notice is served.

(3) In the case of emergency remedial action under section 40, the charge may be recovered from the person served with the notice required by subsection (7) of that section.

(4) In the case of—

(a)   a prohibition order under section 20 or 21,
(b)   an emergency prohibition order under section 43, or
(c)   a demolition order under section 265 of the Housing Act 1985 (c 68),

the charge may be recovered from any person on whom a copy of the order is served as an owner of the premises.

(5) A demand for payment of the charge must be served on the person from whom the authority seek to recover it.

(6) The demand becomes operative, if no appeal is brought against the underlying notice or order, at the end of the period of 21 days beginning with the date of service of the demand.

(7) If such an appeal is brought and a decision is given on the appeal which confirms the underlying notice or order, the demand becomes operative at the time when—

(a)   the period within which an appeal to the Lands Tribunal may be brought expires without such an appeal having been brought, or
(b)   a decision is given on such an appeal which confirms the notice or order.

(8) For the purposes of subsection (7)—

    (a)   the withdrawal of an appeal has the same effect as a decision which confirms the notice or order, and

    (b)   references to a decision which confirms the notice or order are to a decision which confirms it with or without variation.

(9) As from the time when the demand becomes operative, the sum recoverable by the authority is, until recovered, a charge on the premises concerned.

(10) The charge takes effect at that time as a legal charge which is a local land charge.

(11) For the purpose of enforcing the charge the authority have the same powers and remedies under the Law of Property Act 1925 (c 20) and otherwise as if they were mortgagees by deed having powers of sale and lease, of accepting surrenders of leases and of appointing a receiver.

(12) The power of appointing a receiver is exercisable at any time after the end of the period of one month beginning with the date on which the charge takes effect.

(13) The appropriate national authority may by regulations prescribe the form of, and the particulars to be contained in, a demand for payment of any charge under section 49.

Repeals

51   Repeal of power to improve existing enforcement procedures

Omit section 86 of the Housing Grants, Construction and Regeneration Act 1996 (c 53) (power to improve existing enforcement procedures in relation to unfitness for human habitation etc).

52   Repeal of provisions relating to demolition of obstructive buildings

Omit sections 283 to 288 of the Housing Act 1985 (c 68) (demolition of obstructive buildings).

53   Miscellaneous repeals etc in relation to fire hazards

(1) In the London Building Acts (Amendment) Act 1939 (c xcvii)—

    (a)   omit section 35(1)(c)(i) (protection against fire in certain old buildings let in flats or tenements);

    (b)   in section 36(1) (projecting shops in which persons are employed or sleep) omit "or sleep"; and

    (c)   in section 37(1) (means of access to roofs), in paragraph (b) for the words from "except" onwards substitute "except to the extent that it is occupied for residential purposes;".

(2) In the County of Merseyside Act 1980 (c x) omit section 48 (means of escape from fire) and section 49(1) and (2) (maintenance of means of escape from fire).

(3) In the Building Act 1984 (c 55) omit section 72(6)(a) (means of escape from fire in case of certain buildings let in flats or tenements).

(4) In the Leicestershire Act 1985 (c xvii) omit section 54(6)(a) (means of escape from fire in case of certain buildings used as flats or tenements).

Index

54   Index of defined expressions: Part 1

The following table shows where expressions used in this Part are defined or otherwise explained.

Expression	Provision of this Act
Appropriate national authority	Section 261(1)
Building containing one or more flats	Section 1(5)
Category 1 hazard	Section 2(1)
Category 2 hazard	Section 2(1)
Common parts	Section 1(5)
Compliance with improvement notice	Section 30(2)
District of local housing authority	Section 261(6)
Dwelling	Section 1(5), (6)
External common parts	Section 1(5)
Flat	Section 1(5) to (7)
Hazard	Section 2(1)
Hazard awareness notice	Section 28(2) or 29(2)
Health	Section 2(5)
HMO	Section 1(5), (6) (and see also section 1(8))
Improvement notice	Section 11(2) or 12(2)
Lease, lessee etc	Section 262(1) to (4)
Local housing authority	Section 261(2) to (5)
Occupier (and related expressions)	Section 262(6)
Owner	Section 262(7)
Person having control	Section 263(1) and (2)
Person managing	Section 263(3) and (4)
Prohibition order	Section 20(2) or 21(2)
Remedial action	Section 11(8)
Residential premises	Section 1(4)
Residential property tribunal	Section 229
Specified premises, in relation to an improvement notice	Section 13(5)

Specified premises, in relation to a prohibition order	Section 22(10)
Tenancy, tenant	Section 262(1) to (5)
Unoccupied HMO accommodation	Section 1(5) (and see also section 1(8)).

PART 2
LICENSING OF HOUSES IN MULTIPLE OCCUPATION

Introductory

55 Licensing of HMOs to which this Part applies

(1) This Part provides for HMOs to be licensed by local housing authorities where—

    (a)   they are HMOs to which this Part applies (see subsection (2)), and

    (b)   they are required to be licensed under this Part (see section 61(1)).

(2) This Part applies to the following HMOs in the case of each local housing authority—

    (a)   any HMO in the authority's district which falls within any prescribed description of HMO, and

    (b)   if an area is for the time being designated by the authority under section 56 as subject to additional licensing, any HMO in that area which falls within any description of HMO specified in the designation.

(3) The appropriate national authority may by order prescribe descriptions of HMOs for the purposes of subsection (2)(a).

(4) The power conferred by subsection (3) may be exercised in such a way that this Part applies to all HMOs in the district of a local housing authority.

(5) Every local housing authority have the following general duties—

    (a)   to make such arrangements as are necessary to secure the effective implementation in their district of the licensing regime provided for by this Part;

    (b)   to ensure that all applications for licences and other issues falling to be determined by them under this Part are determined within a reasonable time; and

    (c)   to satisfy themselves, as soon as is reasonably practicable, that there are no Part 1 functions that ought to be exercised by them in relation to the premises in respect of which such applications are made.

(6) For the purposes of subsection (5)(c)—

    (a)   "Part 1 function" means any duty under section 5 to take any course of action to which that section applies or any power to take any course of action to which section 7 applies; and

    (b)   the authority may take such steps as they consider appropriate (whether or not involving an inspection) to comply with their duty under subsection (5)(c) in relation to each of the premises in question, but they must in any event comply with it within the period of 5 years beginning with the date of the application for a licence.

Designation of additional licensing areas

56 Designation of areas subject to additional licensing

(1) A local housing authority may designate either—

(a) the area of their district, or
(b) an area in their district,

as subject to additional licensing in relation to a description of HMOs specified in the designation, if the requirements of this section are met.

(2) The authority must consider that a significant proportion of the HMOs of that description in the area are being managed sufficiently ineffectively as to give rise, or to be likely to give rise, to one or more particular problems either for those occupying the HMOs or for members of the public.

(3) Before making a designation the authority must—

(a) take reasonable steps to consult persons who are likely to be affected by the designation; and
(b) consider any representations made in accordance with the consultation and not withdrawn.

(4) The power to make a designation under this section may be exercised in such a way that this Part applies to all HMOs in the area in question.

(5) In forming an opinion as to the matter mentioned in subsection (2), the authority must have regard to any information regarding the extent to which any codes of practice approved under section 233 have been complied with by persons managing HMOs in the area in question.

(6) Section 57 applies for the purposes of this section.

57 Designations under section 56: further considerations

(1) This section applies to the power of a local housing authority to make designations under section 56.

(2) The authority must ensure that any exercise of the power is consistent with the authority's overall housing strategy.

(3) The authority must also seek to adopt a co-ordinated approach in connection with dealing with homelessness, empty properties and anti-social behaviour affecting the private rented sector, both—

(a) as regards combining licensing under this Part with other courses of action available to them, and
(b) as regards combining such licensing with measures taken by other persons.

(4) The authority must not make a particular designation under section 56 unless—

(a) they have considered whether there are any other courses of action available to them (of whatever nature) that might provide an effective method of dealing with the problem or problems in question, and

(b) they consider that making the designation will significantly assist them to deal with the problem or problems (whether or not they take any other course of action as well).

(5) In this Act "anti-social behaviour" means conduct on the part of occupiers of, or visitors to, residential premises—

(a) which causes or is likely to cause a nuisance or annoyance to persons residing, visiting or otherwise engaged in lawful activities in the vicinity of such premises, or

(b) which involves or is likely to involve the use of such premises for illegal purposes.

58 Designation needs confirmation or general approval to be effective

(1) A designation of an area as subject to additional licensing cannot come into force unless—

(a) it has been confirmed by the appropriate national authority; or

(b) it falls within a description of designations in relation to which that authority has given a general approval in accordance with subsection (6).

(2) The appropriate national authority may either confirm, or refuse to confirm, a designation as it considers appropriate.

(3) If the appropriate national authority confirms a designation, the designation comes into force on the date specified for this purpose by that authority.

(4) That date must be no earlier than three months after the date on which the designation is confirmed.

(5) A general approval may be given in relation to a description of designations framed by reference to any matters or circumstances.

(6) Accordingly a general approval may (in particular) be given in relation to—

(a) designations made by a specified local housing authority;

(b) designations made by a local housing authority falling within a specified description of such authorities;

(c) designations relating to HMOs of a specified description.

"Specified" means specified by the appropriate national authority in the approval.

(7) If, by virtue of a general approval, a designation does not need to be confirmed before it comes into force, the designation comes into force on the date specified for this purpose in the designation.

(8) That date must be no earlier than three months after the date on which the designation is made.

59 Notification requirements relating to designations

(1) This section applies to a designation—

    (a)   when it is confirmed under section 58, or

    (b)   (if it is not required to be so confirmed) when it is made by the local housing authority.

(2) As soon as the designation is confirmed or made, the authority must publish in the prescribed manner a notice stating—

    (a)   that the designation has been made,

    (b)   whether or not the designation was required to be confirmed and either that it has been confirmed or that a general approval under section 58 applied to it (giving details of the approval in question),

    (c)   the date on which the designation is to come into force, and

    (d)   any other information which may be prescribed.

(3) After publication of a notice under subsection (2), and for as long as the designation is in force, the local housing authority must make available to the public in accordance with any prescribed requirements—

    (a)   copies of the designation, and

    (b)   such information relating to the designation as is prescribed.

(4) In this section "prescribed" means prescribed by regulations made by the appropriate national authority.

60 Duration, review and revocation of designations

(1) Unless previously revoked under subsection (4), a designation ceases to have effect at the time that is specified for this purpose in the designation.

(2) That time must be no later than five years after the date on which the designation comes into force.

(3) A local housing authority must from time to time review the operation of any designation made by them.

(4) If following a review they consider it appropriate to do so, the authority may revoke the designation.

(5) If they do revoke the designation, the designation ceases to have effect at the time that is specified by the authority for this purpose.

(6) On revoking a designation the authority must publish notice of the revocation in such manner as is prescribed by regulations made by the appropriate national authority.

HMOs required to be licensed

61 Requirement for HMOs to be licensed

(1) Every HMO to which this Part applies must be licensed under this Part unless—

- (a) a temporary exemption notice is in force in relation to it under section 62, or
- (b) an interim or final management order is in force in relation to it under Chapter 1 of Part 4.

(2) A licence under this Part is a licence authorising occupation of the house concerned by not more than a maximum number of households or persons specified in the licence.

(3) Sections 63 to 67 deal with applications for licences, the granting or refusal of licences and the imposition of licence conditions.

(4) The local housing authority must take all reasonable steps to secure that applications for licences are made to them in respect of HMOs in their area which are required to be licensed under this Part but are not.

(5) The appropriate national authority may by regulations provide for—

- (a) any provision of this Part, or
- (b) section 263 (in its operation for the purposes of any such provision),

to have effect in relation to a section 257 HMO with such modifications as are prescribed by the regulations.

A "section 257 HMO" is an HMO which is a converted block of flats to which section 257 applies.

(6) In this Part (unless the context otherwise requires)—

- (a) references to a licence are to a licence under this Part,
- (b) references to a licence holder are to be read accordingly, and
- (c) references to an HMO being (or not being) licensed under this Part are to its being (or not being) an HMO in respect of which a licence is in force under this Part.

[(7) In this Part the "person having control" in respect of a section 257 HMO is—

- *(a) in relation to an HMO in respect of which no person has been granted a long lease of a flat within the HMO, the person who receives the rack rent for the HMO, whether on his own account or as an agent or trustee of another person;*
- *(b) in relation to an HMO in respect of which a person has been granted a long lease of a flat within the HMO, the person who falls within the first paragraph of subsection (8) to apply, taking paragraph (a) of that subsection first, paragraph (b) next, and so on.]*

[(8) A person falls within this subsection if the person—

(a) has acquired the right to manage the HMO under Part 2 of the Commonhold and Leasehold Reform Act 2002;

(b) has been appointed by the Leasehold Valuation Tribunal under section 24 of the Landlord and Tenant Act 1987;

(c) is the person who is the lessee of the whole of the HMO under a lease between him and a head lessor or the freeholder, or is the freeholder of the HMO; or

(d) has been appointed to manage the HMO by the freeholder, by a head lessor of the whole of the HMO, or by a person who has acquired the right to manage the HMO under Part 2 of the Commonhold and leasehold Reform Act 2002.]

[(9) In this section "long lease" means a lease that—

(a) is granted for a term certain exceeding 21 years, whether or not it is (or may become terminable) before the end of that term; or

(b) is for a term fixed by law under a grant with a covenant or obligation for perpetual renewal, other than a lease by sub-demise from one which is not a long lease,

and neither the lease nor any superior lease contains a provision enabling the lessor or superior lessor to terminate the tenancy, other than by forfeiture, before the end of that term.]

Amendment—Modified, in relation to a house in multiple occupation to which s 257 hereof applies, by the Houses in Multiple Occupation (Certain Converted Blocks of Flats) (Modifications to the Housing Act 2004 and Transitional Provisions for section 257 HMOs) (England) Regulations 2007, SI 2007/1904, regs 2, 3.

62 Temporary exemption from licensing requirement

(1) This section applies where a person having control of or managing an HMO which is required to be licensed under this Part (see section 61(1)) but is not so licensed, notifies the local housing authority of his intention to take particular steps with a view to securing that the house is no longer required to be licensed.

(2) The authority may, if they think fit, serve on that person a notice under this section ("a temporary exemption notice") in respect of the house.

(3) If a temporary exemption notice is served under this section, the house is (in accordance with sections 61(1) and 85(1)) not required to be licensed either under this Part or under Part 3 during the period for which the notice is in force.

(4) A temporary exemption notice under this section is in force—

(a) for the period of 3 months beginning with the date on which it is served, or

(b) (in the case of a notice served by virtue of subsection (5)) for the period of 3 months after the date when the first notice ceases to be in force.

(5) If the authority—

(a)   receive a further notification under subsection (1), and

(b)   consider that there are exceptional circumstances that justify the service of a second temporary exemption notice in respect of the house that would take effect from the end of the period of 3 months applying to the first notice,

the authority may serve a second such notice on the person having control of or managing the house (but no further notice may be served by virtue of this subsection).

(6) If the authority decide not to serve a temporary exemption notice in response to a notification under subsection (1), they must without delay serve on the person concerned a notice informing him of—

(a)   the decision,

(b)   the reasons for it and the date on which it was made,

(c)   the right to appeal against the decision under subsection (7), and

(d)   the period within which an appeal may be made under that subsection.

(7) The person concerned may appeal to a residential property tribunal against the decision within the period of 28 days beginning with the date specified under subsection (6) as the date on which it was made.

(8) Such an appeal—

(a)   is to be by way of a re-hearing, but

(b)   may be determined having regard to matters of which the authority were unaware.

(9) The tribunal—

(a)   may confirm or reverse the decision of the authority, and

(b)   if it reverses the decision, must direct the authority to serve a temporary exemption notice that comes into force on such date as the tribunal directs.

Grant or refusal of licences

63 Applications for licences

(1) An application for a licence must be made to the local housing authority.

(2) The application must be made in accordance with such requirements as the authority may specify.

(3) The authority may, in particular, require the application to be accompanied by a fee fixed by the authority.

(4) The power of the authority to specify requirements under this section is subject to any regulations made under subsection (5).

(5) The appropriate national authority may by regulations make provision about the making of applications under this section.

(6) Such regulations may, in particular—

(a)   specify the manner and form in which applications are to be made;
(b)   require the applicant to give copies of the application, or information about it, to particular persons;
(c)   specify the information which is to be supplied in connection with applications;
(d)   specify the maximum fees which are to be charged (whether by specifying amounts or methods for calculating amounts);
(e)   specify cases in which no fees are to be charged or fees are to be refunded.

(7) When fixing fees under this section, the local housing authority may (subject to any regulations made under subsection (5)) take into account—

(a)   all costs incurred by the authority in carrying out their functions under this Part, and
(b)   all costs incurred by them in carrying out their functions under Chapter 1 of Part 4 in relation to HMOs (so far as they are not recoverable under or by virtue of any provision of that Chapter).

64   Grant or refusal of licence

(1) Where an application in respect of an HMO is made to the local housing authority under section 63, the authority must either—

(a)   grant a licence in accordance with subsection (2), or
(b)   refuse to grant a licence.

(2) If the authority are satisfied as to the matters mentioned in subsection (3), they may grant a licence either—

(a)   to the applicant, or
(b)   to some other person, if both he and the applicant agree.

(3) The matters are—

(a)   *that the house is reasonably suitable for occupation by not more than the maximum number of households or persons mentioned in subsection (4) or that it can be made so suitable by the imposition of conditions under section 67;*
(b)   that the proposed licence holder—
  (i)   is a fit and proper person to be the licence holder, and
  (ii)   is, out of all the persons reasonably available to be the licence holder in respect of the house, the most appropriate person to be the licence holder;
(c)   that the proposed manager of the house is either—
  (i)   the person having control of the house, or
  (ii)   a person who is an agent or employee of the person having control of the house;
(d)   that the proposed manager of the house is a fit and proper person to be the manager of the house; and
(e)   that the proposed management arrangements for the house are otherwise satisfactory.

(4) The maximum number of households or persons referred to in subsection (3)(a) is –]

  (a)   the maximum number specified in the application, or
  (b)   some other maximum number decided by the authority.

  [(4) When deciding whether the proposed licence holder is a fit and proper person to be the licence holder the local housing authority must take into consideration whether that person has control of the HMO and the extent to which he has control over it."]

(5) Sections 65 and 66 apply for the purposes of this section.

Amendment—Subs (4) modified, in relation to a house in multiple occupation to which s 257 hereof applies, by the Houses in Multiple Occupation (Certain Converted Blocks of Flats) (Modifications to the Housing Act 2004 and Transitional Provisions for section 257 HMOs) (England) Regulations 2007, SI 2007/1904, regs 2, 4.

65   Tests as to suitability for multiple occupation

[(1) The local housing authority cannot be satisfied that the house is reasonably suitable for occupation as a section 257 HMO if they consider that—

  (a)   the common parts of the HMO; or
  (b)   any flat within the HMO other than a flat let on a long lease,

fail to meet prescribed standards.";

  (b)   after subsection (1) add—

  "(1A) Where a house becomes a section 257 HMO as a result of conversion works carried out on the house after 1st October 2007, any flat within the HMO in respect of which a long lease is granted after that date shall be treated for the purpose of subsection (1) as though no such lease has been granted unless—

    (a)   the local housing authority are satisfied that the appropriate building standards have been met in relation to that flat; or
    (b)   the local housing authority are satisfied that the lease has been granted by a person other than the freeholder or head lessor of the whole of the HMO.";
    (c)   omit subsection (2);
    (d)   in paragraph (a) of subsection (4) omit "number,"; and
    (e)   after subsection (4) add—
    "(5) In this section "long lease" has the same meaning as in section 61(9).]

[(1) The local housing authority cannot be satisfied for the purposes of section 64(3)(a) that the house is reasonably suitable for occupation by a particular maximum number of households or persons if they consider that it fails to meet prescribed standards for occupation by that number of households or persons.]

(2) But the authority may decide that the house is not reasonably suitable for occupation by a particular maximum number of households or persons even if it does meet prescribed standards for occupation by that number of households or persons.

(3) In this section "prescribed standards" means standards prescribed by regulations made by the appropriate national authority.

(4) The standards that may be so prescribed include—

    (a)   standards as to the number, type and quality of—
        (i)   bathrooms, toilets, washbasins and showers,
        (ii) areas for food storage, preparation and cooking, and
        (iii) laundry facilities,
        which should be available in particular circumstances; and
    (b)   standards as to the number, type and quality of other facilities or equipment which should be available in particular circumstances.

Amendment—Sub-s (1) modified, in relation to a house in multiple occupation to which s 257 hereof applies, by the Houses in Multiple Occupation (Certain Converted Blocks of Flats) (Modifications to the Housing Act 2004 and Transitional Provisions for section 257 HMOs) (England) Regulations 2007, SI 2007/1904, regs 2, 5.

66   Tests for fitness etc and satisfactory management arrangements

(1) In deciding for the purposes of section 64(3)(b) or (d) whether a person ("P") is a fit and proper person to be the licence holder or (as the case may be) the manager of the house, the local housing authority must have regard (among other things) to any evidence within subsection (2) or (3).

(2) Evidence is within this subsection if it shows that P has—

    (a)   committed any offence involving fraud or other dishonesty, or violence or drugs, or any offence listed in Schedule 3 to the Sexual Offences Act 2003 (c 42) (offences attracting notification requirements);
    (b)   practised unlawful discrimination on grounds of sex, colour, race, ethnic or national origins or disability in, or in connection with, the carrying on of any business;
    (c)   contravened any provision of the law relating to housing or of landlord and tenant law; or
    (d)   acted otherwise than in accordance with any applicable code of practice approved under section 233.

(3) Evidence is within this subsection if—

    (a)   it shows that any person associated or formerly associated with P (whether on a personal, work or other basis) has done any of the things set out in subsection (2)(a) to (d), and
    (b)   it appears to the authority that the evidence is relevant to the question whether P is a fit and proper person to be the licence holder or (as the case may be) the manager of the house.

(4) For the purposes of section 64(3)(b) the local housing authority must assume, unless the contrary is shown, that the person having control of the house is a more appropriate person to be the licence holder than a person not having control of it.

(5) In deciding for the purposes of section 64(3)(e) whether the proposed management arrangements for the house are otherwise satisfactory, the local housing authority must have regard (among other things) to the considerations mentioned in subsection (6).

(6) The considerations are—

    (a)   whether any person proposed to be involved in the management of the house has a sufficient level of competence to be so involved;

    (b)   whether any person proposed to be involved in the management of the house (other than the manager) is a fit and proper person to be so involved; and

    (c)   whether any proposed management structures and funding arrangements are suitable.

(7) Any reference in section 64(3)(c)(i) or (ii) or subsection (4) above to a person having control of the house, or to being a person of any other description, includes a reference to a person who is proposing to have control of the house, or (as the case may be) to be a person of that description, at the time when the licence would come into force.

67 Licence conditions

(1) A licence may include such conditions as the local housing authority consider appropriate for regulating all or any of the following—

    (a)   the management, use and occupation of the house concerned, and

    (b)   its condition and contents.

[(1A) For the purposes of section 67(1) a licence may not include a condition that regulates the use, occupation or contents of any part of an HMO unless the condition relates to a matter over which it would be reasonable to expect the licence holder, in all the circumstances, to exercise control.]

(2) Those conditions may, in particular, include (so far as appropriate in the circumstances)—

    (a)   conditions imposing restrictions or prohibitions on the use or occupation of particular parts of the house by persons occupying it;

    (b)   conditions requiring the taking of reasonable and practicable steps to prevent or reduce anti-social behaviour by persons occupying or visiting the house;

    (c)   conditions requiring facilities and equipment to be made available in the house for the purpose of meeting standards prescribed under section 65;

    (d)   conditions requiring such facilities and equipment to be kept in repair and proper working order;

    (e)   conditions requiring, in the case of any works needed in order for any such facilities or equipment to be made available or to meet any such standards, that the works are carried out within such period or periods as may be specified in, or determined under, the licence;

(f)   conditions requiring the licence holder or the manager of the house to attend training courses in relation to any applicable code of practice approved under section 233.

(3) A licence must include the conditions required by Schedule 4.

(4) As regards the relationship between the authority's power to impose conditions under this section and functions exercisable by them under or for the purposes of Part 1 ("Part 1 functions")—

(a)   the authority must proceed on the basis that, in general, they should seek to identify, remove or reduce category 1 or category 2 hazards in the house by the exercise of Part 1 functions and not by means of licence conditions;

(b)   this does not, however, prevent the authority from imposing licence conditions relating to the installation or maintenance of facilities or equipment within subsection (2)(c) above, even if the same result could be achieved by the exercise of Part 1 functions;

(c)   the fact that licence conditions are imposed for a particular purpose that could be achieved by the exercise of Part 1 functions does not affect the way in which Part 1 functions can be subsequently exercised by the authority.

(5) A licence may not include conditions imposing restrictions or obligations on a particular person other than the licence holder unless that person has consented to the imposition of the restrictions or obligations.

(6) A licence may not include conditions requiring (or intended to secure) any alteration in the terms of any tenancy or licence under which any person occupies the house.

Amendment—Subs (1) modified, in relation to a house in multiple occupation to which s 257 hereof applies, by the Houses in Multiple Occupation (Certain Converted Blocks of Flats) (Modifications to the Housing Act 2004 and Transitional Provisions for section 257 HMOs) (England) Regulations 2007, SI 2007/1904, regs 2, 6.

68   Licences: general requirements and duration

(1) A licence may not relate to more than one HMO.

(2) A licence may be granted before the time when it is required by virtue of this Part but, if so, the licence cannot come into force until that time.

(3) A licence—

(a)   comes into force at the time that is specified in or determined under the licence for this purpose, and

(b)   unless previously terminated by subsection (7) or revoked under section 70, continues in force for the period that is so specified or determined.

(4) That period must not end more than 5 years after—

(a)   the date on which the licence was granted, or

(b) if the licence was granted as mentioned in subsection (2), the date when the licence comes into force.

(5) Subsection (3)(b) applies even if, at any time during that period, the HMO concerned subsequently ceases to be one to which this Part applies.

(6) A licence may not be transferred to another person.

(7) If the holder of the licence dies while the licence is in force, the licence ceases to be in force on his death.

(8) However, during the period of 3 months beginning with the date of the licence holder's death, the house is to be treated for the purposes of this Part and Part 3 as if on that date a temporary exemption notice had been served in respect of the house under section 62.

(9) If, at any time during that period ("the initial period"), the personal representatives of the licence holder request the local housing authority to do so, the authority may serve on them a notice which, during the period of 3 months after the date on which the initial period ends, has the same effect as a temporary exemption notice under section 62.

(10) Subsections (6) to (8) of section 62 apply (with any necessary modifications) in relation to a decision by the authority not to serve such a notice as they apply in relation to a decision not to serve a temporary exemption notice.

Variation and revocation of licences

69 Variation of licences

(1) The local housing authority may vary a licence—

(a) if they do so with the agreement of the licence holder, or
(b) if they consider that there has been a change of circumstances since the time when the licence was granted.

For this purpose "change of circumstances" includes any discovery of new information.

(2) Subsection (3) applies where the authority—

(a) are considering whether to vary a licence under subsection (1)(b); and
(b) are considering—
  (i)   what number of households or persons is appropriate as the maximum number authorised to occupy the HMO to which the licence relates, or
  (ii) the standards applicable to occupation by a particular number of households or persons.

(3) The authority must apply the same standards in relation to the circumstances existing at the time when they are considering whether to vary the licence as were applicable at the time when it was granted.

This is subject to subsection (4).

(4) If the standards—

(a) prescribed under section 65, and

(b) applicable at the time when the licence was granted,

have subsequently been revised or superseded by provisions of regulations under that section, the authority may apply the new standards.

(5) A variation made with the agreement of the licence holder takes effect at the time when it is made.

(6) Otherwise, a variation does not come into force until such time, if any, as is the operative time for the purposes of this subsection under paragraph 35 of Schedule 5 (time when period for appealing expires without an appeal being made or when decision to vary is confirmed on appeal).

(7) The power to vary a licence under this section is exercisable by the authority either—

(a) on an application made by the licence holder or a relevant person, or

(b) on the authority's own initiative.

(8) In subsection (7) "relevant person" means any person (other than the licence holder)—

(a) who has an estate or interest in the HMO concerned (but is not a tenant under a lease with an unexpired term of 3 years or less), or

(b) who is a person managing or having control of the house (and does not fall within paragraph (a)), or

(c) on whom any restriction or obligation is imposed by the licence in accordance with section 67(5).

70 Revocation of licences

(1) The local housing authority may revoke a licence—

(a) if they do so with the agreement of the licence holder;

(b) in any of the cases mentioned in subsection (2) (circumstances relating to licence holder or other person);

(c) in any of the cases mentioned in subsection (3) (circumstances relating to HMO concerned); or

(d) in any other circumstances prescribed by regulations made by the appropriate national authority.

(2) The cases referred to in subsection (1)(b) are as follows—

(a) where the authority consider that the licence holder or any other person has committed a serious breach of a condition of the licence or repeated breaches of such a condition;

(b) where the authority no longer consider that the licence holder is a fit and proper person to be the licence holder; and

(c) where the authority no longer consider that the management of the house is being carried on by persons who are in each case fit and proper persons to be involved in its management.

Section 66(1) applies in relation to paragraph (b) or (c) above as it applies in relation to section 64(3)(b) or (d).

(3) The cases referred to in subsection (1)(c) are as follows—

    (a) where the HMO to which the licence relates ceases to be an HMO to which this Part applies; and

    (b) where the authority consider at any time that, were the licence to expire at that time, they would, for a particular reason relating to the structure of the HMO, refuse to grant a new licence to the licence holder on similar terms in respect of it.

(4) Subsection (5) applies where the authority are considering whether to revoke a licence by virtue of subsection (3)(b) on the grounds that the HMO is not reasonably suitable for the number of households or persons specified in the licence as the maximum number authorised to occupy the house.

(5) The authority must apply the same standards in relation to the circumstances existing at the time when they are considering whether to revoke the licence as were applicable at the time when it was granted.

This is subject to subsection (6).

(6) If the standards—

    (a) prescribed under section 65, and

    (b) applicable at the time when the licence was granted,

have subsequently been revised or superseded by provisions of regulations under that section, the authority may apply the new standards.

(7) A revocation made with the agreement of the licence holder takes effect at the time when it is made.

(8) Otherwise, a revocation does not come into force until such time, if any, as is the operative time for the purposes of this subsection under paragraph 35 of Schedule 5 (time when period for appealing expires without an appeal being made or when decision to vary is confirmed on appeal).

(9) The power to revoke a licence under this section is exercisable by the authority either—

    (a) on an application made by the licence holder or a relevant person, or

    (b) on the authority's own initiative.

(10) In subsection (9) "relevant person" means any person (other than the licence holder)—

    (a) who has an estate or interest in the HMO concerned (but is not a tenant under a lease with an unexpired term of 3 years or less), or

    (b) who is a person managing or having control of that house (and does not fall within paragraph (a)), or

    (c) on whom any restriction or obligation is imposed by the licence in accordance with section 67(5).

Procedure and appeals

71   Procedural requirements and appeals against licence decisions

Schedule 5 (which deals with procedural requirements relating to the grant, refusal, variation or revocation of licences and with appeals against licence decisions) has effect for the purposes of this Part.

Enforcement

72   Offences in relation to licensing of HMOs

(1) A person commits an offence if he is a person having control of or managing an HMO which is required to be licensed under this Part (see section 61(1)) but is not so licensed.

(2) A person commits an offence if—

   (a)   he is a person having control of or managing an HMO which is licensed under this Part,

   (b)   he knowingly permits another person to occupy the house, and

   (c)   the other person's occupation results in the house being occupied by more households or persons than is authorised by the licence.

(3) A person commits an offence if—

   (a)   he is a licence holder or a person on whom restrictions or obligations under a licence are imposed in accordance with section 67(5), and

   (b)   he fails to comply with any condition of the licence.

(4) In proceedings against a person for an offence under subsection (1) it is a defence that, at the material time—

   (a)   a notification had been duly given in respect of the house under section 62(1), or

   (b)   an application for a licence had been duly made in respect of the house under section 63,

and that notification or application was still effective (see subsection (8)).

(5) In proceedings against a person for an offence under subsection (1), (2) or (3) it is a defence that he had a reasonable excuse—

   (a)   for having control of or managing the house in the circumstances mentioned in subsection (1), or

   (b)   for permitting the person to occupy the house, or

   (c)   for failing to comply with the condition,

as the case may be.

(6) A person who commits an offence under subsection (1) or (2) is liable on summary conviction to a fine not exceeding £20,000.

(7) A person who commits an offence under subsection (3) is liable on summary conviction to a fine not exceeding level 5 on the standard scale.

(8) For the purposes of subsection (4) a notification or application is "effective" at a particular time if at that time it has not been withdrawn, and either—

    (a)   the authority have not decided whether to serve a temporary exemption notice, or (as the case may be) grant a licence, in pursuance of the notification or application, or

    (b)   if they have decided not to do so, one of the conditions set out in subsection (9) is met.

(9) The conditions are—

    (a)   that the period for appealing against the decision of the authority not to serve or grant such a notice or licence (or against any relevant decision of a residential property tribunal) has not expired, or

    (b)   that an appeal has been brought against the authority's decision (or against any relevant decision of such a tribunal) and the appeal has not been determined or withdrawn.

(10) In subsection (9) "relevant decision" means a decision which is given on an appeal to the tribunal and confirms the authority's decision (with or without variation).

73   Other consequences of operating unlicensed HMOs: rent repayment orders

(1) For the purposes of this section an HMO is an "unlicensed HMO" if—

    (a)   it is required to be licensed under this Part but is not so licensed, and

    (b)   neither of the conditions in subsection (2) is satisfied.

(2) The conditions are—

    (a)   that a notification has been duly given in respect of the HMO under section 62(1) and that notification is still effective (as defined by section 72(8));

    (b)   that an application for a licence has been duly made in respect of the HMO under section 63 and that application is still effective (as so defined).

(3) No rule of law relating to the validity or enforceability of contracts in circumstances involving illegality is to affect the validity or enforceability of—

    (a)   any provision requiring the payment of rent or the making of any other periodical payment in connection with any tenancy or licence of a part of an unlicensed HMO, or

    (b)   any other provision of such a tenancy or licence.

(4) But amounts paid in respect of rent or other periodical payments payable in connection with such a tenancy or licence may be recovered in accordance with subsection (5) and section 74.

(5) If—

(a)   an application in respect of an HMO is made to a residential property tribunal by the local housing authority or an occupier of a part of the HMO, and

(b)   the tribunal is satisfied as to the matters mentioned in subsection (6) or (8),

the tribunal may make an order (a "rent repayment order") requiring the appropriate person to pay to the applicant such amount in respect of the housing benefit paid as mentioned in subsection (6)(b), or (as the case may be) the periodical payments paid as mentioned in subsection (8)(b), as is specified in the order (see section 74(2) to (8)).

(6) If the application is made by the local housing authority, the tribunal must be satisfied as to the following matters—

(a)   that, at any time within the period of 12 months ending with the date of the notice of intended proceedings required by subsection (7), the appropriate person has committed an offence under section 72(1) in relation to the HMO (whether or not he has been charged or convicted),

(b)   that housing benefit has been paid (to any person) in respect of periodical payments payable in connection with the occupation of a part or parts of the HMO during any period during which it appears to the tribunal that such an offence was being committed, and

(c)   that the requirements of subsection (7) have been complied with in relation to the application.

(7) Those requirements are as follows—

(a)   the authority must have served on the appropriate person a notice (a "notice of intended proceedings")—
  (i)   informing him that the authority are proposing to make an application under subsection (5),
  (ii)   setting out the reasons why they propose to do so,
  (iii) stating the amount that they will seek to recover under that subsection and how that amount is calculated, and
  (iv)   inviting him to make representations to them within a period specified in the notice of not less than 28 days;

(b)   that period must have expired; and

(c)   the authority must have considered any representations made to them within that period by the appropriate person.

(8) If the application is made by an occupier of a part of the HMO, the tribunal must be satisfied as to the following matters—

(a)   that the appropriate person has been convicted of an offence under section 72(1) in relation to the HMO, or has been required by a rent repayment order to make a payment in respect of housing benefit paid in connection with occupation of a part or parts of the HMO,

(b)   that the occupier paid, to a person having control of or managing the HMO, periodical payments in respect of occupation of part of the

HMO during any period during which it appears to the tribunal that such an offence was being committed in relation to the HMO, and

(c) that the application is made within the period of 12 months beginning with—

   (i)   the date of the conviction or order, or

   (ii) if such a conviction was followed by such an order (or vice versa), the date of the later of them.

(9) Where a local housing authority serve a notice of intended proceedings on any person under this section, they must ensure—

(a) that a copy of the notice is received by the department of the authority responsible for administering the housing benefit to which the proceedings would relate; and

(b) that that department is subsequently kept informed of any matters relating to the proceedings that are likely to be of interest to it in connection with the administration of housing benefit.

(10) In this section—

   ["the appropriate person", in relation to any payment of housing benefit or periodical payments payable in connection with occupation of a part of a section 257 HMO means the person who at the time when such benefit or payments were made was the person—

   (a)   having control of the HMO; and

   (b)   entitled to receive on his own account periodical payments in connection with such occupation of the part of the HMO in respect of which the payment or housing benefit relates."];

   "the appropriate person", in relation to any payment of housing benefit or periodical payment payable in connection with occupation of a part of an HMO, means the person who at the time of the payment was entitled to receive on his own account periodical payments payable in connection with such occupation;

   "housing benefit" means housing benefit provided by virtue of a scheme under section 123 of the Social Security Contributions and Benefits Act 1992 (c 4);

   "occupier", in relation to any periodical payment, means a person who was an occupier at the time of the payment, whether under a tenancy or licence or otherwise (and "occupation" has a corresponding meaning);

   "periodical payments" means periodical payments in respect of which housing benefit may be paid by virtue of regulation 10 of the Housing Benefit (General) Regulations 1987 (SI 1987/1971) or any corresponding provision replacing that regulation;

   ["rent" does not include ground rent, service charges or insurance charges paid under the terms of a lease in respect of a flat within a section 257 HMO.]

(11) For the purposes of this section an amount which—

(a) is not actually paid by an occupier but is used by him to discharge the whole or part of his liability in respect of a periodical payment (for example, by offsetting the amount against any such liability), and

(b) is not an amount of housing benefit,

is to be regarded as an amount paid by the occupier in respect of that periodical payment.

Amendment—Subs (10) modified, in relation to a house in multiple occupation to which s 257 hereof applies, by the Houses in Multiple Occupation (Certain Converted Blocks of Flats) (Modifications to the Housing Act 2004 and Transitional Provisions for section 257 HMOs) (England) Regulations 2007, SI 2007/1904, regs 2, 7.

74 Further provisions about rent repayment orders

(1) This section applies in relation to rent repayment orders made by residential property tribunals under section 73(5).

(2) Where, on an application by the local housing authority, the tribunal is satisfied—

(a) that a person has been convicted of an offence under section 72(1) in relation to the HMO, and

(b) that housing benefit was paid (whether or not to the appropriate person) in respect of periodical payments payable in connection with occupation of a part or parts of the HMO during any period during which it appears to the tribunal that such an offence was being committed in relation to the HMO,

the tribunal must make a rent repayment order requiring the appropriate person to pay to the authority an amount equal to the total amount of housing benefit paid as mentioned in paragraph (b).

This is subject to subsections (3), (4) and (8).

(3) If the total of the amounts received by the appropriate person in respect of periodical payments payable as mentioned in paragraph (b) of subsection (2) ("the rent total") is less than the total amount of housing benefit paid as mentioned in that paragraph, the amount required to be paid by virtue of a rent repayment order made in accordance with that subsection is limited to the rent total.

(4) A rent repayment order made in accordance with subsection (2) may not require the payment of any amount which the tribunal is satisfied that, by reason of any exceptional circumstances, it would be unreasonable for that person to be required to pay.

(5) In a case where subsection (2) does not apply, the amount required to be paid by virtue of a rent repayment order under section 73(5) is to be such amount as the tribunal considers reasonable in the circumstances.

This is subject to subsections (6) to (8).

(6) In such a case the tribunal must, in particular, take into account the following matters—

(a) the total amount of relevant payments paid in connection with occupation of the HMO during any period during which it appears to the tribunal that an offence was being committed by the appropriate person in relation to the HMO under section 72(1);

(b) the extent to which that total amount—

    (i) consisted of, or derived from, payments of housing benefit, and

    (ii) was actually received by the appropriate person;

(c) whether the appropriate person has at any time been convicted of an offence under section 72(1) in relation to the HMO;

(d) the conduct and financial circumstances of the appropriate person; and

(e) where the application is made by an occupier, the conduct of the occupier.

(7) In subsection (6) "relevant payments" means—

(a) in relation to an application by a local housing authority, payments of housing benefit or periodical payments payable by occupiers;

(b) in relation to an application by an occupier, periodical payments payable by the occupier, less any amount of housing benefit payable in respect of occupation of the part of the HMO occupied by him during the period in question.

(8) A rent repayment order may not require the payment of any amount which—

(a) (where the application is made by a local housing authority) is in respect of any time falling outside the period of 12 months mentioned in section 73(6)(a); or

(b) (where the application is made by an occupier) is in respect of any time falling outside the period of 12 months ending with the date of the occupier's application under section 73(5);

and the period to be taken into account under subsection (6)(a) above is restricted accordingly.

(9) Any amount payable to a local housing authority under a rent repayment order—

(a) does not, when recovered by the authority, constitute an amount of housing benefit recovered by them, and

(b) until recovered by them, is a legal charge on the HMO which is a local land charge.

(10) For the purpose of enforcing that charge the authority have the same powers and remedies under the Law of Property Act 1925 (c 20) and otherwise as if they were mortgagees by deed having powers of sale and lease, and of accepting surrenders of leases and of appointing a receiver.

(11) The power of appointing a receiver is exercisable at any time after the end of the period of one month beginning with the date on which the charge takes effect.

(12) If the authority subsequently grant a licence under this Part or Part 3 in respect of the HMO to the appropriate person or any person acting on his behalf, the conditions contained in the licence may include a condition requiring the licence holder—

    (a)   to pay to the authority any amount payable to them under the rent repayment order and not so far recovered by them; and

    (b)   to do so in such instalments as are specified in the licence.

(13) If the authority subsequently make a management order under Chapter 1 of Part 4 in respect of the HMO, the order may contain such provisions as the authority consider appropriate for the recovery of any amount payable to them under the rent repayment order and not so far recovered by them.

(14) Any amount payable to an occupier by virtue of a rent repayment order is recoverable by the occupier as a debt due to him from the appropriate person.

(15) The appropriate national authority may by regulations make such provision as it considers appropriate for supplementing the provisions of this section and section 73, and in particular—

    (a)   for securing that persons are not unfairly prejudiced by rent repayment orders (whether in cases where there have been over-payments of housing benefit or otherwise);

    (b)   for requiring or authorising amounts received by local housing authorities by virtue of rent repayment orders to be dealt with in such manner as is specified in the regulations.

(16) Section 73(10) and (11) apply for the purposes of this section as they apply for the purposes of section 73.

75   Other consequences of operating unlicensed HMOs: restriction on terminating tenancies

[(1) No section 21 notice may be given in relation to a shorthold tenancy of a part of an unlicensed HMO so long as it remains such an HMO.]

[(1)   No section 21 notice may be given in relation to a shorthold tenancy of a flat in an unlicensed section 257 HMO by the person having control of the HMO so long as it remains such an HMO.]

(2) In this section—

    a "section 21 notice" means a notice under section 21(1)(b) or (4)(a) of the Housing Act 1988 (c 50) (recovery of possession on termination of shorthold tenancy);

    a "shorthold tenancy" means an assured shorthold tenancy within the meaning of Chapter 2 of Part 1 of that Act;

    "unlicensed HMO" has the same meaning as in section 73 of this Act.

[(3) Subsection (1) does not affect the right of any person (other than the person having control of a section 257 HMO) to serve a section 21 notice in respect of a shorthold tenancy of a flat in such an HMO.]

Amendment—Subs (1) modified, in relation to a house in multiple occupation to which s 257 hereof applies, by the Houses in Multiple Occupation (Certain Converted Blocks of Flats) (Modifications to the Housing Act 2004 and Transitional Provisions for section 257 HMOs) (England) Regulations 2007, SI 2007/1904, regs 2, 8.

Supplementary provisions

76 Transitional arrangements relating to introduction and termination of licensing

(1) Subsection (2) applies where—

- (a) an order under section 55(3) which prescribes a particular description of HMOs comes into force; or
- (b) a designation under section 56 comes into force in relation to HMOs of a particular description.

(2) This Part applies in relation to the occupation by persons or households of such HMOs on or after the coming into force of the order or designation even if their occupation began before, or in pursuance of a contract made before, it came into force.

This is subject to subsections (3) to (5).

(3) Subsection (4) applies where—

- (a) an HMO which is licensed under this Part, or a part of such an HMO, is occupied by more households or persons than the number permitted by the licence; and
- (b) the occupation of all or any of those households or persons began before, or in pursuance of a contract made before, the licence came into force.

(4) In proceedings against a person for an offence under section 72(2) it is a defence that at the material time he was taking all reasonable steps to try to reduce the number of households or persons occupying the house to the number permitted by the licence.

(5) Subsection (4) does not apply if the licence came into force immediately after a previous licence in respect of the same HMO unless the occupation in question began before, or in pursuance of a contract made before, the coming into force of the original licence.

(6) An order under section 270 may make provision as regards the licensing under this Part of HMOs—

- (a) which are registered immediately before the appointed day under a scheme to which section 347 (schemes containing control provisions) or 348B (schemes containing special control provisions) of the Housing Act 1985 (c 68) applies, or
- (b) in respect of which applications for registration under such a scheme are then pending.

(7) In subsection (6) "the appointed day" means the day appointed for the coming into force of section 61.

77 Meaning of "HMO"

In this Part—

(a) "HMO" means a house in multiple occupation as defined by sections 254 to 259, and

(b) references to an HMO include (where the context permits) any yard, garden, outhouses and appurtenances belonging to, or usually enjoyed with, it (or any part of it).

78 Index of defined expressions: Part 2

The following table shows where expressions used in this Part are defined or otherwise explained.

Expression	Provision of this Act
Anti-social behaviour	Section 57(5)
Appropriate national authority	Section 261(1)
Category 1 hazard	Section 2(1)
Category 2 hazard	Section 2(1)
District of local housing authority	Section 261(6)
HMO	Section 77
HMO to which this Part applies	Section 55(2)
Licence and licence holder	Section 61(6)
Licence (to occupy premises)	Section 262(9)
Local housing authority	Section 261(2) to (5)
Modifications	Section 250(7)
Occupier (and related expressions)	Section 262(6)
Person having control	Section 263(1) and (2) (and see also section [61(7)])
Person having estate or interest	Section 262(8)
Person managing	Section 263(3)
Person involved in management	Section 263(5)
Residential property tribunal	Section 229
Tenant	Section 262(1) to (5).

Amendment—Modified, in relation to a house in multiple occupation to which s 257 hereof applies, by the Houses in Multiple Occupation (Certain Converted Blocks of Flats) (Modifications to the Housing Act 2004 and Transitional Provisions for section 257 HMOs) (England) Regulations 2007, SI 2007/1904, regs 2, 9.

PART 3
SELECTIVE LICENSING OF OTHER RESIDENTIAL ACCOMMODATION

Introductory

79 Licensing of houses to which this Part applies

(1) This Part provides for houses to be licensed by local housing authorities where—

(a) they are houses to which this Part applies (see subsection (2)), and

(b) they are required to be licensed under this Part (see section 85(1)).

(2) This Part applies to a house if—

(a) it is in an area that is for the time being designated under section 80 as subject to selective licensing, and

(b) the whole of it is occupied either—
   (i) under a single tenancy or licence that is not an exempt tenancy or licence under subsection (3) or (4), or
   (ii) under two or more tenancies or licences in respect of different dwellings contained in it, none of which is an exempt tenancy or licence under subsection (3) or (4).

(3) A tenancy or licence is an exempt tenancy or licence if it is granted by a body which is registered as a social landlord under Part 1 of the Housing Act 1996 (c 52).

(4) In addition, the appropriate national authority may by order provide for a tenancy or licence to be an exempt tenancy or licence—

(a) if it falls within any description of tenancy or licence specified in the order; or

(b) in any other circumstances so specified.

(5) Every local housing authority have the following general duties—

(a) to make such arrangements as are necessary to secure the effective implementation in their district of the licensing regime provided for by this Part; and

(b) to ensure that all applications for licences and other issues falling to be determined by them under this Part are determined within a reasonable time.

Designation of selective licensing areas

80 Designation of selective licensing areas

(1) A local housing authority may designate either—

(a) the area of their district, or

(b) an area in their district,

as subject to selective licensing, if the requirements of subsections (2) and (9) are met.

(2) The authority must consider that—

(a) the first or second set of general conditions mentioned in subsection (3) or (6), or

(b) any conditions specified in an order under subsection (7) as an additional set of conditions,

are satisfied in relation to the area.

(3) The first set of general conditions are—

(a) that the area is, or is likely to become, an area of low housing demand; and

(b) that making a designation will, when combined with other measures taken in the area by the local housing authority, or by other persons together with the local housing authority, contribute to the improvement of the social or economic conditions in the area.

(4) In deciding whether an area is, or is likely to become, an area of low housing demand a local housing authority must take into account (among other matters)—

(a) the value of residential premises in the area, in comparison to the value of similar premises in other areas which the authority consider to be comparable (whether in terms of types of housing, local amenities, availability of transport or otherwise);

(b) the turnover of occupiers of residential premises;

(c) the number of residential premises which are available to buy or rent and the length of time for which they remain unoccupied.

(5) The appropriate national authority may by order amend subsection (4) by adding new matters to those for the time being mentioned in that subsection.

(6) The second set of general conditions are—

(a) that the area is experiencing a significant and persistent problem caused by anti-social behaviour;

(b) that some or all of the private sector landlords who have let premises in the area (whether under leases or licences) are failing to take action to combat the problem that it would be appropriate for them to take; and

(c) that making a designation will, when combined with other measures taken in the area by the local housing authority, or by other persons together with the local housing authority, lead to a reduction in, or the elimination of, the problem.

"Private sector landlord" does not include a registered social landlord within the meaning of Part 1 of the Housing Act 1996 (c 52).

(7) The appropriate national authority may by order provide for any conditions specified in the order to apply as an additional set of conditions for the purposes of subsection (2).

(8) The conditions that may be specified include, in particular, conditions intended to permit a local housing authority to make a designation for the purpose of dealing with one or more specified problems affecting persons occupying Part 3 houses in the area.

"Specified" means specified in an order under subsection (7).

(9) Before making a designation the local housing authority must—

    (a)   take reasonable steps to consult persons who are likely to be affected by the designation; and

    (b)   consider any representations made in accordance with the consultation and not withdrawn.

(10) Section 81 applies for the purposes of this section.

81   Designations under section 80: further considerations

(1) This section applies to the power of a local housing authority to make designations under section 80.

(2) The authority must ensure that any exercise of the power is consistent with the authority's overall housing strategy.

(3) The authority must also seek to adopt a co-ordinated approach in connection with dealing with homelessness, empty properties and anti-social behaviour, both—

    (a)   as regards combining licensing under this Part with other courses of action available to them, and

    (b)   as regards combining such licensing with measures taken by other persons.

(4) The authority must not make a particular designation under section 80 unless—

    (a)   they have considered whether there are any other courses of action available to them (of whatever nature) that might provide an effective method of achieving the objective or objectives that the designation would be intended to achieve, and

    (b)   they consider that making the designation will significantly assist them to achieve the objective or objectives (whether or not they take any other course of action as well).

82   Designation needs confirmation or general approval to be effective

(1) A designation of an area as subject to selective licensing cannot come into force unless—

    (a)   it has been confirmed by the appropriate national authority; or

(b)   it falls within a description of designations in relation to which that authority has given a general approval in accordance with subsection (6).

(2) The appropriate national authority may either confirm, or refuse to confirm, a designation as it considers appropriate.

(3) If the appropriate national authority confirms a designation, the designation comes into force on a date specified for this purpose by that authority.

(4) That date must be no earlier than three months after the date on which the designation is confirmed.

(5) A general approval may be given in relation to a description of designations framed by reference to any matters or circumstances.

(6) Accordingly a general approval may (in particular) be given in relation to—

(a)   designations made by a specified local housing authority;
(b)   designations made by a local housing authority falling within a specified description of such authorities;
(c)   designations relating to Part 3 houses of a specified description.

"Specified" means specified by the appropriate national authority in the approval.

(7) If, by virtue of a general approval, a designation does not need to be confirmed before it comes into force, the designation comes into force on the date specified for this purpose in the designation.

(8) That date must be no earlier than three months after the date on which the designation is made.

(9) Where a designation comes into force, this Part applies in relation to the occupation by persons of houses in the area on or after the coming into force of the designation even if their occupation began before, or in pursuance of a contract made before, it came into force.

83   Notification requirements relating to designations

(1) This section applies to a designation—

(a)   when it is confirmed under section 82, or
(b)   (if it is not required to be so confirmed) when it is made by the local housing authority.

(2) As soon as the designation is confirmed or made, the authority must publish in the prescribed manner a notice stating—

(a)   that the designation has been made,
(b)   whether or not the designation was required to be confirmed and either that it has been confirmed or that a general approval under section 82 applied to it (giving details of the approval in question),
(c)   the date on which the designation is to come into force, and

(d)   any other information which may be prescribed.

(3) After publication of a notice under subsection (2), and for as long as the designation is in force, the local housing authority must make available to the public in accordance with any prescribed requirements—

(a)   copies of the designation, and
(b)   such information relating to the designation as is prescribed.

(4) In this section "prescribed" means prescribed by regulations made by the appropriate national authority.

84   Duration, review and revocation of designations

(1) Unless previously revoked under subsection (4), a designation ceases to have effect at the time that is specified for this purpose in the designation.

(2) That time must be no later than five years after the date on which the designation comes into force.

(3) A local housing authority must from time to time review the operation of any designation made by them.

(4) If following a review they consider it appropriate to do so, the authority may revoke the designation.

(5) If they do revoke the designation, the designation ceases to have effect on the date that is specified by the authority for this purpose.

(6) On revoking a designation, the authority must publish notice of the revocation in such manner as is prescribed by regulations made by the appropriate national authority.

Houses required to be licensed

85   Requirement for Part 3 houses to be licensed

(1) Every Part 3 house must be licensed under this Part unless—

(a)   it is an HMO to which Part 2 applies (see section 55(2)), or
(b)   a temporary exemption notice is in force in relation to it under section 86, or
(c)   a management order is in force in relation to it under Chapter 1 or 2 of Part 4.

(2) A licence under this Part is a licence authorising occupation of the house concerned under one or more tenancies or licences within section 79(2)(b).

(3) Sections 87 to 90 deal with applications for licences, the granting or refusal of licences and the imposition of licence conditions.

(4) The local housing authority must take all reasonable steps to secure that applications for licences are made to them in respect of houses in their area which are required to be licensed under this Part but are not so licensed.

(5) In this Part, unless the context otherwise requires—

(a) references to a Part 3 house are to a house to which this Part applies (see section 79(2)),
(b) references to a licence are to a licence under this Part,
(c) references to a licence holder are to be read accordingly, and
(d) references to a house being (or not being) licensed under this Part are to its being (or not being) a house in respect of which a licence is in force under this Part.

86 Temporary exemption from licensing requirement

(1) This section applies where a person having control of or managing a Part 3 house which is required to be licensed under this Part (see section 85(1)) but is not so licensed, notifies the local housing authority of his intention to take particular steps with a view to securing that the house is no longer required to be licensed.

(2) The authority may, if they think fit, serve on that person a notice under this section ("a temporary exemption notice") in respect of the house.

(3) If a temporary exemption notice is served under this section, the house is (in accordance with section 85(1)) not required to be licensed under this Part during the period for which the notice is in force.

(4) A temporary exemption notice under this section is in force—

(a) for the period of 3 months beginning with the date on which it is served, or
(b) (in the case of a notice served by virtue of subsection (5)) for the period of 3 months after the date when the first notice ceases to be in force.

(5) If the authority—

(a) receive a further notification under subsection (1), and
(b) consider that there are exceptional circumstances that justify the service of a second temporary exemption notice in respect of the house that would take effect from the end of the period of 3 months applying to the first notice,

the authority may serve a second such notice on the person having control of or managing the house (but no further notice may be served by virtue of this subsection).

(6) If the authority decide not to serve a temporary exemption notice in response to a notification under subsection (1), they must without delay serve on the person concerned a notice informing him of—

(a) the decision,
(b) the reasons for it and the date on which it was made,
(c) the right to appeal against the decision under subsection (7), and
(d) the period within which an appeal may be made under that subsection.

(7) The person concerned may appeal to a residential property tribunal against the decision within the period of 28 days beginning with the date specified under subsection (6) as the date on which it was made.

(8) Such an appeal—

    (a)   is to be by way of a re-hearing, but

    (b)   may be determined having regard to matters of which the authority were unaware.

(9) The tribunal—

    (a)   may confirm or reverse the decision of the authority, and

    (b)   if it reverses the decision, must direct the authority to issue a temporary exemption notice with effect from such date as the tribunal directs.

Grant or refusal of licences

87 Applications for licences

(1) An application for a licence must be made to the local housing authority.

(2) The application must be made in accordance with such requirements as the authority may specify.

(3) The authority may, in particular, require the application to be accompanied by a fee fixed by the authority.

(4) The power of the authority to specify requirements under this section is subject to any regulations made under subsection (5).

(5) The appropriate national authority may by regulations make provision about the making of applications under this section.

(6) Such regulations may, in particular—

    (a)   specify the manner and form in which applications are to be made;

    (b)   require the applicant to give copies of the application, or information about it, to particular persons;

    (c)   specify the information which is to be supplied in connection with applications;

    (d)   specify the maximum fees which may be charged (whether by specifying amounts or methods for calculating amounts);

    (e)   specify cases in which no fees are to be charged or fees are to be refunded.

(7) When fixing fees under this section, the local housing authority may (subject to any regulations made under subsection (5)) take into account—

    (a)   all costs incurred by the authority in carrying out their functions under this Part, and

    (b)   all costs incurred by them in carrying out their functions under Chapter 1 of Part 4 in relation to Part 3 houses (so far as they are not recoverable under or by virtue of any provision of that Chapter).

88 Grant or refusal of licence

(1) Where an application in respect of a house is made to the local housing authority under section 87, the authority must either—

    (a)   grant a licence in accordance with subsection (2), or

    (b)   refuse to grant a licence.

(2) If the authority are satisfied as to the matters mentioned in subsection (3), they may grant a licence either—

    (a)   to the applicant, or

    (b)   to some other person, if both he and the applicant agree.

(3) The matters are—

    (a)   that the proposed licence holder—

        (i)   is a fit and proper person to be the licence holder, and

        (ii)   is, out of all the persons reasonably available to be the licence holder in respect of the house, the most appropriate person to be the licence holder;

    (b)   that the proposed manager of the house is either—

        (i)   the person having control of the house, or

        (ii)   a person who is an agent or employee of the person having control of the house;

    (c)   that the proposed manager of the house is a fit and proper person to be the manager of the house; and

    (d)   that the proposed management arrangements for the house are otherwise satisfactory.

(4) Section 89 applies for the purposes of this section.

89 Tests for fitness etc and satisfactory management arrangements

(1) In deciding for the purposes of section 88(3)(a) or (c) whether a person ("P") is a fit and proper person to be the licence holder or (as the case may be) the manager of the house, the local housing authority must have regard (among other things) to any evidence within subsection (2) or (3).

(2) Evidence is within this subsection if it shows that P has—

    (a)   committed any offence involving fraud or other dishonesty, or violence or drugs, or any offence listed in Schedule 3 to the Sexual Offences Act 2003 (c 42) (offences attracting notification requirements);

    (b)   practised unlawful discrimination on grounds of sex, colour, race, ethnic or national origins or disability in, or in connection with, the carrying on of any business; or

    (c)   contravened any provision of the law relating to housing or of landlord and tenant law.

(3) Evidence is within this subsection if—

   (a)   it shows that any person associated or formerly associated with P (whether on a personal, work or other basis) has done any of the things set out in subsection (2)(a) to (c), and

   (b)   it appears to the authority that the evidence is relevant to the question whether P is a fit and proper person to be the licence holder or (as the case may be) the manager of the house.

(4) For the purposes of section 88(3)(a) the local housing authority must assume, unless the contrary is shown, that the person having control of the house is a more appropriate person to be the licence holder than a person not having control of it.

(5) In deciding for the purposes of section 88(3)(d) whether the proposed management arrangements for the house are otherwise satisfactory, the local housing authority must have regard (among other things) to the considerations mentioned in subsection (6).

(6) The considerations are—

   (a)   whether any person proposed to be involved in the management of the house has a sufficient level of competence to be so involved;

   (b)   whether any person proposed to be involved in the management of the house (other than the manager) is a fit and proper person to be so involved; and

   (c)   whether any proposed management structures and funding arrangements are suitable.

(7) Any reference in section 88(3)(b)(i) or (ii) or subsection (4) above to a person having control of the house, or to being a person of any other description, includes a reference to a person who is proposing to have control of the house, or (as the case may be) to be a person of that description, at the time when the licence would come into force.

90   Licence conditions

(1) A licence may include such conditions as the local housing authority consider appropriate for regulating the management, use or occupation of the house concerned.

(2) Those conditions may, in particular, include (so far as appropriate in the circumstances)—

   (a)   conditions imposing restrictions or prohibitions on the use or occupation of particular parts of the house by persons occupying it;

   (b)   conditions requiring the taking of reasonable and practicable steps to prevent or reduce anti-social behaviour by persons occupying or visiting the house.

(3) A licence may also include—

(a) conditions requiring facilities and equipment to be made available in the house for the purpose of meeting standards prescribed for the purposes of this section by regulations made by the appropriate national authority;

(b) conditions requiring such facilities and equipment to be kept in repair and proper working order;

(c) conditions requiring, in the case of any works needed in order for any such facilities or equipment to be made available or to meet any such standards, that the works are carried out within such period or periods as may be specified in, or determined under, the licence.

(4) A licence must include the conditions required by Schedule 4.

(5) As regards the relationship between the authority's power to impose conditions under this section and functions exercisable by them under or for the purposes of Part 1 ("Part 1 functions")—

(a) the authority must proceed on the basis that, in general, they should seek to identify, remove or reduce category 1 or category 2 hazards in the house by the exercise of Part 1 functions and not by means of licence conditions;

(b) this does not, however, prevent the authority from imposing (in accordance with subsection (3)) licence conditions relating to the installation or maintenance of facilities or equipment within subsection (3)(a) above, even if the same result could be achieved by the exercise of Part 1 functions;

(c) the fact that licence conditions are imposed for a particular purpose that could be achieved by the exercise of Part 1 functions does not affect the way in which Part 1 functions can be subsequently exercised by the authority.

(6) A licence may not include conditions imposing restrictions or obligations on a particular person other than the licence holder unless that person has consented to the imposition of the restrictions or obligations.

(7) A licence may not include conditions requiring (or intended to secure) any alteration in the terms of any tenancy or licence under which any person occupies the house.

91 Licences: general requirements and duration

(1) A licence may not relate to more than one Part 3 house.

(2) A licence may be granted before the time when it is required by virtue of this Part but, if so, the licence cannot come into force until that time.

(3) A licence—

(a) comes into force at the time that is specified in or determined under the licence for this purpose, and

(b) unless previously terminated by subsection (7) or revoked under section 93, continues in force for the period that is so specified or determined.

(4) That period must not end more than 5 years after—

(a)   the date on which the licence was granted, or

(b)   if the licence was granted as mentioned in subsection (2), the date when the licence comes into force.

(5) Subsection (3)(b) applies even if, at any time during that period, the house concerned subsequently ceases to be a Part 3 house or becomes an HMO to which Part 2 applies (see section 55(2)).

(6) A licence may not be transferred to another person.

(7) If the holder of the licence dies while the licence is in force, the licence ceases to be in force on his death.

(8) However, during the period of 3 months beginning with the date of the licence holder's death, the house is to be treated for the purposes of this Part as if on that date a temporary exemption notice had been served in respect of the house under section 86.

(9) If, at any time during that period ("the initial period"), the personal representatives of the licence holder request the local housing authority to do so, the authority may serve on them a notice which, during the period of 3 months after the date on which the initial period ends, has the same effect as a temporary exemption notice under section 86.

(10) Subsections (6) to (8) of section 86 apply (with any necessary modifications) in relation to a decision by the authority not to serve such a notice as they apply in relation to a decision not to serve a temporary exemption notice.

Variation and revocation of licences

92   Variation of licences

(1) The local housing authority may vary a licence—

(a)   if they do so with the agreement of the licence holder, or

(b)   if they consider that there has been a change of circumstances since the time when the licence was granted.

For this purpose "change of circumstances" includes any discovery of new information.

(2) A variation made with the agreement of the licence holder takes effect at the time when it is made.

(3) Otherwise, a variation does not come into force until such time, if any, as is the operative time for the purposes of this subsection under paragraph 35 of Schedule 5 (time when period for appealing expires without an appeal being made or when decision to vary is confirmed on appeal).

(4) The power to vary a licence under this section is exercisable by the authority either—

(a)   on an application made by the licence holder or a relevant person, or

(b)   on the authority's own initiative.

(5) In subsection (4) "relevant person" means any person (other than the licence holder)—

(a)   who has an estate or interest in the house concerned (but is not a tenant under a lease with an unexpired term of 3 years or less), or

(b)   who is a person managing or having control of the house (and does not fall within paragraph (a)), or

(c)   on whom any restriction or obligation is imposed by the licence in accordance with section 90(6).

93   Revocation of licences

(1) The local housing authority may revoke a licence—

(a)   if they do so with the agreement of the licence holder,

(b)   in any of the cases mentioned in subsection (2) (circumstances relating to licence holder or other person),

(c)   in any of the cases mentioned in subsection (3) (circumstances relating to house concerned), or

(d)   in any other circumstances prescribed by regulations made by the appropriate national authority.

(2) The cases referred to in subsection (1)(b) are as follows—

(a)   where the authority consider that the licence holder or any other person has committed a serious breach of a condition of the licence or repeated breaches of such a condition;

(b)   where the authority no longer consider that the licence holder is a fit and proper person to be the licence holder; and

(c)   where the authority no longer consider that the management of the house is being carried on by persons who are in each case fit and proper persons to be involved in its management.

Section 89(1) applies in relation to paragraph (b) or (c) above as it applies in relation to section 88(3)(a) or (c).

(3) The cases referred to in subsection (1)(c) are as follows—

(a)   where the house to which the licence relates ceases to be a Part 3 house;

(b)   where a licence has been granted under Part 2 in respect of the house;

(c)   where the authority consider at any time that, were the licence to expire at that time, they would, for a particular reason relating to the structure of the house, refuse to grant a new licence to the licence holder on similar terms in respect of it.

(4) A revocation made with the agreement of the licence holder takes effect at the time when it is made.

(5) Otherwise, a revocation does not come into force until such time, if any, as is the operative time for the purposes of this subsection under paragraph 35 of

Schedule 5 (time when period for appealing expires without an appeal being made or when decision to vary is confirmed on appeal).

This is subject to subsection (6).

(6) A revocation made in a case within subsection (3)(b) cannot come into force before such time as would be the operative time for the purposes of subsection (5) under paragraph 35 of Schedule 5 on the assumption that paragraph 35 applied—

    (a)   to an appeal against the Part 2 licence under paragraph 31 of the Schedule as it applies to an appeal under paragraph 32 of the Schedule, and

    (b)   to the period for appealing against the Part 2 licence mentioned in paragraph 33(1) of the Schedule as it applies to the period mentioned in paragraph 33(2) of the Schedule.

(7) The power to revoke a licence under this section is exercisable by the authority either—

    (a)   on an application made by the licence holder or a relevant person, or

    (b)   on the authority's own initiative.

(8) In subsection (7) "relevant person" means any person (other than the licence holder)—

    (a)   who has an estate or interest in the house concerned (but is not a tenant under a lease with an unexpired term of 3 years or less), or

    (b)   who is a person managing or having control of the house (and does not fall within paragraph (a)), or

    (c)   on whom any restriction or obligation is imposed by the licence in accordance with section 90(6).

Procedure and appeals

94   Procedural requirements and appeals against licence decisions

Schedule 5 (which deals with procedural requirements relating to the grant, refusal, variation or revocation of licences and with appeals against licence decisions) has effect for the purposes of this Part.

Enforcement

95   Offences in relation to licensing of houses under this Part

(1) A person commits an offence if he is a person having control of or managing a house which is required to be licensed under this Part (see section 85(1)) but is not so licensed.

(2) A person commits an offence if—

    (a)   he is a licence holder or a person on whom restrictions or obligations under a licence are imposed in accordance with section 90(6), and

    (b)   he fails to comply with any condition of the licence.

(3) In proceedings against a person for an offence under subsection (1) it is a defence that, at the material time—

(a) a notification had been duly given in respect of the house under section 62(1) or 86(1), or

(b) an application for a licence had been duly made in respect of the house under section 87,

and that notification or application was still effective (see subsection (7)).

(4) In proceedings against a person for an offence under subsection (1) or (2) it is a defence that he had a reasonable excuse—

(a) for having control of or managing the house in the circumstances mentioned in subsection (1), or

(b) for failing to comply with the condition,

as the case may be.

(5) A person who commits an offence under subsection (1) is liable on summary conviction to a fine not exceeding £20,000.

(6) A person who commits an offence under subsection (2) is liable on summary conviction to a fine not exceeding level 5 on the standard scale.

(7) For the purposes of subsection (3) a notification or application is "effective" at a particular time if at that time it has not been withdrawn, and either—

(a) the authority have not decided whether to serve a temporary exemption notice, or (as the case may be) grant a licence, in pursuance of the notification or application, or

(b) if they have decided not to do so, one of the conditions set out in subsection (8) is met.

(8) The conditions are—

(a) that the period for appealing against the decision of the authority not to serve or grant such a notice or licence (or against any relevant decision of a residential property tribunal) has not expired, or

(b) that an appeal has been brought against the authority's decision (or against any relevant decision of such a tribunal) and the appeal has not been determined or withdrawn.

(9) In subsection (8) "relevant decision" means a decision which is given on an appeal to the tribunal and confirms the authority's decision (with or without variation).

96 Other consequences of operating unlicensed houses: rent repayment orders

(1) For the purposes of this section a house is an "unlicensed house" if—

(a) it is required to be licensed under this Part but is not so licensed, and

(b) neither of the conditions in subsection (2) is satisfied.

(2) The conditions are—

(a) that a notification has been duly given in respect of the house under section 62(1) or 86(1) and that notification is still effective (as defined by section 95(7));

(b) that an application for a licence has been duly made in respect of the house under section 87 and that application is still effective (as so defined).

(3) No rule of law relating to the validity or enforceability of contracts in circumstances involving illegality is to affect the validity or enforceability of—

(a) any provision requiring the payment of rent or the making of any other periodical payment in connection with any tenancy or licence of the whole or a part of an unlicensed house, or

(b) any other provision of such a tenancy or licence.

(4) But amounts paid in respect of rent or other periodical payments payable in connection with such a tenancy or licence may be recovered in accordance with subsection (5) and section 97.

(5) If—

(a) an application in respect of a house is made to a residential property tribunal by the local housing authority or an occupier of the whole or part of the house, and

(b) the tribunal is satisfied as to the matters mentioned in subsection (6) or (8),

the tribunal may make an order (a "rent repayment order") requiring the appropriate person to pay to the applicant such amount in respect of the housing benefit paid as mentioned in subsection (6)(b), or (as the case may be) the periodical payments paid as mentioned in subsection (8)(b), as is specified in the order (see section 97(2) to (8)).

(6) If the application is made by the local housing authority, the tribunal must be satisfied as to the following matters—

(a) that, at any time within the period of 12 months ending with the date of the notice of intended proceedings required by subsection (7), the appropriate person has committed an offence under section 95(1) in relation to the house (whether or not he has been charged or convicted),

(b) that housing benefit has been paid (to any person) in respect of periodical payments payable in connection with the occupation of the whole or any part or parts of the house during any period during which it appears to the tribunal that such an offence was being committed, and

(c) that the requirements of subsection (7) have been complied with in relation to the application.

(7) Those requirements are as follows—

(a) the authority must have served on the appropriate person a notice (a "notice of intended proceedings")—

    (i)   informing him that the authority are proposing to make an application under subsection (5),

    (ii)   setting out the reasons why they propose to do so,

    (iii) stating the amount that they will seek to recover under that subsection and how that amount is calculated, and

    (iv) inviting him to make representations to them within a period specified in the notice of not less than 28 days;

  (b)   that period must have expired; and

  (c)   the authority must have considered any representations made to them within that period by the appropriate person.

(8) If the application is made by an occupier of the whole or part of the house, the tribunal must be satisfied as to the following matters—

  (a)   that the appropriate person has been convicted of an offence under section 95(1) in relation to the house, or has been required by a rent repayment order to make a payment in respect of housing benefit paid in connection with occupation of the whole or any part or parts of the house,

  (b)   that the occupier paid, to a person having control of or managing the house, periodical payments in respect of occupation of the whole or part of the house during any period during which it appears to the tribunal that such an offence was being committed in relation to the house, and

  (c)   that the application is made within the period of 12 months beginning with—

    (i)   the date of the conviction or order, or

    (ii)   if such a conviction was followed by such an order (or vice versa), the date of the later of them.

(9) Where a local housing authority serve a notice of intended proceedings on any person under this section, they must ensure—

  (a)   that a copy of the notice is received by the department of the authority responsible for administering the housing benefit to which the proceedings would relate; and

  (b)   that that department is subsequently kept informed of any matters relating to the proceedings that are likely to be of interest to it in connection with the administration of housing benefit.

(10) In this section—

"the appropriate person", in relation to any payment of housing benefit or periodical payment payable in connection with occupation of the whole or a part of a house, means the person who at the time of the payment was entitled to receive on his own account periodical payments payable in connection with such occupation;

"housing benefit" means housing benefit provided by virtue of a scheme under section 123 of the Social Security Contributions and Benefits Act 1992 (c 4);

"occupier", in relation to any periodical payment, means a person who was an occupier at the time of the payment, whether under a tenancy or licence (and "occupation" has a corresponding meaning);

"periodical payments" means periodical payments in respect of which housing benefit may be paid by virtue of regulation 10 of the Housing Benefit (General) Regulations 1987 (SI 1987/1971) or any corresponding provision replacing that regulation.

(11) For the purposes of this section an amount which—

(a) is not actually paid by an occupier but is used by him to discharge the whole or part of his liability in respect of a periodical payment (for example, by offsetting the amount against any such liability), and

(b) is not an amount of housing benefit,

is to be regarded as an amount paid by the occupier in respect of that periodical payment.

97 Further provisions about rent repayment orders

(1) This section applies in relation to orders made by residential property tribunals under section 96(5).

(2) Where, on an application by the local housing authority, the tribunal is satisfied—

(a) that a person has been convicted of an offence under section 95(1) in relation to the house, and

(b) that housing benefit was paid (whether or not to the appropriate person) in respect of periodical payments payable in connection with occupation of the whole or any part or parts of the house during any period during which it appears to the tribunal that such an offence was being committed in relation to the house,

the tribunal must make a rent repayment order requiring the appropriate person to pay to the authority an amount equal to the total amount of housing benefit paid as mentioned in paragraph (b).

This is subject to subsections (3), (4) and (8).

(3) If the total of the amounts received by the appropriate person in respect of periodical payments payable as mentioned in paragraph (b) of subsection (2) ("the rent total") is less than the total amount of housing benefit paid as mentioned in that paragraph, the amount required to be paid by virtue of a rent repayment order made in accordance with that subsection is limited to the rent total.

(4) A rent repayment order made in accordance with subsection (2) may not require the payment of any amount which the tribunal is satisfied that, by reason of any exceptional circumstances, it would be unreasonable for that person to be required to pay.

(5) In a case where subsection (2) does not apply, the amount required to be paid by virtue of a rent repayment order under section 96(5) is to be such amount as the tribunal considers reasonable in the circumstances.

This is subject to subsections (6) to (8).

(6) In such a case the tribunal must, in particular, take into account the following matters—

    (a)   the total amount of relevant payments paid in connection with occupation of the house during any period during which it appears to the tribunal that an offence was being committed by the appropriate person in relation to the house under section 95(1);

    (b)   the extent to which that total amount—

        (i)   consisted of, or derived from, payments of housing benefit, and

        (ii)   was actually received by the appropriate person;

    (c)   whether the appropriate person has at any time been convicted of an offence under section 95(1) in relation to the house;

    (d)   the conduct and financial circumstances of the appropriate person; and

    (e)   where the application is made by an occupier, the conduct of the occupier.

(7) In subsection (6) "relevant payments" means—

    (a)   in relation to an application by a local housing authority, payments of housing benefit or periodical payments payable by occupiers;

    (b)   in relation to an application by an occupier, periodical payments payable by the occupier, less any amount of housing benefit payable in respect of occupation of the house, or (as the case may be) the part of it occupied by him, during the period in question.

(8) A rent repayment order may not require the payment of an amount which—

    (a)   (where the application is made by a local housing authority) is in respect of any time falling outside the period of 12 months mentioned in section 96(6)(a); or

    (b)   (where the application is made by an occupier) is in respect of any time falling outside the period of 12 months ending with the date of the occupier's application under section 96(5);

and the period to be taken into account under subsection (6)(a) above is restricted accordingly.

(9) Any amount payable to a local housing authority under a rent repayment order—

    (a)   does not, when recovered by the authority, constitute an amount of housing benefit recovered by them, and

    (b)   is, until recovered by them, a legal charge on the house which is a local land charge.

(10) For the purpose of enforcing that charge the authority have the same powers and remedies under the Law of Property Act 1925 (c 20) and otherwise as if they were mortgagees by deed having powers of sale and lease, and of accepting surrenders of leases and of appointing a receiver.

(11) The power of appointing a receiver is exercisable at any time after the end of the period of one month beginning with the date on which the charge takes effect.

(12) If the authority subsequently grant a licence under Part 2 or this Part in respect of the house to the appropriate person or any person acting on his behalf, the conditions contained in the licence may include a condition requiring the licence holder—

    (a)   to pay to the authority any amount payable to them under the rent repayment order and not so far recovered by them; and

    (b)   to do so in such instalments as are specified in the licence.

(13) If the authority subsequently make a management order under Chapter 1 of Part 4 in respect of the house, the order may contain such provisions as the authority consider appropriate for the recovery of any amount payable to them under the rent repayment order and not so far recovered by them.

(14) Any amount payable to an occupier by virtue of a rent repayment order is recoverable by the occupier as a debt due to him from the appropriate person.

(15) The appropriate national authority may by regulations make such provision as it considers appropriate for supplementing the provisions of this section and section 96, and in particular—

    (a)   for securing that persons are not unfairly prejudiced by rent repayment orders (whether in cases where there have been over-payments of housing benefit or otherwise);

    (b)   for requiring or authorising amounts received by local housing authorities by virtue of rent repayment orders to be dealt with in such manner as is specified in the regulations.

(16) Section 96(10) and (11) apply for the purposes of this section as they apply for the purposes of section 96.

98   Other consequences of operating unlicensed houses: restriction on terminating tenancies

(1) No section 21 notice may be given in relation to a shorthold tenancy of the whole or part of an unlicensed house so long as it remains such a house.

(2) In this section—

    a "section 21 notice" means a notice under section 21(1)(b) or (4)(a) of the Housing Act 1988 (c 50) (recovery of possession on termination of shorthold tenancy);

    a "shorthold tenancy" means an assured shorthold tenancy within the meaning of Chapter 2 of Part 1 of that Act;

    "unlicensed house" has the same meaning as in section 96 of this Act.

Supplementary provisions

99   Meaning of "house" etc

In this Part—

"dwelling" means a building or part of a building occupied or intended to be occupied as a separate dwelling;

"house" means a building or part of a building consisting of one or more dwellings;

and references to a house include (where the context permits) any yard, garden, outhouses and appurtenances belonging to, or usually enjoyed with, it (or any part of it).

100   Index of defined expressions: Part 3

The following table shows where expressions used in this Part are defined or otherwise explained.

Expression	*Provision of this Act*
Anti-social behaviour	Section 57(5)
Appropriate national authority	Section 261(1)
Category 1 hazard	Section 2(1)
Category 2 hazard	Section 2(1)
District of local housing authority	Section 261(6)
Dwelling	Section 99
House	Section 99
Licence and licence holder	Section 85(5)
Licence (to occupy premises)	Section 262(9)
Local housing authority	Section 261(2) to (5)
Occupier (and related expressions)	Section 262(6)
Part 3 house	Section 85(5), together with section 79(2)
Person having control	Section 263(1) and (2) (and see also section 89(7))
Person having estate or interest	Section 262(8)
Person managing	Section 263(3)
Person involved in management	Section 263(5)
Residential property tribunal	Section 229
Tenant	Section 262(1) to (5)

PART 4
ADDITIONAL CONTROL PROVISIONS IN RELATION TO RESIDENTIAL ACCOMMODATION

Chapter 1
Interim and Final Management Orders

Introductory

101   Interim and final management orders: introductory

(1) This Chapter deals with the making by a local housing authority of—

   (a)   an interim management order (see section 102), or
   (b)   a final management order (see section 113),

in respect of an HMO or a Part 3 house.

(2) Section 103 deals with the making of an interim management order in respect of a house to which that section applies.

(3) An interim management order is an order (expiring not more than 12 months after it is made) which is made for the purpose of securing that the following steps are taken in relation to the house—

   (a)   any immediate steps which the authority consider necessary to protect the health, safety or welfare of persons occupying the house, or persons occupying or having an estate or interest in any premises in the vicinity, and
   (b)   any other steps which the authority think appropriate with a view to the proper management of the house pending the grant of a licence under Part 2 or 3 in respect of the house or the making of a final management order in respect of it (or, if appropriate, the revocation of the interim management order).

(4) A final management order is an order (expiring not more than 5 years after it is made) which is made for the purpose of securing the proper management of the house on a long-term basis in accordance with a management scheme contained in the order.

(5) In this Chapter any reference to "the house", in relation to an interim or final management order (other than an order under section 102(7)), is a reference to the HMO or Part 3 house to which the order relates.

(6) Subsection (5) has effect subject to sections 102(8) and 113(7) (exclusion of part occupied by resident landlord).

(7) In this Chapter "third party", in relation to a house, means any person who has an estate or interest in the house (other than an immediate landlord and any person who is a tenant under a lease granted under section 107(3)(c) or 116(3)(c)).

Interim management orders: making and operation of orders

102 Making of interim management orders

(1) A local housing authority—

   (a) are under a duty to make an interim management order in respect of a house in a case within subsection (2) or (3), and
   (b) have power to make an interim management order in respect of a house in a case within subsection (4) or (7).

(2) The authority must make an interim management order in respect of a house if—

   (a) it is an HMO or a Part 3 house which is required to be licensed under Part 2 or Part 3 (see section 61(1) or 85(1)) but is not so licensed, and
   (b) they consider either—
      (i)   that there is no reasonable prospect of its being so licensed in the near future, or
      (ii) that the health and safety condition is satisfied (see section 104).

(3) The authority must make an interim management order in respect of a house if—

   (a) it is an HMO or a Part 3 house which is required to be licensed under Part 2 or Part 3 and is so licensed,
   (b) they have revoked the licence concerned but the revocation is not yet in force, and
   (c) they consider either—
      (i)   that, on the revocation coming into force, there will be no reasonable prospect of the house being so licensed in the near future, or
      (ii) that, on the revocation coming into force, the health and safety condition will be satisfied (see section 104).

(4) The authority may make an interim management order in respect of a house if—

   (a) it is an HMO other than one that is required to be licensed under Part 2, and
   (b) on an application by the authority to a residential property tribunal, the tribunal by order authorises them to make such an order, either in the terms of a draft order submitted by them or in those terms as varied by the tribunal;

and the authority may make such an order despite any pending appeal against the order of the tribunal (but this is without prejudice to any order that may be made on the disposal of any such appeal).

(5) The tribunal may only authorise the authority to make an interim management order under subsection (4) if it considers that the health and safety condition is satisfied (see section 104).

(6) In determining whether to authorise the authority to make an interim management order in respect of an HMO under subsection (4), the tribunal must have regard to the extent to which any applicable code of practice approved under section 233 has been complied with in respect of the HMO in the past.

(7) The authority may make an interim management order in respect of a house if—

(a) it is a house to which section 103 (special interim management orders) applies, and

(b) on an application by the authority to a residential property tribunal, the tribunal by order authorises them to make such an order, either in the terms of a draft order submitted by them or in those terms as varied by the tribunal;

and the authority may make such an order despite any pending appeal against the order of the tribunal (but this is without prejudice to any order that may be made on the disposal of any such appeal).

Subsections (2) to (6) of section 103 apply in relation to the power of a residential property tribunal to authorise the making of an interim management order under this subsection.

(8) The authority may make an interim management order which is expressed not to apply to a part of the house that is occupied by a person who has an estate or interest in the whole of the house.

In relation to such an order, a reference in this Chapter to "the house" does not include the part so excluded (unless the context requires otherwise, such as where the reference is to the house as an HMO or a Part 3 house).

(9) Nothing in this section requires or authorises the making of an interim management order in respect of a house if—

(a) an interim management order has been previously made in respect of it, and

(b) the authority have not exercised any relevant function in respect of the house at any time after the making of the interim management order.

(10) In subsection (9) "relevant function" means the function of—

(a) granting a licence under Part 2 or 3,

(b) serving a temporary exemption notice under section 62 or section 86, or

(c) making a final management order under section 113.

103 Special interim management orders

(1) This section applies to a house if the whole of it is occupied either—

(a) under a single tenancy or licence that is not an exempt tenancy or licence under section 79(3) or (4), or

(b)   under two or more tenancies or licences in respect of different dwellings contained in it, none of which is an exempt tenancy or licence under section 79(3) or (4).

(2) A residential property tribunal may only authorise the authority to make an interim management order in respect of such a house under section 102(7) if it considers that both of the following conditions are satisfied.

(3) The first condition is that the circumstances relating to the house fall within any category of circumstances prescribed for the purposes of this subsection by an order under subsection (5).

(4) The second condition is that the making of the order is necessary for the purpose of protecting the health, safety or welfare of persons occupying, visiting or otherwise engaging in lawful activities in the vicinity of the house.

(5) The appropriate national authority may by order—

(a)   prescribe categories of circumstances for the purposes of subsection (3),
(b)   provide for any of the provisions of this Act to apply in relation to houses to which this section applies, or interim or final management orders made in respect of them, with any modifications specified in the order.

(6) The categories prescribed by an order under subsection (5) are to reflect one or more of the following—

(a)   the first or second set of general conditions mentioned in subsection (3) or (6) of section 80, or
(b)   any additional set of conditions specified under subsection (7) of that section,

but (in each case) with such modifications as the appropriate national authority considers appropriate to adapt them to the circumstances of a single house.

(7) In this section "house" has the same meaning as in Part 3 (see section 99).

(8) In this Chapter—

(a)   any reference to "the house", in relation to an interim management order under section 102(7), is a reference to the house to which the order relates, and
(b)   any such reference includes (where the context permits) a reference to any yard, garden, outhouses and appurtenances belonging to, or usually enjoyed with, it (or any part of it).

104   The health and safety condition

(1) This section explains what "the health and safety condition" is for the purposes of section 102.

(2) The health and safety condition is that the making of an interim management order is necessary for the purpose of protecting the health, safety

or welfare of persons occupying the house, or persons occupying or having an estate or interest in any premises in the vicinity.

(3) A threat to evict persons occupying a house in order to avoid the house being required to be licensed under Part 2 may constitute a threat to the welfare of those persons for the purposes of subsection (2).

This does not affect the generality of that subsection.

(4) The health and safety condition is not to be regarded as satisfied for the purposes of section 102(2)(b)(ii) or (3)(c)(ii) where both of the conditions in subsections (5) and (6) are satisfied.

(5) The first condition is that the local housing authority either—

(a)   (in a case within section 102(2)(b)(ii)) are required by section 5 (general duty to take enforcement action in respect of category 1 hazards) to take a course of action within subsection (2) of that section in relation to the house, or

(b)   (in a case within section 102(3)(c)(ii)) consider that on the revocation coming into force they will be required to take such a course of action.

(6) The second condition is that the local housing authority consider that the health, safety or welfare of the persons in question would be adequately protected by taking that course of action.

105   Operation of interim management orders

(1) This section deals with the time when an interim management order comes into force or ceases to have effect.

(2) The order comes into force when it is made, unless it is made under section 102(3).

(3) If the order is made under section 102(3), it comes into force when the revocation of the licence comes into force.

(4) The order ceases to have effect at the end of the period of 12 months beginning with the date on which it is made, unless it ceases to have effect at some other time as mentioned below.

(5) If the order provides that it is to cease to have effect on a date falling before the end of that period, it accordingly ceases to have effect on that date.

(6) If the order is made under section 102(3)—

(a)   it must include a provision for determining the date on which it will cease to have effect, and

(b)   it accordingly ceases to have effect on the date so determined.

(7) That date must be no later than 12 months after the date on which the order comes into force.

(8) Subsections (9) and (10) apply where—

(a) a final management order ("the FMO") has been made under section 113 so as to replace the order ("the IMO"), but

(b) the FMO has not come into force because of an appeal to a residential property tribunal under paragraph 24 of Schedule 6 against the making of the FMO.

(9) If—

(a) the house would (but for the IMO being in force) be required to be licensed under Part 2 or 3 of this Act (see section 61(1) or 85(1)), and

(b) the date on which—

(i) the FMO,

(ii) any licence under Part 2 or 3, or

(iii) another interim management order,

comes into force in relation to the house (or part of it) following the disposal of the appeal is later than the date on which the IMO would cease to have effect apart from this subsection,

the IMO continues in force until that later date.

(10) If, on the application of the authority, the tribunal makes an order providing for the IMO to continue in force, pending the disposal of the appeal, until a date later than that on which the IMO would cease to have effect apart from this subsection, the IMO accordingly continues in force until that later date.

(11) This section has effect subject to sections 111 and 112 (variation or revocation of orders by authority) and to the power of revocation exercisable by a residential property tribunal on an appeal made under paragraph 24 or 28 of Schedule 6.

106 Local housing authority's duties once interim management order in force

(1) A local housing authority who have made an interim management order in respect of a house must comply with the following provisions as soon as practicable after the order has come into force.

(2) The authority must first take any immediate steps which they consider to be necessary for the purpose of protecting the health, safety or welfare of persons occupying the house, or persons occupying or having an estate or interest in any premises in the vicinity.

(3) The authority must also take such other steps as they consider appropriate with a view to the proper management of the house pending—

(a) the grant of a licence or the making of a final management order in respect of the house as mentioned in subsection (4) or (5), or

(b) the revocation of the interim management order as mentioned in subsection (5).

(4) If the house would (but for the order being in force) be required to be licensed under Part 2 or 3 of this Act (see section 61(1) or 85(1)), the authority must, after considering all the circumstances of the case, decide to take one of the following courses of action—

    (a)   to grant a licence under that Part in respect of the house, or

    (b)   to make a final management order in respect of it under section 113(1).

(5) If subsection (4) does not apply to the house, the authority must, after considering all the circumstances of the case, decide to take one of the following courses of action—

    (a)   to make a final management order in respect of the house under section 113(3), or

    (b)   to revoke the order under section 112 without taking any further action.

(6) In the following provisions, namely—

    (a)   subsections (3) and (4), and

    (b)   section 101(3)(b),

the reference to the grant of a licence under Part 2 or 3 in respect of the house includes a reference to serving a temporary exemption notice under section 62 or section 86 in respect of it (whether or not a notification is given under subsection (1) of that section).

(7) For the avoidance of doubt, the authority's duty under subsection (3) includes taking such steps as are necessary to ensure that, while the order is in force, reasonable provision is made for insurance of the house against destruction or damage by fire or other causes.

107 General effect of interim management orders

(1) This section applies while an interim management order is in force in relation to a house.

(2) The rights and powers conferred by subsection (3) are exercisable by the authority in performing their duties under section 106(1) to (3) in respect of the house.

(3) The authority—

    (a)   have the right to possession of the house (subject to the rights of existing occupiers preserved by section 124(3));

    (b)   have the right to do (and authorise a manager or other person to do) in relation to the house anything which a person having an estate or interest in the house would (but for the order) be entitled to do;

    (c)   may create one or more of the following—

        (i)   an interest in the house which, as far as possible, has all the incidents of a leasehold, or

        (ii)   a right in the nature of a licence to occupy part of the house.

(4) But the authority may not under subsection (3)(c) create any interest or right in the nature of a lease or licence unless consent in writing has been given by the person who (but for the order) would have power to create the lease or licence in question.

(5) The authority—

    (a)   do not under this section acquire any estate or interest in the house, and

    (b)   accordingly are not entitled by virtue of this section to sell, lease, charge or make any other disposition of any such estate or interest;

but, where the immediate landlord of the house or part of it (within the meaning of section 109) is a lessee under a lease of the house or part, the authority is to be treated (subject to paragraph (a)) as if they were the lessee instead.

(6) Any enactment or rule of law relating to landlords and tenants or leases applies in relation to—

    (a)   a lease in relation to which the authority are to be treated as the lessee under subsection (5), or

    (b)   a lease to which the authority become a party under section 124(4),

as if the authority were the legal owner of the premises (but this is subject to section 124(7) to (9)).

(7) None of the following, namely—

    (a)   the authority, or

    (b)   any person authorised under subsection (3)(b),

is liable to any person having an estate or interest in the house for anything done or omitted to be done in the performance (or intended performance) of the authority's duties under section 106(1) to (3) unless the act or omission is due to the negligence of the authority or any such person.

(8) References in any enactment to housing accommodation provided or managed by a local housing authority do not include a house in relation to which an interim management order is in force.

(9) An interim management order which has come into force is a local land charge.

(10) The authority may apply to the Chief Land Registrar for the entry of an appropriate restriction in the register of title in respect of such an order.

(11) In this section "enactment" includes an enactment comprised in subordinate legislation (within the meaning of the Interpretation Act 1978 (c 30)).

108 General effect of interim management orders: leases and licences granted by authority

(1) This section applies in relation to any interest or right created by the authority under section 107(3)(c).

(2) For the purposes of any enactment or rule of law—

    (a)   any interest created by the authority under section 107(3)(c)(i) is to be treated as if it were a legal lease, and

    (b)   any right created by the authority under section 107(3)(c)(ii) is to be treated as if it were a licence to occupy granted by the legal owner of the premises,

despite the fact that the authority have no legal estate in the premises (see section 107(5)(a)).

(3) Any enactment or rule of law relating to landlords and tenants or leases accordingly applies in relation to any interest created by the authority under section 107(3)(c)(i) as if the authority were the legal owner of the premises.

(4) References to leases and licences—

    (a)   in this Chapter, and

    (b)   in any other enactment,

accordingly include (where the context permits) interests and rights created by the authority under section 107(3)(c).

(5) The preceding provisions of this section have effect subject to—

    (a)   section 124(7) to (9), and

    (b)   any provision to the contrary contained in an order made by the appropriate national authority.

(6) In section 107(5)(b) the reference to leasing does not include the creation of interests under section 107(3)(c)(i).

(7) In this section—

    "enactment" has the meaning given by section 107(11);

    "legal lease" means a term of years absolute (within section 1(1)(b) of the Law of Property Act 1925 (c 20)).

109 General effect of interim management orders: immediate landlords, mortgagees etc

(1) This section applies in relation to—

    (a)   immediate landlords, and

    (b)   other persons with an estate or interest in the house,

while an interim management order is in force in relation to a house.

(2) A person who is an immediate landlord of the house or a part of it—

    (a)   is not entitled to receive—

    (i)   any rents or other payments from persons occupying the house or part which are payable to the local housing authority by virtue of section 124(4), or

    (ii)   any rents or other payments from persons occupying the house or part which are payable to the authority by virtue of any leases or licences granted by them under section 107(3)(c);

(b)   may not exercise any rights or powers with respect to the management of the house or part; and

(c)   may not create any of the following—

    (i)   any leasehold interest in the house or part (other than a lease of a reversion), or

    (ii)   any licence or other right to occupy it.

(3) However (subject to subsection (2)(c)) nothing in section 107 or this section affects the ability of a person having an estate or interest in the house to make any disposition of that estate or interest.

(4) Nothing in section 107 or this section affects—

(a)   the validity of any mortgage relating to the house or any rights or remedies available to the mortgagee under such a mortgage, or

(b)   the validity of any lease of the house or part of it under which the immediate landlord is a lessee, or any superior lease, or (subject to section 107(5)) any rights or remedies available to the lessor under such a lease,

except to the extent that any of those rights or remedies would prevent the local housing authority from exercising their power under section 107(3)(c).

(5) In proceedings for the enforcement of any such rights or remedies the court may make such order as it thinks fit as regards the operation of the interim management order (including an order quashing it).

(6) For the purposes of this Chapter, as it applies in relation to an interim management order, a person is an "immediate landlord" of the house or a part of it if—

(a)   he is an owner or lessee of the house or part, and

(b)   (but for the order) he would be entitled to receive the rents or other payments from persons occupying the house or part which are payable to the local housing authority by virtue of section 124(4).

110   Financial arrangements while order is in force

(1) This section applies to relevant expenditure of a local housing authority who have made an interim management order.

(2) "Relevant expenditure" means expenditure reasonably incurred by the authority in connection with performing their duties under section 106(1) to (3) in respect of the house (including any premiums paid for insurance of the premises).

(3) Rent or other payments which the authority have collected or recovered, by virtue of this Chapter, from persons occupying the house may be used by the authority to meet—

(a)   relevant expenditure, and

(b)   any amounts of compensation payable to a third party by virtue of a decision of the authority under section 128.

(4) The authority must pay to such relevant landlord, or to such relevant landlords in such proportions, as they consider appropriate—

(a)   any amount of rent or other payments collected or recovered as mentioned in subsection (3) that remains after deductions to meet relevant expenditure and any amounts of compensation payable as mentioned in that subsection, and

(b)   (where appropriate) interest on that amount at a reasonable rate fixed by the authority,

and such payments are to be made at such intervals as the authority consider appropriate.

(5) The interim management order may provide for—

(a)   the rate of interest which is to apply for the purposes of paragraph (b) of subsection (4); and

(b)   the intervals at which payments are to be made under that subsection.

Paragraph 24(3) of Schedule 6 enables an appeal to be brought where the order does not provide for both of those matters.

(6) The authority must—

(a)   keep full accounts of their income and expenditure in respect of the house; and

(b)   afford to each relevant landlord, and to any other person who has an estate or interest in the house, all reasonable facilities for inspecting, taking copies of and verifying those accounts.

(7) A relevant landlord may apply to a residential property tribunal for an order—

(a)   declaring that an amount shown in the accounts as expenditure of the authority does not constitute expenditure reasonably incurred by the authority as mentioned in subsection (2);

(b)   requiring the authority to make such financial adjustments (in the accounts and otherwise) as are necessary to reflect the tribunal's declaration.

(8) In this section—

"expenditure" includes administrative costs;

"relevant landlord" means any person who is an immediate landlord of the house or part of it;

"rent or other payments" means rents or other payments payable under leases or licences or in respect of furniture within section 126(1).

Interim management orders: variation and revocation

111 Variation of interim management orders

(1) The local housing authority may vary an interim management order if they consider it appropriate to do so.

(2) A variation does not come into force until such time, if any, as is the operative time for the purposes of this subsection under paragraph 31 of Schedule 6 (time when period for appealing expires without an appeal being made or when decision to vary is confirmed on appeal).

(3) The power to vary an order under this section is exercisable by the authority either—

    (a)   on an application made by a relevant person, or
    (b)   on the authority's own initiative.

(4) In this section "relevant person" means—

    (a)   any person who has an estate or interest in the house or part of it (but is not a tenant under a lease with an unexpired term of 3 years or less), or
    (b)   any other person who (but for the order) would be a person managing or having control of the house or part of it.

112 Revocation of interim management orders

(1) The local housing authority may revoke an interim management order in the following cases—

    (a)   if the order was made under section 102(2) or (3) and the house has ceased to be an HMO to which Part 2 applies or a Part 3 house (as the case may be);
    (b)   if the order was made under section 102(2) or (3) and a licence granted by them in respect of the house is due to come into force under Part 2 or Part 3 on the revocation of the order;
    (c)   if a final management order has been made by them in respect of the house so as to replace the order;
    (d)   if in any other circumstances the authority consider it appropriate to revoke the order.

(2) A revocation does not come into force until such time, if any, as is the operative time for the purposes of this subsection under paragraph 31 of Schedule 6 (time when period for appealing expires without an appeal being made or when decision to revoke is confirmed on appeal).

(3) The power to revoke an order under this section is exercisable by the authority either—

    (a)   on an application made by a relevant person, or
    (b)   on the authority's own initiative.

(4) In this section "relevant person" means—

(a) any person who has an estate or interest in the house or part of it (but is not a tenant under a lease with an unexpired term of 3 years or less), or

(b) any other person who (but for the order) would be a person managing or having control of the house or part of it.

Final management orders: making and operation of orders

113 Making of final management orders

(1) A local housing authority who have made an interim management order in respect of a house under section 102 ("the IMO")—

    (a) have a duty to make a final management order in respect of the house in a case within subsection (2), and

    (b) have power to make such an order in a case within subsection (3).

(2) The authority must make a final management order so as to replace the IMO as from its expiry date if—

    (a) on that date the house would be required to be licensed under Part 2 or 3 of this Act (see section 61(1) or 85(1)), and

    (b) the authority consider that they are unable to grant a licence under Part 2 or 3 in respect of the house that would replace the IMO as from that date.

(3) The authority may make a final management order so as to replace the IMO as from its expiry date if—

    (a) on that date the house will not be one that would be required to be licensed as mentioned in subsection (2)(a), and

    (b) the authority consider that making the final management order is necessary for the purpose of protecting, on a long-term basis, the health, safety or welfare of persons occupying the house, or persons occupying or having an estate or interest in any premises in the vicinity.

(4) A local housing authority who have made a final management order in respect of a house under this section ("the existing order")—

    (a) have a duty to make a final management order in respect of the house in a case within subsection (5), and

    (b) have power to make such an order in a case within subsection (6).

(5) The authority must make a new final management order so as to replace the existing order as from its expiry date if—

    (a) on that date the condition in subsection (2)(a) will be satisfied in relation to the house, and

    (b) the authority consider that they are unable to grant a licence under Part 2 or 3 in respect of the house that would replace the existing order as from that date.

(6) The authority may make a new final management order so as to replace the existing order as from its expiry date if—

(a) on that date the condition in subsection (3)(a) will be satisfied in relation to the house, and

(b) the authority consider that making the new order is necessary for the purpose of protecting, on a long-term basis, the health, safety or welfare of persons within subsection (3)(b).

(7) The authority may make a final management order which is expressed not to apply to a part of the house that is occupied by a person who has an estate or interest in the whole of the house.

In relation to such an order, a reference in this Chapter to "the house" does not include the part so excluded (unless the context requires otherwise, such as where the reference is to the house as an HMO or a Part 3 house).

(8) In this section "expiry date", in relation to an interim or final management order, means—

(a) where the order is revoked, the date as from which it is revoked, and

(b) otherwise the date on which the order ceases to have effect under section 105 or 114;

and nothing in this section applies in relation to an interim or final management order which has been revoked on an appeal under Part 3 of Schedule 6.

114   Operation of final management orders

(1) This section deals with the time when a final management order comes into force or ceases to have effect.

(2) The order does not come into force until such time (if any) as is the operative time for the purposes of this subsection under paragraph 27 of Schedule 6 (time when period for appealing expires without an appeal being made or when order is confirmed on appeal).

(3) The order ceases to have effect at the end of the period of 5 years beginning with the date on which it comes into force, unless it ceases to have effect at some other time as mentioned below.

(4) If the order provides that it is to cease to have effect on a date falling before the end of that period, it accordingly ceases to have effect on that date.

(5) Subsections (6) and (7) apply where—

(a) a new final management order ("the new order") has been made so as to replace the order ("the existing order"), but

(b) the new order has not come into force because of an appeal to a residential property tribunal under paragraph 24 of Schedule 6 against the making of that order.

(6) If—

(a) the house would (but for the existing order being in force) be required to be licensed under Part 2 or 3 of this Act (see section 61(1) or 85(1)), and

(b) the date on which—
  (i) the new order, or
  (ii) any licence under Part 2 or 3, or
  (iii) a temporary exemption notice under section 62 or 86,
  comes into force in relation to the house (or part of it) following the disposal of the appeal is later than the date on which the existing order would cease to have effect apart from this subsection,

the existing order continues in force until that later date.

(7) If, on the application of the authority, the tribunal makes an order providing for the existing order to continue in force, pending the disposal of the appeal, until a date later than that on which it would cease to have effect apart from this subsection, the existing order accordingly continues in force until that later date.

(8) This section has effect subject to sections 121 and 122 (variation or revocation of orders) and to the power of revocation exercisable by a residential property tribunal on an appeal made under paragraph 24 or 28 of Schedule 6.

115 Local housing authority's duties once final management order in force

(1) A local housing authority who have made a final management order in respect of a house must comply with the following provisions once the order has come into force.

(2) The local housing authority must take such steps as they consider appropriate with a view to the proper management of the house in accordance with the management scheme contained in the order (see section 119).

(3) The local housing authority must from time to time review—

  (a) the operation of the order and in particular the management scheme contained in it, and
  (b) whether keeping the order in force in relation to the house (with or without making any variations under section 121) is the best alternative available to them.

(4) If on a review the authority consider that any variations should be made under section 121, they must proceed to make those variations.

(5) If on a review the authority consider that either—

  (a) granting a licence under Part 2 or 3 in respect of the house, or
  (b) revoking the order under section 122 and taking no further action,

is the best alternative available to them, the authority must grant such a licence or revoke the order (as the case may be).

(6) For the avoidance of doubt, the authority's duty under subsection (2) includes taking such steps as are necessary to ensure that, while the order is in force, reasonable provision is made for insurance of the house against destruction or damage by fire or other causes.

116   General effect of final management orders

(1) This section applies while a final management order is in force in relation to a house.

(2) The rights and powers conferred by subsection (3) are exercisable by the authority in performing their duty under section 115(2) in respect of the house.

(3) The authority—

(a)   have the right to possession of the house (subject to the rights of existing and other occupiers preserved by section 124(3) and (6));

(b)   have the right to do (and authorise a manager or other person to do) in relation to the house anything which a person having an estate or interest in the house would (but for the order) be entitled to do;

(c)   may create one or more of the following—

(i)   an interest in the house which, as far as possible, has all the incidents of a leasehold, or

(ii)   a right in the nature of a licence to occupy part of the house.

(4) The powers of the authority under subsection (3)(c) are restricted as follows—

(a)   they may not create any interest or right in the nature of a lease or licence—

(i)   which is for a fixed term expiring after the date on which the order is due to expire, or

(ii)   (subject to paragraph (b)) which is terminable by notice to quit, or an equivalent notice, of more than 4 weeks,

unless consent in writing has been given by the person who would (but for the order) have power to create the lease or licence in question;

(b)   they may create an interest in the nature of an assured shorthold tenancy without any such consent so long as it is created before the beginning of the period of 6 months that ends with the date on which the order is due to expire.

(5) The authority—

(a)   do not under this section acquire any estate or interest in the house, and

(b)   accordingly are not entitled by virtue of this section to sell, lease, charge or make any other disposition of any such estate or interest;

but, where the immediate landlord of the house or part of it (within the meaning of section 118) is a lessee under a lease of the house or part, the authority is to be treated (subject to paragraph (a)) as if they were the lessee instead.

(6) Any enactment or rule of law relating to landlords and tenants or leases applies in relation to—

(a)   a lease in relation to which the authority are to be treated as the lessee under subsection (5), or

(b)   a lease to which the authority become a party under section 124(4), as if the authority were the legal owner of the premises (but this is subject to section 124(7) to (9)).

(7) None of the following, namely—

  (a) the authority, or
  (b) any person authorised under subsection (3)(b),

is liable to any person having an estate or interest in the house for anything done or omitted to be done in the performance (or intended performance) of the authority's duty under section 115(2) unless the act or omission is due to the negligence of the authority or any such person.

(8) References in any enactment to housing accommodation provided or managed by a local housing authority do not include a house in relation to which a final management order is in force.

(9) A final management order which has come into force is a local land charge.

(10) The authority may apply to the Chief Land Registrar for the entry of an appropriate restriction in the register in respect of such an order.

(11) In this section "enactment" includes an enactment comprised in subordinate legislation (within the meaning of the Interpretation Act 1978 (c 30)).

117 General effect of final management orders: leases and licences granted by authority

(1) This section applies in relation to any interest or right created by the authority under section 116(3)(c).

(2) For the purposes of any enactment or rule of law—

  (a) any interest created by the authority under section 116(3)(c)(i) is to be treated as if it were a legal lease, and
  (b) any right created by the authority under section 116(3)(c)(ii) is to be treated as if it were a licence to occupy granted by the legal owner of the premises,

despite the fact that the authority have no legal estate in the premises (see section 116(5)(a)).

(3) Any enactment or rule of law relating to landlords and tenants or leases accordingly applies in relation to any interest created by the authority under section 116(3)(c)(i) as if the authority were the legal owner of the premises.

(4) References to leases and licences—

  (a) in this Chapter, and
  (b) in any other enactment,

accordingly include (where the context permits) interests and rights created by the authority under section 116(3)(c).

(5) The preceding provisions of this section have effect subject to—

(a) section 124(7) to (9), and
(b) any provision to the contrary contained in an order made by the appropriate national authority.

(6) In section 116(5)(b) the reference to leasing does not include the creation of interests under section 116(3)(c)(i).

(7) In this section—

"enactment" has the meaning given by section 116(11);
"legal lease" means a term of years absolute (within section 1(1)(b) of the Law of Property Act 1925 (c 20)).

118   General effect of final management orders: immediate landlords, mortgagees etc

(1) This section applies in relation to—

(a) immediate landlords, and
(b) other persons with an estate or interest in the house,

while a final management order is in force in relation to a house.

(2) A person who is an immediate landlord of the house or a part of it—

(a) is not entitled to receive—
   (i) any rents or other payments from persons occupying the house or part which are payable to the local housing authority by virtue of section 124(4), or
   (ii) any rents or other payments from persons occupying the house or part which are payable to the authority by virtue of any leases or licences granted by them under section 107(3)(c) or 116(3)(c);
(b) may not exercise any rights or powers with respect to the management of the house or part; and
(c) may not create any of the following—
   (i) any leasehold interest in the house or part (other than a lease of a reversion), or
   (ii) any licence or other right to occupy it.

(3) However (subject to subsection (2)(c)) nothing in section 116 or this section affects the ability of a person having an estate or interest in the house to make any disposition of that estate or interest.

(4) Nothing in section 116 or this section affects—

(a) the validity of any mortgage relating to the house or any rights or remedies available to the mortgagee under such a mortgage, or
(b) the validity of any lease of the house or part of it under which the immediate landlord is a lessee, or any superior lease, or (subject to section 116(5)) any rights or remedies available to the lessor under such a lease,

except to the extent that any of those rights or remedies would prevent the local housing authority from exercising their power under section 116(3)(c).

(5) In proceedings for the enforcement of any such rights or remedies the court may make such order as it thinks fit as regards the operation of the final management order (including an order quashing it).

(6) For the purposes of this Chapter, as it applies in relation to a final management order, a person is an "immediate landlord" of the house or a part of it if—

 (a) he is an owner or lessee of the house or part, and

 (b) (but for the order) he would be entitled to receive the rents or other payments from persons occupying the house or part which are payable to the authority by virtue of section 124(4).

119 Management schemes and accounts

(1) A final management order must contain a management scheme.

(2) A "management scheme" is a scheme setting out how the local housing authority are to carry out their duty under section 115(2) as respects the management of the house.

(3) A management scheme is to be divided into two parts.

(4) Part 1 of the scheme is to contain a plan giving details of the way in which the authority propose to manage the house, which must (in particular) include—

 (a) details of any works that the authority intend to carry out in connection with the house;

 (b) an estimate of the capital and other expenditure to be incurred by the authority in respect of the house while the order is in force;

 (c) the amount of rent or other payments that the authority will seek to obtain having regard to the condition or expected condition of the house at any time while the order is in force;

 (d) the amount of any compensation that is payable to a third party by virtue of a decision of the authority under section 128 in respect of any interference in consequence of the final management order with the rights of that person;

 (e) provision as to the payment of any such compensation;

 (f) provision as to the payment by the authority to a relevant landlord, from time to time, of amounts of rent or other payments that remain after the deduction of—

  (i) relevant expenditure, and

  (ii) any amounts of compensation payable as mentioned in paragraph (d);

 (g) provision as to the manner in which the authority are to pay to a relevant landlord, on the termination of the final management order, any amounts of rent or other payments that remain after the deduction of—

  (i) relevant expenditure, and

  (ii) any amounts of compensation payable as mentioned in paragraph (d);

(h)   provision as to the manner in which the authority are to pay, on the termination of the final management order, any outstanding balance of compensation payable to a third party.

(5) Part 1 of the scheme may also state—

(a)   the authority's intentions as regards the use of rent or other payments to meet relevant expenditure;

(b)   the authority's intentions as regards the payment to a relevant landlord (where appropriate) of interest on amounts within subsection (4)(f) and (g);

(c)   that section 129(2) or (4) is not to apply in relation to an interim or (as the case may be) final management order that immediately preceded the final management order, and that instead the authority intend to use any balance or amount such as is mentioned in that subsection to meet—

    (i)   relevant expenditure incurred during the currency of the final management order, and

    (ii)   any compensation that may become payable to a third party;

(d)   that section 129(3) or (5) is not to apply in relation to an interim or (as the case may be) final management order that immediately preceded the final management order ("the order"), and that instead the authority intend to use rent or other payments collected during the currency of the order to reimburse the authority in respect of any deficit or amount such as is mentioned in that subsection;

(e)   the authority's intentions as regards the recovery from a relevant landlord, with or without interest, of any amount of relevant expenditure that cannot be reimbursed out of the total amount of rent or other payments.

(6) Part 2 of the scheme is to describe in general terms how the authority intend to address the matters which caused them to make the final management order and may, for example, include—

(a)   descriptions of any steps that the authority intend to take to require persons occupying the house to comply with their obligations under any lease or licence or under the general law;

(b)   descriptions of any repairs that are needed to the property and an explanation as to why those repairs are necessary.

(7) The authority must—

(a)   keep full accounts of their income and expenditure in respect of the house; and

(b)   afford to each relevant landlord, and to any other person who has an estate or interest in the house, all reasonable facilities for inspecting, taking copies of and verifying those accounts.

(8) In this section—

"relevant expenditure" means expenditure reasonably incurred by the authority in connection with performing their duties under section 115(2) in respect of the house (including any reasonable administrative costs and any premiums paid for insurance of the premises);

"relevant landlord" means any person who is an immediate landlord of the house or part of it;

"rent or other payments" means rent or other payments—

    (a)   which are payable under leases or licences or in respect of furniture within section 126(1), and

    (b)   which the authority have collected or recovered by virtue of this Chapter.

(9) In the provisions of this Chapter relating to varying, revoking or appealing against decisions relating to a final management order, any reference to such an order includes (where the context permits) a reference to the management scheme contained in it.

120 Enforcement of management scheme by relevant landlord

(1) An affected person may apply to a residential property tribunal for an order requiring the local housing authority to manage the whole or part of a house in accordance with the management scheme contained in a final management order made in respect of the house.

(2) On such an application the tribunal may, if it considers it appropriate to do so, make an order—

    (a)   requiring the local housing authority to manage the whole or part of the house in accordance with the management scheme, or

    (b)   revoking the final management order as from a date specified in the tribunal's order.

(3) An order under subsection (2) may—

    (a)   specify the steps which the authority are to take to manage the whole or part of the house in accordance with the management scheme,

    (b)   include provision varying the final management order,

    (c)   require the payment of money to an affected person by way of damages.

(4) In this section "affected person" means—

    (a)   a relevant landlord (within the meaning of section 119), and

    (b)   any third party to whom compensation is payable by virtue of a decision of the authority under section 128.

Final management orders: variation and revocation

121 Variation of final management orders

(1) The local housing authority may vary a final management order if they consider it appropriate to do so.

(2) A variation does not come into force until such time, if any, as is the operative time for the purposes of this subsection under paragraph 31 of Schedule 6 (time when period for appealing expires without an appeal being made or when decision to vary is confirmed on appeal).

(3) The power to vary an order under this section is exercisable by the authority either—

   (a)   on an application made by a relevant person, or

   (b)   on the authority's own initiative.

(4) In this section "relevant person" means—

   (a)   any person who has an estate or interest in the house or part of it (but is not a tenant under a lease with an unexpired term of 3 years or less), or

   (b)   any other person who (but for the order) would be a person managing or having control of the house or part of it.

122   Revocation of final management orders

(1) The local housing authority may revoke a final management order in the following cases—

   (a)   if the order was made under section 113(2) or (5) and the house has ceased to be an HMO to which Part 2 applies or a Part 3 house (as the case may be);

   (b)   if the order was made under section 113(2) or (5) and a licence granted by them in respect of the house is due to come into force under Part 2 or Part 3 as from the revocation of the order;

   (c)   if a further final management order has been made by them in respect of the house so as to replace the order;

   (d)   if in any other circumstances the authority consider it appropriate to revoke the order.

(2) A revocation does not come into force until such time, if any, as is the operative time for the purposes of this subsection under paragraph 31 of Schedule 6 (time when period for appealing expires without an appeal being made or when decision to vary is confirmed on appeal).

(3) The power to revoke an order under this section is exercisable by the authority either—

   (a)   on an application made by a relevant person, or

   (b)   on the authority's own initiative.

(4) In this section "relevant person" means—

   (a)   any person who has an estate or interest in the house or part of it (but is not a tenant under a lease with an unexpired term of 3 years or less), or

   (b)   any other person who (but for the order) would be a person managing or having control of the house or part of it.

Interim and final management orders: procedure and appeals

123 Procedural requirements and appeals

Schedule 6 (which deals with procedural requirements relating to the making, variation or revocation of interim and final management orders and with appeals against decisions relating to such orders) has effect.

Interim and final management orders: other general provisions

124 Effect of management orders: occupiers

(1) This section applies to existing and new occupiers of a house in relation to which an interim or final management order is in force.

(2) In this section—

"existing occupier" means a person who, at the time when the order comes into force, either—

   (a)   (in the case of an HMO or a Part 3 house) is occupying part of the house and does not have an estate or interest in the whole of the house, or

   (b)   (in the case of a Part 3 house) is occupying the whole of the house,

but is not a new occupier within subsection (6);

"new occupier" means a person who, at a time when the order is in force, is occupying the whole or part of the house under a lease or licence granted under section 107(3)(c) or 116(3)(c).

(3) Sections 107 and 116 do not affect the rights or liabilities of an existing occupier under a lease or licence (whether in writing or not) under which he is occupying the whole or part of the house at the commencement date.

(4) Where the lessor or licensor under such a lease or licence—

   (a)   has an estate or interest in the house, and

   (b)   is not an existing occupier,

the lease or licence has effect while the order is in force as if the local housing authority were substituted in it for the lessor or licensor.

(5) Such a lease continues to have effect, as far as possible, as a lease despite the fact that the rights of the local housing authority, as substituted for the lessor, do not amount to an estate in law in the premises.

(6) Section 116 does not affect the rights or liabilities of a new occupier who, in the case of a final management order, is occupying the whole or part of the house at the time when the order comes into force.

(7) The provisions which exclude local authority lettings from the Rent Acts, namely—

   (a)   sections 14 to 16 of the Rent Act 1977 (c 42), and

(b)   those sections as applied by Schedule 2 to the Rent (Agriculture) Act 1976 (c 80) and section 5(2) to (4) of that Act,

do not apply to a lease or agreement under which an existing or new occupier is occupying the whole or part of the house.

(8) Section 1(2) of, and paragraph 12 of Part 1 of Schedule 1 to, the Housing Act 1988 (c 50) (which exclude local authority lettings from Part 1 of that Act) do not apply to a lease or agreement under which an existing or new occupier is occupying the whole or part of the house.

(9) Nothing in this Chapter has the result that the authority are to be treated as the legal owner of any premises for the purposes of—

(a)   section 80 of the Housing Act 1985 (c 68) (the landlord condition for secure tenancies); or

(b)   section 124 of the Housing Act 1996 (c 52) (introductory tenancies).

(10) If, immediately before the coming into force of an interim or final management order, an existing occupier was occupying the whole or part of the house under—

(a)   a protected or statutory tenancy within the meaning of the Rent Act 1977 (c 42),

(b)   a protected or statutory tenancy within the meaning of the Rent (Agriculture) Act 1976 (c 80), or

(c)   an assured tenancy or assured agricultural occupancy within the meaning of Part 1 of the Housing Act 1988 (c 50),

nothing in this Chapter prevents the continuance of that tenancy or occupancy or affects the continued operation of any of those Acts in relation to the tenancy or occupancy after the coming into force of the order.

(11) In this section "the commencement date" means the date on which the order came into force (or, if that order was preceded by one or more orders under this Chapter, the date when the first order came into force).

125   Effect of management orders: agreements and legal proceedings

(1) An agreement or instrument within subsection (2) has effect, while an interim or final management order is in force, as if any rights or liabilities of the immediate landlord under the agreement or instrument were instead rights or liabilities of the local housing authority.

(2) An agreement or instrument is within this subsection if—

(a)   it is effective on the commencement date,

(b)   one of the parties to it is a person who is the immediate landlord of the house or a part of the house ("the relevant premises"),

(c)   it relates to the house, whether in connection with—

(i)   any management activities with respect to the relevant premises, or

(ii)   the provision of any services or facilities for persons occupying those premises, or otherwise,

(d)   it is specified for the purposes of this subsection in the order or falls within a description of agreements or instruments so specified, and

(e)   the authority serve a notice in writing on all the parties to it stating that subsection (1) is to apply to it.

(3) An agreement or instrument is not within subsection (2) if—

(a)   it is a lease within section 107(5) or 116(5), or

(b)   it relates to any disposition by the immediate landlord which is not precluded by section 109(2) or 118(2), or

(c)   it is within section 124(4).

(4) Proceedings in respect of any cause of action within subsection (5) may, while an interim or final management order is in force, be instituted or continued by or against the local housing authority instead of by or against the immediate landlord.

(5) A cause of action is within this subsection if—

(a)   it is a cause of action (of any nature) which accrued to or against the immediate landlord of the house or a part of the house before the commencement date,

(b)   it relates to the house as mentioned in subsection (2)(c),

(c)   it is specified for the purposes of this subsection in the order or falls within a description of causes of action so specified, and

(d)   the authority serve a notice in writing on all interested parties stating that subsection (4) is to apply to it.

(6) If, by virtue of this section, the authority become subject to any liability to pay damages in respect of anything done (or omitted to be done) before the commencement date by or on behalf of the immediate landlord of the house or a part of it, the immediate landlord is liable to reimburse to the authority an amount equal to the amount of the damages paid by them.

(7) In this section—

"agreement" includes arrangement;

"the commencement date" means the date on which the order comes into force (or, if that order was preceded by one or more orders under this Chapter, the date when the first order came into force);

"management activities" includes repair, maintenance, improvement and insurance.

126   Effect of management orders: furniture

(1) Subsection (2) applies where, on the date on which an interim or final management order comes into force, there is furniture in the house which a person occupying the house has the right to use in consideration of periodical payments to a person who is an immediate landlord of the house or a part of it (whether the payments are included in the rent payable by the occupier or not).

(2) The right to possession of the furniture against all persons other than the occupier vests in the local housing authority on that date and remains vested in the authority while the order is in force.

(3) The local housing authority may renounce the right to possession of the furniture conferred by subsection (2) if—

  (a)   an application in writing has been made to them for the purpose by the person owning the furniture, and
  (b)   they renounce the right by notice in writing served on that person not less than two weeks before the notice takes effect.

(4) If the authority's right to possession of furniture conferred by subsection (2) is a right exercisable against more than one person interested in the furniture, any of those persons may apply to a residential property tribunal for an adjustment of their respective rights and liabilities as regards the furniture.

(5) On such an application the tribunal may make an order for such an adjustment of rights and liabilities, either unconditionally or subject to such terms and conditions, as it considers appropriate.

(6) The terms and conditions may, in particular, include terms and conditions about the payment of money by a party to the proceedings to another party to the proceedings by way of compensation, damages or otherwise.

(7) In this section "furniture" includes fittings and other articles.

127   Management orders: power to supply furniture

(1) The local housing authority may supply the house to which an interim or final management order relates with such furniture as they consider to be required.

(2) For the purposes of section 110 or a management scheme under section 119, any expenditure incurred by the authority under this section constitutes expenditure incurred by the authority in connection with performing their duty under section 106(3) or 115(2).

(3) In this section "furniture" includes fittings and other articles.

128   Compensation payable to third parties

(1) If a third party requests them to do so at any time, the local housing authority must consider whether an amount by way of compensation should be paid to him in respect of any interference with his rights in consequence of an interim or final management order.

(2) The authority must notify the third party of their decision as soon as practicable.

(3) Where the local housing authority decide under subsection (1) that compensation ought to be paid to a third party in consequence of a final

management order, they must vary the management scheme contained in the order so as to specify the amount of the compensation to be paid and to make provision as to its payment.

129 Termination of management orders: financial arrangements

(1) This section applies where an interim or final management order ceases to have effect for any reason.

(2) If, on the termination date for an interim management order, the total amount of rent or other payments collected or recovered as mentioned in section 110(3) exceeds the total amount of—

    (a)   the local housing authority's relevant expenditure, and

    (b)   any amounts of compensation payable to third parties by virtue of decisions of the authority under section 128,

the authority must, as soon as practicable after the termination date, pay the balance to such relevant landlord, or to such relevant landlords in such proportions, as they consider appropriate.

(3) If, on the termination date for an interim management order, the total amount of rent or other payments collected or recovered as mentioned in section 110(3) is less than the total amount of—

    (a)   the authority's relevant expenditure, and

    (b)   any amounts of compensation payable as mentioned in subsection (2)(b),

the difference is recoverable by the authority from such relevant landlord, or such relevant landlords in such proportions, as they consider appropriate.

(4) If, on the termination date for a final management order, any amount is payable to—

    (a)   a third party, or

    (b)   any relevant landlord in accordance with the management scheme under section 119,

that amount must be paid to that person by the local housing authority in the manner provided by the scheme.

(5) If, on the termination date for a final management order, any amount is payable to the local housing authority in accordance with the management scheme, that amount is recoverable by the local housing authority—

    (a)   from such relevant landlord, or

    (b)   from such relevant landlords in such proportions,

as is provided by the scheme.

(6) The provisions of any of subsections (2) to (5) do not, however, apply in relation to the order if—

    (a)   the order is followed by a final management order, and

(b)   the management scheme contained in that final management order
       provides for that subsection not to apply in relation to the order (see
       section 119(5)(c) and (d)).

(7) Any sum recoverable by the authority under subsection (3) or (5) is, until
recovered, a charge on the house.

(8) The charge takes effect on the termination date for the order as a legal
charge which is a local land charge.

(9) For the purpose of enforcing the charge the authority have the same powers
and remedies under the Law of Property Act 1925 (c 20) and otherwise as if
they were mortgagees by deed having powers of sale and lease, of accepting
surrenders of leases and of appointing a receiver.

(10) The power of appointing a receiver is exercisable at any time after the end
of the period of one month beginning with the date on which the charge takes
effect.

(11) If the order is to be followed by a licence granted under Part 2 or 3 in
respect of the house, the conditions contained in the licence may include a
condition requiring the licence holder—

(a)   to repay to the authority any amount recoverable by them under
       subsection (3) or (5), and
(b)   to do so in such instalments as are specified in the licence.

(12) In this section—

   "relevant expenditure" has the same meaning as in section 110;
   "relevant landlord" means a person who was the immediate landlord of the
      house or part of it immediately before the termination date or his
      successor in title for the time being;
   "rent or other payments" means rents or other payments payable under
      leases or licences or in respect of furniture within section 126(1);
   "the termination date" means the date on which the order ceases to have
      effect.

130   Termination of management orders: leases, agreements and proceedings

(1) This section applies where—

(a)   an interim or final management order ceases to have effect for any
       reason, and
(b)   the order is not immediately followed by a further order under this
       Chapter.

(2) As from the termination date—

(a)   a lease or licence in which the local housing authority was substituted
       for another party by virtue of section 124(4) has effect with the
       substitution of the original party, or his successor in title, for the
       authority; and

    (b)   an agreement which (in accordance with section 108 or 117) has effect as a lease or licence granted by the authority under section 107 or 116 has effect with the substitution of the relevant landlord for the authority.

(3) If the relevant landlord is a lessee, nothing in a superior lease imposes liability on him or any superior lessee in respect of anything done before the termination date in pursuance of the terms of an agreement to which subsection (2)(b) applies.

(4) If the condition in subsection (5) is met, any other agreement entered into by the authority in the performance of their duties under section 106(1) to (3) or 115(2) in respect of the house has effect, as from the termination date, with the substitution of the relevant landlord for the authority.

(5) The condition is that the authority serve a notice on the other party or parties to the agreement stating that subsection (4) applies to the agreement.

(6) If the condition in subsection (7) is met—

    (a)   any rights or liabilities that were rights or liabilities of the authority immediately before the termination date by virtue of any provision of this Chapter or under any agreement to which subsection (4) applies are rights or liabilities of the relevant landlord instead, and

    (b)   any proceedings instituted or continued by or against the authority by virtue of any such provision or agreement may be continued by or against the relevant landlord instead,

as from the termination date.

(7) The condition is that the authority serve a notice on all interested parties stating that subsection (6) applies to the rights or liabilities or (as the case may be) the proceedings.

(8) If by virtue of this section a relevant landlord becomes subject to any liability to pay damages in respect of anything done (or omitted to be done) before the termination date by or on behalf of the authority, the authority are liable to reimburse to the relevant landlord an amount equal to the amount of the damages paid by him.

(9) Where two or more persons are relevant landlords in relation to different parts of the house, any reference in this section to "the relevant landlord" is to be taken to refer to such one or more of them as is determined by agreement between them or (in default of agreement) by a residential property tribunal on an application made by any of them.

(10) This section applies to instruments as it applies to agreements.

(11) In this section—

    "agreement" includes arrangement;
    "relevant landlord" means a person who was the immediate landlord of the house immediately before the termination date or his successor in title for the time being;

"the termination date" means the date on which the order ceases to have effect.

131   Management orders: power of entry to carry out work

(1) The right mentioned in subsection (2) is exercisable by the local housing authority, or any person authorised in writing by them, at any time when an interim or final management order is in force.

(2) That right is the right at all reasonable times to enter any part of the house for the purpose of carrying out works, and is exercisable as against any person having an estate or interest in the house.

(3) Where part of a house is excluded from the provisions of an interim or final management order under section 102(8) or 113(7), the right conferred by subsection (1) is exercisable as respects that part so far as is reasonably required for the purpose of carrying out works in the part of the house which is subject to the order.

(4) If, after receiving reasonable notice of the intended action, any occupier of the whole or part of the house prevents any officer, employee, agent or contractor of the local housing authority from carrying out work in the house, a magistrates" court may order him to permit to be done on the premises anything which the authority consider to be necessary.

(5) A person who fails to comply with an order of the court under subsection (4) commits an offence.

(6) A person who commits an offence under subsection (5) is liable on summary conviction to a fine not exceeding level 5 on the standard scale.

Chapter 2
Interim and Final Empty Dwelling Management Orders

Introductory

132   Empty dwelling management orders: introductory

(1) This Chapter deals with the making by a local housing authority of—

  (a)   an interim empty dwelling management order (an "interim EDMO"), or
  (b)   a final empty dwelling management order (a "final EDMO"),

in respect of a dwelling.

(2) An interim EDMO is an order made to enable a local housing authority, with the consent of the relevant proprietor, to take steps for the purpose of securing that a dwelling becomes and continues to be occupied.

(3) A final EDMO is an order made, in succession to an interim EDMO or a previous final EDMO, for the purpose of securing that a dwelling is occupied.

(4) In this Chapter—

(a) "dwelling" means—
  (i)   a building intended to be occupied as a separate dwelling, or
  (ii) a part of a building intended to be occupied as a separate dwelling which may be entered otherwise than through any non-residential accommodation in the building;

(b) any reference to "the dwelling", in relation to an interim EDMO or a final EDMO, is a reference to the dwelling to which the order relates;

(c) "relevant proprietor", in relation to a dwelling, means—
  (i)   if the dwelling is let under one or more leases with an unexpired term of 7 years or more, the lessee under whichever of those leases has the shortest unexpired term; or
  (ii) in any other case, the person who has the freehold estate in the dwelling;

(d) "third party", in relation to a dwelling, means any person who has an estate or interest in the dwelling (other than the relevant proprietor and any person who is a tenant under a lease granted under paragraph 2(3)(c) or 10(3)(c) of Schedule 7); and

(e) any reference (however expressed) to rent or other payments in respect of occupation of a dwelling, includes any payments that the authority receive from persons in respect of unlawful occupation of the dwelling.

(5) In subsection (4)(c), the reference to an unexpired term of 7 years or more of a lease of a dwelling is—

(a) in relation to a dwelling in respect of which the local housing authority are considering making an interim EDMO, a reference to the unexpired term of the lease at the time the authority begin taking steps under section 133(3),

(b) in relation to a dwelling in respect of which an interim EDMO has been made, a reference to the unexpired term of the lease at the time the application for authorisation to make the interim EDMO was made under subsection (1) of that section, or

(c) in relation to a dwelling in respect of which a local housing authority are considering making or have made a final EDMO, a reference to the unexpired term of the lease at the time the application for authorisation to make the preceding interim EDMO was made under subsection (1) of that section.

"Preceding interim EDMO", in relation to a final EDMO, means the interim EDMO that immediately preceded the final EDMO or, where there has been a succession of final EDMOs, the interim EDMO that immediately preceded the first of them.

(6) Schedule 7 (which makes further provision regarding EDMOs) has effect.

Interim empty dwelling management orders

133 Making of interim EDMOs

(1) A local housing authority may make an interim EDMO in respect of a dwelling if—

(a)   it is a dwelling to which this section applies, and
(b)   on an application by the authority to a residential property tribunal, the tribunal by order authorises them under section 134 to make such an order, either in the terms of a draft order submitted by them or in those terms as varied by the tribunal.

(2) This section applies to a dwelling if—

(a)   the dwelling is wholly unoccupied, and
(b)   the relevant proprietor is not a public sector body.

"Wholly unoccupied" means that no part is occupied, whether lawfully or unlawfully.

(3) Before determining whether to make an application to a residential property tribunal for an authorisation under section 134, the authority must make reasonable efforts—

(a)   to notify the relevant proprietor that they are considering making an interim EDMO in respect of the dwelling under this section, and
(b)   to ascertain what steps (if any) he is taking, or is intending to take, to secure that the dwelling is occupied.

(4) In determining whether to make an application to a residential property tribunal for an authorisation under section 134, the authority must take into account the rights of the relevant proprietor of the dwelling and the interests of the wider community.

(5) The authority may make an interim EDMO in respect of the dwelling despite any pending appeal against the order of the tribunal (but this is without prejudice to any order that may be made on the disposal of any such appeal).

(6) An application to a residential property tribunal under this section for authorisation to make an interim EDMO in respect of a dwelling may include an application for an order under paragraph 22 of Schedule 7 determining a lease or licence of the dwelling.

(7) In this section "public sector body" means a body mentioned in any of paragraphs (a) to (f) of paragraph 2(1) of Schedule 14.

(8) Part 1 of Schedule 6 applies in relation to the making of an interim EDMO in respect of a dwelling as it applies in relation to the making of an interim management order in respect of a house, subject to the following modifications—

(a)   paragraph 7(2) does not apply;
(b)   paragraph 7(4)(c) is to be read as referring instead to the date on which the order is to cease to have effect in accordance with paragraph 1(3) and (4) or 9(3) to (5) of Schedule 7;
(c)   in paragraph 7(6)—
       (i)   paragraph (a) is to be read as referring instead to Part 4 of Schedule 7; and
       (ii)   paragraph (b) does not apply;

(d)   paragraph 8(4) is to be read as defining "relevant person" as any person who, to the knowledge of the local housing authority, is a person having an estate or interest in the dwelling (other than a person who is a tenant under a lease granted under paragraph 2(3)(c) of Schedule 7).

134 Authorisation to make interim EDMOs

(1) A residential property tribunal may authorise a local housing authority to make an interim EDMO in respect of a dwelling to which section 133 applies if the tribunal—

    (a)   is satisfied as to the matters mentioned in subsection (2), and

    (b)   is not satisfied that the case falls within one of the prescribed exceptions.

(2) The matters as to which the tribunal must be satisfied are—

    (a)   that the dwelling has been wholly unoccupied for at least 6 months or such longer period as may be prescribed,

    (b)   that there is no reasonable prospect that the dwelling will become occupied in the near future,

    (c)   that, if an interim order is made, there is a reasonable prospect that the dwelling will become occupied,

    (d)   that the authority have complied with section 133(3), and

    (e)   that any prescribed requirements have been complied with.

(3) In deciding whether to authorise a local housing authority to make an interim EDMO in respect of a dwelling, the tribunal must take into account—

    (a)   the interests of the community, and

    (b)   the effect that the order will have on the rights of the relevant proprietor and may have on the rights of third parties.

(4) On authorising a local housing authority to make an interim EDMO in respect of a dwelling, the tribunal may, if it thinks fit, make an order requiring the authority (if they make the EDMO) to pay to any third party specified in the order an amount of compensation in respect of any interference in consequence of the order with the rights of the third party.

(5) The appropriate national authority may by order—

    (a)   prescribe exceptions for the purposes of subsection (1)(b),

    (b)   prescribe a period of time for the purposes of subsection (2)(a), and

    (c)   prescribe requirements for the purposes of subsection (2)(e).

(6) An order under subsection (5)(a) may, in particular, include exceptions in relation to—

    (a)   dwellings that have been occupied solely or principally by the relevant proprietor who is at the material time temporarily resident elsewhere;

    (b)   dwellings that are holiday homes or that are otherwise occupied by the relevant proprietor or his guests on a temporary basis from time to time;

(c)   dwellings undergoing repairs or renovation;
(d)   dwellings in respect of which an application for planning permission or building control approval is outstanding;
(e)   dwellings which are genuinely on the market for sale or letting;
(f)   dwellings where the relevant proprietor has died not more than the prescribed number of months before the material time.

(7) In this section—

"building control approval" means approval for the carrying out of any works under building regulations;
"planning permission" has the meaning given by section 336(1) of the Town and Country Planning Act 1990 (c 8);
"prescribed" means prescribed by an order under subsection (5);
"wholly unoccupied" means that no part is occupied, whether lawfully or unlawfully.

135 Local housing authority's duties once interim EDMO in force

(1) A local housing authority who have made an interim EDMO in respect of a dwelling must comply with the following provisions as soon as practicable after the order has come into force (see paragraph 1 of Schedule 7).

(2) The authority must take such steps as they consider appropriate for the purpose of securing that the dwelling becomes and continues to be occupied.

(3) The authority must also take such other steps as they consider appropriate with a view to the proper management of the dwelling pending—

(a)   the making of a final EDMO in respect of the dwelling under section 136, or
(b)   the revocation of the interim EDMO.

(4) If the local housing authority conclude that there are no steps which they could appropriately take under the order for the purpose of securing that the dwelling becomes occupied, the authority must either—

(a)   make a final EDMO in respect of the dwelling under section 136, or
(b)   revoke the order under paragraph 7 of Schedule 7 without taking any further action.

(5) For the avoidance of doubt, the authority's duty under subsection (3) includes taking such steps as are necessary to ensure that, while the order is in force, reasonable provision is made for insurance of the dwelling against destruction or damage by fire or other causes.

Final empty dwelling management orders

136 Making of final EDMOs

(1) A local housing authority may make a final EDMO to replace an interim EDMO made under section 133 if—

(a) they consider that, unless a final EDMO is made in respect of the dwelling, the dwelling is likely to become or remain unoccupied;

(b) where the dwelling is unoccupied, they have taken all such steps as it was appropriate for them to take under the interim EDMO with a view to securing the occupation of the dwelling.

(2) A local housing authority may make a new final EDMO so as to replace a final EDMO made under this section if—

(a) they consider that unless a new final EDMO is made in respect of the dwelling, the dwelling is likely to become or remain unoccupied; and

(b) where the dwelling is unoccupied, they have taken all such steps as it was appropriate for them to take under the existing final EDMO with a view to securing the occupation of the dwelling.

(3) In deciding whether to make a final EDMO in respect of a dwelling, the authority must take into account—

(a) the interests of the community, and

(b) the effect that the order will have on the rights of the relevant proprietor and may have on the rights of third parties.

(4) Before making a final EDMO under this section, the authority must consider whether compensation should be paid by them to any third party in respect of any interference in consequence of the order with the rights of the third party.

(5) Part 1 of Schedule 6 applies in relation to the making of a final EDMO in respect of a dwelling as it applies in relation to the making of a final management order in respect of a house, subject to the following modifications—

(a) paragraph 7(2) does not apply;

(b) paragraph 7(4)(c) is to be read as referring instead to the date on which the order is to cease to have effect in accordance with paragraph 1(3) and (4) or 9(3) to (5) of Schedule 7;

(c) in paragraph 7(6)—

(i) paragraph (a) is to be read as referring to Part 4 of Schedule 7, and

(ii) paragraph (b) is to be read as referring instead to paragraph 27(2) of Schedule 7;

(d) paragraph 7(6) in addition is to be read as requiring the notice under paragraph 7(5) also to contain—

(i) the decision of the authority as to whether to pay compensation to any third party,

(ii) the amount of any such compensation to be paid, and

(iii) information about the right of appeal against the decision under paragraph 34 of Schedule 7;

(e) paragraph 8(4) is to be read as defining "relevant person" as any person who, to the knowledge of the local housing authority, is a person having an estate or interest in the dwelling (other than a person who is a tenant under a lease granted under paragraph 2(3)(c) or 10(3)(c) of Schedule 7).

137 Local housing authority's duties once final EDMO in force

(1) A local housing authority who have made a final EDMO in respect of a dwelling must comply with the following provisions once the order has come into force (see paragraph 9 of Schedule 7).

(2) The authority must take such steps as they consider appropriate for the purpose of securing that the dwelling is occupied.

(3) The authority must also take such other steps as they consider appropriate with a view to the proper management of the dwelling in accordance with the management scheme contained in the order (see paragraph 13 of Schedule 7).

(4) The authority must from time to time review—

    (a)   the operation of the order and in particular the management scheme contained in it,

    (b)   whether, if the dwelling is unoccupied, there are any steps which they could appropriately take under the order for the purpose of securing that the dwelling becomes occupied, and

    (c)   whether keeping the order in force in relation to the dwelling (with or without making any variations under paragraph 15 of Schedule 7) is necessary to secure that the dwelling becomes or remains occupied.

(5) If on a review the authority consider that any variations should be made under paragraph 15 of Schedule 7, they must proceed to make those variations.

(6) If the dwelling is unoccupied and on a review the authority conclude that either—

    (a)   there are no steps which they could appropriately take as mentioned in subsection (4)(b), or

    (b)   keeping the order in force is not necessary as mentioned in subsection (4)(c),

they must proceed to revoke the order.

(7) For the avoidance of doubt, the authority's duty under subsection (3) includes taking such steps as are necessary to ensure that, while the order is in force, reasonable provision is made for insurance of the dwelling against destruction or damage by fire or other causes.

Compensation

138 Compensation payable to third parties

(1) A third party may, while an interim EDMO is in force in respect of a dwelling, apply to a residential property tribunal for an order requiring the

local housing authority to pay to him compensation in respect of any interference in consequence of the order with his rights in respect of the dwelling.

(2) On such an application, the tribunal may, if it thinks fit, make an order requiring the authority to pay to the third party an amount by way of compensation in respect of any such interference.

(3) If a third party requests them to do so at any time, the local housing authority must consider whether an amount by way of compensation should be paid to him in respect of any interference in consequence of a final EDMO with his rights.

(4) The authority must notify the third party of their decision as soon as practicable.

(5) Where the local housing authority decide under subsection (3) that compensation ought to be paid to a third party, they must vary the management scheme contained in the order so as to specify the amount of the compensation to be paid and to make provision as to its payment.

Chapter 3
Overcrowding Notices

139 Service of overcrowding notices

(1) This Chapter applies to any HMO—

    (a)   in relation to which no interim or final management order is in force; and

    (b)   which is not required to be licensed under Part 2.

[(1A) This Chapter also applies, in the case of a section 257 HMO which is required to be licensed under Part 2, to any flat within that HMO in respect of which a long lease has been granted and over which the licence holder cannot reasonably be expected to exercise control.]

[(1B) In subsection (1A) "long lease" means a lease that—

    (a)   is granted for a term certain exceeding 21 years, whether or not it is (or may become terminable) before the end of that term; or

    (b)   is for a term fixed by law under a grant with a covenant or obligation for perpetual renewal, other than a lease by sub-demise from one which is not a long lease,

and neither the lease nor any superior lease contains a provision enabling the lessor or superior lessor to terminate the tenancy, other than by forfeiture, before the end of that term.]

(2) The local housing authority may serve an overcrowding notice on one or more relevant persons if, having regard to the rooms available, it considers that an excessive number of persons is being, or is likely to be, accommodated in the HMO concerned.

(3) The authority must, at least 7 days before serving an overcrowding notice—

    (a) inform in writing every relevant person (whether or not the person on whom the authority is to serve the notice) of their intention to serve the notice; and

    (b) ensure that, so far as is reasonably possible, every occupier of the HMO concerned is informed of the authority's intention.

(4) The authority must also give the persons informed under subsection (3) an opportunity of making representations about the proposal to serve an overcrowding notice.

(5) An overcrowding notice becomes operative, if no appeal is brought under section 143, at the end of the period of 21 days from the date of service of the notice.

(6) If no appeal is brought under section 143, an overcrowding notice is final and conclusive as to matters which could have been raised on such an appeal.

(7) A person who contravenes an overcrowding notice commits an offence and is liable on summary conviction to a fine not exceeding level 4 on the standard scale.

(8) In proceedings for an offence under subsection (7) it is a defence that the person had a reasonable excuse for contravening the notice.

(9) In this section "relevant person" means a person who is, to the knowledge of the local housing authority—

    (a) a person having an estate or interest in the HMO concerned, or

    (b) a person managing or having control of it.

Amendment—Subs (1) modified, in relation to a house in multiple occupation to which s 257 hereof applies, by the Houses in Multiple Occupation (Certain Converted Blocks of Flats) (Modifications to the Housing Act 2004 and Transitional Provisions for section 257 HMOs) (England) Regulations 2007, SI 2007/1904, reg 11.

140 Contents of overcrowding notices

(1) An overcrowding notice must state in relation to each room in the HMO concerned—

    (a) what the local housing authority consider to be the maximum number of persons by whom the room is suitable to be occupied as sleeping accommodation at any one time; or

    (b) that the local housing authority consider that the room is unsuitable to be occupied as sleeping accommodation.

(2) An overcrowding notice may specify special maxima applicable where some or all of the persons occupying a room are under such age as may be specified in the notice.

(3) An overcrowding notice must contain—

    (a) the requirement prescribed by section 141 (not to permit excessive number of persons to sleep in the house in multiple occupation); or

(b) the requirement prescribed by section 142 (not to admit new residents if number of persons is excessive).

(4) The local housing authority may at any time—

(a) withdraw an overcrowding notice which has been served on any person and which contains the requirement prescribed by section 142, and

(b) serve on him instead an overcrowding notice containing the requirement prescribed by section 141.

141 Requirement as to overcrowding generally

(1) The requirement prescribed by this section is that the person on whom the notice is served must refrain from—

(a) permitting a room to be occupied as sleeping accommodation otherwise than in accordance with the notice; or

(b) permitting persons to occupy the HMO as sleeping accommodation in such numbers that it is not possible to avoid persons of opposite sexes who are not living together as husband and wife sleeping in the same room.

(2) For the purposes of subsection (1)(b)—

(a) children under the age of 10 are to be disregarded; and

(b) it must be assumed that the persons occupying the HMO as sleeping accommodation sleep only in rooms for which a maximum is set by the notice and that the maximum set for each room is not exceeded.

142 Requirement as to new residents

(1) The requirement prescribed by this section is that the person on whom the notice is served must refrain from—

(a) permitting a room to be occupied by a new resident as sleeping accommodation otherwise than in accordance with the notice; or

(b) permitting a new resident to occupy any part of the HMO as sleeping accommodation if that is not possible without persons of opposite sexes who are not living together as husband and wife sleeping in the same room.

(2) In subsection (1) "new resident" means a person who was not an occupier of the HMO immediately before the notice was served.

(3) For the purposes of subsection (1)(b)—

(a) children under the age of 10 are to be disregarded; and

(b) it must be assumed that the persons occupying any part of the HMO as sleeping accommodation sleep only in rooms for which a maximum is set by the notice and that the maximum set for each room is not exceeded.

143   Appeals against overcrowding notices

(1) A person aggrieved by an overcrowding notice may appeal to a residential property tribunal within the period of 21 days beginning with the date of service of the notice.

(2) Such an appeal—

(a)   is to be by way of a re-hearing, but
(b)   may be determined having regard to matters of which the authority were unaware.

(3) On an appeal the tribunal may by order confirm, quash or vary the notice.

(4) If an appeal is brought, the notice does not become operative until—

(a)   a decision is given on the appeal which confirms the notice and the period within which an appeal to the Lands Tribunal may be brought expires without any such appeal having been brought; or
(b)   if an appeal is brought to the Lands Tribunal, a decision is given on the appeal which confirms the notice.

(5) For the purposes of subsection (4)—

(a)   the withdrawal of an appeal has the same effect as a decision which confirms the notice appealed against; and
(b)   references to a decision which confirms the notice are to a decision which confirms it with or without variation.

(6) A residential property tribunal may allow an appeal to be made to it after the end of the period mentioned in subsection (1) if it is satisfied that there is good reason for the failure to appeal before the end of that period (and for any delay since then in applying for permission to appeal out of time).

144   Revocation and variation of overcrowding notices

(1) The local housing authority may at any time, on the application of a relevant person—

(a)   revoke an overcrowding notice; or
(b)   vary it so as to allow more people to be accommodated in the HMO concerned.

(2) The applicant may appeal to a residential property tribunal if the local housing authority—

(a)   refuse an application under subsection (1); or
(b)   do not notify the applicant of their decision within the period of 35 days beginning with the making of the application (or within such further period as the applicant may in writing allow).

(3) An appeal under subsection (2) must be made within—

(a)   the period of 21 days beginning with the date when the applicant is notified by the authority of their decision to refuse the application, or

(b)   the period of 21 days immediately following the end of the period (or further period) applying for the purposes of paragraph (b) of that subsection,

as the case may be.

(4) Section 143(2) applies to such an appeal as it applies to an appeal under that section.

(5) On an appeal the tribunal may revoke the notice or vary it in any manner in which it might have been varied by the local housing authority.

(6) A residential property tribunal may allow an appeal to be made to it after the end of the 21-day period mentioned in subsection (3)(a) or (b) if it is satisfied that there is good reason for the failure to appeal before the end of that period (and for any delay since then in applying for permission to appeal).

(7) In this section "relevant person" means—

(a)   any person who has an estate or interest in the HMO concerned, or
(b)   any other person who is a person managing or having control of it.

Chapter 4
Supplementary Provisions

145   Supplementary provisions

(1) The appropriate national authority may by regulations make such provision as it considers appropriate for supplementing the provisions of Chapter 1 or 2 in relation to cases where a local housing authority are to be treated as the lessee under a lease under—

(a)   section 107(5) or 116(5), or
(b)   paragraph 2(6) or 10(6) of Schedule 7.

(2) Regulations under this section may, in particular, make provision—

(a)   as respects rights and liabilities in such cases of—
    (i)   the authority,
    (ii)   the person who (apart from the relevant provision mentioned in subsection (1)) is the lessee under the lease, or
    (iii) other persons having an estate or interest in the premises demised under the lease;
(b)   requiring the authority to give copies to the person mentioned in paragraph (a)(ii) of notices and other documents served on them in connection with the lease;
(c)   for treating things done by or in relation to the authority as done by or in relation to that person, or vice versa.

146   Interpretation and modification of this Part

(1) In this Part—

"HMO" means a house in multiple occupation as defined by sections 254 to 259,

"Part 3 house" means a house to which Part 3 of this Act applies (see section 79(2)),

and any reference to an HMO or Part 3 house includes (where the context permits) a reference to any yard, garden, outhouses and appurtenances belonging to, or usually enjoyed with, it (or any part of it).

(2) For the purposes of this Part "mortgage" includes a charge or lien, and "mortgagee" is to be read accordingly.

(3) The appropriate national authority may by regulations provide for—

(a) any provision of this Part, or

(b) section 263 (in its operation for the purposes of any such provision),

to have effect in relation to a section 257 HMO with such modifications as are prescribed by the regulations.

(4) A "section 257 HMO" is an HMO which is a converted block of flats to which section 257 applies.

147 Index of defined expressions: Part 4

The following table shows where expressions used in this Part are defined or otherwise explained.

Expression	Provision of this Act
Appropriate national authority	Section 261(1)
Dwelling	Section 132(4)(a) and (b)
Final EDMO	Section 132(1)(b)
Final management order	Section 101(4)
Health	Section 2(5)
HMO	Section 146(1)
The house	Section 101(5) or 103(8)
Immediate landlord	Section 109(6) or 118(6)
Interim EDMO	Section 132(1)(a)
Interim management order	Section 101(3)
Landlord	Section 262(3)
Lease, lessee, etc	Section 262(1) to (4)
Licence (to occupy premises)	Section 262(9)
Local housing authority	Section 261(2) to (5)
Modifications	Section 250(7)
Mortgage, mortgagee	Section 146(2)
Occupier (and related expressions)	Section 262(6)
Owner	Section 262(7)

Expression	Provision of this Act
Part 3 house	Section 146(1)
Person having control	Section 263(1) and (2)
Person having estate or interest	Section 262(8)
Person managing	Section 263(3)
Relevant proprietor	Section 132(4)(c) and (5)
Rent or other payments (in Chapter 2)	Section 132(4)(e)
Residential property tribunal	Section 229
Tenancy, tenant, etc	Section 262(1) to (5)
Third party (in Chapter 1)	Section 101(7)
Third party (in Chapter 2)	Section 132(4)(d).

PART 7
SUPPLEMENTARY AND FINAL PROVISIONS

Residential property tribunals

229 Residential property tribunals

(1) Any jurisdiction conferred on a residential property tribunal by or under any enactment is exercisable by a rent assessment committee constituted in accordance with Schedule 10 to the Rent Act 1977 (c 42).

(2) When so constituted for exercising any such jurisdiction a rent assessment committee is known as a residential property tribunal.

(3) The appropriate national authority may by order make provision for and in connection with conferring on residential property tribunals, in relation to such matters as are specified in the order, such jurisdiction as is so specified.

(4) An order under subsection (3) may modify an enactment (including this Act).

(5) In this section "enactment" includes an enactment comprised in subordinate legislation (within the meaning of the Interpretation Act 1978 (c 30)).

230 Powers and procedure of residential property tribunals

(1) A residential property tribunal exercising any jurisdiction by virtue of any enactment has, in addition to any specific powers exercisable by it in exercising that jurisdiction, the general power mentioned in subsection (2).

(2) The tribunal's general power is a power by order to give such directions as the tribunal considers necessary or desirable for securing the just, expeditious and economical disposal of the proceedings or any issue raised in or in connection with them.

(3) In deciding whether to give directions under its general power a tribunal must have regard to—

(a) the matters falling to be determined in the proceedings,

(b) any other circumstances appearing to the tribunal to be relevant, and

(c) the provisions of the enactment by virtue of which it is exercising jurisdiction and of any other enactment appearing to it to be relevant.

(4) A tribunal may give directions under its general power whether or not they were originally sought by a party to the proceedings.

(5) When exercising jurisdiction under this Act, the directions which may be given by a tribunal under its general power include (where appropriate)—

(a) directions requiring a licence to be granted under Part 2 or 3 of this Act;

(b) directions requiring any licence so granted to contain such terms as are specified in the directions;

(c) directions requiring any order made under Part 4 of this Act to contain such terms as are so specified;

(d) directions that any building or part of a building so specified is to be treated as if an HMO declaration had been served in respect of it on such date as is so specified (without there being any right to appeal against it under section 255(9));

(e) directions requiring the payment of money by one party to the proceedings to another by way of compensation, damages or otherwise.

(6) Nothing in any enactment conferring specific powers on a residential property tribunal is to be regarded as affecting the operation of the preceding provisions of this section.

(7) Schedule 13 (residential property tribunals: procedure) has effect.

(8) Section 229(5) applies also for the purposes of this section and Schedule 13.

231 Appeals from residential property tribunals

(1) A party to proceedings before a residential property tribunal may appeal to the Lands Tribunal from a decision of the residential property tribunal.

(2) But the appeal may only be made—

(a) with the permission of the residential property tribunal or the Lands Tribunal, and

(b) within the time specified by rules under section 3(6) of the Lands Tribunal Act 1949 (c 42).

(3) On the appeal—

(a) the Lands Tribunal may exercise any power which was available to the residential property tribunal, and

(b) a decision of the Lands Tribunal may be enforced in the same way as a decision of the residential property tribunal.

(4) Section 11(1) of the Tribunals and Inquiries Act 1992 (c 53) (appeals from certain tribunals to High Court) does not apply to any decision of a residential property tribunal.

(5) For the purposes of section 3(4) of the Lands Tribunal Act 1949 (which enables a person aggrieved by a decision of the Lands Tribunal to appeal to the Court of Appeal) a residential property tribunal is not to be regarded as an aggrieved person.

Register of licences and management orders

232 Register of licences and management orders

(1) Every local housing authority must establish and maintain a register of—

   (a) all licences granted by them under Part 2 or 3 which are in force;
   (b) all temporary exemption notices served by them under section 62 or section 86 which are in force; and
   (c) all management orders made by them under Chapter 1 or 2 of Part 4 which are in force.

(2) The register may, subject to any requirements that may be prescribed, be in such form as the authority consider appropriate.

(3) Each entry in the register is to contain such particulars as may be prescribed.

(4) The authority must ensure that the contents of the register are available at the authority's head office for inspection by members of the public at all reasonable times.

(5) If requested by a person to do so and subject to payment of such reasonable fee (if any) as the authority may determine, a local housing authority must supply the person with a copy (certified to be true) of the register or of an extract from it.

(6) A copy so certified is prima facie evidence of the matters mentioned in it.

(7) In this section "prescribed" means prescribed by regulations made by the appropriate national authority.

Codes of practice and management regulations relating to HMOs etc

233 Approval of codes of practice with regard to the management of HMOs etc

(1) The appropriate national authority may by order—

   (a) approve a code of practice (whether prepared by that authority or another person) laying down standards of conduct and practice to be followed with regard to the management of houses in multiple occupation or of excepted accommodation;
   (b) approve a modification of such a code; or
   (c) withdraw the authority's approval of such a code or modification.

(2) Before approving a code of practice or a modification of a code of practice under this section the appropriate national authority must take reasonable steps to consult—

(a) persons involved in the management of houses in multiple occupation or (as the case may be) excepted accommodation of the kind in question and persons occupying such houses or accommodation, or

(b) persons whom the authority considers to represent the interests of those persons.

(3) The appropriate national authority may only approve a code of practice or a modification of a code if satisfied that—

(a) the code or modification has been published (whether by the authority or by another person) in a manner that the authority considers appropriate for the purpose of bringing the code or modification to the attention of those likely to be affected by it; or

(b) arrangements have been made for the code or modification to be so published.

(4) The appropriate national authority may approve a code of practice which makes different provision in relation to different cases or descriptions of case (including different provision for different areas).

(5) A failure to comply with a code of practice for the time being approved under this section does not of itself make a person liable to any civil or criminal proceedings.

(6) In this section "excepted accommodation" means such description of living accommodation falling within any provision of Schedule 14 (buildings which are not HMOs for purposes of provisions other than Part 1) as is specified in an order under subsection (1).

234 Management regulations in respect of HMOs

(1) The appropriate national authority may by regulations make provision for the purpose of ensuring that, in respect of every house in multiple occupation of a description specified in the regulations—

(a) there are in place satisfactory management arrangements; and

(b) satisfactory standards of management are observed.

(2) The regulations may, in particular—

(a) impose duties on the person managing a house in respect of the repair, maintenance, cleanliness and good order of the house and facilities and equipment in it;

(b) impose duties on persons occupying a house for the purpose of ensuring that the person managing the house can effectively carry out any duty imposed on him by the regulations.

(3) A person commits an offence if he fails to comply with a regulation under this section.

(4) In proceedings against a person for an offence under subsection (3) it is a defence that he had a reasonable excuse for not complying with the regulation.

(5) A person who commits an offence under subsection (3) is liable on summary conviction to a fine not exceeding level 5 on the standard scale.

Information provisions

235 Power to require documents to be produced

(1) A person authorised in writing by a local housing authority may exercise the power conferred by subsection (2) in relation to documents reasonably required by the authority—

    (a)   for any purpose connected with the exercise of any of the authority's functions under any of Parts 1 to 4 in relation to any premises, or

    (b)   for the purpose of investigating whether any offence has been committed under any of those Parts in relation to any premises.

(2) A person so authorised may give a notice to a relevant person requiring him—

    (a)   to produce any documents which—

        (i)   are specified or described in the notice, or fall within a category of document which is specified or described in the notice, and

        (ii)   are in his custody or under his control, and

    (b)   to produce them at a time and place so specified and to a person so specified.

(3) The notice must include information about the possible consequences of not complying with the notice.

(4) The person to whom any document is produced in accordance with the notice may copy the document.

(5) No person may be required under this section to produce any document which he would be entitled to refuse to provide in proceedings in the High Court on grounds of legal professional privilege.

(6) In this section "document" includes information recorded otherwise than in legible form, and in relation to information so recorded, any reference to the production of a document is a reference to the production of a copy of the information in legible form.

(7) In this section "relevant person" means, in relation to any premises, a person within any of the following paragraphs—

    (a)   a person who is, or is proposed to be, the holder of a licence under Part 2 or 3 in respect of the premises, or a person on whom any obligation or restriction under such a licence is, or is proposed to be, imposed,

    (b)   a person who has an estate or interest in the premises,

    (c)   a person who is, or is proposing to be, managing or having control of the premises,

(d) a person who is, or is proposing to be, otherwise involved in the management of the premises,

(e) a person who occupies the premises.

236 Enforcement of powers to obtain information

(1) A person commits an offence if he fails to do anything required of him by a notice under section 235.

(2) In proceedings against a person for an offence under subsection (1) it is a defence that he had a reasonable excuse for failing to comply with the notice.

(3) A person who commits an offence under subsection (1) is liable on summary conviction to a fine not exceeding level 5 on the standard scale.

(4) A person commits an offence if he intentionally alters, suppresses or destroys any document which he has been required to produce by a notice under section 235.

(5) A person who commits an offence under subsection (4) is liable—

(a) on summary conviction, to a fine not exceeding the statutory maximum;

(b) on conviction on indictment, to a fine.

(6) In this section "document" includes information recorded otherwise than in legible form, and in relation to information so recorded—

(a) the reference to the production of a document is a reference to the production of a copy of the information in legible form, and

(b) the reference to suppressing a document includes a reference to destroying the means of reproducing the information.

237 Use of information obtained for certain other statutory purposes

(1) A local housing authority may use any information to which this section applies—

(a) for any purpose connected with the exercise of any of the authority's functions under any of Parts 1 to 4 in relation to any premises, or

(b) for the purpose of investigating whether any offence has been committed under any of those Parts in relation to any premises.

(2) This section applies to any information which has been obtained by the authority in the exercise of functions under—

(a) section 134 of the Social Security Administration Act 1992 (c 5) (housing benefit), or

(b) Part 1 of the Local Government Finance Act 1992 (c 14) (council tax).

238 False or misleading information

(1) A person commits an offence if—

   (a)   he supplies any information to a local housing authority in connection with any of their functions under any of Parts 1 to 4 or this Part,

   (b)   the information is false or misleading, and

   (c)   he knows that it is false or misleading or is reckless as to whether it is false or misleading.

(2) A person commits an offence if—

   (a)   he supplies any information to another person which is false or misleading,

   (b)   he knows that it is false or misleading or is reckless as to whether it is false or misleading, and

   (c)   he knows that the information is to be used for the purpose of supplying information to a local housing authority in connection with any of their functions under any of Parts 1 to 4 or this Part.

(3) A person who commits an offence under subsection (1) or (2) is liable on summary conviction to a fine not exceeding level 5 on the standard scale.

(4) In this section "false or misleading" means false or misleading in any material respect.

Enforcement

239 Powers of entry

(1) Subsection (3) applies where the local housing authority consider that a survey or examination of any premises is necessary and any of the following conditions is met—

   (a)   the authority consider that the survey or examination is necessary in order to carry out an inspection under section 4(1) or otherwise to determine whether any functions under any of Parts 1 to 4 or this Part should be exercised in relation to the premises;

   (b)   the premises are (within the meaning of Part 1) specified premises in relation to an improvement notice or prohibition order;

   (c)   a management order is in force under Chapter 1 or 2 of Part 4 in respect of the premises.

(2) Subsection (3) also applies where the proper officer of the local housing authority considers that a survey or examination of any premises is necessary in order to carry out an inspection under section 4(2).

(3) Where this subsection applies—

   (a)   a person authorised by the local housing authority (in a case within subsection (1)), or

   (b)   the proper officer (in a case within subsection (2)),

may enter the premises in question at any reasonable time for the purpose of carrying out a survey or examination of the premises.

(4) If—

(a) an interim or final management order is in force under Chapter 1 of Part 4 in respect of any premises consisting of part of a house ("the relevant premises"), and

(b) another part of the house is excluded from the order by virtue of section 102(8) or 113(7),

the power of entry conferred by subsection (3) is exercisable in relation to any premises comprised in that other part so far as is necessary for the purpose of carrying out a survey or examination of the relevant premises.

(5) Before entering any premises in exercise of the power conferred by subsection (3), the authorised person or proper officer must have given at least 24 hours" notice of his intention to do so—

(a) to the owner of the premises (if known), and
(b) to the occupier (if any).

(6) Subsection (7) applies where the local housing authority consider that any premises need to be entered for the purpose of ascertaining whether an offence has been committed under section 72, 95 or 234(3).

(7) A person authorised by the local housing authority may enter the premises for that purpose—

(a) at any reasonable time, but
(b) without giving any prior notice as mentioned in subsection (5).

(8) A person exercising the power of entry conferred by subsection (3) or (7) may do such of the following as he thinks necessary for the purpose for which the power is being exercised—

(a) take other persons with him;
(b) take equipment or materials with him;
(c) take measurements or photographs or make recordings;
(d) leave recording equipment on the premises for later collection;
(e) take samples of any articles or substances found on the premises.

(9) An authorisation for the purposes of this section—

(a) must be in writing; and
(b) must state the particular purpose or purposes for which the entry is authorised.

(10) A person authorised for the purposes of this section must, if required to do so, produce his authorisation for inspection by the owner or any occupier of the premises or anyone acting on his behalf.

(11) If the premises are unoccupied or the occupier is temporarily absent, a person exercising the power of entry conferred by subsection (3) or (7) must leave the premises as effectively secured against trespassers as he found them.

(12) In this section "occupier", in relation to premises, means a person who occupies the premises, whether for residential or other purposes.

240   Warrant to authorise entry

(1) This section applies where a justice of the peace is satisfied, on a sworn information in writing, that admission to premises specified in the information is reasonably required for any of the purposes mentioned in subsection (2) by a person—

(a)   employed by, or

(b)   acting on the instructions of,

the local housing authority.

(2) The purposes are—

(a)   surveying or examining premises in order to carry out an inspection under section 4(1) or (2) or otherwise to determine whether any functions under any of Parts 1 to 4 or this Part should be exercised in relation to the premises;

(b)   surveying or examining premises—

(i)   which are (within the meaning of Part 1) specified premises in relation to an improvement notice or prohibition order, or

(ii)   in respect of which a management order is in force under Chapter 1 or 2 of Part 4;

(c)   ascertaining whether an offence has been committed under section 72, 95 or 234(3).

(3) The justice may by warrant under his hand authorise the person mentioned in subsection (1) to enter on the premises for such of those purposes as may be specified in the warrant.

(4) But the justice must not grant the warrant unless he is satisfied—

(a)   that admission to the premises has been sought in accordance with section 239(5) or (7) but has been refused;

(b)   that the premises are unoccupied or that the occupier is temporarily absent and it might defeat the purpose of the entry to await his return; or

(c)   that application for admission would defeat the purpose of the entry.

(5) The power of entry conferred by a warrant under this section includes power to enter by force (if necessary).

(6) Subsection (8) of section 239 applies to the person on whom that power is conferred as it applies to a person exercising the power of entry conferred by subsection (3) or (7) of that section.

(7) A warrant under this section must, if so required, be produced for inspection by the owner or any occupier of the premises or anyone acting on his behalf.

(8) If the premises are unoccupied or the occupier is temporarily absent, a person entering under the authority of a warrant under this section must leave the premises as effectively secured against trespassers as he found them.

(9) A warrant under this section continues in force until the purpose for which the entry is required is satisfied.

(10) In a case within section 239(4)(a) and (b), the powers conferred by this section are exercisable in relation to premises comprised in the excluded part of the house as well as in relation to the relevant premises.

(11) In this section "occupier", in relation to premises, means a person who occupies the premises, whether for residential or other purposes.

241 Penalty for obstruction

(1) A person who obstructs a relevant person in the performance of anything which, by virtue of any of Parts 1 to 4 or this Part, that person is required or authorised to do commits an offence.

(2) In proceedings against a person for an offence under subsection (1) it is a defence that he had a reasonable excuse for obstructing the relevant person.

(3) A person who commits an offence under subsection (1) is liable on summary conviction to a fine not exceeding level 4 on the standard scale.

(4) In this section "relevant person" means an officer of a local housing authority or any person authorised to enter premises by virtue of any of Parts 1 to 4 or section 239 or 240.

242 Additional notice requirements for protection of owners

(1) This section applies where an owner of premises gives a notice to the local housing authority for the purposes of this section informing them of his interest in the premises.

(2) The authority must give him notice of any action taken by them under any of Parts 1 to 4 or this Part in relation to the premises.

Authorisations

243 Authorisations for enforcement purposes etc

(1) This section applies to any authorisation given for the purposes of any of the following provisions—

(a) section 131 (management orders: power of entry to carry out work),
(b) section 235 (power to require documents to be produced),
(c) section 239 (powers of entry),
(d) paragraph 3(4) of Schedule 3 (improvement notices: power to enter to carry out work), and
(e) paragraph 25 of Schedule 7 (EDMOs: power of entry to carry out work).

(2) Any such authorisation must be given by the appropriate officer of the local housing authority.

(3) For the purposes of this section a person is an "appropriate officer" of a local housing authority, in relation to an authorisation given by the authority, if either—

    (a)   he is a deputy chief officer of the authority (within the meaning of section 2 of the Local Government and Housing Act 1989 (c 42)), and

    (b)   the duties of his post consist of or include duties relating to the exercise of the functions of the authority in connection with which the authorisation is given,

or he is an officer of the authority to whom such a deputy chief officer reports directly, or is directly accountable, as respects duties so relating.

Documents

244 Power to prescribe forms

(1) The appropriate national authority may by regulations prescribe the form of any notice, statement or other document which is required or authorised to be used under, or for the purposes of, this Act.

(2) The power conferred by this section is not exercisable where specific provision for prescribing the form of a document is made elsewhere in this Act.

245 Power to dispense with notices

(1) The appropriate national authority may dispense with the service of a notice which is required to be served by a local housing authority under this Act if satisfied that it is reasonable to do so.

(2) A dispensation may be given either before or after the time at which the notice is required to be served.

(3) A dispensation may be given either unconditionally or on such conditions (whether as to the service of other notices or otherwise) as the appropriate national authority considers appropriate.

(4) Before giving a dispensation under this section, the appropriate national authority shall, in particular, have regard to the need to ensure, so far as possible, that the interests of any person are not prejudiced by the dispensation.

246 Service of documents

(1) Subsection (2) applies where the local housing authority is, by virtue of any provision of Parts 1 to 4 or this Part, under a duty to serve a document on a person who, to the knowledge of the authority, is—

    (a)   a person having control of premises,
    (b)   a person managing premises, or
    (c)   a person having an estate or interest in premises,

or a person who (but for an interim or final management order under Chapter 1 of Part 4) would fall within paragraph (a) or (b).

(2) The local housing authority must take reasonable steps to identify the person or persons falling within the description in that provision.

(3) A person having an estate or interest in premises may for the purposes of any provision to which subsections (1) and (2) apply give notice to the local housing authority of his interest in the premises.

(4) The local housing authority must enter a notice under subsection (3) in its records.

(5) A document required or authorised by any of Parts 1 to 4 or this Part to be served on a person as—

    (a)   a person having control of premises,

    (b)   a person managing premises,

    (c)   a person having an estate or interest in premises, or

    (d)   a person who (but for an interim or final management order under Chapter 1 of Part 4) would fall within paragraph (a) or (b),

may, if it is not practicable after reasonable enquiry to ascertain the name or address of that person, be served in accordance with subsection (6).

(6) A person having such a connection with any premises as is mentioned in subsection (5)(a) to (d) is served in accordance with this subsection if—

    (a)   the document is addressed to him by describing his connection with the premises (naming them), and

    (b)   delivering the document to some person on the premises or, if there is no person on the premises to whom it can be delivered, by fixing it, or a copy of it, to some conspicuous part of the premises.

(7) Subsection (1)(c) or (5)(c) applies whether the provision requiring or authorising service of the document refers in terms to a person having an estate or interest in premises or instead refers to a class of person having such an estate or interest (such as owners, lessees or mortgagees).

(8) Where under any provision of Parts 1 to 4 or this Part a document is to be served on—

    (a)   the person having control of premises,

    (b)   the person managing premises, or

    (c)   the owner of premises,

and more than one person comes within the description in the provision, the document may be served on more than one of those persons.

(9) Section 233 of the Local Government Act 1972 (c 70) (service of notices by local authorities) applies in relation to the service of documents for any purposes of this Act by the authorities mentioned in section 261(2)(d) and (e) of this Act as if they were local authorities within the meaning of section 233.

(10) In this section—

    (a)   references to a person managing premises include references to a person authorised to permit persons to occupy premises; and

(b) references to serving include references to similar expressions (such as giving or sending).

(11) In this section—

"document" includes anything in writing;
"premises" means premises however defined.

247 Licences and other documents in electronic form

(1) A local housing authority may, subject to subsection (3), issue a licence to a person under Part 2 or 3 by transmitting the text of the licence to him by electronic means, provided the text—

(a) is received by him in legible form, and
(b) is capable of being used for subsequent reference.

(2) A local housing authority may, subject to subsection (3), serve a relevant document on a person by transmitting the text of the document to him in the way mentioned in subsection (1).

(3) The recipient, or the person on whose behalf the recipient receives the document, must have indicated to the local housing authority the recipient's willingness to receive documents transmitted in the form and manner used.

(4) An indication for the purposes of subsection (3)—

(a) must be given to the local housing authority in such manner as they may require;
(b) may be a general indication or one that is limited to documents of a particular description;
(c) must state the address to be used and must be accompanied by such other information as the local housing authority require for the making of the transmission; and
(d) may be modified or withdrawn at any time by a notice given to the local housing authority in such manner as they may require.

(5) In this section any reference to serving includes a reference to similar expressions (such as giving or sending).

(6) In this section—

"document" includes anything in writing; and
"relevant document" means any document which a local housing authority are, by virtue of any provision of Parts 1 to 4 or this Part, under a duty to serve on any person.

248 Timing and location of things done electronically

(1) The Secretary of State may by regulations make provision specifying, for the purposes of any of Parts 1 to 4 or this Part, the manner of determining—

(a) the times at which things done under any of Parts 1 to 4 or this Part by means of electronic communications networks are done;

(b)   the places at which things done under any of Parts 1 to 4 or this Part by means of such networks are done; and

(c)   the places at which things transmitted by means of such networks are received.

(2) The Secretary of State may by regulations make provision about the manner of proving in any legal proceedings—

(a)   that something done by means of an electronic communications network satisfies any requirements of any of Parts 1 to 4 or this Part for the doing of that thing; and

(b)   the matters mentioned in subsection (1)(a) to (c).

(3) Regulations under this section may provide for such presumptions to apply (whether conclusive or not) as the Secretary of State considers appropriate.

(4) In this section "electronic communications network" has the meaning given by section 32 of the Communications Act 2003 (c 21).

249 Proof of designations

(1) This subsection applies in respect of a copy of—

(a)   a designation under section 56 (designation of an area as subject to additional licensing), or

(b)   a designation under section 80 (designation of an area as subject to selective licensing),

which purports to be made by a local housing authority.

(2) A certificate endorsed on such a copy and purporting to be signed by the proper officer of the authority stating the matters set out in subsection (3) is prima facie evidence of the facts so stated without proof of the handwriting or official position of the person by whom it purports to be signed.

(3) Those matters are—

(a)   that the designation was made by the authority,

(b)   that the copy is a true copy of the designation, and

(c)   that the designation did not require confirmation by the confirming authority, or that on a specified date the designation was confirmed by the confirming authority.

Other supplementary provisions

250 Orders and regulations

(1) Any power of the Secretary of State or the National Assembly for Wales to make an order or regulations under this Act is exercisable by statutory instrument.

(2) Any power of the Secretary of State or the National Assembly for Wales to make an order or regulations under this Act—

   (a)   may be exercised so as to make different provision for different cases or descriptions of case or different purposes or areas; and

   (b)   includes power to make such incidental, supplementary, consequential, transitory, transitional or saving provision as the Secretary of State or (as the case may be) the National Assembly for Wales considers appropriate.

(3) The Secretary of State must consult the National Assembly for Wales before making any regulations under Part 5 which relate to residential properties in Wales.

(4) Subject to subsections (5) and (6), any order or regulations made by the Secretary of State under this Act are to be subject to annulment in pursuance of a resolution of either House of Parliament.

(5) Subsection (4) does not apply to any order under section 270 or paragraph 3 of Schedule 10.

(6) Subsection (4) also does not apply to—

   (a)   any order under section 55(3) which makes the provision authorised by section 55(4),

   (b)   any order under section 80(5) or (7),

   (c)   any order under section 216 or 229(3),

   (d)   any order under section 265(2) which modifies any provision of an Act,

   (e)   any regulations under section 254(6),

   (f)   any regulations under paragraph 3 of Schedule 4 or orders under paragraph 11 of Schedule 10, or

   (g)   any regulations made by virtue of paragraph 11(3)(b) or 12(3)(b) of Schedule 13;

and no such order or regulations may be made by the Secretary of State (whether alone or with other provisions) unless a draft of the statutory instrument containing the order or regulations has been laid before, and approved by a resolution of, each House of Parliament.

(7) In this Act "modify", in the context of a power to modify an enactment by order or regulations, includes repeal (and "modifications" has a corresponding meaning).

251   Offences by bodies corporate

(1) Where an offence under this Act committed by a body corporate is proved to have been committed with the consent or connivance of, or to be attributable to any neglect on the part of—

   (a)   a director, manager, secretary or other similar officer of the body corporate, or

   (b)   a person purporting to act in such a capacity,

he as well as the body corporate commits the offence and is liable to be proceeded against and punished accordingly.

(2) Where the affairs of a body corporate are managed by its members, subsection (1) applies in relation to the acts and defaults of a member in connection with his functions of management as if he were a director of the body corporate.

252 Power to up-rate level of fines for certain offences

(1) Subsection (2) applies if the Secretary of State considers that there has been a change in the value of money since the relevant date.

(2) The Secretary of State may by order substitute for the sum or sums for the time being specified in any provision mentioned in subsection (3) such other sum or sums as he considers to be justified by the change.

(3) The provisions are—

    (a)   section 32(2)(b);
    (b)   section 35(6);
    (c)   section 72(6); and
    (d)   section 95(5).

(4) In subsection (1) "the relevant date" means—

    (a)   the date of the passing of this Act; or
    (b)   where the sums specified in a provision mentioned in subsection (3) have been substituted by an order under subsection (2), the date of that order.

(5) Nothing in an order under subsection (2) affects the punishment for an offence committed before the order comes into force.

253 Local inquiries

The appropriate national authority may, for the purposes of the execution of any of the authority's functions under this Act, cause such local inquiries to be held as the authority considers appropriate.

Meaning of "house in multiple occupation"

254 Meaning of "house in multiple occupation"

(1) For the purposes of this Act a building or a part of a building is a "house in multiple occupation" if—

    (a)   it meets the conditions in subsection (2) ("the standard test");
    (b)   it meets the conditions in subsection (3) ("the self-contained flat test");
    (c)   it meets the conditions in subsection (4) ("the converted building test");
    (d)   an HMO declaration is in force in respect of it under section 255; or
    (e)   it is a converted block of flats to which section 257 applies.

(2) A building or a part of a building meets the standard test if—

(a) it consists of one or more units of living accommodation not consisting of a self-contained flat or flats;

(b) the living accommodation is occupied by persons who do not form a single household (see section 258);

(c) the living accommodation is occupied by those persons as their only or main residence or they are to be treated as so occupying it (see section 259);

(d) their occupation of the living accommodation constitutes the only use of that accommodation;

(e) rents are payable or other consideration is to be provided in respect of at least one of those persons" occupation of the living accommodation; and

(f) two or more of the households who occupy the living accommodation share one or more basic amenities or the living accommodation is lacking in one or more basic amenities.

(3) A part of a building meets the self-contained flat test if—

(a) it consists of a self-contained flat; and

(b) paragraphs (b) to (f) of subsection (2) apply (reading references to the living accommodation concerned as references to the flat).

(4) A building or a part of a building meets the converted building test if—

(a) it is a converted building;

(b) it contains one or more units of living accommodation that do not consist of a self-contained flat or flats (whether or not it also contains any such flat or flats);

(c) the living accommodation is occupied by persons who do not form a single household (see section 258);

(d) the living accommodation is occupied by those persons as their only or main residence or they are to be treated as so occupying it (see section 259);

(e) their occupation of the living accommodation constitutes the only use of that accommodation; and

(f) rents are payable or other consideration is to be provided in respect of at least one of those persons" occupation of the living accommodation.

(5) But for any purposes of this Act (other than those of Part 1) a building or part of a building within subsection (1) is not a house in multiple occupation if it is listed in Schedule 14.

(6) The appropriate national authority may by regulations—

(a) make such amendments of this section and sections 255 to 259 as the authority considers appropriate with a view to securing that any building or part of a building of a description specified in the regulations is or is not to be a house in multiple occupation for any specified purposes of this Act;

(b) provide for such amendments to have effect also for the purposes of definitions in other enactments that operate by reference to this Act;

    (c)   make such consequential amendments of any provision of this Act, or any other enactment, as the authority considers appropriate.

(7) Regulations under subsection (6) may frame any description by reference to any matters or circumstances whatever.

(8) In this section—

    "basic amenities" means—
        (a)   a toilet,
        (b)   personal washing facilities, or
        (c)   cooking facilities;

    "converted building" means a building or part of a building consisting of living accommodation in which one or more units of such accommodation have been created since the building or part was constructed;
    "enactment" includes an enactment comprised in subordinate legislation (within the meaning of the Interpretation Act 1978 (c 30);
    "self-contained flat" means a separate set of premises (whether or not on the same floor)—
        (a)   which forms part of a building;
        (b)   either the whole or a material part of which lies above or below some other part of the building; and
        (c)   in which all three basic amenities are available for the exclusive use of its occupants.

255 HMO declarations

(1) If a local housing authority are satisfied that subsection (2) applies to a building or part of a building in their area, they may serve a notice under this section (an "HMO declaration") declaring the building or part to be a house in multiple occupation.

(2) This subsection applies to a building or part of a building if the building or part meets any of the following tests (as it applies without the sole use condition)—

    (a)   the standard test (see section 254(2)),
    (b)   the self-contained flat test (see section 254(3)), or
    (c)   the converted building test (see section 254(4)),

and the occupation, by persons who do not form a single household, of the living accommodation or flat referred to in the test in question constitutes a significant use of that accommodation or flat.

(3) In subsection (2) "the sole use condition" means the condition contained in—

    (a)   section 254(2)(d) (as it applies for the purposes of the standard test or the self-contained flat test), or
    (b)   section 254(4)(e),

as the case may be.

(4) The notice must—

- (a) state the date of the authority's decision to serve the notice,
- (b) be served on each relevant person within the period of seven days beginning with the date of that decision,
- (c) state the day on which it will come into force if no appeal is made under subsection (9) against the authority's decision, and
- (d) set out the right to appeal against the decision under subsection (9) and the period within which an appeal may be made.

(5) The day stated in the notice under subsection (4)(c) must be not less than 28 days after the date of the authority's decision to serve the notice.

(6) If no appeal is made under subsection (9) before the end of that period of 28 days, the notice comes into force on the day stated in the notice.

(7) If such an appeal is made before the end of that period of 28 days, the notice does not come into force unless and until a decision is given on the appeal which confirms the notice and either—

- (a) the period within which an appeal to the Lands Tribunal may be brought expires without such an appeal having been brought, or
- (b) if an appeal to the Lands Tribunal is brought, a decision is given on the appeal which confirms the notice.

(8) For the purposes of subsection (7), the withdrawal of an appeal has the same effect as a decision which confirms the notice appealed against.

(9) Any relevant person may appeal to a residential property tribunal against a decision of the local housing authority to serve an HMO declaration.

The appeal must be made within the period of 28 days beginning with the date of the authority's decision.

(10) Such an appeal—

- (a) is to be by way of a re-hearing, but
- (b) may be determined having regard to matters of which the authority were unaware.

(11) The tribunal may—

- (a) confirm or reverse the decision of the authority, and
- (b) if it reverses the decision, revoke the HMO declaration.

(12) In this section and section 256 "relevant person", in relation to an HMO declaration, means any person who, to the knowledge of the local housing authority, is—

- (a) a person having an estate or interest in the building or part of the building concerned (but is not a tenant under a lease with an unexpired term of 3 years of less), or
- (b) a person managing or having control of that building or part (and not falling within paragraph (a)).

256 Revocation of HMO declarations

(1) A local housing authority may revoke an HMO declaration served under section 255 at any time if they consider that subsection (2) of that section no longer applies to the building or part of the building in respect of which the declaration was served.

(2) The power to revoke an HMO declaration is exercisable by the authority either—

    (a)   on an application made by a relevant person, or

    (b)   on the authority's own initiative.

(3) If, on an application by such a person, the authority decide not to revoke the HMO declaration, they must without delay serve on him a notice informing him of—

    (a)   the decision,

    (b)   the reasons for it and the date on which it was made,

    (c)   the right to appeal against it under subsection (4), and

    (d)   the period within which an appeal may be made under that subsection.

(4) A person who applies to a local housing authority for the revocation of an HMO declaration under subsection (1) may appeal to a residential property tribunal against a decision of the authority to refuse to revoke the notice.

The appeal must be made within the period of 28 days beginning with the date specified under subsection (3) as the date on which the decision was made.

(5) Such an appeal—

    (a)   is to be by way of a re-hearing, but

    (b)   may be determined having regard to matters of which the authority were unaware.

(6) The tribunal may—

    (a)   confirm or reverse the decision of the authority, and

    (b)   if it reverses the decision, revoke the HMO declaration.

257 HMOs: certain converted blocks of flats

(1) For the purposes of this section a "converted block of flats" means a building or part of a building which—

    (a)   has been converted into, and

    (b)   consists of,

self-contained flats.

(2) This section applies to a converted block of flats if—

    (a)   building work undertaken in connection with the conversion did not comply with the appropriate building standards and still does not comply with them; and

    (b)   less than two-thirds of the self-contained flats are owner-occupied.

(3) In subsection (2) "appropriate building standards" means—

    (a)   in the case of a converted block of flats—

        (i)   on which building work was completed before 1st June 1992 or which is dealt with by regulation 20 of the Building Regulations 1991 (SI 1991/2768), and

        (ii)   which would not have been exempt under those Regulations,

    building standards equivalent to those imposed, in relation to a building or part of a building to which those Regulations applied, by those Regulations as they had effect on 1st June 1992; and

    (b)   in the case of any other converted block of flats, the requirements imposed at the time in relation to it by regulations under section 1 of the Building Act 1984 (c 55).

(4) For the purposes of subsection (2) a flat is "owner-occupied" if it is occupied—

    (a)   by a person who has a lease of the flat which has been granted for a term of more than 21 years,

    (b)   by a person who has the freehold estate in the converted block of flats, or

    (c)   by a member of the household of a person within paragraph (a) or (b).

(5) The fact that this section applies to a converted block of flats (with the result that it is a house in multiple occupation under section 254(1)(e)), does not affect the status of any flat in the block as a house in multiple occupation.

(6) In this section "self-contained flat" has the same meaning as in section 254.

258   HMOs: persons not forming a single household

(1) This section sets out when persons are to be regarded as not forming a single household for the purposes of section 254.

(2) Persons are to be regarded as not forming a single household unless—

    (a)   they are all members of the same family, or

    (b)   their circumstances are circumstances of a description specified for the purposes of this section in regulations made by the appropriate national authority.

(3) For the purposes of subsection (2)(a) a person is a member of the same family as another person if—

    (a)   those persons are married to each other or live together as husband and wife (or in an equivalent relationship in the case of persons of the same sex);

    (b)   one of them is a relative of the other; or

    (c)   one of them is, or is a relative of, one member of a couple and the other is a relative of the other member of the couple.

(4) For those purposes—

(a) a "couple" means two persons who are married to each other or otherwise fall within subsection (3)(a);

(b) "relative" means parent, grandparent, child, grandchild, brother, sister, uncle, aunt, nephew, niece or cousin;

(c) a relationship of the half-blood shall be treated as a relationship of the whole blood; and

(d) the stepchild of a person shall be treated as his child.

(5) Regulations under subsection (2)(b) may, in particular, secure that a group of persons are to be regarded as forming a single household only where (as the regulations may require) each member of the group has a prescribed relationship, or at least one of a number of prescribed relationships, to any one or more of the others.

(6) In subsection (5) "prescribed relationship" means any relationship of a description specified in the regulations.

259   HMOs: persons treated as occupying premises as only or main residence

(1) This section sets out when persons are to be treated for the purposes of section 254 as occupying a building or part of a building as their only or main residence.

(2) A person is to be treated as so occupying a building or part of a building if it is occupied by the person—

(a) as the person's residence for the purpose of undertaking a full-time course of further or higher education;

(b) as a refuge, or

(c) in any other circumstances which are circumstances of a description specified for the purposes of this section in regulations made by the appropriate national authority.

(3) In subsection (2)(b) "refuge" means a building or part of a building managed by a voluntary organisation and used wholly or mainly for the temporary accommodation of persons who have left their homes as a result of—

(a) physical violence or mental abuse, or

(b) threats of such violence or abuse,

from persons to whom they are or were married or with whom they are or were co-habiting.

260   HMOs: presumption that sole use condition or significant use condition is met

(1) Where a question arises in any proceedings as to whether either of the following is met in respect of a building or part of a building—

(a) the sole use condition, or

(b) the significant use condition,

it shall be presumed, for the purposes of the proceedings, that the condition is met unless the contrary is shown.

(2) In this section—

    (a)   "the sole use condition" means the condition contained in—

        (i)   section 254(2)(d) (as it applies for the purposes of the standard test or the self-contained flat test), or

        (ii)   section 254(4)(e),

    as the case may be; and

    (b)   "the significant use condition" means the condition contained in section 255(2) that the occupation of the living accommodation or flat referred to in that provision by persons who do not form a single household constitutes a significant use of that accommodation or flat.

Other general interpretation provisions

261 Meaning of "appropriate national authority", "local housing authority" etc

(1) In this Act "the appropriate national authority" means—

    (a)   in relation to England, the Secretary of State; and

    (b)   in relation to Wales, the National Assembly for Wales.

(2) In this Act "local housing authority" means, in relation to England—

    (a)   a unitary authority;

    (b)   a district council so far as it is not a unitary authority;

    (c)   a London borough council;

    (d)   the Common Council of the City of London (in its capacity as a local authority);

    (e)   the Sub-Treasurer of the Inner Temple or the Under-Treasurer of the Middle Temple (in his capacity as a local authority); and

    (f)   the Council of the Isles of Scilly.

(3) In subsection (2) "unitary authority" means—

    (a)   the council of a county so far as it is the council for an area for which there are no district councils;

    (b)   the council of any district comprised in an area for which there is no county council.

(4) In this Act "local housing authority" means, in relation to Wales, a county council or a county borough council.

(5) References in this Act to "the local housing authority", in relation to land, are to the local housing authority in whose district the land is situated.

(6) References in this Act to the district of a local housing authority are to the area of the council concerned, that is to say—

    (a)   in the case of a unitary authority, the area or district;

(b)   in the case of a district council so far as it is not a unitary authority, the district;

(c)   in the case of an authority within subsection (2)(c) to (f), the London borough, the City of London, the Inner or Middle Temple or the Isles of Scilly (as the case may be); and

(d)   in the case of a Welsh county council or a county borough council, the Welsh county or county borough.

(7) Section 618 of the Housing Act 1985 (c 68) (committees and members of Common Council of City of London) applies in relation to this Act as it applies in relation to that Act.

262   Meaning of "lease", "tenancy", "occupier" and "owner" etc

(1) In this Act "lease" and "tenancy" have the same meaning.

(2) Both expressions include—

(a)   a sub-lease or sub-tenancy; and

(b)   an agreement for a lease or tenancy (or sub-lease or sub-tenancy).

And see sections 108 and 117 and paragraphs 3 and 11 of Schedule 7 (which also extend the meaning of references to leases).

(3) The expressions "lessor" and "lessee" and "landlord" and "tenant" and references to letting, to the grant of a lease or to covenants or terms, are to be construed accordingly.

(4) In this Act "lessee" includes a statutory tenant of the premises; and references to a lease or to a person to whom premises are let are to be construed accordingly.

(5) In this Act any reference to a person who is a tenant under a lease with an unexpired term of 3 years or less includes a statutory tenant as well as a tenant under a yearly or other periodic tenancy.

(6) In this Act "occupier", in relation to premises, means a person who—

(a)   occupies the premises as a residence, and

(b)   (subject to the context) so occupies them whether as a tenant or other person having an estate or interest in the premises or as a licensee;

and related expressions are to be construed accordingly.

This subsection does not apply for the purposes of Part 5 and has effect subject to any other provision defining "occupier" for any purposes of this Act.

(7) In this Act "owner", in relation to premises—

(a)   means a person (other than a mortgagee not in possession) who is for the time being entitled to dispose of the fee simple of the premises whether in possession or in reversion; and

(b)   includes also a person holding or entitled to the rents and profits of the premises under a lease of which the unexpired term exceeds 3 years.

(8) In this Act "person having an estate or interest", in relation to premises, includes a statutory tenant of the premises.

(9) In this Act "licence", in the context of a licence to occupy premises—

    (a)   includes a licence which is not granted for a consideration, but

    (b)   excludes a licence granted as a temporary expedient to a person who entered the premises as a trespasser (whether or not, before the grant of the licence, another licence to occupy those or other premises had been granted to him);

and related expressions are to be construed accordingly.

And see sections 108 and 117 and paragraphs 3 and 11 of Schedule 7 (which also extend the meaning of references to licences).

263 Meaning of "person having control" and "person managing" etc

(1) In this Act "person having control", in relation to premises, means (unless the context otherwise requires) the person who receives the rack-rent of the premises (whether on his own account or as agent or trustee of another person), or who would so receive it if the premises were let at a rack-rent.

[(1A) Subsection (1) does not apply to any reference in Parts 2 or 4 to "person having control" where the reference relates to a person having control of a section 257 HMO.

(1B) Any reference in Part 4 to a person having control in respect of a section 257 HMO has the same meaning as in section 61(7).]

(2) In subsection (1) "rack-rent" means a rent which is not less than two-thirds of the full net annual value of the premises.

(3) In this Act "person managing" means, in relation to premises, the person who, being an owner or lessee of the premises—

    (a)   receives (whether directly or through an agent or trustee) rents or other payments from—

        (i)   in the case of a house in multiple occupation, persons who are in occupation as tenants or licensees of parts of the premises; and

        (ii)   in the case of a house to which Part 3 applies (see section 79(2)), persons who are in occupation as tenants or licensees of parts of the premises, or of the whole of the premises; or

    (b)   would so receive those rents or other payments but for having entered into an arrangement (whether in pursuance of a court order or otherwise) with another person who is not an owner or lessee of the premises by virtue of which that other person receives the rents or other payments;

and includes, where those rents or other payments are received through another person as agent or trustee, that other person.

(4) In its application to Part 1, subsection (3) has effect with the omission of paragraph (a)(ii).

(5) References in this Act to any person involved in the management of a house in multiple occupation or a house to which Part 3 applies (see section 79(2)) include references to the person managing it.

Amendment—Subs (1) modified, in relation to a house in multiple occupation to which s 257 hereof applies, by the Houses in Multiple Occupation (Certain Converted Blocks of Flats) (Modifications to the Housing Act 2004 and Transitional Provisions for section 257 HMOs) (England) Regulations 2007, SI 2007/1904, reg 12.

264 Calculation of numbers of persons

(1) The appropriate national authority may prescribe rules with respect to the calculation of numbers of persons for the purposes of—

(a) any provision made by or under this Act which is specified in the rules, or

(b) any order or licence made or granted under this Act of any description which is so specified.

(2) The rules may provide—

(a) for persons under a particular age to be disregarded for the purposes of any such calculation;

(b) for persons under a particular age to be treated as constituting a fraction of a person for the purposes of any such calculation.

(3) The rules may be prescribed by order or regulations.

Final provisions

265 Minor and consequential amendments

(1) Schedule 15 (which contains minor and consequential amendments) has effect.

(2) The Secretary of State may by order make such supplementary, incidental or consequential provision as he considers appropriate—

(a) for the general purposes, or any particular purpose, of this Act; or

(b) in consequence of any provision made by or under this Act or for giving full effect to it.

(3) An order under subsection (2) may modify any enactment (including this Act).

"Enactment" includes an enactment comprised in subordinate legislation (within the meaning of the Interpretation Act 1978 (c 30)).

(4) The power conferred by subsection (2) is also exercisable by the National Assembly for Wales in relation to provision dealing with matters with respect to which functions are exercisable by the Assembly.

(5) Nothing in this Act affects the generality of the power conferred by this section.

266 Repeals

Schedule 16 (which contains repeals) has effect.

267 Devolution: Wales

In Schedule 1 to the National Assembly for Wales (Transfer of Functions) Order 1999 (SI 1999/672) references to the following Acts are to be treated as references to those Acts as amended by virtue of this Act—

    (a)   the Housing Act 1985 (c 68);

    (b)   the Housing Act 1988 (c 50);

    (c)   the Housing Act 1996 (c 52).

268 The Isles of Scilly

(1) This Secretary of State may by order provide that, in its application to the Isles of Scilly, this Act is have effect with such modifications as are specified in the order.

(2) Where a similar power is exercisable under another Act in relation to provisions of that Act which are amended by this Act, the power is exercisable in relation to those provisions as so amended.

269 Expenses

There shall be paid out of money provided by Parliament—

    (a)   any expenditure incurred by the Secretary of State by virtue of this Act;

    (b)   any increase attributable to this Act in the sums payable out of money so provided under any other enactment.

270 Short title, commencement and extent

(1) This Act may be cited as the Housing Act 2004.

(2) The following provisions come into force on the day on which this Act is passed—

    (a)   sections 2, 9, 161 to 164, 176, 190, 208, 216, 233, 234, 244, 248, 250, 252, 264, 265(2) to (5), 267 to 269 and this section, and

    (b)   any other provision of this Act so far as it confers any power to make an order or regulations which is exercisable by the Secretary of State or the National Assembly for Wales.

Subsections (3) to (7) have effect subject to paragraph (b).

(3) The following provisions come into force at the end of the period of two months beginning with the day on which this Act is passed—

    (a)   sections 180, 182 to 189, 195 to 207, 209 to 211, 217, 218, 219, 222, 224, 245 to 247, 249, 251 and 253 to 263,

    (b)   Schedule 9,

    (c)   Schedule 11, except paragraphs 15 and 16, and

(d)   Schedule 14.

(4) The provisions listed in subsection (5) come into force—

    (a)   where they are to come into force in relation only to Wales, on such day as the National Assembly for Wales may by order appoint, and

    (b)   otherwise, on such day as the Secretary of State may by order appoint.

(5) The provisions referred to in subsection (4) are—

    (a)   Part 1 (other than sections 2 and 9),

    (b)   Parts 2 to 4,

    (c)   sections 179, 181, 191 to 194, 212 to 215, 220, 221, 223, 225, 226, 227, 229 to 232, 235 to 243, 265(1) and 266,

    (d)   Schedule 10,

    (e)   paragraphs 15 and 16 of Schedule 11, and

    (f)   Schedules 13, 15 and 16.

(6) Part 5 (other than sections 161 to 164 and 176) comes into force on such day as the Secretary of State may by order appoint.

(7) Section 228 and Schedule 12 come into force on such day as the National Assembly for Wales may by order appoint.

(8) Different days may be appointed for different purposes or different areas under subsection (4), (6) or (7).

(9) The Secretary of State may by order make such provision as he considers necessary or expedient for transitory, transitional or saving purposes in connection with the coming into force of any provision of this Act.

(10) The power conferred by subsection (9) is also exercisable by the National Assembly for Wales in relation to provision dealing with matters with respect to which functions are exercisable by the Assembly

(11) Subject to subsections (12) and (13), this Act extends to England and Wales only.

(12) Any amendment or repeal made by this Act has the same extent as the enactment to which it relates, except that any amendment or repeal in—

    the Mobile Homes Act 1983 (c 34), or
    the Crime and Disorder Act 1998 (c 37),
      extends to England and Wales only.

(13) This section extends to the whole of the United Kingdom.

Schedule 1
Procedue and Appeals Relating to Improvement Notices

Section 18

PART 1
SERVICE OF IMPROVEMENT NOTICES

Service of improvement notices: premises licensed under Part 2 or 3

1

(1) This paragraph applies where the specified premises in the case of an improvement notice are—

(a)   a dwelling which is licensed under Part 3 of this Act, or
(b)   an HMO which is licensed under Part 2 or 3 of this Act.

(2) The local housing authority must serve the notice on the holder of the licence under that Part.

Service of improvement notices: premises which are neither licensed under Part 2 or 3 nor flats

2

(1) This paragraph applies where the specified premises in the case of an improvement notice are—

(a)   a dwelling which is not licensed under Part 3 of this Act, or
(b)   an HMO which is not licensed under Part 2 or 3 of this Act,

and which (in either case) is not a flat.

(2) The local housing authority must serve the notice—

(a)   (in the case of a dwelling) on the person having control of the dwelling;
(b)   (in the case of an HMO) either on the person having control of the HMO or on the person managing it.

Service of improvement notices: flats which are not licensed under Part 2 or 3

3

(1) This paragraph applies where any specified premises in the case of an improvement notice are—

(a)   a dwelling which is not licensed under Part 3 of this Act, or
(b)   an HMO which is not licensed under Part 2 or 3 of this Act,

and which (in either case) is a flat.

(2) In the case of dwelling which is a flat, the local housing authority must serve the notice on a person who—

(a) is an owner of the flat, and

(b) in the authority's opinion ought to take the action specified in the notice.

(3) In the case of an HMO which is a flat, the local housing authority must serve the notice either on a person who—

(a) is an owner of the flat, and

(b) in the authority's opinion ought to take the action specified in the notice,

or on the person managing the flat.

Service of improvement notices: common parts

4

(1) This paragraph applies where any specified premises in the case of an improvement notice are—

(a) common parts of a building containing one or more flats; or

(b) any part of such a building which does not consist of residential premises.

(2) The local housing authority must serve the notice on a person who—

(a) is an owner of the specified premises concerned, and

(b) in the authority's opinion ought to take the action specified in the notice.

(3) For the purposes of this paragraph a person is an owner of any common parts of a building if he is an owner of the building or part of the building concerned, or (in the case of external common parts) of the particular premises in which the common parts are comprised.

Service of copies of improvement notices

5

(1) In addition to serving an improvement notice in accordance with any of paragraphs 1 to 4, the local housing authority must serve a copy of the notice on every other person who, to their knowledge—

(a) has a relevant interest in any specified premises, or

(b) is an occupier of any such premises.

(2) A "relevant interest" means an interest as freeholder, mortgagee or lessee.

(3) For the purposes of this paragraph a person has a relevant interest in any common parts of a building if he has a relevant interest in the building or part of the building concerned, or (in the case of external common parts) in the particular premises in which the common parts are comprised.

(4) The copies required to be served under sub-paragraph (1) must be served within the period of seven days beginning with the day on which the notice is served.

PART 2
SERVICE OF NOTICES RELATING TO REVOCATION OR VARIATION OF IMPROVEMENT NOTICES

Notice of revocation or variation

6

(1) This paragraph applies where the local housing authority decide to revoke or vary an improvement notice.

(2) The authority must serve—

    (a)   a notice under this paragraph, and

    (b)   copies of that notice,

on the persons on whom they would be required under Part 1 of this Schedule to serve an improvement notice and copies of it in respect of the specified premises.

(3) Sub-paragraph (4) applies if, in so doing, the authority serve a notice under this paragraph on a person who is not the person on whom the improvement notice was served ("the original recipient").

(4) The authority must serve a copy of the notice under this paragraph on the original recipient unless they consider that it would not be appropriate to do so.

(5) The documents required to be served under sub-paragraph (2) must be served within the period of seven days beginning with the day on which the decision is made.

7

A notice under paragraph 6 must set out—

    (a)   the authority's decision to revoke or vary the improvement notice;

    (b)   the reasons for the decision and the date on which it was made;

    (c)   if the decision is to vary the notice—

        (i)   the right of appeal against the decision under Part 3 of this Schedule, and

        (ii) the period within which an appeal may be made (see paragraph 14(2)).

Notice of refusal to revoke or vary notice

8

(1) This paragraph applies where the local housing authority refuse to revoke or vary an improvement notice.

(2) The authority must serve—

   (a)   a notice under this paragraph, and
   (b)   copies of that notice,

on the persons on whom they would be required to serve an improvement notice and copies of it under Part 1 of this Schedule.

(3) Sub-paragraph (4) applies if, in so doing, the authority serve a notice under this paragraph on a person who is not the person on whom the improvement notice was served ("the original recipient").

(4) The authority must serve a copy of the notice under this paragraph on the original recipient unless they consider that it would not be appropriate to do so.

(5) The documents required to be served under sub-paragraph (2) must be served within the period of seven days beginning with the day on which the decision is made.

9

A notice under paragraph 8 must set out—

   (a)   the authority's decision not to revoke or vary the improvement notice;
   (b)   the reasons for the decision and the date on which it was made;
   (c)   the right of appeal against the decision under Part 3 of this Schedule; and
   (d)   the period within which an appeal may be made (see paragraph 14(2)).

PART 3
APPEALS RELATING TO IMPROVEMENT NOTICES

Appeal against improvement notice

10

(1) The person on whom an improvement notice is served may appeal to a residential property tribunal against the notice.

(2) Paragraphs 11 and 12 set out two specific grounds on which an appeal may be made under this paragraph, but they do not affect the generality of sub-paragraph (1).

11

(1) An appeal may be made by a person under paragraph 10 on the ground that one or more other persons, as an owner or owners of the specified premises, ought to—

   (a)   take the action concerned, or
   (b)   pay the whole or part of the cost of taking that action.

(2) Where the grounds on which an appeal is made under paragraph 10 consist of or include the ground mentioned in sub-paragraph (1), the appellant must serve a copy of his notice of appeal on the other person or persons concerned.

12

(1) An appeal may be made by a person under paragraph 10 on the ground that one of the courses of action mentioned in sub-paragraph (2) is the best course of action in relation to the hazard in respect of which the notice was served.

(2) The courses of action are—

(a)   making a prohibition order under section 20 or 21 of this Act;

(b)   serving a hazard awareness notice under section 28 or 29 of this Act; and

(c)   making a demolition order under section 265 of the Housing Act 1985 (c 68).

Appeal against decision relating to variation or revocation of improvement notice

13

(1) The relevant person may appeal to a residential property tribunal against—

(a)   a decision by the local housing authority to vary an improvement notice, or

(b)   a decision by the authority to refuse to revoke or vary an improvement notice.

(2) In sub-paragraph (1) "the relevant person" means—

(a)   in relation to a decision within paragraph (a) of that provision, the person on whom the notice was served;

(b)   in relation to a decision within paragraph (b) of that provision, the person who applied for the revocation or variation.

Time limit for appeal

14

(1) Any appeal under paragraph 10 must be made within the period of 21 days beginning with the date on which the improvement notice was served in accordance with Part 1 of this Schedule.

(2) Any appeal under paragraph 13 must be made within the period of 28 days beginning with the date specified in the notice under paragraph 6 or 8 as the date on which the decision concerned was made.

(3) A residential property tribunal may allow an appeal to be made to it after the end of the period mentioned in sub-paragraph (1) or (2) if it is satisfied that

there is a good reason for the failure to appeal before the end of that period (and for any delay since then in applying for permission to appeal out of time).

Powers of residential property tribunal on appeal under paragraph 10

15

(1) This paragraph applies to an appeal to a residential property tribunal under paragraph 10.

(2) The appeal—

(a)   is to be by way of a re-hearing, but

(b)   may be determined having regard to matters of which the authority were unaware.

(3) The tribunal may by order confirm, quash or vary the improvement notice.

(4) Paragraphs 16 and 17 make special provision in connection with the grounds of appeal set out in paragraphs 11 and 12.

16

(1) This paragraph applies where the grounds of appeal consist of or include that set out in paragraph 11.

(2) On the hearing of the appeal the tribunal may—

(a)   vary the improvement notice so as to require the action to be taken by any owner mentioned in the notice of appeal in accordance with paragraph 11; or

(b)   make such order as it considers appropriate with respect to the payment to be made by any such owner to the appellant or, where the action is taken by the local housing authority, to the authority.

(3) In the exercise of its powers under sub-paragraph (2), the tribunal must take into account, as between the appellant and any such owner—

(a)   their relative interests in the premises concerned (considering both the nature of the interests and the rights and obligations arising under or by virtue of them);

(b)   their relative responsibility for the state of the premises which gives rise to the need for the taking of the action concerned; and

(c)   the relative degree of benefit to be derived from the taking of the action concerned.

(4) Sub-paragraph (5) applies where, by virtue of the exercise of the tribunal's powers under sub-paragraph (2), a person other than the appellant is required to take the action specified in an improvement notice.

(5) So long as that other person remains an owner of the premises to which the notice relates, he is to be regarded for the purposes of this Part as the person on whom the notice was served (in place of any other person).

17

(1) This paragraph applies where the grounds of appeal consist of or include that set out in paragraph 12.

(2) When deciding whether one of the courses of action mentioned in paragraph 12(2) is the best course of action in relation to a particular hazard, the tribunal must have regard to any guidance given to the local housing authority under section 9.

(3) Sub-paragraph (4) applies where—

    (a)   an appeal under paragraph 10 is allowed against an improvement notice in respect of a particular hazard; and

    (b)   the reason, or one of the reasons, for allowing the appeal is that one of the courses of action mentioned in paragraph 12(2) is the best course of action in relation to that hazard.

(4) The tribunal must, if requested to do so by the appellant or the local housing authority, include in its decision a finding to that effect and identifying the course of action concerned.

Powers of residential property tribunal on appeal under paragraph 13

18

(1) This paragraph applies to an appeal to a residential property tribunal under paragraph 13.

(2) Paragraph 15(2) applies to such an appeal as it applies to an appeal under paragraph 10.

(3) The tribunal may by order confirm, reverse or vary the decision of the local housing authority.

(4) If the appeal is against a decision of the authority to refuse to revoke an improvement notice, the tribunal may make an order revoking the notice as from a date specified in the order.

"The operative time" for the purposes of section 15(5)

19

(1) This paragraph defines "the operative time" for the purposes of section 15(5) (operation of improvement notices).

(2) If an appeal is made under paragraph 10 against an improvement notice which is not suspended, and a decision on the appeal is given which confirms the notice, "the operative time" is as follows—

    (a)   if the period within which an appeal to the Lands Tribunal may be brought expires without such an appeal having been brought, "the operative time" is the end of that period;

(b)   if an appeal to the Lands Tribunal is brought, "the operative time" is the time when a decision is given on the appeal which confirms the notice.

(3) If an appeal is made under paragraph 10 against an improvement notice which is suspended, and a decision is given on the appeal which confirms the notice, "the operative time" is as follows—

(a)   the time that would be the operative time under sub-paragraph (2) if the notice were not suspended, or

(b)   if later, the time when the suspension ends.

(4) For the purposes of sub-paragraph (2) or (3)—

(a)   the withdrawal of an appeal has the same effect as a decision which confirms the notice, and

(b)   references to a decision which confirms the notice are to a decision which confirms it with or without variation.

"The operative time" for the purposes of section 16(7)

20

(1) This paragraph defines "the operative time" for the purposes of section 16(7) (postponement of time when a variation of an improvement notice comes into force).

(2) If no appeal is made under paragraph 13 before the end of the period of 28 days mentioned in paragraph 14(2), "the operative time" is the end of that period.

(3) If an appeal is made under paragraph 13 before the end of that period and a decision is given on the appeal which confirms the variation, "the operative time" is as follows—

(a)   if the period within which an appeal to the Lands Tribunal may be brought expires without such an appeal having been brought, "the operative time" is the end of that period;

(b)   if an appeal to the Lands Tribunal is brought, "the operative time" is the time when a decision is given on the appeal which confirms the variation.

(4) For the purposes of sub-paragraph (3)—

(a)   the withdrawal of an appeal has the same effect as a decision which confirms the variation, and

(b)   references to a decision which confirms the variation are to a decision which confirms it with or without variation.

Schedule 2
Procedure and Appeals Relating to Prohibition Orders

Section 27

PART 1
SERVICE OF COPIES OF PROHIBITION ORDERS

Service on owners and occupiers of dwelling or HMO which is not a flat

1

(1) This paragraph applies to a prohibition order where the specified premises are a dwelling or HMO which is not a flat.

(2) The authority must serve copies of the order on every person who, to their knowledge, is—

    (a)   an owner or occupier of the whole or part of the specified premises;

    (b)   authorised to permit persons to occupy the whole or part of those premises; or

    (c)   a mortgagee of the whole or part of those premises.

(3) The copies required to be served under sub-paragraph (2) must be served within the period of seven days beginning with the day on which the order is made.

(4) A copy of the order is to be regarded as having been served on every occupier in accordance with sub-paragraphs (2)(a) and (3) if a copy of the order is fixed to some conspicuous part of the specified premises within the period of seven days mentioned in sub-paragraph (3).

Service on owners and occupiers of building containing flats etc

2

(1) This paragraph applies to a prohibition order where the specified premises consist of or include the whole or any part of a building containing one or more flats or any common parts of such a building.

(2) The authority must serve copies of the order on every person who, to their knowledge, is—

    (a)   an owner or occupier of the whole or part of the building;

    (b)   authorised to permit persons to occupy the whole or part of the building; or

    (c)   a mortgagee of the whole or part of the building.

(3) Where the specified premises consist of or include any external common parts of such a building, the authority must, in addition to complying with sub-paragraph (2), serve copies of the order on every person who, to their knowledge, is an owner or mortgagee of the premises in which the common parts are comprised.

(4) The copies required to be served under sub-paragraph (2) or (3) must be served within the period of seven days beginning with the day on which the order is made.

(5) A copy of the order is to be regarded as having been served on every occupier in accordance with sub-paragraphs (2)(a) and (4) if a copy of the order is fixed to some conspicuous part of the building within the period of seven days mentioned in sub-paragraph (4).

PART 2
SERVICE OF NOTICES RELATING TO REVOCATION OR VARIATION OF PROHIBITION ORDERS

Notice of revocation or variation

3

(1) This paragraph applies where the local housing authority decide to revoke or vary a prohibition order.

(2) The authority must serve a notice under this paragraph on each of the persons on whom they would be required under Part 1 of this Schedule to serve copies of a prohibition order in respect of the specified premises.

(3) The notices required to be served under sub-paragraph (2) must be served within the period of seven days beginning with the day on which the decision is made.

(4) Paragraph 1(4) applies in relation to the service of notices on occupiers in accordance with sub-paragraphs (2) and (3) as it applies in relation to the service on them of copies of a prohibition order in accordance with paragraph 1(2)(a) and (3).

4

A notice under paragraph 3 must set out—

    (a)   the authority's decision to revoke or vary the order;
    (b)   the reasons for the decision and the date on which it was made;
    (c)   if the decision is to vary the order—
        (i)   the right of appeal against the decision under Part 3 of this Schedule; and
        (ii)   the period within which an appeal may be made (see paragraph 10(2)).

Notice of refusal to revoke or vary order

5

(1) This paragraph applies where the local housing authority refuse to revoke or vary a prohibition order.

(2) The authority must serve a notice under this paragraph on each of the persons on whom they would be required under Part 1 of this Schedule to serve copies of a prohibition order in respect of the specified premises.

(3) The notices required to be served under sub-paragraph (2) must be served within the period of seven days beginning with the day on which the decision is made.

(4) Paragraph 1(4) applies in relation to the service of notices on occupiers in accordance with sub-paragraphs (2) and (3) as it applies in relation to the service on them of copies of a prohibition order in accordance with paragraph 1(2)(a) and (3).

6

A notice under paragraph 5 must set out—

    (a)   the authority's decision not to revoke or vary the notice;
    (b)   the reasons for the decision and the date on which it was made;
    (c)   the right of appeal against the decision under Part 3 of this Schedule; and
    (d)   the period within which an appeal may be made (see paragraph 10(2)).

PART 3
APPEALS RELATING TO PROHIBITION ORDERS

Appeal against prohibition order

7

(1) A relevant person may appeal to a residential property tribunal against a prohibition order.

(2) Paragraph 8 sets out a specific ground on which an appeal may be made under this paragraph, but it does not affect the generality of sub-paragraph (1).

8

(1) An appeal may be made by a person under paragraph 7 on the ground that one of the courses of action mentioned in sub-paragraph (2) is the best course of action in relation to the hazard in respect of which the order was made.

(2) The courses of action are—

    (a)   serving an improvement notice under section 11 or 12 of this Act;
    (b)   serving a hazard awareness notice under section 28 or 29 of this Act;
    (c)   making a demolition order under section 265 of the Housing Act 1985 (c 68).

Appeal against decision relating to revocation or variation of prohibition order

9

A relevant person may appeal to a residential property tribunal against—

(a) a decision by the local housing authority to vary a prohibition order, or

(b) a decision by the authority to refuse to revoke or vary a prohibition order.

Time limit for appeal

10

(1) Any appeal under paragraph 7 must be made within the period of 28 days beginning with the date specified in the prohibition order as the date on which the order was made.

(2) Any appeal under paragraph 9 must be made within the period of 28 days beginning with the date specified in the notice under paragraph 3 or 5 as the date on which the decision concerned was made.

(3) A residential property tribunal may allow an appeal to be made to it after the end of the period mentioned in sub-paragraph (1) or (2) if it is satisfied that there is a good reason for the failure to appeal before the end of that period (and for any delay since then in applying for permission to appeal out of time).

Powers of residential property tribunal on appeal under paragraph 7

11

(1) This paragraph applies to an appeal to a residential property tribunal under paragraph 7.

(2) The appeal—

(a) is to be by way of a re-hearing, but

(b) may be determined having regard to matters of which the authority were unaware.

(3) The tribunal may by order confirm, quash or vary the prohibition order.

(4) Paragraph 12 makes special provision in connection with the ground of appeal set out in paragraph 8.

12

(1) This paragraph applies where the grounds of appeal consist of or include that set out in paragraph 8.

(2) When deciding whether one of the courses of action mentioned in paragraph 8(2) is the best course of action in relation to a particular hazard, the tribunal must have regard to any guidance given to the local housing authority under section 9.

(3) Sub-paragraph (4) applies where—

(a)   an appeal under paragraph 7 is allowed against a prohibition order made in respect of a particular hazard; and

(b)   the reason, or one of the reasons, for allowing the appeal is that one of the courses of action mentioned in paragraph 8(2) is the best course of action in relation to that hazard.

(4) The tribunal must, if requested to do so by the appellant or the local housing authority, include in its decision a finding to that effect and identifying the course of action concerned.

Powers of residential property tribunal on appeal under paragraph 9

13

(1) This paragraph applies to an appeal to a residential property tribunal under paragraph 9.

(2) Paragraph 11(2) applies to such an appeal as it applies to an appeal under paragraph 7.

(3) The tribunal may by order confirm, reverse or vary the decision of the local housing authority.

(4) If the appeal is against a decision of the authority to refuse to revoke a prohibition order, the tribunal may make an order revoking the prohibition order as from a date specified in its order.

"The operative time" for the purposes of section 24(5)

14

(1) This paragraph defines "the operative time" for the purposes of section 24(5) (operation of prohibition orders).

(2) If an appeal is made under paragraph 7 against a prohibition order which is not suspended, and a decision on the appeal is given which confirms the order, "the operative time" is as follows—

(a)   if the period within which an appeal to the Lands Tribunal may be brought expires without such an appeal having been brought, "the operative time" is the end of that period;

(b)   if an appeal to the Lands Tribunal is brought, "the operative time" is the time when a decision is given on the appeal which confirms the order.

(3) If an appeal is made under paragraph 7 against a prohibition order which is suspended, and a decision is given on the appeal which confirms the order, "the operative time" is as follows—

    (a)   the time that would be the operative time under sub-paragraph (2) if the order were not suspended, or

    (b)   if later, the time when the suspension ends.

(4) For the purposes of sub-paragraph (2) or (3)—

    (a)   the withdrawal of an appeal has the same effect as a decision which confirms the notice, and

    (b)   references to a decision which confirms the order are to a decision which confirms it with or without variation.

"The operative time" for the purposes of section 25(7)

15

(1) This paragraph defines "the operative time" for the purposes of section 25(7) (revocation or variation of prohibition orders).

(2) If no appeal is made under paragraph 9 before the end of the period of 28 days mentioned in paragraph 10(2), "the operative time" is the end of that period.

(3) If an appeal is made under paragraph 10 within that period and a decision is given on the appeal which confirms the variation, "the operative time" is as follows—

    (a)   if the period within which an appeal to the Lands Tribunal may be brought expires without such an appeal having been brought, "the operative time" is the end of that period;

    (b)   if an appeal to the Lands Tribunal is brought, "the operative time" is the time when a decision is given on the appeal which confirms the variation.

(4) For the purposes of sub-paragraph (3)—

    (a)   the withdrawal of an appeal has the same effect as a decision which confirms the variation, and

    (b)   references to a decision which confirms the variation are to a decision which confirms it with or without variation.

Meaning of "relevant person"

16

(1) In this Part of this Schedule "relevant person", in relation to a prohibition order, means a person who is—

    (a)   an owner or occupier of the whole or part of the specified premises,

    (b)   authorised to permit persons to occupy the whole or part of those premises, or

(c)   a mortgagee of the whole or part of those premises.

(2) If any specified premises are common parts of a building containing one or more flats, then in relation to those specified premises, "relevant person" means every person who is an owner or mortgagee of the premises in which the common parts are comprised.

Schedule 3
Improvement Notices: Enforcement Action by Local Housing Authorities

Section 31

PART 1
ACTION TAKEN BY AGREEMENT

Power to take action by agreement

1

(1) The local housing authority may, by agreement with the person on whom an improvement notice has been served, take any action which that person is required to take in relation to any premises in pursuance of the notice.

(2) For that purpose the authority have all the rights which that person would have against any occupying tenant of, and any other person having an interest in, the premises (or any part of the premises).

(3) In this paragraph—

"improvement notice" means an improvement notice which has become operative under Chapter 2 of Part 1 of this Act;

"occupying tenant", in relation to any premises, means a person (other than an owner-occupier) who—

(a)   occupies or is entitled to occupy the premises as a lessee;

(b)   is a statutory tenant of the premises;

(c)   occupies the premises under a restricted contract;

(d)   is a protected occupier within the meaning of the Rent (Agriculture) Act 1976 (c 80); or

(e)   is a licensee under an assured agricultural occupancy;

"owner-occupier", in relation to any premises, means the person who occupies or is entitled to occupy the premises as owner or lessee under a long tenancy (within the meaning of Part 1 of the Leasehold Reform Act 1967 (c 88)).

Expenses of taking action by agreement

2

Any action taken by the local housing authority under paragraph 1 is to be taken at the expense of the person on whom the notice is served.

PART 2
POWER TO TAKE ACTION WITHOUT AGREEMENT

Power to take action without agreement

3

(1) The local housing authority may themselves take the action required to be taken in relation to a hazard by an improvement notice if sub-paragraph (2) or (3) applies.

(2) This sub-paragraph applies if the notice is not complied with in relation to that hazard.

(3) This sub-paragraph applies if, before the end of the period which under section 30(2) is appropriate for completion of the action specified in the notice in relation to the hazard, they consider that reasonable progress is not being made towards compliance with the notice in relation to the hazard.

(4) Any person authorised in writing by the authority may enter any part of the specified premises for the purposes of the taking of any action which the authority are authorised to take under this paragraph.

(5) The right of entry conferred by sub-paragraph (4) may be exercised at any reasonable time.

(6) Any reference in this Part of this Schedule (of whatever nature) to a local housing authority entering any premises under this paragraph is a reference to their doing so in accordance with sub-paragraph (4).

(7) In this paragraph "improvement notice" means an improvement notice which has become operative under Chapter 2 of Part 1 of this Act.

Notice requirements in relation to taking action without agreement

4

(1) The local housing authority must serve a notice under this paragraph before they enter any premises under paragraph 3 for the purpose of taking action in relation to a hazard.

(2) The notice must identify the improvement notice to which it relates and state—

(a)   the premises and hazard concerned;
(b)   that the authority intend to enter the premises;
(c)   the action which the authority intend to take on the premises; and
(d)   the power under which the authority intend to enter the premises and take the action.

(3) The notice must be served on the person on whom the improvement notice was served, and a copy of the notice must be served on any other person who is an occupier of the premises.

(4) The notice and any such copy must be served sufficiently in advance of the time when the authority intend to enter the premises as to give the recipients reasonable notice of the intended entry.

(5) A copy of the notice may also be served on any owner of the premises.

Obstruction of action taken without agreement

5

(1) If, at any relevant time—

 (a) the person on whom the notice under paragraph 4 was served is on the premises for the purpose of carrying out any works, or
 (b) any workman employed by that person, or by any contractor employed by that person, is on the premises for such a purpose,

that person is to be taken to have committed an offence under section 241(1).

(2) In proceedings for such an offence it is a defence that there was an urgent necessity to carry out the works in order to prevent danger to persons occupying the premises.

(3) In sub-paragraph (1) "relevant time" means any time—

 (a) after the end of the period of 7 days beginning with the date of service of the notice under paragraph 4, and
 (b) when any workman or contractor employed by the local housing authority is taking action on the premises which has been mentioned in the notice in accordance with paragraph 4(2)(c).

Expenses in relation to taking action without agreement

6

(1) Part 3 of this Schedule applies with respect to the recovery by the local housing authority of expenses incurred by them in taking action under paragraph 3.

(2) Sub-paragraph (3) applies where, after a local housing authority have given notice under paragraph 4 of their intention to enter premises and take action, the action is in fact taken by the person on whom the improvement notice is served.

(3) Any administrative and other expenses incurred by the authority with a view to themselves taking the action are to be treated for the purposes of Part 3 of this Schedule as expenses incurred by them in taking action under paragraph 3.

PART 3
RECOVERY OF CERTAIN EXPENSES

Introductory

7

This Part of this Schedule applies for the purpose of enabling a local housing authority to recover expenses reasonably incurred by them in taking action under paragraph 3.

Recovery of expenses

8

(1) The expenses are recoverable by the local housing authority from the person on whom the improvement notice was served ("the relevant person").

(2) Where the relevant person receives the rent of the premises as agent or trustee for another person, the expenses are also recoverable by the local housing authority from the other person, or partly from him and partly from the relevant person.

(3) Sub-paragraph (4) applies where the relevant person proves in connection with a demand under paragraph 9—

   (a) that sub-paragraph (2) applies, and
   (b) that he has not, and since the date of the service on him of the demand has not had, in his hands on behalf of the other person sufficient money to discharge the whole demand of the local housing authority.

(4) The liability of the relevant person is limited to the total amount of the money which he has, or has had, in his hands as mentioned in sub-paragraph (3)(b).

(5) Expenses are not recoverable under this paragraph so far as they are, by any direction given by a residential property tribunal on an appeal to the tribunal under paragraph 11, recoverable under an order of the tribunal.

Service of demand

9

(1) A demand for expenses recoverable under paragraph 8, together with interest in accordance with paragraph 10, must be served on each person from whom the local housing authority are seeking to recover them.

(2) If no appeal is brought, the demand becomes operative at the end of the period of 21 days beginning with the date of service of the demand.

(3) A demand which becomes operative under sub-paragraph (2) is final and conclusive as to matters which could have been raised on an appeal.

(4) Paragraph 11 deals with appeals against demands.

Interest

10

Expenses in respect of which a demand is served carry interest, at such reasonable rate as the local housing authority may determine, from the date of service until payment of all sums due under the demand.

Appeals

11

(1) A person on whom a demand for the recovery of expenses has been served may appeal to a residential property tribunal against the demand.

(2) An appeal must be made within the period of 21 days beginning with the date of service of the demand or copy of it under paragraph 9.

(3) A residential property tribunal may allow an appeal to be made to it after the end of the period mentioned in sub-paragraph (2) if it is satisfied that there is a good reason for the failure to appeal before the end of that period (and for any delay since then in applying for permission to appeal out of time).

(4) Where the demand relates to action taken by virtue of paragraph 3(3), an appeal may be brought on the ground that reasonable progress was being made towards compliance with the improvement notice when the local housing authority gave notice under paragraph 4 of their intention to enter and take the action.

This does not affect the generality of sub-paragraph (1).

(5) The tribunal may, on an appeal, make such order confirming, quashing or varying the demand as it considers appropriate.

(6) A demand against which an appeal is brought becomes operative as follows—

(a) if a decision is given on the appeal which confirms the demand and the period within which an appeal to the Lands Tribunal may be brought expires without such an appeal having been brought, the demand becomes operative at end of that period;

(b) if an appeal to the Lands Tribunal is brought and a decision is given on the appeal which confirms the demand, the demand becomes operative at the time of that decision.

(7) For the purposes of sub-paragraph (6)—

(a) the withdrawal of an appeal has the same effect as a decision which confirms the demand, and

(b) references to a decision which confirms the demand are to a decision which confirms it with or without variation.

(8) No question may be raised on appeal under this paragraph which might have been raised on an appeal against the improvement notice.

Expenses and interest recoverable from occupiers

12

(1) Where a demand becomes operative by virtue of paragraph 9(2) or 11(6), the local housing authority may serve a recovery notice on any person—

- (a) who occupies the premises concerned, or part of those premises, as the tenant or licensee of the person on whom the demand was served under paragraph 9(1); and
- (b) who, by virtue of his tenancy or licence, pays rent or any sum in the nature of rent to the person on whom the demand was served.

(2) A recovery notice is a notice—

- (a) stating the amount of expenses recoverable by the local housing authority; and
- (b) requiring all future payments by the tenant or licensee of rent or sums in the nature of rent (whether already accrued due or not) to be made direct to the authority until the expenses recoverable by the authority, together with any accrued interest on them, have been duly paid.

(3) In the case of a demand which was served on any person as agent or trustee for another person ("the principal"), sub-paragraph (1) has effect as if the references in paragraphs (a) and (b) to the person on whom the demand was served were references to that person or the principal.

(4) The effect of a recovery notice, once served under sub-paragraph (1), is to transfer to the local housing authority the right to recover, receive and give a discharge for the rent or sums in the nature of rent.

(5) This is subject to any direction to the contrary contained in a further notice served by the local housing authority on the tenant or licensee.

(6) In addition, the right to recover, receive and give a discharge for any rent or sums in the nature of rent is postponed to any right in respect of that rent or those sums which may at any time be vested in a superior landlord by virtue of a notice under section 6 of the Law of Distress Amendment Act 1908 (c 53).

Expenses and interest to be a charge on the premises

13

(1) Until recovered, the expenses recoverable by the local housing authority, together with any accrued interest on them, are a charge on the premises to which the improvement notice related.

(2) The charge takes effect when the demand for the expenses and interest becomes operative by virtue of paragraph 9(2) or 11(6).

(3) For the purpose of enforcing the charge, the local housing authority have the same powers and remedies, under the Law of Property Act 1925 (c 20) and otherwise, as if they were mortgagees by deed having powers of sale and lease, of accepting surrenders of leases and of appointing a receiver.

(4) The power of appointing a receiver is exercisable at any time after the end of one month beginning with the date when the charge takes effect.

Recovery of expenses and interest from other persons profiting from taking of action

14

(1) Sub-paragraph (2) applies if, on an application to a residential property tribunal, the local housing authority satisfy the tribunal that—

    (a)   the expenses and interest have not been and are unlikely to be recovered; and

    (b)   a person is profiting by the taking of the action under paragraph 3 in respect of which the expenses were incurred in that he is obtaining rents or other payments which would not have been obtainable if the number of persons living in the premises was limited to that appropriate for the premises in their state before the action was taken.

(2) The tribunal may, if satisfied that the person concerned has had proper notice of the application, order him to make such payments to the local housing authority as the tribunal considers to be just.

Schedule 4
Licences under Parts 2 and 3: Mandatory Conditions

Sections 67 and 90

Conditions to be included in licences under Part 2 or 3

1

(1) A licence under Part 2 or 3 must include the following conditions [but in the case of a licence under Part 2, this is subject to sub-paragraph (6)].

(2) Conditions requiring the licence holder, if gas is supplied to the house, to produce to the local housing authority annually for their inspection a gas safety certificate obtained in respect of the house within the last 12 months.

(3) Conditions requiring the licence holder—

    (a)   to keep electrical appliances and furniture made available by him in the house in a safe condition;

    (b)   to supply the authority, on demand, with a declaration by him as to the safety of such appliances and furniture.

(4) Conditions requiring the licence holder—

    (a)   to ensure that smoke alarms are installed in the house and to keep them in proper working order;

    (b)   to supply the authority, on demand, with a declaration by him as to the condition and positioning of such alarms.

(5) Conditions requiring the licence holder to supply to the occupiers of the house a written statement of the terms on which they occupy it.

[(6) The conditions contained in sub-paragraphs (2) to (5) apply only in relation to any part of a section 257 HMO over which the licence holder exercises control, or over which it would be reasonable to expect that he would exercise control.]

Amendment—Para 1 modified, in relation to a house in multiple occupation to which s 257 hereof applies, by the Houses in Multiple Occupation (Certain Converted Blocks of Flats) (Modifications to the Housing Act 2004 and Transitional Provisions for section 257 HMOs) (England) Regulations 2007, SI 2007/1904, regs 2, 10.

Additional conditions to be included in licences under Part 3

2

A licence under Part 3 must include conditions requiring the licence holder to demand references from persons who wish to occupy the house.

Power to prescribe conditions

3

The appropriate national authority may by regulations amend this Schedule so as to alter (by the addition or removal of conditions) the conditions which must be included—

(a) in a licence under Part 2 or 3, or
(b) only in a licence under one of those Parts.

Interpretation

4

In this Schedule "the house" means the HMO or Part 3 house in respect of which the licence is granted.

Schedule 5
Licences Under Parts 2 and 3: Procedure and Appeals

Sections 71 and 94

PART 1
PROCEDURE RELATING TO GRANT OR REFUSAL OF LICENCES

Requirements before grant of licence

1

Before granting a licence, the local housing authority must—

   (a)   serve a notice under this paragraph, together with a copy of the proposed licence, on the applicant for the licence and each relevant person, and

   (b)   consider any representations made in accordance with the notice and not withdrawn.

2

The notice under paragraph 1 must state that the authority are proposing to grant the licence and set out—

   (a)   the reasons for granting the licence,

   (b)   the main terms of the licence, and

   (c)   the end of the consultation period.

3

(1) This paragraph applies if, having considered representations made in accordance with a notice under paragraph 1 or this paragraph, the local housing authority propose to grant a licence with modifications.

(2) Before granting the licence the authority must—

   (a)   serve a notice under this paragraph on the applicant for the licence and each relevant person, and

   (b)   consider any representations made in accordance with the notice and not withdrawn.

4

The notice under paragraph 3 must set out—

   (a)   the proposed modifications,

   (b)   the reasons for them, and

   (c)   the end of the consultation period.

Requirements before refusal to grant licence

5

Before refusing to grant a licence, the local housing authority must—

   (a)   serve a notice under this paragraph on the applicant for the licence and each relevant person, and

   (b)   consider any representations made in accordance with the notice and not withdrawn.

6

The notice under paragraph 5 must state that the local housing authority are proposing to refuse to grant the licence and set out—

   (a)   the reasons for refusing to grant the licence, and

   (b)   the end of the consultation period.

Requirements following grant or refusal of licence

7

(1) This paragraph applies where the local housing authority decide to grant a licence.

(2) The local housing authority must serve on the applicant for the licence (and, if different, the licence holder) and each relevant person—

  (a)   a copy of the licence, and
  (b)   a notice setting out—
    (i)   the reasons for deciding to grant the licence and the date on which the decision was made,
    (ii)   the right of appeal against the decision under Part 3 of this Schedule, and
    (iii) the period within which an appeal may be made (see paragraph 33(1)).

(3) The documents required to be served under sub-paragraph (2) must be served within the period of seven days beginning with the day on which the decision is made.

8

(1) This paragraph applies where the local housing authority refuse to grant a licence.

(2) The local housing authority must serve on the applicant for the licence and each relevant person a notice setting out—

  (a)   the authority's decision not to grant the licence,
  (b)   the reasons for the decision and the date on which it was made,
  (c)   the right of appeal against the decision under Part 3 of this Schedule, and
  (d)   the period within which an appeal may be made (see paragraph 33(1)).

(3) The notices required to be served under sub-paragraph (2) must be served within the period of seven days beginning with the day on which the decision is made.

Exceptions from requirements in relation to grant or refusal of licences

9

The requirements of paragraph 3 (and those of paragraph 1) do not apply if the local housing authority—

  (a)   have already served a notice under paragraph 1 but not paragraph 3 in relation to the proposed licence, and
  (b)   consider that the modifications which are now being proposed are not material in any respect.

10

The requirements of paragraph 3 (and those of paragraph 1) do not apply if the local housing authority—

(a) have already served notices under paragraphs 1 and 3 in relation to the matter concerned, and

(b) consider that the further modifications which are now being proposed do not differ in any material respect from the modifications in relation to which a notice was last served under paragraph 3.

11

Paragraphs 5, 6 and 8 do not apply to a refusal to grant a licence on particular terms if the local housing authority are proposing to grant the licence on different terms.

Meaning of "the end of the consultation period"

12

(1) In this Part of this Schedule "the end of the consultation period" means the last day for making representations in respect of the matter in question.

(2) The end of the consultation period must be—

(a) in the case of a notice under paragraph 1 or 5, a day which is at least 14 days after the date of service of the notice; and

(b) in the case of a notice under paragraph 3, a day which is at least 7 days after the date of service of the notice.

(3) In sub-paragraph (2) "the date of service" of a notice means, in a case where more than one notice is served, the date on which the last of the notices is served.

Meaning of "licence" and "relevant person"

13

(1) In this Part of this Schedule "licence" means a licence under Part 2 or 3 of this Act.

(2) In this Part of this Schedule "relevant person", in relation to a licence under Part 2 or 3 of this Act, means any person (other than a person excluded by sub-paragraph (3))—

(a) who, to the knowledge of the local housing authority concerned, is—

(i) a person having an estate or interest in the HMO or Part 3 house in question, or

(ii) a person managing or having control of that HMO or Part 3 house (and not falling within sub-paragraph (i)), or

(b) on whom any restriction or obligation is or is to be imposed by the licence in accordance with section 67(5) or 90(6).

(3) The persons excluded by this sub-paragraph are—

(a)   the applicant for the licence and (if different) the licence holder, and

(b)   any tenant under a lease with an unexpired term of 3 years or less.

PART 2
PROCEDURE RELATING TO VARIATION OR REVOCATION OF LICENCES

Variation of licences

14

Before varying a licence, the local housing authority must—

(a)   serve a notice under this paragraph on the licence holder and each relevant person, and

(b)   consider any representations made in accordance with the notice and not withdrawn.

15

The notice under paragraph 14 must state that the local housing authority are proposing to make the variation and set out—

(a)   the effect of the variation,

(b)   the reasons for the variation, and

(c)   the end of the consultation period.

16

(1) This paragraph applies where the local housing authority decide to vary a licence.

(2) The local housing authority must serve on the licence holder and each relevant person—

(a)   a copy of the authority's decision to vary the licence, and

(b)   a notice setting out—

(i)   the reasons for the decision and the date on which it was made,

(ii)   the right of appeal against the decision under Part 3 of this Schedule, and

(iii) the period within which an appeal may be made (see paragraph 33(2)).

(3) The documents required to be served under sub-paragraph (2) must be served within the period of seven days beginning with the day on which the decision is made.

Exceptions from requirements of paragraph 14

17

The requirements of paragraph 14 do not apply if—

    (a)   the local housing authority consider that the variation is not material, or

    (b)   the variation is agreed by the licence holder and the local housing authority consider that it would not be appropriate to comply with the requirements of that paragraph.

18

The requirements of paragraph 14 do not apply if the local housing authority—

    (a)   have already served a notice under that paragraph in relation to a proposed variation, and

    (b)   consider that the variation which is now being proposed is not materially different from the previous proposed variation.

Refusal to vary a licence

19

Before refusing to vary a licence, the local housing authority must—

    (a)   serve a notice under this paragraph on the licence holder and each relevant person, and

    (b)   consider any representations made in accordance with the notice and not withdrawn.

20

The notice under paragraph 19 must state that the authority are proposing to refuse to vary the licence and set out—

    (a)   the reasons for refusing to vary the licence, and

    (b)   the end of the consultation period.

21

(1) This paragraph applies where the local housing authority refuse to vary a licence.

(2) The authority must serve on the licence holder and each relevant person a notice setting out—

    (a)   the authority's decision not to vary the licence,

    (b)   the reasons for the decision and the date on which it was made,

    (c)   the right of appeal against the decision under Part 3 of this Schedule, and

    (d)   the period within which an appeal may be made (see paragraph 33(2)).

(3) The documents required to be served under sub-paragraph (2) must be served within the period of seven days beginning with the day on which the decision is made.

Revocation of licences

22

Before revoking a licence, the local housing authority must—

(a) serve a notice on the licence holder under this paragraph and each relevant person, and

(b) consider any representations made in accordance with the notice and not withdrawn.

23

The notice under paragraph 22 must state that the authority are proposing to revoke the licence and set out—

(a) the reasons for the revocation, and

(b) the end of the consultation period.

24

(1) This paragraph applies where the local housing authority decide to revoke a licence.

(2) The authority must serve on the licence holder and each relevant person—

(a) a copy of the authority's decision to revoke the licence, and

(b) a notice setting out—

(i) the reasons for the decision and the date on which it was made,

(ii) the right of appeal against the decision under Part 3 of this Schedule, and

(iii) the period within which an appeal may be made (see paragraph 33(2)).

(3) The documents required to be served under sub-paragraph (2) must be served within the period of seven days beginning with the day on which the decision is made.

Exception from requirements of paragraph 22

25

The requirements of paragraph 22 do not apply if the revocation is agreed by the licence holder and the local housing authority consider that it would not be appropriate to comply with the requirements of that paragraph.

Refusal to revoke a licence

26

Before refusing to revoke a licence, the local housing authority must—

    (a)   serve a notice under this paragraph on the licence holder and each relevant person, and

    (b)   consider any representations made in accordance with the notice and not withdrawn.

27

The notice under paragraph 26 must state that the authority are proposing to refuse to revoke the licence and set out—

    (a)   the reasons for refusing to revoke the licence, and

    (b)   the end of the consultation period.

28

(1) This paragraph applies where the local housing authority refuse to revoke a licence.

(2) The authority must serve on the licence holder and each relevant person a notice setting out—

    (a)   the authority's decision not to revoke the licence,

    (b)   the reasons for the decision and the date on which it was made,

    (c)   the right of appeal against the decision under Part 3 of this Schedule, and

    (d)   the period within which an appeal may be made (see paragraph 33(2)).

(3) The notices required to be served under sub-paragraph (2) must be served within the period of seven days beginning with the day on which the decision is made.

Meaning of "the end of the consultation period"

29

(1) In this Part of this Schedule "the end of the consultation period" means the last day on which representations may be made in respect of the matter in question.

(2) That date must be at least 14 days after the date of service of the notice in question.

(3) In sub-paragraph (2) "the date of service" of a notice means, in a case where more than one notice is served, the date on which the last of the notices is served.

Meaning of "licence" and "relevant person"

30

(1) In this Part of this Schedule "licence" means a licence under Part 2 or 3 of this Act.

(2) In this Part of this Schedule "relevant person", in relation to a licence under Part 2 or 3 of this Act, means any person (other than a person excluded by sub-paragraph (3))—

    (a)   who, to the knowledge of the local housing authority concerned, is—
        (i)   a person having an estate or interest in the HMO or Part 3 house in question, or
        (ii)   a person managing or having control of that HMO or Part 3 house (and not falling within sub-paragraph (i)), or
    (b)   on whom any restriction or obligation is or is to be imposed by the licence in accordance with section 67(5) or 90(6).

(3) The persons excluded by this sub-paragraph are—

    (a)   the licence holder, and
    (b)   any tenant under a lease with an unexpired term of 3 years or less.

PART 3
APPEALS AGAINST LICENCE DECISIONS

Right to appeal against refusal or grant of licence

31

(1) The applicant or any relevant person may appeal to a residential property tribunal against a decision by the local housing authority on an application for a licence—

    (a)   to refuse to grant the licence, or
    (b)   to grant the licence.

(2) An appeal under sub-paragraph (1)(b) may, in particular, relate to any of the terms of the licence.

Right to appeal against decision or refusal to vary or revoke licence

32

(1) The licence holder or any relevant person may appeal to a residential property tribunal against a decision by the local housing authority—

    (a)   to vary or revoke a licence, or
    (b)   to refuse to vary or revoke a licence.

(2) But this does not apply to the licence holder in a case where the decision to vary or revoke the licence was made with his agreement.

Time limits for appeals

33

(1) Any appeal under paragraph 31 against a decision to grant, or (as the case may be) to refuse to grant, a licence must be made within the period of 28 days beginning with the date specified in the notice under paragraph 7 or 8 as the date on which the decision was made.

(2) Any appeal under paragraph 32 against a decision to vary or revoke, or (as the case may be) to refuse to vary or revoke, a licence must be made within the period of 28 days beginning with the date specified in the notice under paragraph 16, 21, 24 or 28 as the date on which the decision was made.

(3) A residential property tribunal may allow an appeal to be made to it after the end of the period mentioned in sub-paragraph (1) or (2) if it is satisfied that there is a good reason for the failure to appeal before the end of that period (and for any delay since then in applying for permission to appeal out of time).

Powers of residential property tribunal hearing appeal

34

(1) This paragraph applies to appeals to a residential property tribunal under paragraph 31 or 32.

(2) An appeal—

    (a)   is to be by way of a re-hearing, but

    (b)   may be determined having regard to matters of which the authority were unaware.

(3) The tribunal may confirm, reverse or vary the decision of the local housing authority.

(4) On an appeal under paragraph 31 the tribunal may direct the authority to grant a licence to the applicant for the licence on such terms as the tribunal may direct.

"The operative time" for the purposes of section 69(6), 70(8), 92(3) or 93(5)

35

(1) This paragraph defines "the operative time" for the purposes of—

    (a)   section 69(6) or 70(8) (variation or revocation of licence under Part 2 of this Act), or

    (b)   section 92(3) or 93(5) (variation or revocation of licence under Part 3 of this Act).

(2) If the period of 28 days mentioned in paragraph 33(2) has expired without an appeal having been made under paragraph 32, "the operative time" is the end of that period.

(3) If an appeal is made under paragraph 32 within that period and a decision is given on the appeal which confirms the variation or revocation, "the operative time" is as follows—

(a) if the period within which an appeal to the Lands Tribunal may be brought expires without such an appeal having been brought, "the operative time" is the end of that period;

(b) if an appeal to the Lands Tribunal is brought, "the operative time" is the time when a decision is given on the appeal which confirms the variation or revocation.

(4) For the purposes of sub-paragraph (3)—

(a) the withdrawal of an appeal has the same effect as a decision confirming the variation or revocation appealed against; and

(b) references to a decision which confirms a variation are to a decision which confirms it with or without variation.

Meaning of "licence" and "relevant person"

36

(1) In this Part of this Schedule "licence" means a licence under Part 2 or 3 of this Act.

(2) In this Part of this Schedule "relevant person", in relation to a licence under Part 2 or 3 of this Act, means any person (other than a person excluded by sub-paragraph (3))—

(a) who is—

    (i) a person having an estate or interest in the HMO or Part 3 house concerned, or

    (ii) a person managing or having control of that HMO or Part 3 house (and not falling within sub-paragraph (i)), or

(b) on whom any restriction or obligation is or is to be imposed by the licence in accordance with section 67(5) or 90(6).

(3) The persons excluded by this sub-paragraph are—

(a) the applicant for the licence and (if different) the licence holder, and

(b) any tenant under a lease with an unexpired term of 3 years or less.

Schedule 6
Management Orders: Procedure and Appeals

Section 123

PART 1
PROCEDURE RELATING TO MAKING OF MANAGEMENT ORDERS

Requirements before making final management order

1

Before making a final management order, the local housing authority must—

(a) serve a copy of the proposed order, together with a notice under this paragraph, on each relevant person; and

(b) consider any representations made in accordance with the notice and not withdrawn.

2

The notice under paragraph 1 must state that the authority are proposing to make a final management order and set out—

(a) the reasons for making the order;

(b) the main terms of the proposed order (including those of the management scheme to be contained in it); and

(c) the end of the consultation period.

3

(1) This paragraph applies if, having considered representations made in accordance with a notice under paragraph 1 or this paragraph, the local housing authority propose to make a final management order with modifications.

(2) Before making the order, the authority must—

(a) serve a notice under this paragraph on each relevant person; and

(b) consider any representations made in accordance with the notice and not withdrawn.

4

The notice under paragraph 3 must set out—

(a) the proposed modifications;

(b) the reasons for them; and

(c) the end of the consultation period.

Exceptions from requirements relating to making of final management order

5

The requirements of paragraph 3 (and those of paragraph 1) do not apply if the local housing authority—

(a) have already served notice under paragraph 1 but not paragraph 3 in relation to the proposed final management order; and

(b) consider that the modifications which are now being proposed are not material in any respect.

6

The requirements of paragraph 3 (and those of paragraph 1) do not apply if the local housing authority—

(a) have already served notices under paragraphs 1 and 3 in relation to the matter concerned; and

(b) consider that the further modifications which are now being proposed do not differ in any material respect from the modifications in relation to which a notice was last served under paragraph 3.

Requirements following making of interim or final management order

7

(1) This paragraph applies where the local housing authority make an interim management order or a final management order.

(2) As soon as practicable after the order is made, the authority must serve on the occupiers of the house—

(a) a copy of the order, and

(b) a notice under this sub-paragraph.

(3) Those documents are to be regarded as having been served on the occupiers if they are fixed to a conspicuous part of the house.

(4) The notice under sub-paragraph (2) must set out—

(a) the reasons for making the order and the date on which it was made,

(b) the general effect of the order, and

(c) the date on which the order is to cease to have effect in accordance with section 105(4) and (5) or 114(3) and (4) (or, if applicable, how the date mentioned in section 105(6) is to be determined),

and (if it is a final management order) give a general description of the way in which the house is to be managed by the authority in accordance with the management scheme contained in the order.

(5) The authority must also serve a copy of the order, together with a notice under this sub-paragraph, on each relevant person.

(6) The notice under sub-paragraph (5) must comply with sub-paragraph (4) and also contain information about—

    (a)   the right of appeal against the order under Part 3 of this Schedule, and

    (b)   the period within which any such appeal may be made (see paragraph 25(2)).

(7) The documents required to be served on each relevant person under sub-paragraph (5) must be served within the period of seven days beginning with the day on which the order is made.

Meaning of "the end of the consultation period" and "relevant person"

8

(1) In this Part of this Schedule "the end of the consultation period" means the last day for making representations in respect of the matter in question.

(2) The end of the consultation period must be—

    (a)   in the case of a notice under paragraph 1, a day which is at least 14 days after the date of service of the notice; and

    (b)   in the case of a notice under paragraph 3, a day which is at least 7 days after the date of service of the notice.

(3) In sub-paragraph (2) "the date of service" of a notice means, in a case where more than one notice is served, the date on which the last of the notices is served.

(4) In this Part of this Schedule "relevant person" means any person who, to the knowledge of the local housing authority, is—

    (a)   a person having an estate or interest in the house or part of it (but who is not a tenant under a lease with an unexpired term of 3 years or less), or

    (b)   any other person who (but for the order) would be a person managing or having control of the house or part of it.

PART 2
PROCEDURE RELATING TO VARIATION OR REVOCATION OF MANAGEMENT ORDERS

Variation of management orders

9

Before varying an interim or final management order, the local housing authority must—

    (a)   serve a notice under this paragraph on each relevant person, and

    (b)   consider any representations made in accordance with the notice and not withdrawn.

10

The notice under paragraph 9 must state that the authority are proposing to make the variation and specify—

    (a)   the effect of the variation,

    (b)   the reasons for the variation, and

    (c)   the end of the consultation period.

11

(1) This paragraph applies where the local housing authority decide to vary an interim or final management order.

(2) The local housing authority must serve on each relevant person—

    (a)   a copy of the authority's decision to vary the order, and

    (b)   a notice setting out—

        (i)   the reasons for the decision and the date on which it was made,

        (ii)   the right of appeal against the decision under Part 3 of this Schedule, and

        (iii)   the period within which an appeal may be made (see paragraph 29(2)).

(3) The documents required to be served on each relevant person under sub-paragraph (2) must be served within the period of seven days beginning with the day on which the decision is made.

Exceptions from requirements of paragraph 9

12

The requirements of paragraph 9 do not apply if the local housing authority consider that the variation is not material.

13

The requirements of paragraph9 do not apply if the local housing authority—

    (a)   have already served a notice under that paragraph in relation to a proposed variation; and

    (b)   consider that the variation which is now being proposed is not materially different from the previous proposed variation.

Refusal to vary interim or final management order

14

Before refusing to vary an interim or final management order, the local housing authority must—

    (a)   serve a notice under this paragraph on each relevant person, and

    (b)   consider any representations made in accordance with the notice and not withdrawn.

15

The notice under paragraph 14 must state that the authority are proposing to refuse to make the variation and set out—

    (a)   the reasons for refusing to make the variation, and

    (b)   the end of the consultation period.

16

(1) This paragraph applies where the local housing authority refuse to vary an interim or final management order.

(2) The authority must serve on each relevant person a notice setting out—

    (a)   the authority's decision not to vary the order;

    (b)   the reasons for the decision and the date on which it was made;

    (c)   the right of appeal against the decision under Part 3 of this Schedule; and

    (d)   the period within which an appeal may be made (see paragraph 29(2)).

(3) The notices required to be served on each relevant person under sub-paragraph (2) must be served within the period of seven days beginning with the day on which the decision is made.

Revocation of management orders

17

Before revoking an interim or final management order, the local housing authority must—

    (a)   serve a notice under this paragraph on each relevant person, and

    (b)   consider any representations made in accordance with the notice and not withdrawn.

18

The notice under paragraph 17 must state that the authority are proposing to revoke the order and specify—

    (a)   the reasons for the revocation, and

    (b)   the end of the consultation period.

19

(1) This paragraph applies where the local housing authority decide to revoke an interim or final management order.

(2) The authority must serve on each relevant person—

    (a)   a copy of the authority's decision to revoke the order; and

    (b)   a notice setting out—

        (i)   the reasons for the decision and the date on which it was made;

(ii) the right of appeal against the decision under Part 3 of this Schedule; and

(iii) the period within which an appeal may be made (see paragraph 29(2)).

(3) The documents required to be served on each relevant person under sub-paragraph (2) must be served within the period of seven days beginning with the day on which the decision is made.

Refusal to revoke management order

20

Before refusing to revoke an interim or final management order, the local housing authority must—

(a) serve a notice under this paragraph on each relevant person; and

(b) consider any representations made in accordance with the notice and not withdrawn.

21

The notice under paragraph 20 must state that the authority are proposing to refuse to revoke the order and set out—

(a) the reasons for refusing to revoke the order, and

(b) the end of the consultation period.

22

(1) This paragraph applies where the local housing authority refuse to revoke an interim or final management order.

(2) The authority must serve on each relevant person a notice setting out—

(a) the authority's decision not to revoke the order;

(b) the reasons for the decision and the date on which it was made;

(c) the right of appeal against the decision under Part 3 of this Schedule; and

(d) the period within which an appeal may be made (see paragraph 29(2)).

(3) The notices required to be served on each relevant person under sub-paragraph (2) must be served within the period of seven days beginning with the day on which the decision is made.

Meaning of "the end of the consultation period" and "relevant person"

23

(1) In this Part of this Schedule "the end of the consultation period" means the last day for making representations in respect of the matter in question.

(2) The end of the consultation period must be a day which is at least 14 days after the date of service of the notice.

(3) In sub-paragraph (2) "the date of service" of a notice means, in a case where more than one notice is served, the date on which the last of the notices is served.

(4) In this Part of this Schedule "relevant person" means any person who, to the knowledge of the local housing authority, is—

- (a) a person having an estate or interest in the house or part of it (but who is not a tenant under a lease with an unexpired term of 3 years or less), or
- (b) any other person who (but for the order) would be a person managing or having control of the house or part of it.

PART 3
APPEALS AGAINST DECISIONS RELATING TO MANAGEMENT ORDERS

Right to appeal against making of order etc

24

(1) A relevant person may appeal to a residential property tribunal against—

- (a) a decision of the local housing authority to make an interim or final management order, or
- (b) the terms of such an order (including, if it is a final management order, those of the management scheme contained in it).

(2) Except to the extent that an appeal may be made in accordance with sub-paragraphs (3) and (4), sub-paragraph (1) does not apply to an interim management order made under section 102(4) or (7) or in accordance with a direction given under paragraph 26(5).

(3) An appeal may be made under sub-paragraph (1)(b) on the grounds that the terms of an interim management order do not provide for one or both of the matters mentioned in section 110(5)(a) and (b) (which relate to payments of surplus rent etc).

(4) Where an appeal is made under sub-paragraph (1)(b) only on those grounds—

- (a) the appeal may be brought at any time while the order is in force (with the result that nothing in sub-paragraph (5) or paragraph 25 applies in relation to the appeal); and
- (b) the powers of the residential property tribunal under paragraph 26 are limited to determining whether the order should be varied by the tribunal so as to include a term providing for the matter or matters in question, and (if so) what provision should be made by the term.

(5) If no appeal is brought against an interim or final management order under this paragraph within the time allowed by paragraph 25 for making such an appeal, the order is final and conclusive as to the matters which could have been raised on appeal.

Time limits for appeals under paragraph 24

25

(1) This paragraph applies in relation to an appeal under paragraph 24 in respect of an interim or final management order.

(2) Any such appeal must be made within the period of 28 days beginning with the date specified in the notice under paragraph 7(5) as the date on which the order was made.

(3) A residential property tribunal may allow an appeal to be made to it after the end of the period mentioned in sub-paragraph (2) if it is satisfied that there is a good reason for the failure to appeal before the end of that period (and for any delay since then in applying for permission to appeal out of time).

Powers of residential property tribunal on appeal under paragraph 24

26

(1) This paragraph applies to an appeal to a residential property tribunal under paragraph 24 in respect of an interim or final management order.

(2) The appeal—

    (a)   is to be by way of a re-hearing, but
    (b)   may be determined having regard to matters of which the authority were unaware.

(3) The tribunal may confirm or vary the order or revoke it—

    (a)   (in the case of an interim management order) as from a date specified in the tribunal's order, or
    (b)   (in the case of a final management order) as from the date of the tribunal's order.

(4) If—

    (a)   the tribunal revokes an interim or final management order,
    (b)   it appears to the tribunal that, on the revocation of the order, the house will be required to be licensed under Part 2 or 3 of this Act, and
    (c)   the tribunal does not give a direction under sub-paragraph (5) or (6),

the tribunal must direct the local housing authority to grant such a licence to such person and on such terms as the tribunal may direct.

(5) If the tribunal revokes a final management order, the tribunal may direct the local housing authority to make an interim management order in respect of the house or part of it on such terms as the tribunal may direct.

This applies despite section 102(9).

(6) If the tribunal revokes a final management order, the tribunal may direct the local housing authority to serve a temporary exemption notice under section 62 or 86 in respect of the house that comes into force on such date as the tribunal directs.

(7) The revocation of an interim management order by the tribunal does not affect the validity of anything previously done in pursuance of the order.

"The operative time" for the purposes of section 114(2)

27

(1) This paragraph defines "the operative time" for the purposes of section 114(2).

(2) If no appeal is made under paragraph 24 before the end of the period of 28 days mentioned in paragraph 25(2), "the operative time" is the end of that period.

(3) If an appeal is made under paragraph 24 before the end of that period, and a decision is given on the appeal which confirms the order, "the operative time" is as follows—

    (a)   if the period within which an appeal to the Lands Tribunal may be brought expires without such an appeal having been brought, "the operative time" is the end of that period;

    (b)   if an appeal to the Lands Tribunal is brought, "the operative time" is the time when a decision is given on the appeal which confirms the order.

(4) For the purposes of sub-paragraph (3)—

    (a)   the withdrawal of an appeal has the same effect as a decision which confirms the order, and

    (b)   references to a decision which confirms the order are to a decision which confirms it with or without variation.

Right to appeal against decision or refusal to vary or revoke interim management order

28

A relevant person may appeal to a residential property tribunal against—

    (a)   a decision of a local housing authority to vary or revoke an interim or final management order, or

    (b)   a refusal of a local housing authority to vary or revoke an interim or final management order.

Time limits for appeals under paragraph 28

29

(1) This paragraph applies in relation to an appeal under paragraph 28 against a decision to vary or revoke, or (as the case may be) to refuse to vary or revoke, an interim or final management order.

(2) Any such appeal must be made before the end of the period of 28 days beginning with the date specified in the notice under paragraph 11, 16, 19 or 22 as the date on which the decision concerned was made.

(3) A residential property tribunal may allow an appeal to be made to it after the end of the period mentioned in sub-paragraph (2) if it is satisfied that there is a good reason for the failure to appeal before the end of that period (and for any delay since then in applying for permission to appeal out of time).

Powers of residential property tribunal on appeal under paragraph 28

30

(1) This paragraph applies to an appeal to a residential property tribunal under paragraph 28 against a decision to vary or revoke, or (as the case may be) to refuse to vary or revoke, an interim or final management order.

(2) Paragraph 26(2) applies to such an appeal as it applies to an appeal under paragraph 24.

(3) The tribunal may confirm, reverse or vary the decision of the local housing authority.

(4) If the appeal is against a decision of the authority to refuse to revoke the order, the tribunal may make an order revoking the order as from a date specified in its order.

"The operative time" for the purposes of section 111(2), 112(2), 121(2) or 122(2)

31

(1) This paragraph defines "the operative time" for the purposes of—

  (a) section 111(2) or 112(2) (variation or revocation of interim management order), or
  (b) section 121(2) or 122(2) (variation or revocation of final management order).

(2) If no appeal is made under paragraph 28 before the end of the period of 28 days mentioned in paragraph 29(2), "the operative time" is the end of that period.

(3) If an appeal is made under paragraph 28 within that period, and a decision is given on the appeal which confirms the variation or revocation, "the operative time" is as follows—

(a) if the period within which an appeal to the Lands Tribunal may be brought expires without such an appeal having been brought, "the operative time" is the end of that period;

(b) if an appeal to the Lands Tribunal is brought, "the operative time" is the time when a decision is given on the appeal which confirms the variation or revocation.

(4) For the purposes of sub-paragraph (3)—

(a) the withdrawal of an appeal has the same effect as a decision which confirms the variation or revocation appealed against; and

(b) references to a decision which confirms a variation are to a decision which confirms it with or without variation.

Right to appeal against decision in respect of compensation payable to third parties

32

(1) This paragraph applies where a local housing authority have made a decision under section 128 as to whether compensation should be paid to a third party in respect of any interference with his rights in consequence of an interim or final management order.

(2) The third party may appeal to a residential property tribunal against—

(a) a decision by the authority not to pay compensation to him, or

(b) a decision of the authority so far as relating to the amount of compensation that should be paid.

Time limits for appeals under paragraph 32

33

(1) This paragraph applies in relation to an appeal under paragraph 32 against a decision of a local housing authority not to pay compensation to a third party or as to the amount of compensation to be paid.

(2) Any such appeal must be made within the period of 28 days beginning with the date the authority notifies the third party under section 128(2).

(3) A residential property tribunal may allow an appeal to be made to it after the end of the period mentioned in sub-paragraph (2) if it is satisfied that there is good reason for the failure to appeal before the end of that period (and for any delay since then in applying for permission to appeal out of time).

Powers of residential property tribunal on appeal under paragraph 32

34

(1) This paragraph applies in relation to an appeal under paragraph 32 against a decision of a local housing authority not to pay compensation to a third party or as to the amount of compensation to be paid.

(2) The appeal—

(a)   is to be by way of re-hearing, but

(b)   may be determined having regard to matters of which the authority were unaware.

(3) The tribunal may confirm, reverse or vary the decision of the local housing authority.

(4) Where the tribunal reverses or varies a decision of the authority in respect of a final management order, it must make an order varying the management scheme contained in the final management order accordingly.

Meaning of "relevant person"

35

In this Part of this Schedule "relevant person" means—

(a)   any person who has an estate or interest in the house or part of it (but is not a tenant under a lease with an unexpired term of 3 years or less), or

(b)   any other person who (but for the order) would be a person managing or having control of the house or part of it.

Schedule 7
Further Provisions Regarding Empty Dwelling Management Orders

Section 132

PART 1
INTERIM EDMOS

Operation of interim EDMOs

1

(1) This paragraph deals with the time when an interim EDMO comes into force or ceases to have effect.

(2) The order comes into force when it is made.

(3) The order ceases to have effect at the end of the period of 12 months beginning with the date on which it is made, unless it ceases to have effect at some other time as mentioned below.

(4) If the order provides that it is to cease to have effect on a date falling before the end of that period, it accordingly ceases to have effect on that date.

(5) Sub-paragraphs (6) and (7) apply where—

(a)   a final EDMO ("the final EDMO") has been made under section 136 so as to replace the order ("the interim EDMO"), but

(b)   the final EDMO has not come into force because of an appeal to a residential property tribunal under paragraph 26 against the making of the final EDMO.

(6) If the date on which the final EDMO comes into force in relation to the dwelling following the disposal of the appeal is later than the date on which the interim EDMO would cease to have effect apart from this sub-paragraph, the interim EDMO continues in force until that later date.

(7) If, on the application of the authority, the tribunal makes an order providing for the interim EDMO to continue in force, pending the disposal of the appeal, until a date later than that on which the interim EDMO would cease to have effect apart from this sub-paragraph, the interim EDMO accordingly continues in force until that later date.

(8) This paragraph has effect subject to paragraphs 6 and 7 (variation or revocation of orders by authority) and to the power of revocation exercisable by a residential property tribunal on an appeal made under paragraph 30.

General effect of interim EDMOs

2

(1) This paragraph applies while an interim EDMO is in force in relation to a dwelling.

(2) The rights and powers conferred by sub-paragraph (3) are exercisable by the authority in performing their duties under section 135(1) to (3) in respect of the dwelling.

(3) The authority—

(a)   have the right to possession of the dwelling (subject to the rights of existing occupiers preserved by paragraph 18(3));

(b)   have the right to do (and authorise a manager or other person to do) in relation to the dwelling anything which the relevant proprietor of the dwelling would (but for the order) be entitled to do;

(c)   may create one or more of the following—

(i)   an interest in the dwelling which, as far as possible, has all the incidents of a leasehold, or

(ii)   a right in the nature of a licence to occupy part of the dwelling;

(d)   may apply to a residential property tribunal for an order under paragraph 22 determining a lease or licence of the dwelling.

(4) But the authority may not under sub-paragraph (3)(c) create any interest or right in the nature of a lease or licence unless—

(a)   consent in writing has been given by the relevant proprietor of the dwelling, and

(b)   where the relevant proprietor is a lessee under a lease of the dwelling, the interest or right is created for a term that is less than the term of that lease.

(5) The authority—

    (a)   do not under this paragraph acquire any estate or interest in the dwelling, and

    (b)   accordingly are not entitled by virtue of this paragraph to sell, lease, charge or make any other disposition of any such estate or interest.

(6) But, where the relevant proprietor of the dwelling is a lessee under a lease of the dwelling, the authority are to be treated (subject to sub-paragraph (5)(a)) as if they were the lessee instead.

(7) Any enactment or rule of law relating to landlords and tenants or leases applies in relation to—

    (a)   a lease in relation to which the authority are to be treated as the lessee under sub-paragraph (6), or

    (b)   a lease to which the authority become a party under paragraph 4(2),

as if the authority were the legal owner of the premises (but this is subject to paragraph 4(4) to (6)).

(8) None of the following, namely—

    (a)   the authority, or

    (b)   any person authorised under sub-paragraph (3)(b),

is liable to any person having an estate or interest in the dwelling for anything done or omitted to be done in the performance (or intended performance) of the authority's duties under section 135(1) to (3) unless the act or omission is due to negligence of the authority or any such person.

(9) An interim EDMO which has come into force is a local land charge.

(10) The authority may apply to the Chief Land Registrar for the entry of an appropriate restriction in the register of title in respect of such an order.

(11) In this paragraph "enactment" includes an enactment comprised in subordinate legislation (within the meaning of the Interpretation Act 1978 (c 30)).

General effect of interim EDMOs: leases and licences granted by authority

3

(1) This paragraph applies in relation to any interest or right created by the authority under paragraph 2(3)(c).

(2) For the purposes of any enactment or rule of law—

    (a)   any interest created by the authority under paragraph 2(3)(c)(i) is to be treated as if it were a legal lease, and

    (b)   any right created by the authority under paragraph 2(3)(c)(ii) is to be treated as if it were a licence to occupy granted by the legal owner of the dwelling, despite the fact that the authority have no legal estate in the dwelling (see paragraph 2(5)(a)).

(3) Any enactment or rule of law relating to landlords and tenants or leases accordingly applies in relation to any interest created by the authority under paragraph 2(3)(c)(i) as if the authority were the legal owner of the dwelling.

(4) References to leases and licences—

    (a)   in this Chapter, and

    (b)   in any other enactment,

accordingly include (where the context permits) interests and rights created by the authority under paragraph 2(3)(c).

(5) The preceding provisions of this paragraph have effect subject to—

    (a)   paragraph 4(4) to (6), and

    (b)   any provision to the contrary contained in an order made by the appropriate national authority.

(6) In paragraph 2(5)(b) the reference to leasing does not include the creation of interests under paragraph 2(3)(c)(i).

(7) In this paragraph—

    "enactment" has the meaning given by paragraph 2(11);

    "legal lease" means a term of years absolute (within section 1(1)(b) of the Law of Property Act 1925 (c 20)).

General effect of interim EDMOs: relevant proprietor, mortgagees etc

4

(1) This paragraph applies in relation to—

    (a)   the relevant proprietor, and

    (b)   other persons with an estate or interest in the dwelling,

while an interim EDMO is in force in relation to a dwelling.

(2) Where the relevant proprietor is a lessor or licensor under a lease or licence of the dwelling, the lease or licence has effect while the order is in force as if the local housing authority were substituted in it for the lessor or licensor.

(3) Such a lease continues to have effect, as far as possible, as a lease despite the fact that the rights of the local housing authority, as substituted for the lessor, do not amount to an estate in law in the dwelling.

(4) The provisions mentioned in sub-paragraph (5) do not apply to a lease or licence within sub-paragraph (2).

(5) The provisions are—

    (a)   the provisions which exclude local authority lettings from the Rent Acts, namely—

        (i)   sections 14 to 16 of the Rent Act 1977 (c 42), and

(ii) those sections as applied by Schedule 2 to the Rent (Agriculture) Act 1976 (c 80) and section 5(2) to (4) of that Act; and

(b) section 1(2) of, and paragraph 12 of Part 1 of Schedule 1 to, the Housing Act 1988 (c 50) (which exclude local authority lettings from Part 1 of that Act).

(6) Nothing in this Chapter has the result that the authority are to be treated as the legal owner of any premises for the purposes of—

(a) section 80 of the Housing Act 1985 (c 68) (the landlord condition for secure tenancies); or

(b) section 124 of the Housing Act 1996 (c 52) (introductory tenancies).

(7) The relevant proprietor of the dwelling—

(a) is not entitled to receive any rents or other payments made in respect of occupation of the dwelling;

(b) may not exercise any rights or powers with respect to the management of the dwelling; and

(c) may not create any of the following—

(i) any leasehold interest in the dwelling or a part of it (other than a lease of a reversion), or

(ii) any licence or other right to occupy it.

(8) However (subject to sub-paragraph (7)(c)) nothing in paragraph 2 or this paragraph affects the ability of a person having an estate or interest in the dwelling to make any disposition of that estate or interest.

(9) Nothing in paragraph 2 or this paragraph affects—

(a) the validity of any mortgage relating to the dwelling or any rights or remedies available to the mortgagee under such a mortgage, or

(b) the validity of any lease of the dwelling under which the relevant proprietor is a lessee, or any superior lease, or (subject to paragraph 2(6)) any rights or remedies available to the lessor under such a lease,

except to the extent that any of those rights or remedies would prevent the local housing authority from exercising their power under paragraph 2(3)(c).

(10) In proceedings for the enforcement of any such rights or remedies the court may make such order as it thinks fit as regards the operation of the interim EDMO (including an order quashing it).

Financial arrangements while order is in force

5

(1) This paragraph applies to relevant expenditure of a local housing authority who have made an interim EDMO.

(2) "Relevant expenditure" means—

(a) expenditure incurred by the authority with the consent of the relevant proprietor, or

(b) any other expenditure reasonably incurred by the authority,

in connection with performing their duties under section 135(1) to (3) in respect of the dwelling (including any premiums paid for insurance of the premises).

(3) Rent or other payments which the authority have collected or recovered, by virtue of this Chapter, from persons occupying or having the right to occupy the dwelling may be used by the authority to meet—

(a) relevant expenditure, and

(b) any amounts of compensation payable to a third party by virtue of an order under section 134(4) or 138(2) or to a dispossessed landlord or tenant by virtue of an order under paragraph 22(5).

(4) The authority must pay to the relevant proprietor—

(a) any amount of rent or other payments collected or recovered as mentioned in sub-paragraph (3) that remains after deductions to meet relevant expenditure and any amounts of compensation payable as mentioned in that sub-paragraph, and

(b) (where appropriate) interest on that amount at a reasonable rate fixed by the authority,

and such payments are to be made at such intervals as the authority consider appropriate.

(5) The interim EDMO may provide for—

(a) the rate of interest which is to apply for the purposes of paragraph (b) of sub-paragraph (4); and

(b) the intervals at which payments are to be made under that sub-paragraph.

Paragraph 26(1)(c) enables an appeal to be brought where the order does not provide for both of those matters.

(6) The authority must—

(a) keep full accounts of their income and expenditure in respect of the dwelling; and

(b) afford to the relevant proprietor, and to any other person who has an estate or interest in the dwelling, all reasonable facilities for inspecting, taking copies of and verifying those accounts.

(7) The relevant proprietor may apply to a residential property tribunal for an order—

(a) declaring that an amount shown in the accounts as expenditure of the authority does not constitute relevant expenditure (see sub-paragraph (2));

(b) requiring the authority to make such financial adjustments (in the accounts and otherwise) as are necessary to reflect the tribunal's declaration.

(8) In this paragraph—

"dispossessed landlord or tenant" means a person who was a lessor, lessee, licensor or licensee under a lease or licence determined by an order under paragraph 22;

"expenditure" includes administrative costs.

Variation or revocation of interim EDMOs

6

(1) The local housing authority may vary an interim EDMO if they consider it appropriate to do so.

(2) A variation does not come into force until such time, if any, as is the operative time for the purposes of this sub-paragraph under paragraph 33 (time when period for appealing expires without an appeal being made or when decision to vary is confirmed on appeal).

(3) The power to vary an order under this paragraph is exercisable by the authority either—

- (a) on an application made by a relevant person, or
- (b) on the authority's own initiative.

(4) In this paragraph "relevant person" means any person who has an estate or interest in the dwelling (other than a person who is a tenant under a lease granted under paragraph 2(3)(c)).

7

(1) The local housing authority may revoke an interim EDMO in the following cases—

- (a) where the authority conclude that there are no steps which they could appropriately take for the purpose of securing that the dwelling is occupied (see section 135(4));
- (b) where the authority are satisfied that—
  - (i) the dwelling will either become or continue to be occupied, despite the order being revoked, or
  - (ii) that the dwelling is to be sold;
- (c) where a final EDMO has been made by the authority in respect of the dwelling so as to replace the order;
- (d) where the authority conclude that it would be appropriate to revoke the order in order to prevent or stop interference with the rights of a third party in consequence of the order; and
- (e) where in any other circumstances the authority consider it appropriate to revoke the order.

(2) But, in a case where the dwelling is occupied, the local housing authority may not revoke an interim EDMO under sub-paragraph (1)(b), (d) or (e) unless the relevant proprietor consents.

(3) A revocation does not come into force until such time, if any, as is the operative time for the purposes of this sub-paragraph under paragraph 33 (time when period for appealing expires without an appeal being made or when decision to revoke is confirmed on appeal).

(4) The power to revoke an order under this paragraph is exercisable by the authority either—

(a) on an application made by a relevant person, or

(b) on the authority's own initiative.

(5) Where a relevant person applies to the authority for the revocation of an order under this paragraph, the authority may refuse to revoke the order unless the relevant proprietor (or some other person) agrees to pay to the authority any deficit such as is mentioned in paragraph 23(4).

(6) In this paragraph "relevant person" means any person who has an estate or interest in the dwelling (other than a person who is a tenant under a lease granted under paragraph 2(3)(c)).

8

(1) Part 2 of Schedule 6 applies in relation to the variation or revocation of an interim EDMO as it applies in relation to the variation or revocation of an interim management order.

(2) But Part 2 of that Schedule so applies as if—

(a) references to the right of appeal under Part 3 of the Schedule and to paragraph 29(2) were to the right of appeal under Part 4 of this Schedule and to paragraph 31(2) of this Schedule, and

(b) paragraph 23(4) defined "relevant person" as any person who, to the knowledge of the local housing authority, is a person having an estate or interest in the dwelling (other than a person who is a tenant under a lease granted under paragraph 2(3)(c) of this Schedule).

PART 2
FINAL EDMOS

Operation of final EDMOs

9

(1) This paragraph deals with the time when a final EDMO comes into force or ceases to have effect.

(2) The order does not come into force until such time (if any) as is the operative time for the purposes of this sub-paragraph under paragraph 29 (time when period for appealing expires without an appeal being made or when order is confirmed on appeal).

(3) The order ceases to have effect at the end of the period of 7 years beginning with the date on which it comes into force, unless it ceases to have effect at some other time as mentioned below.

(4) If the order provides that it is to cease to have effect on a date falling before the end of that period, it accordingly ceases to have effect on that date.

(5) If—

    (a)   the order provides that it is to cease to have effect on a date falling after the end of that period, and

    (b)   the relevant proprietor of the dwelling has consented to that provision,

the order accordingly ceases to have effect on that date.

(6) Sub-paragraphs (7) and (8) apply where—

    (a)   a new final EDMO ("the new order") has been made so as to replace the order ("the existing order"), but

    (b)   the new order has not come into force because of an appeal to a residential property tribunal under paragraph 26 against the making of that order.

(7) If the date on which the new order comes into force in relation to the dwelling following the disposal of the appeal is later than the date on which the existing order would cease to have effect apart from this sub-paragraph, the existing order continues in force until that later date.

(8) If, on the application of the authority, the tribunal makes an order providing for the existing order to continue in force, pending the disposal of the appeal, until a date later than that on which it would cease to have effect apart from this sub-paragraph, the existing order accordingly continues in force until that later date.

(9) This paragraph has effect subject to paragraphs 15 and 16 (variation or revocation of orders) and to the power of revocation exercisable by a residential property tribunal on an appeal made under paragraph 26 or 30.

General effect of final EDMOs

10

(1) This paragraph applies while a final EDMO is in force in relation to a dwelling.

(2) The rights and powers conferred by sub-paragraph (3) are exercisable by the authority in performing their duties under section 137(1) to (3) in respect of the dwelling.

(3) The authority—

    (a)   have the right to possession of the dwelling (subject to the rights of existing and other occupiers preserved by paragraph 18(3) and (4));

(b)   have the right to do (and authorise a manager or other person to do) in relation to the dwelling anything which the relevant proprietor of the dwelling would (but for the order) be entitled to do;

(c)   may create one or more of the following—

    (i)   an interest in the dwelling which, as far as possible, has all the incidents of a leasehold, or

    (ii)   a right in the nature of a licence to occupy part of the dwelling;

(d)   may apply to a residential property tribunal for an order under paragraph 22 determining a lease or licence of the dwelling.

(4) The powers of the authority under sub-paragraph (3)(c) are restricted as follows—

(a)   they may not create any interest or right in the nature of a lease or licence—

    (i)   which is for a fixed term expiring after the date on which the order is due to expire, or

    (ii)   (subject to paragraph (b)) which is terminable by notice to quit, or an equivalent notice, of more than 4 weeks,

    unless consent in writing has been given by the relevant proprietor;

(b)   they may create an interest in the nature of an assured shorthold tenancy without any such consent so long as it is created before the beginning of the period of 6 months that ends with the date on which the order is due to expire.

(5) The authority—

(a)   do not under this paragraph acquire any estate or interest in the dwelling, and

(b)   accordingly are not entitled by virtue of this paragraph to sell, lease, charge or make any other disposition of any such estate or interest.

(6) But, where the relevant proprietor of the dwelling is a lessee under a lease of the dwelling, the authority are to be treated (subject to sub-paragraph (5)(a)) as if they were the lessee instead.

(7) Any enactment or rule of law relating to landlords and tenants or leases applies in relation to—

(a)   a lease in relation to which the authority are to be treated as the lessee under sub-paragraph (6), or

(b)   a lease to which the authority become a party under paragraph 12(2),

as if the authority were the legal owner of the premises (but this is subject to paragraph 12(4) to (6)).

(8) None of the following, namely—

(a)   the authority, or

(b)   any person authorised under sub-paragraph (3)(b),

is liable to any person having an estate or interest in the dwelling for anything done or omitted to be done in the performance (or intended performance) of the authority's duties under section 137(1) to (3) unless the act or omission is due to negligence of the authority or any such person.

(9) A final EDMO which has come into force is a local land charge.

(10) The authority may apply to the Chief Land Registrar for the entry of an appropriate restriction in the register in respect of such an order.

(11) In this paragraph "enactment" includes an enactment comprised in subordinate legislation (within the meaning of the Interpretation Act 1978 (c 30)).

General effect of final EDMOs: leases and licences granted by authority

11

(1) This paragraph applies in relation to any interest or right created by the authority under paragraph 10(3)(c).

(2) For the purposes of any enactment or rule of law—

    (a)   any interest created by the authority under paragraph 10(3)(c)(i) is to be treated as if it were a legal lease, and

    (b)   any right created by the authority under paragraph 10(3)(c)(ii) is to be treated as if it were a licence to occupy granted by the legal owner of the dwelling,

despite the fact that the authority have no legal estate in the dwelling (see paragraph 10(5)(a)).

(3) Any enactment or rule of law relating to landlords and tenants or leases accordingly applies in relation to any interest created by the authority under paragraph 10(3)(c)(i) as if the authority were the legal owner of the dwelling.

(4) References to leases and licences—

    (a)   in this Chapter, and

    (b)   in any other enactment,

accordingly include (where the context permits) interests and rights created by the authority under paragraph 10(3)(c).

(5) The preceding provisions of this paragraph have effect subject to—

    (a)   paragraph 12(4) to (6), and

    (b)   any provision to the contrary contained in an order made by the appropriate national authority.

(6) In paragraph 10(5)(b) the reference to leasing does not include the creation of interests under paragraph 10(3)(c)(i).

(7) In this paragraph—

    "enactment" has the meaning given by paragraph 10(11);

    "legal lease" means a term of years absolute (within section 1(1)(b) of the Law of Property Act 1925 (c 20)).

General effect of final EDMOs: relevant proprietor, mortgagees etc

12

(1) This paragraph applies in relation to—

    (a)   the relevant proprietor, and

    (b)   other persons with an estate or interest in the dwelling,

while a final EDMO is in force in relation to a dwelling.

(2) Where the relevant proprietor is a lessor or licensor under a lease or licence of the dwelling, the lease or licence has effect while the order is in force as if the local housing authority were substituted in it for the lessor or licensor.

(3) Such a lease continues to have effect, as far as possible, as a lease despite the fact that the rights of the local housing authority, as substituted for the lessor, do not amount to an estate in law in the dwelling.

(4) The provisions mentioned in sub-paragraph (5) do not apply to a lease or licence within sub-paragraph (2).

(5) The provisions are—

    (a)   the provisions which exclude local authority lettings from the Rent Acts, namely—

        (i)   sections 14 to 16 of the Rent Act 1977 (c 42), and

        (ii)   those sections as applied by Schedule 2 to the Rent (Agriculture) Act 1976 (c 80) and section 5(2) to (4) of that Act; and

    (b)   section 1(2) of, and paragraph 12 of Part 1 of Schedule 1 to, the Housing Act 1988 (c 50) (which exclude local authority lettings from Part 1 of that Act).

(6) Nothing in this Chapter has the result that the authority are to be treated as the legal owner of any premises for the purposes of—

    (a)   section 80 of the Housing Act 1985 (c 68) (the landlord condition for secure tenancies); or

    (b)   section 124 of the Housing Act 1996 (c 52) (introductory tenancies).

(7) The relevant proprietor of the dwelling—

    (a)   is not entitled to receive any rents or other payments made in respect of occupation of the dwelling;

    (b)   may not exercise any rights or powers with respect to the management of the dwelling; and

    (c)   may not create any of the following—

        (i)   any leasehold interest in the dwelling or a part of it (other than a lease of a reversion), or

        (ii)   any licence or other right to occupy it.

(8) However (subject to sub-paragraph (7)(c)) nothing in paragraph 10 or this paragraph affects the ability of a person having an estate or interest in the dwelling to make any disposition of that estate or interest.

(9) Nothing in paragraph 10 or this paragraph affects—

    (a)   the validity of any mortgage relating to the dwelling or any rights or remedies available to the mortgagee under such a mortgage, or

    (b)   the validity of any lease of the dwelling under which the relevant proprietor is a lessee, or any superior lease, or (subject to paragraph 10(6)) any rights or remedies available to the lessor under such a lease;

except to the extent that any of those rights or remedies would prevent the local housing authority from exercising their power under paragraph 10(3)(c).

(10) In proceedings for the enforcement of any such rights or remedies the court may make such order as it thinks fit as regards the operation of the final EDMO (including an order quashing it).

Management scheme and accounts

13

(1) A final EDMO must contain a management scheme.

(2) A "management scheme" is a scheme setting out how the local housing authority are to carry out their duties under section 137(1) to (3) as respects the dwelling.

(3) The scheme is to contain a plan giving details of the way in which the authority propose to manage the dwelling, which must (in particular) include—

    (a)   details of any works that the authority intend to carry out in connection with the dwelling;

    (b)   an estimate of the capital and other expenditure to be incurred by the authority in respect of the dwelling while the order is in force;

    (c)   the amount of rent which, in the opinion of the authority, the dwelling might reasonably be expected to fetch on the open market at the time the management scheme is made;

    (d)   the amount of rent or other payments that the authority will seek to obtain;

    (e)   the amount of any compensation that is payable to a third party by virtue of a decision of the authority under section 136(4) or 138(3) in respect of any interference in consequence of the final EDMO with the rights of that person;

    (f)   provision as to the payment of any such compensation and of any compensation payable to a dispossessed landlord or tenant by virtue of an order under paragraph 22(5);

    (g)   where the amount of rent payable to the authority in respect of the dwelling for a period is less than the amount of rent mentioned in paragraph (c) in respect of a period of the same length, provision as to the following—

        (i)   the deduction from the difference of relevant expenditure and any amounts of compensation payable to a third party or dispossessed landlord or tenant;

     (ii)   the payment of any remaining amount to the relevant proprietor;

     (iii) the deduction from time to time of any remaining amount from any amount that the authority are entitled to recover from the proprietor under paragraph 23(5) or (6);

  (h)   provision as to the payment by the authority to the relevant proprietor from time to time of amounts of rent or other payments that remain after the deduction of—

     (i)   relevant expenditure, and

     (ii)   any amount of compensation payable to a third party or dispossessed landlord or tenant;

  (i)   provision as to the manner in which the authority are to pay to the relevant proprietor, on the termination of the final EDMO, the balance of any amounts of rent or other payments that remain after the deduction of relevant expenditure and any amounts of compensation payable to a third party or dispossessed landlord or tenant;

  (j)   provision as to the manner in which the authority are to pay, on the termination of the final EDMO, any outstanding amount of compensation payable to a third party or dispossessed landlord or tenant.

(4) The scheme may also state—

  (a)   the authority's intentions as regards the use of rent or other payments to meet relevant expenditure;

  (b)   the authority's intentions as regards the payment to the relevant proprietor (where appropriate) of interest on amounts within sub-paragraph (3)(h) and (i);

  (c)   that paragraph 23(2) or, where the relevant proprietor consents, paragraph 23(3)(c) is not to apply in relation to an interim EDMO or (as the case may be) final EDMO that immediately preceded the final EDMO, and that instead the authority intend to use any balance such as is mentioned in that sub-paragraph to meet—

     (i)   relevant expenditure incurred during the currency of that final EDMO, and

     (ii)   any compensation that may become payable to a third party or a dispossessed landlord or tenant;

  (d)   that paragraph 23(4) to (6) are not to apply in relation to an interim EDMO or, where the relevant proprietor consents, a final EDMO that immediately preceded the final EDMO, and that instead the authority intend to use rent or other payments collected during the currency of that final EDMO to reimburse the authority in respect of any deficit such as is mentioned in paragraph 23(4);

  (e)   the authority's intentions as regards the recovery from the relevant proprietor, with or without interest, of any amount of relevant expenditure incurred under a previous interim EDMO or final EDMO that the authority are entitled to recover from the proprietor under paragraph 23(5) or (6).

(5) The authority must—

(a) keep full accounts of their income and expenditure in respect of the dwelling; and

(b) afford to the relevant proprietor, and to any other person who has an estate or interest in the dwelling, all reasonable facilities for inspecting, taking copies of and verifying those accounts.

(6) In this paragraph—

"dispossessed landlord or tenant" means a person who was a lessor, lessee, licensor or licensee under a lease or licence determined by an order under paragraph 22;

"relevant expenditure" means—

(a) expenditure incurred by the authority with the consent of the relevant proprietor, or

(b) any other expenditure reasonably incurred by the authority, in connection with performing their duties under section 135(1) to (3) or 137(1) to (3) in respect of the dwelling (including any reasonable administrative costs and any premiums paid for insurance of the premises);

"rent or other payments" means rent or other payments collected or recovered, by virtue of this Chapter, from persons occupying or having the right to occupy the dwelling.

(7) In any provision of this Chapter relating to varying, revoking or appealing against decisions relating to a final EDMO, any reference to such an order includes (where the context permits) a reference to the management scheme contained in it.

Application to residential property tribunal in respect of breach of management scheme

14

(1) An affected person may apply to a residential property tribunal for an order requiring the local housing authority to manage a dwelling in accordance with the management scheme contained in a final EDMO made in respect of the dwelling.

(2) On such an application the tribunal may, if it considers it appropriate to do so, make an order—

(a) requiring the authority to manage the dwelling in accordance with the management scheme, or

(b) revoking the final EDMO as from a date specified in the tribunal's order.

(3) An order under sub-paragraph (2) may—

(a) set out the steps which the authority are to take to manage the dwelling in accordance with the management scheme,

(b) include provision varying the final EDMO, and

(c)   require the payment of money to an affected person by way of damages.

(4) In this paragraph "affected person" means—

(a)   the relevant proprietor, and

(b)   any third party to whom compensation is payable by virtue of an order under section 134(4) or 138(2) or a decision of the authority under section 136(4) or 138(3) or who was a lessor, lessee, licensor or licensee under a lease or licence determined by an order of the residential property tribunal under paragraph 22 and to whom compensation is payable by virtue of an order under sub-paragraph (5) of that paragraph.

Variation or revocation of final EDMOs

15

(1) The local housing authority may vary a final EDMO if they consider it appropriate to do so.

(2) A variation does not come into force until such time, if any, as is the operative time for the purposes of this sub-paragraph under paragraph 33 (time when period for appealing expires without an appeal being made or when decision to vary is confirmed on appeal).

(3) The power to vary an order under this paragraph is exercisable by the authority either—

(a)   on an application made by a relevant person, or

(b)   on the authority's own initiative.

(4) In this paragraph "relevant person" means any person who has an estate or interest in the dwelling (other than a person who is a tenant under a lease granted under paragraph 2(3)(c) or 10(3)(c)).

16

(1) The local housing authority may revoke a final EDMO in the following cases—

(a)   where the authority conclude that there are no steps which they could appropriately take as mentioned in section 137(4)(b) or that keeping the order in force is not necessary as mentioned in section 137(4)(c);

(b)   where the authority are satisfied that—

(i)   the dwelling will either become or continue to be occupied, despite the order being revoked, or

(ii)   that the dwelling is to be sold;

(c)   where a further final EDMO has been made by the authority in respect of the dwelling so as to replace the order;

(d)   where the authority conclude that it would be appropriate to revoke the order in order to prevent or stop interference with the rights of a third party in consequence of the order; and

(e)   where in any other circumstances the authority consider it appropriate to revoke the order.

(2) But, in a case where the dwelling is occupied, the local housing authority may not revoke a final EDMO under sub-paragraph (1)(b), (d) or (e) unless the relevant proprietor consents.

(3) A revocation does not come into force until such time, if any, as is the operative time for the purposes of this sub-paragraph under paragraph 33 (time when period for appealing expires without an appeal being made or when decision to revoke is confirmed on appeal).

(4) The power to revoke an order under this paragraph is exercisable by the authority either—

(a)   on an application made by a relevant person, or
(b)   on the authority's own initiative.

(5) Where a relevant person applies to the authority for the revocation of an order under this paragraph, the authority may refuse to revoke the order unless the relevant proprietor (or some other person) agrees to pay to the authority any deficit such as is mentioned in paragraph 23(4).

(6) In this paragraph "relevant person" means any person who has an estate or interest in the dwelling (other than a person who is a tenant under a lease granted under paragraph 2(3)(c) or 10(3)(c)).

17

(1) Part 2 of Schedule 6 applies in relation to the variation or revocation of a final EDMO as it applies in relation to the variation or revocation of a final management order.

(2) But Part 2 of that Schedule so applies as if—

(a)   references to the right of appeal under Part 3 of the Schedule and to paragraph 29(2) were to the right of appeal under Part 4 of this Schedule and to paragraph 31(2) of this Schedule, and
(b)   paragraph 23(4) defined "relevant person" as any person who, to the knowledge of the local housing authority, is a person having an estate or interest in the dwelling (other than a person who is a tenant under a lease granted under paragraph 2(3)(c) or 10(3)(c) of this Schedule).

PART 3
INTERIM AND FINAL EDMOS: GENERAL PROVISIONS (OTHER THAN PROVISIONS RELATING TO APPEALS)

Effect of EDMOs: persons occupying or having a right to occupy the dwelling

18

(1) This paragraph applies to existing and new occupiers of a dwelling in relation to which an interim EDMO or final EDMO is in force.

(2) In this paragraph—

    "existing occupier" means a person other than the relevant proprietor who, at the time when the order comes into force—

        (a)   has the right to occupy the dwelling, but

        (b)   is not a new occupier within sub-paragraph (4);

    "new occupier" means a person who, at a time when the order is in force, is occupying the dwelling under a lease or licence granted under paragraph 2(3)(c) or 10(3)(c).

(3) Paragraphs 2 and 10 do not affect the rights or liabilities of an existing occupier under a lease or licence (whether in writing or not) under which he has the right to occupy the dwelling at the commencement date.

(4) Paragraph 10 does not affect the rights and liabilities of a new occupier who, in the case of a final EDMO, is occupying the dwelling at the time when the order comes into force.

(5) The provisions mentioned in sub-paragraph (6) do not apply to a lease or agreement under which a new occupier has the right to occupy or is occupying the dwelling.

(6) The provisions are—

        (a)   the provisions which exclude local authority lettings from the Rent Acts, namely—

             (i)   sections 14 to 16 of the Rent Act 1977 (c 42), and

             (ii)   those sections as applied by Schedule 2 to the Rent (Agriculture) Act 1976 (c 80) and section 5(2) to (4) of that Act; and

        (b)   section 1(2) of, and paragraph 12 of Part 1 of Schedule 1 to, the Housing Act 1988 (c 50) (which exclude local authority lettings from Part 1 of that Act).

(7) If, immediately before the coming into force of an interim EDMO or final EDMO, an existing occupier had the right to occupy the dwelling under—

        (a)   a protected or statutory tenancy within the meaning of the Rent Act 1977,

        (b)   a protected or statutory tenancy within the meaning of the Rent (Agriculture) Act 1976, or

        (c)   an assured tenancy or assured agricultural occupancy within the meaning of Part 1 of the Housing Act 1988,

nothing in this Chapter (except an order under paragraph 22 determining a lease or licence) prevents the continuance of that tenancy or occupancy or affects the continued operation of any of those Acts in relation to the tenancy or occupancy after the coming into force of the order.

(8) In this paragraph "the commencement date" means the date on which the order came into force (or, if that order was preceded by one or more orders under this Chapter, the date when the first order came into force).

Effect of EDMOs: agreements and legal proceedings

19

(1) An agreement or instrument within sub-paragraph (2) has effect, while an interim EDMO or final EDMO is in force, as if any rights or liabilities of the relevant proprietor under the agreement or instrument were instead rights or liabilities of the local housing authority.

(2) An agreement or instrument is within this sub-paragraph if—

- (a) it is effective on the commencement date,
- (b) one of the parties to it is the relevant proprietor of the dwelling,
- (c) it relates to the dwelling, whether in connection with any management activities with respect to it, or otherwise,
- (d) it is specified for the purposes of this sub-paragraph in the order or falls within a description of agreements or instruments so specified, and
- (e) the authority serve a notice in writing on all the parties to it stating that sub-paragraph (1) is to apply to it.

(3) An agreement or instrument is not within sub-paragraph (2) if—

- (a) it is a lease or licence within paragraph 2(6) or 10(6), or
- (b) it relates to any disposition by the relevant proprietor which is not precluded by paragraph 4(7) or 12(7).

(4) Proceedings in respect of any cause of action within sub-paragraph (5) may, while an interim EDMO or final EDMO is in force, be instituted or continued by or against the local housing authority instead of by or against the relevant proprietor.

(5) A cause of action is within this sub-paragraph if—

- (a) it is a cause of action (of any nature) which accrued to or against the relevant proprietor of the dwelling before the commencement date,
- (b) it relates to the dwelling as mentioned in sub-paragraph (2)(c),
- (c) it is specified for the purposes of this sub-paragraph in the order or falls within a description of causes of action so specified, and
- (d) the authority serve a notice in writing on all interested parties stating that sub-paragraph (4) is to apply to it.

(6) If, by virtue of this paragraph, the authority become subject to any liability to pay damages in respect of anything done (or omitted to be done) before the commencement date by or on behalf of the relevant proprietor of the dwelling, the relevant proprietor is liable to reimburse to the authority an amount equal to the amount of damages paid by them.

(7) In this paragraph—

"agreement" includes arrangement;
"the commencement date" means the date on which the order comes into force (or, if that order was preceded by one or more orders under this Chapter, the date when the first order came into force);

"management activities" includes repair, maintenance, improvement and insurance.

Effect of EDMOs: furniture

20

(1) Sub-paragraph (2) applies where, on the date on which an interim EDMO or final EDMO comes into force, there is furniture owned by the relevant proprietor in the dwelling.

(2) Subject to sub-paragraphs (3) and (4), the right to possession of the furniture against all persons vests in the local housing authority on that date and remains vested in the authority while the order is in force.

(3) The right of the local housing authority under sub-paragraph (2) to possession of the furniture is subject to the rights of any person who, on the date on which the interim EDMO or final EDMO comes into force, has the right to possession of the dwelling.

(4) Where—

    (a)   the local housing authority have the right to possession of the furniture under sub-paragraph (2), and

    (b)   they have not granted a right to possession of the furniture to any other person,

they must, on a request by the relevant proprietor, give up possession of the furniture to him.

(5) The local housing authority may renounce the right to possession of the furniture conferred by sub-paragraph (2) by serving notice on the relevant proprietor not less than two weeks before the renunciation is to have effect.

(6) Where the local housing authority renounce the right to possession of the furniture under sub-paragraph (5), they must make appropriate arrangements for storage of the furniture at their own cost.

(7) In this paragraph "furniture" includes fittings and other articles.

EDMOs: power to supply furniture

21

(1) The local housing authority may supply the dwelling to which an interim EDMO or final EDMO relates with such furniture as they consider to be required.

(2) For the purposes of paragraph 5 or paragraph 13, any expenditure incurred by the authority under this paragraph constitutes expenditure incurred by the authority in connection with performing their duties under section 135(1) to (3) or 137(1) to (3).

(3) In this paragraph "furniture" includes fittings and other articles.

Power of a residential property tribunal to determine certain leases and licences

22

(1) A residential property tribunal may make an order determining a lease or licence to which this paragraph applies if—

   (a)   the case falls within sub-paragraph (3) or (4), and

   (b)   the tribunal are satisfied that the dwelling is not being occupied and that the local housing authority need to have the right to possession of the dwelling in order to secure that the dwelling becomes occupied.

(2) This paragraph applies to the following leases and licences of a dwelling—

   (a)   a lease of the dwelling in respect of which the relevant proprietor is the lessor,

   (b)   a sub-lease of any such lease, and

   (c)   a licence of the dwelling.

(3) A case falls within this sub-paragraph if—

   (a)   an interim or final EDMO is in force in respect of the dwelling, and

   (b)   the local housing authority have applied under paragraph 2(3)(d) or 10(3)(d) for an order determining the lease or licence.

(4) A case falls within this sub-paragraph if—

   (a)   the local housing authority have applied to the residential property tribunal under section 133 for an order authorising them to make an interim EDMO in respect of the dwelling and an order determining the lease or licence, and

   (b)   the residential property tribunal has decided to authorise the authority to make an interim EDMO in respect of the dwelling.

(5) An order under this paragraph may include provision requiring the local housing authority to pay such amount or amounts to one or more of the lessor, lessee, licensor or licensee by way of compensation in respect of the determination of the lease or licence as the tribunal determines.

(6) Where—

   (a)   a final EDMO is in force in respect of a dwelling, and

   (b)   the tribunal makes an order requiring the local housing authority to pay an amount of compensation to a lessor, lessee, licensor or licensee in respect of the determination of a lease or licence of the dwelling,

the tribunal must make an order varying the management scheme contained in the final EDMO so as to make provision as to the payment of that compensation.

Termination of EDMOs: financial arrangements

23

(1) This paragraph applies where an interim EDMO or final EDMO ceases to have effect for any reason.

(2) If, on the termination date for an interim EDMO, the total amount of rent or other payments collected or recovered as mentioned in paragraph 5(3) exceeds the total amount of—

    (a)   the authority's relevant expenditure, and

    (b)   any amounts of compensation payable to third parties by virtue of orders under section 134(4) or 138(2) or decisions of the authority under section 136(4) or 138(3),

the authority must, as soon as possible after the termination date, pay the balance to the relevant proprietor.

(3) If, on the termination date for a final EDMO, any balance is payable to—

    (a)   a third party,

    (b)   a dispossessed landlord or tenant, or

    (c)   the relevant proprietor,

in accordance with the management scheme under paragraph 13, that amount must be paid to that person by the local housing authority in the manner provided by the scheme.

(4) Sub-paragraphs (5) and (6) apply where, on the termination date for an interim EDMO or final EDMO, the total amount of rent or other payments collected or recovered as mentioned in paragraph 5(3) is less than the total amount of the authority's relevant expenditure together with any such amounts of compensation as are mentioned in sub-paragraph (2)(b) above.

(5) The authority may recover from the relevant proprietor—

    (a)   the amount of any relevant expenditure (not exceeding the deficit mentioned in sub-paragraph (4)) which he has agreed in writing to pay either as a condition of revocation of the order or otherwise, and

    (b)   where the relevant proprietor is a tenant under a lease in respect of the dwelling, the amount of any outstanding service charges payable under the lease.

(6) In the case of an interim EDMO ceasing to have effect, the authority may recover the deficit mentioned in sub-paragraph (4) from the relevant proprietor if, in their opinion, he unreasonably refused to consent to the creation of an interest or right as mentioned in paragraph 2(3)(c) while the order was in force.

(7) The provisions of any of sub-paragraphs (2) to (6) do not, however, apply in relation to the order if—

    (a)   the order is followed by a final EDMO, and

(b)   the management scheme contained in that final EDMO provides for those sub-paragraphs not to apply in relation to the order (see paragraph 13(4)(c) and (d)).

(8) Any sum recoverable by the authority under sub-paragraph (5) or (6) is, until recovered, a charge on the dwelling.

(9) The charge takes effect on the termination date for the order as a legal charge which is a local land charge.

(10) For the purpose of enforcing the charge the authority have the same powers and remedies under the Law of Property Act 1925 (c 20) and otherwise as if they were mortgagees by deed having powers of sale and lease, of accepting surrenders of leases and of appointing a receiver.

(11) The power of appointing a receiver is exercisable at any time after the end of the period of one month beginning with the date on which the charge takes effect.

(12) In this paragraph—

"dispossessed landlord or tenant" means a person who was a lessor, lessee, licensor or licensee under a lease or licence determined by an order under paragraph 22;
"relevant expenditure" has the same meaning as in paragraph 5 (in relation to an interim EDMO) or paragraph 13 (in relation to a final EDMO);
"service charge" has the meaning given by section 18 of the Landlord and Tenant Act 1985 (c 70);
"the termination date" means the date on which the order ceases to have effect.

Termination of EDMOs: leases, agreements and proceedings

24

(1) This paragraph applies where—

(a)   an interim EDMO or final EDMO ceases to have effect for any reason, and
(b)   the order is not immediately followed by a further order under this Chapter.

(2) As from the termination date, an agreement which (in accordance with paragraph 3 or 11) has effect as a lease or licence granted by the authority under paragraph 2 or 10 has effect with the substitution of the relevant proprietor for the authority.

(3) If the relevant proprietor is a lessee, nothing in a superior lease imposes liability on him or any superior lessee in respect of anything done before the termination date in pursuance of the terms of an agreement to which sub-paragraph (2) applies.

(4) If the condition in sub-paragraph (5) is met, any other agreement entered into by the authority in the performance of their duties under section 135(1) to

(3) or 137(1) to (3) in respect of the dwelling has effect, as from the termination date, with the substitution of the relevant proprietor for the authority.

(5) The condition is that the authority serve a notice on the other party or parties to the agreement stating that sub-paragraph (4) applies to the agreement.

(6) If the condition in sub-paragraph (7) is met—

(a) any rights or liabilities that were rights or liabilities of the authority immediately before the termination date by virtue of any provision of this Chapter, or under any agreement to which sub-paragraph (4) applies, are rights or liabilities of the relevant proprietor instead, and

(b) any proceedings instituted or continued by or against the authority by virtue of any such provision or agreement may be continued by or against the relevant proprietor instead,

as from the termination date.

(7) The condition is that the authority serve a notice on all interested parties stating that sub-paragraph (6) applies to the rights or liabilities or (as the case may be) the proceedings.

(8) If by virtue of this paragraph a relevant proprietor becomes subject to any liability to pay damages in respect of anything done (or omitted to be done) before the termination date by or on behalf of the authority, the authority are liable to reimburse to the relevant proprietor an amount equal to the amount of the damages paid by him.

(9) This paragraph applies to instruments as it applies to agreements.

(10) In this paragraph—

"agreement" includes arrangement;
"the termination date" means the date on which the order ceases to have effect.

EDMOs: power of entry to carry out work

25

(1) The right mentioned in sub-paragraph (2) is exercisable by the local housing authority, or any person authorised in writing by them, at any time when an interim EDMO or final EDMO is in force.

(2) That right is the right at all reasonable times to enter any part of the dwelling for the purpose of carrying out works, and is exercisable as against any person having an estate or interest in the dwelling.

(3) If, after receiving reasonable notice of the intended action, any occupier of the dwelling prevents any officer, employee, agent or contractor of the local housing authority from carrying out work in the dwelling, a magistrates" court may order him to permit to be done on the premises anything which the authority consider to be necessary.

(4) A person who fails to comply with an order of the court under sub-paragraph (3) commits an offence.

(5) A person who commits an offence under sub-paragraph (4) is liable on summary conviction to a fine not exceeding level 5 on the standard scale.

PART 4
APPEALS

Appeals: decisions relating to EDMOs

26

(1) A relevant person may appeal to a residential property tribunal against—

(a)   a decision of the local housing authority to make a final EDMO,

(b)   the terms of a final EDMO (including the terms of the management scheme contained in it), or

(c)   the terms of an interim EDMO on the grounds that they do not provide for one or both of the matters mentioned in paragraph 5(5)(a) and (b) (which relate to payments of surplus rent etc).

(2) Where an appeal is made under sub-paragraph (1)(c)—

(a)   the appeal may be brought at any time while the order is in force (with the result that nothing in sub-paragraph (3) or paragraph 27 applies in relation to the appeal); and

(b)   the powers of the residential property tribunal under paragraph 28 are limited to determining whether the order should be varied by the tribunal so as to include a term providing for the matter or matters in question, and (if so) what provision should be made by the term.

(3) If no appeal is brought under this paragraph in respect of a final EDMO within the time allowed by paragraph 27 for making such an appeal, the order is final and conclusive as to the matters which could have been raised on appeal.

Appeals: time limits for appeals under paragraph 26

27

(1) This paragraph applies in relation to an appeal under paragraph 26 in respect of a final EDMO.

(2) Any such appeal must be made within the period of 28 days beginning with the date specified in the notice under paragraph 7(5) of Schedule 6 (as applied by section 136(5)) as the date on which the order was made.

(3) A residential property tribunal may allow an appeal to be made to it after the end of the period mentioned in sub-paragraph (2) if it is satisfied that there is a good reason for the failure to appeal before the end of that period (and for any delay since then in applying for permission to appeal out of time).

Appeals: powers of residential property tribunal on appeal under paragraph 26

28

(1) This paragraph applies to an appeal to a residential property tribunal under paragraph 26 in respect of an interim EDMO or a final EDMO.

(2) The appeal—

    (a)   is to be by way of a re-hearing, but

    (b)   may be determined having regard to matters of which the authority were unaware.

(3) The tribunal may—

    (a)   in the case of an interim EDMO, vary the order as mentioned in paragraph 26(2)(b), or

    (b)   in the case of a final EDMO, confirm or vary the order or revoke it as from the date of the tribunal's order.

"The operative time" for the purposes of paragraph 9(2)

29

(1) This paragraph defines "the operative time" for the purposes of paragraph 9(2).

(2) If no appeal is made under paragraph 26 before the end of the period of 28 days mentioned in paragraph 27(2), "the operative time" is the end of that period.

(3) If an appeal is made under paragraph 26 before the end of that period, and a decision is given on the appeal which confirms the order, "the operative time" is as follows—

    (a)   if the period within which an appeal to the Lands Tribunal may be brought expires without such an appeal having been brought, "the operative time" is the end of that period;

    (b)   if an appeal to the Lands Tribunal is brought, "the operative time" is the time when a decision is given on the appeal which confirms the order.

(4) For the purposes of sub-paragraph (3)—

    (a)   the withdrawal of an appeal has the same effect as a decision which confirms the order, and

    (b)   references to a decision which confirms the order are to a decision which confirms it with or without variation.

Right to appeal against decision or refusal to vary or revoke EDMO

30

A relevant person may appeal to a residential property tribunal against—

(a) a decision of a local housing authority to vary or revoke an interim EDMO or a final EDMO, or

(b) a refusal of a local housing authority to vary or revoke an interim EDMO or a final EDMO.

Time limits for appeals under paragraph 30

31

(1) This paragraph applies in relation to an appeal under paragraph 30 against a decision to vary or revoke, or (as the case may be) to refuse to vary or revoke, an interim EDMO or a final EDMO.

(2) Any such appeal must be made before the end of the period of 28 days beginning with the date specified in the notice under paragraph 11, 16, 19 or 22 of Schedule 6 (as applied by paragraph 8 or 17 of this Schedule (as the case may be)) as the date on which the decision concerned was made.

(3) A residential property tribunal may allow an appeal to be made to it after the end of the period mentioned in sub-paragraph (2) if it is satisfied that there is a good reason for the failure to appeal before the end of that period (and for any delay since then in applying for permission to appeal out of time).

Powers of residential property tribunal on appeal under paragraph 30

32

(1) This paragraph applies to an appeal to a residential property tribunal under paragraph 30 against a decision to vary or revoke, or (as the case may be) to refuse to vary or revoke, an interim EDMO or final EDMO.

(2) The appeal—

(a) is to be by way of a re-hearing, but

(b) may be determined having regard to matters of which the authority were unaware.

(3) The tribunal may confirm, reverse or vary the decision of the local housing authority.

(4) If the appeal is against a decision of the authority to refuse to revoke the order, the tribunal may make an order revoking the order as from a date specified in its order.

"The operative time" for the purposes of paragraphs 6, 7, 15 and 16

33

(1) This paragraph defines "the operative time" for the purposes of—

(a) paragraph 6(2) or 7(3) (variation or revocation of interim EDMO), or

(b) paragraph 15(2) or 16(3) (variation or revocation of final EDMO).

(2) If no appeal is made under paragraph 30 before the end of the period of 28 days mentioned in paragraph 31(2), "the operative time" is the end of that period.

(3) If an appeal is made under paragraph 30 before the end of that period, and a decision is given on the appeal which confirms the variation or revocation, "the operative time" is as follows—

(a)   if the period within which an appeal to the Lands Tribunal may be brought expires without such an appeal having been brought, "the operative time" is the end of that period;

(b)   if an appeal to the Lands Tribunal is brought, "the operative time" is the time when a decision is given on the appeal which confirms the variation or revocation.

(4) For the purposes of sub-paragraph (3)—

(a)   the withdrawal of an appeal has the same effect as a decision which confirms the variation or revocation appealed against; and

(b)   references to a decision which confirms a variation are to a decision which confirms it with or without variation.

Right to appeal against decision in respect of compensation payable to third parties

34

(1) This paragraph applies where a local housing authority have made a decision under section 136(4) or 138(3) as to whether compensation should be paid to a third party in respect of any interference with his rights in consequence of a final EDMO.

(2) The third party may appeal to a residential property tribunal against—

(a)   a decision by the authority not to pay compensation to him, or

(b)   a decision of the authority so far as relating to the amount of compensation that should be paid.

Time limits for appeals under paragraph 34

35

(1) This paragraph applies in relation to an appeal under paragraph 34 against a decision of a local housing authority not to pay compensation to a third party or as to the amount of compensation to be paid.

(2) Any such appeal must be made—

(a)   where the decision is made before the final EDMO is made, within the period of 28 days beginning with the date specified in the notice under paragraph 7(5) of Schedule 6 (as applied by section 136(5)) as the date on which the order was made, or

(b) in any other case, within the period of 28 days beginning with the date the authority notifies the third party under section 138(4).

(3) A residential property tribunal may allow an appeal to be made to it after the end of the period mentioned in sub-paragraph (2) if it is satisfied that there is good reason for the failure to appeal before the end of that period (and for any delay since then in applying for permission to appeal out of time).

Powers of residential property tribunal on appeal under paragraph 34

36

(1) This paragraph applies in relation to an appeal under paragraph 34 against a decision of a local housing authority not to pay compensation to a third party or as to the amount of compensation to be paid.

(2) The appeal—

(a) is to be by way of re-hearing, but
(b) may be determined having regard to matters of which the authority were unaware.

(3) The tribunal may confirm, reverse or vary the decision of the local housing authority.

(4) Where the tribunal reverses or varies the decision of the authority, it must make an order varying the management scheme contained in the final EDMO accordingly.

Meaning of "relevant person" for the purposes of this Part

37

In this Part of this Schedule "relevant person" means any person who has an estate or interest in the dwelling (other than a person who is a tenant under a lease granted under paragraph 2(3)(c) or 10(3)(c)).

Schedule 9
New Schedule 5a to the Housing Act 1985: Initial Demolition Notices

Section 183

"Schedule 5a
Initial Demolition Notices

Section 138A

Initial demolition notices

1

(1) For the purposes of this Schedule an "initial demolition notice" is a notice served on a secure tenant—

(a)   stating that the landlord intends to demolish the dwelling-house or (as the case may be) the building containing it ("the relevant premises"),

(b)   setting out the reasons why the landlord intends to demolish the relevant premises,

(c)   specifying the period within which he intends to demolish those premises, and

(d)   stating that, while the notice remains in force, he will not be under any obligation to make such a grant as is mentioned in section 138(1) in respect of any claim made by the tenant to exercise the right to buy in respect of the dwelling-house.

(2) An initial demolition notice must also state—

(a)   that the notice does not prevent—

(i)   the making by the tenant of any such claim, or

(ii)   the taking of steps under this Part in connection with any such claim up to the point where section 138(1) would otherwise operate in relation to the claim, or

(iii)   the operation of that provision in most circumstances where the notice ceases to be in force, but

(b)   that, if the landlord subsequently serves a final demolition notice in respect of the dwelling-house, the right to buy will not arise in respect of it while that notice is in force and any existing claim will cease to be effective.

(3) If, at the time when an initial demolition notice is served, there is an existing claim to exercise the right to buy in respect of the dwelling-house, the notice shall—

(a)   state that section 138C confers a right to compensation in respect of certain expenditure, and

(b)   give details of that right to compensation and of how it may be exercised.

(4) The period specified in accordance with sub-paragraph (1)(c) must not—

(a)   allow the landlord more than what is, in the circumstances, a reasonable period to carry out the proposed demolition of the relevant premises (whether on their own or as part of a scheme involving the demolition of other premises); or

(b)   in any case expire more than five years after the date of service of the notice on the tenant.

Period of validity of initial demolition notice

2

(1) For the purposes of this Schedule an initial demolition notice—

(a)   comes into force in respect of the dwelling-house concerned on the date of service of the notice on the tenant, and

(b)   ceases to be so in force at the end of the period specified in accordance with paragraph 1(1)(c),

but this is subject to compliance with the conditions mentioned in sub-paragraph (2) (in a case to which they apply) and to paragraph 3.

(2) The conditions in sub-paragraphs (6) and (7) of paragraph 13 of Schedule 5 (publicity for final demolition notices) shall apply in relation to an initial demolition notice as they apply in relation to a final demolition notice.

(3) The notice mentioned in paragraph 13(7) (as it applies in accordance with sub-paragraph (2) above) must contain the following information—

- (a) sufficient information to enable identification of the premises that the landlord intends to demolish,
- (b) the reasons why the landlord intends to demolish those premises,
- (c) the period within which the landlord intends to demolish those premises,
- (d) the date when any initial demolition notice or notices relating to those premises will cease to be in force, unless revoked or otherwise terminated under or by virtue of paragraph 3 below,
- (e) that, during the period of validity of any such notice or notices, the landlord will not be under any obligation to make such a grant as is mentioned in section 138(1) in respect of any claim to exercise the right to buy in respect of any dwelling-house contained in those premises,
- (f) that there may be a right to compensation under section 138C in respect of certain expenditure incurred in respect of any existing claim.

Revocation or termination of initial demolition notices

3

(1) Paragraph 15(4) to (7) of Schedule 5 (revocation notices) shall apply in relation to an initial demolition notice as they apply in relation to a final demolition notice.

(2) If a compulsory purchase order has been made for the purpose of enabling the landlord to demolish the dwelling-house in respect of which he has served an initial demolition notice (whether or not it would enable him to demolish any other premises as well) and—

- (a) a relevant decision within sub-paragraph (3)(a) becomes effective while the notice is in force, or
- (b) a relevant decision within sub-paragraph (3)(b) becomes final while the notice is in force,

the notice ceases to be in force as from the date when the decision becomes effective or final.

(3) A "relevant decision" is—

- (a) a decision under Part 2 of the Acquisition of Land Act 1981 to confirm the order with modifications, or not to confirm the whole or part of the order, or
- (b) a decision of the High Court to quash the whole or part of the order under section 24 of that Act,

where the effect of the decision is that the landlord will not be able, by virtue of that order, to carry out the demolition of the dwelling-house.

(4) A relevant decision within sub-paragraph (3)(a) becomes effective—

(a) at the end of the period of 16 weeks beginning with the date of the decision, if no application for judicial review is made in respect of the decision within that period, or

(b) if such an application is so made, at the time when—

(i) a decision on the application which upholds the relevant decision becomes final, or

(ii) the application is abandoned or otherwise ceases to have effect.

(5) A relevant decision within sub-paragraph (3)(b), or a decision within sub-paragraph (4)(b), becomes final—

(a) if not appealed against, at the end of the period for bringing an appeal, or

(b) if appealed against, at the time when the appeal (or any further appeal) is disposed of.

(6) An appeal is disposed of—

(a) if it is determined and the period for bringing any further appeal has ended, or

(b) if it is abandoned or otherwise ceases to have effect.

(7) Where an initial demolition notice ceases to be in force under sub-paragraph (2), the landlord must, as soon as is reasonably practicable, serve a notice on the tenant which informs him—

(a) that the notice has ceased to be in force as from the date in question, and

(b) of the reason why it has ceased to be in force.

(8) If, while an initial demolition notice is in force in respect of a dwelling-house, a final demolition notice comes into force under paragraph 13 of Schedule 5 in respect of that dwelling-house, the initial demolition notice ceases to be in force as from the date when the final demolition notice comes into force.

(9) In such a case the final demolition notice must state that it is replacing the initial demolition notice.

Restriction on serving further demolition notices

4

(1) This paragraph applies where an initial demolition notice ("the relevant notice") has (for any reason) ceased to be in force in respect of a dwelling-house without it being demolished.

(2) No further initial demolition notice may be served in respect of the dwelling-house during the period of 5 years following the time when the relevant notice ceases to be in force, unless—

(a) it is served with the consent of the Secretary of State, and

(b) it states that it is so served.

(3) Subject to sub-paragraph (4), no final demolition notice may be served in respect of the dwelling-house during the period of 5 years following the time when the relevant notice ceases to be in force, unless—

(a) it is served with the consent of the Secretary of State, and

(b) it states that it is so served.

(4) Sub-paragraph (3) does not apply to a final demolition notice which is served at a time when an initial demolition notice served in accordance with sub-paragraph (2) is in force.

(5) The Secretary of State's consent under sub-paragraph (2) or (3) may be given subject to compliance with such conditions as he may specify.

Service of notices

5

Paragraph 16 of Schedule 13 (service of notices) applies in relation to notices under this Schedule as it applies in relation to notices under paragraph 13 or 15 of that Schedule.

Interpretation

6

(1) In this Schedule any reference to the landlord, in the context of a reference to the demolition or intended demolition of any premises, includes a reference to a superior landlord.

(2) In this Schedule—

> "final demolition notice" means a final demolition notice served under paragraph 13 of Schedule 5;
> "premises" means premises of any description;
> "scheme" includes arrangements of any description."

Schedule 13
Residential Property Tribunals: Procedure

Section 230

Procedure regulations

1

(1) The appropriate national authority may make regulations about the procedure of residential property tribunals.

(2) Nothing in the following provisions of this Schedule affects the generality of sub-paragraph (1).

(3) In those provisions—

> "procedure regulations" means regulations under this paragraph;
> "tribunal" means a residential property tribunal.

Appeals

2

(1) Procedure regulations may include provision, in relation to applications to tribunals—

    (a)   about the form of such applications and the particulars to be contained in them,

    (b)   requiring the service of notices of such applications, and

    (c)   in the case of applications under section 102(4) or (7) or 133(1), requiring the service of copies of the draft orders submitted with the applications.

(2) Procedure regulations may include provision, in relation to appeals to tribunals—

    (a)   about the form of notices of appeal and the particulars to be contained in them, and

    (b)   requiring the service of copies of such notices.

(3) Procedure regulations may include provision dispensing with the service of the notices or copies mentioned in sub-paragraph (1)(b) or (2)(b) in such cases of urgency as are specified in the regulations.

Transfers

3

(1) This paragraph applies where, in any proceedings before a court, there falls for determination a question which a tribunal would have jurisdiction to determine on an application or appeal to the tribunal.

(2) The court—

    (a)   may by order transfer to the tribunal so much of the proceedings as relate to the determination of that question, and

    (b)   may then dispose of all or any remaining proceedings, or adjourn the disposal of all or any remaining proceedings pending the determination of that question by the tribunal, as it thinks fit.

(3) When the tribunal has determined the question, the court may give effect to the determination in an order of the court.

(4) Rules of court may prescribe the procedure to be followed in a court in connection with or in consequence of a transfer under this paragraph.

(5) Procedure regulations may prescribe the procedure to be followed in a tribunal consequent on a transfer under this paragraph.

(6) Nothing in this Act affects any power of a court to make an order that could be made by a tribunal (such as an order quashing a licence granted or order made by a local housing authority) in a case where—

    (a)   the court has not made a transfer under this paragraph, and

(b) the order is made by the court in connection with disposing of any proceedings before it.

Parties etc

4

(1) Procedure regulations may include provision enabling persons to be joined as parties to the proceedings.

(2) Procedure regulations may include provision enabling persons who are not parties to proceedings before a tribunal to make oral or written representations to the tribunal.

Information

5

(1) Procedure regulations may include—

    (a) provision relating to the supply of information and documents by a party to the proceedings, and

    (b) in particular any provision authorised by the following provisions of this paragraph.

(2) The regulations may include provision for requiring, or empowering the tribunal to require, a party to proceedings before a tribunal—

    (a) to supply to the tribunal information or documents specified, or of a description specified, in the regulations or in an order made by the tribunal;

    (b) to supply to any other party copies of any information or documents supplied to the tribunal;

    (c) to supply any such information, documents or copies by such time as is specified in or determined in accordance with the regulations or order.

(3) The regulations may also include provision—

    (a) for granting a party to the proceedings such disclosure or inspection of documents, or such right to further information, as might be granted by a county court;

    (b) for requiring persons to attend to give evidence and produce documents;

    (c) for authorising the administration of oaths to witnesses.

(4) The regulations may include provision empowering a tribunal to dismiss, or allow, the whole or part of an appeal or application in a case where a party to the proceedings has failed to comply with—

    (a) a requirement imposed by regulations made by virtue of this paragraph, or

    (b) an order of the tribunal made by virtue of any such regulations.

Pre-trial reviews etc

6

(1) Procedure regulations may include provision for the holding of a pre-trial review (on the application of a party to the proceedings or on the tribunal's own initiative).

(2) Procedure regulations may provide for functions of a tribunal in relation to, or at, a pre-trial review to be exercised by a single qualified member of the panel.

(3) Procedure regulations may provide for other functions as to preliminary or incidental matters to be exercised by a single qualified member of the panel.

(4) For the purposes of this paragraph—

    (a) a person is a qualified member of the panel if he was appointed to it by the Lord Chancellor; and

    (b) "the panel" means the panel provided for in Schedule 10 to the Rent Act 1977 (c 42).

Interim orders

7

Procedure regulations may include provision empowering tribunals to make orders, on an interim basis—

    (a) suspending, in whole or in part, the effect of any decision, notice, order or licence which is the subject matter of proceedings before them;

    (b) granting any remedy which they would have had power to grant in their final decisions.

Additional relief

8

(1) Procedure regulations may include provision as to—

    (a) any additional relief which tribunals may grant in respect of proceedings before them; and

    (b) the grounds on which such relief may be granted.

(2) In this paragraph "additional relief" means relief additional to any relief specifically authorised by any provision of Parts 1 to 4 of this Act.

Dismissal

9

Procedure regulations may include provision empowering tribunals to dismiss applications, appeals or transferred proceedings, in whole or in part, on the ground that they are—

(a)   frivolous or vexatious, or

(b)   otherwise an abuse of process.

Determination without hearing

10

(1) Procedure regulations may include provision for the determination of applications, appeals or transferred proceedings without an oral hearing.

(2) Procedure regulations may include provision enabling a single qualified member of the panel to decide whether an oral hearing is appropriate in a particular case.

(3) Procedure regulations may provide for a single qualified member of the panel to make determinations without an oral hearing.

(4) For the purposes of this paragraph—

(a)   a person is a qualified member of the panel if he was appointed to it by the Lord Chancellor; and

(b)   "the panel" means the panel provided for in Schedule 10 to the Rent Act 1977 (c 42).

Fees

11

(1) Procedure regulations may include provision requiring the payment of fees in respect of applications, appeals or transfers of proceedings to, or oral hearings by, tribunals.

(2) The fees payable shall be such as are specified in or determined in accordance with procedure regulations.

(3) But the fee (or, where fees are payable in respect of both an application, appeal or transfer and an oral hearing, the aggregate of the fees) payable by a person in respect of any proceedings must not exceed—

(a)   £500, or

(b)   such other amount as may be specified in procedure regulations.

(4) Procedure regulations may empower a tribunal to require a party to proceedings before it to reimburse another party to the proceedings the whole or any part of any fees paid by him.

(5) Procedure regulations may provide for the reduction or waiver of fees by reference to the financial resources of the party by whom they are to be paid or met.

(6) If they do so they may apply, subject to such modifications as may be specified in the regulations, any other statutory means-testing regime as it has effect from time to time.

Costs

12

(1) A tribunal may determine that a party to proceedings before it is to pay the costs incurred by another party in connection with the proceedings in any circumstances falling within sub-paragraph (2).

(2) The circumstances are where—

   (a) he has failed to comply with an order made by the tribunal;
   (b) in accordance with regulations made by virtue of paragraph 5(4), the tribunal dismisses, or allows, the whole or part of an application or appeal by reason of his failure to comply with a requirement imposed by regulations made by virtue of paragraph 5;
   (c) in accordance with regulations made by virtue of paragraph 9, the tribunal dismisses the whole or part of an application or appeal made by him to the tribunal; or
   (d) he has, in the opinion of the tribunal, acted frivolously, vexatiously, abusively, disruptively or otherwise unreasonably in connection with the proceedings.

(3) The amount which a party to proceedings may be ordered to pay in the proceedings by a determination under this paragraph must not exceed—

   (a) £500, or
   (b) such other amount as may be specified in procedure regulations.

(4) A person may not be required to pay costs incurred by another person in connection with proceedings before a tribunal, except—

   (a) by a determination under this paragraph, or
   (b) in accordance with provision made by any enactment other than this paragraph.

Enforcement

13

Procedure regulations may provide for decisions of tribunals to be enforceable, with the permission of a county court, in the same way as orders of such a court.

Schedule 14
Buildings which are not HMOs for Purposes of this Act (excluding Part 1)

Section 254

Introduction: buildings (or parts) which are not HMOs for purposes of this Act (excluding Part 1)

1

(1) The following paragraphs list buildings which are not houses in multiple occupation for any purposes of this Act other than those of Part 1.

(2) In this Schedule "building" includes a part of a building.

Buildings controlled or managed by public sector bodies etc

2

(1) A building where the person managing or having control of it is—

   (a)   a local housing authority,

   (b)   a body which is registered as a social landlord under Part 1 of the Housing Act 1996 (c 52),

   (c)   a police authority established under section 3 of the Police Act 1996 (c 16),

   (d)   the Metropolitan Police Authority established under section 5B of that Act,

   (e)   a fire and rescue authority, or

   (f)   a health service body within the meaning of section 4 of the National Health Service and Community Care Act 1990 (c 19).

(2) In sub-paragraph (1)(e) "fire and rescue authority" means a fire and rescue authority under the Fire and Rescue Services Act 2004 (c 21).

Buildings regulated otherwise than under this Act

3

Any building whose occupation is regulated otherwise than by or under this Act and which is of a description specified for the purposes of this paragraph in regulations made by the appropriate national authority.

Buildings occupied by students

4

(1) Any building—

   (a)   which is occupied solely or principally by persons who occupy it for the purpose of undertaking a full-time course of further or higher education at a specified educational establishment or at an educational establishment of a specified description, and

(b) where the person managing or having control of it is the educational establishment in question or a specified person or a person of a specified description.

(2) In sub-paragraph (1) "specified" means specified for the purposes of this paragraph in regulations made by the appropriate national authority.

(3) Sub-paragraph (4) applies in connection with any decision by the appropriate national authority as to whether to make, or revoke, any regulations specifying—

(a) a particular educational establishment, or
(b) a particular description of educational establishments.

(4) The appropriate national authority may have regard to the extent to which, in its opinion—

(a) the management by or on behalf of the establishment in question of any building or buildings occupied for connected educational purposes is in conformity with any code of practice for the time being approved under section 233 which appears to the authority to be relevant, or
(b) the management of such buildings by or on behalf of establishments of the description in question is in general in conformity with any such code of practice,

as the case may be.

(5) In sub-paragraph (4) "occupied for connected educational purposes", in relation to a building managed by or on behalf of an educational establishment, means occupied solely or principally by persons who occupy it for the purpose of undertaking a full-time course of further or higher education at the establishment.

Buildings occupied by religious communities

5

(1) Any building which is occupied principally for the purposes of a religious community whose principal occupation is prayer, contemplation, education or the relief of suffering.

(2) This paragraph does not apply in the case of a converted block of flats to which section 257 applies.

Buildings occupied by owners

6

(1) Any building which is occupied only by persons within the following paragraphs—

(a) one or more persons who have, whether in the whole or any part of it, either the freehold estate or a leasehold interest granted for a term of more than 21 years;

(b)   any member of the household of such a person or persons;
(c)   no more than such number of other persons as is specified for the purposes of this paragraph in regulations made by the appropriate national authority.

(2) This paragraph does not apply in the case of a converted block of flats to which section 257 applies, except for the purpose of determining the status of any flat in the block.

Buildings occupied by two persons

7

Any building which is occupied only by two persons who form two households.

Appendix 2

STATUTORY INSTRUMENTS

CONTENTS

HOUSING HEALTH AND SAFETY RATING SYSTEM (ENGLAND) REGULATIONS 2005

(2005/3208)

Made 17th November 2005

Laid before Parliament 28th November 2005

Coming into force 6th April 2006

1 Citation, commencement and application

(1) These Regulations may be cited as the Housing Health and Safety Rating System (England) Regulations 2005 and shall come into force on 6th April 2006.

(2) These Regulations apply in relation to residential premises in England only.

2 Interpretation

In these Regulations—

"the Act" means the Housing Act 2004;
"harm" means harm which is within any of Classes I to IV as set out in Schedule 2 to these Regulations;

"inspector" means a person carrying out an inspection under section 4 of the Act (inspections by local housing authorities to see whether a category 1 or 2 hazard exists); and except in regulation 6(7)(e), "occupier" includes potential occupier.

3 Prescribed descriptions of hazard

(1) A hazard is of a prescribed description for the purposes of the Act where the risk of harm is associated with the occurrence of any of the matters or circumstances listed in Schedule 1.

(2) In Schedule 1, a reference to a matter or circumstance is, unless otherwise stated, to a matter or circumstance in or, as the case may be, at the dwelling or HMO in question, or in any building or land in the vicinity of the dwelling or HMO.

4 Prescribed fire hazard

For the purposes of section 10 of the Act a category 1 or 2 hazard is a prescribed fire hazard if the risk of harm is associated with exposure to uncontrolled fire and associated smoke.

5 Inspections

An inspector must—

  (a) have regard to any guidance for the time being given under section 9 of the Act in relation to the inspection of residential premises;
  (b) inspect any residential premises with a view to preparing an accurate record of their state and condition; and
  (c) prepare and keep such a record in written or in electronic form.

6 Seriousness of hazards

(1) Where, following an inspection of residential premises under section 4 of the Act, the inspector—

  (a) determines that a hazard of a prescribed description exists; and
  (b) considers, having regard to any guidance for the time being given under section 9 of the Act in relation to the assessment of hazards, that it is appropriate to calculate the seriousness of that hazard,

the seriousness of that hazard shall be calculated in accordance with paragraphs (2) to (4) of this regulation.

(2) The inspector shall assess the likelihood, during the period of 12 months beginning with the date of the assessment, of a relevant occupier suffering any harm as a result of that hazard as falling within one of the range of ratios of likelihood set out in column 1 of Table 1.

Table 1

Column 1	Column 2

Range of ratios of likelihood	Representative scale point of range
Less likely than 1 in 4200	5600
1 in 4200 to 1 in 2400	3200
1 in 2400 to 1 in 1300	1800
1 in 1300 to 1 in 750	1000
1 in 750 to 1 in 420	560
1 in 420 to 1 in 240	320
1 in 240 to 1 in 130	180
1 in 130 to 1 in 75	100
1 in 75 to 1 in 42	56
1 in 42 to 1 in 24	32
1 in 24 to 1 in 13	18
1 in 13 to 1 in 7.5	10
1 in 7.5 to 1 in 4	6
1 in 4 to 1 in 2.5	3
1 in 2.5 to 1 in 1.5	2
More likely than 1 in 1.5	1

(3)   The inspector shall assess which of the four classes of harm (set out in Schedule 2) a relevant occupier is most likely to suffer during the period mentioned in paragraph (2).

(4)   The inspector shall—

    (a)   assess the possibility of each of the other classes of harm occurring as a result of that hazard, as falling within one of the range of percentages of possibility set out in column 1 of Table 2;

    (b)   record each possibility so assessed as the corresponding RSPRR set out in column 2 of Table 2; and

    (c)   record the possibility (which shall be known, for the purposes of the formula in paragraph (5), as the RSPPR) of the most likely class of harm occurring as a percentage calculated using the following formula—

$$100\% - (A + B + C)$$

Where—

A is the RSPPR recorded under sub paragraph (b) as the second most likely class of harm;

B is the RSPPR recorded under sub paragraph (b) as the third most likely class of harm; and

C is the RSPPR recorded under sub paragraph (b) as the fourth most likely class of harm.

Table 2

Column 1	Column 2
Range of percentages of possibility	*Representative scale point of the percentage range (RSPPR)*
Below 0.05%	0%
0.05 to 0.15%	0.1%
0.15% to 0.3%	0.2%
0.3% to 0.7%	0.5%
0.7% to 1.5%	1%
1.5% to 3%	2.2%
3% to 7%	4.6%
7% to 15%	10%
15% to 26%	21.5%
26% to 38 %	31.6%
Above 38%	46.4%

(5) When the inspector has assessed likelihood under paragraph (2) and assessed the possibility of each harm occurring under paragraph (3), the seriousness of that hazard shall be expressed by a numerical score calculated using the following formula—

$$S1 + S2 + S3 + S4$$

Where—

$$S1\ 10000 \times (1 / L) \times O1$$
$$S2\ 1000 \times (1 / L) \times O2$$
$$S3\ 300 \times (1 / L) \times O3$$
$$S4\ 10 \times (1 / L) \times O4$$

(6) For the purposes of the formula in paragraph (5)—

(a) L is the representative scale point of range in column 2 of Table 1 corresponding to the range that has been recorded under paragraph (2);

(b) O1 is the RSPPR recorded under paragraph (4) in relation to Class I harm;

(c) O2 is the RSPPR recorded under paragraph (4) in relation to Class II harm;

(d) O3 is the RSPPR recorded under paragraph (4) in relation to Class III harm;

(e) O4 is the RSPPR recorded under paragraph (4) in relation to Class IV harm.

(7) In this regulation—

"relevant occupier" means, where the risk of harm concerned is associated with the occurrence of any of the matters or circumstances listed in—

(a) paragraph 1 of Schedule 1, an occupier under the age of 15 years;

(b)   paragraph 2, 3 or 6(a) of Schedule 1, an occupier aged 65 years or over;

(c)   paragraph 7 of Schedule 1, an occupier under the age of 3 years;

(d)   paragraph 8 of Schedule 1, an occupier aged 60 years or over who has been exposed to radon since birth;

(e)   paragraph 11 of Schedule 1, the actual occupier;

(f)   paragraph 17, 22, 23 or 25 of Schedule 1, an occupier under the age of 5 years;

(g)   paragraph 19, 20, 21, 24 or 28 of Schedule 1, an occupier aged 60 years or over;

(h)   paragraph 26—

    (i)   except where a collision is with low architectural features, an occupier under the age of 5 years, and

    (ii)   where a collision is with low architectural features, an occupier aged 16 years or over;

(i)   any other paragraph of Schedule 1, any occupier; and

"RSPPR" means the representative scale point of the percentage range.

(8)   In making assessments under this regulation, an inspector shall have regard to any guidance for the time being given under section 9 of the Act.

7   Prescribed bands

For the purposes of the Act a hazard falls within a band identified by a letter in column 1 of Table 3 where it achieves a numerical score calculated in accordance with regulation 6(5) which is within the range corresponding to that letter in column 2 of that Table.

Table 3

Column 1 *Band*	Column 2 *Numerical Score Range*
A	5000 or more
B	2000 to 4999
C	1000 to 1999
D	500 to 999
E	200 to 499
F	100 to 199
G	50 to 99
H	20 to 49
I	10 to 19
J	9 or less

8   Category of hazard

For the purposes of the Act—

(a)   a hazard falling within band A, B or C of Table 3 is a category 1 hazard; and

(b)   a hazard falling within any other band in that Table is a category 2 hazard.

Signed on behalf of the First Secretary of State

Kay Andrews

Parliamentary Under Secretary of State

Office of the Deputy Prime Minister

17th November 2005

Schedule 1
Matters and Circumstances

Regulation 3(1)

Damp and mould growth

1

Exposure to house dust mites, damp, mould or fungal growths.

Excess cold

2

Exposure to low temperatures.

Excess heat

3

Exposure to high temperatures.

Asbestos and MMF

4

Exposure to asbestos fibres or manufactured mineral fibres.

Biocides

5

Exposure to chemicals used to treat timber and mould growth.

Carbon monoxide and fuel combustion products

6

Exposure to—

(a)   carbon monoxide;
(b)   nitrogen dioxide;
(c)   sulphur dioxide and smoke.

Lead

7

The ingestion of lead.

Radiation

8

Exposure to radiation.

Uncombusted fuel gas

9

Exposure to uncombusted fuel gas.

Volatile organic compounds

10

Exposure to volatile organic compounds.

Crowding and space

11

A lack of adequate space for living and sleeping.

Entry by intruders

12

Difficulties in keeping the dwelling or HMO secure against unauthorised entry.

Lighting

13

A lack of adequate lighting.

Noise

14

Exposure to noise.

Domestic hygiene, pests and refuse

15

(1) Poor design, layout or construction such that the dwelling or HMO cannot readily be kept clean.

(2) Exposure to pests.

(3) An inadequate provision for the hygienic storage and disposal of household waste.

Food safety

16

An inadequate provision of facilities for the storage, preparation and cooking of food.

Personal hygiene, sanitation and drainage

17

An inadequate provision of—

    (a)   facilities for maintaining good personal hygiene;
    (b)   sanitation and drainage.

Water supply

18

An inadequate supply of water free from contamination, for drinking and other domestic purposes.

Falls associated with baths etc

19

Falls associated with toilets, baths, showers or other washing facilities.

Falling on level surfaces etc

20

Falling on any level surface or falling between surfaces where the change in level is less than 300 millimetres.

Falling on stairs etc

21

Falling on stairs, steps or ramps where the change in level is 300 millimetres or more.

Falling between levels

22

Falling between levels where the difference in levels is 300 millimetres or more.

Electrical hazards

23

Exposure to electricity.

Fire

24

Exposure to uncontrolled fire and associated smoke.

Flames, hot surfaces etc

25

Contact with—

    (a)   controlled fire or flames;
    (b)   hot objects, liquid or vapours.

Collision and entrapment

26

Collision with, or entrapment of body parts in, doors, windows or other architectural features.

Explosions

27

An explosion at the dwelling or HMO.

Position and operability of amenities etc

28

The position, location and operability of amenities, fittings and equipment.

Structural collapse and falling elements

29

The collapse of the whole or part of the dwelling or HMO.

Schedule 2
Classes of Harm

Regulation 2

Class I

1

A Class I harm is such extreme harm as is reasonably foreseeable as a result of the hazard in question, including—

(a) death from any cause;
(b) lung cancer;
(c) mesothelioma and other malignant tumours;
(d) permanent paralysis below the neck;
(e) regular severe pneumonia;
(f) permanent loss of consciousness;
(g) 80% burn injuries.

Class II

2

A Class II harm is such severe harm as is reasonably foreseeable as a result of the hazard in question, including—

(a) cardio-respiratory disease;
(b) asthma;
(c) non-malignant respiratory diseases;
(d) lead poisoning;
(e) anaphylactic shock;
(f) cryptosporidiosis;
(g) legionnaires disease;
(h) myocardial infarction;
(i) mild stroke;
(j) chronic confusion;
(k) regular severe fever;
(l) loss of a hand or foot;
(m) serious fractures;
(n) serious burns;
(o) loss of consciousness for days.

Class III

3

A Class III harm is such serious harm as is reasonably foreseeable as a result of the hazard in question, including—

(a) eye disorders;
(b) rhinitis;
(c) hypertension;
(d) sleep disturbance;
(e) neuropsychological impairment;
(f) sick building syndrome;
(g) regular and persistent dermatitis, including contact dermatitis;
(h) allergy;
(i) gastro-enteritis;
(j) diarrhoea;
(k) vomiting;
(l) chronic severe stress;
(m) mild heart attack;
(n) malignant but treatable skin cancer;
(o) loss of a finger;
(p) fractured skull and severe concussion;
(q) serious puncture wounds to head or body;
(r) severe burns to hands;
(s) serious strain or sprain injuries;
(t) regular and severe migraine.

Class IV

4

A Class IV harm is such moderate harm as is reasonably foreseeable as a result of the hazard in question, including—

(a) pleural plaques;
(b) occasional severe discomfort;
(c) benign tumours;
(d) occasional mild pneumonia;
(e) broken finger;
(f) slight concussion;
(g) moderate cuts to face or body;
(h) severe bruising to body;
(i) regular serious coughs or colds.

HOUSING (EMPTY DWELLING MANAGEMENT ORDERS) (PRESCRIBED EXCEPTIONS AND REQUIREMENTS) (ENGLAND) ORDER 2006

(2006/367)

Made 15th February 2006

Laid before Parliament 22nd February 2006

Coming into force 6th April 2006

The Secretary of State, in exercise of the powers conferred by section 134(5)(a) and (c) and (6) of the Housing Act 2004, makes the following Order:

1   Citation, commencement and application

(1)   This Order may be cited as The Housing (Empty Dwelling Management Orders) (Prescribed Exceptions and Requirements) (England) Order 2006 and shall come into force on 6th April 2006.

(2)   This Order shall apply in England only.

2   Interpretation

In this Order "the Act" means the Housing Act 2004.

3   Prescribed exceptions

For the purposes of section 134(1)(b) of the Act a dwelling falls within a prescribed exception if—

    (a)   it has been occupied solely or principally by the relevant proprietor and is wholly unoccupied because—
        (i)   he is temporarily resident elsewhere;
        (ii)   he is absent from the dwelling for the purpose of receiving personal care by reason of old age, disablement, illness, past or present alcohol or drug dependence or past or present mental disorder;
        (iii)   he is absent from the dwelling for the purpose of providing, or better providing, personal care for a person who requires such care by reason of old age, disablement, illness, past or present alcohol or drug dependence or past or present mental disorder; or
        (iv)   he is a serving member of the armed forces and he is absent from the dwelling as a result of such service;
    (b)   it is used as a holiday home (whether or not it is let as such on a commercial basis) or is otherwise occupied by the relevant proprietor or his guests on a temporary basis from time to time;

(c)   it is genuinely on the market for sale or letting;

(d)   it is comprised in an agricultural holding within the meaning of the Agricultural Holdings Act 1986 or a farm business tenancy within the meaning of the Agricultural Tenancies Act 1995;

(e)   it is usually occupied by an employee of the relevant proprietor in connection with the performance of his duties under the terms of his contract of employment;

(f)   it is available for occupation by a minister of religion as a residence from which to perform the duties of his office;

(g)   it is subject to a court order freezing the property of the relevant proprietor;

(h)   it is prevented from being occupied as a result of a criminal investigation or criminal proceedings;

(i)   it is mortgaged, where the mortgagee, in right of the mortgage, has entered into and is in possession of the dwelling; or

(j)   the person who was the relevant proprietor of it has died and six months has not elapsed since the grant of representation was obtained in respect of such person.

4 Prescribed requirements

(1) For the purpose of section 134(2)(e) of the Act the prescribed requirements with which a local housing authority must comply are that—

(a)   it must make reasonable efforts to establish from the relevant proprietor whether he considers that any of the exceptions contained in article 3 apply to the dwelling;

(b)   it must provide to the residential property tribunal—

    (i)   details of the efforts they have made to notify the relevant proprietor that they are considering making an interim empty dwelling management order in respect of his dwelling, as required under section 133(3)(a) of the Act;

    (ii)   details of the enquiries they have made to ascertain what steps (if any) the relevant proprietor is taking, or is intending to take, to secure that the dwelling is occupied, as required under section 133(3)(b) of the Act;

    (iii)   details of any advice and assistance they have provided to the relevant proprietor with a view to the relevant proprietor securing that the dwelling is occupied;

    (iv)   all information they have that suggests that the dwelling may fall within one of the exceptions described in article 3, whether available from the authority's own enquiries or from representations made to it by the relevant proprietor; and

    (v)   the classification of the dwelling for council tax purposes under the Local Government Finance Act 1992; and

(c)   where the relevant proprietor—

    (i)   has undertaken or is undertaking repairs, maintenance or improvement works; or

    (ii)   has applied to a local planning authority or other authority for permission to make structural alterations or additions to the dwelling and he awaits the decision of a relevant authority on the application,

it must give reasons to the tribunal why it considers that an empty dwelling management order is required to secure occupation of the dwelling.

(2) For the purpose of paragraph (1)(c)(ii) a relevant authority is—

    (a)   the authority to whom the relevant proprietor has made the application; or,

    (b)   where that authority has made a decision against which the relevant proprietor or another person has appealed, the person or body that determines the appeal.

Signed by the authority of the First Secretary of State

Kay Andrews

Parliamentary Under Secretary of State

Office of the Deputy Prime Minister

15th February 2006

SELECTIVE LICENSING OF HOUSES (SPECIFIED EXEMPTIONS) (ENGLAND) ORDER 2006

(2006/370)

Made 15th February 2006

Laid before Parliament 22nd February 2006

Coming into force 6th April 2006

The Secretary of State, in exercise of the powers conferred by section 79(4) of the Housing Act 2004, makes the following Order:

1 Citation, commencement and application

(1) This Order may be cited as The Selective Licensing of Houses (Specified Exemptions) (England) Order 2006 and shall come into force on 6th April 2006.

(2) This Order applies to houses in England only.

2 Exempt tenancies or licences for the purposes ofPart 3of the Housing Act 2004

(1) A tenancy or licence of a house or a dwelling contained in a house is an exempt tenancy or licence for the purposes of Part 3 of the Housing Act 2004 ("the Act") if it falls within any of the following descriptions—

    (a) a tenancy or licence of a house or dwelling that is subject to a prohibition order made under section 20 of the Act whose operation has not been suspended in accordance with section 23 of the Act;

    (b) a tenancy described in any of the following provisions of Part 1 of Schedule 1 to the Housing Act 1988, which cannot be an assured tenancy by virtue of section 1(2) of that Act—

        (i) paragraph 4 (business tenancies);

        (ii) paragraph 5 (licensed premises);

        (iii) paragraph 6 (tenancies of agricultural land); or

        (iv) paragraph 7 (tenancies of agricultural holdings etc);

    (c) a tenancy or licence of a house or a dwelling that is managed or controlled by—

        (i) a local housing authority;

        (ii) a police authority established under section 3 of the Police Act 1996;

        (iii) the Metropolitan Police Authority established under section 5B of the Police Act 1996;

        (iv) a fire and rescue authority under the Fire and Rescue Services Act 2004; or

        (v) a health service body within the meaning of section 4 of the National Health Service and Community Care Act 1990;

    (d) a tenancy or licence of a house which is not a house in multiple occupation for any purposes of the Act (except Part 1) by virtue of—

        (i) paragraph 3 of Schedule 14 to the Act (buildings regulated otherwise than under the Act); or

        (ii) paragraph 4(1) of that Schedule (buildings occupied by students);

    (e) a tenancy of a house or a dwelling where—

        (i) the full term of the tenancy is more than 21 years;

        (ii) the lease does not contain a provision enabling the landlord to determine the tenancy, other than by forfeiture, earlier than at end of the term; and

        (iii) the house or dwelling is occupied by a person to whom the tenancy was granted or his successor in title or any members of such person's family;

    (f) a tenancy or licence of a house or a dwelling granted by a person to a person who is a member of his family where—

        (i) the person to whom the tenancy or licence is granted occupies the house or dwelling as his only or main residence;

        (ii) the person granting the tenancy or licence is the freeholder or the holder of a lease of the house or dwelling the full term of which is more than 21 years; and

    (iii)   the lease referred to in sub-paragraph (ii) does not contain a provision enabling the landlord to determine the tenancy, other than by forfeiture, earlier than at end of the term;

(g)   a tenancy or licence that is granted to a person in relation to his occupancy of a house or a dwelling as a holiday home; or

(h)   a tenancy or licence under the terms of which the occupier shares any accommodation with the landlord or licensor or a member of the landlord's or licensor's family.

(2)   For the purposes of this article—

(a)   a person is a member of the same family as another person if—
    (i)   those persons live as a couple;
    (ii)   one of them is the relative of the other; or
    (iii)   one of them is, or is a relative of, one member of a couple and the other is a relative of the other member of the couple;

(b)   "couple" means two persons who are married to each other or live together as husband and wife (or in an equivalent relationship in the case of persons of the same sex);

(c)   "relative" means parent, grandparent, child, grandchild, brother, sister, uncle, aunt, nephew, niece or cousin;

(d)   a relationship of the half-blood is to be treated as a relationship of the whole blood;

(e)   a stepchild of a person is to be treated as his child;

(f)   an occupier shares accommodation with another person if he has the use of an amenity in common with that person (whether or not also in common with others); and

(g)   "amenity" includes a toilet, personal washing facilities, a kitchen or a living room but excludes any area used for storage, a staircase, corridor or other means of access.

Signed by authority of the First Secretary of State

Kay Andrews

Parliamentary Under Secretary of State

Office of the Deputy Prime Minister

15th February 2006

LICENSING OF HOUSES IN MULTIPLE OCCUPATION (PRESCRIBED DESCRIPTIONS) (ENGLAND) ORDER 2006

(2006/371)

Made 15th February 2006

Laid before Parliament 22nd February 2006

Coming into force 6th April 2006

The Secretary of State, in exercise of the powers conferred by section 55(3) of the Housing Act 2004, makes the following Order:

1 Citation, commencement and application

(1) This Order may be cited as The Licensing of Houses in Multiple Occupation (Prescribed Descriptions) (England) Order 2006 and shall come into force on 6th April 2006.

(2) This Order applies to any HMO in England, other than a converted block of flats to which section 257 of the Act applies.

2 Interpretation

In this Order—

  (a) "the Act" means the Housing Act 2004; and
  (b) "business premises" means premises, or any part of premises, which are not, or are not used in connection with, and as an integral part of, living accommodation.

3 Description of HMOs prescribed by the Secretary of State

(1) An HMO is of a prescribed description for the purpose of section 55(2)(a) of the Act where it satisfies the conditions described in paragraph (2).

(2) The conditions referred to in paragraph (1) are that—

  (a) the HMO or any part of it comprises three storeys or more;
  (b) it is occupied by five or more persons; and
  (c) it is occupied by persons living in two or more single households.

(3) The following storeys shall be taken into account when calculating whether the HMO or any part of it comprises three storeys or more—

  (a) any basement if—
    (i)   it is used wholly or partly as living accommodation;
    (ii) it has been constructed, converted or adapted for use wholly or partly as living accommodation;
    (iii) it is being used in connection with, and as an integral part of, the HMO; or
    (iv) it is the only or principal entry into the HMO from the street.
  (b) any attic if—
    (i)   it is used wholly or partly as living accommodation;
    (ii) it has been constructed, converted or adapted for use wholly or partly as living accommodation, or
    (iii) it is being used in connection with, and as an integral part of, the HMO;
  (c) where the living accommodation is situated in a part of a building above business premises, each storey comprising the business premises;

(d)   where the living accommodation is situated in a part of a building below business premises, each storey comprising the business premises;

(e)   any mezzanine floor not used solely as a means of access between two adjoining floors if—

     (i)   it is used wholly or mainly as living accommodation; or

     (ii)   it is being used in connection with, and as an integral part of, the HMO; and

(f)   any other storey that is used wholly or partly as living accommodation or in connection with, and as an integral part of, the HMO.

Signed by authority of the First Secretary of State

Kay Andrews

Parliamentary Under Secretary of State

Office of the Deputy Prime Minister

15th February 2006

LICENSING AND MANAGEMENT OF HOUSES IN MULTIPLE OCCUPATION AND OTHER HOUSES (MISCELLANEOUS PROVISIONS) (ENGLAND) REGULATIONS 2006

(2006/373)

Made 15th February 2006

Laid before Parliament 22nd February 2006

Coming into force 6th April 2006

The Secretary of State, in exercise of the powers conferred by sections 59(2), (3) and (4), 60(6), 63(5) and (6), 65(3) and (4), 83(2) and (4), 84(6), 87(5) and (6), 232(3) and (7), 250(2), 258(2)(b), (5) and (6) 259(2)(c) of, and paragraphs 3 and 6(1)(c) of Schedule 14 to the Housing Act 2004, makes the following Regulations:

1   Citation, commencement and application

(1)   These Regulations may be cited as The Licensing and Management of Houses in Multiple Occupation and Other Houses (Miscellaneous Provisions) (England) Regulations 2006 and shall come into force on 6th April 2006.

(2)   These Regulations apply in relation to any HMO in England, ... and to any house in England to which Part 3 of the Act applies.

2 Interpretation

In these Regulations "the Act" means the Housing Act 2004[; and "section 257 HMO" means an HMO which is a converted block of flats to which section 257 of the Act applies].

3 Persons to be regarded as forming a single household for the purposes of section 254 of the Act: employees

(1)   Where—

- (a)   a person ("person A") occupies living accommodation in a building or part of a building; and
- (b)   another person ("person B") and any member of person B's family living with him occupy living accommodation in the same building or part,

those persons are only to be regarded as forming a single household for the purposes of section 254 of the Act if their circumstances are those described in paragraph (2).

(2)   The circumstances are that—

- (a)   Person A carries out work or performs a service of an exclusively domestic nature for person B or such a member of person B's family;
- (b)   Person A's living accommodation is supplied to him by person B or by such a member of person B's family as part of the consideration for carrying out the work or performing the service; and
- (c)   person A does not pay any rent or other consideration in respect of his living accommodation (other than carrying out the work or performance of the service).

(3)   Work or a service usually carried out or performed by any of the following is to be regarded as work or service of a domestic nature for the purpose of paragraph (2)(a)—

- (a)   au pair;
- (b)   nanny;
- (c)   nurse;
- (d)   carer;
- (e)   governess;
- (f)   servant, including maid, butler, cook or cleaner;
- (g)   chauffeur;
- (h)   gardener;
- (i)   secretary; or
- (j)   personal assistant.

(4)   Where person A and person B are to be regarded as forming a single household under paragraph (1) any member of person A's family occupying the living accommodation with him is to be regarded as forming a single household with person A, person B and any member of person B's family living with him for the purpose of section 254 of the Act.

4 Other persons to be regarded as forming a single household for the purposes of section 254 of the Act

(1)   Where a person receiving care and his carer occupy living accommodation in the same building or part of a building, they are to be regarded as forming a single household for the purposes of section 254 of the Act if—

(a)   the carer is an adult placement carer approved under the Adult Placement Schemes (England) Regulations 2004; and

(b)   the carer provides care in that living accommodation for not more than three service users under the terms of a scheme permitted by those Regulations.

(2)   Where a person and his foster parent occupy living accommodation in the same building or part of a building, they are to be regarded as forming a single household for the purposes of section 254 of the Act if that person is placed with the foster parent under the provisions of the Fostering Services Regulations 2002.

(3)   The terms "adult placement carer" and "service users" have the meanings given to those expressions in the regulations referred to in paragraph (1)(a).

5 Persons treated as occupying premises as their only or main residence for the purposes of section 254 of the Act

(1)   A person is to be treated as occupying a building or part of a building as his only or main residence for the purposes of section 254 of the Act if he is—

(a)   a migrant worker or a seasonal worker—
   (i)   whose occupation of the building or part is made partly in consideration of his employment within the United Kingdom, whether or not other charges are payable in respect of that occupation; and
   (ii)   where the building or part is provided by, or on behalf of, his employer or an agent or employee of his employer; or

(b)   an asylum seeker or a dependent of an asylum seeker who has been provided with accommodation under section 95 of the Immigration and Asylum Act 1999 and which is funded partly or wholly by the National Asylum Support Service.

(2)   In this regulation—

(a)   "a migrant worker" is—
   (i)   a person who is a national of a member State of the European Economic Area or Switzerland who has taken up an activity as an employed person in the United Kingdom under Council Regulation (EEC) No 1612/68 on Freedom of Movement for Workers Within the Community, as extended by the EEA Agreement or the Switzerland Agreement; or

(ii)   any person who has a permit indicating, in accordance with the immigration rules, that a person named in it is eligible, though not a British citizen, for entry into the United Kingdom for the purpose of taking employment;

(b)   "EEA agreement" means the agreement on the European Economic Area signed at Oporto on 2nd May 1992, as adjusted by the Protocol signed at Brussels on 17th March 1993;

(c)   "Switzerland agreement" means the agreement between the European Community and its Member States of the one part and the Swiss Confederation of the other on the Free Movement of Persons signed at Luxembourg on 21st June 1999 and which came into force on 1st June 2002;

(d)   "seasonal worker" means a person who carries out for an employer or undertaking employment of a seasonal character—

    (i)   the nature of which depends on the cycle of the seasons and recurs automatically each year; and

    (ii)   the duration of which cannot exceed eight months;

(e)   "immigration rules" means the rules for the time being laid down as mentioned in section 3(2) of the Immigration Act 1971 and

(f)   "asylum seeker" has the meaning given to that expression in section 94 of Immigration and Asylum Act 1999.

6   Buildings that are not HMOs for the purposes of the Act (excluding Part 1)

(1)   A building is of a description specified for the purposes of paragraph 3 of Schedule 14 to the Act (buildings regulated otherwise than under the Act which are not HMOs for purposes of the Act (excluding Part 1)) where its occupation is regulated by or under any of the enactments listed in Schedule 1.

(2)   The number of persons specified for the purposes of paragraph 6(1)(c) of Schedule 14 to the Act is two.

7   Applications for licences under Part 2 or 3 of the Act

(1)   An application for a licence under section 63 (application for HMO licence) or 87 (application for licence of Part 3 house) of the Act ("an application") must include a statement in the form specified in paragraph 1of Schedule 2

(2)   An applicant must supply as a part of his application—

(a)   the information contained in paragraph 2 of Schedule 2; and

(b)   the information relating to the proposed licence holder or proposed manager of the HMO or house specified in paragraph 3 of that Schedule.

(3)   An applicant must—

(a)   supply with the application completed and signed declarations in the form specified in paragraph 4 of Schedule 2; and

(b)   sign the application.

(4)   Where the applicant proposes that another person should be the licence holder, both the applicant and the proposed licence holder must comply with the requirements in paragraph (3).

(5)   The applicant must give the following information about the application to every relevant person—

- (a)   the name, address, telephone number and any e-mail address or fax number of the applicant;
- (b)   the name, address, telephone number and any e-mail address or fax number of the proposed licence holder (if he is not the applicant);
- (c)   the type of application by reference to it being made in respect of an HMO that must be licensed under Part 2 or in respect of a house that must be licensed under Part 3 of the Act;
- (d)   the address of the HMO or house to which the application relates;
- (e)   the name and address of the local housing authority to which the application is made; and
- (f)   the date on which the application is, or is to be, made.

(6)   Nothing in paragraph (5) precludes an applicant from supplying a copy of the application, or other information about the application, to a relevant person.

(7)   A local housing authority must refund an applicant in full any fee that he has paid in respect of an application as soon as reasonably practicable after it learns that at the time the fee was paid—

- (a)   in the case of an application for a licence under Part 2 of the Act, the house was not an HMO, or was not an HMO that was required to be licensed; or
- (b)   in the case of an application for a licence under Part 3 of the Act, the house was a house that was not required to be licensed under Part 2 or 3 of the Act.

(8)   Paragraph (7) applies whether or not the local housing authority, pursuant to the application, granted a licence for the HMO or house when it was not required to be licensed.

(9)   For the purposes of this regulation a "relevant person" is any person (other than a person to whom paragraph (10) applies)—

- (a)   who, to the knowledge of the applicant, is—
  - (i)   a person having an estate or interest in the HMO or house that is the subject of the application, or
  - (ii)   a person managing or having control of that HMO or house (and not falling within paragraph (i)); or
- (b)   where the applicant proposes in the application that conditions should be in the licence imposing a restrictions or obligation on any person (other than the licence holder, that person.

(10)   This paragraph applies to any tenant under a lease with an unexpired term of three years or less.

[8   Prescribed standards for deciding the suitability of a house for multiple occupation by a particular maximum number of households or persons]

[(1)   The standards prescribed for HMOs other than section 257 HMOs for the purpose of section 65 of the Act (tests as to suitability of HMO for multiple occupation) are those set out in Schedule 3.

(2)   The standards prescribed for section 257 HMOs for the purpose of section 65 of the Act are—

  (a)   that all bathrooms and toilets contained in each flat must be of an adequate size and layout, and all wash-hand basins must be suitably located and be fit for purpose, having regard to the age and character of the HMO, the size and layout of each flat and its existing provision for wash-hand basins, toilets and bathrooms;

  (b)   those standards set out in paragraph 4(1) of Schedule 3, in so far as it is reasonably practicable to comply with them; and

  (c)   those standards set out in paragraph 5 of Schedule 3.]

9   Publication requirements relating to designations under Part 2 or 3 of the Act

(1)   A local housing authority that is required under section 59(2) or 83(2) of the Act to publish a notice of a designation of an area for the purpose of Part 2 or 3 of the Act must do so in the manner prescribed by paragraph (2).

(2)   Within 7 days after the date on which the designation was confirmed or made the local housing authority must—

  (a)   place the notice on a public notice board at one or more municipal buildings within the designated area, or if there are no such buildings within the designated area, at the closest of such buildings situated outside the designated area;

  (b)   publish the notice on the authority's internet site; and

  (c)   arrange for its publication in at least two local newspapers circulating in or around the designated area—

    (i)   in the next edition of those newspapers; and

    (ii)   five times in the editions of those newspapers following the edition in which it is first published, with the interval between each publication being no less than two weeks and no more than three weeks.

(3)   Within 2 weeks after the designation was confirmed or made the local housing authority must send a copy of the notice to—

  (a)   any person who responded to the consultation conducted by it under section 56(3) or 80(9) of the Act;

  (b)   any organisation which, to the reasonable knowledge of the authority—

    (i)   represents the interests of landlords or tenants within the designated area; or

    (ii)   represents managing agents, estate agents or letting agents within the designated area; and

(c)   every organisation within the local housing authority area that the local housing authority knows or believes provides advice on landlord and tenant matters, including—

    (i)   law centres;

    (ii)   citizens" advice bureaux;

    (iii)   housing advice centres; and

    (iv)   homeless persons" units.

(4)   In addition to the information referred to in section 59(2)(a), (b) and(c) or 83(2)(a), (b) and(c), the notice must contain the following information—

(a)   a brief description of the designated area;

(b)   the name, address, telephone number and e-mail address of—

    (i)   the local housing authority that made the designation;

    (ii)   the premises where the designation may be inspected; and

    (iii)   the premises where applications for licences and general advice may be obtained;

(c)   a statement advising any landlord, person managing or tenant within the designated area to seek advice from the local housing authority on whether their property is affected by the designation; and

(d)   a warning of the consequences of failing to licence a property that is required to be licensed, including the criminal sanctions.

10 Publication requirements relating to the revocation of designations made under Part 2 or 3 of the Act

(1)   A local housing authority that is required under section 60(6) or 84(6) of the Act to publish a notice of revocation of a designation of an area for the purposes of Part 2 or 3 of the Act, must do so in the manner prescribed by paragraph (2).

(2)   Within 7 days after revoking a designation the local housing authority must—

(a)   place a notice on a public notice board at one or more municipal buildings within the designated area, or if there are no such buildings within the designated area, at the closest of such buildings situated outside the designated area;

(b)   publish the notice on the authority's internet site; and

(c)   arrange for the publication of the notice in at least two local newspapers circulating in or around the designated area in the next edition of those newspapers.

(3)   The notice must contain the following information—

(a)   a brief description of the area to which the designation being revoked relates;

(b)   a summary of the reasons for the revocation;

(c)   the date from which the revocation takes effect;

(d)   the name, address, telephone number and e-mail address—

    (i)   of the local housing authority that revoked the designation; and

    (ii)   where the revocation may be inspected.

11 Registers of Licences

(1) The following particulars are prescribed for each entry in a register established and maintained under section 232(1)(a) of the Act in respect of a licence granted under Part 2 (HMOs) or 3 (selective licensing) of the Act which is in force—

   (a)   the name and address of the licence holder;

   (b)   the name and address of the person managing the licensed HMO or house;

   (c)   the address of the licensed HMO or house;

   (d)   a short description of the licensed HMO or house;

   (e)   a summary of the conditions of the licence;

   (f)   the commencement date and duration of the licence;

   (g)   summary information of any matter concerning the licensing of the HMO or house that has been referred to a residential property tribunal or to the Lands Tribunal; and

   (h)   summary information of any decision of the tribunals referred to in sub-paragraph (g) that relate to the licensed HMO or house, together with the reference number allocated to the case by the tribunal.

(2) [Subject to paragraph (3), the] following additional particulars are prescribed for each entry in a register established and maintained under section 232(1)(a) of the Act in respect of a licence granted under Part 2 of the Act which is in force—

   (a)   the number of storeys comprising the licensed HMO;

   (b)   the number of rooms in the licensed HMO providing—

      (i)   sleeping accommodation; and

      (ii)   living accommodation;

   (c)   in the case of a licensed HMO consisting of flats—

      (i)   the number of flats that are self contained; and

      (ii)   the number of flats that are not self contained;

   (d)   a description of shared amenities including the numbers of each amenity; and

   (e)   the maximum number of persons or households permitted to occupy the licensed HMO under the conditions of the licence.

[(3) The particulars mentioned in sub-paragraphs (b), (c)(ii), (d) and (e) of paragraph (2) are not prescribed for any entry in a register referred to in that paragraph in respect of a licence granted in relation to a section 257 HMO.]

12 Registers of temporary exemption notices

(1) The following particulars are prescribed for each entry in a register established and maintained under section 232(1)(b) of the Act in respect of a temporary exemption notice served under section 62 or 86 of the Act which is in force—

   (a)   the name and address of the person notifying the local housing authority under section 62(1) or section 86(1) of the Act;

(b)   the address of the HMO or house in respect of which the local housing authority has served the temporary exemption notice and any reference number allocated to it by the authority;

(c)   a summary of the effect of the notice;

(d)   details of any previous temporary exemption notices that have been served in relation to the same HMO or house for a period immediately preceding the current temporary exemption notice;

(e)   a statement of the particular steps that the person referred to in sub-paragraph (a) intends to take with a view to securing that the HMO or house is no longer required to be licensed;

(f)   the date on which the local housing authority served the temporary exemption notice and the date on which it ceases to be in force;

(g)   summary information of any matter concerning the HMO or house that has been referred to a residential property tribunal or to the Lands Tribunal; and

(h)   summary information of any decision of the tribunals referred to in sub-paragraph (g) that relate to the HMO or house together with the reference number allocated to the case by the tribunal.

13   Registers of management orders

(1) The following particulars are prescribed for each entry in a register established and maintained under section 232(1)(c) of the Act in respect of a management order made under section 102(2), (3), (4) or (7) or 113(1) or (6) of the Act—

(a)   the address of the HMO or house to which the order relates and any reference number allocated to it by the local housing authority;

(b)   a short description of the HMO or house;

(c)   the date on which the order comes into force;

(d)   a summary of the reasons for making the order;

(e)   a summary of the terms of the order and the type of order made;

(f)   summary information of any application concerning the HMO or house that has been made to a residential property tribunal or to the Lands Tribunal; and

(g)   summary information of any decision of the tribunals referred to in sub-paragraph (f) that relate to the HMO or house, together with the reference number allocated to the case by the tribunal.

(2) [Subject to paragraph (4), the] following additional particulars are prescribed for each entry in a register established and maintained under section 232(1)(c) of the Act in respect of a management order made under section 102(2), (3), (4) or (7) or 113(1) or (6) of the Act which is in force—

(a)   the number of storeys comprising the HMO;

(b)   the number of rooms in the HMO providing—

      (i)   sleeping accommodation; and

      (ii)   living accommodation;

(c)   in the case of an HMO consisting of flats—

      (i)   the number of flats that are self contained;

   (ii)   the number of flats that are not self contained;

   (iii)   a description of shared amenities including the numbers of each amenity;

   (iv)   the maximum number of households permitted to occupy the HMO; and

   (v)   the maximum number of persons permitted to occupy the HMO.

(3) The following particulars are prescribed for each entry in a register established and maintained under section 232(1)(c) of the Act in respect of an empty dwelling management order made under section 133(1) or 136(1) or (2) of the Act—

   (a)   the address of the dwelling to which the order relates and any reference number allocated to it by the local housing authority;

   (b)   a short description of the dwelling;

   (c)   the date on which the order comes into force;

   (d)   a summary of the reasons for making the order;

   (e)   a summary of the terms of the order;

   (f)   summary information of any application concerning the dwelling that has been made to a residential property tribunal or to the Lands Tribunal; and

   (g)   summary information of any decision of the tribunals referred to in sub-paragraph (f) that relate to the dwelling, together with the reference number allocated to the case by the tribunal.

[(4) The particulars mentioned in sub-paragraphs (b) and (c)(ii) to (v) of paragraph (2) are not prescribed for any entry referred to in that paragraph in respect of a management order made in relation to a section 257 HMO.]

Signed by authority of the First Secretary of State

Kay Andrews

Parliamentary Under Secretary of State

Office of the Deputy Prime Minister

15th February 2006

Buildings which are Not HMOs for Any Purpose of the Act (Excluding Part 1)

Schedule 1

Regulation 6(1)

The enactments referred to in regulation 13(1) are—

   (h)   sections 87, 87A, 87B, 87C and 87D of the Children Act 1989;

   (i)   section 43(4) of the Prison Act 1952;

   (j)   section 34 of the Nationality, Immigration and Asylum Act 2002;

   (k)   The Secure Training Centre Rules 1998;

   (l)   The Prison Rules 1999;

   (m)   The Young Offender Institute Rules 2000;

   (n)   The Detention Centre Rules 2001;

(o) The Criminal Justice and Court Services Act 2000 (Approved Premises) Regulations 2001;

(p) The Care Homes Regulations 2001;

(q) The Children's Homes Regulations 2001; and

(r) The Residential Family Centres Regulations 2002;

Content of Applications under Sections 63 and 87 of the Act

Schedule 2

Regulation 7(1), (2) and (3)

1

The form of statement mentioned in regulation 7(1) is:

"You must let certain persons know in writing that you have made this application or give them a copy of it. The persons who need to know about it are—

any mortgagee of the property to be licensed

any owner of the property to which the application relates (if that is not you) ie the freeholder and any head lessors who are known to you

any other person who is a tenant or long leaseholder of the property or any part of it (including any flat) who is known to you other than a statutory tenant or other tenant whose lease or tenancy is for less than three years (including a periodic tenancy)

the proposed licence holder (if that is not you)

the proposed managing agent (if any) (if that is not you)

any person who has agreed that he will be bound by any conditions in a licence if it is granted.

You must tell each of these persons—

your name, address telephone number and e-mail address or fax number (if any)

the name, address, telephone number and e-mail address or fax number (if any) of the proposed licence holder (if it will not be you)

whether this is an application for an HMO licence under Part 2 or for a house licence under Part 3 of the Housing Act 2004

the address of the property to which the application relates

the name and address of the local housing authority to which the application will be made

the date the application will be submitted"

2

(1) The information mentioned in regulation 7(2)(a) is—

(a) the name, address, telephone number and e-mail address of—

(i) the applicant;

(ii) the proposed licence holder;

(iii) the person managing the HMO or house;

(iv) the person having control of the HMO or house; and

(v)   any person who has agreed to be bound by a condition contained in the licence;

(b)   the address of the HMO or house for which the application is being made;

(c)   the approximate age of the original construction of the HMO or house (using the categories before 1919, 1919-45, 1945-64, 1965-80 and after 1980);

(d)   the type of HMO or house for which the application is being made, by reference to one of the following categories—

    (i)   house in single occupation;

    (ii)   house in multiple occupation;

    (iii)   flat in single occupation;

    (iv)   flat in multiple occupation;

    (v)   a house converted into and comprising only of self contained flats;

    (vi)   a purpose built block of flats; or

    (vii)   other;

(e)   details of other HMOs or houses that are licensed under Part 2 or 3 of the Act in respect of which the proposed licence holder is the licence holder, whether in the area of the local housing authority to which the application is made or in the area of any other local housing authority;

(f)   the following information about the HMO or house for which the application is being made[, except in respect of an application in respect of a section 257 HMO]—

    (i)   the number of storeys comprising the HMO or house and the levels on which those storeys are situated;

    (ii)   the number of separate letting units;

    (iii)   the number of habitable rooms (excluding kitchens);

    (iv)   the number of bathrooms and shower rooms;

    (v)   the number of toilets and wash basins;

    (vi)   the number of kitchens;

    (vii)   the number of sinks;

    (viii) the number of households occupying the HMO or house;

    (ix)   the number of people occupying the HMO or house;

    (x)   details of fire precautions equipment, including the number and location of smoke alarms;

    (xi)   details of fire escape routes and other fire safety [information] provided to occupiers;

    (xii)   a declaration that the furniture in the HMO or house that is provided under the terms of any tenancy or licence meets any safety requirements contained in any enactment; and

    (xiii) a declaration that any gas appliances in the HMO or house meet any safety requirements contained in any enactment;

[(g)   where the application is being made in respect of a section 257 HMO, the following information—

    (i)   the number of storeys comprising the HMO and the levels on which those storeys are situated;

   (ii)   the number of self-contained flats and, of those, the number—
- (aa) that the applicant believes to be subject to a lease of over 21 years; and
- (bb) over which he cannot reasonably be able to exercise control;

  (iii)   in relation to each self-contained flat that is not owner-occupied and which is under the control of or being managed by the proposed licence holder, and in relation to the common parts of the HMO—
- (aa) details of fire precautions equipment, including the number and location of smoke alarms;
- (bb) details of fire escape routes and other fire safety information provided to occupiers; and
- (cc) a declaration that the furniture in the HMO or house that is provided under the terms of any tenancy or licence meets any safety requirements contained in any enactment; and

  (iv)   a declaration that any gas appliances in any parts of the HMO over which the proposed licence holder can reasonably be expected to exercise control meet any safety requirements contained in any enactment].

3

The information mentioned in regulation 7(2)(b) is—

(a) details of any unspent convictions that may be relevant to the proposed licence holder's fitness to hold a licence, or the proposed manager's fitness to manage the HMO or house, and, in particular any such conviction in respect of any offence involving fraud or other dishonesty, or violence or drugs or any offence listed in Schedule 3 to the Sexual Offences Act 2003;

(b) details of any finding by a court or tribunal against the proposed licence holder or manager that he has practised unlawful discrimination on grounds of sex, colour, race, ethnic or national origin or disability in, or in connection with, the carrying on of any business;

(c) details of any contravention on the part of the proposed licence holder or manager of any provision of any enactment relating to housing, public health, environmental health or landlord and tenant law which led to civil or criminal proceedings resulting in a judgement being made against him.

(d) information about any HMO or house the proposed licence holder or manager owns or manages or has owned or managed which has been the subject of—
- (i) a control order under section 379 of the Housing Act 1985 in the five years preceding the date of the application; or
- (ii) any appropriate enforcement action described in section 5(2) of the Act.

(e) information about any HMO or house the proposed licence holder or manager owns or manages or has owned or managed for which a local housing authority has refused to grant a licence under Part 2 or 3 of the Act, or has revoked a licence in consequence of the licence holder breaching the conditions of his licence; and

(f)   information about any HMO or house the proposed licence holder or manager owns or manages or has owned or managed that has been the subject of an interim or final management order under the Act.

4

The form of declaration mentioned in regulation 7(3)(a) is as follows—

I/we declare that the information contained in this application is correct to the best of my/our knowledge. I/We understand that I/we commit an offence if I/we supply any information to a local housing authority in connection with any of their functions under any of Parts 1 to 4 of the Housing Act 2004 that is false or misleading and which I/we know is false or misleading or am/are are reckless as to whether it is false or misleading.

Signed (all applicants)

Dated

I/We declare that I/We have served a notice of this application on the following persons who are the only persons known to me/us that are required to be informed that I/we have made this application:

Name	Address	Description of the person's interest in the property or the application	Date of service

Prescribed Standards for Deciding the Suitability for Occupation of an HMO by a Particular Maximum Number of Households or Persons

Schedule 3

Regulation 8

Heating

1

Each unit of living accommodation in an HMO must be equipped with adequate means of space heating.

Washing Facilities

2

[(1)   Where all or some of the units of living accommodation in an HMO do not contain bathing and toilet facilities for the exclusive use of each individual household—

(a)   there must be an adequate number of bathrooms, toilets and wash-hand basins suitable for personal washing) for the number of persons sharing those facilities; and

(b)   where reasonably practicable there must be a wash hand basin with appropriate splash back in each unit other than a unit in which a sink has been provided as mentioned in paragraph 4(1),

having regard to the age and character of the HMO, the size and layout of each flat and its existing provision for wash-hand basins, toilets and bathrooms.]

(3)   All baths, showers and wash hand basins in an HMO must be equipped with taps providing an adequate supply of cold and constant hot water.

(4)   All bathrooms in an HMO must be suitably and adequately heated and ventilated.

(5)   All bathrooms and toilets in an HMO must be of an adequate size and layout.

(6)   All baths, toilets and wash hand basins in an HMO must be fit for the purpose.

(7)   All bathrooms and toilets in an HMO must be suitably located in or in relation to the living accommodation in the HMO.

Kitchens

3

Where all or some of the units of accommodation within the HMO do not contain any facilities for the cooking of food—

(a)   there must be a kitchen, suitably located in relation to the living accommodation, and of such layout and size and equipped with such facilities so as to adequately enable those sharing the facilities to store, prepare and cook food;

(b)   the kitchen must be equipped with the following equipment, which must be fit for the purpose and supplied in a sufficient quantity for the number of those sharing the facilities—

(i)   sinks with draining boards;

(ii)   an adequate supply of cold and constant hot water to each sink supplied;

(iii) installations or equipment for the cooking of food;

(iv)   electrical sockets;

(v)   worktops for the preparation of food;

(vi)   cupboards for the storage of food or kitchen and cooking utensils;

(vii)   refrigerators with an adequate freezer compartment (or, where the freezer compartment is not adequate, adequate separate freezers);

(viii)   appropriate refuse disposal facilities; and

(ix)   appropriate extractor fans, fire blankets and fire doors.

Units of living accommodation without shared basic amenities

4

(1)   Where a unit of living accommodation contains kitchen facilities for the exclusive use of the individual household, and there are no other kitchen facilities available for that household, that unit must be provided with—

(a)   adequate appliances and equipment for the cooking of food;

(b)   a sink with an adequate supply of cold and constant hot water;

(c)   a work top for the preparation of food;

(d)   sufficient electrical sockets;

(e)   a cupboard for the storage of kitchen utensils and crockery; and

(f)   a refrigerator.

[(1A)   The standards referred to in paragraphs (a) and (f) of sub-paragraph (1) shall not apply in relation to a unit of accommodation where—

(a)   the landlord is not contractually bound to provide such appliances or equipment;

(b)   the occupier of the unit of accommodation is entitled to remove such appliances or equipment from the HMO; or

(c)   the appliances or equipment are otherwise outside the control of the landlord.]

(2)   Where there are no adequate shared washing facilities provided for a unit of living accommodation as mentioned in paragraph 2, an enclosed and adequately laid out and ventilated room with a toilet and bath or fixed shower supplying adequate cold and constant hot water must be provided for the exclusive use of the occupiers of that unit either—

(a)   within the living accommodation; or

(b)   within reasonable proximity to the living accommodation

Fire precautionary facilities

5

Appropriate fire precaution facilities and equipment must be provided of such type, number and location as is considered necessary.

RESIDENTIAL PROPERTY TRIBUNAL (FEES) (ENGLAND) REGULATIONS 2006

(2006/830)

Made 17th March 2006

Laid before Parliament 23rd March 2006

Coming into force 13th April 2006

The First Secretary of State, in exercise of the powers conferred by paragraphs 1 and 11 of Schedule 13 to the Housing Act 2004, makes the following Regulations:

1 Citation, commencement and interpretation

(1) These Regulations may be cited as the Residential Property Tribunal (Fees) (England) Regulations 2006 and shall come into force on 13th April 2006.

(2) In these Regulations—

"the Act" means the Housing Act 2004;
"the 1985 Act" means the Housing Act 1985;
"tribunal" means a residential property tribunal.

2 Application

These Regulations apply in relation to appeals and applications of any of the descriptions specified in regulation 3 made after 6th April 2006 in respect of premises in England.

3 Fees

(1) Subject to regulation 5(2), a fee of £150 shall be payable for—

    (a) an appeal to a tribunal under—
        (i) section 22(9) of the Act (refusal to approve use of premises subject to a prohibition order);
        (ii) paragraph 10 of Schedule 1 to the Act (improvement notice);
        (iii) paragraph 13 of Schedule 1 to the Act (refusal to revoke or vary an improvement notice);
        (iv) paragraph 7 of Schedule 2 to the Act (prohibition order);
        (v) paragraph 9 of Schedule 2 to the Act (refusal to revoke or vary a prohibition order);
        (vi) paragraph 11 of Schedule 3 to the Act (improvement notice: demand for recovery of expenses);
        (vii) paragraph 32 of Schedule 5 to the Act (HMO licensing: decision or refusal to vary or revoke licence);
        (viii) paragraph 32 of Schedule 6 to the Act (management order: third party compensation);

(ix)   paragraph 26(1)(a) and (b) of Schedule 7 to the Act (final EDMO);

(x)   paragraph 30 of Schedule 7 to the Act (decision or refusal to revoke or vary an interim or final EDMO);

(xi)   paragraph 34(2) of Schedule 7 to the Act (EDMO: third party compensation);

(xii)   section 269(1) of the 1985 Act (demolition orders);

(b)   an application to a tribunal under—

   (i)   section 126(4) of the Act (effect of management orders: furniture);

   (ii)   under section 138 of the Act (compensation payable to third parties);

   (iii)   section 318(1) of the 1985 Act (power of the tribunal to authorise execution of works on unfit premises or for improvement).

(2)   Subject to paragraph (3) and regulation 5(2), a fee of £150 shall be payable for an appeal to a tribunal under one or more of the following provisions—

(a)   section 62(7) of the Act (HMO licensing: refusal to grant temporary exemption notice);

(b)   section 86(7) of the Act (selective licensing: refusal to grant temporary exemption notice);

(c)   paragraph 31 of Schedule 5 to the Act (grant or refusal of licence);

(d)   paragraph 24 of Schedule 6 to the Act (interim and final management order);

(e)   paragraph 28 of Schedule 6 to the Act (decision or refusal to vary or revoke a management order).

(3)   No fee is payable where an appeal under sub-paragraph (1)(b) of paragraph 24 of Schedule 6 to the Act is made on the grounds set out in sub-paragraph (4) of that paragraph.

4 Payment of fees

Any fee payable under regulation 3 must accompany the appeal or application and must be paid by a cheque made payable to, or postal order drawn in favour of, the Office of the Deputy Prime Minister.

5 Liability to pay fee and waiver of fees

(1)   The appellant or applicant shall be liable to pay any fee payable under regulation 3.

(2)   No fee is payable under regulation 3 where, on the date that the appeal or application is made, the appellant or applicant (as the case may be) or his partner is in receipt of—

(a)   either of the following benefits under Part 7 of the Social Security Contributions and Benefits Act 1992—

   (i)   income support; or

   (ii)   housing benefit;

(b)   an income-based jobseeker's allowance within the meaning of section 1 of the Jobseekers Act 1995;

(c)   a working tax credit under Part 1 of the Tax Credits Act 2002 to which paragraph (3) applies;

(d)   a guarantee credit under the State Pensions Credit Act 2002.

(3)   This paragraph applies where—

  (a)   either—

    (i)   there is a disability element or severe disability element (or both) to the tax credit received by the person or his partner; or

    (ii)   the person or his partner is also in receipt of child tax credit; and

  (b)   the gross annual income taken into account for the calculation of the working tax credit is £14, 213 or less.

(4)   In this regulation "partner", in relation to a person, means—

  (a)   where the person is a member of a couple, the other member of that couple; or

  (b)   where the person is polygamously married to two or more members of his household, any such member.

(5)   In paragraph (4), "couple" means—

  (a)   a man and woman who are married to each other and are members of the same household;

  (b)   a man and woman who are not married to each other but are living together as husband and wife;

  (c)   two people of the same sex who are civil partners of each other and are members of the same household; or

  (d)   two people of the same sex who are not civil partners of each other but are living together as if they were civil partners,

and for the purposes of sub-paragraph (d), two people of the same sex are to be regarded as living together as if they were civil partners if, but only if, they would be regarded as living together as husband and wife were they instead two people of the opposite sex.

6   Reimbursement of fees

(1)   Subject to paragraph (2), in relation to any appeal or application in respect of which a fee is payable under regulation 3, a tribunal may require any party to the appeal or application to reimburse any other party to the extent of the whole or part of any fee paid by him in respect of the appeal or application.

(2)   A tribunal shall not require a party to make such reimbursement if, at the time the tribunal is considering whether or not to do so, the tribunal is satisfied that the party or his partner is in receipt of assistance of any description mentioned in regulation 5(2).

Signed by authority of the First Secretary of State

Kay Andrews

Parliamentary Under Secretary of State

Office of the Deputy Prime Minister

17th March 2006

RESIDENTIAL PROPERTY TRIBUNAL PROCEDURE (ENGLAND) REGULATIONS 2006

(2006/831)

Made 17th March 2006

Laid before Parliament 23rd March 2006

Coming into force 13th April 2006

The First Secretary of State makes the following Regulations in exercise of the powers conferred by section 250(2)(a) of and Schedule 13 to the Housing Act 2004.

In accordance with section 8 of the Tribunals and Inquiries Act 1992 he has consulted with the Council on Tribunals.

1   Citation and commencement

(1)   These Regulations may be cited as the Residential Property Tribunal Procedure (England) Regulations 2006.

(2)   These Regulations shall come into force on 13th April 2006.

2   Interpretation

In these Regulations—

"the Act" means the Housing Act 2004;

"the 1985 Act" means the Housing Act 1985;

"application" means an application or appeal to a tribunal under the Act or Part 9 of the 1985 Act and "applicant" bears a corresponding meaning;

"case management conference" means a pre-trial review or any other meeting held by a tribunal for the purpose of managing the proceedings in respect of an application;

"the Fees Regulations" means the Residential Property Tribunals (Fees) (England) Regulations 2006;

"IMO authorisation application" means an application for authorisation to make an interim management order;

"interested person" means in relation to a particular application—

   (a)   a person other than the applicant who would have been entitled under the Act or the 1985 Act (as the case may be) to make the application;

(b)   a person to whom notice of the application must be given by the applicant in accordance with the following provisions of the Act—

(i)   section 73(7);

(ii)   section 96(7);

(iii)   paragraph 11(2) of Schedule 1; or

(iv)   paragraph 14(2) of Schedule 3;

(c)   a person to whom the tribunal must give the opportunity of being heard in accordance with the following provisions of the Act—

(i)   section 34(4); or

(ii)   section 317(2);

(d)   the LHA where it is not a party to the application;

"LHA" means the local housing authority;

"premises" means the dwelling or building to which the application relates;

"the respondent" means, in respect of an application to which a paragraph of the Schedule to these Regulations applies, the person or persons, or one of the persons, specified in sub-paragraph (3) of that paragraph;

"statement of reasons" means a statement of reasons prepared by the LHA under section 8 of the Act (reasons for decision to take enforcement action); and

"tribunal" means a residential property tribunal, and "the tribunal" in relation to an application means the tribunal by which the application is to be determined.

3   Application

These Regulations apply to proceedings of residential property tribunals for determining applications in respect of premises in England made—

(a)   under the Act;

(b)   under section 318(1) of the 1985Act in respect of applications made on or after 6th April 2006; or

(c)   under any of sections 269(1), 272(1) or (2)(a), 272(2)(b), or 317(1) of the 1985 Act in respect of demolition orders made on or after 6th April 2006.

4   The overriding objective

(1)   When a tribunal—

(a)   exercises any power under these Regulations; or

(b)   interprets any regulation,

it must seek to give effect to the overriding objective of dealing fairly and justly with applications which it is to determine.

(2)   Dealing with an application fairly and justly includes—

(a)   dealing with it in ways which are proportionate to the complexity of the issues and to the resources of the parties;

(b) ensuring, so far as practicable, that the parties are on an equal footing procedurally and are able to participate fully in the proceedings;

(c) assisting any party in the presentation of his case without advocating the course he should take;

(d) using the tribunal's special expertise effectively; and

(e) avoiding delay, so far as is compatible with proper consideration of the issues.

5 Request for extension of time to make an application

(1) This regulation applies where a person makes a request to a tribunal for permission to make an application after the end of the period stipulated in the Act as the period within which the application must be made.

(2) A request to which this regulation applies must—

(a) be in writing;

(b) give reasons for the failure to make the application before the end of that period and for any further delay since then;

(c) include a statement that the person making the request believes that the facts stated in it are true; and

(d) be dated and signed.

(3) Where a request mentioned in paragraph (1) is made, the applicant must at the same time send the completed application to which the request relates to the tribunal.

6 Particulars of application

(1) An application must be in writing and must include the following particulars—

(a) the applicant's name and address;

(b) the name and address of the respondent where known to the applicant, or where not known a description of the respondent's connection with the premises;

(c) the address of the premises;

(d) the applicant's connection with the premises;

(e) the applicant's reasons for making the application including the remedy sought;

(f) where known to the applicant, the name and address of any interested person;

(g) a statement that the applicant believes that the facts stated in the application are true; and

(h) in respect of each application to which a paragraph in the Schedule to these Regulations applies, the documents specified in sub-paragraph (2) of that paragraph.

(2) Any of the particulars required by paragraph (1) may be dispensed with or relaxed if the tribunal is satisfied that—

(a) the particulars and documents included with an application are sufficient to establish that the application is one which may be made to a tribunal; and

(b) no prejudice will be, or is likely to be, caused to any party to the application.

(3) A single qualified member of the panel may exercise the power conferred by paragraph (2).

7 Acknowledgement and notification of application by tribunal

(1) As soon as practicable after receiving the application, the tribunal must—

(a) send an acknowledgement of receipt to the applicant; and

(b) send a copy of the application and of each document accompanying it to the respondent.

(2) Except in a case to which regulation 9 applies, the tribunal must also send to the respondent a notice specifying the date by which he must send the reply mentioned in regulation 8.

(3) The date specified in the notice must not be less than 14 days after the date specified in the notice as the date on which it was made.

8 Reply by respondent

(1) This regulation applies where a respondent receives the notice mentioned in regulation 7(2).

(2) Where this regulation applies the respondent must by the date specified in that notice send to the tribunal a written reply acknowledging receipt of the copy documents sent in accordance with regulation 7(1)(b) and stating—

(a) whether or not he intends to oppose the application;

(b) where not already included in the application, the name and address of each interested person known to the respondent; and

(c) the address to which documents should be sent for the purposes of the proceedings.

9 Urgent IMO authorisation applications

(1) This regulation applies where the LHA requests a tribunal to deal with an IMO authorisation application as a matter of urgency.

(2) Where it appears to the tribunal, on the basis of information accompanying the application, that the exceptional circumstances mentioned in paragraph (3) exist, it may order that an oral hearing (an "urgent oral hearing") shall be held without complying with the notice requirements of regulation 25.

(3) The exceptional circumstances are that—

(a) there is an immediate threat to the health and safety of the occupiers of the house or to persons occupying or having an estate or interest in any premises in the vicinity of the house; and

(b)   by making the interim management order as soon as possible (together where applicable with such other measures as the LHA intends to take) the LHA will be able to take immediate appropriate steps to arrest or significantly reduce the threat.

(4)   The tribunal must as soon as practicable notify the parties and each interested person whose name and address have been notified to it—

(a)   that the application is being dealt with as a matter of urgency under this regulation;

(b)   of the reasons why it appears to the tribunal that the exceptional circumstances exist;

(c)   of any requirement to be satisfied by a party before the hearing; and

(d)   of the date on which the urgent oral hearing will be held.

(5)   The date of the hearing must be not less than 4 days after the date that notification of the urgent oral hearing is sent.

(6)   At the urgent oral hearing the tribunal must—

(a)   if it is satisfied upon hearing evidence that the exceptional circumstance do exist, determine the application; or

(b)   if it is not so satisfied—

     (i)   adjourn the hearing; and

     (ii)   give such directions as it considers appropriate.

(7)   A single qualified member of the panel may—

(a)   exercise the power conferred by paragraph (2); and

(b)   decide the date of the urgent oral hearing.

(8)   Where the tribunal orders an urgent oral hearing the notice provisions contained in the following regulations shall not apply to the application—

(a)   regulation 21(5) (notice for an inspection); and

(b)   regulation 25(3) and (4) (notice of hearing).

10   Request to be treated as an applicant or respondent

(1)   A person ("the potential party") may make a request to the tribunal to be joined as a party to the proceedings.

(2)   Any request under paragraph (1)—

(a)   may be made without notice;

(b)   must be in writing;

(c)   must give reasons for the request; and

(d)   must specify whether the potential party wishes to be treated as—

     (i)   an applicant; or

     (ii)   a respondent.

(3)   As soon as practicable after reaching its decision whether to grant or refuse a request under paragraph (1), the tribunal must—

(a)   notify the potential party of the decision and the reasons for it; and

(b)   send a copy of the notification to the existing parties.

(4)   Any potential party whose request under paragraph (1) is granted must be treated as an applicant or respondent for the purposes of regulations 4, 9, 11, 13 to 37 and 39 to 41.

(5)   In the regulations mentioned in paragraph (4) any reference to an applicant or a respondent must be construed as including a person treated as such under this regulation, and any reference to a party must be construed as including any such person.

(6)   A single qualified member of the panel may grant or refuse a request under paragraph (1).

11   Determining applications together

(1)   This regulation applies where separate applications have been made which in the opinion of the tribunal—

(a)   involve related issues concerning the same premises; or
(b)   are made in respect of two or more premises in which the same parties have interests and as to which similar or related issues fall to be determined.

(2)   Where paragraph (1) applies, the tribunal may order that—

(a)   some or all of those applications; or
(b)   particular issues or matters raised in the applications,

shall be determined together.

12   Payment of fees

Where a fee which is payable under the Fees Regulations is not paid within a period of 14 days from the date on which the application is received, the application shall be treated as withdrawn unless the tribunal is satisfied that there are reasonable grounds not to do so.

13   Representatives

(1)   This regulation applies where a party or an interested person makes a request in writing to the tribunal for information or documents to be supplied to his representative.

(2)   A request mentioned in paragraph (1) must contain the name and address of the representative.

(3)   Where this regulation applies any duty of the tribunal under these Regulations to supply any information or document shall be satisfied by sending or giving it to the representative.

14   Supply of information and documents to interested persons

(1)   Where the tribunal is notified of the name and address of an interested person, it must ensure that as soon as is practicable he is supplied with—

(a) a copy of the application;

(b) an explanation of the procedure for applying to be joined as an applicant or respondent; and

(c) any other information or document which the tribunal considers appropriate.

(2) The tribunal may ensure the supply of information or documents under paragraph (1) by—

(a) itself supplying the interested person with the information or documents; or

(b) requiring a party to do so by an order made under regulation 16(2).

(3) Where information and documents are supplied to an interested person in accordance with paragraph (1) but—

(a) he responds to the tribunal but is not joined as a party under regulation 10; or

(b) he does not so respond,

the tribunal shall not be under any further duty to ensure the supply of information or documents to that person.

15 Supply of documents by tribunal

(1) Before determining an application, the tribunal must take all reasonable steps to ensure that each of the parties is supplied with—

(a) a copy of any document relevant to the proceedings (or sufficient extracts from or particulars of the document) which has been received from any other party or from an interested person (other than a document already in his possession or one of which he has previously been supplied with a copy); and

(b) a copy of any document which embodies the results of any relevant enquiries made by or for the tribunal for the purposes of the proceedings.

(2) At a hearing, if a party has not previously received a relevant document or a copy of, or sufficient extracts from or particulars of, a relevant document, then unless—

(a) that person consents to the continuation of the hearing; or

(b) the tribunal considers that that person has a sufficient opportunity to deal with the matters to which the document relates without an adjournment of the hearing,

the tribunal must adjourn the hearing for a period which it considers will give that person a sufficient opportunity to deal with those matters.

16 Supply of information and documents by parties

(1) Subject to paragraph (5), the tribunal may make an order requiring a party to supply to the tribunal any information or document which it is in the power of that party to supply and which is specified, or of a description specified, in the order.

(2) The tribunal may make an order requiring a party to supply to another party or to an interested person copies of any documents supplied or to be supplied to the tribunal under paragraph (1).

(3) A party who is subject to an order made under paragraph (1) or (2) must supply such information, documents or copies by such time as may be specified in, or determined in accordance with, the order.

(4) Subject to paragraph (5) the tribunal may make an order requiring any person to attend an oral hearing to give evidence and produce any documents specified, or of a description specified, in the order which it is in the power of that person to produce.

(5) Paragraphs (1) and (4) do not apply in relation to any document which a person could not be compelled to produce on the trial of an action in a court of law in England.

(6) A single qualified member of the panel may make an order under paragraph(1), (2) or (4) which is—

    (a)   preliminary to an oral hearing; or
    (b)   preliminary or incidental to a determination.

17 Failure to comply with an order to supply information and documents

Where a party has failed to comply with an order made under regulation 16(1), (2) or (4) the tribunal may make an order dismissing or allowing the whole or part of the application.

18 Determination without a hearing

(1) Subject to paragraphs (2) and (6) the tribunal may determine an application without an oral hearing if it has given the parties not less than 14 days" notice in writing of its intention to do so.

(2) At any time before the application is determined—

    (a)   the applicant or the respondent may request an oral hearing; or
    (b)   the tribunal may give notice to the parties that it intends to hold an oral hearing.

(3) Where a request is made or a notice given under paragraph (2) the tribunal must give notice of a hearing in accordance with regulation 25.

(4) A determination without an oral hearing may be made in the absence of any representations by the respondent.

(5) A single qualified member of the panel may decide whether an oral hearing is or is not appropriate to determine an application.

(6) This regulation does not apply to an application to which regulation 9 (urgent IMO authorisation applications) applies.

19 Interim orders

(1) A tribunal may make an order on an interim basis (an "interim order")—

    (a) suspending, in whole or in part, the effect of any decision, notice, order or licence which is the subject matter of proceedings before it; or

    (b) for the time being granting any remedy which it would have had power to grant in its final decision.

(2) Where the tribunal makes an interim order without first giving the parties the opportunity to make representations with regard to making it, a party may request that the interim order be varied or set aside.

(3) Any such request may be made—

    (a) orally at a case management conference or hearing;

    (b) in writing; or

    (c) by such other means as the tribunal may permit.

(4) An interim order must be recorded as soon as possible in a document which, except in the case of an order made with the consent of all parties, must give reasons for the decision to make the order.

(5) This regulation does not apply to an IMO authorisation application.

20 Directions

(1) A party may request the tribunal to give directions by order under its general power in section 230(2) of the Housing Act 2004.

(2) A party to whom a direction is addressed may request the tribunal to vary it or set it aside.

(3) A request referred to in paragraph (1) or (2) may be made—

    (a) orally at a case management conference or hearing;

    (b) in writing; or

    (c) by such other means as the tribunal may permit.

(4) The party making the request must specify the directions which are sought and the reasons for seeking them.

(5) A single qualified member of the panel may give a procedural direction as to any matter which is—

    (a) preliminary to an oral hearing; or

    (b) preliminary or incidental to a determination.

(6) In paragraph (5)(a), "procedural direction" means any direction other than one of those set out in paragraphs (a) to (e) of section 230(5) of the Act.

21   Inspection of premises and neighbourhood

(1)   Subject to paragraph (3) the tribunal may inspect—

    (a)   the premises;

    (b)   any other premises inspection of which may assist the tribunal in determining the application;

    (c)   the locality of the premises.

(2)   Subject to paragraph (3)—

    (a)   the tribunal must give the parties an opportunity to attend an inspection; and

    (b)   a member of the Council on Tribunals who is acting in that capacity may attend any inspection.

(3)   The making of and attendance at an inspection is subject to any necessary consent being obtained.

(4)   Where there is an oral hearing, an inspection may be carried out before, during, or after the hearing.

(5)   Subject to paragraph (6), the tribunal must give the parties not less than 14 days notice of the date, time and place of the inspection.

(6)   Any of the requirements for notice in paragraph (5) may be dispensed with or relaxed if the tribunal is satisfied that the parties have received sufficient notice.

(7)   Where an inspection is made after the close of an oral hearing, the tribunal may reopen the hearing on account of any matter arising from the inspection, after giving reasonable notice of the date, time and place of the reopened hearing to the parties.

22   Expert evidence

(1)   In this regulation "expert" means an independent expert who is not an employee of a party.

(2)   Subject to paragraph (4) a party may adduce expert evidence, and in doing so must—

    (a)   provide the tribunal with a written summary of the evidence; and

    (b)   supply a copy of that written summary to each other party at least 7 days before—

        (i)   the date of the relevant oral hearing notified in relation to the application under regulation 25; or

        (ii)   the date notified under regulation 18 upon which the application will be determined without an oral hearing.

(3)   An expert's written summary of his evidence must—

    (a)   be addressed to the tribunal;

    (b)   include details of the expert's qualifications;

(c)   contain a statement that the expert understands and has complied with his duty to assist the tribunal on the matters within his expertise, overriding any obligation to the person from whom the expert has received instructions or by whom he is employed or paid.

(4)   Where the tribunal gives a direction, under its general power in section 230(2) of the Act, that a party may not adduce expert evidence without its permission, it may specify as a condition of that permission that—

(a)   the expert's evidence must be limited to such matters as the tribunal directs;

(b)   the expert must attend a hearing to give oral evidence; or

(c)   the parties must jointly instruct the expert.

23   Case management conference

(1)   The tribunal may hold a case management conference.

(2)   The tribunal must give the parties not less than 7 days" notice of the date, time and place of the case management conference.

(3)   At the case management conference the tribunal may order the parties to take such steps or do such things as appear to it to be necessary or desirable for securing the just, expeditious and economical determination of the application.

(4)   The tribunal may postpone or adjourn a case management conference.

(5)   A party may be represented at a case management conference.

(6)   The functions of the tribunal under this regulation may be exercised by a single qualified member of the panel.

24   Other case management powers

(1)   The tribunal may—

(a)   reduce the time appointed by or under these Regulations for doing any act where all parties agree the reduction in question;

(b)   extend the time appointed by or under these Regulations for doing any act, even if the time appointed has expired, where—
  (i)   it would not be reasonable to expect the person in question to comply or have complied within that time; or
  (ii)   not to extend the time would result in substantial injustice;

(c)   permit the use of telephone, video link, or any other method of communication—
  (i)   to make representations to the tribunal; or
  (ii)   for the purposes of a case management conference or hearing;

(d)   require any person giving written evidence to include with that evidence a signed statement that he believes the facts stated in the evidence are true;

(e)   take any other step or make any other decision which the tribunal considers necessary or desirable for the purpose of managing the case.

(2)   The tribunal may exercise its powers under these Regulations in response to a request to do so or on its own initiative.

(3)   A single qualified member of the panel may exercise the powers under this regulation as to any matter which is preliminary to—

    (a)   an oral hearing; or

    (b)   a determination which is to be made without an oral hearing.

25   Notice of hearing

(1)   A hearing shall be on the date and at the time and place appointed by the tribunal.

(2)   The tribunal must give notice to the parties of the appointed date, time and place of the hearing.

(3)   Subject to paragraph (4) notice of the hearing must be given not less than 21 days before the appointed date.

(4)   In exceptional circumstances the tribunal may, without the agreement of the parties, give less than 21 days" notice of the appointed date, time and place of the hearing; but any such notice must be given as soon as practicable before the appointed date and the notice must specify what the exceptional circumstances are.

26   Postponement of hearing

(1)   Subject to paragraph (3) the tribunal may postpone an oral hearing.

(2)   The tribunal must give reasonable notice to the parties of the time and date to which a hearing is postponed

(3)   Where postponement has been requested by a party the tribunal must not postpone the hearing except where it considers it is reasonable to do so having regard to—

    (a)   the grounds for the request;

    (b)   the time at which the request is made; and

    (c)   the convenience of the parties.

27   Hearing

(1)   At a hearing—

    (a)   the tribunal shall (subject to these regulations) determine the procedure and conduct;

    (b)   any person appearing before the tribunal may do so either in person or by his representative;

    (c)   the parties shall be entitled to—

        (i)   give relevant evidence;

        (ii)   call witnesses;

        (iii)   question any witness; and

      (iv)   address the tribunal on the evidence and law and generally on the subject matter of the application; and

  (d)   the tribunal may receive evidence of any fact which seems to it to be relevant, even if the evidence would be inadmissible in proceedings before a court of law, and must not refuse to admit any evidence presented in due time which is admissible at law and is relevant and necessary and has not been improperly obtained.

(2)   At a hearing the tribunal may, if it is satisfied that it is just and reasonable to do so, permit a party to rely on reasons not previously stated and on evidence not previously available or not previously adduced.

(3)   The tribunal may adjourn a hearing, but if this is done at the request of a party it must consider that it is reasonable to do so having regard to—

  (a)   the grounds for the request;

  (b)   the time at which the request is made; and

  (c)   the convenience of the parties.

28 Hearing in public or private

(1)   A hearing must be in public except where the tribunal is satisfied that in the circumstances of the case and subject to the overriding objective the hearing should be held in private.

(2)   The tribunal may decide under paragraph (1) that—

  (a)   part only of the hearing must be in private; or

  (b)   any of the following matters must not be made public—

      (i)   information about the proceedings before the tribunal;

      (ii)   the names and identifying characteristics of persons concerned in the proceedings; or

      (iii)   specified evidence given in the proceedings.

29 Persons entitled to be present at a hearing held in private

(1)   Subject to paragraphs (2) and (3) the following persons shall be entitled to attend a hearing held in private and to be present at the tribunal's deliberations with respect to the determination of the application—

  (a)   a president or chair or other panel member not forming part of the tribunal for the purpose of the hearing;

  (b)   a member of the Council on Tribunals who is acting in that capacity;

  (c)   the staff of the Tribunal Service;

  (d)   any other person permitted by the tribunal with the consent of the parties.

(2)   None of the persons specified in paragraph (1) may take any part in the hearing or such deliberations.

(3)   The tribunal may admit persons to a hearing held in private on such terms and conditions as it considers appropriate.

30 Failure of a party to appear at a hearing

Where a party fails to appear at a hearing the tribunal may proceed with the hearing if—

  (a) it is satisfied that notice has been given to that party in accordance with these Regulations; and
  (b) it is not satisfied that there is a good reason for the failure to appear.

31 Decisions of the Tribunal in determining applications

(1) This regulation applies to the decision determining an application.

(2) If a hearing was held, the decision may be given orally at the end of the hearing.

(3) A decision must, in every case, be recorded in a document as soon as practicable after the decision has been made.

(4) A decision given or recorded in accordance with paragraph (2) or (3) need not record the reasons for the decision.

(5) The reasons for the decision must be recorded in a document as soon as practicable after the decision has been given or recorded.

(6) A document recording a decision or the reasons for a decision (a "decision document"), must be signed and dated by an appropriate person.

(7) An appropriate person may, by means of a certificate signed and dated by him, correct any clerical mistakes in a decision document or any errors arising in it from an accidental slip or omission.

(8) In this regulation "appropriate person" means—

  (a) the Chair of the tribunal; or
  (b) in the event of his absence or incapacity, another member of the tribunal.

(9) A copy of any decision document, and a copy of any correction certified under paragraph (7) must be sent to each party.

32 Costs

The tribunal must not make a determination under paragraph 12 of Schedule 13 to the Act in respect of a party without first giving that party an opportunity of making representations to the tribunal.

33 Withdrawal of application

(1) Subject to paragraph (3) an applicant ("the withdrawing party") may withdraw the whole or part of his application in accordance with paragraph (2) at any time before determination of the application.

(2) The withdrawing party must notify withdrawal of his application by a signed and dated notice supplied to the tribunal—

(a) sufficiently identifying the application or part of the application which is withdrawn;

(b) stating whether any part of the application, and if so what, remains to be determined; and

(c) confirming that a copy of the notice of the withdrawal has been supplied to all other parties and stating the date on which this was done.

(3) In any of the circumstances set out in paragraph (4), withdrawal of the application shall not take effect until one of the courses of action in paragraph (5) has been carried out.

(4) The circumstances mentioned in paragraph (3) are that—

(a) an interim order in favour of a party has been made;

(b) a party has given an undertaking to the tribunal;

(c) payment to the withdrawing party has been ordered whether by way of compensation, damages, costs, reimbursement of fees or otherwise;

(d) a party has requested an order for reimbursement of fees; or

(5) The courses of action mentioned in paragraph (3) are that—

(a) the withdrawing party has sent to the tribunal a written statement signed by all other parties setting out how any of the circumstances in sub-paragraphs (a) to (d) of paragraph (4) which apply to the case are to be dealt with; or

(b) the withdrawing party has given notice of the intended withdrawal to all parties and—

(i) the withdrawing party has requested the tribunal to give directions as to the conditions on which the withdrawal may be made; and

(ii) the tribunal has given such directions.

(6) In giving directions under paragraph (5)(b)(ii) the tribunal may impose such conditions as it considers appropriate.

(7) A single qualified member may give directions under paragraph (5)(b)(ii).

34 Enforcement

Any decision of the tribunal may, with the permission of the county court, be enforced in the same way as orders of such a court.

35 Permission to appeal

(1) In this regulation "to appeal" means to make an appeal from a decision of the tribunal to the Lands Tribunal and "appellant" bears a corresponding meaning.

(2) Where a party makes a request to the tribunal for permission to appeal to the Lands Tribunal from a decision of the tribunal the request may be made—

(a) orally at the hearing at which the decision is announced by the tribunal; or

(b) subsequently in writing to the office of the tribunal.

(3) A request for permission to appeal must be made within the period of 21 days starting with the date specified in the decision notice as the date on which reasons for the decision were given.

(4) Where a request for permission to appeal is made in writing it must be signed by the appellant or the appellant's representative and must—

    (a) state the name and address of the appellant and of any representative of the appellant;

    (b) identify the decision and the tribunal to which the request for leave relates; and

    (c) state the grounds on which the appellant intends to rely in the appeal.

(5) The decision of the tribunal on a request for permission to appeal must be recorded in writing together with the reasons for it, and the tribunal must send a copy of the decision and reasons to the appellant and to the other parties to the application which is the subject of the appeal.

(6) A notification under paragraph (5) must, as appropriate, include a statement of any relevant statutory provision, rule or guidance relating to any further request to the Lands Tribunal for permission to appeal and of the time and place for making the further request or for giving notice of appeal.

36 Assistance to participants

(1) In this regulation "participant" means a party or witness or other person taking part in proceedings relating to an application or to whom an order of the tribunal is addressed.

(2) If a participant is unable to read or speak or understand the English language, the tribunal must make arrangements for him to be provided, free of charge, with the necessary translations and assistance of an interpreter to enable his effective participation in the proceedings.

(3) If a participant is without hearing or speech, the tribunal must make arrangements for him to be provided, free of charge, with the services of a sign language interpreter, lip speaker, or palantypist, to enable his effective participation in the proceedings.

(4) A participant shall be entitled to assistance under this regulation whether or not he is represented.

(5) A participant who requires assistance under this regulation must at the earliest opportunity notify the requirement to the tribunal.

37 Requirements for supply of notices and documents

(1) Any document or notice required or authorised by these Regulations to be supplied to any person, whether by the tribunal, a party, or any other person, shall be duly supplied to that person—

(a) if it is sent to his proper address by first class post or by special delivery, or by recorded delivery;

(b) if it is delivered by any other means to his proper address;

(c) subject to paragraph (2), if with his written consent it is sent to him—

    (i) by fax, email or other electronic communication which produces a text received in legible form;

    (ii) by a private document delivery service.

(2) For the purposes of paragraph (1)(c) a person's legal representative shall be deemed to have given written consent if the reference or address for the means of fax or electronic communication or private document delivery system is shown on the legal representative's notepaper.

(3) A person's proper address for the purposes of paragraph (1) is—

(a) in the case of the tribunal, the address of the office of the tribunal;

(b) in the case of an incorporated company or other body registered in the United Kingdom, the address of the registered or principal office of the company or body;

(c) in the case of any other person the usual or last known address of that person.

(4) This paragraph applies where—

(a) an intended recipient of a document or notice—

    (i) cannot be found after all diligent enquiries have been made;

    (ii) has died and has no personal representative; or

    (iii) is out of the United Kingdom; or

(b) for any other reason a notice or other document cannot readily be supplied in accordance with these Regulations.

(5) Where paragraph (4) applies, the tribunal may—

(a) dispense with supplying the notice or other document; or

(b) give directions for substituted service in such other form (whether by advertisement in a newspaper or otherwise) or manner as the tribunal thinks fit.

(6) Where it is required under the Act or these Regulations that a party must provide evidence that he has supplied any person with a document, a party may satisfy the requirement by providing a signed certificate confirming that the document was served in accordance with the requirements of this regulation.

38 Time

Where the time specified by these Regulations for doing any act expires on a Saturday or Sunday or public holiday, it shall be treated as expiring on the next following day which is not a Saturday or Sunday or public holiday.

39 Frivolous and vexatious applications

(1) Subject to paragraph (2), where it appears to the tribunal that an application is frivolous or vexatious or otherwise an abuse of process, the tribunal may dismiss the application in whole or in part.

(2) Before dismissing an application under paragraph (1) the tribunal must give notice of its intention to do so to the applicant in accordance with paragraph (3).

(3) Any notice under paragraph (2) must state—

    (a)   that the tribunal is minded to dismiss the application;

    (b)   the grounds on which it is minded to dismiss the application;

    (c)   the date (being not less than 21 days after the date that the notice was sent) before which the applicant may be heard by the tribunal on the question of whether the application should be dismissed.

(4) An application may not be dismissed under paragraph (1) unless—

    (a)   the applicant makes no request to the tribunal before the date mentioned in paragraph (3)(c) or

    (b)   where the applicant makes such a request, the tribunal has heard the applicant and the respondent, or such of them as attend the hearing, on the question of the dismissal of the application.

40 Irregularities

Any irregularity resulting from failure by a party to comply with any provision of these Regulations or of any direction of the tribunal before the tribunal has determined the application shall not of itself render the proceedings void.

41 Signature of documents

Where these Regulations require a document to be signed, that requirement shall be satisfied—

    (a)   if the signature is either written or produced by computer or other mechanical means; and

    (b)   the name of the signatory appears beneath the signature in such a way that he may be identified.

Signed by the authority of the First Secretary of State

Kay Andrews

Parliamentary Under Secretary of State

Office of the Deputy Prime Minister

17th March 2006

Additional Details with Regard to Certain Applications

regulation 2 and 6

Applications relating to improvement notices

1

(1) This paragraph applies to an application under paragraph 10(1) of Schedule 1 to the Act (appeal against improvement notice) other than an application referred to in paragraph 2.

(2) The specified documents are—

    (a)   a copy of the improvement notice (including any schedule to it);

    (b)   the statement of reasons; and

    (c)   where the ground or one of the grounds of the application is that one of the courses of action mentioned in paragraph 12(2) of Schedule 1 to the Act is the best course of action in relation to the hazard, a statement identifying that course of action with the applicant's reasons for considering it the best course.

(3) The specified respondent is the LHA.

2

(1) This paragraph applies to an application under paragraph 10 of Schedule 1 to the Act which consists of or includes the ground set out in paragraph 11(1) of that Schedule (ground of appeal relating to other persons).

(2) The specified documents are—

    (a)   a copy of the improvement notice (including any schedule to it);

    (b)   the statement of reasons;

    (c)   where one of the grounds of the application is that another course of action mentioned in paragraph 12(2) of Schedule 1 to the Act is the best course of action in relation to the hazard, a statement identifying that course of action with the applicant's reasons for considering it the best course;

    (d)   the name and address of any person who as an owner of the premises, in the applicant's opinion ought to take the action required by the improvement notice or pay the whole or part of the costs of taking that action("the other owner");

    (e)   proof of service of a copy of the application on the other owner; and

    (f)   a statement containing the following details—

        (i)   the nature of the other owner's interest in the premises;

        (ii)   the reason the applicant considers the other owner ought to take the action concerned or pay the whole or part of the cost of taking that action; and

        (iii)   where the ground of the application is that the other owner ought to pay the whole or part of the cost of taking the action, the estimated cost of taking the action and the proportion of that cost which the applicant considers the other owner ought to pay.

(3) The specified respondent is the LHA.

3

(1) This paragraph applies to an application under paragraph 13(1) of Schedule 1 to the Act (appeal against LHA's decision to vary or refuse to vary or revoke an improvement notice).

(2) The specified documents are—

    (a) a copy of the improvement notice (including any schedule to it);

    (b) the statement of reasons; and

    (c) a copy of the LHA's decision to vary or refuse to vary or revoke (including any documentation issued by the LHA in connection with its notice of decision).

(3) The specified respondent is the LHA.

4

(1) This paragraph applies to an application under—

    (a) paragraph 11(1) of Schedule 3 to the Act (appeal against demand by the LHA for recovery of expenses incurred by LHA in taking action where improvement notice has been served); and

    (b) that paragraph as applied with modifications by section 42 of the Act (an appeal against a demand by the LHA for recovery of expenses incurred by taking emergency remedial action).

(2) The specified documents are—

    (a) a copy of the improvement notice or (as the case may be) the notice of emergency remedial action (including any schedule to it);

    (b) the statement of reasons notice;

    (c) a copy of the notice served by the LHA under paragraph 4 of Schedule 3 to the Act (notice of LHA's intention to enter premises to carry out specified actions without agreement);

    (d) a copy of the LHA's demand for expenses; and

    (e) where the application is made on the ground mentioned in paragraph 11(4) of that Schedule, details of the progress relied upon as being made towards compliance with the notice.

(3) The specified respondent is the LHA.

Applications relating to prohibition orders

5

(1) This paragraph applies to an application under section 22(9) of the Act (appeal against LHA's refusal to give approval of particular use under section 22(4)).

(2) The specified documents are—

(a) a copy of the prohibition order (including any schedule to it);
(b) the statement of reasons; and
(c) notice of the LHA's decision to refuse a particular use of the whole or part of the premises.

(3) The specified respondent is the LHA.

6

(1) This paragraph applies to an application under section 34(2) of the Act (application by lessor or lessee for order determining or varying lease where a prohibition order has become operative).

(2) The specified documents are—

(a) a copy of the prohibition order (including any schedule to it);
(b) the statement of reasons;
(c) a copy of the relevant lease; and
(d) a statement of the name and address of any other party to the lease and of any party to an inferior lease.

(3) The specified respondent is the other party to the lease.

7

(1) This paragraph applies to an application under paragraph 7(1) of Schedule 2 to the Act (appeal against prohibition order).

(2) The specified documents are—

(a) a copy of the prohibition order (including any schedule to it);
(b) the statement of reasons; and
(c) where one of the grounds of the application is that one of the courses of action mentioned in paragraph 8(2) of Schedule 2 to the Act is the best course of action in relation to the hazard, a statement identifying that course of action with the applicant's reasons for considering it the best course.

(3) The specified respondent is the LHA.

8

(1) This paragraph applies to an application under paragraph 9(1) of Schedule 2 to the Act (appeal against LHA's decision to vary or refuse to vary or revoke a prohibition order).

(2)   The specified documents are—

(a)   a copy of the prohibition order (including any schedule to it);
(b)   the statement of reasons; and
(c)   a copy of the LHA's decision to vary or refuse to vary or revoke (including any documentation issued by the LHA in connection with its notice of decision).

(3)   The specified respondent is the LHA.

Applications relating to emergency remedial action

9

(1)   This paragraph applies to an application under section 45(1) of the Act (appeal by person upon whom a notice under section 41 of the Act has been served against LHA's decision to take emergency remedial action).

(2)   The specified documents are—

(a)   a copy of the notice of emergency remedial action (including any schedule to it); and
(b)   the statement of reasons.

(3)   The specified respondent is the LHA.

10

(1)   This paragraph applies to an application under section 45(2) of the Act (appeal by relevant person against emergency prohibition order).

(2)   The specified documents are—

(a)   a copy of the notice of emergency prohibition order made under section 43 of the Act (including any schedule to it); and
(b)   the statement of reasons.

(3)   The specified respondent is the LHA.

11

(1)   This paragraph applies to an application under—

(a)   paragraph 14 of Schedule 3 to the Act (application by LHA for order for recovery of expenses and interest from person profiting from the taking of action without agreement); and
(b)   that paragraph as applied with modifications by section 42 of the Act.

(2)   The specified documents are—

(a)   a copy of the notice of the improvement notice or, as the case may be, the notice of emergency remedial action (including any schedule to it);
(b)   the statement of reasons;
(c)   a copy of the demand for expenses served under paragraph 9 of that Schedule;

(d)   a copy of any notice served under paragraph 12 of that Schedule; and

(e)   proof of service of notice of the application on the person concerned as mentioned in paragraph 14(2) of that Schedule.

(3)   The specified respondent is the person from whom the LHA seeks to recover expenses and interest.

Applications relating to demolition orders

12

(1)   This paragraph applies to an application under section 269(1) of the 1985 Act (appeal by person aggrieved by demolition order).

(2)   The specified documents are—

(a)   a copy of the demolition order made under section 265 of the 1985 Act (including any schedule to it); and

(b)   the statement of reasons; and

(c)   where the ground or one of the grounds of the application is that one of the courses of action mentioned in section 269A(2) of the 1985 Act is the best course of action in relation to the hazard, a statement identifying that course of action with the applicant's reasons for considering it the best course.

(3)   The specified respondent is the LHA.

13

(1)   This paragraph applies to an application under section 272(1) or (2)(a) of the 1985 Act (application in connection with recovery of LHA's expenses in executing demolition order under section 271 of the 1985 Act including determination of contributions by joint owners).

(2)   The specified documents are—

(a)   a copy of the demolition order made under section 265 of the 1985 Act (including any schedule to it);

(b)   the statement of reasons; and

(c)   a statement of—

     (i)   the expenses incurred by the LHA under section 271 of the 1985 Act (execution of demolition order);

     (ii)   the amount (if any) realised by the sale of materials; and

     (iii)   the amount the LHA seeks to recover from an owner of the premises.

(3)   The specified respondent is the owner of the premises.

14

(1)   This paragraph applies to an application under section 272(2)(b) of the 1985 Act (application by owner of premises for determination of contribution to LHA's expenses to be paid by another owner).

(2)   The specified documents are—

(a)   a copy of the demolition order made under section 265 of the 1985 Act (including any schedule to it);

(b)   the statement of reasons; and

(c)   a statement of—

(i)   the owners" respective interests in the premises; and

(ii)   their respective obligations and liabilities in respect of maintenance and repair under any covenant or agreement, whether express or implied.

(3)   The specified respondent is the owner from whom the applicant seeks a contribution to the LHA's expenses.

15

(1)   This paragraph applies to an application under section 317(1) of the 1985 Act (application by lessor or lessee of premises in respect of which demolition order has become operative, for an order varying or determining lease).

(2)   The specified documents are—

(a)   a copy of the demolition order made under section 265 of the 1985 Act (including any schedule to it);

(b)   the statement of reasons;

(c)   a copy of the relevant lease; and

(d)   a statement of the name and address of any other party to the lease and of any party to an inferior lease.

(3)   The specified respondent is the other party to the lease.

Application relating to work on unfit premises

16

(1)   This paragraph applies to an application under section 318(1) of the 1985 Act (application by person with interest in premises for authorisation by tribunal of execution of works on unfit premises or for improvement).

(2)   The specified documents are—

(a)   details of the work which the applicant proposes to carry out including—

(i)   names and addresses of proposed contractors where relevant;

(ii)   an estimate of the costs of the work; and

(iii)   a timetable for starting and completing the work;

(b)   where the application is made on the ground mentioned in section 318(1)(b) of the 1985 Act, details of—

(i)   the scheme of improvement or reconstruction which the applicant wishes to carry out; and

(ii)   the LHA's approval of the scheme.

(c)   a statement of the financial standing of the applicant including disclosure of funds available to meet the estimated costs of the work;

(d)   where the application includes a request for an order determining a lease held from the applicant or a derivative lease, a copy of that lease.

(3)   The specified respondents are—

(a)   the person with a right to possession of the premises;
(b)   the owner of the premises.

Applications relating to HMO licensing

17

(1)   This paragraph applies to an application under section 62(7) of the Act (appeal against refusal by LHA to serve a temporary exemption notice).

(2)   The specified documents are—

(a)   a copy of the notification to the LHA under section 62(1) of the Act; and
(b)   a copy of the LHA's decision notice under section 62(6) of the Act.

(3)   The specified respondent is the LHA.

18

(1)   This paragraph applies to an application under section 73(5) of the Act (application by LHA or occupier for rent repayment order).

(2)   The specified documents are—

(a)   where the application is made by the LHA—
  (i)   a copy of the notice of intending proceedings under section 73(7);
  (ii)   a copy of any representation received in respect of the notice;
  (iii)   either—
    (aa)   a statement containing the details relied on in making the allegation that an offence under section 72(1) of the Act was committed; or
    (bb)   where the LHA relies on the provisions of section 74 of the Act, proof that the appropriate person has been convicted of an offence under section 72(1) of the Act; and
  (iv)   a document showing the housing benefit paid by the LHA in connection with occupation of the premises during the period in which it is alleged such an offence was committed; or
(b)   where the application is made by an occupier—
  (i)   evidence that the appropriate person has been convicted of an offence under section 72(1) of the Act or has been required by a rent repayment order to make a payment in respect of housing benefit; and
  (ii)   evidence that the occupier has paid periodical payments in respect of occupation of the premises during a period which it is alleged that such an offence was being committed.

(3)   The specified respondent is the appropriate person.

19

(1)   This paragraph applies to an application under section 255(9) of the Act (appeal against decision of LHA to serve an HMO declaration).

(2)   The specified document is a copy of the HMO declaration.

(3)   The specified respondent is the LHA.

20

(1)   This paragraph applies to an application under section 256(4) of the Act (appeal against decision of LHA to refuse to revoke HMO declaration).

(2)   The specified documents are—

(a)   a copy of the HMO declaration; and
(b)   a copy of the LHA's notice of decision not to revoke the HMO declaration.

(3)   The specified respondent is the LHA.

21

(1)   This paragraph applies to an application under paragraph 31(1) of Schedule 5 to the Act (appeal against decision by LHA to grant, or refuse to grant, a licence under Part 2 of the Act, or against any of the terms of the licence).

(2)   The specified documents are—

(a)   where the application relates to the grant or terms of a licence—
  (i)   a copy of the LHA's notices under paragraphs 1 and 7 of Schedule 5, and of any notice under paragraph 3 of that Schedule; and
  (ii)   a copy of the licence; and
(b)   where the application relates to a refusal to grant a licence, a copy of the LHA's notices under paragraphs 5 and 8 of that Schedule.

(3)   The specified respondent is the LHA.

22

(1)   This paragraph applies to an application under paragraph 32(1) of Schedule 5 to the Act (appeal by licence holder or any relevant person against decision by LHA with regard to the variation or revocation of licence).

(2)   The specified documents are—

(a)   where the application relates to a decision to vary a licence, a copy of the LHA's notices under paragraphs 14 and 16 of Schedule 5;
(b)   where the application relates to refusal to vary a licence, a copy of the LHA's notices under paragraphs 19 and 21 of that Schedule;

(c) where the application relates to a decision to revoke a licence, a copy of the LHA's notices under paragraphs 22 and 24 of that Schedule;

(d) where the application relates to refusal to revoke a licence, a copy of the LHA's notices under paragraphs 26 and 28 of that Schedule; and

(e) in all cases a copy of the licence.

(3) The specified respondent is the LHA.

Applications relating to selective licensing of other residential accommodation

23

(1) This paragraph applies to an application under section 86(7) of the Act (appeal against refusal by the LHA to serve a temporary exemption notice).

(2) The specified documents are—

(a) a copy of the notification to the LHA under section 86(1) of the Act; and

(b) a copy of the LHA's decision notice under section 86(6) of the Act.

(3) The specified respondent is the LHA.

24

(1) This paragraph applies to an application under section 96(5) of the Act (application by LHA or occupier for a rent repayment order).

(2) The specified documents are—

(a) where the application is made by the LHA—

　　(i) a copy of the notice of intended proceedings under section 96(7);

　　(ii) a copy of any representation received in respect of the notice;

　　(iii) either—

　　　　(aa) a statement containing the details relied on in making the allegation that an offence under section 95(1) of the Act was committed; or

　　　　(bb) where the LHA relies on the provisions of section 97 of the Act, proof that the appropriate person has been convicted of an offence under section 95(1) of the Act; and

　　(iv) a document showing the housing benefit paid by the LHA in connection with occupation of the premises during the period in which it is alleged such an offence was committed; or

(b) where the application is made by an occupier—

　　(i) evidence that the appropriate person has been convicted of an offence under section 95(1) of the Act or has been required by a rent repayment order to make a payment in respect of housing benefit; and

　　(ii) evidence that the occupier has paid periodical payments in respect of occupation of the premises for a period during which it is alleged that such an offence was being committed.

(3) The specified respondent is the appropriate person.

25

(1) This paragraph applies to an application under paragraph 31 of Schedule 5 to the Act (appeal against decision by LHA to grant or refuse licence under Part 3 or relating to terms of licence).

(2) The specified documents are—

  (a) where the application relates to the grant or terms of a licence—
      (i)   a copy of the LHA's notices under paragraphs 1 and 7 of Schedule 5, and of any notice under paragraph 3 of that Schedule; and
      (ii) a copy of the licence; and
  (b) where the application relates to a refusal to grant a licence, a copy of the LHA's notices under paragraphs 5 and 8 of that Schedule.

(3) The specified respondent is the LHA.

26

(1) This paragraph applies to an application under paragraph 32(1) of Schedule 5 to the Act (appeal by licence holder or relevant person against decision by LHA relating to variation or revocation of licence).

(2) The specified documents are—

  (a) where the application relates to a decision to vary a licence, a copy of the LHA's notices under paragraphs 14 and 16 of Schedule 5;
  (b) where the application relates to refusal to vary a licence, a copy of the LHA's notices under paragraphs 19 and 21 of that Schedule;
  (c) where the application relates to a decision to revoke a licence, a copy of the LHA's notices under paragraphs 22 and 24 of that Schedule;
  (d) where the application relates to refusal to revoke a licence, a copy of the LHA's notices under paragraphs 26 and 28 of that Schedule; and
  (e) in any case a copy of the licence.

(3) The specified respondent is the LHA.

Applications relating to interim and final management orders

27

(1) This paragraph applies to an application under section 102(4) of the Act (LHA application for authorisation to make an interim management order).

(2) The specified documents are—

  (a) a copy of the draft order;
  (b) a statement of matters relevant to the tribunal's consideration of—
      (i)   whether the health and safety condition in section 104 of the Act is satisfied; and
      (ii) the extent to which any applicable code of practice approved under section 233 of the Act has been complied with; and

    (iii)   where the LHA requests that the application be dealt with as a matter of urgency under regulation 9, a statement giving sufficient details to enable the tribunal to form an opinion as to whether the exceptional circumstances mentioned in paragraph (3) of that regulation appear to exist.

(3)   The specified respondent is a relevant person as defined in paragraph 8(4) and paragraph 35 of the Act.

28

(1)   This paragraph applies to an application under section 102(7) of the Act (LHA application for authorisation to make an interim management order in respect of a house to which section 103 of the Act applies).

(2)   The specified documents are—

    (a)   a copy of the draft order;

    (b)   a statement of matters relevant to the tribunal's consideration as to whether the conditions in section 103(3) and (4) are satisfied; and

    (c)   where the LHA requests that the application be dealt with as a matter of urgency under regulation 9, a statement giving sufficient details to enable the tribunal to form an opinion as to whether the exceptional circumstances mentioned in paragraph (3) of that regulation appear to exist.

(3)   The specified respondent is a relevant person as defined in paragraph 8(4) and paragraph 35 of Schedule 6 to the Act.

29

(1)   This paragraph applies to an application under section 105(10) of the Act (LHA application for order that an interim management order continue in force pending disposal of appeal).

(2)   The specified documents are—

    (a)   a copy of the interim management order; and

    (b)   a copy of the notice of appeal under paragraph 24 of Schedule 6 to the Act against the making of a final management order.

(3)   The specified respondent is the applicant who has made the relevant appeal.

30

(1)   This paragraph applies to an application under section 110(7) of the Act (application by relevant landlord for order regarding financial arrangements while interim management order in force).

(2)   The specified documents are—

    (a)   a copy of the interim management order;

(b)   a copy of the accounts kept by the LHA in accordance with section 110(6).

(3)   The specified respondent is the LHA.

31

(1)   This paragraph applies to an application under section 114(7) of the Act (LHA application for order that existing final management order continue in force pending disposal of appeal against new final management order).

(2)   The specified documents are—

(a)   a copy of the existing final management order;
(b)   a copy of the new final management order made in order to replace it; and
(c)   a copy of the notice of appeal under paragraph 24 of Schedule 6 to the Act against the making of the new final management order.

(3)   The specified respondent is the applicant who has made the relevant appeal.

32

(1)   This paragraph applies to an application under section 120(1) of the Act (application by an affected person for order that LHA manage in accordance with management scheme in final management order).

(2)   The specified document is a copy of the final management order which contains the management scheme to which the application relates.

(3)   The specified respondent is the LHA.

33

(1)   This paragraph applies to an application under section 126(4) of the Act (application for adjustment of rights and liabilities with regard to furniture vested in LHA while management order in force).

(2)   The specified documents are—

(a)   a copy of the relevant management order; and
(b)   a statement giving details of the respective rights and liabilities (including ownership) of the persons interested in the furniture.

(3)   The specified respondent is the other person interested in the furniture.

34

(1)   This paragraph applies to an application under section 130(9) of the Act (application to determine who is "the relevant landlord" for the purposes of section 130 on termination of management order).

(2)   The specified document is a copy of the management order.

(3)   The specified respondent is the other relevant landlord.

35

(1) This paragraph applies to an application under paragraph 24 of Schedule 6 to the Act (appeal against making of a management order, or against the terms of the order or of associated management scheme).

(2) The specified documents are—

   (a)   a copy of the management order (including the management scheme);

   (b)   a copy of the notice served by the LHA under paragraph 7(2)(b) of Schedule 6 to the Act;

   (c)   where the application relates to the terms of the management order, a statement specifying each term to which objection is made, with reasons for the objection; and

   (d)   where the application is made on the ground specified in paragraph 24(3) of Schedule 6 to the Act, a statement of the matters in section 110(5) (which relates to payments of surplus rents etc) relevant to that ground.

(3)   The specified respondent is the LHA.

36

(1) This paragraph applies to an application under paragraph 28 of Schedule 6 to the Act (appeal against LHA's decision or refusal to vary or revoke management order).

(2)   The specified documents are—

   (a)   where the application relates to a decision to vary a management order, a copy of the LHA's notices under paragraphs 9 and 11 of Schedule 6;

   (b)   where the application relates to refusal to vary a management order, a copy of the LHA's notices under paragraphs 14 and 16 of that Schedule;

   (c)   where the application relates to a decision to revoke a management order, a copy of the LHA's notices under paragraphs 17 and 19 of that Schedule; and

   (d)   where the application relates to refusal to revoke a management order, a copy of the LHA's notices under paragraphs 20 and 22 of that Schedule; and

   (e)   in any case—

      (i)   a copy of the management order; and

      (ii)   a copy of the notice served by the LHA under paragraph 7(2)(b) of Schedule 6 to the Act.

(3)   The specified respondent is the LHA.

37

(1) This paragraph applies to an application under paragraph 32(2) of Schedule 6 to the Act (appeal by third party against LHA's decision under section 128 of the Act regarding compensation payable to third parties).

(2)   The specified documents are—

(a)   a copy of the management order (including the management scheme);
(b)   a copy of the LHA's notification of its decision to the third party in accordance with section 128(2) of the Act; and
(c)   a statement giving full details of—
  (i)   the rights in respect of which it is claimed that there has been interference in consequence of the management order; and
  (ii)   the amount of compensation claimed in respect of that interference.

(3)   The specified respondent is the LHA.

Applications in relation to empty dwelling management orders

38

(1)   This paragraph applies to an application under section 133(1) of the Act (LHA application for authorisation to make interim EDMO).

(2)   The specified documents are—

(a)   a copy of the draft interim EDMO;
(b)   a statement of evidence—
  (i)   in respect of the matters as to which the tribunal must be satisfied under section 134(2) of the Act;
  (ii)   of the LHA's consideration of the rights and interests specified in section 133(4) of the Act; and
(c)   where the LHA in accordance with section 133(3) of the Act notified the relevant proprietor that it was considering making an interim EDMO, a copy of the notification.

(3)   The specified respondent is the relevant proprietor.

39

(1)   This paragraph applies to an application under section 138(1) of the Act (application while interim EDMO in force for order that the LHA pay compensation to third party for interference with rights).

(2)   The specified documents are—

(a)   a copy of the interim EDMO (including the management scheme);
(b)   a copy of the LHA's notification of its decision to the third party in accordance with section 138(4) of the Act; and
(c)   a statement giving full details of—
  (i)   the rights in respect of which it is claimed that there has been interference in consequence of the interim EDMO; and
  (ii)   the amount of compensation claimed in respect of that interference.

(3)   The specified respondent is the LHA.

40

(1) This paragraph applies to an application under paragraph 1(7) of Schedule 7 to the Act (LHA application for order that interim EDMO continue in force pending disposal of appeal under paragraph 26 of that Schedule).

(2) The specified documents are—

    (a)   a copy of the interim EDMO; and

    (b)   a copy of the notice of appeal under paragraph 26 of Schedule 7 to the Act against the making of an interim EDMO.

(3) The specified respondent is the applicant who has made the relevant appeal.

41

(1) This paragraph applies to an application under paragraph 2(3)(d) or paragraph 10(3)(d) of Schedule 7 to the Act (LHA's application for order under paragraph 22 of that Schedule determining a lease or licence while interim or final EDMO is in force).

(2) The specified documents are—

    (a)   a copy of the interim or final EDMO (including any management scheme);

    (b)   a copy of the relevant lease or licence, or if not available evidence of the existence of the lease or licence; and

    (c)   a statement containing the following details—

        (i)   the name and address where known of any lessor, lessee, sub-lessor, sub-lessee or licensee;

        (ii)   evidence of matters in respect of which the tribunal must be satisfied under paragraph 22(1)(b) of Schedule 7 to the Act; and

        (iii)   the amount of compensation (if any) which the LHA is willing to pay in respect of the determination of the lease or licence, including details of how such compensation has been calculated.

(3) The specified respondents are the parties to the lease or licence.

42

(1) This paragraph applies to an application under paragraph 5(7) of Schedule 7 to the Act (application by relevant proprietor for order in connection with financial arrangements while interim EDMO in force).

(2) The specified documents are—

    (a)   a copy of the interim EDMO; and

    (b)   a copy of the accounts kept by the LHA in accordance with paragraph 5(6) of Schedule 7 to the Act.

(3) The specified respondent is the LHA.

43

(1) This paragraph applies to an application under paragraph 9(8) of Schedule 7 to the Act (application by LHA for order that final EDMO should continue in force pending disposal of an appeal under paragraph 26).

(2) The specified documents are—

(a) a copy of the interim EDMO; and
(b) a copy of the notice of appeal under paragraph 26 of Schedule 7 to the Act against the making of a final EDMO.

(3) The specified respondent is the applicant who has made the relevant appeal.

44

(1) This paragraph applies to an application under paragraph 14(1) of Schedule 7 to the Act (application by a affected person for order that LHA manage dwelling in accordance with management scheme in final EDMO).

(2) The specified document is a copy of the final EDMO (including the management scheme).

(3) The specified respondent is the LHA.

45

(1) This paragraph applies to an application under paragraph 26(1) of Schedule 7 to the Act (appeal against LHA's decision to make final EDMO or against terms of the order or of associated management scheme).

(2) The specified documents are—

(a) a copy of the final EDMO (including the management scheme);
(b) where the application relates to the terms of the management order, a statement specifying each term to which objection is made, with reasons for the objection; and
(c) where the application is made on the ground specified in paragraph 26(1)(c) of Schedule 6 to the Act, a statement of the matters in paragraph 5(5)(a) and (b) (which relate to payments of surplus rents etc) relevant to that ground.

(3) The specified respondent is the LHA.

46

(1) This paragraph applies to an application under paragraph 30 of Schedule 7 to the Act (appeal against LHA's decision or refusal to vary or revoke interim or final EDMO).

(2) The specified documents are—

(a)   where the application relates to a decision to vary an interim or final EDMO, a copy of the LHA's notices under paragraphs 9 and 11 of Schedule 6 to the Act (as applied by paragraph 17 of Schedule 7);

(b)   where the application relates to refusal to vary an interim or final EDMO, a copy of the LHA's notices under paragraphs 14 and 16 of that Schedule;

(c)   where the application relates to a decision to revoke an interim or final EDMO, a copy of the LHA's notices under paragraphs 17 and 19 of that Schedule; and

(d)   where the application relates to refusal to revoke an interim or final EDMO, a copy of the LHA's notices under paragraphs 20 and 22 of that Schedule; and

(e)   in any case a copy of the interim or final EDMO (as the case may be).

(3)   The specified respondent is the LHA.

47

(1)   This paragraph applies to an application under paragraph 34(2) of Schedule 7 to the Act (appeal against LHA's decision under section 136(4) or 138(3) of the Act in respect of compensation payable to third parties for interference with rights in consequence of final EDMO).

(2)   The specified documents are—

(a)   a copy of the final EDMO (including the management scheme);

(b)   where the third party has requested compensation under section 138 of the Act, a copy of the LHA's notification of its decision to the third party in accordance with subsection (4) of that section; and

(c)   a statement giving full details of—

(i)   the rights in respect of which it is claimed that there has been interference in consequence of the final EDMO; and

(ii)   the amount of compensation claimed in respect of that interference.

(3)   The specified respondent is the LHA.

Applications in relation to overcrowding notices

48

(1)   This paragraph applies to an application under section 143(1) of the Act (appeal by a person aggrieved by overcrowding notice).

(2)   The specified document is a copy of the overcrowding notice, or a statement by the applicant explaining the circumstances by reason of which he is not able to provide a copy of this notice.

(3)   The specified respondent is the LHA.

49

(1) This paragraph applies to an application under section 144(2) (appeal by relevant person against LHA's refusal to revoke or vary an overcrowding notice, or against failure by the LHA to respond in time to an application to revoke or vary it).

(2) The specified documents are—

    (a) a copy of the overcrowding notice;
    (b) where the LHA refused to vary an overcrowding notice, a copy of the LHA's decision.

(3) The specified respondent is the LHA.

LICENSING AND MANAGEMENT OF HOUSES IN MULTIPLE OCCUPATION (ADDITIONAL PROVISIONS) (ENGLAND) REGULATIONS 2007

(2007/1903)

Made 28th June 2007

Laid before Parliament 10th July 2007

Coming into force 1st October 2007

The Secretary of State, in exercise of the powers conferred by sections 63(5) and (6), 65(3) and (4), 87(5) and (6), 232(3) and (7) and 234 of the Housing Act 2004, makes the following Regulations:

1 Citation, commencement and application

(1) These Regulations may be cited as the Licensing and Management of Houses in Multiple Occupation (Additional Provisions) (England) Regulations 2007 and shall come into force on 1st October 2007.

(2) Regulations 2 to 11 apply to any HMO in England which is an HMO to which section 257 of the Housing Act 2004 applies and regulation 12 applies to any HMO in England to which Part 2 of that Act (licensing of houses in multiple occupation) applies.

2 Interpretation

In these Regulations—

    (a) "the Act" means the Housing Act 2004;
    (b) "fixtures, fittings or appliances" are—
        (i) lighting, space heating or water heating appliances;
        (ii) toilets, baths, showers, sinks, or wash basins or any cupboards, shelving or fittings supplied in a bathroom or lavatory;

(iii) cupboards, shelving or appliances used for the storage, preparation or cooking of food; and

(iv) washing machines or other laundry appliances; and

(c) "the manager", in relation to an HMO, means the person managing the HMO.

3   Manager's duties: general

(1) Regulations 4 to 10 shall apply subject to the following limitations—

(a) the manager's duty shall only apply in relation to such parts of the HMO over which it would be reasonable to expect the licence holder, in all the circumstances, to exercise control; and

(b) the manager's duty to maintain or keep in repair is to be construed as requiring a standard of maintenance or repair that is reasonable in all the circumstances, taking account of the age, character and prospective life of the house and the locality in which it is situated.

(2) Nothing in regulations 4 to 10 shall—

(a) require or authorise anything to be done in connection with the water supply or drainage or the supply of gas or electricity otherwise than in accordance with any enactment; or

(b) oblige the manager to take, in connection with those matters, any action which is the responsibility of a local authority or any other person, other than such action as may be necessary to bring the matter promptly to the attention of the authority or person concerned.

4   Duty of manager to provide information to occupier

The manager must ensure that his name, address and any telephone contact number are clearly displayed in a prominent position in the common parts of the HMO so that they may be seen by all occupiers.

5   Duty of manager to take safety measures

(1) The manager must ensure that all means of escape from fire in the HMO are—

(a) kept free from obstruction; and

(b) maintained in good order and repair.

(2) The manager must ensure that any fire fighting equipment and fire alarms are maintained in good working order.

(3) The manager must ensure that all notices indicating the location of means of escape from fire are displayed in positions within the common parts of the HMO that enable them to be clearly visible to all the occupiers.

(4) The manager must take all such measures as are reasonably required to protect the occupiers of the HMO from injury, having regard to—

(a) the design of the HMO;

(b) the structural conditions in the HMO; and

    (c)   the number of flats or occupiers in the HMO.

(5) In performing the duty imposed by paragraph (4) the manager must in particular—

    (a)   in relation to any roof or balcony that is unsafe, either ensure that it is made safe or take all reasonable measures to prevent access to it for so long as it remains unsafe; and

    (b)   in relation to any window the sill of which is at or near floor level, ensure that bars or other such safeguards as may be necessary are provided to protect the occupiers against the danger of accidents which may be caused in connection with such windows.

6 Duty of manager to maintain water supply and drainage

(1) The manager must ensure that the water supply and drainage system serving the HMO is maintained in good, clean and working condition and in particular he must ensure that—

    (a)   any tank, cistern or similar receptacle used for the storage of water for drinking or other domestic purposes is kept in a good, clean and working condition, with a cover kept over it to keep the water in a clean and proper condition; and

    (b)   any water fitting which is liable to damage by frost is protected from frost damage.

(2) The manager must not unreasonably cause or permit the water or drainage supply that is used by any occupier at the HMO to be interrupted.

(3) In this regulation "water fitting" means a pipe, tap, cock, valve, ferrule, meter, cistern, bath, water closet or soil pan used in connection with the supply or use of water, but the reference in this definition to a pipe does not include an overflow pipe or the mains supply pipe.

7 Duty of manager to supply and maintain gas and electricity

(1) The manager must supply to the local housing authority within 7 days of receiving a request in writing from that authority the latest gas appliance test certificate it has received in relation to the testing of any gas appliance at the HMO by a recognised engineer.

(2) In paragraph (1), "recognised engineer" means an engineer recognised by the Council of Registered Gas Installers as being competent to undertake such testing.

(3) The manager must—

    (a)   ensure that every fixed electrical installation is inspected and tested at intervals not exceeding five years by a person qualified to undertake such inspection and testing;

    (b)   obtain a certificate from the person conducting that test, specifying the results of the test; and

(c)   supply that certificate to the local housing authority within 7 days of receiving a request in writing for it from that authority.

(4)   The manager must not unreasonably cause the gas or electricity supply that is used by any occupier within the HMO to be interrupted.

8   Duty of manager to maintain common parts, fixtures, fittings and appliances

(1)   The manager must ensure that all common parts of the HMO are—

(a)   maintained in good and clean decorative repair;
(b)   maintained in a safe and working condition; and
(c)   kept reasonably clear from obstruction.

(2)   In performing the duty imposed by paragraph (1), the manager must in particular ensure that—

(a)   all handrails and banisters are at all times kept in good repair;
(b)   such additional handrails or banisters as are necessary for the safety of the occupiers of the HMO are provided;
(c)   any stair coverings are safely fixed and kept in good repair;
(d)   all windows and other means of ventilation within the common parts are kept in good repair;
(e)   the common parts are fitted with adequate light fittings that are available for use at all times by every occupier of the HMO; and
(f)   subject to paragraph (3), fixtures, fittings or appliances used in common by two or more households within the HMO are maintained in good and safe repair and in clean working order.

(3)   The duty imposed by paragraph (2)(f) does not apply in relation to fixtures, fittings or appliances that the occupier is entitled to remove from the HMO or which are otherwise outside the control of the manager.

(4)   The manager must ensure that—

(a)   outbuildings, yards and forecourts which are used in common by two or more households living within the HMO are maintained in repair, clean condition and good order;
(b)   any garden belonging to the HMO is kept in a safe and tidy condition; and
(c)   boundary walls, fences and railings (including any basement area railings), in so far as they belong to the HMO, are kept and maintained in good and safe repair so as not to constitute a danger to occupiers.

(5)   If any part of the HMO is not in use the manager shall ensure that such part, including any passage and staircase directly giving access to it, is kept reasonably clean and free from refuse and litter.

(6)   In this regulation—

(a)"common parts" means—

(i)   the entrance door to the HMO and the entrance doors leading to each unit of living accommodation within the HMO; and

(ii) all such parts of the HMO as comprise staircases, lifts, passageways, corridors, halls, lobbies, entrances, balconies, porches and steps that are used by the occupiers of the units of living accommodation within the HMO to gain access to the entrance doors of their respective unit of living accommodation.

9   Duty of manager to maintain living accommodation

(1)   Subject to paragraph (4), the manager must ensure that each unit of living accommodation within the HMO and any furniture supplied with it are in clean condition at the beginning of a person's occupation of it.

(2)   Subject to paragraphs (3) and (4), the manager must ensure, in relation to each part of the HMO that is used as living accommodation, that—

(a)   the internal structure is maintained in good repair;

(b)   any fixtures, fittings or appliances within the part are maintained in good repair and in clean working order; and

(c)   every window and other means of ventilation are kept in good repair.

(3)   The duties imposed under paragraph (2) do not require the manager to carry out any repair the need for which arises in consequence of use by the occupier of his living accommodation otherwise than in a tenant-like manner.

(4)   The duties imposed under paragraphs (1) and (2) do not apply in relation to furniture, fixtures, fittings or appliances that the occupier is entitled to remove from the HMO or which are otherwise outside the control of the manager.

(5)   For the purpose of this regulation a person shall be regarded as using his living accommodation otherwise than in a tenant-like manner where he fails to treat the property in accordance with the covenants or conditions contained in his lease or licence or otherwise fails to conduct himself as a reasonable tenant or licensee would do.

10   Duty to provide waste disposal facilities

The manager must—

(a)   ensure that sufficient bins or other suitable receptacles are provided that are adequate for the requirements of each household occupying the HMO for the storage of refuse and litter pending their disposal; and

(b)   make such further arrangements for the disposal of refuse and litter from the HMO as may be necessary, having regard to any service for such disposal provided by the local authority.

11   Duties of occupiers of HMOs

Every occupier of the HMO must—

(a) conduct himself in a way that will not hinder or frustrate the manager in the performance of his duties;

(b) allow the manager, for any purpose connected with the carrying out of any duty imposed on him by these Regulations, at all reasonable times to enter any living accommodation or other place occupied by that person;

(c) provide the manager, at his request, with such information as he may reasonably require for the purpose of carrying out any such duty;

(d) take reasonable care to avoid causing damage to anything which the manager is under a duty to supply, maintain or repair under these Regulations;

(e) store and dispose of litter in accordance with the arrangements made by the manager under regulation 10; and

(f) comply with the reasonable instructions of the manager in respect of any means of escape from fire, the prevention of fire and the use of fire equipment.

12 Amendments to the Licensing and Management of Houses in Multiple Occupation and Other Houses (Miscellaneous Provisions) (England) Regulations 2006

(1) The Licensing and Management of Houses in Multiple Occupation and Other Houses (Miscellaneous Provisions) (England) Regulations 2006 are amended as follows.

(2) In regulation 1(2) (application) omit the words "other than a converted block of flats to which section 257 of the Act applies,".

(3) In regulation 2 (interpretation) after "2004" insert—

"; and "section 257 HMO" means an HMO which is a converted block of flats to which section 257 of the Act applies".

(4) For regulation 8 (prescribed standards for deciding the suitability of a house for multiple occupation by a particular maximum number of households or persons) substitute—

"8 Prescribed standards for deciding the suitability of a house for multiple occupation by a particular maximum number of households or persons

(1) The standards prescribed for HMOs other than section 257 HMOs for the purpose of section 65 of the Act (tests as to suitability of HMO for multiple occupation) are those set out in Schedule 3.

(2) The standards prescribed for section 257 HMOs for the purpose of section 65 of the Act are—

(a) that all bathrooms and toilets contained in each flat must be of an adequate size and layout, and all wash-hand basins must be suitably located and be fit for purpose, having regard to the age and character of the HMO, the size and layout of each flat and its existing provision for wash-hand basins, toilets and bathrooms;

(b) those standards set out in paragraph 4(1) of Schedule 3, in so far as it is reasonably practicable to comply with them; and

    (c)   those standards set out in paragraph 5 of Schedule 3.''

(5) In regulation 11 (registers of licences)—

    (a)   in paragraph (2) for "The" substitute "Subject to paragraph (3), the"; and

    (b)   after paragraph (2) insert—

    "(3) The particulars mentioned in sub-paragraphs (b), (c)(ii), (d) and (e) of paragraph (2) are not prescribed for any entry in a register referred to in that paragraph in respect of a licence granted in relation to a section 257 HMO."

(6) In regulation 13 (registers of management orders)—

    (a)   in paragraph (2) for "The" substitute "Subject to paragraph (4), the"; and

    (b)   after paragraph (3) add—

    "(4) The particulars mentioned in sub-paragraphs (b) and (c)(ii) to (v) of paragraph (2) are not prescribed for any entry referred to in that paragraph in respect of a management order made in relation to a section 257 HMO.".

(7) In Schedule 2 (content of applications under sections 63 and 87 of the Act)—

    (a)   in paragraph 2(1)(f)—
        (i)   after "for which the application is being made" insert ", except in respect of an application in respect of a section 257 HMO";
        (ii)   in paragraph (f)(xi) for "training" substitute "information";
    (b)   after paragraph 2(1)(f) insert—

    "(g) where the application is being made in respect of a section 257 HMO, the following information—

        (i)   the number of storeys comprising the HMO and the levels on which those storeys are situated;
        (ii)   the number of self-contained flats and, of those, the number—
            (aa)   that the applicant believes to be subject to a lease of over 21 years; and
            (bb)   over which he cannot reasonably be able to exercise control;
        (iii)   in relation to each self-contained flat that is not owner-occupied and which is under the control of or being managed by the proposed licence holder, and in relation to the common parts of the HMO—
            (aa)   details of fire precautions equipment, including the number and location of smoke alarms;
            (bb)   details of fire escape routes and other fire safety information provided to occupiers; and
            (cc)   a declaration that the furniture in the HMO or house that is provided under the terms of any tenancy or licence meets any safety requirements contained in any enactment; and
        (iv)   a declaration that any gas appliances in any parts of the HMO over which the proposed licence holder can reasonably be expected to exercise control meet any safety requirements contained in any enactment."

(8) In Schedule 3 (prescribed standards for deciding the suitability for occupation of an HMO by a particular maximum number of households or persons)—

(a)   for paragraph 2(1) and (2) substitute—

"2

(1)   Where all or some of the units of living accommodation in an HMO do not contain bathing and toilet facilities for the exclusive use of each individual household—

    (a)   there must be an adequate number of bathrooms, toilets and wash-hand basins suitable for personal washing) for the number of persons sharing those facilities; and

    (b)   where reasonably practicable there must be a wash hand basin with appropriate splash back in each unit other than a unit in which a sink has been provided as mentioned in paragraph 4(1),

having regard to the age and character of the HMO, the size and layout of each flat and its existing provision for wash-hand basins, toilets and bathrooms."; and

(b)   after paragraph 4(1), insert—

"(1A)   The standards referred to in paragraphs (a) and (f) of sub-paragraph (1) shall not apply in relation to a unit of accommodation where—

    (a)   the landlord is not contractually bound to provide such appliances or equipment;

    (b)   the occupier of the unit of accommodation is entitled to remove such appliances or equipment from the HMO; or

    (c)   the appliances or equipment are otherwise outside the control of the landlord."

Signed by authority of the Secretary of State for Communities and Local Government

Kay Andrews

Parliamentary Under Secretary of State

Department for Communities and Local Government

28th June 2007

Appendix 3

HOUSING HEALTH AND SAFETY RATING SYSTEM

ENFORCEMENT GUIDANCE

Housing Act 2004

Part 1: Housing Conditions

Structure of the Guidance

This guidance is arranged as follows:

Emergency remedial action
Emergency prohibition order
Appeals against emergency measures
Decision to serve a hazard awareness notice
Demolition orders
Clearance areas
Powers to charge for enforcement action
PART 6 APPLICATION OF HHSRS IN HMOS
Link with licensing
Factors to consider in HMOs
Targeting action in HMOs
Consultation with fire and rescue authorities
PART 7 OTHER ISSUES
Powers of access
Use of premises for temporary housing accommodation
Disrepair
Mortgage lenders in possession

Part 1
Purpose of the Guidance

1.1 This guidance is given to local housing authorities in England by the Secretary of State under section 9 of the Housing Act 2004 (referred to in this guidance as "the Act"). They are required to have regard to it in exercising their duties and powers under Part 1 of the Act. The guidance is intended to help authorities decide which is the appropriate enforcement action under section 5 of the Act and how they should exercise their discretionary powers under section 7.

1.2 The guidance replaces that given in Annex B to DOE Circular 17/96[1] and DOE Circular 12/92[2]. It should also be read in conjunction with the Housing Health and Safety Rating System (England) Regulations 2005 (SI 2005 No. 3208) ("the Regulations"), and the Housing Health and Safety Rating System Operating Guidance, given under section 9(1)(a) of the Act ("the Operating Guidance")[3].

1.3 The housing fitness enforcement powers set out in the Housing Act 1985 (referred to in this guidance as "the 1985 Act"), including the separate provisions for Houses in Multiple Occupation (HMOs), have been replaced or (in the case of demolition and clearance) modified by the new system set out in Part 1 of the Act. The new system is structured around an evidence based risk assessment procedure, the Housing Health and

---

[1] Private Sector Renewal: a Strategic Approach, December 1996.
[2] Houses in Multiple Occupation; Guidance to Local Housing Authorities on Standards of Fitness under section 352 of the Housing Act 1985, May 1992.
[3] Housing Health and Safety Rating System Operating Guidance 2006.

Safety Rating System (HHSRS), on which local authorities must base their decisions on the action to take to deal with poor housing conditions, from 6th April 2006.

1.4 The new system, and the powers available to local authorities, apply to all types of residential premises, including HMOs, purpose built blocks of flats and buildings comprising converted flats. Although local authorities cannot take statutory enforcement action against themselves in respect of their own stock they will be expected to use HHSRS to assess the condition of their stock and to ensure their housing meets the Decent Home Standard.

1.5 Part 2 of the Act introduces the licensing of certain HMOs and the Management Regulations to which all HMOs will be subject. See Part 6 of this guidance.

1.6 Formal statutory action begun under the 1985 Act, from the service of a statutory notice, other than a "minded-to" notice, should continue under the provisions of that Act. Aside from such cases, authorities will be expected to deal with hazards to health or safety in all types of residential premises through the new system, and to follow its procedures through to a conclusion. Authorities will need to take a view on notices that have not been formally complied with but where no compliance proceedings have been initiated. Historical cases that have been lying dormant would best be dealt with under the new system should the premises once again give rise to concerns.

Part 2
Taking a strategic approach

Keeping housing conditions under review

2.1 Section 3 of the Act requires local authorities to consider the housing conditions in their district with a view to determining what action to take under the Act, which includes their duties and powers to deal with hazards identified under HHSRS or provide financial assistance for home repair and improvement. This duty reflects the Government's approach to local housing strategies. The purpose of the review is to ensure that a local authority maintains a current awareness of the state of the housing stock in its area, so that it can come to well-informed judgements as to the action it needs to take. At present authorities are not required to produce reports at particular intervals, although the Secretary of State does have the power to require them to keep and supply records if necessary.

2.2 Authorities will need to take a view of the spread of hazards in the local housing stock that have come to their attention, and prioritise action on those with the most serious impact on health or safety. It might be an inappropriate diversion of resources and effort to deal with modest hazards when there is evidence of more serious hazards elsewhere. This does not mean that authorities should make only sparing use of their discretionary powers. On the contrary, they will be able to deal systematically with premises found to have less serious hazards, scheduling action to deal with the most serious problems first, and less serious ones over a longer time frame, as appropriate. Authorities should act consistently. The decision to take enforcement action will require a judgement as to the necessity for intervention, given the authority's priorities and wider renewal policies and, where appropriate, their knowledge of a landlord and his or her compliance history.

2.3 Where practicable, authorities should consult neighbouring authorities in respect of areas of housing or estates that straddle local authority boundaries. They should also consider what liaison is required with Registered Social Landlords (RSLs) who are improving their stock to make them decent, and whose stock crosses local authority boundaries. Informal working with RSLs is seen as preferable to resorting to formal enforcement measures where the landlord has a timetable for making the stock decent. However, occupiers should not be left for long periods in unsafe housing. (See also Part 5, "Decision to suspend an improvement notice or prohibition order".)

Financial assistance

2.4 The Regulatory Reform (Housing Assistance) Order 2002 (SI 2002 No. 1860), which came into force on 18 July 2002, introduced a general power for local authorities to provide financial assistance. The Order provides authorities with a good degree of flexibility in devising a strategy to deal with poor condition private sector housing, both in terms of the policy tools available to them, and in terms of their ability to work in partnership with others. In exercising their powers under the Order, local authorities should have regard to their enforcement duties and powers under Part 1 of the Act in conjunction with the renewal guidance issued in the ODPM Housing Renewal Circular 05/2003 (June 2003).

2.5 Authorities should also consider the availability of other sources of funding and assistance, in particular to improve energy efficiency and tackle fuel poverty. Further information on working with local partnerships is contained in the renewal guidance.

Identifying the need for action

2.6 Where, in the light of the review of housing conditions under section 3, or following a complaint or for any other reason, the authority considers it appropriate to inspect premises to determine whether a category 1 or 2 hazard exists, the authority must arrange for an inspection. While there is not an express duty on local authorities to inspect properties where they think there might be hazards, sections 3 and 4 of the Act, when taken together, imply that an authority should have good reason not to investigate further.

2.7 Inspections may also need to be carried out where official complaints about the condition of residential premises are made to the proper officer of the authority. Official complaints are those made by a justice of the peace or a parish or community council and when such a complaint is made the duty to inspect falls on the Proper Officer. Where, following an official complaint, the inspector concludes that there are hazards on the premises, or that an area should be dealt with as a clearance area, he must report to the authority without delay and the authority must consider his report as soon as possible.

2.8 Authorities will need to prioritise inspections and in doing so may have regard to their wider housing strategies and the individual circumstances of the case before them. Local authorities may feel that priority should be given to complaints or referrals from sources such as social services child protection teams, the police, the fire and rescue authority and Warm Front managers, and also from other occupiers, directly or indirectly through local councillors.

2.9 It is good practice for the authority to carry out as full an inspection of the premises as possible, as it is important for enforcement action to be supported by all the relevant evidence. The Regulations require an accurate record to be prepared and kept of the inspection in written or electronic form. The assessment of any hazard, following the inspection of the premises, must be carried out in accordance with the Regulations.

2.10 In summary, local authorities might identify the need to act to deal with hazards in a number of ways, including:
- as a result of a review under section 3 of the Act, which leads to an inspection under section 4 of the Act;
- as a result of any other inspection under section 4 of the Act, ie as a result of an official complaint or other request for enforcement action;
- under a fuel poverty or energy efficiency strategy;
- as a result of a Neighbourhood Renewal Assessment;
- in the light of a strategy for multiply occupied buildings established in conjunction with the fire and rescue authority;
- in the light of a request for financial assistance by the owner or tenant to improve the property.

Fuel poverty and energy efficiency strategies

2.11 There are a wide range of energy efficiency programmes, some of which are provided by energy suppliers and others through Government funding. The Warm Front scheme is the Government's main tool for tackling fuel poverty in private sector housing in England. Warm Front provides a grant of up to £2,700 (or £4,000 where oil central heating has been recommended) to install a range of heating and insulation measures (including central heating, loft and cavity wall insulation and draught proofing) to householders in receipt of certain benefits. In addition, the Energy Efficiency Commitment (EEC) is an obligation on energy suppliers to deliver improvements in energy efficiency in housing through the provision of energy efficiency measures and advice. Other grants or offers may be available through local authorities or utility companies. Information on where these grants are available can be obtained from the Energy Saving Trust (www.est.org.uk).

2.12 Local authorities should consider an HHSRS inspection where the property is to be considered for improvements under any strategies to deal with fuel poverty, to improve energy efficiency or to increase the proportion of vulnerable people living in decent homes. Additionally, where an owner or landlord refuses a Warm Front grant or declines to reply to enquiries by scheme managers, or where a private landlord declines to co-operate with an approach from an energy supplier under EEC, the authority should treat such information from a scheme manager or energy supplier as an indication that an inspection may be necessary to establish whether anything needs to be done to protect the occupant from excess cold, or damp and mould affecting the property. Authorities should bear in mind that any action taken under the HHSRS must be in relation to a hazard. It will not be in relation, directly, to alleviating fuel poverty or improving energy efficiency, though this may be the outcome.

Neighbourhood Renewal Assessment Process (NRA)

2.13 A revised Neighbourhood Renewal Assessment Guidance Manual was issued in September 2004. The NRA is a systematic approach to assessing local areas prior to regeneration or renewal. It comprises a series of steps which provide a thorough appraisal method for considering alternative courses of action. A summary of the NRA Guidance can be found on the ODPM website. The full NRA Guidance can be obtained from the ODPM publications sales centre (see address on inside cover).

2.14 The NRA process will continue to be recommended as a method for considering the most appropriate course of action, not only in large or small-scale assessments but also in the assessment of individual properties. Authorities should therefore ensure that their policy responses are adequate and appropriate for the range of outcomes that can arise from the NRA process. However, the introduction of HHSRS means that authorities will also need to build into their housing strategy a policy on the extent to which they will intervene to make use of their powers in Part 1 of the Act.

Formal and informal enforcement action

2.15 The Housing Renewal circular emphasises the importance of private sector strategies which encourage co-operation between the local authority and the community to help keep homes in good repair. Over time, successful housing strategies should lead to a reduced need for formal enforcement action to deal with properties that fall below acceptable standards. Nonetheless, enforcement is a legitimate element of a housing renewal strategy.

2.16 Authorities are likely to find formal enforcement particularly important in the case of rented properties and HMOs in the private sector, where some of the worst housing conditions are to be found (though poor conditions in any part of the housing stock should not go unaddressed). Enforcement policies should take account of the circumstances and views of tenants, landlords and owners. Policies should also provide for consultation social services, tenancy support, housing needs and housing management officers, where there are vulnerable occupants, for the purposes of agreeing a suitable approach to hazards.

2.17 Local authorities are encouraged to adopt the Enforcement Concordat, which provides a basis for fair, practical and consistent enforcement. It is based on the principle that anyone likely to be subject to formal enforcement action should receive clear explanations of what they need to do to comply and have an opportunity to resolve difficulties before formal action is taken. The current Concordat can be found on the Cabinet Office website.

2.18 Where an owner or landlord agrees to take the action required by the authority it might be appropriate to wait before serving a notice unless the owner fails to start the work within a reasonable time. The authority will need to take its own view of what is reasonable in the circumstances. Where RSLs have a programme of works to make their stock decent, it would also be appropriate to liaise with the landlord over any works necessary to deal with category 1 and 2 hazards in advance of the planned improvements. An alternative approach where a landlord agrees to take remedial action quickly and the authority is confident that this will be done, would be for authorities to use the hazard awareness notice procedure. This would provide a way of recording the action, and would provide evidence should the landlord fail to carry out remedial works or carry them out inadequately. (See Part 5, "Hazard awareness notices".)

2.19 However, there may be circumstances in which authorities do not wish to delay in beginning formal enforcement action. This is likely to arise where the authority considers that there is a high risk to the health or safety of the occupant, and there are concerns that the owner or landlord will not co-operate. This may include cases where the HHSRS assessment reveals category 2 hazards and where the current occupants are vulnerable, or where occupancy factors (for example in hostels for special groups) appear to the authority to increase the risk.

2.20 Accreditation schemes or housing forums are a useful means of working informally with private sector landlords. A number of local authorities have already begun to develop closer working relationships with individual private landlords through such arrangements. They enable authorities to provide support to landlords and to raise the standards of management and property condition. Landlords will also benefit from better access to information on their obligations in relation to tenants and can receive help in dealing with problems which arise with tenants and properties.

Decent Homes

2.21 The Government is committed to ensuring that every social sector tenant will be living in a decent home by 2010. It is also committed to increasing the proportion of vulnerable households living in decent homes in the private sector. The decent homes standard is a minimum standard that triggers action, not one to which dwellings are improved. The detailed definition and implementation guidance can be found on the ODPM website. A decent home is one which:
- does not contain a category 1 hazard;
- is in a reasonable state of repair;
- has reasonably modern facilities and services;
- provides a reasonable degree of thermal comfort.

2.22 The decent home standard is not an enforcement standard, and authorities do not have powers to require owners to comply. They should however have regard to it in giving advice to owners or in considering financial assistance. As RSLs are included in the commitment to make all social housing decent by 2010, authorities should have regard to the compliance of a particular property, or the timetable within which compliance is planned, in considering the action to take. However, significant hazards should not be ignored, and occupiers should not be left for long periods in unhealthy or unsafe housing. (See also Part 5, "Decision to suspend an improvement notice or prohibition order".)

Part 3
Assessing Hazards

Housing Health and Safety Rating System (HHSRS)

3.1 The new hazard based rating system introduces a more flexible enforcement framework which means that authorities can now take action against a much broader range of housing conditions, from very severe to relatively minor hazards.

3.2 Local authorities must inspect properties to determine whether there are category 1 or 2 hazards, using the method prescribed by the Regulations. Separate guidance to authorities on the use of HHSRS to assess and rate the severity of hazards has been given by the Secretary of State under section 9(1)(a) of the Act and is referred to in this guidance as the "operating guidance". Following the method prescribed by the Regulations and having regard to the operating guidance, local authority environmental health practitioners may assess the severity of the risks associated with any hazards in or at the premises.

3.3 Authorities will be expected to ensure that their officers and other surveyors contracted by them are familiar with HHSRS, the Regulations and guidance. It is for authorities themselves to ensure that their officers and agents have the skills to perform their functions efficiently on behalf of the authority. Most environmental health practitioners will have experience in risk assessment procedures. They will also be familiar with surveying techniques, will be able to identify deficiencies and appreciate their potential harmful effects on the health or safety of current or potential occupants.

3.4 Assessment of hazards is a two-stage process, addressing first the likelihood of an occurrence and then the range of probable harm outcomes. These two factors are combined using a standard method to give a score in respect of each hazard. HHSRS does not provide a single score for the dwelling as a whole or, in the case of multiply occupied buildings, for the building as a whole. The scores from different hazards are not intended to be aggregated. However, the presence of a number of individual category 2 hazards may be a factor in an authority's decision to take action. In specific cases, authorities will need to form a view whether a number of hazards justify the use of their powers. This needs to be approached with consistency and reflected in the authority's enforcement strategy as the action to be taken following the assessment is not determined by the score alone.

3.5 Assessing hazards is only the first part of the process leading to action. The score does not determine subsequent action. Action to remove a hazard is based on a three-stage consideration:
(a) the hazard score determined under HHSRS;
(b) whether the authority, in the light of the score, has a duty or discretion to act; and
(c) the authority's judgement as to the most appropriate means of dealing with the hazard, taking account of both potential and actual vulnerable occupants.

Part 4
Action Following Hazard Assessment

Local authority duties and powers

4.1 The Act gives local authorities powers to intervene where they consider housing conditions to be unacceptable, on the basis of the impact of hazards on the health or safety of the most vulnerable potential occupant. Before taking formal enforcement action they should follow the principles of the Enforcement Concordat.

4.2 The Act puts authorities under a general duty to take appropriate action in relation to a category 1 hazard. Where they have a general duty to act, they must take the most appropriate of the following courses of action:
- serve an improvement notice in accordance with section 11;
- make a prohibition order in accordance with section 20;
- serve a hazard awareness notice in accordance with section 28;
- take emergency remedial action under section 40 or make an emergency prohibition order under section 43;
- make a demolition order under section 265 of the Housing Act 1985 as amended;
- declare a clearance area by virtue of section 289 of the 1985 Act as amended.

4.3 Authorities cannot simultaneously take more than one of these actions – for example make a prohibition order and serve an improvement notice dealing with the same hazard in the same premises. The authority must therefore ensure they have thoroughly considered the most appropriate action. However, the authority can take a different course of action, or the same course again, if the action already taken has not proved satisfactory. Emergency measures are the exception. Emergency remedial action followed by an improvement notice or a prohibition order is a single course of action.

4.4 Authorities have similar powers to deal with category 2 hazards (see section 7 of the Act). However, emergency measures cannot be used in respect of category 2 hazards, and authorities cannot make a demolition order, or declare a clearance area in response to a category 2 hazard unless the circumstances are such as have been prescribed in regulations. No such Regulations have been made in England at the time this guidance is given.

4.5 It is for authorities to decide which course of action is the best in all the circumstances. See Part 5, "Enforcement options". They should also consider whether it would be appropriate for them or other enforcement agencies to act under other legislation.

Reasons for decision

4.6 Section 8 of the Act places a duty on local authorities to give a statement of reasons for their decision to take a particular course of enforcement action. This provision is designed to meet concerns that the absence of a duty on local authorities to give reasons might fail to comply with Article 6 of the European Convention on Human Rights – the right to a fair hearing.

4.7 Authorities must prepare a statement of their reasons for their decision and provide a copy of that statement to accompany the notices, copies of notices, and copies of orders which they are required to serve under Part 1 and relevant provisions of the 1985 Act. There is no requirement for authorities to provide a copy of their inspection report with the statement but there is nothing to prevent them from doing so if they consider that it would be helpful.

4.8 The requirement to give a statement extends to the declaration of a clearance area. In these cases the statement of reasons must be published as soon as possible after the passing of the resolution declaring that the area be defined as a clearance area under section 289 of the 1985 Act, and in such manner as the authority consider appropriate.

Taking account of the current occupant and other factors influencing priority

4.9 The assessment of hazards under HHSRS is based on the risk to the *potential occupant who is most vulnerable to that hazard*. However, in determining what action to take, authorities should use their judgement to take account of the current occupant. This does not mean that action should always be based on the vulnerability of the current occupant. Action can be taken whether or not a person at most risk to the hazard is living in the dwelling or is a regular visitor to it. The authority should consider the turnover of tenancies. Where they consider that a wide range of occupants might potentially occupy the premises in future they may take the view that action in respect of the current condition of the premises is justified. (See also paragraph 4.14.)

4.10 In general, the severest risks arising from the hazards identified by the authority are likely to trigger enforcement action. This would be justified by the need to tackle poor housing conditions and would be consistent with the principle that people in their homes should not be exposed to unacceptable levels of risk. However, there could be a limited range of circumstances in which such action might be disproportionate. For example, a hazard might be significant only in relation to a category of occupant who was not in residence and would not reasonably be expected to live there in the medium to long term. Therefore, even in the case of a category 1 hazard there is a broad range of responses. Action might be necessary over a short timescale; an owner or landlord could be given longer time to make repairs; action might be suspended and changes of occupation monitored; or where it appears unlikely that vulnerable occupants will occupy the premises in the medium to long term (perhaps because they are let by an educational body to their students) it may be that hazard awareness advice is appropriate. Even in the case of student tenancies however, hazards may be a threat to young and fit people. Some student accommodation is let out during vacations. Much will depend on the extent to which students and their visitors are exposed to any hazards.

4.11 Authorities should consider carefully how occupancy factors and management in HMOs might compromise safety. There are also some groups of people who are not among the vulnerable groups considered by the hazard assessment but may nevertheless be at risk, for example in the case of hostels housing people with alcohol or drug dependency, or where people are housed temporarily, or in circumstances over which they have no control, or are unfamiliar with facilities. In these circumstances, once a hazard has been assessed, the authority would be justified in considering the express use of such accommodation and whether accommodation targeted at specific groups provides a safe environment.

4.12 For category 1 hazards an improvement notice will be an appropriate means of mitigating a hazard, where works of mitigation are practicable and the occupants are vulnerable . However, occupancy factors may suggest to the authority that some other form of action is appropriate. Occupancy factors may also suggest that action can be suspended pending a future change of circumstances.

4.13 As suggested above, a factor which may weigh with authorities is the control that occupiers have over their living conditions and their ability to finance and carry out remedial action. Authorities should weigh up all the circumstances when considering what action to take in respect of owner-occupiers. Early consultation on the HHSRS enforcement regime showed that a majority of authorities considered the regime should be tenure neutral. There is a risk of challenge if an authority takes action in tenanted property where it would not take similar action in owner occupied property in similar circumstances.

4.14 One of the factors authorities may wish to consider alongside the vulnerability of the occupant is the risk of the exclusion of vulnerable groups of people from the private rented sector. Authorities should weigh the evidence of the HHSRS assessment against the benefits of the retention of accommodation which might house vulnerable people. Gradual improvements to a property might be one solution, with care taken to minimise risk and inconvenience taken in the interim.

4.15 Authorities should also take some account of the views of occupants. Where there are concerns about vulnerable occupants, authorities should consult other relevant agencies to agree an appropriate response to hazards, such as social services, child protection teams, and the police.

Multiple hazards

4.16 Authorities have a general power under section 7 to take enforcement action in relation to category 2 hazards. But aside from hazards which are at the upper range, in band D for example, residential property may contain a number of more modestly rated hazards which appear to create a more serious situation when looked at together. There may for example be a minor hazard to health from damp in the bathroom ceiling, plus a moderate fall hazard from a loose but not actually broken handrail on the stairs, plus a food hygiene hazard from old-fashioned preparation facilities in the kitchen. In this example, the hazards do not combine in any measurable way. However the situation in the property may be considered unsatisfactory because the occupants encounter one hazard after another as they move around. Such a property may be perceived as less safe than one with a single high-scoring hazard.

4.17 There may be pressure on authorities, particularly from tenants, to act against a number of moderate hazards on the grounds that they present a picture of a run-down property, even though no single hazard is evidence of a serious risk to health and safety. HHSRS is designed to deal with all hazards, no matter how serious, which arise from deficiencies in and around the home. Therefore, even minor category 2 hazards need not go un-addressed if the local authority considers that it is appropriate in all the circumstances to take action in relation to those hazards. Authorities can use their powers to deal with single or multiple category 2 hazards. More generally, authorities may also decide that they will always act on certain bands of category 2 hazards.

Building Regulations

4.18 Satisfying the requirements of the current Building Regulations, the supporting Approved Documents and relevant standards and Codes of Practices will usually achieve the Ideal for the majority of hazards as described in the operating guidance. In a few cases, the Ideal might be at a higher level than Building Regulations require. In practice, the difference will be negligible and is extremely unlikely to result in enforcement action.

4.19 Work to mitigate hazards may need to comply with the current Building Regulations where major improvements are carried out, or windows are replaced. A house built under the Building Regulations as a single family dwelling may need additional works if it is to be used as an HMO. Where the Building Regulations will apply to the works of improvement, separate approval will need to be sought by the owner.

Empty property

4.20 As the hazard score is based on the most vulnerable potential occupant, HHSRS can be used to assess an empty property. Property condition may be a factor in an authority's empty property strategy, and they may decide to target properties, in part, because of their condition so that the property can be improved at the same time as it is brought back into use for housing. But authorities will need to take care that, aside from the intention to bring housing back into use, they deal with hazards in an empty property in an appropriate way. For example, should an improvement notice be issued when a house has been unoccupied for some time and the owner has no intention of letting it? If there is no occupant there will be less risk of an accident or ill health. Should the authority intend to carry out works itself it may do so with the co-operation of the owner. Where such co-operation is not forthcoming, Part 7 of the Act contains provisions that enable authorities to gain access. (See Part 7 of this guidance, "Powers of access").

4.21 Aside from the authority's empty property strategy, where category 1 hazards have been identified in two units of accommodation – either in the same building or in separate premises – and one of the units is unoccupied whereas the other is occupied, the fact that the property is occupied raises the priority for intervention.

Guidance on specific hazards

Radiation

4.22 The average hazard scores provided in the operating guidance are based on the member of the vulnerable group who has had a lifetime exposure to the radon level under consideration. When deciding the most appropriate course of action, authorities should take into account, so far as they can, the likelihood of past and likely future exposure to radon of the actual occupants. Past exposure will be partly dependent on the location of the current occupant's previous homes and the length of time resident there. Maps showing radon levels in England are available from the Health Protection Agency. In considering future exposure, it should not automatically be assumed that the current occupants will move and that their radon exposure in the future will be less than in their current dwelling.

Space and crowding

4.23 Authorities should take note that in assessing this hazard only the risk to the current occupiers is considered.

4.24 There are other statutory provisions in relation to overcrowding and the numbers permitted to occupy residential premises. The overcrowding provisions in Part 10 of the 1985 Act define overcrowding in housing accommodation other than HMOs and provide authorities with certain powers to act. An Order under section 216 of the Act may disapply or amend the standards in Part 10. It may also disapply or amend sections 139 to 144 of the Act, under which local authorities may control overcrowding in HMOs not subject to mandatory licensing. Section 216 of the Act also enables the Secretary of State to prescribe the factors that local authorities should take into account in making determinations.

4.25 Authorities are advised, as a first step, to assess the health and safety implications of overcrowding and to consider the appropriateness of action under Part 1 of the Act. Such action would need to be based on the evidence of the harmful impact of overcrowding in relation to the household's needs. A wide range of factors is relevant to the space and crowding hazard, including the number, sizes and layout of rooms. If authorities choose to use their Part 1 powers it will not normally be appropriate to make parallel use of the Part 10 provisions. Concerns over the provision of facilities in HMOs not subject to licensing which do not give rise to health and safety issues might still be addressed under sections 139 to144 of the Act, should authorities consider that they should act to influence the provision of amenities in such HMOs.

Nitrogen dioxide and carbon monoxide

4.26 Authorities should be aware of research published in October 2004 commissioned by the Department of Trade and Industry and the Health and Safety Executive which suggests that, under certain conditions, levels of some pollutants in the home from gas appliances may exceed outdoor air quality standards. Further information on nitrogen dioxide and carbon monoxide can be found on the website of the Committee on the Medical Effects of Air Pollutants.[4]

Part 5
Enforcement options

5.1   As noted above, the Act provides authorities with a range of enforcement options to address hazards:
   - improvement notices;
   - prohibition orders;
   - hazard awareness notices;
   - emergency remedial action or emergency prohibition orders (not available for category 2 hazards);
   - demolition orders (not available for category 2 hazards);
   - clearance areas (not available for category 2 hazards).

5.2   The first three enforcement options are available for both category 1 and category 2 hazards. There may be circumstances when, given similar

---

4   www.advisorybodies.doh.gov.uk.

conditions in different dwellings, the authority might decide to respond differently to similar hazards or in a similar way towards different types of hazard. An authority might respond to a category 1 hazard in some dwellings by requiring works of improvement while in another by prohibiting occupation (or by suspending action). The action authorities choose to take must be the most appropriate course of action in relation to the hazard in all the circumstances.

5.3 Schedules 1 and 2 to the Act make provision for the service of, and appeal against, improvement notices, hazard awareness notices and prohibition orders. Schedule 3 deals with enforcement action being taken by local authorities and the recovery of their expenses. As regards service of demolition orders, see section 268 of the 1985 Act. Clearance procedures remain in sections 289-298 of the1985 Act.

Decision to serve an improvement notice

5.4 An improvement notice under section 11 or 12 of the Act is a possible response to a category 1 or a category 2 hazard. Under section 11, action must as a minimum remove the category 1 hazard but may extend beyond this. For example, an authority may wish to ensure that a category 1 hazard is not likely to reoccur within 12 months, or is reduced to category 2, or both. Such work would need to be reasonable in relation to the hazard and it might be unreasonable to require work which goes considerably beyond what is necessary to remove a hazard.

5.5 Authorities should try to ensure that any works required to mitigate a hazard are carried out to a standard that prevents building elements deteriorating. It would be a false economy to allow work which only temporarily reduces a category 1 hazard to, say, a band D category 2 hazard. It is worth bearing in mind that a duty on the authority may arise again should conditions deteriorate. Authorities should avoid taking enforcement action which results in "patch and mend" repairs.

5.6 An improvement notice may relate to more than one category 1 hazard. Where there are multiple hazards, including category 2 hazards, the same notice can require action to deal with both category 1 and 2 hazards.

5.7 An improvement notice must contain the information set out in section 13. It must specify:
- whether the notice is served under s11 or s12;
- the nature of the hazard and the premises on which it exists;
- the deficiency giving rise to the hazard;
- the premises in relation to which remedial action is to be taken and the nature of that remedial action;
- the date when the action is to be started;
- the periods in which the action is to be completed.

The notice must also contain information about the right to appeal.

5.8 Authorities should take care to ensure that the requirements as to the contents of notices are complied with, not only in the interests of the person on whom the notice is served, but also to reduce the risk of appeals on the grounds that the notice has not been properly served.

5.9 A notice cannot require remedial works to start within 28 days of the service of the notice. Where a landlord has been asked to carry out works in more than one property, consideration should be given to staggering start times to enable the landlord to organise the work. As more than one hazard can be dealt with in the same notice, the notice can specify different deadlines for completion of the various actions required, allowing less time to tackle serious hazards and longer time for the less serious hazards. This is reasonable and appropriate where all the hazards are sufficiently serious to be the subject of an improvement notice. However, it might be more appropriate to deal with lesser hazards by a separate improvement notice or a hazard awareness notice so that they do not remain the subject of outstanding action.

5.10 An improvement notice must be revoked when the notice has been complied with. It may also be revoked or varied in other circumstances. The authority may need to make a judgement that, although the terms of the notice itself may not have been fully complied with, the hazard has ceased to be a category 1 hazard and they do not intend to take further action. Where a notice deals with more than one category 1 or 2 hazard, or a combination of categories of hazards, the notice can be revoked in relation to certain hazards and varied in relation to the rest. A notice can also be varied by agreement.

5.11 Where an improvement notice has been served an authority should consider whether it is appropriate to offer financial assistance or advice to the owner, landlord or tenant, for example on the availability of Disabled Facilities Grant. It should also consider the circumstances and wishes of tenants and owner-occupiers, including the extent to which they are able to carry out or tolerate repairs. Where in the opinion of the authority, remedial works would lead to a high probability of serious health consequences for occupants, this is a factor which might lead them to suspend the action or to issue a hazard awareness notice.

5.12 An appeal can be made to a residential property tribunal against an improvement notice by the person on whom the notice was served. In particular, an appeal can be made on the grounds that someone else ought to take the action or pay the costs, or that an improvement notice was not the most appropriate option. Appeals can also be made in relation to the variation or revocation of the notice. Any appeal must be made within 21 days from the service of the notice.

Works in default and action by authorities with owner's agreement

5.13 Section 31 and Schedule 3 to the Act enable authorities to take the action required by an improvement notice itself, with or without the agreement of the person on whom the notice was served. The need to act with agreement may arise where a category 1 hazard exists and remedial action is required without undue delay, but the owner is not in a position to carry out the works or arrange for the work to be done, perhaps for financial reasons. Authorities may have to carry out works without agreement where a notice has not been complied with.

5.14 Where the authority takes action with the agreement of the person served with the improvement notice the works are to be taken at his expense. Where the authority takes action without agreement, it may recover expenses reasonably incurred, with interest. Such expenses may be made a charge on the property. Schedule 3 also deals with appeals against the recovery of expenses.

Decision to make a prohibition order

5.15 A prohibition order under section 20 or 21 of the Act is a possible response to a category 1 or a category 2 hazard. It may prohibit the use of part or all of the premises for some or all purposes, or occupation by particular numbers or descriptions of people.

5.16 A prohibition order must contain the information set out in section 22. It must specify:
- whether the order is made under section 20 or 21;
- the nature of the hazard and the residential premises on which it exists;
- the deficiency giving rise to the hazard;
- the premises in relation to which prohibitions are imposed;
- any remedial action that would result in the order being revoked.

The notice must also contain information about the right to appeal.

5.17 An authority can be asked to approve a use of the premises, and that approval should not be unreasonably withheld. Any such refusal must be notified to the applicant within 7 days of the date of the decision to refuse.

5.18 An order becomes operative 28 days after it is made, unless the order is appealed. Copies of the order must be served on everyone who, to the authority's knowledge, is an owner, occupier, is authorised to permit occupation, or a mortgage lender in relation to the whole or part of the premises. Copies must be served within 7 days of the making of the order. The requirement in respect of occupiers may be met by fixing a copy of the order to a conspicuous part of the premises.

5.19 A prohibition order in relation to a category 1 hazard must be revoked if the authority is satisfied that the hazard in respect of which the order was made no longer exists. An order in respect of a category 1 hazard can also be revoked if the authority is satisfied that there are special circumstances making it appropriate to revoke the order. For example, the authority may need to take a view on whether any work to remove a hazard might lead them to reconsider their original decision. An order in relation to a category 2 hazard may be revoked if it is appropriate to do so. An authority may revoke or vary a prohibition order either in response to an application from any person on whom a copy of the order was required to be served, or on their own initiative.

5.20 An appeal can be made to a residential property tribunal against an order by an owner, occupier, a person authorised to permit occupation, or a mortgage lender in relation to the whole or part of the premises, on the specific ground that an order is not the most appropriate option, or on general grounds. The appeal must be made within 28 days from the date the order was made. An appeal can also be made against a decision on the revocation or variation of an order. There is a right of appeal against an authority's refusal to permit the use of the premises for any other purpose while the prohibition order is in operation, within 28 days of the date on which the decision was made.

5.21 An Order might be appropriate:
- where the conditions present a serious threat to health or safety but where remedial action is considered unreasonable or impractical for cost or other reasons. These other reasons may include cases where work cannot be carried out to remedy a serious hazard with the tenant in residence. The landlord may not be able to rehouse the tenant, though the authority may consider offering temporary or permanent alternative accommodation to the tenant to assist in progressing remedial works;
- to specify the maximum number of persons who occupy a dwelling where it is too small for the household's needs, in particular the number of bedrooms (action to deal with future occupation could be taken through the use of a suspended order);
- to control the number of persons who occupy a dwelling where there are insufficient facilities (e.g. personal washing facilities, sanitary facilities, or food preparation or cooking facilities) for the numbers in occupation (a suspended order could deal with future occupation);
- to prohibit the use of a dwelling by a specified group (until such time as improvements have been carried out), where a dwelling is hazardous to some people, but relatively safe for occupation by others. The specified group relates to the class of people for whom the risk arising from the hazard is greater than for any other group, for example, elderly people or those with young children;
- in an HMO, to prohibit the use of specified dwelling units or of common parts.

5.22 It is important to bear in mind that prohibition orders are intended to deal with health and safety matters, whereas the separate provisions dealing with non-licensed HMOs in Part 4 of the Act are available where action is required to limit the number of occupants in relation to the inadequacy of amenities. (See Part 6 of this guidance.)

5.23 When considering serving a prohibition order, the local authority should also:

- have regard to the risk of exclusion of vulnerable people from the accommodation;

- consider whether the premises are a listed building or a building protected by notice pending listing. Where improvement is not the most appropriate course of action, serving a prohibition order in respect of a listed or protected building should always be considered in preference to demolition (aside from whether consent would be forthcoming for demolition). The authority will need to balance the gain from preservation of the listed building in anticipation of future remedial works against the problems that might result in a vacant property in poor condition deteriorating further;

- take account of the position of the premises in relation to neighbouring buildings. Where improvement is not the most appropriate course of action and demolition would have an adverse effect on the stability of neighbouring buildings, prohibition of the whole or part of the building may be the only realistic option;

- irrespective of any proposals the owner may have, consider the potential alternative uses of the premises;

- take into account the existence of a conservation or renewal area and of any proposals generally for the area in which the premises are situated. Short term prohibition may be an option if the long term objective is revitalisation of the area;

- consider the effect of complete prohibition on the well being of the local community and the appearance of the locality;

- consider the availability of local accommodation for rehousing any displaced occupants. Rehousing in such cases is for the authority to consider, particularly where they may have a duty to provide accommodation. It is unrealistic to expect a landlord owning a small number of properties to re-house the tenant. Landlords have no legal responsibility to re-house their tenants as a result of action by the authority, although the tenant may be able to seek redress;

- consider whether it is appropriate to offer financial advice or assistance.

Decision to suspend an improvement notice or prohibition order

5.24 Normally, an improvement notice becomes operative 21 days after service of the notice, while a prohibition order becomes operative after 28 days. However, an authority may suspend the action specified in an improvement notice or a prohibition order. The notice may specify an event that triggers the end of the suspension, such as non-compliance with an undertaking given to the authority, or a change of occupancy. Suspension may be appropriate where the hazard is not sufficiently minor to be addressed by a hazard awareness notice but the current occupiers are not members of a vulnerable group. However, in this kind of circumstance, authorities will need to judge whether a risk exists which warrants a programme of improvement over a more relaxed timescale.

5.25 The authority should consider the likely turnover of tenants at the property. To suspend the action of a notice may not be appropriate where there has been quick turnover in occupancy. In these circumstances the authority should consider the likelihood that a range of occupants will be housed in the property in the coming 12 months.

5.26 Suspension may be appropriate where enforcement can safely be postponed while a more strategic approach to area renewal is considered, including where landlords have a programme to make their stock decent. It may also be appropriate in the case of accommodation occupied during term time by students. It may be possible to time the operation of the order to coincide with the accommodation being vacated. In the case of category 1 hazards, the authority will need to consider very carefully whether a suspended notice is an appropriate way of responding.

5.27 Typically, an event that might trigger the re-activation of a suspended notice would be a change of occupancy, where an occupier considered less vulnerable to the hazard is replaced by one who is more vulnerable. The authority needs to know who is living in a property and consider the kind of circumstances that would be a reasonable trigger. The circumstances that will trigger the action must be specified in the notice. The notice might require an owner or landlord to notify the authority of a change of occupancy to ensure that the notice can be reviewed. The use of a suspended order is appropriate to deal with future occupation.

5.28 Authorities will need to establish appropriate procedures regarding notification, and the consequences of failure by owners to notify them of a change in circumstances. Authorities should ensure that the owner is clear about the circumstances that will trigger the notice or order. As failure to notify is not an offence, authorities may want in future to take immediate enforcement in relation to landlords who have failed to notify them in the past.

5.29 Authorities should consider any request by a tenant to suspend action, or to replace the action by the issue of a hazard awareness notice. But they should also consider the other factors given in this guidance.

Review of suspended improvement notices and prohibition orders

5.30 The authority must review suspended notices and orders not later than 12 months after the date the notice was served or the order was made, but they can do so earlier. They should also decide the method of the review, which could be a further visit and inspection of the property, or an assessment of reliable information collected on the dwelling.

Emergency measures

5.31 Local authorities have discretion to take emergency enforcement action against hazards which present an imminent risk of serious harm to occupiers. In such circumstances, authorities will themselves take remedial action to remove a hazard and recover reasonable expenses, or they will be able to prohibit the use of all or part of a property. The owner of a property will be able to appeal, but any appeal will not prevent the action from being taken or the prohibition being put into effect. These provisions may only be used where there is a category 1 hazard; the hazard involves an imminent risk of harm to any of the occupiers of those or other residential premises; and no management order is in force under Part 4.

Emergency remedial action

5.32 Where the requirements of section 40(1) are fulfilled, an authority may enter the premises at any time to take emergency remedial action. The action will consist of whatever remedial action the authority considers necessary to remove an imminent risk of serious harm. Action may be taken in respect of more than one hazard in the same premises. It is a matter of judgement as to whether emergency action should be taken. The same deficiency, for example in relation to heating, is likely to be a greater cause for concern in winter than in summer.

5.33 The authority may apply to a Justice of the Peace for a warrant to enter premises to take emergency remedial action. A warrant may only be granted where the Justice of the Peace is satisfied there are reasonable grounds to believe the authority would not gain admission without a warrant.

5.34 The authority must serve a notice of emergency remedial action within 7 days of taking that action. The notice must specify:
- the nature of the hazard and the residential premises on which it exists;
- the deficiency giving rise to the hazard;
- the premises in relation to which emergency remedial action has been or is to be taken, and the nature of the action;
- the power under which the remedial action was or is to be taken;
- the date when the action was or is to be started.

The notice must also contain information about the right to appeal.

Emergency prohibition orders

5.35 Where the conditions of section 43(1) are fulfilled, an authority may enter the premises at any time to make an emergency prohibition order, prohibiting the use of all or any part of the premises with immediate effect. The order must specify:
- the nature of the hazard and the residential premises on which it exists;
- the premises in relation to which prohibitions are imposed;
- any remedial action which would result in the order being revoked.

The order must also contain information about the right to appeal.

5.36 An emergency prohibition order is served on the day it is made. It will be for the authority to consider whether subsequent action by the owner gives grounds to revoke or vary the order. Once issued, an emergency prohibition order can be reviewed and varied or revoked in the same way as ordinary prohibition orders.

Appeals against emergency measures

5.37 A person served with a notice of emergency remedial action can appeal against the action taken, whilst any person who was served with a copy of an emergency prohibition order can appeal against such an order. Appeals are made to a residential property tribunal and must be made within 28 days of the date emergency remedial action is to be started or the date an emergency prohibition order is made. The tribunal may allow late appeals if it considers there are good reasons for the delay.

Decision to serve a hazard awareness notice

5.38 A hazard awareness notice under section 29 of the Act may be a reasonable response to a less serious hazard, where the authority wishes to draw attention to the desirability of remedial action.

5.39 A hazard awareness notice under section 28 is also a possible response to a category 1 hazard as long as no management order is in place under Part 4. There may be circumstances where works of improvement, or prohibition of the use of the whole or part of the premises, are not practicable or reasonable, in which case a hazard awareness notice might be appropriate.

5.40 A hazard awareness notice must specify:
- the nature of the hazard and the residential premises on which it exists;
- the deficiency giving rise to the hazard;
- the premises on which the deficiency exists;

- the authority's reasons for deciding to serve the notice, including their reasons for deciding that serving the notice is the most appropriate course of action;
- the details of any remedial action which the authority considers would be practicable and appropriate to take.

5.41 This procedure does not require further action by the person served with the notice, though the authority should consider monitoring any hazard awareness notices that it serves.

5.42 There is no provision for an appeal against a hazard awareness notice and there is no requirement to register these notices as a local land charge. The advisory nature of the procedure, with no follow-up to determine whether the advice has been acted upon, makes an appeal process or a land charge inappropriate. If an authority considers that the hazard is sufficiently serious to require a local land charge, it should not adopt this procedure.

5.43 Authorities may wish to use the hazard awareness notice procedure without issuing an improvement notice where an owner or landlord has agreed to take remedial action and the authority is confident the work will be done in reasonable time. This might be a way of recording and monitoring the action and would provide evidence should the remedial works not be carried out, or be carried out inadequately. The service of a hazard awareness notice does not prevent further formal action, should an unacceptable hazard remain.

Demolition orders

5.44 Demolition orders remain available under Part 9 of the 1985 Act as amended. They are a possible response to a category 1 hazard where this is the appropriate course of action, unless the premises are a listed building. In deciding whether to make a demolition order an authority should:
- take into account the availability of local accommodation for rehousing the occupants;
- take into account the demand for, and sustainability of, the accommodation if the hazard was remedied;
- consider the prospective use of the cleared site;
- consider the local environment, the suitability of the area for continued residential occupation and the impact of a cleared site on the appearance and character of the neighbourhood.

5.45 The authority must serve a copy of the order on every person who, to their knowledge is an owner or occupier, is authorised to permit occupation or is a mortgage lender in relation to the whole or part of the premises, within 7 days from the date the order was made. The requirement in relation to occupiers will be met if a copy has been fixed to a conspicuous part of the premises. An aggrieved person may appeal against a demolition order to the residential property tribunal within 21 days from the service of the order.

5.46 It is possible to substitute a demolition order with a prohibition order if proposals are submitted for the use of the premises other than for human habitation.

Clearance areas

5.47 The provisions of Part 9 of the 1985 Act are retained in respect of clearance areas, with changes to align them with the provisions of the new legislation. An authority can declare an area a clearance area if it is satisfied that each of the residential buildings in the area contains one or more category 1 hazards (*or* that these buildings are dangerous or harmful to the health or safety of the inhabitants as a result of their bad arrangement or the narrowness or bad arrangement of the streets); and any other buildings in the area are dangerous or harmful to the health of the inhabitants. In a building containing flats, two or more of those flats must contain a category 1 hazard before a clearance area can be declared.

5.48 A local authority should consider the desirability of clearance in the context of proposals for the wider neighbourhood of which the dwelling forms part. In deciding whether to declare the area in which hazardous dwellings are situated to be a clearance area, a local authority should have regard to:

- the likely long-term demand for residential accommodation;
- the degree of concentration of dwellings containing serious and intractable hazards within the area;
- the density of the buildings and street pattern around which they are arranged;
- the overall availability of housing accommodation in the wider neighbourhood in relation to housing needs and demands;
- the proportion of dwellings free of hazards and other, non-residential, premises in sound condition which would also need to be cleared to arrive at a suitable site;
- whether it would be necessary to acquire land surrounding or adjoining the proposed clearance area; and whether added land can be acquired by agreement with the owners;
- the existence of any listed buildings protected by notice pending listing – listed and protected buildings should only be included in a clearance area in exceptional circumstances and only when building consent has been given;
- the results of statutory consultations;
- the arrangements necessary for rehousing the displaced occupants and the extent to which occupants are satisfied with those arrangements;

- the impact of clearance on, and the scope for relocating, commercial premises;
- the suitability of the proposed after-use(s) of the site having regard to its shape and size, the needs of the wider neighbourhood and the socio-economic benefits which the after-use(s) would bring, the degree of support by the local residents and the extent to which such used would attract private investment into the area.

5.49 Clearance may be a feature of plans to redevelop areas where there is low demand for housing or other reasons for development. Where the reasons for redevelopment are not primarily related to housing condition, the powers in the Act will not be the most appropriate. Local authorities may therefore have to make a compelling case that clearance is necessary for the 'well being' of residents. As an alternative to declaring a clearance area, an authority could consider use of compulsory purchase powers.

Powers to charge for enforcement action

5.50 The Act enables local authorities to make a reasonable charge as a means of recovering certain expenses incurred in serving an improvement notice, making a prohibition order, serving a hazard awareness notice, taking emergency remedial action, making an emergency prohibition order, or making a demolition order. The expenses are in connection with the inspection of the premises, the subsequent consideration of any action to be taken and the service of notices. Authorities will be able to charge for each course of action including, where emergency remedial action is taken, for any subsequent notices.

5.51 This provision does not relate to the cost of any remedial action taken by the authority either with or without agreement. These are separate charges covered by section 31 and Schedule 3 to the Act.

5.52 The Act provides for the appropriate national authority to set a maximum charge to be made by authorities. No such maximum has been set in England and the Secretary of State has no current plans to do so. Authorities are reminded that they should charge only the reasonable costs of enforcement. In deciding whether to exercise their powers to make a charge and the level of any charge, authorities should take account of the personal circumstances of the person or persons against whom the enforcement action is being taken. The degree to which authorities consider personal circumstances is at their discretion, having regard to the resources available to them. Section 50 of the Act sets out the powers available to a local authority for recovering any charge they make under their section 49 powers.

Part 6
Application of HHSRS in HMOs

Link with licensing

6.1 The HMO licensing regime provides local authorities with procedures to assess the fitness of a person to be a licence-holder, potential management arrangements of the premises and suitability of the property for the number of occupants, including the provision of relevant and adequate equipment and facilities at the property. An assessment under HHSRS is *not* part of the licensing procedure.

6.2 Under section 55 of the Act, authorities are required to satisfy themselves as soon as practicable and not later than 5 years after an application for a licence has been received that there are no Part 1 functions that ought to be exercised by them in relation to premises in respect of which the licensing application is made. It is not intended that authorities should always carry out a comprehensive inspection in every HMO. But the licensing process may bring to light properties which the authority wants to prioritise in order to mitigate possible hazards. It would be for the authority to decide on the extent to which an inspection of the dwelling is necessary, subject to section 4 of the Act. (See Part 2, "Identifying the need for action".)

6.3 Where all matters in relation to the application for a licence listed in section 64(3) of the Act are satisfied, the authority should not unreasonably delay the grant of a licence pending its consideration of its duties or powers under Part 1. (See however, paragraphs 6.4 and 6.5.) Any works necessary to mitigate a hazard should follow the procedures set out in Part 1. Although it is possible to attach conditions to a licence requiring such works to be carried out, section 67(4) provides that authorities should proceed on the basis that generally they should exercise Part 1 functions to identify, remove or reduce category 1 or 2 hazards in the house in preference to imposing licence conditions.

6.4 Separate action under HHSRS may restrict the number of occupants under a prohibition order, for example because of fire hazard. Licensing decisions in relation to the maximum number of occupants who may occupy the HMO will not always be influenced by a prohibition under Part 1. However, where the authority considers that the condition of an HMO is such that it might take action under Part 1 to prohibit the use of an HMO or restrict occupancy, it would be justified in considering this process a priority and proceeding with any licence application subsequently.

6.5 Management regulations under section 234 of the Act impose duties on landlords and managers of HMOs (whether or not subject to licensing). Though there are no notice serving powers under section 234, the authority can prosecute landlords for breach of the regulations. In considering such action, authorities should consider whether they should also or alternatively take action in relation to such facilities by exercising their powers under Part 1.

Factors to consider in HMOs

6.6 HHSRS covers the whole range of hazards stemming from physical factors likely to be experienced in all types of housing, including HMOs. This type of accommodation has long been regarded as being of higher risk to health and safety than dwellings built for and containing single households. It is essential to prioritise intervention, and resources, wherever these higher risks are found. In HMOs, hazards are assessed for each individual unit of accommodation and the shared facilities and common parts attributable to that unit. Each assessment will reflect the contribution of conditions in the common parts. The same enforcement tools will be appropriate to HMOs as to other sorts of housing. However, additional guidance is contained in the operating guidance on the application of HHSRS in HMOs.

6.7 Where, following the issue of a statutory notice or order, an HMO reverts to single occupancy, the authority should consider whether a different course of action is now more appropriate. Following a change of circumstances the authority will need to consider whether the impact of any hazard has diminished, and whether the same or different, or any, action is required. The authority should also consider whether any notices or orders should be revoked or varied.

Targeting action in HMOs

6.8 Hazards in HMOs are assessed in relation to individual dwelling units – for the purposes of the Act these will be "dwellings". Deficiencies are likely to arise in shared facilities and common parts as well as in the living units and the Act enables action to be taken in relation to any part of the building and for notices to be served on a range of people where there is joint or separate responsibility.

6.9 A deficiency in shared facilities or common parts giving rise to a hazard can be dealt with in a notice served on the person responsible for those parts of the building. A deficiency relating to the structure can normally be dealt with in a notice served on the person who owns the building. A notice can always be served on a superior landlord if this is where ultimate responsibility lies.

6.10 It may occasionally be necessary to make a choice in dealing with hazards. Where there is a category 1 hazard and a category 2 hazard arising from the same deficiencies, the category 1 hazard alone need be dealt with.

6.11 Authorities cannot simultaneously take more than one form of action – for example make a prohibition order and serve an improvement notice – dealing with the same hazard in the same premises. However, where the same deficiencies in an HMO give rise to more than one hazard, each hazard can be dealt with at the same time and by way of different enforcement action. Works to the units or common parts could form part of an overall package by combining the hazards on the same notice, where appropriate. Improvement notices could include category 1 and 2 hazards. They must however be served on the appropriate person(s) and this may determine the number of notices served in relation to the HMO.

Consultation with fire and rescue authorities

6.12 The Regulatory Reform (Fire Safety) Order 2005 (SI 2005 No. 1541) will rationalise existing fire safety legislation, including the Fire Precautions Act 1971, and bring it into one regime. Guidance will be issued under the Order.

6.13 Section 10 of the Act requires local housing authorities to consult the local fire and rescue authority before taking enforcement action in respect of a prescribed fire hazard in an HMO or in the common parts of a building containing flats. The form of the consultation is not prescribed. Where emergency measures are to be taken in relation to a prescribed fire hazard the housing authority must consult the fire and rescue authority before taking those measures as far as is practicable.

6.14 Effective communication between the two enforcement agencies is essential for the successful operation of both Part 1 functions and Part 2 licensing functions. Where an inspection or assessment of the property shows the occupants to be at a high risk, there should be an agreed procedure in place for informing the fire and rescue authority of that risk so that the fire and rescue authority may develop appropriate intervention tactics for dealing with an incident at the property.

6.15 It is important therefore that protocols are established between fire and rescue authorities and local authorities to set out good working practice and create failsafe lines of communication between them in relation to Part 1.

6.16 In general, protocols should cover the agreed method of consultation and the time allowed for a response and should agree other administrative procedures so that it is not necessary in all cases for the authorities to make joint visits to premises. Agreements about this might be based on their respective knowledge of properties in the area.

6.17 It is not expected that consultation will re-examine the HHSRS assessment of the hazard or attempt to apply considerations that fall outside the scope of the HHSRS assessment and enforcement guidance.

But it is important for housing authorities to liaise closely with the fire and rescue authority in respect of HMOs, and in particular over any action that needs to be taken, or conditions that have to be met, under any Part of the Act. The views of the fire and rescue authority should include the proposed remedial action and whether it is sufficient in providing an adequate means to fight fire and escape in case of fire. The housing authority is expected to take a holistic approach to the property, taking into account matters such as security and overcrowding. The final decision to serve a notice or make an order under housing legislation lies with the housing authority, and it may have to defend its decision before a residential property tribunal.

6.18 The extent to which consultation should include the assessment of fire risks in properties which are not subject to proposed enforcement action is a matter for local agreements between local housing authorities and fire and rescue authorities.

6.19 In considering the form of local protocols, authorities may wish to consider as a model any existing protocols that may have been agreed at a national or regional level between housing and building control bodies and fire and rescue authorities or other professional bodies.

Part 7
Other issues

Powers of access

7.1 Section 239 of the Act gives a local authority power of entry to properties in pursuance of its duties under Part 1 of the Act when certain conditions are met. In particular, this enables authorities, where it is necessary to carry out an inspection under section 4, to see whether a category 1 or 2 hazard exists.

7.2 Representatives of the authority must have written authorisation which sets out the purpose for which the entry is authorised and must give at least 24 hours notice to the owner or occupier of the premises they intend to enter. Authorisation must also be given by the appropriate officer of the authority. Section 243 requires that the authorisation is given by a deputy chief officer within the meaning of section 2 of the Local Government and Housing Act 1989 whose duties consist of or include the exercise of functions relevant to the authorisation. Permission under this section does not include a power to use force to obtain entry. Section 240 enables a justice of the peace to issue a warrant for admission to premises. This includes power to enter by force if necessary. This power is only applicable, however, when entry under section 239 has been refused; or the property is empty and immediate access is necessary; or prior warning of entry is likely to negate the purpose of access.

7.3 The powers of entry allow authorities to leave recording equipment, but such equipment must be relevant to their enforcement powers, for example to record levels of radon or other harmful gases or particles. The equipment may need to be left in working order and collected after a period of time. The authority needs reasonable grounds to leave the recording equipment.

7.4 Local authorities also have powers in section 235 to require the production of documents reasonably required to enable them to carry their enforcement functions.

Use of premises for temporary housing accommodation

7.5 Instead of making a prohibition order or a demolition order, the authority can make a determination under section 300(1) or (2) of the 1985 Act (as amended by paragraph 20 of Schedule 15 to the Act), enabling it to purchase the property if it is capable of providing adequate accommodation for temporary housing use. Authorities should not consider a property to be adequate for temporary housing if it contains category 1 hazards in respect of which they would find it impracticable to carry out remedial work to make conditions acceptable for potential occupants particularly vulnerable to the hazards. Following a determination the property can then be bought by agreement with the owner, or through compulsory purchase. This power is not available in relation to a listed building. Aside from this power, authorities can seek to acquire land for housing purposes under section 17 of the 1985 Act.

7.6 Under section 301 of the 1985 Act an authority may also retain property acquired for clearance for temporary housing use where it can be improved to an adequate standard. Again, authorities should not consider a property to be adequate if it contains category 1 hazards in respect of which they would find it impracticable to carry out remedial work to make conditions acceptable for potential occupants particularly vulnerable to the hazards.

7.7 For further guidance on housing CPOs see the current guidance issued by the ODPM.[5]

Disrepair

7.8 Disrepair is likely to contribute to a number of hazards that can be assessed under HHSRS. These include hazards from cold, falls, fire, damp and mould growth, electrical hazards, entry by intruders, and structural failure. The HHSRS operating guidance illustrates the kinds of disrepair

---

[5] Compulsory Purchase Orders, ODPM Circular 02/2003, February 2003.

that can give rise to these hazards and against which authorities will have either a duty or a discretionary power to take action according to their severity.

7.9 Authorities should consider whether minor disrepair, and conditions giving rise to discomfort, is a priority, given the spread of hazards they may encounter in the local stock. Authorities can consider the use of financial assistance and other non-enforcement tools to encourage owners to deal with minor disrepair.

7.10 Authorities may wish to ensure that hazards are dealt with where they contain deficiencies to building elements which might deteriorate. Such action might ensure that the deficiencies which gave rise to hazards do not recur over at least the next 12 months. Intervention may therefore be justified in the case of a hazard in a low band where deterioration is likely to occur and result subsequently in a hazard in a higher band.

Mortgage lenders in possession

7.11 Where a local authority takes enforcement action the notice requires the person on whom it is served – normally the owner or landlord – to take the remedial action specified. The Act makes provision for a change in circumstance so that the original recipient of a notice is no longer responsible for complying with it. This is likely to arise where an owner or landlord has sold the property or where a mortgage lender has taken possession of it. In such cases, the action required by a notice can be enforced on the successor. The exception is where the person on whom the notice was originally served has already incurred a liability – e.g. he has been fined for non-compliance or obstruction – he retains that liability despite the subsequent transfer of responsibility.

7.12 Liability should not take new owners unawares, as improvement notices and prohibition orders are land charges and will be revealed by the local search. But in these and in other cases the local authority has discretion to vary or revoke a notice and may very well do so where it considers that it is safe to take no further action, for example in an unoccupied property. Where a house is in an unsafe condition – though empty, there may be dangers to passers-by or to visitors – the authority may still require the new owners, including a mortgage lender, to make the house safe.

7.13 In most cases a mortgage lender is likely to secure the property following repossession and may carry out checks on its condition to ensure that it is safe eg slates are not likely to fall off and endanger passers-by. Nevertheless, authorities are advised to discuss the situation with a mortgage lender who has taken possession of a property before continuing with enforcement action.

INDEX

References are to paragraph numbers.